WHERE SHOULD WE TAKE THE KIDS?

THE NORTHEAST
by Elin McCoy

Fodor's Travel Publications, Inc.

New York • Toronto • London • Sydney • Auckland

www.fodors.com

Copyright

Third Edition

ISBN 0–679–00203–0

**Fodor's Where Should We Take the Kids?
The Northeast**

EDITOR: Tania Inowlocki
Editorial Production: Stacey Kulig
Creative Director: Fabrizio La Rocca
Cover Photograph: Paul D'Innocenzo
Design: Guido Caroti
Production/Manufacturing: Mike Costa

Foreword

While every care has been taken to ensure
the accuracy of the information in this guide,
the passage of time will always bring change,
and consequently Fodor's cannot accept
responsibility for errors that may occur. All
prices and opening times quoted here are
based on information supplied to us at press
time. Hours and admission fees may change,
however, and the prudent traveler will avoid
inconvenience by calling ahead.

Fodor's wants to hear about your travel
experiences, both pleasant and unpleasant.
Send your letters to Editor, *Where Should
We Take the Kids? The Northeast,* 201 East
50th Street, New York, NY 10022—and
have a wonderful trip!

Also check out Fodor's Web site at
www.fodors.com.

Special Sales

Contents

Author's Acknowledgments

This book could not have been written without the cooperation of the many families—both friends and friends of friends—who shared their travel experiences in the Northeast with me. Very special thanks are due to Matthew Wool, whose research and help on Chapter 8 were essential. I'd also like to single out Rebecca Ballard; Robbie Barnett; Sarah Jane and Krystyna Chelminski; Nancy Cherosnik; Mira Felner and Joshua Cutler; Abby and Eliza Fitzgerald; Mary Kay, Michael, and Matthew Flowers; Dan Ford; Sally, Stephen, Betsy, and Eric Fortlouis; Pam, John, Will, and Noah Gasner; Candace Gianetti; Betsy Goff; Bob and Carol Goldfeld; Betsy Hart and Marty O'Tolle plus M. J., Teresa, and Emily; Susan Cohen and Peter, Jacob, and Kate Hellman; Jane and Andrew Holt; Sari Jubein; Nancy, Alison, Danny, Brendan, and John Kinchla; Susan, Eliza, and Caroline Kinsolving; Sue Kirber; Mark, Geri, Matt, and Dana Kupersmith; Larry Lindner; Justin McCabe and Jared Hudson; Carroll, Mike, Alexander, and Olivia Macdonald; Jim and Eileen McKay; Juliana May; Kristin Mellen-Smith; Wenda Harris Millard and her two kids; Vita, Arthur, and Owen Muir; Kathleen Heenan and Nicholas, Caitlin, and Jonathan Olmstead; Michelle Phelan and her two kids; Louise and Curtis Read; Connie, David, Andrea, and Sarah Rosengarten; Nancy and Malcolm Sandberg; Rosellen, Bob, Brian, and Michael Schnurr; Wendy and Brian Seeley; Frances and Peter Shocket; Judy and Jasper Speicher; Eddie Udel and his family; Tina Ujlaki and Nicholas and Chloe Marmet; the Van Hemerts; Sarah Van Fleet; Vanessa, Zoe, and Bridget Wool; Roberta, Jason, Matthew, and Richard Wool; Sally Zunino and her kids. I'm also grateful to the staff at Fodor's for their efforts on this book. My agent, Joan Raines, deserves many thanks, too. Last but not least, to John and Gavin, my heartfelt thanks for meals cooked, chapters read, and trips taken.

Dedication

To the memory of my parents, Margaret and J. L. McCoy, who taught me the basics about family travel.

Why the Northeast

This is one of the best areas in the United States for family travel because such a wide variety of landscape, culture, history, and activity that's appropriate for families is packed into a small space just right for short trips or long. You and your kids can swim in warm ocean bays edged by perfect sand beaches, climb a mountain or ascend the world's most famous skyscraper, camp in the wilderness, or visit unique historic sites of America's beginnings, like Paul Revere's House.

The Northeast is our home territory. In this book, I include all six states in New England (Connecticut, Maine, Massachusetts, New Hampshire, Rhode Island, and Vermont) and the eastern half of New York State (New York City, Long Island, as well as the Hudson Valley, the Catskills, and the Adirondacks).

How to Use This Book

ORGANIZATION

Part I, Openers, covers general strategies to make family travel fun and rewarding for both parents and kids as well as basic information on getting there, and what to expect in the way of weather and seasons in the Northeast.

Part II, Pleasures, is organized by subjects—from the most fascinating museums for kids (and why) to exciting opportunities for outdoor action adventures. If your kids are intrigued by science museums, for example, you can compare the Museum of Science in Boston with New York's Hall of Science and others included in Chapter 3 to see which they might like best.

Part III, Places, outlines what you need to know for visiting eight geographic areas in the Northeast most interesting for kids: the area's two biggest cities—Boston and New York; what my family considers the three best seaside resorts—Block Island, Nantucket, and Cape Cod; and the mountains and hills of the Adirondacks in New York State, the Berkshires in Massachusetts, and the White Mountains of New Hampshire. Each of these areas offers a wide variety of things to do and see no matter what your kids' ages and interests—which is why they make such great family destinations. Each chapter includes the top kid-pleasing sights and stuff to do, the most family-friendly hotels, and restaurants that welcome kids. Of course the Northeast is teeming with things to do, and the eight specific destinations we thought to consider in greater depth in this section are by no means the only spots we recommend. There are dozens of itineraries that can be custom-made for your family. If your child loves dinosaurs and mummies, check out the listings in our museums chapter. Around the attractions you choose, a whole vacation can be planned. In addition to the information we provide, you can contact local tourist offices for dining and lodging recommendations.

At the end of the book are two directories—the Directory of Resources, which includes helpful toll-free numbers for visitor bureaus, car-rental agencies, and hotel chains, and the Directory of Attractions, which provides location-finder information.

As anyone who has traveled with kids knows, spots that appeal to 3-year-olds rarely interest teens, and vice versa. On the basis of my experience with my son and friends' experiences with their kids aged infant–15, I assess sports, sights, hotels, restaurants, and more for their appeal to different age groups.

ICONS AND SYMBOLS

(**👫 1–6**) Recommended ages

🏠 Address, telephone number, cost, opening times

The following abbreviations are used: AE, American Express; D, Discover; DC, Diners Club; MC, MasterCard; and V, Visa.

DINING AND LODGING

Price charts appear in the beginning of each Eats and Where to Stay section.

HOTEL FACILITIES

Available facilities are always listed—but I don't specify whether they cost extra: When pricing accommodations, always ask what's included.

Assume that hotels operate on the European Plan (EP, with no meals) unless noted that they use the Full American Plan (FAP, with all meals), the Modified American Plan (MAP, with breakfast and dinner daily), the Continental Plan (CP, with a Continental breakfast daily), or are all-inclusive (all meals and most activities).

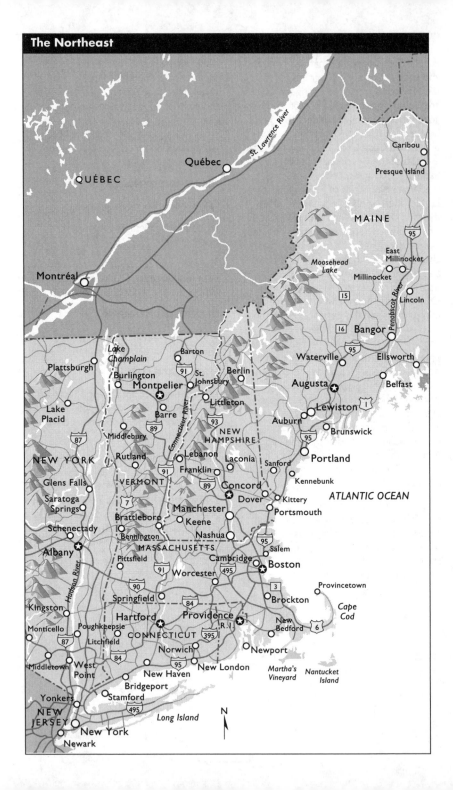

The Northeast

PART I

OPENERS

Information and Tips for Traveling with Children

ARE WE THERE YET?
GETTING STARTED IN THE NORTHEAST

My view of family travel is firmly rooted in my own childhood in western New York State and the Midwest. I am the child of parents who loved nothing better than climbing into the car on Friday night and heading off on a travel adventure for the weekend. For my sister and me a family vacation was a chance to step out of our normal daily routine (stay up late, eat ice cream every night) and have the exclusive attention of our parents, who, as we drove, listened to poems we wrote, shared tales of their own childhoods, and occasionally astonished us with their knowledge of some fascinating, obscure fact. Their main rules were simple: no fighting in the backseat and only one souvenir that cost more than $1 on each trip.

Now there are three of us who travel together: my husband, John, a painter and writer, my son, Gavin, and me, though on many excursions through the years our small band has also included cousins and friends, Cub Scouts and classmates. Our home base has been the Northeast—first in New York City, then in the small town in rural northwestern Connecticut where we now live—for more than 20 years. Over the past 19 years of short and long vacations with Gavin and some of his friends, John and I have most often discovered the pleasures *parents* glean from such travel scenarios when we could take the same relaxed attitude toward travel with kids as my parents did. This translated into being flexible, seeing the funny side of problems, and looking at things from a kid's perspective, whatever that was at different ages.

Then too, kids have the gift of instant friendships that make you part of a wider family community; Gavin's exuberance and questions have resulted more than once in an after-dinner invitation into the kitchen of a Chinese restaurant to meet the chef's family and try a few special treats. At playground and park stops we invariably met families who shared with us the name of the best local restaurant for kids, the most interesting biking spot, a tiny, just-opened bird sanctuary. Choosing activities that appeal to kids opens up new possibilities for you, too.

Traveling with a kid's perspective affects how you plan, where you go, where you stay, what you see and do when you get there, where and what you eat, and how you schedule a day's activities so that kids—and you—have fun. A morning in a museum can be boring, but not if you choose one that has displays of dinosaurs or real skeletons you can touch or an old boat where you can play lobsterman or dress up in a knight's armor and chain mail. Sightseeing as an end in itself is rarely a turn-on for any kids under 12. They want views of Quechee Gorge to culminate in action—like hiking down to the gorge itself on a narrow path for a swim or 15 minutes of tossing rocks into the stream.

Every family has its own set of likes and dislikes, and this book reflects ours and those of our friends, who were able to fill in our gaps. Lighthouses and forts have always appealed to us—and Gavin—more than historic houses; we're hikers and canoers more than bicyclists and horseback riders; as a family we prefer small hotels to big ones, and John and I have always heaved a sigh of relief that Gavin likes Chinese dim sum as much as fast food. We also have our individual passions. John is more a museum goer than a sports watcher (except for tennis). For me no trip is complete without a visit to a bookstore and a hike. Gavin's interests, like all kids', changed and evolved as he grew from toddler to teenager: Skiing is a constant, but going to baseball games has not been; big machines and animals in zoos weren't the delight to him at 12 that they were when he was 6; a week in a city with a chance to skateboard and people-watch was more exciting to him at 14 than a week of camping and hiking in the mountains. Our vacations have had to evolve, too. The 25 tips below are ones that have helped make our vacations and those of other traveling families we know work over a period of years.

One last thought: We've learned, not without effort, to give up the myth of the perfect vacation. Things will go wrong; kids will not coexist with you or each other in complete harmony; not all your planned activities will be as wonderful or exciting as you thought. But—hey—surprise! You can have fun anyway.

Gearing Up to Go

When to Go

New England and New York State are year-round destinations; the best seasons for visiting different areas depend on what you want to do. Summer, favored by most families with school-age kids, is pleasantly warm in mountain and coastal regions but often muggy and very hot in cities. (Summer temperatures in northern coastal and mountain regions can vary by as much as 40°F, however.) Even so, both New York and Boston attract families with a host of street fairs, festivals, and free outdoor entertainment. Memorial Day is the start of the summer season at mountain and beach resort areas, when festivals and outdoor concerts begin and seasonal museums open; serious sum-mer tourist traffic usually commences only with the Fourth of July weekend. Fall, when leaves begin to turn, is the most colorful season in the countryside. Be warned that many hotels and inns are booked far in advance for leaf peepers and that rates in places such as New Hampshire's White Mountains are the very highest of the year. By the end of October, however, leaves are off the trees, hunting season begins, and the landscape is gray and bleak, so November is not a good month for family hiking. The early fall at beach resorts is lovely; if your kids are preschoolers this is an ideal vacation time as the water is still warm, but crowds disappear after Labor Day. In the Northeast's cities, fall is exciting: clear weather, pleasant temperatures, and new programs at museums and theaters. Winter is for downhill and cross-country skiing—and every state but Rhode Island is home to ski resorts that have snowmaking equipment. In December cities offer much entertainment specifically for kids and families, but they're usually not very pleasant from January through March—as reflected by hotel rates. March is sugaring-off time in northern states. The spring is variable: You may see blizzards as late as April; otherwise it's mud season; avoid outdoor activities in the northern woods for the last two weeks in May and usually into early June because of black-fly season.

Before You Go

Before you go, you can do a number of things to improve the chances for your trip's success.

● When choosing a destination, take into account the ages, likes, and dislikes of every member of the family, starting with the youngest—and including your own. If your 5-year-old gets bored with a constant round of museums or your teenager goes into a funk because he's cooped up with younger kids for days, no one will have a good time. Make sure the trip includes something special for everyone.

● Get your kids actively involved in planning your trip from the very beginning—that way older kids have a stake in making it work and you have a chance to allay younger kids' natural wariness of the unknown. Besides, it's fun. After poring over brochures and books (see Boning Up: Books and Videos, below), we each make a list of what we want to see and do. When Gavin was little, he used felt-tip markers to circle pictures of what appealed to him. From this we planned out what to do each day.

● Give kids information about travel time and where you are staying in kid terms (i.e., it will take about as long as to drive to Grandma and Grandpa's), and don't take anything for granted with little kids. A family we know discussed their trip to a cottage in Cape Cod with their three kids for weeks, but as they climbed into the car, their 3-year-old wondered aloud nervously whether a cottage was "like cottage cheese."

● Start small. Try a one-night camp-out in the backyard or a nearby state park before committing yourself to a weeklong trip, an afternoon hike as a trial run for a vacation in the mountains, a local museum visit before a weekend grand museum jaunt.

● Choose places to stay where families are welcome so you don't feel as though you have to apologize when your kids act like kids. We always pick somewhere with a pool if it's affordable.

● If your kids are under 8, pick one spot to stay and content yourself with occasional short day trips from there. It's hard for kids to adjust to new surroundings every night, and packing and repacking all their gear isn't much fun for parents either.

● Bring and plan small surprises you know your kids will like: new toys and books, an ice cream picnic, an hour at a mall en route, fanny packs they've admired with $5 or $10 inside.

● Agree on a few basic behavior rules ahead of time and stick to them on your trip. This includes deciding what you plan to do to minimize sibling fights.

● With little kids, take pretend trips before you go. Gavin and his best friends loved packing a small suitcase, setting up rows of chairs as a plane, cutting up paper for play tickets, and taking turns being waiter and customer in a restaurant. Use this as an opportunity to warn kids about what to expect—that the plane may rock, for example.

Boning Up: Books and Videos Before You Go

Four good books on general travel strategies with kids are *Trouble-Free Travel with Children* (updated edition, 1996) by Vicki Lansky (available from Practical Parenting, 15245 Minnetonka Blvd., Minnetonka, MN 55345-1510, tel. 800/255–3379, fax 612/

912–0105); *How to Take Great Trips with Your Kids* by Sanford and Joan Portnoy (The Harvard Common Press, 1995); *The Pennywhistle Traveling with Kids Book* by Meredith Brokaw, Annie Gilbar, and Jill Weber (Fireside, 1995); and, if you're traveling with a baby, *Baby Maneuvers* by Ericka Lutz (Macmillan, 1997).

Getting kids interested in and knowledgeable about your travel destination in advance contributes to their enthusiasm for the trip and usually (we've found, anyway) makes it more successful because kids love seeing in person things they recognize from a book or movie. (I've also included specific book and video suggestions in individual chapters.) Available from *The Family Travel Guides Catalog* (Carousel Press, Box 6038, Berkeley, CA 94706-0038, tel. 510/527–5849) is a great resource: *Books on the Move: A Read-About-It-Go-There Guide to America's Best Family Destinations*, which lists dozens of children's titles (including fiction) related to many destinations in New England and topics such as animals, sports, nature, geography, and so on. To receive a catalog of general and specialized travel guides that includes books of games, send a self-addressed envelope with 55¢ for postage to the address listed above.

To help little kids grasp some basics: *Dinosaur's Travel: A Guide for Families on the Go* by Laurie Krasny Brown and Marc Brown (Little, Brown; ages 3–8) covers aspects of vacationing such as getting ready for a trip, sleeping in an unfamiliar bed, and more, all from a kid's perspective; *Arthur's Family Vacation* by Marc Brown (Little, Brown; ages 3–8) is a humorous look at a vacation that includes six days of rain and how everyone had fun anyway. *In the Back Seat* by Deborah Durland Desaix (Farrar Straus & Giroux, ages 4–8) is a tale of how two kids combat boredom on a car trip. When my son was little, we also read books about whatever kind of transportation we would be using: *Your First Airplane Trip* by Pat and Joel Ross and *The Car Trip* by Helen Oxenbury (avail-

able at libraries) are two we particularly liked.

For kids ages 7–12: *The Amazing Backseat Book-A-Ma-Thing* (Klutz, 1998) contains 33 game boards in a book; *KidsTravel: A Backseat Survival Kit* (Klutz, 1994) includes game ideas, a tablet, dice, markers, and more; and *Travel Fun: A DK First Activity Pack* (Dorling Kindersley, 1996) contains game boards, game and activity ideas, and a traveler's log book. Also check out the four inexpensive *Travel Game Packs* put out by Creative Child Press.

A trip to the library will turn up a surprising number of books for all ages related to some aspect of your trip. Some examples: If you're visiting Salem, Massachusetts, you might want to read books about witches and the history of the witch trials; if you're going to Maine, books about lobsters, lighthouses, and the classic *One Morning in Maine* (Robert McCloskey, Viking). Three books for kids in the 4–8 range that we've liked paint vivid pictures of outdoor action adventures: *Three Days on a River in a Red Canoe* by Vera Williams (Greenwillow), detailed enough to be a guide for planning a canoe trip; *Amelia Bedelia Goes Camping* by Peggy Parish (Avon), a humorous camping story for beginning readers; and *Tomorrow on Rocky Pond* by Lynn Reiser (Greenwillow), about an idyllic family fishing excursion.

Many resorts send short videos. Even if they sound like ads, they'll help kids picture where they're going. In our house, a screening of the hilarious *National Lampoon's Family Vacation* with Chevy Chase was a good starting point for discussion about how to ensure our trip didn't end up like that. Check individual chapters for videos that provide a preview of a specific location, such as New York City. Films based on events in American history or set in 18th- or 19th-century America (*The Last of the Mohicans*, for example) are good bets as they convey the flavor of the Northeast's past. Watching a movie such as *Free Willy* may interest your kids in whales in general and, by extension, a whale-watching trip.

One valuable—and highly recommended—additional resource is *Family Travel Times* (Box 14326, Washington, DC 20044-4326, tel. 888/822–4388, fax 212/477–5173; $39 for 6 bimonthly issues), a national newsletter that offers a wealth of helpful tips and up-to-date advice on traveling with children as well as periodic features on destinations in the Northeast. Subscribers also have access to a free, weekly call-in advisory service.

The Internet

The World Wide Web is another good source of useful information. Besides individual state tourism sites (*see* Directory of Resources, *below*), I recommend the following general family travel sites. The Family Travel Network on America Online (kid-travel@aol.com) is the largest site so far on family travel. The Family Travel Forum newsletter site, www.familytravelforum.com, carries a list of family-friendly travel agents, provides links to many other sites, and lets you post questions for other parents about particular destinations. Disney's family site, www.family.com, also offers great travel tips and information, as does the Travel with Kids section on www.miningco.com. For outdoor adventures with kids, check out www.gorp.com, and for many family-friendly inns in New England try www.inns.com.

Packing

THE ESSENTIALS. Some items we've found useful when traveling with Gavin are: flashlight (with extra batteries), can opener, Swiss army knife (any kind of folding knife will do), sewing kit, and almost the most important thing—all sizes of locking plastic bags, in which we've stashed everything from a wet bathing suit to soap to a snack to a precious collection of acorns. If your kids are little, bring safety plugs for electrical outlets and a small plug-in night-light.

Necessities like batteries, film, and sunscreen lotion are available almost anywhere, but if you end up buying them at shops on the tourist track, prices can be high. If your kids are still in diapers, buy them (along with wipes) at local supermarkets—hotel sundry shops usually don't sell them (and if they do they're too expensive). Bring an extra pair of your glasses, contact lenses, or prescription sunglasses, and pack any prescription medications you need regularly.

And we always pack a basic first-aid kit:

- bandages, gauze pads, and tape
- antiseptic cream
- thermometer and petroleum jelly
- needle and tweezers for splinters or removing ticks, plus matches so we can sterilize
- children's acetaminophen
- small first-aid book

INFANTS. Make a list of what you think you'll need for your baby a few weeks, even a month, ahead of time. That way you can add to your stacks of travel stuff gradually, during your baby's naps. Check off items as you go and leave basic necessities, like diapers and things you can't spare to pack away early (baby's favorite toy, for example), for the last minute.

THE ALL-IMPORTANT TOY-AND-BOOK BAG. Once kids turn 3 or so, they're ready to decide what toys and books they want to take—though I always reserved the right to make some suggestions and packed some additional toys in our regular luggage. They're also able to carry most of their treasures themselves in a backpack or lightweight travel bag with lots of flaps, compartments, and zippered pockets. Some of our friends put a mesh bag behind each front seat so kids can see what toys and games they have. If we're going by car, we take a canvas bag of additional books and books on tape that we've borrowed from the library. (If you're traveling by plane, coloring books, playing cards, and kids' magazines are the most you can expect from the airline over and above the set of Junior Captain wings.) The following lists may serve as reminders of the objects children in your family consider essential. These things can mean the difference between major crises and relatively peaceful traveling with infants and toddlers:

• An essential stuffed toy and blanket; old baby rattles and teething toys (tie them with a string to the car seat so kids can drop them and pull them up); song tapes, including nursery rhymes, finger plays, lullabies; a toy telephone.

• Preschoolers and up can create their own pastimes with washable felt-tip markers (crayons often melt if left in the sun); spiral notebooks or a clipboard and paper with a pencil on a string attached; a glue stick; a magic slate; playing cards and book of card games; books (preferably paperbacks), most brand-new but a few old favorites (keep a few of the new ones to dole out later in the trip); cassette tapes—of songs, novels, and children's books (let each kid—especially teens—bring his or her own tape player, tapes, and headset) and extra batteries; Mad Libs (pads of fill-in-the-blank stories that amuse kids from age 7) and fill-in activity books; sticker books, such as the *Where's Waldo Sticker Books* by Martin Handford (Candlewick Press); finger puppets, small toy people, or action figures of some kind; dolls; small cars and trucks; Legos in coffee cans or large zip-shut bags; hand-held video games; travel versions of popular games, such as Battleship, Yahtzee, and checkers; Klutz Press books, which come with jacks, juggling balls, and other toys; modeling compound; Brain Quest packages (each box contains 300 to 1,500 questions and answers designed for a specific age group, from preschoolers through grade 7), especially Brain Quest Extra: For the Car for ages 7–12; Etch-a-Sketch; disposable cameras; crocheting gear—or some other favorite craft; binoculars (for older kids); action toys for rest stops: bubble-liquid sets, Frisbee, inflatable beach ball, baseball bat, gloves, tennis ball, soccer ball, jump ropes.

Getting There

By Plane

Of all the airports in the Northeast, Logan International Airport in Boston (the biggest in New England) is the most kid-friendly. In Terminal C, next to the barbershop, is a special carpeted children's play area with climbing structures built to look like an airplane and a fuel truck, a view of the airfield, and kinetic sculptures; it now also contains a toddler section with a slide and a Children's Museum shop. In Terminal A there's a small play area near Continental Airlines. New York City is served by three major airports; La Guardia and Newark are cleaner and more pleasant and easier to get around with kids than JFK. Bradley International Airport in Windsor Locks, Connecticut, just north of Hartford, is in a central New England location, never crowded, and small. Other major airports are just outside Providence, Rhode Island, and Portland, Maine. It's also possible to fly to many small airports in New Hampshire and Vermont and to Albany, New York.

The February/March issue of *Family Travel Times* details children's services on dozens of airlines ($8; see Gearing up to Go, *above*). Many offer special meals for babies and older children if you request them when you reserve. On Delta flights, for example, kids may get a sugared cereal and bananas for breakfast; pizza, macaroni and cheese, chicken nuggets, or a turkey hot dog for lunch; and spaghetti and meatballs or cheeseburgers for dinner, all served with milk and cookies; jars of baby food are provided for the littlest ones. On United's flights into Boston and New York, McDonald's Happy Meals are the kids' choice; infants get baby food. If the airline has no children's meal, order a fruit plate. Playing cards, coloring books and crayons, games, and puzzles are just some of the in-flight entertainment provided. For useful tips on air travel with children from toddlers to teens, send for the free pamphlet "When Kids Fly" put out by Boston's Logan Airport (Massport Public Information Program, Boutwell One, Logan International Airport, East Boston 02128, tel. 617/561–1800). Be sure to include a self-addressed stamped envelope.

KID DISCOUNTS. When you make plane reservations, be sure to state the ages of your children and ask about discounts and special packages available for families. Though it's no longer the norm, some airlines still offer children's discounts on certain flights, and infants under 2 generally fly free on domestic flights when they're held on a parent's lap.

BABY ON BOARD. If you'd like a bassinet—not available on all airlines—be sure to request one when you make a reservation. You'll need a bulkhead seat for a bassinet, but be warned—the seat trays in the bulkhead usually fold out of your chair arm and are impossible to use with a child on your lap. You can bring an FAA-approved car seat aboard if you've bought a seat for your little one or if there's an unoccupied seat for it (your airline may charge for this—check). If you will want formula or baby food on the flight, be sure to request it when you reserve.

By Train

With room for fidgety kids to roam about, train travel can be a great alternative for vacationing families—so long as you have the time and the trains go where you need to go. Snack bars, rest rooms, and water fountains help kids fend off travel boredom; reclining seats, overhead luggage racks, and even sleeping compartments on long-distance routes make travel hours relatively comfortable. Call Amtrak (tel. 800/872–7245) for information and reservations. Children ages 2–15 ride for half fare on Amtrak when accompanied by an adult paying full fare. Children under 2 ride free.

Amtrak's *Ethan Allen* (New York City's Penn Station to Rutland, Vermont) travels through the Hudson Valley to upstate New York (Saratoga Springs and Glens Falls) before crossing into Vermont; the *Vermonter* (Penn Station to St. Albans) runs up the eastern side of Vermont, providing access to such ski towns as Stowe; the *Adirondack* (Penn Station to Montreal) stops at points in the Adirondacks such as Saratoga Springs and Fort Ticonderoga. Frequent daily service traverses the Northeast Corridor Route from Washington and New York City to Boston, with stops in Connecticut and Rhode Island.

By Car

The Northeast is a compact area with an excellent system of interstate highways. But in summer, especially on Friday and Sunday nights, Route 1 up the coast of Maine, roads on Cape Cod, and highways on Long Island can be bumper to bumper. New York City and Boston are predictably inhospitable to cars.

En Route

En route, here are some strategies for smoother travel.

● Know what travel times work for your kids. Some families prefer traveling at night because their children will sleep.

● Though we've taken marathon car trips, we don't recommend them with kids, even older ones. Break the trip into smaller parts or, better yet, fly as close to your destination as possible, and then rent a car. When you do arrive, keep daily car travel to a minimum.

● Travel in comfortable clothes—sweat suits or T-shirts and shorts are best—and pack a small bag of backup duds that are easy to get to. On summer car trips keep a bag with bathing suits and towels handy for quick dips.

● Don't travel at peak hours on either airplanes or the road if any other option exists;

otherwise tempers, including children's, can fray.

● On airplanes, get on last, rather than first (as most airlines suggest), so your kids can be active as long as possible and haven't tried all the activities they've brought before the plane even takes off.

● If you have kids over the age of 5, you can carry a cache of quarters for the video games and vending machines at highway plazas and gas stations.

● In the car, do not assume that kids over 9 want to sing "100 bottles of beer on the wall" or engage in any other (in Gavin's words) "dopey games" from your own childhood long, long ago. Do assume that whatever music you play will be torture to older kids' ears, especially if they are teenagers. Bring a headset and a small cassette player for each child.

● We stop frequently en route and include short adventures along the way by getting off the interstate to explore a town or arranging our route to pass state parks so we have more attractive spots for picnics and even a swim. This takes longer but is much more fun and ensures that kids arrive at your ultimate destination still enthusiastic.

Great Games for the Road

Most kids we know quickly get down to the basics: "I'm bo-o-o-o-red" and "How much longer before we get there?" One way to counteract that is with car games; the best ones don't require much in the way of equipment or props, relying instead on everyone's quick wits. Listed below are our favorites; some good books of other games are *Glove Compartment Games* (Klutz Press, 1997) for kids ages 9–12; *Family Fun Games on the Go: 150 Games, Activities and Tips for Vacationing Families* by Lisa Stiepock (Hyperion, 1998); *Miles of Smiles: 101 Great Car Games and Activities* by Carole Terwilliger Meyers (Carousel Press, 1992); and *52 Fun Things to Do on the Plane* by Lynn Gordon (Chronicle,

1995). *Are We There Yet?* (available at toy stores and from L. L. Bean, tel. 800/809–7057) is a great card game challenging kids to spot certain things on the road.

2–4 **What's in the Cup?** Take turns dropping a coin, key, crayon, grape, or other small object into a hard plastic cup. Shake it, and then see if anyone can guess what's in it.

4–8 **I Spy.** One child starts by "spying" something, such as a red barn, then announces, "I spy something red." Whoever guesses what it is becomes It next. Limit choices to inside or outside the car.

4–12 **Animal Lookout.** Give points for animals spotted; the winner is the person with the highest total when you arrive at your destination. In our version dogs and cats were worth 1 point; chipmunks and squirrels, 2 points; farm animals (horses, cows, chickens, sheep), 3 points; deer, rabbits, and birds, 5 points; snakes, moose, and other unlikely specimens, 10 points.

4–12 **Collect the Alphabet Game.** We compete to see who can find all the letters of the alphabet, in sequence, first. We permit only one letter for each sign, billboard, license plate, and so on, per player. The letters q and z are the toughies.

4–12 **Pink Toads.** It must answer any question asked of him or her with the phrase "Pink Toads" without laughing. Other players try to provoke laughter by asking what Its favorite breakfast is or what It always takes to bed with him or her or what he or she most hopes to get for a birthday present. Whoever makes It laugh becomes It for the next round. Gavin and his friends found this a much more hilarious game than John and I did. For the most fun, use other silly phrases, changing frequently.

5+ **I'm Taking a Trip.** To us this is a classic. The first person says, "I'm taking a trip and packing an apron." The second person repeats the sentence and adds an item beginning with the letter b, and so on, until someone forgets one item.

(**5+**) **Treasure Hunt**. With your kids, draw up a list of items to look for along the way. A few examples: a hay wagon, a cement mixer, a black dog, a bridge, and a waterfall. Twenty to 30 items are sufficient; if your kids are older, add in a few hard ones, such as a burned-down house or an auto graveyard. En route, check them off as they're spotted.

(**5 – 12**) **Counting Cows**. One person counts the cows in fields on one side of the road; the other person counts those on the opposite side; when you pass a graveyard, the person whose side it is on must bury his or her cows and start again. To keep the game manageable, pick an end point—until you stop for lunch or reach a turnoff.

(**6 – 14**) **Round-Robin Story**. One person begins a tale, stopping after 10 sentences or an agreed-upon time limit (one or two minutes for little kids, longer for older ones). Then another storyteller adds to it, and so on until the last person has to wrap up a conclusion. We found it fun to tape these and play them later.

(**10+**) **Twenty Questions**. You probably know how to play this game, but if not, read on. One player thinks of a person, place, or thing for others to guess. We sometimes mention one clue, as in "I'm thinking of something inside a house" or "I'm thinking of a place in New York City," to make it easy enough for younger kids. The other players can ask up to 20 questions (only if they can be answered with "yes" or "no") to help them guess.

(**10+**) **Ghost**. Both John and I played this challenging game when we were kids, and Gavin likes it as much as we did then. The first player says the first letter of any word with more than four letters, but without saying the word. The next player adds a letter that would fit in a word he has in mind. Then the next player adds another letter, and so on. The point, however, is to add letters without completing any word. Whoever does (or can't think of a letter to add) is given

the letter G. The next time it happens he or she gets an H, and so on until someone completes the word "ghost" and is out of the game. The last player in the game wins.

Once You're There

When You Arrive

A couple of simple decisions can ease your first days at your destination.

● Arrive well before dark, preferably by 4 or 5 o'clock, so kids have time to explore and feel at home before they go to sleep. For us, jumping in a pool for a swim before dinner is the best start to a vacation.

● If you've traveled all day in a car or a plane, set aside most of the next day for action-oriented activities: swimming and digging at a beach, exploring a city park and playground, patting animals at a farm. Picnic instead of eating in restaurants, or splurge the first night by ordering from room service and watching a movie.

Day by Day

Planning loosely and leaving room for spontaneity can improve your stay.

● Plan days to include a variety of activities: a morning at a terrific museum followed by a picnic in a park where kids can feed ducks and climb statues will work better than trying to pack all the museums into one day. Include time at playgrounds, parks, or other green spaces every day, and be back at your hotel or resort early enough for kids to chill out and relax, take a nap, or swim in the pool before dinner.

● Underplan. Schedules that are too tight don't leave time for those serendipities that are the delight of travel. Also, kids love to repeat what they've liked—go back to a great kids' museum, eat at the same restaurant two or three times, walk down a street or stop in a shop again.

- If your older kids are not that keen on historic sites—and there are many in the Northeast—focus on the gruesome ones where a massacre took place, six men were hanged, witches were stoned, skeletons were found. Many school-age kids respond to blood and gore.

- Build in time away from each other on longer vacations. Kids like to spend some time with others their own age instead of just siblings, and vacations should give parents a break, too. Resorts and hotels that have children's programs offer the easiest solution.

Staying Healthy

Anyone traveling in the Northeast needs to be concerned about poison ivy and Lyme disease, a bacterial infection transmitted by some, but not all, deer ticks, which are found on animals but also on tall grass or trees in the deep woods. Deer ticks are very tiny, resembling a small black dot about the size of a pinhead; they are most active during June and July, though prevalent from April through October. If you see one, pull it out gently and slowly with tweezers; be careful not to leave any part of the tick under the skin. Save it in a jar to show your doctor. Minimize your chance of exposure by wearing long, light-color (so ticks are easier to spot) pants tucked into boots, and long-sleeved shirts, using a good insect repellent, and checking clothing and bodies carefully after hiking.

When Kids Have to Wait

Everyone in our family hates waiting in line or being stuck in traffic, and I don't know any kids who handle these situations with grace. The younger they are, the harder it is. Unfortunately, if you visit popular sights (the Statue of Liberty, for example) and resort areas in the Northeast on peak weekends and in summer, you'll have to face these problems sometimes, though lines and traffic will not compare to what our friends

have encountered at Florida's Disney World. Our strategy is as follows. First, avoidance whenever possible. Throughout the book I've indicated the least crowded times for sights where you can expect a wait. As a general rule of thumb, arrive just before opening time on a weekday; for outdoor sights, aim for a cloudy but not actually rainy day. The hours between 11 and 3 on weekends are usually the most crowded no matter where you go, whether beaches or museums; at restaurants the least crowded times are early—11 for lunch; 5:30 to 6 for dinner, which is usually better for little kids anyway. Never visit any popular sight on a free-admission day in summer. Traffic jams are most common on Friday and Sunday nights beginning with the Fourth of July weekend and continuing through Labor Day weekend. Our family decides together in advance how long we are willing to wait to get into an attraction and we discuss how we can entertain ourselves. It's important to know your family's tolerance level, which will depend on both age and temperament. At most sights attendants can generally give you a fairly accurate estimate of waiting time; if it's too long, we leave. Another solution is for one parent to wait in line (this works best for paying entry fees) while the other whisks kids off for a nearby bench picnic or walk. Come prepared with books and game ideas, such as the car games above, and snacks.

Eating Out with Kids

THE PLEASURES OF PICNICS. One of the family trips I most enjoyed as a child was a car tour through New England. My sister and I had extracted a promise from my parents that we could picnic at every meal, including breakfast. They honored this promise even on a drizzly morning; as there was no park near our motel, we ate cereal and milk out of individual boxes while sitting on gravestones under a big overhanging tree. It was the highlight of our trip. When Gavin was little, he, too, considered picnicking the meal mode of choice because it is totally informal, you don't have to wait to be served, and you can jump around, make noise, and do all those things that are not considered "restaurant behavior" in our or any other family. And it's a way to save money.

On warm-weather trips, we usually scheduled a daily lunch picnic outside in a park when Gavin was younger, but indoor picnics in a hotel room really made us feel as though we were on vacation, no matter what the season. A breakfast picnic of cereal and milk, fresh fruit, and boxed juices is easy to assemble (best if you have an in-room refrigerator) and ready more quickly than room service (older kids, however, love ordering by telephone even if they have to wait). The first night you arrive at a hotel or motel is a good time for a dinner picnic of sandwiches, chips, carrot and celery sticks, and cookies; most little kids don't perform well in any kind of restaurant when they're tired and cranky from being cooped up in a car or plane. They welcome the chance to relax and explore the room, closets, and bathroom.

ON THE ROAD. Kids always seem to get hungry long before anything is served on a plane or in a restaurant, so I keep a bag of snacks in the backpack I carry while sightseeing, and let kids choose food to carry in theirs, too. Our family is partial to bite-size crackers and cookies, trail mix, grapes (good when frozen), oranges, small boxes of raisins, granola bars, and pretzels. Bananas get too squishy and apples develop bruises. When Gavin was a toddler, we tied a bagel on a string to his car seat so that he could pull it up and mouth it when he felt like chewing on something. For drinks we favor box juices, individual bottles of mineral water (these are expensive but can be refilled with tap water for hikes), and a few cans of soft drinks. If you freeze juice boxes the night before you leave, they'll stay cold for a long time. All these are easier to handle than pouring from a big jug or thermos while the car is moving (though not as ecologically desirable). For older kids, freeze a plastic squirt or sport bottle half full of water, then add cold water just before you leave.

IN RESTAURANTS. We extend our basic vacation travel principle—that everyone in the family should have fun—to restaurants. This means occasional, sometimes frequent, stops at fast-food restaurants, which have the added advantage of providing large, clean bathrooms that are usually more pleasant than those at service stations. When you're on the road or in doubt, the reliable New England–based restaurant chain Friendly's is particularly welcoming to families. All the restaurants listed in this book welcome children, but if yours are under 3, I advise frequenting those that offer booster seats or high chairs and, whenever possible, sitting in a booth or outdoor café section instead of in the middle of the restaurant's action. Though some do stock crayons for drawing on paper tablecloths, I always carried a restaurant survival kit of crackers and finger food to munch, washable markers and a tablet, and sometimes finger puppets for the wait, as well as a damp washcloth in a zip-shut bag. Our best strategy, however, was not sitting down until the food was on the table. This is easy if you eat in a restaurant in your hotel, as many will allow you to order from your room and tell you when your meal should be ready. Elsewhere, one parent can do the ordering while the other walks around with the kids outside.

In the Northeast, you certainly don't have to stick with fast-food spots to find meals appealing to kids. Many restaurants have special children's menus (usually limited to children age 12 and under), and some allow children to order from the adult menu for half price. One solution that worked for us when Gavin and his friends were older was to stay at a hotel with an elegant restaurant; we ate there and ordered a pizza delivered to our hotel room for the kids. They loved watching whatever they wanted on TV while eating with their fingers—and we were just downstairs in case they needed us.

Where to Stay with Kids

Among the kids I know, many prefer to stay in a chain hotel or motel rather than a very individual hotel. They like to know what to expect—one Howard Johnson's looks much like another, including the restaurants—and let's face it, kids are more comfortable with what's familiar. Many of these hotels and resorts now actively court family business by offering special deals, some of which allow kids to stay free in a room with their parents. Others let families rent adjoining rooms at discounts, which is a great way for parents to have some privacy. You can get the same effect, often for less money, by staying at an all-suite hotel, an increasingly popular choice for families.

Finding bed-and-breakfasts that welcome young children can be difficult. Many are filled with fragile antiques; serve communal breakfasts of fruit, bran muffins, and yogurt (not exactly child-pleasers); and seldom have a TV in the rooms. A few reservation services list B&Bs that welcome children and will match families with accommodations that fit their needs.

Condo rentals are becoming increasingly popular for families because they usually offer you more space for less money and the chance to save even more by cooking your own meals. Best bets for families are those at year-round ski resort areas, which usually offer children's and family programs, family discounts, and a wide variety of sports activities.

See the Directory of Resources *below* for toll-free numbers of prominent chains with properties in the Northeast that have recently offered attractive children's programs and discounts. Telephone numbers for B&B reservation services are also listed.

Saving Memories

Think about ways you can savor your trip after you get home.

• To most kids, part of the fun of travel is buying souvenirs. To keep this habit from becoming too expensive, a Boston family we know lets each child pick out a postcard at every stop. One year they wrote a few lines on each card, which they sent to themselves; when they returned home, they delighted in remembering the places they'd visited and what they most enjoyed at each. Other families encourage their kids to start collections: pencils, key chains, napkins, seashells, rocks, and leaves.

• Part of the fun of a family trip is remembering later the wonderful, awful, and funny things that happened. Encourage kids to put together their own scrapbook and journal of the trip even if they can't write. We always packed a spiral notebook or homemade notebook of stapled construction paper, a glue stick, tape, and locking plastic bags in which to collect souvenirs of the trip, such as a subway token, a special leaf, menus, postcards, napkins, and so on. Each evening Gavin glued everything from that day into his book and dictated (later wrote) a sentence or two. Now it's fun to reread them and laugh—I hope your travels will inspire as many good memories.

PART II

PLEASURES

Top Family Activities and Destinations by Category

HISTORIC STRUCTURES AND FAMOUS SITES
FORTS, LIGHTHOUSES, CASTLES, AND SKYSCRAPERS

The Northeast's landscape is saturated with famous and historic sites, not surprising when you consider that this is where the Pilgrims landed, the American Revolution unfolded, and the industrial revolution came to the states. Take advantage of this cornucopia of exploration possibilities by seeking out places that interest everyone in the family. It's not just the biggest and most famous places that are worth seeing. Smaller houses, forts, and villages are more fun for young children—they don't seem so overwhelming.

The Northeast's historic sites certainly offer an education, but kids absorb more just from taking in the atmosphere of a place. Many sites are staffed by costumed interpreters who invite kids to join in such activities as baking bread, picking crops, and using an old printing press. Reading *Johnny Tremain, The Courage of Sarah Noble, The Witch of Blackbird Pond,* and Jean Fritz's books for young readers about Sam Adams and Paul Revere may spark even more interest. I've mentioned other pre-trip movie and book possibilities under individual sites.

Connecticut

Gillette Castle State Park

(**ALL**) Perched high on a cliff overlooking the Connecticut River, this 24-room, oak-and-fieldstone medieval-looking structure combines the odd, the outrageous, and the tacky—all the more fun for kids to explore, even if some of it is in disrepair. Call before visiting, as renovations of the overgrown walkways and castle begun in 1998 are expected to take 18 months. During that time some areas of the grounds will remain open, but the castle will be closed. When it reopens, guides will resume giving the 15-minute history of the castle every hour on the main floor; it includes amusing stories about eccentric cat- and frog-loving William Gillette, the actor (noted for his portrayal of Sherlock Holmes) who built the castle between 1914 and 1919. Kids can search for Gillette's cat memorabilia (including cat-shape salt and pepper shakers, black cat bookends, and 100 scrapbooks with pictures of cats) in the castle's rooms. You get the best view of the castle coming over the river on the Chester-Hadlyme Ferry. It runs daily (Mon.–Fri. 7 AM–6 PM, weekends 10:30–5; follow Rte. 148 to the river; $2.25 for car and driver, 75¢ each additional person), and the trip takes a mere five minutes.
🏛 *67 River Rd. (off Rte. 82), East Haddam 06423, tel. 860/526–2336. Cost: $4 adults, $2 kids 6–11. Call for hrs.*

Mystic Seaport

(⭐ ALL) A re-creation of a 19th-century coastal village, Mystic Seaport is one of three living-history museums in the Northeast that our family consider must-sees (Plimoth Plantation and Old Sturbridge Village in Massachusetts are the other two). Its 40 riverfront acres contain some 60 shops, homes, and workplaces, including a shipyard and docks filled with historic tall ships and fishing craft. Of the three tall ships you can board, Gavin's favorite is the *Charles W. Morgan*, the last of America's wooden whalers. Another ship to be sure to see is the full-scale re-creation of the 80-ft freedom schooner, *Amistad*, which is being built in the shipyard and will be completed in 2000. Several scenes in the movie *Amistad* were actually filmed at the seaport, and a new exhibit tells the story through props from the film. If your kids are under 8, a stop at the Children's Museum is a must; here kids can dress in sailor's garb, climb into a bunk, peek out a porthole, swab a deck, and climb on rigging. For kids 8 and up, the Discovery Barn encourages adventures like walking out on a yardarm. Plan to spend an entire day at Mystic Seaport—unless your kids are toddlers.

Mystic's one drawback is the lack of protective railings along wharves and waterfront streets. Bringing an energetic and unpredictable 2-year-old may doom you to a day of nervous vigilance and constant hand-grabbing. If you hate crowds, avoid big weekends such as the Fourth of July and consider visiting off-season. During the summer there are activities for kids every day (no extra charge); many special events take place throughout the year, but two stand out for us—the Sea Music Festival in June when musicians perform on the decks of ships and the Lantern Light Tours (for kids 10 and up; $18 adults, $14 kids 5–15) on various December evenings. On these you join in a Victorian Christmas drama in which actors play the parts of townsfolk; kids get to sing along with carolers, be part of the dancing, meet St. Nick, eat gingerbread, and have impromptu conversations with the actors. The cost for special events held in the evening when the Seaport is normally closed varies.

🏛 *Mystic Seaport (1 mi south of I-95 on Rte. 27, Exit 90), Box 6000, Mystic 06355–0990, tel. 860/572–5315 or 888/972–7678. Cost: $16 adults, $8 kids 6–12. Open Apr.–Oct., daily 9—5; Nov.–Mar., daily 10–4.*

Old New-Gate Prison and Copper Mine

(⭐ 7–15) You descend the tunnel stairway into the dark, dank underground chambers and passageways of the Colonial mine (opened in 1707) that in 1776 became the nation's first state prison, housing burglars, horse thieves, and British sympathizers. The guides posted along the way tell stories of prisoners' ingenious escapes. The journey takes about 20 minutes if you don't linger. The atmosphere is cold (bring a sweater) and creepy. The aboveground guardhouse can also be explored, and there are places to picnic and a nature trail around a pond nearby. All explorations are self-guided.

🏛 *Newgate Rd., East Granby 06026, tel. 860/653–3563 or 860/566–3005. Take Exit 40 off I-91 to Rte. 20, then west to East Granby. Cost: $3 adults, $1.50 kids 6–17. Open mid-May–Oct., Wed.–Sun. 10–4:30.*

Sheffield Island Lighthouse

(⭐ 6–13) My husband is fascinated by island lighthouses, but few are open to the public. A regularly scheduled half-hour ferry ride takes you to this one—a two-story cut-stone keeper's house with a two-story lighthouse on top—on a 50-acre island in Long Island Sound. You can walk up to the light room and observation platform, from which you can see the tops of buildings in New York City on a clear day. Most of the island is a National Wildlife Refuge filled with birds; you can picnic and walk, and for $40 per person, you can attend one of their Thursday-night clam-bakes.

🔔 *Sheffield Island ferry service, Norwalk Seaport Association, 132 Water St., South Norwalk 06854, tel. 203/838–9444. From Hope Dock, corner of Washington and North Water Sts. Cost: $10 adults or kids. Open weekends and holidays Memorial Day–June, ferries leave at 10, 12:30, 3; daily July–Labor Day, ferries 9:30 and 1:30 on weekdays, 9:30, 11:30, 1:30, 3:30 on weekends and holidays.*

Maine

Ft. Knox State Park

(👬 3 – 15) Bring flashlights on your visit to Maine's largest fort, an impressive, enormous granite structure poised on a bluff above the Penobscot River; the dark underground tunnel (Long Alley) and massive, now-empty gunpowder storage rooms stemming from it are the most exciting parts to explore. Ask the ranger on duty to tell you how the fort was built in the 1830s to keep the British from sailing up the river during the Aroostook War. In either of the two granite spiral staircases that wind up to the ceiling, you can test out the fort's echo potential. At Civil War encampments held the last weekend of July and August, tents, colorful flags, and soldiers fill the parade ground. Picnic tables, fireplaces, a snack bar, and nature trails are outside the fort.

🔔 *Rte. 174 (just off Rte. 1), Prospect Harbor 04669, tel. 207/469–7719. Cost: $2 adults, 50¢ kids 5–11. Open May–Nov., daily 9–5; Memorial Day–Labor Day, daily 9–sunset.*

Ft. Popham

(👬 4 – 13) For pretending that a flotilla is about to attack and you're defending the coast, unfinished Ft. Popham can't be beat. The 500-ft-long, 30-ft-high granite crescent of archways and spiral staircases was erected during the Civil War to guard the mouth of the Kennebec River and the ship-yards upriver at Bath. It's right on the water at the tip of a flat peninsula, with clear views of boats on both sides. Nearby is an old cannon pointing out to sea. Two miles away is Popham Beach State Park, which has a great 1½-mi-long sand beach.

🔔 *Ft. Popham, Rte. 209, Phippsburg 04562, tel. 207/389–1335. Cost: Free. Open Memorial Day–Sept., daily 9–sunset.*

Ft. William Henry and Colonial Pemaquid State Historic Site

(👬 5 – 12) A round brick-and-stone tower fort is great for climbing (as are the stone walls outside it for jumping off). You can fish from the dock by the small riverside restaurant. In addition, there's an ongoing archaeological excavation of a fishing village that dates back to 1625. A small museum displays a miniature model of the village, plus some 100,000 artifacts (ask for the kids' museum searches for different ages), which helped us picture the original buildings. A resident archaeologist is available most summers to tell you about the history of the village and the three forts built to protect it. The Colonial Pemaquid restaurant next door serves lunch and dinner on a dock and a deck.

🔔 *Entrance on Rte. 130, about 13 mi south of Rte. 1 (no street address), New Harbor 04554, tel. 207/677–2423. Cost: $1 adults. Open Memorial Day–Labor Day, daily 9:30–5.*

Pemaquid Point Lighthouse and Fisherman's Museum

(👬 5 – 15) At the tip of the Pemaquid peninsula stand the charming little lighthouse keeper's house that's now a museum, a grove of tall pointed firs, and a picturesque lighthouse built in 1827. What makes this site so special is the long, ½-mi-wide finger of spectacular exposed rock ledges that leads, almost like a stairway, down to the crashing surf. The rocks form smooth, polished tables, tempting spots for spreading a picnic lunch, and they have just the right number of notches and crevices to make them perfect for climbing. Wear sneakers, avoid wet rocks (they're slippery), and don't go too close to the surf, where a wave can catch kids off balance and pull them into the water.

The lighthouse tower can't be visited, but stop in the adjoining museum for a look at the 28-pound lobster (found in Rhode Island), lobstering equipment, and some old-time photographs.
🏠 *End of Rte. 130, Pemaquid 04554, tel. 207/677–2494 or 207/677–2726. Cost: Park $1 adults, kids 12 and under free; museum donation. Open mid-May–mid-Oct., Mon.–Sat. 10–5, Sun. 11–5.*

Massachusetts

Boston Waterfront

(👫 **ALL**)   To get the full flavor of Boston, you have to walk along the wharves and piers that jut into its busy harbor. On the historic waterfront, renovated and rehabilitated, you can gaze at ferries and cruise boats, sit in cafés and parks, visit the world-class aquarium, and just stroll. The current Central Artery Tunnel construction (it's scheduled for completion in 2004) shouldn't affect the waterfront as it is affecting other parts of the city.

The official HarborWalk route, the blue line prominently marked on the pavement from Christopher Columbus Park to the Children's Museum and across the Congress Street Bridge, takes you past four wharves. If you have young children, start by spending some time at the Christopher Columbus Park playground and fountain. Long Wharf, Boston's oldest, has a breezy small park (perfect for a picnic), where kids can take a look at boats in the harbor through free telescopes. India and Rowes wharves have brick apartment towers and a hotel with cupolas, colonnades, and oddly shaped steps, as well as a ferry terminal and an outdoor café. At the James Hook Lobster

Company next to the Northern Bridge, you can ogle huge lobsters in a saltwater tank. Families munching lunch cluster around the big new harbor seal exhibit (it's free!) in front of the **New England Aquarium** on Central Wharf. *See also* Chapter 4, New England Aquarium.
🏠 *Waterfront between Christopher Columbus Park and Northern Ave. Bridge. Maps at Boston Common Visitor's Center, tel. 617/426–3115, open Mon.–Sat. 8:30–5, Sun. 9–5; or National Park Service Visitor's Center, 15 State St., tel. 617/242–5642, open daily 9–5.*

Bunker Hill Monument

(👫 **6+**)   A towering obelisk marks the site of the first major battle of the American Revolution. The battle, a defeat for the colonists, is most remembered for Col. William Prescott's command to the citizen's militia, "Don't fire till you see the whites of their eyes." You can climb 294 steps to the top for a good view of the city. During the summer—mid-June through the end of August—musket-firing demonstrations take place Thursday through Sunday on the grounds of the monument. In the museum, 15-minute talks and dioramas relate the history of the battle.
🏠 *Breed's Hill, Monument Ave. (Bus 93 from Haymarket), Charlestown 02129, tel. 617/242–5641. Cost: Free. Open daily 9–5; last climb 4:30.*

Cranberry World

(👫 **5 – 13**)   At the Ocean Spray Visitor Center, in the midst of the Massachusetts cranberry bogs, the 45-minute self-guided run-through of everything you ever wanted to know about cranberries ends with tastes of cranberry juice. It's not for everyone, particularly not teens. Little kids, however, can become entranced with the buttons to push on the interactive displays and with the little machine that demonstrates how cranberries are bounced to determine their quality.
🏠 *225 Water St. (overlooking Plymouth Harbor, ¼ mi north of Plymouth Rock), Plymouth*

02360, tel. 508/747–2350. Cost: Free. Open May–Nov., daily 9:30–5:30.

Faneuil Hall Marketplace

(👫 **ALL**) This is what malls aspire to be but aren't. Boutiques, restaurants, food stalls, and flower stands spill out of three refurbished buildings onto cobblestone, traffic-free plazas. The place is filled with color, exotic food aromas, and swarms of adults and kids watching jugglers balance spinning plates, listening to guitarists play the blues, and just chowing down. If you have teens, this is the one place in Boston where I can confidently predict they will be happy.

The copper-domed center building has been known as Quincy Market since the 1830s. Restored in 1976, the inner hall is a prime food stall–browsing territory, where we tried everything from baked beans to gourmet fudge. It's flanked by canopies and pushcarts filled with jewelry and all kinds of stuffed toys. Facing it is colonial Faneuil Hall, where the virtues and drawbacks of the Revolution were debated in town meetings more than 200 years ago. Check out the grasshopper weather vane on top. Threaded throughout the two other buildings are more than 125 shops, restaurants, and food stalls. Pick up a brochure with a map at the information booth in the South Market Building. Walking on cobblestones is tiring. Wear sturdy shoes and think twice about bringing a stroller.
🏛 *Between Congress and Commercial Sts. (Information Booth tel. 617/338–2323: summer, South Market St., Entrance 3; winter, South Canopy, Quincy Market). Limited parking. Free entertainment Apr.–Oct., daily 11–11, more on weekends (schedule at Information Booth); shops open Mon.–Sat. 10–9, Sun. noon–6; restaurants open later.*

Freedom Trail

(👫 **7–15**) The Freedom Trail is a 3-mi self-guided walk that winds its way past 16 of Boston's most important historic sites. Unless your kids are avid American history

buffs, though, visit only the highlights: the Paul Revere House, the Old Granary Burial Ground, the Old South Meetinghouse (renovated in 1997), the USS *Constitution* in Charlestown, and the Old North Church where the enthusiastic guide brings the stories to life (and you can sit in the box pews).
🏛 *Freedom Trail Information Center, Tremont St. side of Boston Common. (Brochures also at National Park Service Visitor's Center, 15 State St., Boston 02109, tel. 617/242–5642.) Open daily 9–5.*

Hammond Castle Museum

(👫 **6–15**) Inventor John Hayes Hammond Jr., who made a fortune from his more than 400 patents (only Thomas Edison held more), built this version of a medieval castle in 1926. It sits on a steep rock ledge above Gloucester Harbor and has a moat, a drawbridge, parapets, and turrets. Like Gillette Castle in Connecticut, it's a mix of the awe-inspiring and the wacky, and it seems to be just what kids have in mind when they imagine living in a castle. Partway up the winding stairway to one 85-ft tower, you can peer into a small but not too creepy dungeon. In the interior courtyard, a deep, curved stone swimming pool was designed so that Dr. Hammond could dive into it from his bedroom window, and pipes in the skylight enabled him to create a mild drizzle or a teeming downpour. On Friday, Saturday, and Sunday for the last three weeks in October, the castle holds an annual haunted house. As even some 9-year-olds were scared, I recommend this event only for kids 10 and up who aren't easily frightened.
🏛 *80 Hesperus Ave. (off Rte. 123), Gloucester 01930, tel. 978/283–2080. Cost: $6 adults, $4 kids 4–12. Open Memorial Day–Oct. 1, daily 10–4, Oct. 2–31 (many special events) and Nov.–Memorial Day, weekends 10–4.*

Hancock Shaker Village

(👫 **8–13**) Hancock, the largest restored Shaker farming community in the Northeast, is one of the few historic sites in the

Berkshires that appeal to kids. The round stone barn and 20 other buildings here have none of the hustle-bustle, almost hectic quality of restorations such as Sturbridge. Guides explain and often demonstrate Shaker traditions, and kids love visiting the laundry to hear about Shaker inventions such as the clothespin. Don't miss the 19th-century water turbine and woodworking shop. You'll find new hands-on activities for kids throughout the village. Depending on the day, you might make cheese and butter in the dairy or use the double-handled rolling pin on pie dough in the kitchen. In the Family Discovery Room, kids can dress up in Shaker clothes, experiment with a quill pen, and try milking the life-size fiberglass cow, Mary Jane (water will come out). There are several annual events—our favorite is the Spring Farm Weekend—with many superb family activities.

🏠 Rte. 20 (at Rte. 41, 5 mi west of Pittsfield), Box 927, Pittsfield 01202, tel. 413/443–0188 or 800/817–1137. Cost: $13.50 adults, $5.50 kids 6–17, $33 family rate. Open Memorial Day–Oct., daily 9:30–5; Apr.–Memorial Day and Nov., adult and family reduced rates, guided tours only daily 10–3.

HMS *Bounty*

(👫 8–15) We're familiar with the story of the 1787 mutiny on the English ship HMS *Bounty* because my father collected books on the subject and shared his knowledge over many dinners. When this replica of the ship, which starred in the 1962 movie along with Marlon Brando and Trevor Howard, moved to Massachusetts in 1993, our visit became almost a pilgrimage. On the 40-minute tour, you're usually greeted by an actor playing Captain Bligh, and then mutiny leader Fletcher Christian takes you below. Each confides his side of the story, which kids may follow better if they've screened the movie first. Be warned that the ship often travels to Nantucket, New Bedford, and other locales for festivals on summer weekends, so be sure to call before visiting to make sure it's in port.

🏠 State Pier, Battleship Cove, Fall River 02722, tel. 508/673–3886 (information from Tall Ship Bounty Foundation, Inc., Box 990, Fall River 02722). Cost: $5 adults, $3 kids 5–12. Open Memorial Day–Labor Day, Sun.–Tues. and Thurs. 10–6, Fri.–Sat. 10–8.

John Hancock Tower Observatory

(👫 5–15) On a clear day you can see to New Hampshire, Vermont, and the Berkshires from this 60-story tower, the tallest in New England. You'll also enjoy a spectacular bird's-eye view of Boston's buildings, parks, bridges, and waters. Boston 1775, a dramatic presentation on the Revolution, played out on a circular, waist-high map model in an adjoining room, is worth seeing (if your kids are over 8).

🏠 John Hancock Tower, 200 Clarendon St. (observatory ticket office, corner Trinity Pl. and St. James Ave.), Boston 02116, tel. 617/572–6429. Cost: $5 adults, $3 students and kids 5–17. Open Apr.–Oct., daily 9 AM–11 PM (last ticket 10 PM); Nov.–Mar., Sun. noon–11.

Lowell National Historical Park

(👫 5–15) It's fitting that the nation's first urban national park is in the nation's first industrial city. The squared-off redbrick mill buildings and peaceful canals of Lowell National Historical Park offer families an unusual perspective on America's industrial revolution through hands-on exhibits, complete with churning noisy machinery and action-oriented tours. The 10-block area in downtown Lowell is a mix of old restored buildings, housing exhibits, and contemporary restaurants and shops. You can explore the park yourself by foot on brick promenades or by turn-of-the-century trolley (year-round and free), or on one of the many guided tours, some by boat through the 5½ mi of canals, others by a combination of boat, trolley, and foot. The park isn't a well-defined geographic area, so stop at the visitor center for the film, a good map, and a list of good lunch spots.

The essential stops: the Boott Cotton Mills Museum, where 88 power looms clatter and vibrate, and the Tsongas Industrial History Center in the same building, where kids can try out looms and play with a model of the canal system during scheduled family programs. If you have kids under 8, keep your time here short and stop in the Children's Corner for a puppet or magic show. The annual Lowell Folk Festival is worth attending.

🏠 *Visitor Center, Market Mills, 246 Market St. (Lowell Connector of I–495 to Exit 5N for Thorndike St., then follow national park signs), Lowell 01852, tel. 978/970–5000. Cost: Boat-and-trolley tour $4 adults, $2 kids 6–16; Boott Museum $4 adults, $2 kids 6–16; Tsongas programs $3 kids over 5. Open daily 8:30–5. Trolleys Mar.–Nov. Boat-and-trolley tour May–Oct.*

Minuteman National Historical Park

(👫 10–15) The heart of this park is the 20-mi winding, hilly road along which the first battles of the Revolution took place. You can drive the route, hopping in and out of the car to visit historic houses and sites, but it's hard to picture the bloody battles at these now peaceful spots. For us the most interesting part was following the wide path to the Old North Bridge, where the "shot heard round the world" was fired. Several visitor centers have maps and staff to answer questions. The Minuteman Center also has a film, exhibits, and a large diorama of the battle fought on April 19, 1775. On your way there you can stop at the Battle Green in Lexington, where the Revolution began. Each year the anniversary is marked with a colorful reenactment.

🏠 *Minuteman Visitors Center, 1 mi from Battle Green, off Rte. 2A, Concord 01742, tel. 781/862–7753. Cost: Free. Open Apr.–Oct., daily 9–5; North Bridge Visitor's Center, 174 Liberty St., Concord 01742, tel. 978/369–6993. Cost: Free. Open all yr, 9:30–4.*

Old Sturbridge Village

(👫 4–13) One of the country's largest living history museums sprawls out over a rolling 200-acre country landscape just like a real rural agricultural community of the 1830s. Shops and houses are clustered around a village green, while a working farm, several mills, a pottery, and a blacksmith shop lie farther out. Costumed interpreters busily engage in 19th-century chores; while talking to the printer and cooper, we felt we had been transported back in time.

There's too much here to do in just one day, and on the map everything looks closer together than it really is. Fortunately a horse-drawn wagon rolls back and forth between the village and the outlying area. Don't miss a session at the district school, even if you have to wait in line. A teacher in period dress treats visitors like pupils, giving you a vivid picture of what a day at school was like in the 1800s. Among the special programs we recommend are the Kids as Craftsmen program and the Family Fun Days. The annual Sheepshearing and Harvest Weekends are great fun for kids, as is the special First Night celebration on New Year's Eve. *A Gathering of Days* by Joan Blos (for ages 8–12) will give your kids a good sense of the period.

🏠 *1 Old Sturbridge Village Rd., Sturbridge 01566, tel. 508/347–3362 or 800/733–1830. Take Massachusetts Turnpike (I–90) to Exit 9, then Rte. 20 West. Cost: $16 adults, $8 kids 6–15, boat ride $3 adults and kids 4 and up. Open Nov.–Dec., daily 10–4; Apr.–Oct., daily 9–5; Jan.–Feb., call for hrs.*

Orchard House

(👫 8–14) Two girls we know who are fans of Louisa May Alcott's *Little Women* delighted in the 45-minute tour of the house the author shared with her father, Bronson. None of the rooms are roped off, so kids can pretend they've come for an afternoon visit. If they've read *Little Women* or seen the 1995 movie, they will undoubtedly spot items that are mentioned. The tour reveals little-known aspects of Alcott's life, such as her involvement in the women's rights movement.

🏠 *399 Lexington Rd., Box 343, Concord 01742, tel. 978/369–4118. Cost: $5.50 adults, $3.50 kids 6–18, $16 family rate. Open Apr.–Oct., Mon.–Sat. 10–4:30, Sun. 1–4:30; Nov.–Mar., weekdays 11–3, Sat. 10–4:30, Sun. 1–4:30.*

Paper House

👫 **5 – 12** All the furniture in the house—lamps, chairs, grandfather clock—is made of paper. The walls are 215 sheets thick, the writing desk is made only from newspaper reports of Charles Lindbergh's 1927 flight, and the bookcase consists of only foreign papers. The project started as a lark back in 1924 and finally drew so many tourists that the owners, a Boston couple, moved into another house next door.

🏠 *50 Pigeon Hill St. (across from Pigeon Cove Post Office), Rockport 01966, tel. 978/546–2629. Cost: Donation. Open mid-May–Oct., daily 10–5.*

Paul Revere's House

👫 **5 – 15** This small, gray-green, lopsided frame structure with tiny diamond-pane windows, in the midst of the larger buildings in Boston's North End, is the house from which the Boston silversmith made his famous ride to warn patriots in Middlesex County that the British were coming. It's the oldest building in Boston. Its cozy size (just four rooms) and crooked walls, and the brick courtyard and tiny garden outside have a special charm. Though you can't touch anything, the museum guides are quick to show you rope supports on the beds, point out Paul Revere's rocker, and tell you about bedbugs in the straw mattresses. It helps to read the information on the kiosk outside or the "Kid's Guide to the Paul Revere House," available for $1.50 from the ticket office, before you go in. Family programs are held Saturday afternoon from May through October.

🏠 *19 North Sq., Boston 02113, tel. 617/523–2338. Cost: $2.50 adults, $1 kids 5–17. Open Apr.–Oct., daily 9:30–5:15; Nov., daily 9:30–4:15; Jan.–Mar., Tues.–Sun. 9:30–4:15.*

Pilgrim Monument and Museum

👫 **6 – 15** The Pilgrims landed first in what's now Provincetown and even stayed here a month and signed the Mayflower Compact before sailing on to Plymouth. With its arches and turrets, the 252-ft-high granite tower built to commemorate the first landing is certainly more impressive than the official rock in Plymouth. The 116 steps (60 ramps) to the very top bring you to a view of dunes, harbor and boats, and, if you squint, Boston's skyscrapers.

🏠 *High-pole Hill on Winslow St., off Bradford St., Provincetown 02657-1125, tel. 508/487–1310. Cost: $5 adults, $3 kids 4–12 (includes monument, museum, and changing special exhibits). Open Apr.—June and Sept.–Nov., daily 9–5; July–Aug., daily 9–7.*

Plimoth Plantation, *Mayflower II,* and Hobbamock's Homesite

👫 **7 – 14** More than at any other such museum in the Northeast, visitors here feel as though they've actually been transported back in time to the year 1627. The essential 12-minute presentation at the visitor center tells you what to expect. Compared to Old Sturbridge and Mystic, this village of 20 humble, thatched-roof dwellings, barns, and storehouses resting on a gentle slope above Cape Cod Bay is simple and untouristy (though sometimes crowded). Paths are rough and dusty, and the smells of hay and farm animals fill the air as you walk around. Each actor (including children) in the village takes on the name, dress, and role of a specific Pilgrim who came from England on the Mayflower. They play their parts so completely that if you ask about anything that happened after

1627, they stay in character, look puzzled, and reply in a variety of dialects. Initially the kids with us felt shy, but they soon discovered that to have the most fun they had to wander into homes and barnyards and chat with the Pilgrims as they baked bread, thatched a roof, repaired a fence, and fed the chickens running around. Soon they were offering to help the Pilgrims, just as though they lived there too.

Be sure to visit Hobbamock's Homesite, a small Indian community of bark houses a short walk away, to see the contrast between the two cultures. Two and a half miles away, moored at State Pier in Plymouth Harbor, is the *Mayflower II*, a too-brightly painted replica of the famous ship, with interpreters who talk about the ship. **⚑** *Warren Ave., Rte. 3A, Plymouth 02362, tel. 508/746–1622 (mailing address: Box 1620, Plymouth 02362). Take Rte. 3 south to Exit 4, then follow signs. Cost: $18.50 adults, $11 kids 6–12; Plimoth Plantation only: $15 adults, $9 kids 6–12; Mayflower II only: June–Nov. $5.75 adults, $3.75 kids 6–12. Open Apr.–June and Sept.–Nov., daily 9–5.*

Plymouth Rock, Plymouth

(**ⵌ 5 – 15**) Though we'd warned Gavin that the rock the Pilgrims supposedly stepped on as they disembarked from the *Mayflower* in 1620 looks quite small (most of it is actually underground, and more than 3,000 pounds was chipped away by tourists in the past), at 9 he was still expecting something akin to the Rock of Gibraltar. Instead the rock has a crack running through it and the date 1620 carved in its side; the white-columned portico and iron bars around it look grander. But if you've come to visit Plimoth Plantation and *Mayflower II*, nearby, it might be worth five minutes so you can say you've seen it—along with the other 1.5 million yearly visitors. **⚑** *Water St. (overlooking harbor, near Mayflower II), Plymouth 02362, no phone. Cost: Free. Open daily, 24-hr access.*

Salem 1630 Pioneer Village

(**ⵌ 5 – 13**) The year in the country's oldest living history village is 1630, when Salem was a Puritan fishing settlement. A small-scale version of Sturbridge Village, it's less well known and less crowded and also has some unusual features, such as replicas of dugout houses—the kind the settlers lived in the first winter—and a few cottages with real thatch. The daily activities kids can join in are simple but fun, like helping to wash clothes in a stream, feeding sheep and goats, and carding wool. You can swim and picnic in the park. A combination ticket includes a visit to the nearby House of Seven Gables. **⚑** *Forest River Park, Salem 01970, tel. 978/744–0991 (mailing address c/o House of Seven Gables Historic Site, 54 Turner St., Salem 01970). Take Rte. 114 to West St., 2 mi from Salem State College. Cost: $5 adults, $3 kids 6–17. Combo ticket: $10 adults, $6 kids 6–17. Open Memorial Day–Oct., Mon.–Sat. 10–5, Sun. noon–5. House of Seven Gables open daily Apr.–June 10–4:30, July–Oct. 9–6, Jan.–Mar. Sun noon–4:30.*

New Hampshire

Fort No. 4

(**ⵌ 4 – 12**) Fort No. 4 gives you a taste of life on the frontier during the French and Indian Wars and a sense of what it was like to be confined and have danger lurking outside. The reproduction of the first tiny settlement at Charlestown, with a 10-ft-high wooden stockade, a lookout tower you can climb into, and simple cabins with dirt floors and lean-tos like the ones in which the original settlers lived, sits on a meadow on the Connecticut River. Costumed guides give cooking, candle-dipping, woodworking, and musket ball–molding demonstrations (on weekends), and barns and a blacksmith shop stand outside the fence. None of this is as impressive as Mystic or Sturbridge or Ft. Ticonderoga, even during one of the occasional militia musters, but its simplicity may be more appealing to young kids. 🏠 *Rte. 11, Springfield Rd., Charlestown 03603, tel. 603/826–5700. Cost: $6 adults, $4 kids 6–11. Open late May–mid-Oct., daily 10–4.*

Strawbery Banke Museum

(👬 **7–14**) At the 42 historic buildings in this 10-acre area of downtown Portsmouth restoration is an ongoing process. You can watch archaeologists, carpenters, gardeners, and others actively at work on projects in different stages of completion. The eight exhibit houses that have interpreters are not all from the same period; each one illustrates a different time period, from the 1600s to the 1950s, so it's fun to compare them and talk with the appropriately costumed role players. Abbots Corner Store harks back to wartime with ration cards; the Schapiro home tells the immigrant story. The visitor center has walking guides and posts times of demonstrations. During the summer (June through August) you can go aboard an old-fashioned sailboat with a folding mast. 🏠 *Marcy and Hancock Sts. (opposite Prescott Park and Portsmouth waterfront), Portsmouth 03802, tel. 603/433–1100 (mailing address: Box 300, Portsmouth 03802). Cost: $12 adults, $8 kids 7–17, $28 family; tickets good for 2 days. Open late Apr.–Nov. 1, daily 10–5.*

New York

Empire State Building

(👬 **ALL**) This 60-year-old skyscraper, a New York City landmark, probably needs no introduction, even to kids. Those who've never been to New York still know it from *King Kong, Sleepless in Seattle,* the IMAX film *Across the Sea of Time,* and countless other movies. Built in 1931, it's no longer the world's tallest building, but to

us its shape has more character than the ubiquitous glass-walled towers. More than 2½ million people visit each year, and you can see 50-mi views and five states on a clear day from the 86th-floor outdoor promenade or the 102nd-floor observatory. We like to come at sunset to watch the city light up. 🏠 *350 5th Ave. at 34th St., New York 10001, tel. 212/736–3100. Cost: $6 adults, $3 kids 5–12. Open daily 9:30 AM–midnight (last elevator up 11:30 PM).*

Farmer's Museum and 19th Century Village

(👬 **5–13**) Compared with such museum villages as Sturbridge and Mystic, the village at the Farmer's Museum, representing a typical upstate New York farming village in the late-19th century, is small, eclectic, and laidback, and it may be more fun for little kids. Sheep, chickens, and geese run around freely. The printer's shop, doctor's office, and so on are staffed by guides giving demonstrations, and now you can watch shoes being made in a shoe shop and workers manufacturing wallpaper by hand pressing. Each year the village is changing as new buildings are added and old ones moved. The museum itself, through which you enter the village, is a huge stone barn, where you can see spinning, weaving, and other demonstrations. Don't miss the stone carving that was passed off by a farmer–con artist as a petrified giant in one of the most famous hoaxes of the 19th century. This is a place to come while you're here to visit the nearby Baseball Hall of Fame (combined tickets are available), not a destination in its own right. 🏠 *Lake Rd. (off Rte. 80, 1 mi north of Cooperstown), Cooperstown 13326, tel. 607/547–1450. Cost: $9 adults, $4 kids 7–12; combined tickets (include Fenimore House Museum and Baseball Hall of Fame) $22 adults, $9.50 kids 7–12. Open Apr.–Nov., daily 10–4 (except closed Mon. Apr. and Nov.); June–Labor Day, daily 9–5; Dec. special events only.*

Ft. Ticonderoga

(👫 2–15) Everything about this restored 18th-century stone fort that figured so prominently in both the French and Indian Wars and the American Revolution struck us as impressive and imposing: the way it sits high, high above the southern end of Lake Champlain; the varied flags flying from the ramparts; its star shape of stone bastions; the dozens of bronze cannon poking out. Kids can watch booming cannon demonstrations and join in the fife and drum corps parades (July and August only). We got a stronger sense of life at a fort here than at any other fort in the Northeast. The 20- to 40-minute tours are a good introduction to the fort's basic structure and history; experienced guides tailor each one to the ages of those in the group. There's much to explore and do—a dungeon, exhibits of muskets, swords, and pistols, an underground bakery, and running on the parade ground.

🏛 Rte. 74, Box 390, Ticonderoga 12883, tel. 518/585–2821. Take I–87 to Exit 28, continue east 18 mi. Cost: $8 adults, $6 kids 7–12. Open early May–June and Sept.–late Oct., daily 9–5; July–Aug., daily 9–6.

Ft. William Henry

(👫 5–15) In the mid-18th century, this now-restored log fortress high above Lake George was an important wilderness outpost in the French and Indian Wars. The massacres that occurred when French troops seized it were the basis for James Fenimore Cooper's Last of the Mohicans. The fort, now owned by a corporation, makes an interesting contrast to the grander stone Ticonderoga farther north, but be warned that it has a hokier, somewhat commercial flavor. The short tour includes musket and cannon firings, a grenadier bomb toss, a musket ball–molding demonstration, and exploration of the underground powder magazine and dungeon. You can also watch the 1930s movie version of is Last of the Mohicans, but most kids will probably prefer the 1992 version—screen it before you come.

🏛 Canada St., Beach Rd., and Rte. 9 entrances, Lake George 12845, tel. 518/668–5471. Cost: $8.50 adults, $6.50 kids 4–11. Open May–mid-June and Labor Day–mid-Oct., daily 10–5; mid-June–Labor Day, daily 9 AM–10 PM.

Philipsburg Manor

(👫 ALL) A working water-powered gristmill that grinds corn and wheat every day, a farmyard of animals, and an old restored barn were the prime attractions for us at this 17th-century historic manor, on the Potanico River near the Hudson River. Once the commercial center of a 52,000-acre estate owned by Frederick Philipse, it shipped flour down the Hudson to New York City. The costumed miller often lets in the water and recruits kids to help pour the corn; the cornmeal can be purchased in the gift shop. Costumed interpreters are stationed throughout to answer questions and perform demonstrations. You may want to combine your visit to Philipsburg with trips to nearby Sleepy Hollow and Van Cortlandt Manor, but if you have time for only one, Philipsburg appeals to the widest age group. A pleasant café serves excellent sandwiches. This is also the place to come on Halloween for spooky stories and a visit to the Old Dutch Church graveyard nearby; apple harvest weekend is also fun.

🏛 Rte. 9 (2 mi north of Tappan Zee Bridge), North Tarrytown 10591, tel. 914/631–8200 (mailing address: Historic Hudson Valley, 150 White Plains Rd., Tarrytown 10591). Cost: $8 adults, $4 kids 6–17. Open Apr.–Dec., Wed.–Mon. 10–4; Mar., weekends 10–4.

Rockefeller Center

(👫 ALL) This complex of buildings and public plazas on 5th Avenue is a great place for strolling around, window-shopping, and people-watching. On the upper level, the Channel Gardens have flowers and pools; water jets spray a gold-leaf statue of Prometheus; and flags of the states and the

United Nations members wave. In winter skaters twirl on the lower level's ice rink. Don't miss the huge Christmas tree during the holidays. The Center also houses Radio City Music Hall and the GE Building (on the west side of the Lower Plaza between 49th and 50th Sts.), where NBC is located. Tours of the NBC Studios leave from the GE Building's lobby Monday through Saturday plus Sunday in summer, every 15 minutes 9:30–4:30. Kids especially like seeing the makeup rooms, special props, and the machinery in the studios.

🏚 *47th–52nd Sts. between 5th and 6th Aves. (Subway B, D, F, or Q to Rockefeller Center), New York, tel. 212/698–2950. Tour cost: $10.*

South Street Seaport Museum and Marketplace

(👫 **ALL**) Unlike Mystic Seaport in Connecticut, the 12-block South Street Seaport district of historic ships and restored buildings in lower Manhattan is both educational and commercial. Much of the Seaport reminds us of what New York must have looked like in the 19th century, when it was one of the great ports of the world. Back then the port must have had a bustling atmosphere; now the action comes from tourists, street performers, and free entertainment during the summer and winter holidays and a shopping mall–marketplace area. Sadly, in recent years the marketplace has gone downhill as interesting boutiques are being replaced by chain stores and restaurants of varying quality. Nevertheless, the South Street Seaport Museum with its historic ships is still going strong and offers enough to see and do to keep a family entertained for an afternoon.

To get a map and find out what's going on, stop at the Museum Visitor Center on Fulton Street or the Pier 16 Ticketbooth. For many kids, including mine, exploring the sailing ships moored at Pier 16, especially the four-masted 347-ft *Peking*, is the highlight. Other good stops: the Maritime Crafts Center to watch craftspeople work on models;

the boatbuilding shop, where small wooden boats are being restored; and the old print shop. The small Children's Center offers excellent hands-on workshops with a maritime focus.

You'll find food choices, from cafés to fast food, in the Food Court in Pier 17.

Steamers, a schooner, and a paddleboat make scheduled sails on the harbor in summer (we like the two-hour regular sails on the historic schooner *Pioneer*—check at the visitor center or call 212/745–8786), and tours of the historic Fulton Fish Market, the oldest fish market in the United States, take place twice a month from April through October. If you can rally the troops by 6 AM for the market tour, you'll see 600 varieties of fish while you soak in the frenetic atmosphere of people, pushcarts, and forklifts. One of our favorite annual events here is the Ship and Boat Model Festival at the beginning of August; you may see as many as 100 models on display and can participate in a model-making workshop. Another favorite exhibit (best for kids 8 and up), New York Unearthed: City Archaeology, is a nearby branch of the museum; we give thumbs up to the simulated ride down through the layers of an archaeological dig of New York City's history.

🏚 *19 Fulton St. (at East River; Subway 2, 3, 4, 5, J, M, or Z to Fulton St. or A or C to Broadway–Nassau), New York 10002, tel. 212/748–8600 (museum) or 212/732–7678 (marketplace). Cost: Museum $6 adults, $4 students with ID, $3 kids 5–12. Open Apr.–Sept., Fri.–Wed. 10–6, Thurs. 10–8; Oct.–Mar., Wed.–Mon. 10–5. South Street Seaport Marketplace open year-round.*

Statue of Liberty

(👫 **4–15**) This symbol of freedom on an island in New York Harbor is probably the best-recognized statue in the world. It was rated among New York's top 10 sights by every kid over 5 on my New York panel, and among the top 10 in the world by several. All insist that for the full effect it's necessary to climb the 354 steps (the equivalent of 22 stories) from the statue's pedestal to the crown. You go in a spiral, so it's easy to get dizzy (if you can move fast enough), especially on the last six or seven flights. Because of crowds, the pace can be agonizingly slow, and the climb has taken as much as two to even four (!) hours. Add to that the fact that in summer the temperature on the staircase has reached 100°F. As a result, in the summer of 1998, only those on the first boat in the morning—1,500 people—were allowed to climb to the top each day. If you plan to climb, bring water! You can ride an elevator to the top of the pedestal (10 stories), where, from the balcony, I think you get the best view of Manhattan. The exhibits at the base of the statue include her original torch and a model of her huge ear.

The ticket office for the ferry is in the center of Castle Clinton, a restored brick fortress in Manhattan's Battery Park. It takes the ferry only a few minutes to get to Liberty Island, where you can debark and visit the statue, then reboard any ferry to go on to Ellis Island, boarding another boat to return. Sounds simple. The problem is the crowds. Ask how long the wait is to get to the crown before you buy your ferry ticket, and if you come in the summer arrive in time for the first boat. Forget a sunny summer weekend, unless you arrive before the ticket office opens at 8:30. Saturday is less crowded than Sunday. In any case, plan on about four hours for your trip. Though there's a cafeteria and a snack bar, bring lunch and have a picnic outside. See also Chapter 3, Ellis Island and Immigration Museum.
🏠 Liberty Island, tel. 212/363–3200; ferry tel. 212/269–5755. Take Subway 1 or 9 to South Ferry or 4 or 5 to Bowling Green and Battery Park, then cross Battery Park to Circle Line office at Castle Clinton. Cost: Ferry $7 adults, $3 kids 3–17. Sept.–May departures daily every 30–45 mins, 9:15–3:30; June, every 20 mins, 9:15–3:30; July–Aug. extended hrs. Ferries also from Liberty State Park, Jersey City, New Jersey, tel. 201/435–9499.

Sleepy Hollow

(👫 6–14) Author Washington Irving, best known for The Legend of Sleepy Hollow and Rip Van Winkle, lived and worked in this romantic 17-room house he described as "full of angles and corners as an old cocked hat." You can enjoy its cozy-cottage, slightly mysterious, fairy-tale quality; a picnic by the swan pond; and the walking path with views of the Hudson River designed by Irving himself. For younger kids, a pre-visit screening of the Disney version of The Legend of Sleepy Hollow can be useful. Special tours for kids 5–10 are conducted every Thursday in August.

Combine a visit here with trips to Philipsburg Manor (3 mi north) and Van Cortlandt Manor (9 mi north), for which an all-in-one ticket is available. In summer, you can take a special boat tour from New York City and New Jersey to Tarrytown, where a waiting bus transports you first to Philipsburg Manor, then to Sleepy Hollow (NY Waterway, tel. 800/533–3779).
🏠 Rte. 9 (1 mi south of Tappan Zee Bridge), Tarrytown 10591, tel. 914/631–8200 (mailing address: Historic Hudson Valley, 150 White Plains Rd., Tarrytown 10591). Cost: $8 adults, $4 kids 6–17. Open Apr.–Dec., Wed.–Mon. 10–4; Mar., weekends 10–4.

Van Cortlandt Manor

(👫 3–14) This estate was occupied by the wealthy Dutch-American Van Cortlandt family for 300 years, and touring the grounds and several buildings gives kids a picture of family life around the time of the American Revolution. During that war, soldiers bivouacked here and left behind graffiti you can still see. At the Ferry House, a tavern on the estate, we learned that the price of accommodations in the 1700s was based on sharing a bed with as many as five strangers. A blacksmith gives demonstrations, the kitchen in the tenant house is sometimes good for a few cookies made from old Dutch recipes, and at special

events kids may dance to fiddle music or be allowed to help mix clay with their bare feet in the brick-making pit. Lovely gardens and brick paths provide exploring space.
🏛 *Croton Point exit off Rte. 9 (9 mi north of Tappan Zee Bridge, accessible by Metro North trains), Croton-on-Hudson 10520, tel. 914/ 631–8200 (mailing address: Historic Hudson Valley, 150 White Plains Rd., Tarrytown 10591). Cost: $8 adults, $4 kids 6–17. Open Apr.–Oct., Wed.–Mon. 10–4; Nov.–Dec., weekends only 10–4.*

West Point (United States Military Academy)

(👫 7–15) America's oldest and most distinguished military academy, perched on bluffs above the Hudson River, is also a historic military site with statues, monuments, cannons, a museum, and restored forts that appeal to many kids. If you can, time a visit to coincide with a football game preceded by dress parades of cadets in colorful uniforms and brass bands. *See also* Chapter 8, Football.
🏛 *U.S. Military Academy, Visitors Center, West Point 10996, tel. 914/938–2638. Take Rte. 9W to Highland Falls, then follow signs. Admission free; tours $5 adults, $2.50 kids under 12. Visitor center open daily 9–4:45.*

World Trade Center and Observation Deck

(👫 ALL) At 110 floors each, these two skyscrapers are New York City's tallest towers. On a clear day the view from the open-air Rooftop Promenade at the top of Two World Trade Center (still the world's highest outdoor observation platform), or the indoor observation deck on the 107th floor, is fantastic. Check the visibility before you buy your tickets, but even if it's a little cloudy it's still fun; kids can look down on clouds clustered around the towers. The ear-popping elevator ride to the top, with the wind howling down the elevator shaft, is also a thrill. The 1997 renovation added three theaters in which you can take a six-minute simulated

helicopter ride around the city (great! say kids on my New York panel) and a neat kinetic ball sculpture.

The plaza between the two towers has shops and restaurants, and there's often free entertainment, some specifically for children, on selected weekends and during the winter holidays.
🏛 *Church St. and Cortlandt St. (Subway 1, 9, or N to Cortlandt St. or A, C, or E to Chambers St.), New York 10047, tel. 212/435–4170 information on events, 212/323–2340 observation center. Cost: $12 adults, $6 kids 6–12. Open daily 9:30 AM–11:30 PM.*

Rhode Island

The Astors' Beechwood

(👫 8+) While seeing the Breakers is a matter of oohing and aahing on a formal tour, visiting the Astors' Beechwood, the summer cottage of "The Mrs. Astor" (as she wished to be called) is like entering a Newport version of the TV series *Upstairs Downstairs* and much more fun for younger kids. Members of the Beechwood Theatre Company assume the roles of the Astors' gossipy servants and eccentric guests getting ready for a dinner hosted by the Mrs. Astor's daughter; they welcome you as a guest, gossiping to you about their mistress as they show you through the mansion. The tour lasts about an hour. On Tuesday nights you can attend an evening of 1890s music and dance.
🏛 *580 Bellevue Ave., Newport 02840, tel. 401/846–3772. Cost: $8.75 adults, $7.25 students with ID, $6.75 kids 6–13, $25 family rate. Open mid-May–Oct., daily 10–5; Nov.– Dec., daily 10–4; Feb.–mid-May, weekends only 10–5; closed Jan.*

The Breakers

(👫 8+) Cornelius Vanderbilt II built his 70-room, four-story summer "cottage," the

Breakers, on the Atlantic Ocean in 1895. No other mansion we've seen in the Northeast is so magnificent. In this American version of a northern Italian palace, gilt and painted ceilings, grand staircases, massive carved archways, ornate paneling, and bathrooms with both salt- and freshwater taps evoke the era appropriately called the Gilded Age. The Children's Cottage is the ultimate fantasy playhouse; even the elaborate furniture is kid-size. During weekends in summer don't miss the wonderful miniature New York Central trains in the stable. You can buy a combination ticket that admits you to additional mansions, but a little of this goes a long way with kids.
🏠 *Ochre Point Ave., Newport 02840, tel. 401/847–1000. Cost: $10 adults, $4 kids 6–11. Open late Mar.–Oct., daily 10–5 (July–Aug., Sat. until 6).*

Flying Horse Carousel, Watch Hill Lighthouse, and Napatree Point

(👫 3–10) In a town full of Victorian houses is the oldest and prettiest merry-go-round in America. It's now a National Historic Landmark and may be the lone site in the Northeast that's just for kids. The horses of the ride have real tails and manes, leather saddles, and agate eyes and swing out on chains when they're in motion, rather than just going up and down on a pole. A short walk away on Lighthouse Road is a charming lighthouse, rocks to climb on, and fishermen to watch. Still farther is Napatree Point, a long sandy spit of land that's one of the nicest beach walks around, especially on the Fourth of July, when all the boats are sailing by.
🏠 *Bay St., Watch Hill, no phone (Chamber of Commerce tel. 800/732–7636). Cost: 50¢. Carousel open June 15–Labor Day, weekdays 1–9, weekends and holidays 11–9: lighthouse, Tues. and Thurs. 1–3.*

Vermont

Ben & Jerry's Ice Cream Factory

(👫 3–15) This factory is where 36 million pints of this ice cream are made each year. If your kids have never seen an ice-cream or candy factory and you're nearby, the short tour and the gift shop—black-and-white cow hats, socks, mugs, sweatshirts, glasses, T-shirts, and so on—are worth a visit. Be prepared for unbelievably corny jokes during the slide show. Don't miss the miniature model of the factory.
🏠 *Rte. 100 (Exit 10 off I–89), Waterbury 05676, tel. 802/244–5641. Cost: $2 adults and kids over 12. Open daily 9–5.*

Billings Farm and Museum

(👫 ALL) This 350-acre historic working dairy farm illustrates to kids what living on a farm was like in the 19th century, in a more personal and intimate way than most other living-history villages. You can walk anywhere you like in the rambling 1890s farmhouse, for example, just as though you were a friend of the family, and join any of the staff in their 19th-century tasks. In the kitchen, where workers (who are not in costume) are always cooking something, kids can peel apples with an old mechanical peeler. In the basement creamery, even toddlers can help make the butter in old-fashioned churns—and taste it spread on crackers. If you come during cider-making season, you can help press and drink. The farm-life museum in four connected barns houses both exhibits and demonstrations.
🏠 *Rte. 12, Woodstock 05091, tel. 802/457–2355. Cost: $7 adults, $1 kids 3–4, $3.50 kids 5–12, $5.50 kids 13–17. Open May–Oct., daily 10–5; Nov.–Dec., call for hrs.*

Rock of Ages Granite Quarry

(👫 6–13) One of the most unusual and imposing sights in the Northeast is the view of the world's largest granite quarry from an observation platform. Huge 40-ton blocks of stone are being carved out by machines, then hauled up from a pit the size of a football field by derricks so big they reminded us of dinosaurs. On the self-guided walking tour the noise assaults you. At the visitor center, besides checking out the exhibits, you can purchase tickets for a 35-minute bus ride (offered weekdays only) right into the work areas farther uphill. Perhaps most interesting of all is watching men and machines polish, shape, and carve the blocks into finished products from the platform above the Craftsman Manufacturing Center (open weekdays 8–3:30) a mile from the visitor center.

🏠 *Exit 6 off I–89, Box 482, Barre 05641, tel. 802/476–3119, ext. 202. Admission free, bus tour $4 adults, $1.50 kids 6–12, kids under 6 free. Visitor center open May–Oct.,* *Mon.–Sat. 8:30–5, Sun. noon–5; bus tour June–mid-Oct., weekdays 9:15–3.*

Vermont Teddy Bear Company

(👫 **1 – 15**) Little kids usually like to see how familiar items are made; this entertaining half-hour factory tour, conducted by local actors, shows how jointed teddy bears are cut out, stuffed, and sewn. Come before 11 or after 3 in summer or you may have to wait as much as an hour. In the shop, jammed with hundreds of teddy bears in different sizes and colors to purchase, kids can even stuff their own bears. On weekends in July and August a tent on the factory grounds offers kid activities.

🏠 *6655 Shelburne Rd., Shelburne 05482, tel. 802/985–3001. Cost: $1 adults and kids over 12. Open Mon.–Sat. 9–6, Sun. 10–5.*

MUSEUMS, PLANETARIUMS, AND HALLS OF FAME
DINOSAURS, MUMMIES, WITCHES, AND ROBOTS

An Italian palazzo filled with paintings, the country's finest dinosaur display, a theater where you can watch a machine create lightning, the world's first nuclear-powered submarine, the history of baseball on three floors: The Northeast's numerous museums cover subjects appealing to both children and adults. The trouble is that if you're not careful about how you see them, kids come to regard museums as those places parents think kids should go to get the required dose of culture and to be "exposed" to the finer things of life.

In our experience, hands-on museums, natural history museums with stuffed animals, and history museums onboard ships are those that most appeal to kids until they're nearly teens. Almost all the museums I've included below have at least some participatory exhibits. A good book that lists many children's museums is *Doing Children's Museums* by Joanne Cleaver (Williamson, 1992).

No matter what their age, pick a museum with at least some objects your kids are already interested in—whether dinosaurs or dolls or robots, or paintings of some of these subjects. Do talk with kids in advance about what you're going to see. If you're visiting an art museum, it's worth reading a book on a particular artist, or *Looking at Pictures: An Introduction to Art for Young People* by Joy Richardson (Harry Abrams, 1997) for kids 8–12 or *Ella's Trip to the Museum* by Elaine Clayton (Crown, 1996) for kids 4–8. We go early, when museums are usually least crowded. When our son was under 6, we used to let him run around outside and blow off steam before going in. Plan on spending no more than two hours before you head for something to eat (less if your kids are under 6). If the museum has no cafeteria, bring snacks or determine the location of the nearest restaurant or coffee shop. Make sure what you want to view will be on display the day you plan to be there.

We stop first at the Information Desk for the following:

• A floor plan and directions to exhibits, bathrooms, and the cafeteria (plus the hours it is least crowded). Nothing so ruins a museum visit for our family as wandering about aimlessly.

• Museum pamphlets or guides for kids or families (ask, as they're not always displayed).

- Tickets for scheduled events—puppet show, discovery room, planetarium, music show—or family tours or workshops. Often these fill up and sell out early in the day. (Generally take only tours designed for kids unless yours are over 10; older kids we know often enjoy self-guided audio tours.)

Games can keep interest from flagging, especially in art and history museums. We have two favorites. In "picture hunt," kids pick out several postcards of related paintings or sculptures in the museum's gift shop when you first come in, then hunt for them in the galleries. Hint: Ask the staff person in the gift shop if these items are on display now. In "animal hunt," kids look for paintings or objects that have some particular item in them—animals or dragons or angels or babies or, hey, even body parts—whatever works.

Connecticut

Barnum Museum

(♛♛ 3–13) This museum about the life of showman P. T. Barnum, who is best known for founding the Barnum and Bailey Circus, "The Greatest Show on Earth," is a must for circus lovers. We immediately head for the third-floor gallery to see the hand-carved, moving miniature five-ring circus, which covers 1,000 square ft, and to marvel at its 3,000 tiny figures. In the Clown Corner, you'll find baggy pants, crazy hats, and makeup mirrors; if you put your face up to them, you can check out how you'd look as a clown. If you can, time your visit to take advantage of their one-Saturday-a-month family program, Breakfast at the Barnum, which includes breakfast and a performance, or combine a visit here with a stop at the Beardsley Zoo or the Discovery Museum. ♨ *820 Main St. (Exit 27 off I–91), Bridgeport 06604, tel. 203/331—1104, 203/331–9881 information. Cost: $5 adults, $3 kids 4–18. Open Tues.–Sat. 10–4:30, Sun. noon–4:30.*

Children's Museum of Southeastern Connecticut

(♛♛ 2–7) Though tiny in comparison with places like the Children's Museum in Boston—the single-story white building covers only 5,000 square ft—this museum has a couple of intriguing and unusual exhibits. One is the small-size working pipe organ in the Discovery Room. A panel of Plexiglas covers the inner pump and valves so kids can view the way air moves the parts to create sounds when they play. Another is the two-man yellow submarine outside; kids can climb into it and even try the intercom. ♨ *409 Main St. (Exit 74 off I–95), Niantic 06357, tel. 860/691–1111. Cost: $3.50, kids under 2 free. Open Mon.–Thurs. and Sat. 9:30–4:30, Fri. 9:30–8, Sun. noon–4. Closed Mon. Sept.–May.*

Discovery Museum

(♛♛ 3+) At the largest and best hands-on museum in Connecticut, in its Challenger Learning Center, you can spend a Saturday being part of a once-a-month simulated space mission. The computer-filled mission-control room looks just like a simplified version of the real ones we've seen on TV, as does the space module joined to it by a long, dark hallway. The morning training session teaches you to work the computer programs, monitors, and video cameras you'll need to use in the afternoon as you work together with other participants, each taking a different role, to perform the mission. Regardless of the emergencies you have to deal with, all missions end successfully. If you don't want to spend a whole day, you can go on a half-hour minimission tour. The Planetarium, totally revamped in 1997, now offers programs geared to specific ages. **🏛** *4450 Park Ave. (Exit 27A off I–95), Bridgeport 06604, tel. 203/372–3521. Cost: $6 adults, $4 kids 3–18; $3 for minimission; $25 for all-day Challenger program. Open Sept.–June, Tues.–Sat. 10–5, Sun. noon–5; July–Aug., Mon.–Sat. 10–5, Sun. noon–5.*

Historic Ship *Nautilus* and Submarine Force Museum

👫 6–15 The first nuclear-powered U.S. submarine floats just outside the entrance to the U.S. Submarine Base in Groton. Only 75 people at a time are allowed aboard, so you'll probably have to wait at least a short time for the self-guided tour unless you get here first thing in the morning or on a weekday. It's hard to believe that 116 men could live in a space just 319 ft long and 28 ft wide, once cruising more than 3,000 mi without surfacing. You carry electronic digital wands to activate narration at each point. In the museum, connected to the submarine by a walkway, the three working periscopes fascinate kids. You can see the sub and nearby U.S. submarine base by boat. Captain Bob's River Rides (tel. 860/445–8111) conducts sightseeing cruises that depart from the Thames Inn & Marina. **🏛** *U.S. Naval Submarine Base (Exit 86 off I–95 to Rte. 12, then left at Crystal Lake Rd.), Groton 06349, tel. 800/343–0079 or 860/694–3174. Cost: Free. Open May 15–Oct. 15, Wed.–Mon. 9–5, Tues. 1–5; Nov.–May 14, Wed.–Mon. 9–5. Closed 1st full wk in May and last wk of Oct.*

Mashantucket Pequot Museum & Research Center

👫 4–15 This huge exhibit and research complex owned by the Mashantucket Pequot Tribal Nation is devoted to the history and culture of several Native American tribes, primarily the Pequots (who also own the nearby Foxwoods Casino). In fact, Native Americans have inhabited this land in southeastern Connecticut for the last 10,000 years; galleries displaying artifacts, photographs, crafts, and enormous dioramas, films and videos, and interactive computer programs trace that history using state-of-the-art technology that wowed us. Traveling through a simulated glacial crevasse, we could feel chilling air and hear the ice creaking; walking around the re-creation of a 16th-century Pequot village, a 22,000-square-ft diorama with life-size, handcrafted figures, you smell the woods and a campfire and hear hundreds of realistic village sounds. Older kids were fascinated by the interactive 3-D computer program you can use to explore a scale-model 17th-century Pequot fort. **🏛** *110 Pequot Trail (Take Rte. 2 East to Rte. 214, then right on Pequot Trail), Box 3180, Mashantucket 06339–3180, tel. 860/396–6800. Cost: $10 adults, $6 kids 6–15. Open daily 10–7.*

Maine

Maine Maritime Museum

👫 4–15 Once there were nearly 100 shipyards on the banks of the Kennebec River. Now these old, white clapboard buildings and the Maritime History Building are a museum filled with exhibits illustrating Maine's nearly 400-year-old shipbuilding, fishing, and lobstering past. In the main building you'll find some hands-on exhibits (you can try tapping out Morse code, for example). At the lobstering exhibit, you can learn exactly how lobster traps work and why lobstermen never paint their boats blue or utter the word "pig" aboard. The best time to come is in summer, when there are demonstrations of seafaring techniques, little kids can play in the giant sandbox ship while you picnic, and you can go aboard the several vessels outdoors. The museum's daylong cruises to explore islands and lighthouses ($25) are best for older, energetic kids.

🏠 *243 Washington St. (Washington St. exit off Rte. 1), Bath 04530, tel. 207/443–1316. Cost: $8 adults, $5.50 kids 7–17, $24 family. Open daily 9:30–5.*

Railway Village

(👫 **3–9**) At this re-created turn-of-the-century museum village you can ride the Boothbay Central, pulled by a real steam-engine locomotive over a narrow-gauge railroad just like the one that used to go through nearby Wiscasset. Stop in the old-fashioned ticket office and take the 1½-mi ride past a little red schoolhouse, a doll museum, a bank, a barbershop, a toy shop, and 25 other buildings. The turn-of-the-century house has great old appliances, radios, and a Victrola. On the village green, you can pet goats in a pen and picnic.
🏠 *Rte. 27, Boothbay 04537, tel. 207/633–4727. Cost: $7 adults, $3 kids 3–12. Open mid-June–Columbus Day, daily 9:30–5; Memorial Day–mid-June, weekends 9:30–5.*

Massachusetts

Basketball Hall of Fame

(👫 **5–15**) Basketball was invented in Springfield in 1891 by Dr. James Naismith for his students at the School for Christian Workers, so it's entirely fitting that this 56,000-square-ft shrine documenting and celebrating all levels of the game, from high-school amateur to international professional, is located here. To us its atmosphere is more intense and action-oriented than that of any other sports museum, and like most other families we left tired and perspiring. Again and again we took the moving sidewalk through the Shoot Out Hall and tried to beat our records for sinking baskets in 15 hoops set at different heights and distances. Next to it is a new-in-1998 two-minute virtual reality game in which you play against Bill Walton in the Boston Garden. And don't miss Bob Lanier's bronzed size-22 basketball shoes.

🏠 *1150 W. Columbus Ave. (Exit 4 off I–91 N or Exit 7 off I–91 S), Springfield 01101, tel. 413/781–6500. Cost: $8 adults, $5 kids 7–14. Open Labor Day–Memorial Day, daily 9–6; Memorial Day–Labor Day, Wed. and Fri.–Sat. 9–8.*

Battleship *Massachusetts*

(👫 **7–15**) This complex of six big and small U.S. Navy warships from World War II is special. If you've ever visited a submarine, skip the tour of the USS *Lionfish*'s bleak, confined quarters. Concentrate instead on the huge USS *Massachusetts*, a World War II battleship nicknamed "Big Mamie," whose main deck is twice the length of a football field. We saw more of what life was like on a ship for the 2,000 men aboard than we could on the *Intrepid* in New York City, because you can explore nine decks on your own (better than taking the tour). You can aim the battleship guns, climb the turrets, and try out one of the 500 navy bunks hung on chains. Make sure you take a brochure with the plan and keep your kids close. Kids under 6 have legs that are too short for some of the climbing. Combine a visit here with one to the New Bedford Whaling Museum.
🏠 *Battleship Cove (Exit 7 off Rte. 24), Fall River 02721, tel. 508/678–1100 or 800/533–3194. Cost: $9 adults, $4.50 kids 6–14. Open daily 9–5.*

Boston Tea Party Ship and Museum

(👫 **4–10**) Most school-age kids know the story of how, in 1773, American revolutionists disguised as Indians crept aboard several ships in Boston Harbor loaded with tea from Britain, smashed the 340 tea chests, and threw them overboard to protest the newly imposed British taxes on tea. The small museum and fairly authentic replica of one of the ships, the *Beaver*, moored beside it, with crew members dressed in typical Colonial attire, seemed an expensive, hokey, and commercial attraction to us.

🏛 *Congress St. Bridge (South Station stop on Red Line T), Boston 02210, tel. 617/338–1773. Cost: $8 adults, $6.40 students 13 and up, $4 kids 4–12. Open Mar.–Memorial Day and Labor Day–Nov., daily 9–5; Memorial Day–Labor Day, daily 9–5:45.*

Children's Museum

(👫 1–12) You can't miss it: A take-out snack bar in the shape of a giant white milk bottle with red trim and awnings stands on the wharf in front of a converted warehouse that houses the very best children's museum in the Northeast, the one that pioneered hands-on exhibits back in 1962 and became the model all the others copied. If you have preschoolers, ask at the Information Desk for the booklet on exploring the museum with kids under 5; there's even a section for kids under 2.

Be sure to take your kids into the two-story Japanese silk merchant's house in which they can discover how a Japanese bathroom differs from their own. This museum is a very popular destination in summer, so I highly recommend obtaining advance tickets from a Ticketmaster outlet (service charge) or the museum box office (no service charge) if you want to visit on a weekend in summer. If your kids are over 7, check out the Computer Museum next door.

🏛 *Museum Wharf, 300 Congress St. (South Station stop on Red Line T), Boston 02210, tel. 617/426–6500; What's Up line, 617/426–8855; Ticketmaster, tel. 508/931–2787. Cost: $7 adults, $6 kids 2–15, $2 1-year-olds, $1 for all Fri. 5–9. Open Labor Day–mid-June, Tues.–Thurs. and weekends 10–5, Fri. 10–9; mid-June–Labor Day, Mon.–Thurs. 10–7, Fri. 10–9, weekends 10–5.*

Computer Museum

(👫 8+) For many kids, these two floors of hands-on, easy-to-use exhibits in the world's only Computer Museum (next to the Children's Museum are like a technological playground. The giant, working walk-through

computer 2000 is the size of a two-story house, with a car-size mouse and a keyboard 50 times larger than life. I used to think it was overrated as a family attraction, but now the exhibit and activities have been upgraded. Still, to us, the two most delightful sections for families are the new-in-1998 Virtual Fish-Tank, where you can design your own fish, tell it how to behave, and then let it loose in a giant fish tank to interact with other fish, and Tools & Toys. These seven jazzily designed environments have several dozen computer stations in which you can do everything from make your own cartoon to use a joystick to compose new songs from digitized sound samples to pretend to be an ant in a simulated ant colony, fending off invaders.

Younger kids need parents to work with them. I'd think twice about bringing kids under 7 here (most of the kids we saw having fun here were over 10), but if you do, be sure to get the flyer "Making the Most of Your Visit with Children," which is available at the Admission Desk. If you are traveling with a teen who's mad about computers, plan on spending most of the day here.

🏛 *Museum Wharf, 300 Congress St. (South Station stop on Red Line T), Boston 02210, tel. 617/426–2800. Cost: $7 adults, $5 kids 5–17; half-price Sun. 3 to closing. Open Sept.–June, Tues.–Sun. 10–5; July–Aug., daily 10–6.*

Essex Shipbuilding Museum

(👫 6–13) From 1650 to 1950 Essex was the Detroit of the shipbuilding industry. More wooden ships were built here than in any other place in the entire world—more than 4,000, mostly two-masted schooners—and this small museum tracks exactly how the ships were built, from the keel up. Kids can try aspects of the building process themselves with real shipbuilding tools at workstations in front of exhibits, or they can explore the active boatyard outside.

🏛 *28–66 Main St., Rte. 133W, Essex 01929, tel. 978/768–7541. Cost: $3 adults, $2.50 kids 12–17. Open Mon.–Sat. 10–5, Sun. 1–5.*

Higgins Armory Museum

(🏃🏃 6–15) The Higgins collection of medieval and Renaissance armor, originally put together in the 1920s and 1930s by steel magnate John Higgins, is even more thrilling for kids than the arms and armor collection at New York City's Metropolitan Museum of Art. When we stood in the Great Hall during one of the regular computerized sound-and-light shows, for example, we heard the clatter of dueling swords. (Unfortunately, these do not always work!) During the engaging presentations (on weekends and daily in summer) kid volunteers are asked up on stage to try on chain mail (over a padded doublet, which answered many kids' questions about what knights wore underneath their armor) and helmets. Don't miss the armor for dogs. 🏛 100 Barber Ave. (Exit 1 off I–90 to Rte. 12N), Worcester 01616, tel. 508/853–6015. Cost: $4.75 adults, $3.75 kids 6–16. Open Tues.–Sat. 10–4, Sun. noon–4.

Isabella Stewart Gardner Museum

(🏃🏃 7+) Just two blocks from Boston's Museum of Fine Arts is a mansion in the style of a Venetian palazzo built in 1903 by the eccentric socialite Isabella Stewart Gardner after her husband's death. Now it houses only her collection of artwork, but for a time the top two floors were also her home. Our favorite place in the museum is the Great Court, a reconstruction of a 15th-century Venetian Gothic palace court with hanging balconies, a mosaic floor, and a glass skylight. (Stop at the Gardner Café, which overlooks the court, for an elegant dessert.) If your kids are curious about Mrs. Gardner, who once walked her pet ocelot down Tremont Street, there's a fine portrait of her, painted by John Singer Sargent, in the third-floor Gothic Room. In 1990, 13 priceless art works were stolen from the museum in the largest art theft ever; they have yet to be recovered. Pick up one of the family "Eyes on Art" packets. A lively jazz concert is held the first Saturday of each month. 🏛 280 The Fenway, Boston 02199, tel. 617/566–1401. Cost: $10 adults, kids under 18 free. Open Tues.–Sun. 11–5.

Museum of Fine Arts

(🏃🏃 8+) The MFA contains gallery after gallery of masterpieces. It has a formal, gray-stone, Greek-columned look, plus a dramatic wing for contemporary art that also holds the cafeteria, which is full of light and open space. Kids like this museum for the silver pieces actually made by Paul Revere and the portraits of Revolutionary War heroes they've read about: George Washington (the famous painting by Gilbert Stuart), Paul Revere, John Hancock, Sam Adams, and John Quincy Adams. The collections of Asian art (visit the Japanese Garden) and Egyptian art are among the most extensive in the world. The Egyptian art galleries, now twice as big, reopened in 1998. The key attraction for kids—the mummies—includes neat animal mummies, and it's more interesting than the mummy display in New York's Metropolitan Museum. The best bets for families are the self-guided tours using one of the "Family Activity" booklets available at the Information Center, and two drop-in programs. Special family activities, including scavenger hunts, art workshops, and games, are planned for kids 4 and up throughout the year. 🏛 465 Huntington Ave. (Ruggles/Museum stop on the E Green Line T), Boston 02115, tel. 617/267–9300. Cost: $10 adults, kids 17 and under free, donation Wed. 4–9:45. Open Mon.–Tues. 10–4:45, Wed.–Fri. 10–9:45 (Thurs.–Fri., west wing only after 5), weekends 10–5:45.

Museum of Science

(🏃🏃 2+) Almost as soon as we entered the largest science museum in the Northeast we got lost in its complicated layout of east and west wings on three floors, which are not all accessible to one another without backtracking. Carrying a floor plan with you is essential. On a plot of land that straddles the Charles River between Boston and Cambridge, this museum of interactive exhibits is a favorite place of all the kids on my Boston panel, including preschoolers, who head for the two-level Discovery Center (open daily 10–4) to touch and hold bones, huge shells, and rocks and to watch mice in glass tanks. But the other 400-plus exhibits are a mixed bag. Concentrate on the Human Body Discovery Space (open daily 10–4), where kids take turns riding on a bike and see the skeleton opposite mimic them; the sound stairs, which play a different note on each step as you walk up; and the Investigate! exhibit, in which kids try thinking like a scientist in activities such as designing and racing a scale-model solar car, and playing around with creating optical illusions in the new (1998) Seeing Is Deceiving section. The two-story Theater of Electricity's Lightning! show (daily 12 and 2, Fri. also at 7) is spectacular but scary to little kids. An Omni Theater and Planetarium have regular shows. And if your kids (or you) are interested in computers, stop by the free Computer Discovery Space (open daily 10–4) near the museum's parking garage.

🏛 *Science Park (Science Park stop on Green Line T), Boston 02114, tel. 617/723–2500. Cost: $9 adults, $7 kids 3–11. Open Labor Day–July 4 Sat.–Thurs. 9–5, Fri. 9–9; July 5–Labor Day, Sat.–Thurs. 9–7, Fri. 9–9.*

EcoTarium

(👫 **3–15**) This large environmental science center on 60 acres has everything from a wildlife center to one of the world's largest kaleidoscopes (you can walk inside and manipulate it) to interactive question-oriented exhibits to a narrow-gauge railroad and nature trails. At press time, the center was improving its previously ho-hum natural-history exhibits. Don't miss the fascinating mathematical toy exhibit or (if your kids are 10 and up) the regular Sky Watch programs at the Norton Observatory, during which you first get acquainted with stars,

planets, or the moon through a planetarium show, then view the same thing from several sizes of telescopes. *See also* Chapter 4, Eco-Tarium.

🏛 *222 Harrington Way (off Rte. 9), Worcester 01604, tel. 508/791–9211. Cost: $6 adults, $4 kids 3–16 and college students with ID; Sky Watch evening program, $12 adults, $6 kids 12 and under. Open Mon.–Sat. 10–5, Sun. noon–5.*

Salem Wax Museum of Witches and Seafarers

(👫 **8+**) It's not one of the official museum stops in Salem, even though its 13 stage sets with 50 figures (not all gruesome) convey different aspects of Salem's colorful past. Among the things that make it more interesting than other such museums is that it has a section where kids can be part of a mock trial or make a gravestone rubbing. Kids fascinated by witches may also want to take the new "Hysteria Path" tour given by real witches through an indoor village, which illustrates the history of witches, but it's not as interesting as it sounds.

🏛 *Derby St., Salem 01970, tel. 978/740–2929. Cost: Museum $4.50 adults, $2.75 kids 6–14. Combined ticket including tour $7.95 adults, $4.50 kids 6–14. Open Nov.–Apr., daily 10–5; May–June and Sept., daily 9–6; July–Aug., Sun.–Thurs. 9–7, Fri.–Sat. 9–9; call ahead for Oct. hrs.*

Salem Witch Museum

(👫 **7+**) Salem was a major seaport from which ships sailed to China and the East Indies in the 17th and 18th centuries, but everyone remembers it for the "witch trials" that took place here in 1692. The museum, an imposing, heavy stone structure that resembles a church, across from the town Common, seems a fittingly solemn setting for the subject from the outside, but it may disappoint you. The exhibits consist of just 13 stage sets with life-size figures built into the walls of the auditorium. The room is dark when you enter for the half-hour presentation that uses the stage sets, sound effects, and narration of accusations, court proceedings, and hangings to dramatize what happened and why. I found all the eerie music and facts gruesome, but older kids in the audience seemed to revel in it all; some little kids were scared and had to leave.

🏛 *Washington Sq. (off Washington St.), Salem 01970, tel. 978/744–1692. Cost: $4.50 adults, $3 kids 6–14. Open Sept.–June, daily 10–5; July–Aug., daily 10–7.*

Sports Museum of New England

(👫 6+) As of 1998, this museum, which celebrates all sports from baseball and candlepin bowling to marathon running and sailing, is in two parts; one is in the nearby city of Lowell, but the larger and more interesting one by far is on the fifth and sixth floors of Boston's FleetCenter (where the Bruins and Celtics play). Besides displaying sports memorabilia, many exhibits at the FleetCenter attempt to tell a story, making the information easier for kids to grasp, while others imaginatively let you take part in the actual experience of playing or watching. At Catching Clemens, for example, you put your face into a catcher's mask, your hand into a glove, call Robert Clemens's pitch, and feel the sting of the ball in your mitt.

🏛 *FleetCenter, 150 Causeway St. (North Station stop on the Green or Orange line T), Boston 02114, tel. 617/624–1234. Cost: $5 adults, $4 kids 6–17. Open Tues.–Sat. 10–5, Sun. noon–5.*

Thornton Burgess Museum

(👫 3–10) If your kids have read the Mother West Wind stories by Thornton Burgess about Reddy Fox, Paddy the Beaver, and other animals, as my son—and my husband before him—did, they may be as taken with this picture-book-perfect museum memorial as we were. Burgess visited his aunt Arabella Eldred Burgess in this typical 19th-century house, where you can look at

original illustrations for Burgess's books (most interesting to adults) and try on animal costumes (most interesting to kids). But what felt most special was sitting under a shady tree for the Story Hour featuring live animals corresponding to those in the stories and feeding swans and ducks on the pond afterward.

🏛 *4 Water St. (edge of Shawme Pond), Sandwich 02537, tel. 508/888–6870. Cost: Donation. Open Apr.–Dec., Mon.–Sat. 10–4, Sun. 1–4; story hr 10:30 Mon., Wed., and Sat. July–Aug. and on some holidays.*

USS *Constitution* and Museum

(👫 4+) At the Charlestown Navy Yard, Boston's number one historical attraction, across the Charles River from Boston proper, we got a real sense of early United States maritime history from just walking around. It's big: The grounds include a National Historical Park Visitor's Center, two ships you can board, a couple of museums, a grand waterfront walk, and more. Much is free. But what we most wanted to see was the USS *Constitution*, nicknamed "Old Ironsides," a wooden 44-gun three-masted ship built in 1797. It got its nickname because during the War of 1812 even British cannonballs bounced off its 2-ft-thick oak hull. (A good book: *The Story of Old Ironsides* by Norman Richards, Children's Press.) On the 20- to 30-minute tour of the ship the sailor guides in 1812 uniforms recount entertaining stories about hardships aboard—such as the fact that men only bathed every five or six months. Also worth touring is the destroyer USS *Cassin Young*. The *Constitution* Museum's exhibits explore the ship's history; check out Life at Sea, where kids can swing in a sailor's hammock, hoist sails, and take a crew member's role in a computerized video of the War of 1812.

🏛 *Charlestown Navy Yard (Bus 93 from Haymarket; tel. 617/222–3200 for schedule), Charlestown 02129, tel. 617/426–1812. Cost: Museum only $4 adults, $2 kids 6–16; admission to Navy Yard free. Open: Ship daily*

9:30–sunset, tours until 3:50; museum Dec.–
Feb. 10–4, Mar.–May and Sept.–Nov. 10–5,
June–Aug. 9–6.

Wenham Museum

(👫 4–13) Seeing the world-class collection of 1,000 dolls made from wood, china,
cloth, rubber, leather, even metal, in this
17th-century house 25 mi north of Boston
is a must for doll lovers. It's the most appealing doll museum I've seen (though it's not all
dolls). The intricate dollhouses are fascinating: A Victorian mansion even has parquet
floors and stained-glass windows. Also in
the museum is a charming Colonial playhouse with dress-up clothes and a great
model railroad room, in which you can
press buttons to make the train work. The
Wenham Tea House across the street is
perfect for an afternoon tea stop.
🏠 132 Main St. (Rte. 1A), Wenham 01984,
tel. 978/468–2377. Cost: $4 adults, $2 kids
3–16. Open weekdays 10–4, weekends 1–4.

Whaling Museum

(👫 6–15) You might want to screen the
movie version of the book *Moby-Dick*
before you come to this museum in the
world's most famous whaling port. Historic
New Bedford is the city from which Captain
Ahab set off on his quest for the great white
whale. Of all the whaling museums in the
Northeast, this one best re-creates that
world for kids. It's not just the collection,
which includes an 89-ft-long model of a full-
rigged whaling bark kids can climb aboard,
and real harpoons and blubber hooks to
touch. It's also that the museum is in what
was once the world's whaling capital. Just
looking at the buildings and wharves nearby
recalls that past. The museum's 22-minute
silent film of an actual whale voyage is
action-packed, but when the fishermen cap-
tured the whale in the end, it upset some 5-
year-olds in the audience. In 2000, the
museum's 65-ft-long blue whale skeleton
will go on display—the only one in the
world the public can view.

🏠 18 Johnny Cake Hill (Exit 15 off I–95 to
Downtown exit, then right on Elm St., left on
Bethel), New Bedford 02740, tel. 508/997–
0046. Cost: $4.50 adults, $3 kids 6–14. Open
daily 9–5 (Memorial Day–Labor Day, Thurs.
until 8).

New Hampshire

Children's Metamorphosis Museum

(👫 1–7) What sets this small children's
museum apart from others its size is how
light and bright and clean it is and the fact
that kids can play with everything they see.
From the outside the museum looks like a
ranch house, and inside it's a series of small
rooms, each with one exhibit, such as the
Rainbow Room of color and light and the
Sticky Room with Velcro boards.
🏠 217 Rockingham Rd., Londonderry
03053, tel. 603/425–2560. Cost: $3.75, kids
under 1 free. Open Tues.–Thurs. and Sat.
9:30–5, Fri. 9:30–8, Sun. 1–5.

Christa McAuliffe Planetarium

(👫 3+) Named for the teacher from
Concord, New Hampshire, who perished
on the *Challenger* space mission, this small
planetarium is one of the most appealing in
the Northeast for kids because of its intimate size (just 92 seats), the way shows
make you feel as though you are traveling
through space (an effect of the Digistar pro-
jector), and the box of interactive buttons
on each seat that allows kids to participate
in choosing what you'll see in the show. A
small area houses an exhibit on Christa
McAuliffe's life. There are special shows for
preschoolers.
🏠 3 Institute Dr. (Exit 15E off I–93), Concord 03301, tel. 603/271–7827. Cost: $6
adults, $3 kids 3–17. Open Tues.–Sun., but hrs
and show times vary; call first. Reservations
advised.

Heritage New Hampshire

(👣 4–13) Strictly speaking, this crash course in 300 years of New Hampshire's history is a commercial attraction, not a museum; the 25 scenes showing different periods and events in the state's history are full of the kinds of special effects kids love. Despite a touristy flavor, it's fairly authentic. When we boarded the ship *Reliance* for our 60-day "voyage" from England to Mason's Grant in the New World, we smelled codfish (it's in a barrel), heard seagulls squawk, saw lightning flash and sails billow, and felt the ship roll while the captain gave us some sobering facts. Not all scenes were quite so involving, and some of the speeches given by mechanized mannequins may impress little kids more than cynical teenagers, but real trout swim in the Amoskeag Falls, and the woodsman carves spoons and gives them to kids as souvenirs. Stop also in the barn to see what artisans are demonstrating; if one is making ice cream or cheese the old-fashioned way, you can get a taste.

🏠 *Rte. 16 (6 mi north of North Conway), Glen 03838, tel. 603/383–4186 recorded info, 603/383–9776. Cost: $10 adults, $4.50 kids 6–12. Open mid-May–mid-Oct., daily 9–5.*

New York

Adirondack Museum

(👣 3+) This outstanding outdoor museum devoted to the social history of the region perches on the side of Blue Mountain. Just dipping in and out of the 23 indoor and outdoor activity areas on this "campus" with spectacular views of lake and mountain gave our family a picture of and feeling for what the Adirondacks were like in the past—from the days of mining and logging camps, fishing, trapping, and boatbuilding, to the Gilded Age in the 19th and early 20th century, when robber barons arrived on private railway cars at their huge log "Great Camps" and upper-class city dwellers took launches to fancy "rustic" hotels on remote islands.

In a massive, wood-columned pavilion in the center of the campus you'll find an old steamboat and the short Marion River Carry locomotive that kids can climb aboard, and there are plenty of hands-on activities, especially during July and August. Our favorites: filling up an old-fashioned pack basket and trying it on to see how heavy it is.

🏠 *Rtes. 28N and 30, Blue Mountain Lake 12812, tel. 518/352–7311. Cost: $10 adults, $6 kids 7–16. Open late May–mid-Oct., daily 9:30–5:30.*

American Museum of Natural History

(👣 ALL) The very best natural history museum in the Northeast—in fact, in the entire country—with 30 million artifacts and specimens displayed on four floors, this is one of the country's must-see museums for families.

The building, set in its own four-block park, has several entrances, but we still like to go in the main one, across from Central Park, because as soon as you walk in, you see the tallest freestanding dinosaur exhibit in the world—a five-story-tall barosaurus rearing up to defend its baby from an allosaurus—right there in the rotunda. For some kids the museum's world-renowned collection of dinosaurs on the fourth floor is *the* highlight. The displays are even more fun for kids; you can touch a dinosaur tooth and measure your head beside one from a Tyrannosaurus. Plan to swing through the new (1998) Hall of Biodiversity, too, to see the rain-forest diorama and the amazing "Spectrum of Life" installation.

Other kids, including mine, still prefer the meticulously crafted lifelike dioramas with stuffed animal specimens. Because the glass goes almost to the floor, even tikes in strollers can see. If you have a toddler or preschooler, spend some time in the dimly lighted Hall of Ocean Life (the blue whale model is suspended from the ceiling), a large self-contained space down a flight of stairs, with dioramas of walruses, seals, and sharks, and a restaurant. The best place to eat with kids, though, is Diner Saurus, a cafeteria that serves french fries in the shape of dinosaurs.

The museum has excellent family workshops every weekend (once we helped carve a Tibetan butter sculpture) and dance, music, and storytelling programs for kids. Also worth seeing are the spectacular features shown daily in the museum's IMAX theater. Much is currently being revamped at the museum. The **Hayden Planetarium**, for example, is now closed for reconstruction and will reopen in early 2000 as part of the new Rose Center for Earth and Space. One part of this center, the Hall of Planet Earth, is scheduled to open in June 1999; a display of 100 giant rocks and information on how to "read" them will illustrate the way the earth evolved.

Central Park W between 77th and 81st Sts. (Subway C or B to 81st St.), tel. 212/769–5100, 212/769–5200. Cost: Suggested donation $8 adults, $4.50 kids 2–12, $6 students with ID. Open Sun.–Thurs. 10–5:45, Fri.–Sat. 10–8:45. To reserve in advance, tel. 212/769–5200. Combination tickets that include the IMAX theater $13 adults, $7 kids 2–12, $9 students with ID; Citypass also accepted.

Brooklyn Children's Museum

👫 0–12 A corrugated-metal tunnel entrance leads into this multilevel hands-on play-and-learn museum, which tells you that this will be an unusual and exuberant place. Though it is small compared with the huge Boston Children's Museum and difficult to get to, it's worth it. Not only is it the oldest children's museum in the country (nearly 100 years old), but it's also unique among those we've been to in terms of imaginative graphics and museum design. The tunnel, lighted by bands of neon, is the museum's core. Kids run up and down the ramp inside it to get to the exhibits, stopping to put

their hands in the raised water trough, complete with waterwheel, that runs down its center. The graphics of the exhibits are particularly wild, like brightly painted stage sets inside an old factory.

Exhibits link the business of a museum with kids' lives and concerns. In Ready, Set, Sleep, kids can try out a life-size re-creation of an Egyptian leather-strap bed or write down bad dreams and push them into the mouth of a wooden monster, Baku, the Dream Eater.

Be sure to check the day's information board: There's an excellent short workshop or program for some age group going on just about every half hour.

145 Brooklyn Ave. (take Subway 3 to Kingston Ave.; walk 6 blocks on Kingston to St. Mark's Ave., then left 1 block), Brooklyn 11213, tel. 718/735–4400. Cost: Suggested donation $3. Open Labor Day–June, Wed.–Fri. 2–5, weekends and holiday wks 10–5; July–Labor Day, Mon., Wed., and Thurs. noon–5, Fri. noon–6:30, weekends 10–5.

Ellis Island and Immigration Museum

👫 8+ Between 1892 and 1954 about 12 million immigrants from all over the world, many fleeing poverty or political or religious persecution, came through the immigration-processing center on Ellis Island, which reopened as a museum in 1990. An estimated 40% of all Americans have at least one relative or ancestor who was among these immigrants. The restored buildings include the great hall where newcomers were questioned as well as 30 exhibit galleries with photographs, maps, posters, and objects telling the story of what happened to them. To us the most moving exhibit was the display of precious items people brought with them, entitled Treasures from Home, which prompted a discussion of what we would take with us if we had to leave our home behind.

Coming here with a grandparent or a relative who actually immigrated and can

explain why he or she came to America would make the experience even more meaningful for kids. Bring a picnic. This is among the most heavily visited national monuments, so go on a weekday after 2:30 to avoid school groups or on the earliest morning boat on a weekend to avoid long lines.
🏛 *Ellis Island, New York 10004, tel. 212/ 363–3200. Take Statue of Liberty boat that stops at both Liberty and Ellis Islands from Battery Park (or Liberty State Park in New Jersey); tickets at Castle Clinton in park, tel. 212/ 269–5755. Cost: $7 adults, $3 kids 3–17; boats depart every 30–40 mins 9:30–3:30, May–Labor Day. Museum free. Open Sept.– June, daily 9:30–5; July–Aug., daily 9:30–5:30.*

Intrepid Sea/Air/ Space Museum

(👪 4–15) When you board the USS *Intrepid*, an aircraft carrier used in World War II that is permanently moored at a pier in the Hudson River, you can see the fastest spy plane in the world and 40 other aircraft, space vehicles, and rockets. This is the world's largest naval museum (owned and maintained by the U.S. Navy). It includes the USS *Growler*, a guided missile submarine, and the USS *Edson*, a destroyer, moored on the other side of the pier.

See the short film in the main exhibit hall, which shows how planes take off and land on a carrier's deck, before you walk around. Inside the carrier several huge halls have displays of photographs, videos, and battleship and airplane models, each focusing on a different war period. Most kids want to head for things you can climb on or peer into, like the cockpit of a fighter plane, or just explore the ship's passageways and walk around the deck looking at the planes.

As you can't explore cabins and the engine room on the *Intrepid*, be sure to take the 25-minute tour of the USS *Edson*. Everything is impressively compact, especially the stacked, curtained bunks for enlisted men with not even enough space to sit up.

The lines for the 20-minute tour of the USS *Growler* submarine have always been long when we've been here. Only 13 people at a time can board, so you'll almost always have to wait at least half an hour.
🏛 *Pier 86, W. 46th St. at 12th Ave. (Subway A, E, or C to 42nd St.; Bus M42 to last stop), New York 10036, tel. 212/245–0072. Cost: $12 adults, $9.50 kids 12–17, $6 kids 6–11, $2 kids 2–5. Also on New York Citypass. Open Oct.–Mar., Wed.–Sun. 10–5; Apr.–Sept., daily 10–5.*

Kaleidoworld

(👪 4+) This is a fascinating and astonishing place to spend a few hours. In a 19th-century barn complex of displays and shops you can take a look at a whole cornucopia of kaleidoscopes, including the world's largest (it's in the *Guinness Book of Records*), which is in a 65-ft tube that was once the silo. The Amazing Starworks, the second-largest kaleidoscope, sort of a kaleidoscopic starship, seemed even more spectacular to us—it uses electronic wizardry to create a sound-and-light show. The Crystal Palace is a fantasyland of giant kaleidoscopes for kids to climb on, play with, and manipulate. And of course there's a shop with the biggest collection of kaleidoscopes for sale in the world.
🏛 *Catskill Corners, Rte. 28, Mt. Tremper, NY 12457, tel. 914/688–5300. Cost: $10 adults, $8 kids under 4'6", family discounts. Kaleidoscope only, $5; Crystal Palace and Starworks only, $6. Open Wed.–Mon. 10–7.*

Liberty Science Center

(👪 5+) Okay, this huge four-story center of more than 250 exciting interactive science exhibits and a six-story IMAX theater isn't really in New York, but it's only a short ferry and bus ride away and worth the trek. There's so much to see and do from the moment you enter that most kids want to spend at least a half a day here. On the main floor, the first thing that grabs you is the 700-pound suspended aluminum geodesic globe that continually expands and contracts. Each of the other three floors has a theme, which makes it easy to find your way around. Upstairs on two is "Health"; some of these exhibits are very similar to those at Boston's Museum of Science. Totally unique is the famous pitch-black Touch Tunnel to crawl through using only your sense of touch as a guide. Even though it only takes about five minutes, it's scary—and not for kids under 7. Floor three is "Environment"; here you can hold your favorite bug at the MicroZoo, watch gigantic hissing cockroaches, and create a 10-ft-high geyser. Our favorite floor was "Invention" (below the main floor), where you can try out a United States Air Force fighter jet simulator actually used to train American pilots. Though a few of the exhibits appeal to the younger set, most of the exhibits at this museum are fairly sophisticated and most fun for kids 7–15. Don't miss having a snack at the glassed-in café; from here you'll have a great view of Lower Manhattan.

🏛 *Liberty State Park, 251 Philip St., Jersey City, New Jersey 07305-4699, tel. 201/200–1000. (NY Waterway ferry, tel. 800/533–3779, leaves from the World Financial Center in New York City; weekdays it arrives at Colgate Center, weekends at Liberty State Park—a free shuttle bus to the museum meets you. Cost: $2. Call for hrs. Or take Path train from World Trade Center or other locations to Grove St. in Jersey City, then free shuttle bus. Or by car, take New Jersey Turnpike south to Exit 14B, then follow signs.) Cost: $10 adults, $9 students, $7 kids 2–12. Open Labor Day–Mar., Tues.–Sun. 9:30–5:30; Apr.–Labor Day, daily 9:30–5:30.*

Metropolitan Museum of Art

(👫 **4+**) The Met is the largest art museum in the western hemisphere and feels like it. With kids, this is one museum where it's essential to get a map, pick only a few exhibits to see, and not stay too long before you head for lunch in the cafeteria or a walk in Central Park behind the museum. Before you go, try to find a copy of *Inside*

the Museum by Joy Richardson (Metropolitan Museum of Art/Harry N. Abrams), a children's book about the Met.

Kids like the full suits of armor in the hall of arms and armor on the first floor. The collection of mummies in the Egyptian galleries is also a hit, but seeing the Temple of Dendur, a real Egyptian temple moved here because it would have been submerged after the Aswan Dam was built, eclipses them for us. Another exhibit we always have to visit is the Ming Dynasty Chinese Garden Court on the second floor. Walking through the circular entrance is like entering an area outside an old Chinese home to discover a tiny goldfish pool, plants, rocks, and seats. At Christmas, don't miss the decorated tree and crèche display in the medieval hall.

Check at the Information Desk for the "Museum Hunt" and family gallery guides. Among the best times to go on weekends are Friday and Saturday evenings, when there are also concerts, and the first thing Sunday morning, but be aware that strollers are not permitted on Sunday. Check at the 81st Street entrance for back carriers. *See also* Chapter 12, Entertainment and the Arts.

🏛 *1000 5th Ave., between 82nd and 84th Sts. (Subway 4, 5, or 6 to 86th St.), New York 10028, tel. 212/535–7710. Cost: Suggested donation $8 adults, $4 students, kids 12 and under free. Open Tues.–Thurs. and Sun. 9:30–5:15, Fri.–Sat. 9:30–8:45.*

Museum of Television and Radio

(👫 **5 – 15**) Unlike the subjects of most museums, TV is something kids consider important in their own lives. What they don't know is its history. The museum's collection of 98,000 TV and radio programs that span broadcast history is bound to contain some of your favorites. But get here early to reserve one of the individual TVs with headphones to watch one. The museum also has exhibits that appeal to kids. One displays masks and costumes from

Star Trek and provides a behind-the-scenes look at characters' makeup. I recommend the Saturday-morning Television Together screenings once a month for kids 4–8 and their parents, annual Children's Television Festival (for kids 4–10), and radio workshops (for kids 8–13) in which they learn how to re-create the sound effects and performances from radio shows of the '30s and '40s.
≜ *25 W. 52nd St. (Subway B, D, F, or Q to Rockefeller Center), New York 10019, tel. 212/621–6600. Cost: $6 adults, $4 students, $3 kids under 13. Open Tues.–Wed. and Sun. noon–6, Thurs. noon–8, Fri. noon–9.*

National Baseball Hall of Fame

(**♀♀ 8+**)   If your kids are baseball fans, this is Mecca—the place they simply have to visit at least once in a lifetime. Everything you ever wanted to see and know about baseball is on these three floors of memorabilia, equipment, clothing, cards, photos, videos, and books, with life-size carved wooden statues of great stars greeting you as you enter. Don't skip the short introductory film of baseball-movie and great-player clips. Half the fun is sitting in ballpark seats in a movie theater painted to look like a stadium while sound effects re-create hawkers' offers of hot dogs and peanuts.

In the records room you can check out how today's players compare with those in the past or call up information about Hall of Famers on video machines. You can see how a baseball is manufactured and admire displays on early Negro baseball leagues and old equipment (baseball gloves used in the mid-1800s looked just like ordinary winter gloves). Not much is hands-on, however. It's best for kids who understand and are crazy about baseball. Don't even consider joining the hordes on July 4 or when the Hall of Fame inductions are held the last weekend in July.
≜ *Main St., Cooperstown 13326, tel. 607/ 547–7200. Cost: $9.50 adults, $4 kids 7–12. Open May–Sept., daily 9–9; Oct.–Apr., daily 9–5.*

New York Hall of Science

(**♀♀ 3 – 15**)   Although it can't compete with Boston's Museum of Science in terms of sheer size, the Hall of Science is one of the 10 best science museums in the United States in terms of the quality of its more than 185 hands-on exhibits. It has the added virtue of feeling encompassable, intimate, and unusually friendly, something due partly to the museum's circular interiors and partly to the group of young high school and college student "explainers," who answer kids' questions, give demonstrations (the most popular is the dissection of a cow's eye), and run workshops. To me, one of the most fun and unique parts of the Hall is the recently built 30,000-square-ft outdoor science playground, the largest of its kind in the western hemisphere, where you can experience the principles of a tensile structure by climbing on the giant space net, try your hand at creating solar energy to make a kinetic sculpture move, and much more. Get here early, though, because only a certain number of kids (over 6) are allowed on the playground at any one time. Older kids give thumbs up to the exhibit SoundSensations, which offers kids the chance to mix tracks, arrange synthesized music sources, and compose and play music with just your shadow. Little kids gravitate to the Preschool Discovery Space for kids under 6. The special exhibits are just about always fascinating, like the one about the brain where you can step inside a 12-times-life-size model of the human brain. Don't miss a turn at the popular bubble table on the main floor, where you can blow human-size bubbles. Our favorite event? The Halloween family sleepover. Nearby is the Queens Wildlife Center, where you'll see North American animals (including bison) from a walking trail that takes only about 20 minutes.
≜ *47–01 111th St. (Subway 7 to 111th St.), Flushing Meadows, Queens 11368, tel. 718/ 699–0005. Cost: $6 adults, $4 kids 3–15; free Thurs.–Fri. 2–5; $5 parking in summer. Open Sept.–June, Mon.–Wed. 9:30–2, Thurs.–Sun. 9:30–5; open July–Aug., daily 9:30–5.*

Old Rhinebeck Aerodrome

(👫 6+) Of the several airplane museums in the Northeast, this one is a favorite because of its colorful but corny weekend air shows. Battles of World War I are reenacted in costume as crowds cheer for the good guys and announcers explain just what is going on. Other demonstrations range from thrilling aerobatics to funny comedy routines, but all of it takes you back to the exciting Red Baron era of flying. Though the walking tour featuring restored airplanes in several hangars is led by enthusiastic guides who can—and will—tell inquisitive kids as much as they want to know, the air shows here are the real treat.

🏠 U.S. 9 (U.S. 9 north from Rhinebeck to Stone Church Rd., then watch for signs), Rhinebeck 12572, tel. 914/758–8610. Cost: Weekdays $5, $2 kids 6–10; weekends $10 adults, $5 kids 6–10. Open mid-May–Oct., daily 10–5; air shows mid-June–mid-Oct., weekends 2–4.

Vermont

Fairbanks Museum and Planetarium

(👫 5 – 13) Remember when natural history museums were vast collections of curious treasures in big old buildings where you felt as though you should whisper? That's just how we felt in the 130-ft-long great hall of this ornate, red sandstone Victorian structure right on Main Street that manages to be wonderfully old-fashioned, cozy, and grandly impressive all at the same time. Four large stuffed bears, including an immense standing Kodiak bear, greet you by the entrance. The exhibits have character: stuffed specimens and strange artifacts neatly displayed behind oak-trimmed glass cases, everything from a giant clam to paper made from the bark of a mulberry tree.

Shows are presented in the small 50-seat planetarium. The weather center in the basement lets you watch weather forecasters prepare maps, consult computer data, and make their broadcast. In summer a children's nature program is staffed by kids 10–15; the August star party and the September Festival of Traditional Crafts are tops.

🏠 Main St., St. Johnsbury 05819, tel. 802/ 748–2372. Cost: $5 adults, $3 kids 5–17, $12 family. Open Sept.–June, Mon.–Sat. 10–4, Sun. 1–5; July–Aug., Mon.–Sat. 10–6, Sun. 1–5.

Montshire Museum of Science

(👫 2+) This is the complete opposite of the Fairbanks Museum. A cathedral-ceilinged, open, modern space on 110 peaceful acres above the Connecticut River, it hums with the noise and activity of kids launching pennies to spiral down into the dark hole of the "gravity well" or checking out CT scans and X rays to see the human body in new ways. Kids can also go on a nature trail. The museum is a miniversion of New Jersey's Liberty Science Center transplanted to the country. Of all their special weekend events, the most unusual is the annual igloo-build held in winter.

🏠 Rte. 10A, Norwich 05055, tel. 802/649– 2200. Cost: $5 adults, $4 kids 3–17. Open daily 10–5.

Shelburne Museum

(👫 5+) Imagine a great collection of all the very best American folk art, artifacts, and architecture gathered up on 45 acres to make one perfect small Vermont village of 37 19th-century houses and shops, a round barn, and a covered bridge, where the smell of one of the finest lilac gardens in New England greets visitors in May. That's the Shelburne Museum. It's slightly stiff and proper, with quilts and weather vanes, dolls and toys, furniture and pewter pitchers, sleighs and carriages. Owl Cottage, the family activity center, offers tours, workshops, and games to involve kids more directly in the historical era. Time a visit for one of their special events, such as the Fourth of July, the last week of July (when the Big Apple Circus performs), or the December Christmas celebration.

🏠 *Rte. 7, Shelburne 05482, tel. 802/985–3346. Cost: $17.50 adults, $7 kids 6–14. Ticket good for 2 days. Open late May–late Oct., daily 10–5 (tour at 1); late Oct.–late May, open only for tour at 1 ($7 adults, $3 kids 6–14).*

ANIMALS AND MARINE LIFE 4
ZOOS, AQUARIUMS, GAME FARMS, AND WILDLIFE SANCTUARIES

Are there any kids who don't like to pet or just watch animals? Not among the ones I know. Even 1-year-olds and young teens put visiting zoos and aquariums high on their lists of favorite things to do. As Gavin was no exception, we've always tried to work in an animal visit on any trip. In the Northeast you have a number of options, from baby animals to pet at a charming farm in New Hampshire to the exotic species at one of the world's greatest zoos (the Bronx Zoo in New York City) and the sea life at several terrific aquariums (in Boston, New York City, and Mystic, Connecticut). But don't neglect smaller places: As befits a region with a long coastline on the Atlantic Ocean, the Northeast has some small aquariums right next to the water that provide opportunities for kids to handle crabs and other shellfish. Inland you'll find everything from a game farm that raises exotic animals and sells them to the country's zoos to science centers that introduce kids to species native to the Northeast such as beavers and deer. Many children's museums have petting areas and small aquariums. In our experience most of the region's wildlife sanctuaries and Audubon centers are more appealing as places to hike than to see animals; I've included here only a couple that have special live-animal exhibits or injured-animal programs that appeal to kids.

Uncomfortable with the image that they just run menageries for viewing animals in cages, zookeepers and aquarium owners in the Northeast have adopted strong conservation policies in the past few years, actively working to preserve and breed endangered species. They're spreading the word with interactive exhibits and educational programs for kids.

Age makes a big difference in the kinds of animals kids are interested in. Toddlers are usually just as excited about feeding chickens in a barnyard as they are about looking at sea lions and giraffes. At age 7 monkeys of all kinds appealed to Gavin, and the idea of petting farm animals was pronounced babyish. By age 14 he was taken with complete environments—like a tropical rain forest—and more concerned about whether a friend was along. For him, as with most other kids, getting to feed, hold, pet, or at least get as close as possible to animals was always the real highlight, so my choices for this chapter are heavily weighted toward places where kids can engage in these activities.

Connecticut

Beardsley Park and Zoological Gardens

(**†† ALL**) The New World Tropics building in Connecticut's only zoo, 36 acres in a 180-acre park, boasts the only South American rain forest in New England. Its four main viewing areas, separated by bamboo and glass walls and lighted by skylights, are home to four different kinds of monkeys, small crocodile-like creatures called caimans, ocelots, toucans, macaws, and other exotic animals. If you stop for a break next to a glass barrier, a curious woolly monkey may even peer through it at you and tap on the glass.

The zoo has been moving its animals from old-style cages to natural habitats and plans a number of buildings for indoor exhibits. Most of the hoofed animals graze in a field set off by a moat, and there's a new, larger tiger exhibit. Little kids we know gravitate toward the children's zoo—a New England farm setting where you can feed unusual species of farm animals and walk through a covered bridge. Behind the greenhouse is a historic carousel to ride ($1).

🏛 *Noble Ave., Bridgeport 06610 (Exit 27A off I–95), tel. 203/394–6565. Cost: $5 adults, $3 kids 3–11; parking $4. Open daily 9–4.*

Maritime Aquarium at Norwalk

(**†† ALL**) This complex in a restored 19th-century redbrick foundry includes a maritime museum, the only IMAX theater in Connecticut, two seagoing boats for cruises, and a working boat shop. Yet on the second floor is its most important attraction: a wonderful aquarium devoted to the marine life of Long Island Sound and the Atlantic Ocean. (An indoor-outdoor seal pool, where kids can watch harbor seals being fed, is to the right of the lobby.) Because it's less well known and smaller than Mystic's aquarium (it has a mere 1,100 specimens), this

aquarium is often less crowded, even on weekends, though this is changing. What's special in this aquarium is the ingenious way the 20 marine environments are arranged: You progress from a shallow salt marsh with sand shrimp and mussels through each successive level of habitat to the depths of the ocean. A 110,000-gallon tank houses the center's sand tiger sharks and sandbar sharks, some of which are 9 ft long. The viewing windows go almost to the floor so that even little kids can easily watch the sharks swim by; a separate exhibit allows you to pet one.

Don't miss the exhibit of otters—the two sisters are very active and playful and can often be seen wrestling—or the ray pool, where you can stroke a live ray's back as it swims by. If you plan to see an IMAX show (for kids over 5), buy your tickets as soon as you arrive or reserve in advance; we've sometimes missed out because they are usually sold out by show time. The two research cruises in the Sound (weekends in May, June, Sept., and Oct., daily in summer) are appropriate for interested older (9 and up) kids; participants get to help collect animals and record data.

🏛 *10 N. Water St. (Exit 14 northbound or 15 southbound off I–95), Norwalk 06854, tel. 203/852–0700. Cost: $7.75 adults, $6.50 kids 2–12; IMAX theater $6 adults, $4.75 kids 2–12; combined tickets $12 adults, $9.50 kids 2–12. Open Sept.–June, daily 10–5; July–Aug., daily 10–6.*

Mystic Marinelife Aquarium

(**†† ALL**) Along with the Mystic Seaport Museum nearby, this great aquarium is one of our favorite places in the Northeast and one of the most interesting modern aquariums in the country, a must-see for traveling families. It's also Connecticut's number one tourist attraction, drawing hordes of people in summer; if you can, come in spring or fall.

Mystic Marinelife has more than 6,000 specimens of sea life and the largest collection of marine mammals in the Northeast—three beluga whales, dolphins, and more than 50 seals and sea lions, including the only Steller's sea lions (the biggest species, now endangered) in North America. You'll see (and hear) the seals and sea lions as you walk around Pribilof's Island outdoor complex, a 2½-acre re-creation of New England, California, and Pacific Northwest rocky coastal habitats. The penguins nearby don't look like the ones from the Antarctic; these are African black-footed penguins who look as though they are flying underwater. We're looking forward to the outdoor beluga whale pool scheduled to open in spring 1999; you'll be able to see animals up close, both above the water and from a below-water viewing station.

The main building is now divided into four main sections, each illustrating different ocean habitats. Hundreds of dancing jellyfish greet you at the entrance; inside kids like to hang around the centerpiece, a huge circular (30,000-gallon) tank, to watch 500 exotic fish and sharks dart in and out of the coral reef. In the section devoted to shoreline habitats, a special machine ingeniously re-creates the sounds of a salt marsh as you see if you can spot the mudskipper, a creature that lives caked in mud with just its eyes bulging out. Now you can get closer to the fish than ever before: In the Upwelling Zones gallery, which shows what it's like thousands of feet below the sea's surface, kids can crawl underneath the exhibit into a cavelike bubble window for a fish-eye view; another curved acrylic window in the California coast exhibit lets you come face-to-face with fish.

Unlike other aquariums in the Northeast, this one is also involved in deep-ocean archaeological expeditions through its Institute for Exploration, headed by scientist Dr. Robert D. Ballard, who discovered *Titanic*. In 1999 you'll be able to take a simulated dive below the ocean surface and see the kind of technology it takes to discover shipwrecks.

At the daily 30-minute shows in the World of the Dolphin theater, you'll see dolphins leap 20 ft into the air, vocalize, swim in formation, and walk on the water on their tails. *See also* Chapter 2, Mystic Seaport.

🏠 *55 Coogan Blvd. (Exit 90 off I-95), Mystic 06355–1997, tel. 860/572–5955. Cost: $13 adults, $8 kids 3–12. Open Labor Day–June, daily 9–5 (grounds close at 6); July–Labor Day, daily 9–6 (grounds close at 7).*

New Britain Youth Museum at Hungerford Park

(👫 3–12) Housed in a restored horse stable set on 27 acres, Hungerford has a range of animals that kids can get close to, from a capuchin monkey to rabbits and tarantulas inside, and geese, turkeys, goats, sheep, ducks, chickens, and even a bull outside. Exhibits focus on teaching respect for animals and on rehabilitating wildlife. Regular animal talks on Saturdays are particularly good, with lots of questions from kids and a chance to touch animals.

🏠 *191 Farmington Ave., Rte. 372, Kensington 06037, tel. 860/827–9064. Cost: $2 adults, $1 kids 2–17. Open Labor Day–mid-June, Tues.–Fri. 1–5, Sat. 10–5; July–Aug., Tues.–Fri. 11–5, Sat. 10–5.*

Science Center of Connecticut

(👫 3–12) The only zoo in Hartford is part of this center filled with many other kinds of science exhibits. The indoor-outdoor Live Animal Center, though very small, is home to 30 different species (including cougars, reptiles, birds, and small mammals) and a touch tank. The talking macaws, who can imitate the way different members of the staff say hello and even the way they sneeze, are hilarious.

🏠 *950 Trout Brook Dr., West Hartford 06119, tel. 860/231–2824. Cost: $6 adults, $5 kids 3–15; planetarium $2 additional. Open Sept.–June, Tues.–Sat. 10–5, Thurs. 10–8, Sun. noon–5; July–Aug., Mon.–Sat. 10–5, Thurs. 10–8, Sun. noon–5.*

Maine

Acadia Zoological Park

(**👫 1 – 12**) The most interesting exhibit at this small collection of 55 species just 16 mi north of Bar Harbor is the large barn full of rain-forest creatures. Black and white colobus monkeys, rare golden lion tamarins (the zoo is part of a worldwide effort to save and reintroduce to the wild this endangered species), lemurs, poison-arrow frogs, 2-inch-long hissing cockroaches, and more inhabit this space. Outside are a tiger, snow leopard, moose, and reindeer and some farm animals to pet, along with a picnic area and a fairly basic playground.
🏠 R.F.D. 1, Box 113 (on Rte. 3), Trenton 04605, tel. 207/667–3244. Cost: $6 adults, $5 kids 3–12. Open May–Columbus Day, daily 9:30–5.

Kelmscott Farms

(**👫 1 – 10**) This unusual 160-year-old farm on a hillside in mid-coast Maine is the closest thing the United States has to England's Farm Parks; most of the more than 200 sheep, goats, pigs, cattle, and poultry here are rare breeds that flourished centuries ago but nearly became extinct. Not that kids need to understand this to enjoy visiting—many of these animals are fun to look at, like the four-horned Jacob breed sheep or the huge, 1-ton Shire horse descended from the English horses that carried armored knights into battle. Frequent summer events include sheepdog competitions, riding demonstrations, regular story hours on weekends, and a two-day Renaissance Festival with jousting matches that wow kids.
🏠 R.R. 2, Box 365, Lincolnville, ME 04849, tel. 207/763–4088 or 207/763–4298. Cost: $5 adults, $3 kids 4–15. Open Tues.–Sun., May–Oct. 10–5, Nov.–Apr. 10–3. Closed Mon.

Maine Department of Marine Resources Public Aquarium

(**👫 2 – 12**) If you're in the area, visit this small (1,800 square ft) but interesting aquarium that introduces people to the marine life of this part of Maine. It's tacked onto a fisheries research lab and resource center and is perched on a lovely point overlooking the ocean. The touch pool, designed by the same people who designed the one at the New England Aquarium, is a three-sided, 16-ft-long naturalistic rocky habitat filled with sea urchins, starfish, periwinkles, and other creatures clinging to rocks that kids can reach in and touch. One adventurous kid we know always wants to pat the huge dogfish and the skate in the open, elevated, 20-ft-long, 1,000-gallon tank in the middle of the room. A standing platform around it enables even 3-year-olds to reach easily into the tank. Most of the fish are indoors, but the large wraparound deck outside with views of boats and the harbor has a few touch tanks and kid activities, like getting to measure a lobster.
🏠 McKown Pt., West Boothbay Harbor 04575, tel. 207/633–9542. Cost: $3 adults, $2.50 kids 5–18. Open Memorial Day–Columbus Day, daily 10–5.

Mt. Desert Oceanarium

(**👫 ALL**) One of the nicest things about this small, cozy, low-key 25-tank aquarium (called "The Living Room") and museum of local marine life is the staff of college students, who wander around the exhibits answering questions and just pointing out something special about whatever you happen to be looking at. Hits here are the touch tank with 12 animals kids can hold and the scallop demonstration. The museum's interactive exhibits about sea life and the fishing industry include games to play to answer questions such as "How does the tide happen?" or "Why is the ocean salty?" This place is jammed on a rainy day; come before 10:30 or after 3.

The same family also runs an oceanarium and a lobster hatchery in Bar Harbor; a combined ticket to all three can be used over a period of several days. At the **Oceanarium,** a combination indoor lobster museum, outdoor salt marsh, and harbor-seal pool, you can find out in an interactive exhibit that you can't squeeze as hard as a lobster can. On the guided walk through the 13-acre salt marsh, you see ponds, lots of birds, and maybe even a great blue heron. Displays in the much-expanded **Lobster Hatchery** on the waterfront (the only one in the U.S.) will tell you everything you ever wanted to know about how Maine lobsters grow. You'll see mothers with eggs on their tails (20,000 eggs on one!), babies at different stages, and more than 30,000 tiny lobsters.

🏠 *Mt. Desert Island Oceanarium: Clark Point Rd. (off Rte. 102), Southwest Harbor 04679, tel. 207/244–7330. Cost: $6 adults, $4.50 kids 4–12. Oceanarium and Lobster Hatchery in Bar Harbor: Rte. 3, Bar Harbor 04609, tel. 207/288–5005. Cost for Bar Harbor Oceanarium: $5.50 adults, $4.75 kids 4–12; Lobster Hatchery $3.95 adults, $2.75 kids; 3-location ticket $11.40 adults, $8.35 kids. Open mid-May–mid-Oct., Mon.–Sat. 9–5.*

Scarborough Marsh Nature Center

(👬 **7+**) In this 3,000-acre marsh, the largest in Maine, we saw snowy egrets, osprey, herons, ducks, gulls, cormorants, river otters, and seals. It's hard to spot some of these creatures; your kids are more likely to see something if you take a naturalist-guided tour. The most enjoyable way to see animals here is to get out on the marsh in one of the center's rental canoes, which only cost $10, including paddles, life jackets, and maps. *See also* Chapter 5, Scarborough Marsh Nature Center.

🏠 *Rte. 9 (south of Portland), Scarborough 04074, tel. 207/883–5100. Cost: Donation requested; naturalist-led tours and programs $4; canoe tours $9 adults, $7 kids under 12. Open mid-June–Labor Day, daily 9:30–5:30.*

Massachusetts

Butterfly Place at Papillon Park

(👬 **4–12**) About 500 butterflies (at least 24 different species) flutter freely in this 3,000-square-ft plant-filled atrium of wood and glass, one of the few butterfly farms in the Northeast. Walking around it, we felt transported to some exotic jungle. A 15-minute video introduces the life cycle of the butterfly, and display cases explain more, but we just enjoyed walking on the brick pathway and asking the staff person on duty for specific information. Check to see whether a school group is scheduled before you come.

🏠 *120 Tyngsboro Rd. (40 mi north of Boston), Westford 01886, tel. 978/392–0955. Cost: $6 adults, $5 kids 3–12. Open Apr.–Columbus Day, daily 10–5.*

Drumlin Farm Education Center and Wildlife Sanctuary

(👬 **2–11**) The horses, pigs, cows, owls, chickens, and special demonstrations are the main attractions at this large working farm and nature center run by the Massachusetts Audubon Society just outside Boston. There's always something special—sheep-shearing, tasting from the organic garden, collecting eggs from the chicken coop. Check out the outdoor New England wildlife exhibits, too. At the hibernation exhibit in winter we peered into fox, skunk, groundhog, and rabbit dens and caught a glimpse of sleeping animals—something we'd never seen anywhere else. There are fields to run in; short, easy trails to hike; ponds for exploring; and a mouse nursery to observe. Alas, no picnicking is allowed.

🏠 *208 S. Great Rd. (Rte. 117), South Lincoln 01773, tel. 781/259–9807. Cost: $6 adults, $4 kids 3–12. Open Tues.–Sun. 9–5 and Mon. holidays.*

Fisheries Aquarium

(🕅 3 – 12) A large tank with eels is one of 16 display tanks with marine specimens in the public aquarium at Woods Hole's Northeast Fisheries Science Center. Our favorite part, however, is the laboratory room behind the scenes, where you can reach into three small, child-height touch tanks and pick up lobsters, starfish, and other creatures; look at tiny specimens under illuminated magnifying glasses; and peer down into the display tanks. Student interns answer questions in summer. The purpose of this center is to help the commercial fish industry, so they provide all sorts of information on local fish, including recipes.

🏛 Albatross and Water Sts., Woods Hole 02543, tel. 508/495–2000 or 508/495–2267. Cost: Free. Open mid-Sept.–mid-June, weekdays 10–4; mid-June–mid-Sept., daily 10–4.

Franklin Park Zoo

(🕅 ALL) This 72-acre enclosed zoo in a huge Boston park is still in the process of being revitalized (as is Franklin Park itself), but now there are many more reasons to make the trek than the world-class African Tropical Forest, one of North America's largest freestanding enclosed tropical forests. Here, as you walk through the gorilla area, put your face against the glass at overlook number two. Chances are a gorilla will amble over, sit on the other side, stare at you, and put his face up to yours. Walking along the meandering path, we saw pygmy hippos underwater, listened to the sound of waterfalls, observed birds building nests, and stopped to watch baboons, crocodiles, and leopards. Now there's much, much more—including a splendidly designed 3-acre lion exhibit, a butterfly greenhouse garden, and an Australian Outback trail where you can walk on the same path the wallabies and kangaroos use. Pierpont Road parking is closest to the Tropical Forest, Blue Hill to the Lion and Antelope exhibits.

🏛 1 Franklin Park Rd. (Rte. 203 East from Rte. 1 to Circuit Dr.), Boston 02121, tel. 617/541–5466. Cost: $6 adults, $3 kids 2–15. Open Oct.–Mar. daily 10–4; Apr.–Sept. weekdays 10–5, weekends and holidays 10–6.

New England Alive Nature Study Center

(🕅 1 – 12) Kids can hold newly hatched chicks and newborn bunnies and feed goats, lambs, and calves at this barnyard and nature center. It's special because it's also a licensed rehabilitation center that treats as many as 700 injured and orphaned animals every year. A mountain lion, turtles, frogs, black bears, snakes, a bobcat, hawks and owls, and more are in natural enclosures, and there's a brook with a waterfall, a pond, flower gardens, a snack bar, and tables with white-and-red-checked tablecloths at which to picnic (you can bring your own or buy from a concession stand). Paved paths are ideal for strollers.

🏛 189 High St. (Rtes. 1A and 133), Ipswich 01938, tel. 978/356–7013. Cost: $5 adults, $3 kids 3–12. Open Apr.–Nov., weekdays 9–5, weekends 9:30–6.

New England Aquarium

(🕅 ALL) One great thing about this world-class aquarium is its easy-to-reach location right on Boston's historic waterfront overlooking the harbor; it's much more accessible to the city than New York's aquarium is to New York. Virtually all the exhibits are inside, including ground-level pools with jackass penguins that bray like donkeys and rockhopper penguins with head feathers that resemble punk hairdos. The most spectacular exhibit is the glass-enclosed, four-story saltwater Giant Ocean Tank (one of the largest in the world) at the center of the building, which brings several species of sharks, huge sea turtles, and hundreds of fish just inches from your face. When the diver descends five times a day to feed them, the fish get excited, gobbling up drifting bits of food, darting here and there, and they even eat from his hand. Kids seem to find just running up and down the ramp that spirals around the tank irresistible. But when the aquarium is crowded, the line of visitors winding up the ramp seems almost claustrophobic—kids press their noses to the windows and don't move on. Crowds are worst between 11 and 3 on weekends and during school vacations.

Another favorite area is the Edge of the Sea hands-on tidal pool, a re-creation of a rocky shore in Maine, where you can learn from encouraging aquarium employees how to turn over a horseshoe crab. Outside the two-level west wing, opened in 1998, are seals to watch for free; inside are changing exhibits, like the one where we gazed at silvery garden eels waving their heads, and crocodiles in a mangrove swamp.

At the sea lion shows aboard the floating pavilion next to the aquarium (admission is included in your aquarium ticket) you'll get wet if you sit in the front rows. From April to October the aquarium also sponsors its own excellent whale-watching expeditions and 45-minute tours of Boston Harbor (best for little kids) on which kids can help pull up lobster traps and look at plankton under microscopes. *See also* Chapter 6, Whale-watching on the *Voyager.*

🏫 *Central Wharf (Aquarium T stop on the Blue Line), Boston 02110, tel. 617/973–5200. Cost: $11 adults, $5.50 kids 3–11. Open July–Labor Day, Mon.–Tues. and Fri. 9–6; Wed.–Thurs. 9–8; weekends and holidays 9–7; Labor Day–June, weekdays 9–5, weekends and holidays 9–6.*

EcoTarium

(👫 2+) This large, three-story building is packed with science exhibits. Its Wildlife Center, affiliated with the Tufts University Wildlife Clinic, acquires only injured animals. It offers talks and interactive programs—such as a workshop on building birdhouses and an exploration of why some animals don't make good pets. Outside, polar bears, bobcats, river otters, and snowy owls live in

fenced enclosures on the center's 60 acres. One of the nicest ways to see them is on the leisurely 20-minute train ride ($1.50) past all the animals. *See also* Chapter 3, Eco-Tarium.

🏫 *222 Harrington Way (off Rte. 9), Worcester 02110, tel. 508/791–9211. Cost: $6 adults, $4 kids 3–16 and college students with ID. Open Mon.–Sat. 10–5, Sun. noon–5.*

Southwick's Wild Animal Farm

(👫 ALL) One of several family-owned game farms in the Northeast, Southwick's has more than 100 different species, including giraffes, rhinos, lions, and tigers, making it the largest zoo in New England. Like New York's Catskill Game Farm, Southwick's doesn't have the atmosphere or conservation-oriented philosophy of the Bronx Zoo and other members of the American Zoological Society. Though it has a country-ish feeling, wide, winding paths good for strollers, a moated elephant exhibit where three elephants roam freely, as well as a new moated area for two lions, some of the animals here are still in old-fashioned small cages with chain-link fencing. There are daily animal shows, elephant rides, and a new playground. Don't miss feeding the llamas and a walk among the herd of deer.

🏫 *2 Southwick St. (off Rte. 16), Mendon 01756, tel. 508/883–9182 or 800/258–9182. Cost: $8.75 adults, $6.75 kids 3–12. Open May–Columbus Day, daily 10–5.*

ZooQuarium

(👫 2 – 12) The owners of this small group of buildings and outdoor environments stress conservation in their exhibits, which focus on aquatic creatures native to the waters of Cape Cod (inside in tanks) and species that flourish in Massachusetts, like bobcats, foxes, raccoons, and so on (outdoors in small but naturalistic environments). All are nonreleasable, rehabilitated animals. There are also llamas, pigs, sheep, and other domestic animals that you can pet. The Children's Discovery Center has displays teaching about different aspects of animal life, like Scoop on Poop. Daily seal and sea lion shows and short live-animal presentations take place all summer.

🏠 674 Rte. 28, West Yarmouth 02673, tel. 508/775–8883. Cost: $7.50 adults, $4.50 kids 2–9. Open Feb.–late June and Sept.–Nov., daily 9:30–5; late June–Labor Day, Mon.–Thurs. 9:30–8, Fri.–Sun. 9:30–6.

New Hampshire

Friendly Farm

(👬 1–7) We spent hours at this charming New England farm with more than 100 baby animals in a barn, henhouse, and fenced pens outdoors during Gavin's first three summers. In the henhouse you'll usually see chicks hatching and you can cuddle a baby chick. Other highlights are the fat sow reclining in dirt as she feeds her tiny pink piglets, a pen of baby bunnies, and the honking geese, who draw a crowd when they hiss and attack each other.

If you can, visit at the beginning of the season and then again later so you can see how much the animals have grown.

🏠 Rte. 101 (½ mi west of Dublin Lake), Dublin 03444, tel. 603/563–8444. Cost: $4.75 adults, $3.75 kids 1–12. Open late Apr.–Labor Day, daily (weather permitting) 10–5; Labor Day–Columbus Day, weekends 10–5.

Science Center of New Hampshire

(👬 3–14) All the animals in this 200-acre complex of indoor and outdoor exhibits devoted to native New Hampshire wildlife have been either orphaned or injured and can no longer survive in the wild. The black bears, bobcats, deer, red foxes, otters, turtles, birds, and other convalescents live in spacious natural woodland and marsh habi-

tat enclosures along an easy-to-walk, ¾-mi exhibit trail. The otter exhibit has an underwater viewing window where we watched these playful creatures swim. There's a real effort here to introduce kids to the science behind these animal and plant environments through interactive exhibits, puzzles, and games. In summer, staff members give regular 15-minute minitalks about animal and plant life. At the Children's Activity Center in a two-story barn, kids 3–8 find out what it feels like to be an animal by going down a groundhog hole, climbing a giant spiderweb, and walking through a two-story hollow tree. The center also offers nature cruises on Squam Lake appropriate for older kids.

🏠 Rte. 113, Box 173, Holderness 03245, tel. 603/968–7194. Cost: $6 adults ($8 July–Aug.), $3 kids 5–15 ($4 July–Aug.). Open May–Oct., daily 9:30–4:30 (live-animal programs July–Aug. only).

New York

Bronx Zoo/International Wildlife Conservation Park

(👬 ALL) Everyone in our family has always loved this internationally famous 265-acre zoo, the oldest and largest in any North American city. You simply won't be able to see all the 4,000 creatures here in a single day. The zoo has self-guided tour maps that show the quickest routes to specific animals. (Your best bet is to call or write for a map before you come.) If your children are toddlers or preschoolers, it's essential to bring a stroller or rent one at a park entrance ($5 plus $20 deposit; you can't take the strollers into buildings). Assume even older kids will need to rest their feet on the Zoo Shuttle, an open-sided tram that follows the perimeter path.

Paved paths from the several parking lots pass large and small outdoor naturalistic habitats that are interspersed with buildings; most of the animals are outdoors. Birds, sea lions, monkeys, the Children's Zoo, and the Zoo Center cluster in the northeastern part of the zoo; African, Asian, and a few South American animals spread out over the western half. We head first to the monorail around Wild Asia because lines waiting to board it grow very long in the afternoon; riding it is as much fun as looking down on the elephants, rhinoceroses, and other Asian creatures you pass. The indoor rain forest in World of Birds is another of our favorites, as is the World of Darkness, which seems quite dark even after your eyes adjust. It's best for kids over 8. Be sure to see the bats and the amazing Naked Mole-Rats exhibit, which has cross-section views of mole-rat tunnel systems; miniature TV cameras provide close-ups. The world's largest—and most elaborate—African rain-forest exhibit, Congo Gorilla Forest, is set to open this spring (1999); the 6½-acre indoor-outdoor exhibit will be home to two family groups of gorillas as well as okapi, mandrill, red river hogs, peacocks, reptiles, fish—35 species and 300 animals in all. Much of the exhibit is designed to minimize the feeling of separation between you and the animals. For example, you'll be able to view lowland gorillas up close and on four sides from inside a huge gallery of glass and then walk through their habitat in a glass tunnel (reinforced glass, of course). Feeding stations are right next to the glass, so expect to be as close as you'll ever be able to get to a gorilla—some little kids might be scared by their proximity. In the Children's Zoo, kids can pet and feed domestic animals and discover what it might feel like to be an animal by climbing a rope spiderweb, trying on a turtle shell, and sitting in the kid-size bird nest. This area is often very crowded on sunny weekends; skip it if your kids are over 9.

One of the zoo's special events really stands out: Every evening for six weeks, beginning just after Thanksgiving to just after New Year's, the Holiday Lights extravaganza features 50 giant animal sculptures, ice carvings, live reindeer, caroling, and visits to animal exhibits.

🏠 *Fordham Rd. (Subway 2 to Pelham Pkwy. or Bus Bx9 and Bx19 to Southern Blvd. entrance or Liberty Lines Express Bus BxM11, call 718/652–8400, from stops on Madison Ave.), Bronx 10460, tel. 718/367–1010 or 718/220–5100. Cost: $7.75 adults, $4 kids 2–12; free Wed.; parking $6; extra charges for Children's Zoo and several other exhibits; 1-yr family membership $58. Reduced prices Nov.– Mar. Open Mar.–Oct., weekdays 10–5, weekends and holidays 10–5:30; Nov.–Feb., daily 10–4:30.*

Catskill Game Farm

👫 **ALL** Seeing, patting, and bottle-feeding baby animals (like young lambs) in the animal nursery are among the highlights of a visit to this 240-acre game farm, the first privately owned zoo in the United States. Kids can walk among, pat, and feed the friendly deer and llamas. Animal food is expensive—$3 for 40 crackers. Among the more than 2,000 animals to see are zebras, African antelopes, crocodiles, rhinos, lions, and bears, and you can get fairly close to all of them, especially those still in old-fashioned cages. Paved pathways ideal for strollers connect all the areas; from the petting zoo you can take a train through the bird section—the best bet with little kids. Exciting and excellent animal shows in summer feature dancing elephants and bicycle-riding bears, and elephant and amusement park rides, all of which reflect a more entertainment-oriented philosophy than the one prevalent at zoos today.

🏠 *400 Game Farm Rd. (off Rte. 32), Catskill 12414, tel. 518/678–9595. Cost: $13.50 adults, $9.50 kids 4–11. Open May–Oct., daily 9–5 (Memorial Day–Labor Day, daily 9–6).*

Central Park Wildlife Conservation Center and Children's Zoo

👫 **0–12** Central Park's 5½-acre zoo is one of the most charming small city zoos I've ever seen, the perfect size for toddlers and preschoolers or just for a one-hour stroll to see animals. The sea lion pool (feeding times are 11:30, 2, and 4) lies at the center (you can glimpse these popular animals without actually going into the zoo). There are Victorian-style green metal fences and gates, walkways, benches, four large, fierce-looking stone eagles, and gardens around it, and buildings and areas representing three different climate zones beyond. A surprising number of animals, from red pandas to penguins, are housed in these miniature environments. The indoor Tropic Zone has a small rain forest; the outdoor Temperate Territory has snow monkeys scampering on an island; the Polar Circle has polar bears in a big pool. Toddlers can see into the pool from a stroller. It's easy for preschoolers to walk around the whole zoo. The new children's zoo is best for the 3-and-under crowd; you'll see goats, rabbits, a Vietnamese potbellied pig as well as an aviary where birds fly free and people are confined. Costumed characters provide information and answer questions. Occasional events, like the Go Batty Halloween celebration, are always well planned.

🏠 *64th St. and 5th Ave., New York 10021, tel. 212/861–6030. Cost: $3.50 adults, 50¢ kids 3–12. Open weekdays 10–5, weekends and holidays 10:30–5:30; Nov.–Mar., daily 10–4:30.*

Jamaica Bay Wildlife Refuge

(👯 **10+**) Kids who are interested in birds will truly appreciate this nearly 10,000-acre tidal wetlands and uplands nature preserve that borders Jamaica Bay on Long Island. Spring and fall are the best times to glimpse migrating birds—the refuge is on a major migration flyway, and its variety of habitats mean you'll see many different kinds of birds. A quarterly program guide gives a schedule of guided walks and programs given by National Park Service rangers.

🏠 *Visitor's Center, Crossbay Blvd., Broad Channel, Queens, tel. 718/318–4340. For information, write to Gateway National Recreation Area, Floyd Bennett Field, Brooklyn 11234, tel. 718/338–3338. Cost: Free. Open daily 8:30–5.*

Long Island Game Farm

(👯 **2–12**) There are not many places to see animals on Long Island; at this combined petting zoo and 45-acre family park that's been around since 1970, kids can cuddle and bottle-feed baby animals at the Nursery and hand-feed deer in Bambiland. They can also see llamas, zebras, camels, monkeys, bears, peacocks, and more. Paved pathways suitable for strollers link the themed sections. Kids we know also head for Old MacDonald's Farm, where farm animals live in a cluster of big red barns, and for the swing rides in the Play Park. Get an overview of all the animals aboard the 1860s train around the park. Kids can touch pythons, lizards, and an iguana at the Animal Wonderland shows.

🏠 *Chapman Blvd. (Exit 70 off Long Island Expwy. [LIE]), Manorville 11949, tel. 516/878–6644. Cost: $11.95 + tax adults, $9.95 + tax kids 2–11. Open mid-Apr.–mid-Oct., weekdays 10–5, weekends 10–6.*

New York Aquarium for Wildlife Conservation

(👯 **ALL**) The best time to visit this aquarium is on a nice day in late spring, summer, or early fall. That's because it's adjacent to the Coney Island boardwalk and beach, and because, unlike the New England Aquarium, the most exciting part of it is outside—the 300-ft-long Pacific rocky coast habitat, Sea Cliffs, a series of five environments where penguins, seals, walruses, and otters live. Even toddlers in strollers can easily see the animals because the all-glass barriers go all the way down to the walkway, and the animals swim right up to them. From inside an adjoining building you have an underwater view of each animal (we saw the fur seals playing and kissing), as well as many other exhibits, including the Living in Water room, where we compared our weight to that of different animals. The shark exhibit is the best we've seen, and you can touch creatures in the Discovery Cove. The aquaview theater has three sea lion and dolphin shows daily; it's big, so nab a seat down front or at the very top where you can see the ocean. This isn't as impressive an aquarium as the revamped one in Mystic, Connecticut, but here you can walk on the beach and try some rides at the nearby amusement parks.

🏠 W. 8th St. off Surf Ave. (Subway F or D to W. 8th St. stop in Brooklyn, then pedestrian overpass), Coney Island, Brooklyn 11224, tel. 718/265–3400. Cost: $8.75 adults, $4.50 kids 2–12. Open Labor Day–Memorial Day, daily 10–5; Memorial Day–Labor Day, weekdays 10–5, weekends and holidays 10–7.

Rhode Island

Roger Williams Park and Zoo

(👯 **ALL**) It's easy to see why the Boston Globe rated this 40-acre haven for 957 domestic and exotic animals the best zoo in New England. In the middle of a beautiful, large park with ponds, lakes, expanses of lawn, and walkways designed in the 19th century, the zoo has charming historic Victorian buildings as well as many recently revamped exhibits. The large animals, including giraffes, zebras, and elephants, are now in outdoor naturalistic settings; the polar bear pool has an underwater viewing window; and the Farmyard's storybook-style signs tell about donkeys, goats, pigs, sheep, and the famous state chicken, the Rhode Island Red.

Visits to several areas are a must. In the two-level Tropical America building a spiral staircase and rope bridge lead to a platform from which to view very active monkeys. The outdoor Asian animal display is a "biopark," in which you see the animals as part of a foreign land; you enter through Marco Polo's sailing ship and "disembark" in Asia, where kids can sit on a camel saddle and under a bedouin awning. At Plains of Africa, the elephants' bath time at 10 AM is a daily event. Combine a visit here with time in the adjacent park, where you can rent a

mini-speedboat, play miniature golf, ride the carousel, or visit the only public planetarium in Rhode Island. Or stop at the zoo before a trip to see the Pawtucket Red Sox.

🏠 1000 Elmwood Ave. (off I–95), Providence 02907, tel. 401/785–3510. Cost: $6 adults, $3.50 kids 3–12; parking free. Open Nov.– Apr., daily 9–4; May–Oct., weekdays 9–5, weekends and holidays 9–6.

Vermont

Billings Farm and Museum

(👯 1–13) This large, historic working dairy farm illustrates what farm life was like in the 19th century. Besides visiting the L-shape dairy and livestock barns and pens that house prize Jersey cows, chickens, oxen, super woolly Southdown sheep, and a newborn calf nursery, you can also wander through a farm-life museum and a rambling 1890s farmhouse, which has an attached dairy bar that serves farm-made ice cream. The kinds of demonstrations and special events you see depend on the weather and the time of year and day you visit—you might see teams of oxen pulling plows and learn how farmers trained these huge animals. The best time to come is in the afternoon. There's lots to do to fill a morning or afternoon here, plus places to picnic.

🏠 Rte. 12, Woodstock 05091, tel. 802/ 457–2355. Cost: $7 adults, $5.50 kids 13– 17, $3.50 kids 5–12, $1 kids 3–4, $18 family. Open May–Oct., daily 10–5; Nov.–Dec., call for hrs.

Shelburne Farms

(👯 2–10) We came on a warm, sunny summer afternoon to see goats, cows, sheep, chickens, and all the usual farm animals at this former estate high above Lake Champlain. It's about a 10-minute walk on a mowed-grass path from the visitor center at the entrance to the Children's Farmyard, an open area bounded by traditional New

England red barns and outbuildings that's designed so kids can run around among the animals, but we rode on a hay wagon along with several families with small children. Before long all the kids were learning how to milk a cow, collect eggs, and make butter. The Farmyard is more appealing to toddlers and preschoolers than is the Billings Farm. At the main barn the farm's prizewinning (and delicious) cheddar cheese is made; you can visit and taste. Skip the slide show and the historic gardens (boring, Mom). An 8-mi walking trail around the property has wonderful views of Lake Champlain from Lone Tree Hill.

🏠 Bay and Harbor Rds. (off Rte. 7), Shelburne 05482, tel. 802/985–8686. Cost: $5 adults, $3 kids 3–14. Open mid-May–mid-Oct., daily 10–4.

UVM Morgan Horse Farm

(👫 4+) The University of Vermont now operates this working farm, one of the centers where purebred Morgan horses were developed in the 19th century. It is worth a stop for kids who are keen horse lovers (especially if they've read Justin Morgan Had a Horse by Marguerite Henry). Stroll around the spacious grounds, hang over a fence to see horses being trained for riding, and poke your head into the Victorian barn to see the horses in their stalls. The 20-minute guided tours of the stables

and the 15-minute video presentation will educate you about this breed. You can't pat or feed the horses, but they will come up to the fence to check you out. The 6 acres of lawns are perfect for picnics, and the gift shop has all sorts of wonderful items for horse-loving kids—wind chimes with horses, horse earrings, good books, and puzzles.

🏠 Morgan Horse Farm Rd., Middlebury 05753, tel. 802/388–2011. Cost: $4 adults, $3 kids 13–19, $1 kids 5–12. Open May–Oct., daily 9–4.

Vermont Institute of Natural Science

(👫 3–15) The focus at this research institute on 77 acres is the study and rehabilitation of raptors. In its Raptor Center you can see more than 26 species of birds, including injured owls, falcons, hawks, and bald eagles, and learn how they were rehabilitated. The most intriguing part to us was the way the large naturalistic flight cages have been customized to suit each bird's injury; to protect birds' feet, branches are wrapped with carpeting. A raptor flight demonstration is held each afternoon. Stop by the Nature Store at the institute and take one of the short, self-guided nature trails.

🏠 Church Hill Rd., Woodstock 05482, tel. 802/457–2779. Cost: $6 adults, $2 kids 5–11. Open May–Oct., daily 10–4; Nov.–Apr., Mon.–Sat. 10–4.

PARKS, SEASHORES, AND NATURE CENTERS
GREEN SPACES, WILDERNESS, BIG ROCKS, AND BOGS

The Northeast has national parks, forests, seashores, wildlife refuges, state parks, and recreation areas, as well as lands that are preserved by national organizations such as the Audubon Society and the Nature Conservancy, all with different purposes:

• **National and state parks** almost always have the most facilities. The largest, like Acadia National Park in Maine, have visitor centers with nature programs and guided hikes for families and kids; campgrounds and picnic areas are well equipped. Even the smaller parks on lakes usually provide a lifeguard, bathhouses, and a snack bar.

• **National and state forests** extend over much larger areas and tend to have fewer amenities. I have to admit that these are what my husband and I prefer, and sometimes my son has agreed.

• **Wilderness areas** in the Northeast are as wild as any in the West; they're for families with older kids who like to backpack, hike, and canoe.

• **National seashores,** like the one on Cape Cod, are similar to national forests in terms of facilities but offer beaches and swimming and have more educational programs.

• **Wildlife refuges and sanctuaries** have been especially attractive to us because we find that our enthusiasm for birds and animals and nature activities rarely wanes, as long as the programs don't get too didactic. For information on National Wildlife Refuges in the Northeast contact the United States Fish and Wildlife Service (Northeast Regional Office, 300 Westgate Center Dr., Hadley, MA 01035, tel. 413/253–8322). Audubon Centers in particular are a wonderful combination of short, well-laid-out hikes, wildlife viewing, and very strong but interesting-to-kids educational programs—we learned how bees swarm at one—that are particularly appealing for a one-day visit. For our family a park has to offer more than woods and a view, and the parks and places listed below reflect that preference.

July and August are the most crowded months in all parks; that's also when most planned activities occur. The early fall is our favorite time to explore woods. (Be aware that Lyme disease, caused by the tiny deer tick, is a problem in the Northeast. When exploring parks during the summer, check yourself and your children daily for ticks.) *See also* Chapter 6 for more specific activities such as camping and hiking and Chapters 11 and 12 *under* Green Spaces for information on city parks.

Connecticut

Connecticut has more than 100 state parks and forests, many quite similar to one another, with the woodland, stream, and pond landscape that characterizes much of Connecticut; you'll find others along the state's two most scenic rivers—the Housatonic and the Connecticut—along the shores of lakes, and at a few saltwater beaches on Long Island Sound. For more information, contact the **Bureau of Outdoor Recreation** (State Parks Division, Connecticut Dept. of Environmental Protection, 79 Elm St., Hartford 06106–5127, tel. 860/424–3200).

Lake Waramaug State Park

(👫 0–12) Lake Waramaug, surrounded by nicely forested hills and lake inns, has a meandering, winding coastline and a road that follows it. The park lies along a sheltered finger of water; shady trees, picnic tables, and grass edge a wide sand beach; across the road and down a bit among the trees are campsites that all have a view of the water. For little kids the swimming area is just the right size; the grassy spots are good places to stand and throw in a fishing line; and the lake is calm enough for easy canoeing and paddle-boating, even with young kids. Rarely crowded except on holiday weekends, the park attracts families and kids. The only drawbacks: Kids have to cross the road to get to the snack bar from the beach, which, in early fall, attracts lots of messy geese.

🏠 *30 Lake Waramaug Rd., New Preston 06777, tel. 860/868–0220. Cost: Free weekdays, $8 nonresident parking fee weekends. Open daily 8–sunset. Facilities: camping, canoe*

and paddleboat rentals, fishing, hiking, picnicking, snack bar, swimming.

Rocky Neck State Park

(👫 2+) Though we prefer the coastal beaches of Rhode Island, Cape Cod, and Long Island, this mile-long crescent beach is our preferred public saltwater swimming site in Connecticut.

🏠 *Rte. 156 (Exit 72 off I–95), Niantic 06357, tel. 860/739–5471. Cost: $5 weekdays, $7 weekends for CT vehicles; $8 weekdays, $12 weekends for out-of-state vehicles. Open daily 8–sunset. Facilities: bathhouses, family campground, fishing, picnicking, snack bar.*

Sharon Audubon Center

(👫 4–12) This 758-acre nature center is essentially rural Connecticut countryside, with woodlands, ponds, stream, marsh, meadow, and swamp crisscrossed by trails and wildlife—a setting that seems to have been perfectly arranged by nature for young kids and families who want to spend an afternoon or the whole day outdoors. Trails cross a boardwalk above a bog, follow the edges of ponds, and pass big rocks on which you can climb. Kids' nature programs are offered on many weekends, and in March families can help collect and make maple syrup (call to check times).

🏠 *Rte. 4, 93 W. Cornwall Rd., Sharon 06069, tel. 860/364–0520. Cost: $3 adults, $1.50 kids under 18. Trails open daily dawn–dusk; museum open Mon.–Sat. 9–5, Sun. 1–5.*

White Memorial Foundation

(👫 3–12) The 4,000 acres of Connecticut's largest nature center and wildlife sanctuary used to be a private estate. What drew our family back weekend after weekend were the easy hikes, the boardwalks over marshy areas where you can view wildlife, ponds where you can catch tadpoles and spot sunning turtles, wide meadows and grassy areas for running and spreading a blanket for a picnic, and excellent family programs. Even if it's not raining, stop in their big new (1997) Nature Museum; besides dioramas of animals and habitats, it also has wonderful ceiling murals of clouds in a blue sky, doorways surrounded with paintings of creatures, and forest sounds wafting through the air. Among the most interesting exhibits are the life-size model of a beaver lodge and, in the children's room, a big snake in a tank as well as items kids can touch.

🏠 *Rte. 202, Litchfield 06759, tel. 860/567–0857. Cost: Grounds free; nature center $4 adults, $2 kids 6–12. Grounds open daily 24 hrs; nature center Apr.–Nov., Mon.–Sat. 9–5, Sun. noon–5; Nov.–Apr., Mon.–Sat. 8:30–4:30, Sun. noon–4. Facilities: bird-watching, camping, cross-country skiing, family programs, fishing, gift shop, hiking, horseback riding, library, nature center, nearby beach.*

Maine

Maine's parks are the most diverse in the Northeast: sandy beaches and rocky promontories along the Atlantic; freshwater lakes inland; and a wilderness of mountains and gorges in the vast, forested, remote northern region. I haven't included any of the state's southern beach state parks; Maine's northern rocky coast, unique in the Northeast, is what we prefer. One warning: No matter where you go, bring insect repellent, especially in June, which is black-fly season. For general information contact the **Maine Bureau of Parks and Lands** (22 State House Station, Augusta 04333–0022, tel. 207/287–3821). The State Department of Conservation publishes "Outdoors in Maine," a map and guide to 30 state parks. Family season passes allowing unlimited day-

time use of Maine's state parks are available for $40 by mail from the Bureau. "On Water, On Wings, In the Woods—A Guide for Maine Wildlife Watchers" contains information on spotting wildlife in state parks ($5.95; Dept. of Inland Fisheries and Wildlife, 284 State St., 41 SHS, Augusta, ME 04333, tel. 207/287-8000). *The Maine Atlas and Gazetteer* (DeLorme Mapping, Box 298, Yarmouth, ME 04096, tel. 207/846–7000) has a complete listing of Maine's city, state, and national parks and recreation areas, plus nature preserves, natural areas, waterfalls, and beaches.

Acadia National Park

👫 2+   Acadia is one of the country's most popular national parks, and it's no wonder: Its 22 square mi, which includes most of Mount Desert Island (and the Schoodic Peninsula, Isle au Haut, and some small islands), captures all that our family loves about Maine's coast—a ragged shoreline of fingers of rock; craggy, towering cliffs with pounding surf at the bottom; fragrant pines; perfect blue lakes; pink granite mountains; and shallow mountain streams. Mount Desert Island's first settlers were the Abnaki Indians. The explorer Samuel de Champlain named it, and Woodrow Wilson set aside much of it as a park in 1919. What makes Mount Desert Island so attractive to us as a place for a family vacation is the unique combination of beautiful scenery, a wide range of activities—you can bike, hike, swim, canoe, ride horseback, camp, and participate in some of the best kids' nature programs around—and proximity to several towns, especially the lively village of Bar Harbor, which is full of shops, museums, and restaurants. Plus, it's an island, and that makes it seem cut off from ordinary life.

Stop first at the visitor center at Hulls Cove. The free 15-minute video gives kids a quick introduction to the park's history, geology, flora, and fauna. Pick up information on hiking trails, campgrounds, and especially the Acadia National Park "Beaver Log," which lists free daily naturalist programs for kids (and adults).

Next, for an overview, drive the 27-mi loop road around one small portion of the park, finishing off with the Cadillac Mountain Summit Road (come back at sunrise to be the first people in the United States to see the sun that day). The views of the whole island and the bay from the top are simply stunning, though on most days this has to be the most densely populated spot on the island.

If your kids are old enough, rent bikes and explore car-free carriage paths; this is a good way to get to more remote spots without hiking. Do take one of the park naturalist cruises; you won't always see a seal (we didn't), but you'll probably see porpoises. The best place to swim is in freshwater Echo Lake, near Southwest Harbor, which has a sandy beach and lifeguards. The water at Sand Beach is so frigid our legs went numb.

Head for the famous sights—Thunder Hole (a chasm that gets its name from the boom of waves rushing in and compressing pockets of trapped air) and Sand Beach—before 10 or after 4:30 and concentrate on hiking on the western side of the island during the middle of the day. The Sierra Club offers a yearly Toddler Tromp camping and hiking experience here for families with small children.

The best guides to the park are *The AMC Guide to Mount Desert Island and Acadia National Park* (Appalachian Mountain Club, 1993) and *An Outdoor Family Guide to Acadia National Park* (Evans, Mountaineer Books). Good descriptions of appropriate hikes for kids in the park are in *Best Hikes with Children in Vermont, New Hampshire & Maine* (Lewis and Lewis, Mountaineer Books). See also Chapter 6, Biking, Camping, Canoeing.
🏠 *Superintendent, Box 177, Bar Harbor 04609, tel. 207/288–3338. Park Headquarters, Rte. 233, Eagle Lake; open daily 8–4:30. Visitor center, Rte. 3, Hulls Cove, tel. 207/288–4932; open mid-Apr.–Oct., daily 8–4:30 (July–Aug, daily 8–6). Cost: $10 per car for 1 wk; camping: Blackwoods $16 (tel. 800/365–*

2267 for reservations), Seawall $11–$14 (no reservations). Park open daily 24 hrs (Cadillac Mt. closed midnight–dawn). Facilities: biking, boat cruises, camping, canoeing, carriage roads, hiking trails, horseback riding, nature programs, rock climbing, swimming.

Baxter State Park

(🏃🏃 **8+**)   This is a place for families who want a great wilderness experience where they can stay in a primitive cabin instead of pitching a tent. It's best for kids who have already done some primitive camping and really love hiking and fishing. Why? Baxter's unspoiled 201,018 acres in Maine's remote northwest region, dominated by mile-high Mt. Katahdin, are as close to wilderness as you'll get in the Northeast. That means no running water, electricity, food, or supplies in the park. On the other hand, it offers some of the best canoeing and fishing in the country on truly pristine ponds and lakes, as well as the chance to see bears, moose, deer, and other wildlife; and you will not find crowds on the easy trails.

The park has only 10 campgrounds, and people start reserving space in January. Call for the forms; telephone reservations are not accepted. The best sites for families are Daicey Pond and Kidney Pond, which have a main gathering building where kids can hang out if it rains and two- to six-person primitive cabins with bunks and mattresses, a stove, a table, and chairs. Both are near many easy trails; Daicey Pond has views of Katahdin. The essential complete guidebook to the park (and other camping possibilities nearby) is *Katahdin: A Guide to Baxter State Park & Katahdin* by Stephen Clark (North Country Press). The park's rangers are particularly helpful and offer many personal services.
🏠 *Baxter Park Headquarters, 64 Balsam Dr., Millinocket 04462, tel. 207/723–5140 or 207/723–9500 (secretary). Cost: $8 per car for nonresidents, free for residents. Camping fees range from $12 to $50 (for 2- to 4-person cabins). Open mid-May–mid-Oct., daily 6 AM–10 PM; mid-Oct.–mid-May, daily dawn–dusk.*

Facilities: backpacking, camping, fishing, hiking, moose watching.

Desert of Maine

(👫 5–14) This unique, 50-acre sandy desert environment surrounded by lush trees and wildflowers has an intriguing story: During the last ice age, glaciers left behind sand and mineral deposits that were eventually covered over with soil, then trees; finally it became farmland. After years of tree-cutting and overgrazing, the topsoil eroded, exposing the sand underneath. Now it's both a natural wonder—a small desert with dunes higher than trees and buildings and occasional sandstorms—and a privately owned tourist attraction. On the sand, it's sometimes more than 100°F; when you step into the pine woods at the desert's edge it's like walking into air-conditioning. Many kids enjoy the gemstone search, but skip the turn-of-the-century museum, with its displays of farm equipment.

🏠 Desert Rd. (Exit 19 off I–95), Freeport 04032, tel. 207/865–6962. Cost: $6.75 adults, $4.75 kids 13–16, $3.75 kids 6–12. Open May 5–Oct. 15, daily 9–6.

Grafton Notch State Park

(👫 7+) Waterfalls and gorges are the attractions of this end of the Mahoosuc range not far from the Sunday River ski resort. Several of these impressive sights are almost roadside stops along Route 26, so they're easy to explore with kids. Both 900-ft-long Mother Walker Falls Gorge and Screw Auger Falls Gorge have natural bridges at their upper end; each has rocks to climb on and pools to wade in. Moose Cave Gorge has large mossy boulders. If you want to hike, head for Table Rock; underneath its ledges are a labyrinth of slab caves and tunnels to explore, but with caution. Don't miss the hike to Step Falls—it's just before the entrance to the park. See also Chapter 6, Hiking (Step Falls).

🏠 Rte. 26 (14 mi north of Bethel), between Upton and Newry, Newry 04261, tel. 207/

824–2912, 207/624–6075 in off-season. Cost: $1 adults, 50¢ kids 5–11. Open mid-May–mid-Oct., daily 9–sunset. Facilities: fishing, hiking, picnicking.

Lily Bay State Park

(👫 5+) On the shores of Moosehead Lake (Maine's largest lake), this park's 924 acres are almost—but not quite—in the wilderness. The spacious, well-laid-out campsites among pine trees make you feel you're in backcountry, but amenities like a playground and a nice small beach with good but cold swimming make it a bit more comfortable. It's best as a center from which to explore the bays and inlets and islands of undeveloped Moosehead Lake. (Though the park has no canoe rentals, several shops will deliver.) The lake is 40 mi long and 10 mi wide, and is surrounded by rugged mountains and dense forest, where some 10,000 moose live. The best time to see them is at dawn or dusk in some of the secluded bogs not too far from the park. From Greenville, you can board the S.S. Katahdin for a boat trip to spectacular Mt. Kineo.

🏠 Beaver Cove, Moosehead Lake (8 mi north of Greenville), Greenville 14441, tel. 207/695–2700. Cost for day use: $2 adults, 50¢ kids 5–11. Camping fee: $12 resident, $16 non-resident. Open early May–mid-Oct., daily 7 AM–11 PM. Facilities: boat launches, camping, canoeing, fishing, freshwater swimming, hiking, moose watching, picnicking.

Mt. Blue State Park

(👫 6+) Mt. Blue is one of those large (more than 4,000 acres) parks that have everything: good campsites, a lake for swimming, a recreation hall, scenic hiking with relatively easy climbs to views of Mt. Washington in New Hampshire, and deep gorges with rocky walls. But it's the unusual ranger-naturalist program here that makes the park so special for kids, especially the trips to pan for gold and hikes on which you stop to pick blueberries growing on the ledges of Bald Mountain. See also Chapter 6, Camping.

🏕 *15 mi off Rte. 2 from Wilton or Dixfield, Weld 04285, tel. 207/585–2347. Cost for day use: $2 adults, 50¢ kids 5–11. Camping fee: $12 resident, $16 non-resident. Open mid-May–Sept., daily 24 hrs. Facilities: boat launch, camping, canoe and boat rentals, freshwater swimming, hiking, nature trails, picnicking.*

Reid State Park

(👫 **ALL**) The park's two long stretches of sand beach and dunes lie at the tip of the Georgetown peninsula, but it's the other natural features that appealed to Gavin. The saltwater lagoon is safe for swimming and deliciously warm compared to the icy Atlantic, so our warm-water-loving family could actually swim. At low tide, we walked on a sandbar to an island in the Sheepscot River and watched shorebirds come in to feed at the far end of the beach by Little River. Only drawback: Parking lots often fill by 11 AM on warm weekends.

🏕 *Rte. 127 (14 mi south of Rte. 1 in Woolwich), Georgetown 05448, tel. 207/371–2303. Cost: $2.50 adults, 50¢ kids 5–11. Open daily 9–sunset. Facilities: bathhouses, fireplaces, fishing, freshwater showers, picnicking, sand beach, snack bar, swimming.*

Scarborough Marsh Nature Center

(👫 **5+**) Scarborough, the largest salt marsh in Maine, encompasses 3,000 acres of tidal marshes, salt creeks, cattails, and marsh grasses that teem with animal and bird life. From a distance, a salt marsh doesn't have the immediate spectacular appeal to kids (at least not to mine) of a waterfall pool or a stretch of sand beach; you need to get close. In most sanctuaries you can't do that. Here you can take part in nature center activities and marsh walks (in one program you can try eating the base of a cattail, which tastes like cucumber) and by renting a canoe. As you glide along the edges of the Dunstan River as it winds through the marsh, you notice all sorts of creatures. Use a paddle to test the water depth and be

sure to head for the sea on an outgoing tide and return on an incoming tide, unless you want to work hard. Bring lots of bug repellent and sunblock, and wear old canvas shoes that you won't mind getting wet and mucky. The 90-minute guided canoe tours are best for older kids. *See also* Chapter 4, Scarborough Marsh Nature Center.

🏕 *Pine Point Rd., Scarborough 04074, tel. 207/883–5100. Cost: Donation requested; tours $4–$9. Nature center open mid-June–Labor Day, daily 9–5. Facilities: canoeing and rentals, guided tours, hiking, kids' nature programs, nature center, nature tours.*

Sebago Lake State Park

(👫 **ALL**) Only 32 mi from Portland, Sebago Lake, the state's second-largest lake, hums with boating and swimming activity. At its north end this 1,300-acre wooded park has one of the only public beaches on the lake (and one of the nicest); it's long, sandy, well supervised, and backed by a shady picnic grove; one camping area is on the waterfront near it. It's easy for families to sail, canoe, windsurf, water-ski, and fish here because of the boat-launching sites and nearby places to rent boats and sailboards. The working lock on the Songo River raises the water so boats from Long Lake can pass into Sebago. As the park is not too far from civilization, it sometimes closes to day users by mid-morning on a hot weekend.

🏕 *RR 1, Box 101 (off U.S. Rte. 302 between Naples and South Casco), Naples 04055, tel. 207/693–6231. Cost for day use: $2.50 adults, 50¢ kids 5–11. Camping fees range from $13 to $17. Open early May–mid-Oct., daily 9–8. Facilities: bathhouses, boating, camping, fishing, hiking, hot showers, kids' nature programs and guided hikes, sand beach, snack bar, swimming.*

White Mountain National Forest

(👫 **7+**) More than 49,000 acres of this forest are in Maine along the New Hampshire border. For a description, see New Hampshire, *below.*

🏕 *Evans Notch Ranger District, RFD 2, Box 2270, Bethel 04217, tel. 207/824–2134.*

Massachusetts

Massachusetts has the ninth-largest forest and park system in the country, with more than 100 state parks and forests. My family gravitates toward parks in the east along the coast, which are mostly beaches, and those in the west in the rounded, forested Berkshire hills. The few I've listed here are only some of our favorites. For further information, contact the Massachusetts Department of Environmental Management (Division of Forests and Parks, 100 Cambridge St., 19th floor, Boston, MA 02202, tel. 617/727–3180) or the Massachusetts Audubon Society (S. Great Rd., Lincoln, MA 01773, tel. 617/259–9500).

Boston Harbor Islands State Park

(👫 **ALL**) It may be apparent by now that our family likes islands. Well, 17 islands in Boston Harbor constitute this park. Part of the fun is going to the largest and most developed, Georges Island, in a water taxi that holds 49 people, then island-hopping on the free daily water taxi to others. On Georges you'll find an old fort, Fort Warren, with tunnels and parapets (bring a flashlight!) to explore on your own (kids must be accompanied by an adult) or on a guided tour. Lovells has good beaches (and lifeguards), walking trails through dunes, and a salt marsh. Both have picnic tables and shade. If you have kids in strollers, you might want to stop on Thompson Island (open to visitors only on weekends), because many of the paths are roadways. Bring a picnic, as there is only a refreshment stand on Georges Island, and no water on any of the others.

🏕 *Water taxis: Boston Harbor Cruises, 67 Long Wharf, Boston 02210 (white ticket booth on wharf beyond Marriott Hotel), tel. 617/*

723–800. Cost: $8 adults, $6 kids 3–11. Open early May–Oct., daily. The islands: Dept. of Environmental Management, 349 Lincoln St., Bldg. 45, Hingham 02043, tel. 617/727–5290. Facilities: camping, fishing, guided walks, hiking, snack bar.

Cape Cod National Seashore

(👫 **ALL**) To our family this 40-mi-long national seashore that extends from Chatham to Provincetown on Cape Cod (the elbow-to-fist portion of the peninsula shaped like a flexed arm) is the ultimate stretch of beach and dunes on the East Coast. Established in 1961 to preserve the Outer Cape's natural resources from commercial development, it encompasses sandy white beaches, nature trails, bicycle paths, rolling dunes as high as 100 ft, salt marshes, and kettle ponds—those deep round dips of freshwater tucked behind ocean beaches. The government owns more than half the land in the seashore; the rest is private or commercial land in the six towns that have boundaries in it. The beach and dune setting offers families a combination of swimming, biking, hiking, canoeing, and extensive naturalist programs. Another bonus is the proximity to charming towns with shopping, baseball, and concerts, which are essential if you have teenagers.

You can stop first at the Salt Pond Visitor's Center just beyond the village of Eastham or the Province Lands Visitor's Center in Provincetown, where you can pick up information and trail maps, see short audiovisual programs about the area, and look at some exhibits. Be sure to get a list of the regular guided walks and canoe trips, demonstrations, children's and evening nature films and programs held at both centers' amphitheaters during the summer; the walks designated for children 5–10 are shorter and more hands-on, with scavenger hunts and games. On the Sunset Campfire Walk guides tell stories around a beach campfire and help the young ones see the shapes in the stars.

For beachcombing, the ocean beaches are best: Sea urchins, sand dollars, and starfish are what you'll find. For swimming, the ocean beaches have the highest, roughest surf (with a strong undertow), good for boogie-boarding and strong, older swimmers; the best ones for younger families are Race Point and protected Herring Cove, the only one facing warmer Cape Cod Bay (both in Provincetown). *See also* Chapter 6, Biking, Fishing, Sailing, and Swimming.

🏠 *National Seashore Headquarters, 99 Marconi Site Rd., Wellfleet 02667, tel. 508/349–3785. Salt Pond Visitor's Center, off Rte. 6, Eastham 02663, tel. 508/255–3421. Open daily mid-Feb.–Jan. 1, 9–4:30 (July–Aug. until 6), weekends only Jan.–mid-Feb. 9–4:30. Province Lands Area Visitor's Center, Race Point Rd., off Rte. 6, Provincetown 02657, tel. 508/487–1256. Open Apr. 15 –Dec. 1, daily 9–4:30 (July–Aug. until 6). Cost: Beach-area parking $7 daily, $20 season pass in summer. Beaches open end of June–Labor Day, daily 9– 4:30 (July–Aug. until 6).*

Halibut Point Reservation and State Park

(👫 **5+**)   Basically this small park at the very top of Cape Ann is a place to picnic and explore. There's an old granite quarry filled with greenish water to walk around (hang on to little kids' hands), blueberries to pick in late July, views of lobstermen hauling up their traps, and huge open sheets of granite to sit on while you admire the view. Some of the park's magnificent tide pools are surrounded by big rocks good for climbing. Take the good 90-minute guided tour Saturday mornings (and other days during the summer) at 10 or pick up a self-guided tour brochure. When visiting: Make sure the kids wear sneakers, bring jackets because it gets windy, and watch out for poison ivy.

🏠 *Gott Ave. (via Rte. 127), Rockport 01966, tel. 978/546–2997. Cost: $2 per car. Open daily 8–8. Facilities: bird-watching, hiking, picnicking.*

Ipswich River Wildlife Sanctuary

(👫 **4+**)   The rockery at the largest Audubon sanctuary in the state is what draws several Boston families on my panel back to these 2,800 acres again and again. The series of stone stairways, tunnels, and bridges built nearly a century ago is an intricate maze of boulders to explore. It took nine years to construct it all; the rocks were hauled here by horse and cart. Set on a section of the Ipswich River, the sanctuary has many other enticing sites—rustic bridges, boardwalks, abundant wildlife, the remains of early Colonial settlements, an observation tower, an island, and a very special Japanese garden.

🏠 *87 Perkins Row (Rte. 1 North to Rte. 97 south at lights; 2nd left onto Perkins Row), Topsfield 01983, tel. 978/887–9264. Cost: $3 adults, $2 kids 3–15. Open Tues.–Sun., trails open dawn–dusk. Facilities: bird-watching, camping and canoeing (members only), hiking, nature programs.*

Mt. Greylock State Reservation

(👫 **6+**)   At 3,491 ft, Mt. Greylock is the highest peak in Massachusetts, a monadnock (single peak) surrounded by 10,000 acres of red spruce and balsam forests, streams, and waterfalls. The Appalachian Trail crosses the park. The woods have a near-wilderness look and feel, but we go for the view, especially during fall foliage time. This isn't just any old view: An 8-mi winding road leads to the summit, and then there are the 89 steps to the top of the war memorial tower for a view of five states on a clear day—you can even see Mt. Monadnock in New Hampshire. A 360-degree map identifies the peaks. The views may not be as spectacular or the summit as high as those of New Hampshire's Mt. Washington, but Greylock is less crowded. At the top, the Appalachian Mountain Club offers guided hikes, slide shows, and several family programs at Bascom Lodge (tel. 413/743–1591), a rustic

stone house where you can stay overnight or just eat lunch, as we did, on the big porch that overlooks the mountains to the west.
🏠 *Rockwell Rd. (MA Turnpike to Exit 2, Rte. 20 West, then Rte. 7 North to Lanesborough; follow signs to visitor center on Rockwell Rd.), Lanesborough 01237, tel. 413/499–4262. Cost: Free. Visitor center open daily 9–5; road to summit open mid-May–mid-Oct., daily dawn–dusk. Facilities: camping, canoeing, cross-country skiing, hiking, naturalist programs, picnicking.*

Natural Bridge State Park

(👫 **7+**)   The natural bridge that extends 30 ft across a gorge 45 ft deep in this tiny state park is a one-of-a-kind site. What was most exciting to Gavin was actually walking across the 15-ft-thick bridge (an easy trek leads to it) and looking down at the rushing water and the length of the gorge. The bridge was formed about 10,000 years ago, during the last ice age, from marble that is 500 million years old; Hudson Brook flowed both down and across and gradually eroded the layers of rock that covered the light-gray marble.
🏠 *Rte. 8 (Rte. 2 to Rte. 8 north, then follow signs), North Adams 01247, tel. 413/663–6312 or 413/663–6392. Cost: $2 per car. Open Memorial Day–July 4 and Labor Day–Columbus Day, daily 10–4:30; July 4–Labor Day weekdays 10–8, weekends 10–6. Facilities: interpretive programs, picnicking.*

Nickerson State Park

(👫 **ALL**)   This 1,955-acre forested state park near the Cape Cod National Seashore is dotted with eight freshwater kettle ponds but has no ocean or bay frontage. Toddlers can splash happily in the calm waters of the kettle ponds (some have lifeguards). Flax Pond is the ideal place for slightly older kids to experiment with boating; you can rent kid-size sailboards (and pedal boats, kayaks, and sailboats). Several ponds are stocked with trout. *See also* Chapter 6, Fishing, Sailing, and Swimming, and Chapter 13.

🏠 *Rte. 6A (Rte. 6 east to Exit 12, Rte. 6A), tel. 508/896–3491. Cost: Free. Camping fee: $6. Open daily 8–8. Facilities: biking, birdwatching, camping, canoeing, fishing, sailing, swimming.*

New Hampshire

What most draws us to this state's green spaces are the White Mountains, higher than any others in the Northeast, including New York's Adirondacks. They offer better views and easier climbs—but they're also more crowded. Many state parks are fairly large, but the White Mountain National Forest dwarfs them all (within the national forest lands, though, there are a number of state parks). Avoid May through mid-June, which is black-fly season. For information on state parks contact New Hampshire Division of Parks (Box 1856, Concord, NH 03302, tel. 603/271–3254, 603/271–3628 for campground reservations). All are open year-round, but services are available from mid-May through mid-October only. All New Hampshire state parks charge a day fee of $2.50 for adults (12 and up). *The New Hampshire Atlas and Gazetteer* (DeLorme Mapping, Box 298, Yarmouth, ME 04096, tel. 207/846–7000) has the most complete listing of parks, state forests, and national areas.

Bear Brook State Park

(👫 **ALL**)   You'll find some highly unusual things here, including a family camping and snowmobile museum complete with tents, RVs, and snowmobiles kids can climb into. This large (9,300-acre), heavily forested park also has ponds and streams for fishing and swimming. You'll see teens biking, families with little kids learning how to canoe on the pond, and kids fishing in the stream. Hikes range from short to serious. The one drawback: The only swimming is in a small pond.
🏠 *Off Rte. 28, Allenstown 03275, tel. 603/ 485–9874. Camping fee: $14. Facilities: biking, boat rentals, camping, canoeing, cross-*

country skiing, fishing, hiking, museums, nature center and trails, park store, picnicking, showers, snowmobiling, swimming.

Crawford Notch State Park

(**👫 5+**) This rugged mountain-pass park near Mt. Washington resembles Franconia Notch State Park (*see below*) in size but is much less crowded, with none of Franconia's commercialism. It, too, has splendid waterfalls visible from the road, but there aren't as many buses and cars parked at the turnoffs, and my husband and I didn't feel as though we were standing in line to look at a tree. To my mind it has the edge in scenery and laid-back, peaceful mountain atmosphere, but many kids prefer Franconia's action and people-watching. The campground has only a few sites spread out in the woods, and the hiking trails are just superb, especially the one to Arethusa Falls, New Hampshire's highest. The one thing it doesn't have is a lake for swimming.

🏠 *Rte. 302 (12 mi north of Bartlett), Harts Location 03596, tel. 603/374–2272. Dry River Campground camping fee: $12. Campground open mid-May–mid-Oct. Facilities: camping, fishing, hiking, information center, snack bar.*

Echo Lake State Park

(**👫 1–15**) Set below White Horse Ledge, a dramatic sheer rock face in the White Mountains, small Echo Lake has a beach and a shallow swimming area good for toddlers as well as a raft for older kids. A 1-mi trail leads around the lake, if you want to walk, but don't miss the road that leads to 700-ft-high Cathedral Ledge, from which we watched rock climbers inching their way up and sky divers descending. Picnic tables and fireplaces are set attractively among pine trees. It's least crowded before noon and after 4.

🏠 *Rte. 302 off Rte. 16, North Conway 03860, tel. 603/356–2672. Open Memorial Day–Labor Day. Facilities: hiking, picnicking, swimming.*

Franconia Notch State Park

(**👫 ALL**) This state park within the White Mountain National Forest may have the most easy-to-get-to famous natural sights in New England, but on weekends it has too many people. Along Route 3, which parallels the Pemigewasset River through the center of the park's 6,440 acres, you can find the Basin, a 20-ft-wide glacial pothole at the bottom of a waterfall; the Flume (tel. 603/745–8391; open mid-May–mid-Oct., daily 9–5; $7 adults, $4 kids 6–12), an 800-ft-long gorge 70 ft deep and only 12 to 20 ft wide, which you can explore on boardwalks and trails; the Old Man of the Mountains, a granite outcropping formed 200 million years ago that resembles a man's face, above Profile Lake (overrated; it's worth two minutes, tops); and the Cannon Aerial Tramway (tel. 603/823–5563; open Memorial Day–June and Labor Day–mid-Oct., daily 9–4:30, July–Labor Day, daily 9–7; $9 adults, $5 kids 6–12), a huge gondola that whisks you to the top of Cannon Mountain in five minutes—it's definitely worth it.

Franconia's other attractions are incredible natural beauty; wonderful family hikes (our favorite is Lonesome Lake); the comfortable, developed Lafayette Campground; a 9-mi biking path; excellent nature programs for kids; swimming in another Echo Lake; and fly-fishing for trout in Profile Lake.

🏠 *Rte. 3, Franconia Notch 03580, tel. 603/745–8391. Lafayette campground camping fee: $14. Facilities: biking, camping, fishing, hiking, nature center and programs, swimming.*

Lost River Reservation

(**👫 7+**) Our family was damp and dirty after we followed the riverbed of the Lost River for ¾ mi through a narrow, steep-walled gorge, caverns, and crevasses formed in the ice age. But this one-hour self-guided tour is definitely fun. You can stick to the boardwalks and bridges by the tumbling falls and skip the caves, but 10-year-olds are likely to want to slither through the Dungeon, a cave where you have to pull yourself through on your stomach. Climbing up and down ladders and stairs and navigating the caves is more involved here than it is at Ausable Chasm or Howe Caverns, which are both in New York. It's important to wear sneakers and it would help to have a flashlight. Forget bringing preschoolers because you'll have to hang on to them every minute. There is a snack bar and picnic area and a lovely nature garden. Tuesday is the least crowded.

🚶 *Rte. 112, Kinsman Notch, North Woodstock 03262, tel. 603/745–8031. Cost: $8 adults, $4.50 kids 6–12. Open mid-May–mid-Oct., daily 9–5 (July–Aug. until 6).*

Mt. Monadnock State Park

(👫 8+) We first spied Mt. Monadnock from far away across a pond while on Route 101 between Keene and Dublin. In eastern terms, it's impressive; a solitary mountain whose upper slopes, unlike those of most other mountains this size (just 3,165 ft) in the Northeast, are bare, craggy rock, burned off by massive fires in the last century. The reason to come to the park is to climb this famous mountain, a national landmark and the second most climbed mountain in the world after Japan's Mt. Fuji. It has been scaled by Thoreau, Emerson, and many other writers and artists. *See also* Chapter 6, Hiking.

🚶 *Off Rte. 124 (4 mi north of Jaffrey), Jaffrey Center 03452, tel. 603/532–8862. Cost for day use: $2.50 kids 12 and up. Camping fee: $12. Facilities: camping, hiking, picnicking, ski touring.*

Mt. Washington State Park

(👫 4+) At the summit of the highest peak in the Northeast (6,288 ft) the record was set for the highest wind speed in the world—231 mi per hour. We could see the Atlantic Ocean from here. (We were lucky; 60% of the time the park is fogged in.) The guided tour of Tip Top House, the huge stone hotel built in the 1800s and now restored, includes many fascinating historical facts about the mountain, but it's for older

kids. If your kids are fascinated by extreme weather, they may be intrigued by the displays in the Sherman Adams Summit Building, which also houses the cafeteria. If you drive up the 8-mi, 12%-grade winding road, you can stop periodically above the tree line to snap photos or explore. Expect it to be 20°F–30°F colder at the summit and very windy. For the most excitement, take the three-hour Cog Railway trip from Mt. Washington Hotel. *See also* Chapter 18.

🚶 *Visitor center at summit: Sargents Purchase 03581, tel. 603/466–3347. Facilities: cafeteria, gift shop, museum. Auto road: Glen House 03581 (off Rte. 16, 8 mi south of Gorham), tel. 603/466–3988. Cost: $15 driver and car (includes audiotape tour), $6 additional adults, $4 kids 5–12. Open mid-May–late Oct., weather permitting. Facilities: cafeteria, gift shop, guided van tours.*

Odiorne Point State Park

(👫 2–15) This 330-acre park, the largest undeveloped stretch of ocean shoreline in New Hampshire, has great views and is one of the best places for tide-pooling on the coast, with hundreds of tide pools to explore (you'll find everything from starfish to shrimp). The Seacoast Science Center, run by the Audubon Society of New Hampshire, houses aquariums and exhibits of the seven habitats found in the park where you can identify the specimens you'll see in the tide pools; the volunteer guides are happy to answer questions. Trails follow the rocky coast and meander through salt marshes and woodlands; some will accommodate mountain bikes and, in winter, many cross-country skiers.

🚶 *Rte. 1A, Rye 03871, tel. 603/436–7406. Park free 8–dusk. Science Center: Cost: $1 over age 5. Open daily 10–5. Facilities: fishing, hiking, picnicking.*

White Mountain National Forest

(👫 ALL) The 774,085 acres of national forest here cover about 80% of the White

Mountains, sprawling through the middle of the state from west to east and into a chunk of Maine. If we want mountain hiking in the Northeast, we'd rather do it on the National Forest's 1,200 mi of trails than anywhere else. The peaks are sharper, higher, rockier, and more vivid, with more open vistas than Vermont's Green Mountains or even the Adirondacks.

For families, the Appalachian Mountain Club's camping programs and comfortable huts in prime scenic locations are especially attractive. The AMC is the source of the best guidebooks and maps for the White Mountains (available at Pinkham Notch Visitor Center or by mail from AMC, Rte. 16, Box 298, Gorham, NH 03581, tel. 800/262–4455, 603/466–2727 for reservations and information). The National Forest also maintains a system of 23 campgrounds (some allow reservations; call 800/280–2267) and primitive huts.

We're hikers, but energetic, athletic teens we know say the National Forest's old roads are great for mountain biking. Swimming here is in icy cold ponds and rivers (no lifeguards); fishing is good, but can't compare with that in the Adirondacks for the sheer number and variety of lakes, ponds, streams, and rivers. The most scenic route through the forest is the east–west Kancamagus Highway, Route 112, from Conway to Lincoln, which is lined with campgrounds. *See also* Chapter 6, Camping and Hiking, and Chapter 18. 🏠 *Forest Supervisor, White Mountain National Forest, 719 Main St., Laconia 03246, tel. 603/528–8721. Cost: Parking permit, $5 for 1 wk, $20 for 1 yr. Permits also at ranger stations. Camping fee: $10–$17. Office open weekdays 8–4:30. Facilities: camping (fee), hiking, picnicking, swimming.*

New York

There is an amazing amount of green parkland in the eastern part of this state, much of it concentrated in the north in huge tracts of forests, high mountains, and lakes that provide some of the best family hiking, canoeing, and fishing in the Northeast—and some of the most remote wilderness outside of Maine. This is the state with the most caves to explore. Its coastline on Long Island is where you'll find parks with perfect sand beaches. For further information contact the New York State Parks, Recreation and Historic Preservation Office (Empire State Plaza, Agency Bldg. 1, Albany 12238, tel. 518/474–0456). For campgrounds in the Adirondacks and the Catskills, contact the Department of Environmental Conservation (50 Wolf Rd., Albany 12233, tel. 518/457–2500). The most complete listing of parks and natural wonders is in *The New York State Atlas and Gazetteer* (DeLorme Mapping, Box 298, Yarmouth, ME 04096, tel. 207/846–7000). The New York State Travel Information Center (1 Commerce Plaza, Albany 12245, tel. 518/474–4116 or 800/225–5697) has a lot of information, including a free, very helpful guide to New York State.

Adirondack Park and Forest Preserve

👫 **4+**   This vast 6-million-acre park, ⅔ of upper New York State, is the Northeast's Yellowstone or Yosemite, though it's much bigger than any national park in the lower 48 states. Unlike other state parks, it is a patchwork of public and private land, a combination of the most remote wilderness east of the Mississippi (except for Maine), the noisy amusement parks and pop-culture activities of Lake George, and developed ski areas like Whiteface Mountain. Motels and restaurants on private land coexist with state-maintained campgrounds and hiking trails, which means families have many more options than they do in the remote reaches of northern Maine. No matter what outdoor activity you are interested in, you can probably do it somewhere in this park, though I wouldn't take a bike trip here because it's so mountainous.

To me, much of the park's landscape and its 42 mountains over 4,000 ft seem rugged, dramatic, and wild. It is a place of mysterious dark forests and the calls of loons, with challenging hiking, climbing, and cross-country skiing best suited to families with kids over 10. What makes this pine-forested range so different from Vermont's Green Mountains and New Hampshire's Whites, however, is the number of lakes and ponds—nearly 3,000— and the hundreds of miles of streams, ideal for family swimming, camping, canoeing, and fishing, even with very young kids.

The park has several distinct regions, nearly all of which are home to significant populations of bears, moose, deer, beavers, and many other animals. If you climb Mt. Marcy, the highest peak, don't expect your family to be alone communing with nature; on the trail and summit it seems as though just about everyone wants to bag the biggest peak.

The two visitor centers, Paul Smiths (just north of Saranac Lake) and Newcomb (about ½ hour from Blue Mountain Lake), have exhibits on the park's colorful history, flora and fauna, and special programs and walks for kids.

The Northway (I–87) runs north and south on the eastern edge of the park. Route 30 is the central north–south road. Route 28 in the south and Routes 3 and 73 in the north are the primary east–west roads. Because of the size and nature of the park, there is no single place to obtain information. There is no entrance fee, though there are parking costs in different areas of the park. For general information, contact the I Love NY Tourism Office. For the best information on camping, as well as hiking trail and canoe maps, write the Department of Environmental Conservation (50 Wolf Rd., Albany 12233, tel. 518/457–2500) and the Adirondack Mountain Club (814 Goggins Rd., Lake George 12845, tel. 518/668–4447 for general information; Box 867, Lake Placid 12946, tel. 518/523–3441 for information on family programs). For an excellent map of the whole park, contact ANCA (183

Broadway, Saranac Lake 12983, tel. 518/891–6200; maps cost $2). *See also* Chapter 6, Camping (Saranac Lake), Canoeing, and Hiking and Chapter 17.

🏠 *Adirondack Park visitor centers: Box 3000, Paul Smiths 12970, tel. 518/327–3000 (Rte. 30, 12 mi north of Saranac Lake); Box 101, Newcomb 12852, tel. 518/582–2000 (Rte. 28N, Exit 29 off I–87). Open daily 9–5. Facilities: backpacking, biking, boating, camping, canoeing, fishing, hiking, rafting, sailing, swimming.*

Ausable Chasm

(🏃 ALL) Don't be put off too much by the tour buses and touristy surroundings; this gorge has drama, especially if you've never been to one before. The layered sandstone cliffs, several hundred feet high and at some points a mere 20 ft apart, were carved out by the swiftly flowing Ausable River 500 million years ago. In the first half of the 1½-mi gorge tour you walk down into and along the gorge itself on natural stone walkways and steps and across the river on steel walkways where you can look down at the falls and rapids below. The second half of the tour consists of a 20-minute raft ride during which you glide along the cool dim section of the Grand Flume, where towering cliffs are only 20 ft apart. Even 3- and 4-year-olds seem to enjoy floating in the rafts, but if the water is high, the ride is only for kids 6 and up. A bus takes you back to the parking lot, where there are picnic tables, a playground, and food.

🏠 *Box 390, Rte. 9 (Exit 34 or 35 off I–87 or I–89 and ferry from Burlington, VT), Ausable Chasm 12911, tel. 518/834–7454. Cost: Raft and walk $19 adults, $17 kids 5–11; walk only $13 adults, $11 kids. Open mid-May–early Oct., daily 9:30–4 (late June–Labor Day until 5).*

Bear Mountain/Harriman State Park

(🏃 ALL) We've always preferred the less-crowded, western section of the park (Harriman) along and off Seven Lakes Parkway, where you'll find more than seven lakes and the most interesting trails. Of the three sand beaches, we head for Lake Tiorati's small one, the least crowded because no buses can park here. Of the 200-odd trails, our favorites are those leading to higher hidden and deserted lakes like Pine Meadow, where we skip stones from long flat ledges that hang over the water. Bear Mountain Park, bordering the Hudson River to the east, is the more civilized area and very crowded on weekends; a distinctly urban crowd hangs around the jammed swimming pool, lunches on the inn's deck, and strolls the walkways by the slightly shabby zoo and along dramatically rocky Hessian Lake, filled with paddleboats. The walkways are good if you're pushing a stroller. Be sure to get a map ($3) from the Administration Building right across the parking lot from the inn. By Sebago Lake are inexpensive, basic cabins (with electricity) that you can rent by the night or week.

🏠 *Palisades Interstate Park Commission (Palisades Pkwy. to Rte. 9W or Rte. 6, or bus from New York City's Port Authority Bus Terminal), Bear Mountain 10911, tel. 914/786–2701. Cost: Parking at Bear Mountain Inn $4, at beaches $5. Camping fee: $13–$16 tent, $50 cabin. Open daily 8:30–dusk; swimming weekdays 10–6, weekends 9–7. Facilities: boating (and rentals), camping, cross-country skiing, fishing, hiking, ice-skating, nature museum, nature programs, swimming (lifeguards), zoo.*

Catskill Park and State Forest Preserve

(👬 **ALL**) It took our family years to discover the Catskills as a green space because our image of it was huge resort hotels with aging crooners singing every night. In truth, it does have many hokey attractions on the kitschy side, which appeal more to a lot of kids than do the magnificent landscapes. The name Catskills refers to the region just west of the central Hudson Valley as well as to a mountain range. The Catskill Park (705,000 acres of public and fairly developed private land) and the Catskill State Forest Preserve

(386,000 unspoiled state-owned acres), like a smaller version of the Adirondacks (lower peaks and fewer lakes), are spread over several counties—Ulster, Sullivan, Delaware, and Greene. All have good hiking, fishing, and tubing on rivers; there are a number of downhill ski areas. We favor the Greene County part of the park, which has 100 waterfalls with pools for swimming. The best family campground and day-use area are by North–South Lakes (Rte. 18, Haines Falls, tel. 518/589–5058; day use fee: $5; camping fee: $18), within easy hiking distance of the state's highest waterfall, Kaaterskill Falls. Ulster's mountains are still said to be haunted by ghosts and goblins of centuries past; in that county we prefer other parks in the Shawangunk Mountains (see Minnewaska State Park, *below*). Sullivan is best for fishing and canoeing. See *also* Chapter 6, Canoeing and Fishing.

🏠 *As with the Adirondack Park, there's no convenient central Catskill Park and Forest Preserve office for information. Check with the I Love NY Tourism Office and, for camping and hiking, the Department of Environmental Conservation and the Adirondack Mountain Club (see Adirondack Park and Forest Preserve, above). Other useful sources of information are Greene County, tel. 800/542–2414; Ulster County, tel. 800/342–5826; Delaware County, tel. 800/642–4443; and Sullivan County, tel. 800/882–2287.*

Fire Island National Seashore

(👬 **4–12**) One of the East Coast's great barrier beaches, Fire Island is simply a 32-mi-long strip of sand, dune, and beach grass no more than a ½ mi wide off Long Island's south shore, between the Great South Bay and the Atlantic. It has good swimming, sand, beach-walking, and not much else, which is why it appeals to us. You can go for the day. We give a slight edge to the Watch Hill Visitor Center, especially for older kids: It's got camping, an 8-mi wilderness area for hiking, and (on the bay side) the most active marina, where kids can watch boats or fish at one end of the cove.

You can get to know the seashore by staying in one of the small resort communities (of the 17, several are very family-oriented, with planned kids' activities) interspersed amid protected land, as we did. Part of the fun was hauling our groceries home in a red wagon because there are no cars or roads, only boardwalks and sandy paths. Don't miss exploring the Sunken Forest (a self-guided trail map is available at Sailors Haven Visitor Center) hidden behind the dunes, where you can walk on boardwalks through a primeval forest that includes 200-year-old holly trees. In contrast to driving on the Long Island Expressway to get to the South Fork, you have to take a ferry to get here. For day trips we go to the beach by the Sailors Haven Visitor Center, which has a lifeguard, a marina, and an easy-to-get-to snack bar on the bay side.

fh *National Park Service, U.S. Dept. of the Interior, Park Headquarters, 120 Laurel St., Patchogue 11772, tel. 516/289–4810. Sailors Haven Visitor Center, tel. 516/597–6183 (ferry from Sayville, tel. 516/589–0810; round-trip $8 adults, $4.50 kids under 11). Watch Hill Visitor Center, tel. 516/597–6455 (ferry from Patchogue, tel. 516/475–1665; round-trip $10 adults, $5.50 kids 2–11). Smith Point West Visitor Center, tel. 516/281–3010 (William Floyd Pkwy. to Smith Point Bridge). Cost: Free. Visitor centers open late June–Labor Day; ferries May–Oct. Facilities: bathhouses, camping, fishing, groceries, kids' activities and programs, picnic tables, snack bars, swimming (lifeguards).*

Howe Caverns/Secret Caverns

(**ii 5–15**) The elevator in the visitor center at Howe Caverns descends 156 ft into the earth to this series of cool limestone caverns, the biggest in the Northeast, carved out by streams millions of years ago. The tour lasts 1¼ hours, so if you or your kids are claustrophobic, think twice before you climb in. The paved walkways are lighted; the colored lights playing across the strange, contorted rock formations make them seem like stage sets for an Indiana Jones movie. It's all very developed and organized. Be sure to listen to the Stone Organ, from which weird sounds emanate. Bring sweaters even in hot weather; the caves are always 52°F and damp. If you want a cave experience that has a more adventurous flavor, head for the smaller Secret Caverns nearby (Cavern Rd., between Rtes. 7 and 20, tel. 518/296–8558). Here you walk down 130 steps to the underground river and see a 100-ft-high waterfall.

fh *Rte. 7 (between Central Bridge and Cobleskill), Howes Cave 12092, tel. 518/296–8900. Cost: $12 adults, $6 kids 7–12. Open daily 9–6.*

Minnewaska State Park

(**ii 6+**) Two glacial lakes, one remote and one not, a misty waterfall where you can see rainbows, easy biking on old carriage roads that pass ruins of old hotels, and good picnic spots are just some of the reasons we'll go back to this relatively undeveloped 11,600-acre park in the Shawangunk Mountains in southern Ulster County.

fh *U.S. 44, New Paltz 12561, tel. 914/255–0752. Cost: $5 per car. Park open mid-May–Labor Day, daily 9–9; swimming area mid-May–Labor Day, daily 10–5:30; Labor Day–mid-May, weekends and holidays 9–5. Facilities: cross-country skiing, hiking, horseback riding, picnic tables, swimming.*

Rhode Island

Although there are green spaces in many parts of this tiny state, the ones that most appeal to us are on or near the ocean along the stretch of coast from Westerly to Narragansett called South County, on the islands of Jamestown and Block Island, and on little headlands and points that reach out from the Newport peninsula. This is the land of white sand beaches, pine barrens, salt ponds, the sound of birds, and mists coming in from the sea. State park beaches tend to be interspersed among town beaches. For general information, check with the Rhode Island Economic Development Corp., Tourism Division (1 W. Exchange St., Providence 02903, tel. 401/222–2601 or 800/556–2484) or the Division of Parks and Recreation (2321 Hartford Ave., Johnston 02919, tel. 401/222–2632). The Rhode Island Travel Guide lists beaches, state parks, sanctuaries, and preserves; for a copy, contact the Rhode Island Economic Development Corp., Tourism Division (see *above*).

Block Island National Wildlife Refuge

(**†† 4 – 12**) Of Block Island's five wildlife refuges—some mainly dunes and grass and beach, some high bluffs and meadows—we especially like this stretch of dunes and grass at the northern tip of the island because it's next to North Lighthouse, which now houses a museum you can visit (ghostly when it's misty out). We also like the fact that it borders another preserve on calm Sachem Pond where you can find crabs, and that it's a primary summer nesting area for gulls by the thousands. Don't go too close, because protective parent gulls may dive at you. All the refuges are administered by the U.S. Fish and Wildlife Service (Box 307, Charlestown 02813, tel. 401/364–9124), which has a brochure with maps and descriptions. The Nature Conservancy (Ocean Ave., New Harbor, across from Deadeye Dick's, tel. 401/466–2129), however, can tell you all you want to know and has trail maps and special kids' walks in this and other areas.

🏠 *Corn Neck Rd., Block Island 02807. Cost: Free. Open daily dawn–dusk.*

Burlingame State Park

(**†† 3 – 14**) This 2,100-acre pinewood park is just across Route 1 from beaches and the Ninigret Wildlife Refuge. The park is a big circle of land covered with skinny, reddish-trunked pines around pretty, freshwater Watchaug Pond, which has a couple of

pleasant small, sandy beaches with nice shade and lifeguards. The woods feel light and open and smell good, and a circular 8-mi trail rings the park. But the only way to use the park is to camp here. The 755 sites (they take no reservations, unfortunately) are particularly clean and well cared for. The best bet for an inexpensive vacation: Camp here, swim and hike here, and make visits to Ninigret Wildlife Refuge and East Beach–Ninigret Conservation Area.

🏠 *75 Burlingame Park Rd., Charlestown 02813, tel. 401/322–7337 or 401/322–7994, picnic area 401/364–8910. For more information, write to the Division of Parks and Recreation (see above). Cost: Camping $12. Open mid-Apr.–Oct., daily 24 hrs. Facilities: basketball, boating, canoe rentals, camping, fishing, freshwater swimming, picnicking, playground, recreation hall with video games, store, volleyball.*

Ft. Adams State Park

(**†† 3+**) Finding a park for watching boats is not as easy as you might think, but sailboats of all sizes and fishing boats regularly pass the narrow neck between this point overlooking Narragansett Bay and Jamestown Island. The beach on the south side of Brenton Cove has a roped-off area for young swimmers, a lifeguard, and lots of green space for running around.

🏠 *Ocean Dr., Newport 02480, tel. 401/847–2400. Cost: $2 residents, $4 nonresidents per car. Open daily dawn–dusk.*

Green Animals

(**†† 2 – 12**) What distinguishes this garden is that it is a garden of topiary—trees and shrubs pruned to create living sculptures. Twenty-one of the 80 shapes are animal figures to hunt for on the mazelike winding paths. It's a humorous search—don't miss the camel.

🏠 *Cory's Lane (off Rte. 114), Portsmouth 02871, tel. 401/847–1000. Cost: $8 adults, $6 students with ID, $3.50 kids 5–11. Open May–Oct., daily 10–5.*

Misquamicut State Beach and Atlantic Beach

(👫 5+) Boom boxes, wall-to-wall people, the smell of suntan lotion—this 7-mi-long beach park has everything East Beach doesn't, including an amusement park with miniature golf, kiddie rides, and a Ferris wheel. For teens who want action, people-watching, and good body surfing, these two beaches are fine places. Opt for a season parking pass if you're staying at least a week. 🏠 Atlantic Ave. (off Rte. 1; follow signs), Westerly 02891, tel. 401/596–9097. Cost: Weekdays, $4 per car resident, $8 nonresident; weekends, $5 resident, $10 nonresident. Open weekdays 9–4, weekends 8:30–4. Facilities: bathhouses, lifeguard, nearby amusement park, snack bar.

Ninigret Conservation Area (East Beach)

(👫 6+) This long barrier of low dunes and a 3½-mi swath of perfect, flat, windswept sand beach lies between Ninigret Pond, Rhode Island's largest salt pond, and Block Island Sound and borders the Ninigret National Wildlife Refuge. Here you can walk along the water's edge without seeing hundreds of people, and play Frisbee or fly a kite without hitting anyone. Though there are no high dunes to climb, small paths lead to the Salt Pond. It's not a place for kids who crave the excitement of lots of action or for families with little kids who must have bathhouses, showers, a snack bar, and lots of other kids. On the other hand, it's never very crowded because there are only 100 parking spaces in the lot. (On weekends, the lot is filled by 8:30 in the morning.) Bring a beach umbrella and plenty of sunblock, as there is no shade, and a cooler with snacks and drinks. If you crave more amenities and more kids, go to 4-mi-long Blue Shutters Town Beach (tel. 401/364–1206), which you pass on East Road and which has a snack bar and showers and even beach-friendly wheelchairs; its parking lot fills about an hour later (Cost: Weekdays, $8, weekends, $10).

🏠 Conservation Area, end of East Beach Rd. (off Rte. 1), Charlestown 12813, tel. 401/322–0450. For more information, write to Division of Parks and Recreation, 2321 Hartford Ave., Johnston 02919, tel. 401/222–2632. Cost: Weekdays, $4 per car resident, $8 nonresident; weekends, $5 resident, $10 nonresident, camping (self-contained vehicle only with permit) $12. Open daily 7 AM–11 PM. Facilities: lifeguard, portable toilets, windsurfing.

Norman Bird Sanctuary

(👫 7–12) This 450-acre bird sanctuary has more diverse terrain than other refuges along the coast, and one of its key attractions is Hanging Rock, a rock formation with views of marsh, pond, and ocean that will appeal to parents. Kids have a chance to scramble up bumpy cliff walls like rock climbers. Legend has it that criminals were once hanged on top. Bring binoculars and a bird book, as birds are easy to spot here, even for noisy kids; there's a constant sound of birdsong and chatter. A museum on the second floor of the large barn displays specimens of local birds, and cages near the main building house a few injured ones. Trail maps are available at the headquarters. 🏠 583 Third Beach Rd., Middletown 02842, tel. 401/846–2577. Cost: $4 adults, $1 kids 3–12. Open Memorial Day–Labor Day, Thurs.–Tues. 9–5, Wed. 9–9; Labor Day–Memorial Day, Tues.–Sun. 9–5. Facilities: bird-watching, hiking, natural history museum, nature programs and expeditions.

Vermont

Vermont's landscape is tamer than New Hampshire's and New York's; the mountains are (mostly) rounder and forested. We usually head for the two large tracts of the Green Mountain National Forest or the large state forests. State parks tend to be small and neat, huddled by a tiny lake or one mountain or along Lake Champlain's shore; many offer on-site naturalists, annual arts and entertainment programs for kids, even cabins and cottages. In 1999 the state park system celebrates its 75th anniversary; there will be many special activities. All state parks charge $2 for adults and $1.50 for kids 4–13 for day use. Vermont Department of Forests, Parks, and Recreation (103 S. Main St., Waterbury 05676, tel. 802/241–3655) publishes "Vermont State Parks & Day Recreation Areas." *The Vermont Atlas and Gazetteer* (DeLorme Mapping, Box 298, Yarmouth, ME 04096, tel. 207/846–7000) has descriptive listings of natural phenomena and a brief listing of all the parks.

Burton Island State Park

(**ii ALL**) Near Canada, in the northernmost part of Lake Champlain, the largest lake in the Northeast (112 mi long), lies 253-acre Burton Island. You can get here only by ferry—something that always appeals to our family. The park is an unusual combination of isolation (no cars or houses on the island), comfortable camping (hot showers), and wonderful boating and fishing, especially if you bring your own boat to keep at the large marina. It's a big enough island not to be boring after one day. The nearby chain of unspoiled Lake Champlain Islands, ideal for exploring by bike, is easy to get to for a day or overnight trip; a ferry from the state park goes to Knight Point on North Hero. The island's woods-and-fields terrain is fairly flat, good for short, easy hikes and bike rides with kids. Kids can roam and explore by themselves, fish in the marina and watch boats, swim at the shale beach with its nice gradual drop, make an Indian dream catcher at the nature center. The only drawback is that there is no sand beach, but you can find one at Knight's Point.

🏠 *Box 123 (Rte. 36 and Point Rd. to Kamp Kill Kare State Park, then passenger ferry), St. Alban's Bay 05481, tel. 802/524–6353. Cost for day use: $2 adults, $1.50 kids 4–13. Camping fee: $13–$17. Open mid-May–Labor Day. Facilities: beach, biking, boating (canoe and rowboat rentals), camping, fishing, marina,* *nature program and trails, picnic tables, playground, swimming.*

Emerald Lake State Park

(**ii 0–13**) Emerald Lake is a busy, family-filled park at the foot of Dorset Mountain, hidden from Route 7. The small, round, placid lake has charm, warm water, a short sand beach with grass and trees near it, and an island of rocks and a couple of trees to swim to. You can stop for the day or camp up on the mountain for several days, especially if you have little kids who want short, easy trails (try the one to the natural bridge) and swimming.

🏠 *RD Box 485 (off Rte. 7 in North Dorset), East Dorset 05253, tel. 802/362–1655. Cost for day use: $2 adults, $1.50 kids 4–13. Camping fee: $13–$17. Open mid-May–mid-Oct. Facilities: boating (and rentals), camping, canoeing, fishing, hiking, picnic tables, playground, snack bar, summer programs, swimming.*

Green Mountain National Forest

(**ii ALL**) Vermont's mountains, green in summer and white in winter, cluster in the center of the state to form a wide, forested ridge with tidy farms on either side. Much of the ridge is covered by the 300,000 acres of the National Forest, which is broken into north and south sections that stretch over two-thirds the length of Vermont and include six wilderness areas. Route 100, the ski road our family knows well, is its boundary to the east, but three ski areas are actually in the forest. In winter the forest is a fine place for cross-country skiing and snowmobiling.

In summer, we find the Green Mountains friendlier and less rugged than New Hampshire's Whites, a place for hiking through trees and picking berries instead of climbing up rock faces (though there's some of that). Hiking, fishing, biking, and camping (and swimming in a few ponds) draw families here. But what we come to explore—and what's most unique—are the forest's special recreation areas, which make backcountry experiences more accessible to families, whether for a day or overnight. Picnic areas at the ends of roads serve as base points, and easy-to-read map brochures highlight features appealing to kids. The White Rocks are a slope of huge shattered quartzite boulders that harbor ice and snow in their crevasses all summer long. Information is available from the Forest Supervisor (Green Mountain National Forest, 231 N. Main St., Rutland 05702, tel. 802/747–6700). The Green Mountain Club (RR 1, Box 650, Waterbury Center 05677, tel. 802/244–7037) publishes hiking guides, brochures, and maps; holds hiking-with-kids outings; and offers advice. *See also* Chapter 6, Hiking. **ᴍ** *For information, contact district office in Manchester (2538 Depot St., Manchester Center 05255, tel. 802/362–2307), Middlebury (Rte. 7, RR 4, Box 1260, Middlebury 05753, tel. 802/388–4362), or Rochester (RR 2, Box 35, Rochester 05767, tel. 802/767–4261). Cost: $5 fee for camping only (Hapgood Pond campground, $13). Facilities: backpacking, camping, canoeing, cross-country skiing, fishing, hiking, picnicking, scenic drives, snowmobiling, swimming, wildlife watching.*

Groton State Forest

(**ᴌᴌ 3 – 15**) Here we've seen beavers, otters, a loon, deer, and even a moose; we didn't spot any black bears, but they inhabit these woods, too. This 25,000-acre forest, only a half-hour drive from St. Johnsbury, Barre, and Montpelier, retains a feeling of true wilderness yet offers families a wide range of outdoor recreational opportunities—developed campgrounds, lakes for swimming, good hiking, and a nature center. Many scenic hikes are under a mile long, ideal for families. The Seyon Recreation Area in the southern part of the forest has a pond where you can do some fly-fishing. *See also* Chapter 6, Camping and Fishing. **ᴍ** *Rte. 232, Groton 05406, tel. 802/584–3827. Cost for day use: $2 adults, $1.50 kids*

4–13. Camping fee: $13–$17. Open May–Oct. Facilities: boating (and rentals), camping, canoeing, cross-country skiing, fly-fishing, hiking, picnic tables, snowmobiling, snowshoeing, summer kids' programs, swimming.

Merck Forest and Farmland Center

(**ᴌᴌ 3 – 12**) A unique combination of old hilltop farm, wildlife sanctuary, environmental education center, and just plain beautiful near-wilderness hilly land with meadows and spectacular views, this 3,130-acre nonprofit foundation is open year-round for day-use or camping. Beyond the visitor center near the entrance there are no cars; a five-minute walk brings you to the working organic farm's barns and lots of animals. More than 28 mi of lovely walking trails through woods and meadows pass scattered shelters and primitive camping cabins equipped with wood-burning stoves (one cabin is in a field by a clump of birch trees), views of the Adirondacks, and a spring-fed swimming and fishing pond. The family nature programs include getting to know llamas or helping to make maple sugar. **ᴍ** *Rte. 315, Rupert 05768, tel. 802/394–7836. Cost: donation. Camping fee: $25 for 2 people, $5 each additional person for shelters; $12 for tent site. Open daily year-round. Facilities: camping, farm, fishing, hiking, nature programs, swimming.*

Quechee Gorge and Quechee State Park

(**ᴌᴌ 6+**) There are two ways to see Vermont's prime natural wonder, a mile-long, 200-ft-wide gorge that's 165 ft deep: Just park and stare down at it and the falls from either side of the bridge or take one of the trails to viewing spots by the Ottauquechee River. My family's vote: the falls from the bridge; the sheer, straight rock walls and rushing water of the gorge from the trails. Quechee's gorge and falls are 5 to 10 times wider than New Hampshire's Flume (which is almost like a deep brook by

comparison) or New York's Ausable Chasm, and the site is less touristy (no charge!). But it doesn't have an extensive network of walkways and bridges in the gorge itself.
🏚 *Gorge: Rte. 4 (Exit 1 off I–89, then west on Rte. 4), Quechee 05059, tel. 802/295–7900. Cost: Free. Open daily. Facilities: gift* *shops, snack bar. State park: 190 Dewey Mills Rd. off Rte. 4 (Exit 1 off I–89, then 3 mi west on Rte. 4), White River Junction 05001, tel. 802/295–2990 mid-May–Columbus Day, 802/886–2434 Columbus Day–mid-May. Cost: $2 adults, $1.50 kids 4–13. Open mid-May–Columbus Day.*

OUTDOOR ACTION IN THE SUN
TREKS, TRAIL RIDES, CANOE TRIPS, AND MORE

Our best vacations and outings, like those of other families we know, nearly always involve some outdoor sports and activities. The Northeast's diverse terrain and coastline have allowed us to try just about any outdoor activity that interests us. We've canoed on lakes and rivers, swum in Atlantic surf and freshwater ponds, played tennis in the shade of mountains, climbed peaks, hiked short paths and long trails, bicycled on backcountry roads, camped on islands, sailed into harbors, picked fruit on farms and mountaintops, and more. We've covered quite a few of our favorites and those of our friends in this chapter, including, in the last section, some ideas for what to do on a rainy day.

We recommend choosing outdoor activities in conjunction with a workshop, guide, or organized program or trip, especially if you're trying something new. On guided hikes where we've joined other families, the kids enjoyed each other's company, and our guide knew the precise places to spot moose and stop to fish, educated us about the natural sights of the area in an entertaining way, and spared us the drudgery of making lunch. For neophyte canoers or kayakers, a guided trip can be safer and more enjoyable than going on your own because you won't have so much to plan and do. Learning to sail or canoe as a family draws everyone together to work as a team and ensures kids (not to mention the adults) will know how to do it safely. More and more such programs have started in the last few years. The famous L. L. Bean Outdoor Discovery School (see Fishing, *below*), for example, now holds excellent parent-child workshops and daylong and overnight sports lessons for kids in such activities as fishing, kayaking, and canoeing; it also offers family trips. One organization that has led exceptional trips in several different categories for years is the Chewonki Foundation (R.R. 2, Box 1200, Wiscasset, ME 04578, tel. 207/882–7323), whose weeklong programs vary from year to year but usually include canoe, kayak, sailing, and hiking trips for families with kids 8 and up (*see* Chapter 9, Chewonki Wilderness Programs *in* Maine).

Satisfying each family member's outdoor activity preferences on one vacation is often difficult. So we welcome another recent trend—the growing number of resorts, especially ski resorts, that offer a wide variety of outdoor adventures in one spot. Several resorts owned by the American Ski Company—Sunday River, Sugarloaf/USA, Killington, Mount Snow, Sugarbush, and Attitash Bear Peak—have new-in-1998 Adventure Centers, which offer hiking, canoeing and kayaking, fishing, mountain biking, and more. Smuggler's Notch (see Chapter 7, Vermont), which caters to skiing families in winter, offers everything from rock climbing to guided hikes to tennis instruction for all ages. At the Telemark Inn your family can sign up for three-day to one-week vacation packages that include a different activity each day (see Llama-Trekking, *below*, and Chapter 9, Maine). And large resorts such as the Balsams (see Chapter 9, New Hampshire), with 15,000 acres, has miles of trails for hiking, mountain biking, and horseback riding as well as a pond where you can learn to fly-fish and one of the best golf courses in the Northeast.

Wilderness with Children *by Michael Hodgson (Stackpole Books, 1992) is a useful book with extensive advice on family camping, canoeing, biking, and skiing, as is* Family Adventures *by Christine Loomis (Fodor's, 1998).*

Apple- and Berry-Picking

Filling up bushels of apples or baskets of berries can be a satisfying and inexpensive outdoor excursion for kids, one that's available in every state in the Northeast. Besides the few unusual places listed below that we've particularly enjoyed, you can also pick at farms and orchards; most states publish lists of "pick your own" producers that you can request from tourist information offices. One warning: Bees, although not usually aggressive, also like berries. If one of your children is allergic, opt for apple-picking.

Connecticut

Buell's Orchards

(🎎 4 – 13) Buell's has an attraction highly appealing to kids, but not quite as healthy as the apples you can pick. It's a candy-apple factory in which a Rube Goldbergesque contraption manages to produce 750,000 of these sticky treats a year. Yes, you can watch and buy samples. Besides blueberry-picking in summer, the old cider mill, the Saturday hayrides out to the apple orchard in fall, and pumpkin-picking, there's a Columbus Day weekend open house with free doughnuts

and cider, and barbecued chicken and hamburgers you can buy.

🏠 108 Crystal Pond Rd., Eastford 06242, tel. 860/974–1150. Open for picking and special events July–Oct.; call for schedule.

Massachusetts

Goodale Orchards

(🎎 2 – 12) Goodale's is a family-friendly New England farm where you feel like spending a whole day. There's an antique barn with a kids' swing, hayrides, a small pond where you can picnic, a barnyard with animals to pet, and a kids' book corner by a big stone fireplace. You can pick strawberries and blueberries in summer, apples in the fall. The prime draw at Goodale's are the terrific cider and homemade cider doughnuts. It also happens to be on the road to Crane's Beach, one of the best beaches in the area.

🏠 Argilla Rd. off Rte. 1A, Ipswich, tel. 978/ 356–5366. Open Apr., weekends 9–6; mid-May–Nov., daily 9–6.

New Hampshire

Pitcher Mountain

(🎎 4 – 12) Just off Route 123, between Marlow and Stoddard, is a turnoff and parking area for the ¼-mi trail to the top of Pitcher Mountain (see Hiking, Walking, and Climbing, below), where you'll find some of the best, most concentrated mountain blueberries in the Northeast. Bring a few plastic containers. Pitcher Mountain is actually private land, so during blueberry season you'll usually find someone in the parking area who'll weigh what you haven't eaten at the summit and charge you an outrageously small sum.

🏔 Rte. 123 between Marlow and Stoddard, no phone. Blueberry season, late July–Aug.

New York

Montgomery Place

(👫 **5 – 12**) More than 5,000 trees fill the orchard on this grand estate above the Hudson River. The estate once belonged to Revolutionary War hero General Richard Montgomery. After you pick apples (you pay by the pound), take some time to check out the views and roam around the trails through gardens, in woodlands, and by waterfalls.

🏔 River Rd. (corner of Rtes. 9G and 199, just outside Rhinebeck), Annandale-on-Hudson 12504, tel. 914/758–5461. Cost: Grounds only $3 per person; house tour $6 adults, $3 kids 5–17. Open Labor Day–mid–Oct., daily 10–6.

Biking

There are three essentials for a pleasant biking excursion in our family. Relatively flat terrain is important. Interesting places to stop and swim, picnic, or climb on rocks, or a goal such as strawberry- or apple-picking keep us going. Minimum car traffic has always been the key to my enjoyment, for reasons obvious to any parent who has watched speeding cars come dangerously close to defenseless bikers at the side of a road. I'm happiest on recreational paths designated just for bicycles or on backcountry

dirt roads. It's hard to separate road and mountain biking because although some biking routes are paved, others, such as dirt roads, are best explored on mountain bikes, and many bike-rental shops rent hybrid bikes designed for both. (For mountain biking off-road, see below.) Besides state parks, a few locations stand out for the sheer number of biking possibilities within a small area as well as the easy availability of rental bikes in all sizes. Some shops do not have a large selection of bikes or helmets in small sizes or passenger seats for toddlers, so you might want to reserve one well in advance for major holiday weekends. Some include helmets in the rental price; others charge extra. One great invention, the Trail-A-Bike, attaches to an adult bike; intended for kids 1–10, these are rented by more and more outfitters. Most states require children 12 and under to wear a helmet when biking, but even if they don't, I advise it, as helmets reduce the risk of serious injury from accidents by as much as 85%.

Few tour companies that plan and guide several-day bicycling tours cater to families with younger kids. Here are two that welcome kids 10 and up. **Vermont Bicycle Touring** (Box 711, Bristol, VT 05443, tel. 802/453–4811 or 800/245–3868; 5-day trip $995 and up per person plus bike rental, discounts for kids) is one of the oldest and best-organized touring companies in the Northeast; it has plenty of small-size bikes. Kids with biking experience do well on its regular tours. **Bike Vermont** specializes in Vermont trips (see Vermont, below).

Maine

Many of Maine's islands, such as the Casco Bay Islands, Vinalhaven, and Isleboro, are ideal for bike exploring, especially for kids over 10, but the one with the most car-free biking is Mount Desert Island. For information on biking in Maine, especially with older kids, see 25 Bicycle Tours in Maine by Howard Stone (Backcountry Publications, 1998).

Acadia National Park

(**☆☆ 5–15**) The park's 57 mi of car-free carriage paths, laid out by landscape architect Frederick Law Olmsted and built in the early 1920s and '30s, pass lakes, rocky coastline, beaches, woods, and the park's prime sights, and cross over 16 stone bridges. The easiest and most level, around Eagle Lake and near Witch Hole Pond (both okay for little kids), have a fine-grained gravel surface suitable for even small road bikes; most of the others have softer surfaces. Roads on the less-trafficked western side of the island and the 7 mi of paved roads on Swan's Island, accessible by ferry (40-minute ride) from Bass Harbor, are even more fun. **Acadia Bike & Coastal Kayaking Company** (48 Cottage St., Bar Harbor 04609, tel. 207/ 288–5483; full day, $14–$17 adults and $9– $12 kids) has a good selection of all types of bikes for children and adults and includes trail maps, advice on the best trails considering your kids' ages, instructions, locks, and helmets in the price. For young kids, it also rents Trail-A-Bikes that can be attached to an adult bike. *See also* Chapter 5.

Massachusetts

Besides bike paths on Cape Cod and Nantucket and Martha's Vineyard, families on my Boston panel like the 14 mi of looped and interlocking paved trails in **Myles Standish State Forest** (tel. 508/866–2526) in South Carver. In the center of the state is the new 8½-mi-long blacktopped **Norwottuck Rail Trail** (tel. 413/586–8706), from Northampton to Amherst, which crosses the Connecticut River on a ½-mi-long bridge (spectacular views) and passes a major mall. Pete's Drive-In, an ice cream shop, is ideally placed at about the halfway point. Best starting place is Northampton; the entrance is at Connecticut River Greenway State Park (Exit 19 off I-91). Bike rentals ($6–$15) across the road at **Golden Harvest** (391 Damon Rd., Northampton 01060, tel. 413/ 586–6246) include helmets and maps. Be aware that there is a law requiring helmets

on children 12 and under. The Massachusetts Office of Tourism maintains lists of bicycle-rental shops, organizations, and state parks with bike trails.

Cape Cod

(**☆☆ 6–15**) To us, the Cape, especially the Lower and Outer Cape from Dennis to Provincetown, is one of the best places for family biking in the Northeast, thanks to the variety of long, relatively easy, and mostly flat bike paths that are never very far from a beach, in case we want to stop for a swim or a picnic. (Even kids with training wheels maneuver them.) Considering the traffic on the Cape during the summer, biking is the most pleasant way to get around, though bike paths can also suffer from crowding. Besides maps and pamphlets available from the Chambers of Commerce in Dennis and Wellfleet, two books detail the best routes: *Short Bike Rides on Cape Cod, Martha's Vineyard, and Nantucket* (Globe Pequot Press, 1991) describes 19 rides on the Cape; *The Cape Cod Bike Book*, available in Cape bookstores and some bike shops or by mail (Box 627, South Dennis 02660; $3.25), is a booklet of both marked and unmarked bike trails. The **Cape Cod Rail Trail**, once a railroad track bed, is now a 25-mi-long paved path that winds through scrub pine forests, cranberry marshes, and fields from South Dennis (beginning at the parking lot off Rte. 134 near Theophilus Smith Rd.) to Eastham, where it ends at the entrance to the Salt Pond Visitor's Center. In Brewster it hooks up with bike paths in Nickerson State Park (trail maps are available at the park office). Though it's wide and safe, warn your kids not to weave suddenly from side to side and to watch out for hikers.

Of the three bike paths in the Cape Cod National Seashore, **Nauset Trail**, which ends at Coast Guard Beach, is the shortest, a little more than 1½ mi. **Province Lands Trail**, a 5½-mi loop that starts in Provincetown, passes dunes and marshes and offers spectacular views. For trail maps, check at Salt Pond Visitor's Center (off Rte. 6, Eastham 02663, tel. 508/255–3421) or Province Lands Area Visitor's Center (Race Point Rd., off Rte. 6, Provincetown, tel. 508/487–1256).

On either side of the **Cape Cod Canal**, a waterway that separates the Cape from mainland Massachusetts, is an easy, straight, wide trail from which you have views of freighters and tugboats. A fish pier along the way and Scusset Beach at the north end provide goals. You might want to stick to the path on just one side, as we found trying to cross the bridges (both busy highways with practically no space for bicyclists) was extremely dangerous. The **Shining Sea Bikeway**, an easy 3½-mi route, follows the coast along the ocean from Falmouth to the Woods Hole ferry parking lot.

Bike-rental shops in every community on the Cape offer bikes on an hourly, half-day, full-day, or weekly basis. Those that follow are conveniently located near a major bike path and have kids' bikes as small as 16 inches, as well as a good supply of small-size helmets, though these cost extra. **Idle Times** (Rte. 6A, Brewster 02631, tel. 508/896–9242; full-day price, $15 adults, $8 kids; helmets $3) is ideally situated at Nickerson State Park just off the Rail Trail. **Arnold's** (329 Commercial St., Provincetown 02657, tel. 508/487–0844; full-day price, $10–$15 adults, $10 kids; helmets $1 adults, free for kids) also rents bikes with training wheels, baby carriers, and trailers that hold two small kids (up to 100 pounds, total) and fasten to the back of an adult bike; the staff is especially friendly. The **Little Capistrano** (Rte. 6, Eastham 02642, tel. 508/255–6515; 2-hr price, $8 adults, $6 kids), right across from the Salt Pond Visitor's Center and by the Rail Trail, offers training wheels and cover seats for babies. **P & M Cycles** (29 Main St., Buzzard's Bay 02532, tel. 508/759–2830; 2-hr price, $10 adults and kids, including helmet), on the bike path along the Cape Cod Canal, has a wide range of bikes and training wheels, baby carriers, and attachable carts for two kids. See also Chapters 5 and 13.

Nantucket

(🚶🚶 **5–15**) Four bike paths, ranging in length from 2½ to 6 mi, lead to beaches and picnic areas and by dunes and ponds. See also Chapter 14, Biking.

Rhode Island

Besides biking on Block Island, which always appeals to our family, Rhode Island families we know recommend the peaceful, low-traffic village of Little Compton and one of the most interesting-to-kids bike paths in the Northeast: the **East Bay Bike Path**. It's a 14½-mi, 10-ft-wide scenic paved bikeway from Bristol to Providence that passes through several state and town parks, by ponds and a carousel, and even close to restaurants. In the "Rhode Island Outdoor Activities Guide," published by the Rhode Island Tourism Division, is a map of the trail and information on bike rentals.

Block Island

(🚶🚶 **9–15**) All kinds of roads and paths suitable for biking, from paved to dirt, traverse the hilly terrain on this island of moors, beaches, and bluffs; we've found traveling by bike is the easiest and most fun-filled way to explore. See also Chapter 15, Biking.

Vermont

Several Vermont communities have paved recreational bike paths that are safe even for younger kids, but so far none of these link together to create loops. For information, contact the Vermont State Department of Forest, Parks and Recreation (Montpelier 05602, tel. 802/241–3655). The **Vermont Department of Tourism and Marketing** (tel. 800/837–6668) puts out "Bicycling in Vermont" brochures for many different regions in the state. One particularly attractive area for family biking is the Lake Champlain Islands, where little-trafficked roads wind past a shaded rocky shoreline and gently rolling pastoral scenery.

Bike Vermont

(**ii** 10+) Two of this experienced bike-touring company's routes—the Saxtons River weekend and the four-day Shelburne trip—are especially good for families because they offer more than just biking. The Shelburne trip, for example, includes a ferry ride across Lake Champlain and a stop at the Shelburne Museum (*see also* Chapter 3).

ii *Box 207, Woodstock, VT 05091, tel. 802/ 457–3553 or 800/257–2226; 2- to 6-day trips. Cost: $315 and up per person.*

Stowe Recreation Path

(**ii** 5 – 15) This 5.3-mi-long scenic path along the West Branch of the Little River seems perfectly designed for kids: It starts in town, isn't too long, crosses 10 bridges, has views of Mt. Mansfield, and passes close enough to McDonald's that we could stop for lunch. It is frequented by hikers, rollerbladers, bicyclists, and people with strollers. **Mountain Bike** (Mountain Rd., Stowe 05662, tel. 802/253–7919; price $7 first hr adults, $5 first hr kids; helmets included) rents bikes as small as 16 inches; they will suggest bike tours and routes for families with older kids.

Camping

We've tried several types of camping experience in the Northeast, from a snug family campground with planned activities and oodles of kids running around to a wilderness site on a remote island with only the sound of a loon for company. When you have young kids, however, a campground equipped with hot showers, a store to bike to, a swimming beach, boats to rent, and some organized nature activities generally make a stay much easier. Changeable weather is the worst aspect of family camping in this region; we've experienced sudden and severe thunderstorms, temperature drops of as much as 40°F in the mountains,

and, on the Maine coast, a wake-up to a thick blanket of fog that lasted most of the day. A highly waterproof tent is essential, as is planning for indoor entertainment. One of the big advantages of the Northeast is how close so many scenic campgrounds are to civilization; if it rains continuously, a movie and shops are not that far away. Private campgrounds and those in some state parks have the most creature comforts; camping in state forests is usually more primitive, but most have a picnic table and fireplace at each site, plus flush toilets.

Listed below are sites we've liked that have something unusual or are particularly scenic. For families just starting out, the Appalachian Mountain Club's (AMC's) family camping programs in huts (*see* New Hampshire in Hiking, *below*) and New York State's Camper Assistance and Beginner Campers programs are ideal. Friends also rave about the AMC's weekend introductions to family backpacking and camping at **Valley View Lodge** in the Catskills (Oliverea, NY, tel. 607/746–2737, reservations 518/624–2056; mailing address: 3 Woolerton St., Delhi, NY 13753 for June–Sept., and Box 366, Long Lake, NY 12847 for Sept.–June) and at **Bascom Lodge** in the Berkshires (Box 1800, Lanesboro, MA 01237, tel. 413/443–0011), for which all you have to bring are sleeping bags; tents and backpacks are for rent (kids are welcome). Throughout the Northeast, campgrounds in national and state parks and forests cost between $9 and $20 per night, depending on location and facilities.

Connecticut

Most state campgrounds are open from mid-April to September 30, with reservations, by mail only, accepted from mid-January. Obtain a "Camping in Connecticut" brochure from the **Bureau of Outdoor Recreation** (CT Dept. of State Parks, 79 Elm St., Hartford 06106, tel. 860/424–3200); then write to the campground of your choice for a camping permit and site map. Besides those listed below, we highly recommend the 78 sites at Lake Waramaug State Park (*see also* Chapter 5), which overlook a lake that's especially great for little-kid swimming. Camping in Connecticut parks fees range from $9 to $12.

Housatonic Meadows State Park

(7 – 15) Sheltered among pine trees above the rushing and beautiful Housatonic River, the campsites at this park in the state's sparsely populated northwest corner make a fine base for family canoeing, rafting, and hiking (there is no swimming). The park is the take-out point for shops in the area that rent watercraft. The Appalachian Trail as well as several short hiking trails pass near the campground, which is also within a few miles' drive of several interesting towns. Only fly-fishing is permitted from the banks of the river in the park. Try to reserve one of the 22 scenic sites right on the water. *Off Rte. 7 just north of town, Cornwall Bridge 06754, tel. 860/672–6772 or 860/ 927–3238. Facilities: 95 sites, canoeing, fishing, flush toilets, hiking, kayaking, showers.*

Rocky Neck State Park

(4 – 15) For beach camping that offers a pleasant retreat from the generally touristy and trafficky coast of Long Island Sound yet still has many comfortable amenities, we'd pick one of Rocky Neck's open or wooded sites. Besides swimming, you can climb on the rocky peninsula that juts into the Sound, fish from a jetty, explore the wooded trails, and join a sing-along at one of the campground's communal bonfire rings. *Box 676 (Exit 18 off I–95), Niantic 06357, tel. 860/739–5471. Facilities: 160 sites, beach, bike paths, concessions, hiking trails, nature programs and guided walks, showers, toilets.*

Maine

The summer season in state park campgrounds lasts from Memorial Day to Labor Day; fees range from $9 to $17 per night plus Maine's 7% lodging tax. Reservations must be made seven nights in advance (tel. 207/287– 3824 or 800/332–1501, fax 207/287–6170). Brochures on the parks are available from the **Bureau of Parks and Lands** (22 S.H.S., Augusta 04333-0022, tel. 207/287–3821). The state renovated showers and other facilities at all state campgrounds.

Acadia Toddler Tromp

(1 – 5) Demanding and noisy, but also curious and social, toddlers are not easy to travel with, let alone take on a camping trip. I wish we'd known about the Sierra Club's annual weeklong base camp on Echo Lake at Acadia National Park when Gavin was little; the camp is designed precisely for the interests and capabilities of families with kids this age. The leader plans the meals and many activities for the six or seven families, so you don't feel exhausted. *See also* Chapter 5, Acadia National Park. *Sierra Club Outing Dept., 85 Second St., San Francisco, CA 94105, tel. 415/977–5522. Cost: $625 adults, $410 kids under 14.*

Lily Bay State Park

(5+) The campground on the shores of Moosehead Lake is a combination of backcountry wilderness and family amenities. *See also* Chapter 5. *Beaver Cove, Moosehead Lake, Greenville 04441, tel. 207/695–2700.*

Mt. Blue State Park

(6+) To take full advantage of Mt. Blue's excellent mountain hiking (many short hikes to summits), swimming, and naturalist programs (they even include gold panning), you have to camp here. Tent sites are a 10-minute walk from the beach; the views of towering Mt. Blue resemble the Paramount Pictures opening peak. Yet because the park is not well known, it is one of the few state camping facilities that usually has openings. *See also* Chapter 5.

🏠 *15 mi from Dixfield off Rte. 142, Weld 02485, tel. 207/585–2347.*

Sebago Lake State Park

(👫 **2 – 15**) The park's campsites spread out through the woods and along the shore of this gigantic lake with beautiful sand beaches and clear water. There's easy access to windsurfing and boating. The Songo Locks, where boats pass into Sebago Lake, fascinate many kids; they're right next to one sector of the campground. *See also* Chapter 5.

🏠 *Off U.S. Rte. 302 (between Naples and South Casco), Naples 04055, tel. 207/693–6321. Facilities: bathhouses, hot showers, snack bar. Open early May–mid-Oct.*

New Hampshire

Appalachian Mountain Club

(👫 **4 – 15**) We love the Appalachian Mountain Club's high mountain huts strung along 56 mi of the Appalachian Trail for "camping" because they feel adventurous yet safe and comfortable. Part of the fun of staying in these large bunkhouses that provide dinner, breakfast, wool blankets, pillows, and hot and cold running water is all the other people staying here. You only need to bring a sleeping bag. The Lonesome Lake and Zealand Falls Huts are the easiest to hike to and attract the most families; Greenleaf Hut is a moderate hike suitable for ages 9 and up. The AMC offers special weekend family camping programs at all three huts and also maintains shelters, primitive tent campgrounds (meaning no showers or nature programs, but also no crowds), and several lodges and hostels in the White Mountains and in Massachusetts, Maine, and Vermont (*see also* Chapter 9). On the Saco River, we like Moose Campground, a combination of riverbank, woods, and open fields, with good swimming; it's a welcome respite from the North Conway crowds only a few miles away. *See also* Chapter 5, White Mountain National Forest.

🏠 *Pinkham Notch Visitor Center, Pinkham's Grant (Box 298, Gorham 03581), tel. 603/466–2727, fax 603/466–3871.*

Lafayette Campground

(👫 **ALL**) Though the campsites are tucked back into the woods and some have a feeling of privacy, the location in the heart of the White Mountains near superlative hiking and the profusion of amenities and attractions are what draw families. A paved, 9-mi bike path runs through it, too. *See also* Chapter 5, Franconia Notch State Park.

🏠 *Franconia Notch State Park, Rte. 3, Franconia Notch 03580, tel. 603/823–9513. Facilities: biking, camping, fishing, hiking, nature center and programs, swimming.*

New York

A microcosm of the entire region, with campsites by perfect ocean beaches as well as in remote wilderness, New York turns out to be a particularly good place for families who are new to camping. The Camper Assistance Program in 36 state parks and the Beginner Campers Program in the Catskills were created for them. A number of state parks also have cabins and primitive lean-tos; some are next to golf courses!

For a brochure on camping in New York's state parks, write: New York Office of Parks and Recreation (1 Empire State Plaza, Albany 12238). Call 518/474–0456 or individual state parks for information for the Camper Assistance Program. Rates for campsites are $10–$13 per day, for cabins, depending on how primitive, $75–$325 per week. For camping in the Catskills or the Adirondacks, write or call: Camping, **New York State Department of Environmental Conservation Summer Recreation** (50 Wolf Rd., Room 623, Albany 12233–5253, tel. 518/457–2500). Most D.E.C. campsites are open from Memorial Day to Labor Day and range in price from $9 to $16, depending on the camp's facilities and the season. Remember that in the Adirondacks you're liable to hear the snuffle of a scavenging bear if you don't suspend your food from a tree limb at least 12 ft above the ground or keep it in a locked car—even if you camp in a developed campground. The most complete listing of parks is in *The New York State Atlas and Gazetteer* (DeLorme Mapping, Box 298, Yarmouth, ME 04096, tel. 800/254–5081). To make a reservation in any New York state campground, call 800/456–2267.

Hither Hills State Park

(**👫 5–15**) This is the only oceanfront campground located in a beach resort area in the entire Northeast. It's also a bargain place to stay at this expensive tip of Long Island. Camping is right in the dunes near a beach with a remote and wild feeling. The only way to get a space is to call the reservation number below at 8 in the morning exactly 90 days before the date you want to arrive. Spots are filled in a mere 20 to 25 minutes. There are amenities and views, but the sites are open, interspersed with low, scrub vegetation. Rough surf and a strong undertow mean swimming here is best for older kids, but nearby, in Montauk Downs State Park, an Olympic-size pool and a little kids' pool are open to campers, as are the tennis courts and golf course. Through the Camper Assistance Program, volunteer expert campers help put up tents, answer questions and give advice, and from time to time teach an especially good nature program.

🏠 *Rte. 217, Montauk 11954, tel. 516/668–2554 (campground information), 800/256–2267 (reservations). Facilities: 165 sites, beach, biking, bathhouse, fishing, hiking, playground, restaurant, showers, store.*

Mongaup Pond Campground

(**👫 3–13**) In the Beginner Campers Program at this campground on a large pond edged with sandy beaches, all you have to bring are clothes and food; a tent, sleeping bags, air mattresses, a camping stove, a cooler, a lantern, day packs, even flashlights and batteries, will be waiting for you, and a

friendly ranger will help you set up your tent. The rangers act as a support group for beginning campers, stopping by periodically to offer advice and encouragement. Everything in this park is on a small-kids' scale: The hiking trails are short and well marked, the pond is calm, the other campers are friendly families with young kids.

🏠 *Off Fish Hatchery Rd. (take Rte. 17 to Exit 96, then 6½ mi northeast to DeBruce, left onto Mongaup Pond Rd. for 3 mi north to sign), Livingston Manor 12758, tel. 914/439–4233 (campground information). Facilities: 163 sites, basketball, boating (and rentals), fireplaces, fishing, hiking, picnic areas, showers, swimming, volleyball. Open mid-May–mid-Dec.*

Saranac Lake and Indian Lake Islands

(**👫 5–15**) The Adirondacks, with myriad lakes, have more developed island campsites that fit my fantasies than anywhere else in the Northeast; 500 campsites are spread over 48 islands on three lakes. Lake George is huge, with powerboating and wave action that are dangerous for family canoers with young kids or those less experienced. Less-trafficked Lower Saranac Lake, our preference, with a host of bays and points that are easy to explore in a canoe, has lovely island campsites and excellent fishing. (The large Fish Creek Ponds Campground on a pond that feeds into the Upper Lake has a children's center and is also good for families, tel. 518/891–4560.) Indian Lake, farther south, also has 55 island campsites (tel. 518/648–5300).

🏠 *NYS Dept. of Environmental Conservation, Rte. 86, Ray Brook 12977, tel. 518/897–1310 for detailed site maps and brochures, 800/456–2267 for reservations.*

Rhode Island

Burlingame State Park

(**👫 ALL**) Other than Nickerson State Park on Cape Cod, I don't know of any large campground (it has 755 sites) that is as well kept and well run as this one. It also has easy access to both fresh and salt water warm enough for swimming. Winding roads loop through open stands of tall pines to level campsites that are spacious, private, and woodsy with cushions of pine needles. Only the campsites by the small campers-only beach on Wachaug Pond feel crowded. Kids of all ages swim, fish from boats on the pond, and ride their bikes on the paved loop roads. Yet the camping area is also an easy 10-minute drive from the long coastline of sandy beaches on the other side of Route 1. Unfortunately, they don't take reservations. **🔥** *75 Burlingame Rd., Charlestown, tel. 401/ 322–7337 or 401/322–7337 (mailing address: Div. Parks & Recreation, 2321 Hart-ford Ave., Johnston, RI 02919). Facilities: biking, boating, fishing, picnicking, fresh- and saltwater swimming, playground, rec hall, store.*

Vermont

A significant number of Vermont's state parks with campgrounds have summer natu-ralist programs, resident naturalists, and summer entertainment series of puppet shows, concerts, and storytellers geared to children, as well as a variety of types of camping from tent ($11–$17 per night) and RV sites to primitive cabins and even cot-tages. The **Department of Forests, Parks and Recreation** (103 S. Main St., Bldg. 10 South, Waterbury 05671, tel. 802/241–3655) has brochures, camping reservation applications, and *The Vermont Campground Guide*, which covers both state forest and private campgrounds. After mid-May call the park directly.

Burton Island State Park

🧒 ALL On Lake Champlain, Burton Island is one of the few state campgrounds with a marina where you can keep any kind—or size—of powerboat and even camp aboard. *See also* Chapter 5. **🔥** *Box 123, St. Alban's Bay 05481, tel. 802/ 524–6353. Take Rte. 36 and Point Rd. to Kamp Kill Kare State Park, then passenger ferry.*

Stillwater State Park

🧒 ALL Of the five campgrounds in Groton State Forest (*see also* Chapter 5), we like this one, where you can camp right on the shores of the lake. Just down the road is a large, interesting nature center, and many of the 22 mi of hiking trails in the state forest start here. Stillwater has a beach, but check out the nearby Boulder Beach area, too, for its sandy beaches, dramatic boulders, great views, and a sand-castle competition. **🔥** *RD 2, Box 332, Groton 05046, tel. 802/ 584–3822. Go 2 mi on Rte. 302, then north on Rte. 232 to Boulder Beach Rd. Facilities: 62 tent/trailer, 17 lean-to sites, boating, hiking, pic-nicking, summer programs, swimming.*

Canoeing, Kayaking, and Paddle Rafting

We're boosters of family canoeing because a canoe is light enough for two people to heft but big enough to hold several people and gear. You can easily nose a canoe into shallow places you want to explore, and you'll be able to be pull it ashore just about anywhere when everyone needs a break. The problem when you take small kids is the lack of stability. We favor smaller lakes that don't attract large motorboats whose wake can swamp us and where strong winds don't whip up waves. (For river canoeing, rent a raft if you have very small, active chil-dren.) Our choices below have canoe-rental shops nearby.

If you've never canoed, it's worth reading *Canoe Tripping with Children*, by David and Judy Harrison (ICS Books, 1990). The best guidebooks to canoeing in the Northeast are published by the Appalachian Mountain Club; the *Quiet Water Canoe Guides* series by Alex Wilson and others contain detailed observations about each pond and lake with much helpful information for families, though not, unfortunately, places near each to rent canoes. The best seasons to canoe are summer and early fall. Carry warmer clothes in a waterproof bag, and don't forget sunscreen, hats, and something to drink.

Kayaks come in several different designs, including two-seaters. Lake-touring kayaks can travel on flat water anywhere canoes can (almost all outfitters below also rent them); sea kayaking (using heavier, more stable boats designed to plow into waves and carry more gear) is a safer way of edging around a rocky coastline, though it's best to go with a guide. In addition to the coast of Mount Desert Island, Maine's Penobscot Bay and the coast of Connecticut near the Thimble Islands are fun to explore. Paddling a kayak can be tricky for kids, so I advise taking a course or going on a guided trip. Kids need to be about 9 or 10 and weigh about 100 pounds to be able to maneuver a kayak properly alone. One marvelous paddling school that teaches kids and runs regular family workshops is Adventure Quest (see in Vermont below). In the Adirondacks, **W.I.L.D. W.A.T.E.R.S.** (Rte. 28, Warrensburg, NY 12885, tel. 518/494–7478 or 800/867–2335) offers regular family canoeing and kayaking clinics, workshops, and guided tours.

Connecticut

Farmington River

(**👫 4 – 15**) This 9-mi section of the Farmington between Avon and Simsbury, peaceful flat water with vistas of lovely old trees, is only waist deep, with sandy banks and a bottom that reminds me of the Saco River's. The first 3 mi make an ideal beginning canoe trip for small children. The Pinchot Sycamore, the tree with the largest circumference in Connecticut (23½ ft), stands near the picnic area at the 3-mi take-out spot. Alongside the river in this section is a paved bicycle path, part of the state's Rails & Trails program. **Huck Finn Adventures** (9 Gemstone Dr., Box 137, Collinsville 06022, tel. 860/693–0385; $45 per canoe per day) specializes in renting canoes (large ones with three or four rows of seats that hold as

many as three kids) and necessary equipment to families and conveniently picks up at 3-mi, 5-mi, and 9-mi intervals. (It also rents bikes; $10–$20 per day.) With small kids and stops for swimming, 3 mi will take a couple of hours.

Housatonic River

(**👫 8 – 15**) A forested, well-traveled 12-mi section of this noted trout river from Falls Village to Cornwall Bridge, which has short stretches of very mild rapids, is one of our favorite daylong canoe and raft runs; the trip takes about four hours if you stop to swim at one of the several good spots. A raft is safest with younger kids. Outfitters insist kids must be at least 7 for either canoes or rafts. **Clarke Outdoors** (163 Rte. 7 West, Cornwall 06796, tel. 860/672–6365) rents canoes ($50 weekends, $45 weekdays), four- and six-person rafts ($25 adults, $15 kids 15 and under weekends, $22 and $12 weekdays), and kayaks ($30; must have experience) by the day, provides life vests and paddles and some brief instruction, transport to the river, and pickup service at Housatonic Meadows State Park.

Maine

Casco Bay

(**👫 9+**) Sea kayaking is a wonderful way to explore the islands and inlets of Maine's rocky coastline, and one of the best and most convenient places to do it is in Casco Bay near Portland. Small and large islands, some inhabited, many not, dot the bay; distances from one to another are short, so kids paddling always have an immediate goal. The other reason to try kayaking here is the **Maine Island Kayak Company** (70 Luther St., Peaks Island, ME 04108, about 20 minutes by ferry from Portland, tel. 207/766–2373 or 800/796–2373), whose tours, courses, and expeditions are exceptional. Their three-day Family Fun trip in the Casco Bay for six to eight people is a good introduction to the sport (Cost: $345 adults, $230 kids in double kayak); they also offer a similar trip in eastern Penobscot Bay that costs slightly more and will design ½-day to six-day custom trips, too. The staff who accompany family trips really like kids and teach skills and environmental awareness at their level.

Massachusetts

Deerfield River

(**👫 10 – 15**) On this river in northwestern Massachusetts, which is also good for rafting (*see also* White Water Rafting, *below*), you'll find an excellent outfitter, **Zoar Outdoors** (Box 245, Charlemont, MA 01339, tel. 800/ 532–7483; 1- to 5-day trips), with long experience teaching kayaking and a great setup for families. Here you'll find a campground, kitchen, showers, outfitter's store, and more. We recommend the two-day parent-child beginner clinic; they also have a one-day course just for kids and run two-day expeditions, including one to the Boston Harbor Islands.

New Hampshire

Connecticut River

(**👫 3 – 15**) A gentle, shallow, and wide river edged with wildflowers and farmland, it forms the border of Vermont and New Hampshire. The 12-mi section from Hartland, Vermont, to just below Cornish, New Hampshire, is particularly pleasant for family canoeing and rafting because the flat water is fast moving (meaning easy paddling), no motorboats are permitted in this section, and a multitude of small islands furnish good picnicking and swimming stops. **North Star Canoes** (Balloch's Crossing, Rte. 12A, R.R. 2, Box 894, Cornish 03745, tel. 603/542– 5802) rents canoes ($12–$20 per person, $5 kids under 8) and six-person rafts (2- person minimum, $12.50–$20 per person), for full and half-day trips, and is also a working farm with animals.

Lake Umbagog

(**👫 8 – 15**) Wildlife abounds in the Lake Umbagog National Wildlife Refuge, a spectacular wilderness area that straddles the New Hampshire/Maine border; you're liable to see moose, eagles, and loons. The huge, shallow, island-strewn lake is prime flatwater canoeing territory, but because strong winds can arise quickly a trip here is for older kids. Several outfitters organize trips here, among them Saco Bound (*see below*); our favorite is the three-day family canoe trip led by the **Appalachian Mountain Club** (Box 298, Gorham, NH 03581, tel. 603/ 466–2727; $223 adults, $100 kids 8–14), which includes an excellent review of paddling and safety skills but also recognizes kids' needs to swim and relax.

Saco River

(**👫 3 – 15**) The Saco between North Conway, New Hampshire, and Hiram Falls, Maine, is the most perfect river I know in the Northeast for a family canoe trip, whether for one day or for several, with small kids or older ones. Inviting sand beaches and rocky ledges on the shore lure swimmers and picnickers. Because of the current, paddling is easy. And in contrast to most rivers, camping is permitted anywhere along the Saco's banks for a stretch of 45 mi from just below Center Conway to the falls at Hiram, Maine. (A fire permit, available from outfitters who rent canoes, is required if you wish to cook at your campsite.) No wonder the Saco is one of the two most popular family canoeing rivers east of the Mississippi. On summer weekends, the best time to come as the water is warm and mosquitoes are less pesty, it can almost get crowded; reserving weekend rentals several weeks in advance is essential. Two good places to enter the river are just below Center Conway and across the border in Fryeburg, Maine. If you have a young teenager, let him or her rent a kayak to paddle alongside you.

Saco Bound (Box 119, Rte. 302, Center Conway 03813, tel. 603/447–2177; and Main St., North Conway 03860, tel. 603/447–3801; $36–$39.50 per day, including shuttle service) has equipment, life jackets, maps, instructions, and shuttle service. A new 3-mi, one-hour introductory trip is just $15; a good day trip is from Saco Bound to the Pig Farm. **Saco River Canoe & Kayak** (188 Main St., Rte. 5, Box 100, Fryeburg, ME 04037, tel. 207/935–2369; $33.50–$52 per day, including shuttle service) rents sturdy, heavy Old Town canoes that are stable and have plenty of space for a family and gear.

New York

The Adirondacks

This region draws us with its many blue island-dotted lakes that connect in long chains. Paddling from island to island also breaks up a trip, whether it's several hours or a day or longer. *Fun on Flatwater—An Introduction to Adirondack Canoeing* by Barbara McMartin (North Country, 1995), written for families, gives key information on 42 easy canoe trips. At many lakeside resorts, use of canoes is free.

Two of the best canoeing spots in this area include the following:

(👫 **4 – 15**) **Blue Mountain Lake**. Small and smooth, yet dotted with islands, this lake surrounded by shoulders of mountains that appear faintly blue from the water seems tame and wild at the same time. Just drifting around the lake is fun, but the 15-mi route through Eagle and Utowana Lakes to the west, which ends up, after a short portage, in Racquette Lake, is easy enough for beginning canoers. **Blue Mountain Outfitters** (Box 144, Blue Mountain Lake 12812, tel. 518/352–7306 or 518/352–7675) rents sturdy Old Town canoes by the day ($20 plus tax) or week ($115 plus tax) and provides life jackets for adults and kids and shuttle service.

(👫 **6 – 15**) **Saranac Lake**. This is really three lakes: Upper, Middle, and Lower. Larger

and in parts wilder than Blue Mountain Lake and with more islands (including some where you can camp; see Camping, *above*), it has a more meandering shoreline to explore. **St. Regis Canoe Outfitters** (Box 318, Lake Clear 12945, tel. 518/891–1838) has experience with families; it runs a regular introduction to canoeing for kids. Canoe rentals, which include life jackets, paddles, and all other equipment, are $39–$49 per day.

Delaware River

(👫 **9 – 15**) Besides the Saco, this wide National Scenic and Recreational River protected by the National Park Service is the most popular waterway in the Northeast for canoeing, kayaking, tubing, and rafting. It has much more drama than the Saco—easy rapids, steep shale cliffs, lush forested mountains, and abundant wildlife—but not such nice sandy beaches, and you have to camp at designated campgrounds. The 79-mi section that borders Pennsylvania has many access points. **Kittatinny Canoes** (Dingmans Ferry, PA 18328, tel. 800/356–2852) has several bases in New York State where you can pick up canoes and rafts ($24–$27 per person per day, under 12 free with parents) and kayaks ($29 per day) and offers special learn-to-canoe days for families.

Vermont

Adventure Quest

(👫 **7+**) Few paddling schools specialize in teaching children; this one in south-central Vermont does. In fact, its founder, Peter Kennedy, is considered one of the best outdoors educators in the country. Family workshops in kayaking (the school also teaches other outdoor skills) are held on rivers around Woodstock, near the school's 40 wooded acres. **Adventure Quest** (Box 184, Woodstock 05091, tel. 802/484–3939; 1-day workshop $250 for up to 4 people) also has special camp programs for kids.

Battenkill River

(**👫 5 – 15**) Known for trout fishing, the Battenkill seems more civilized than the Saco in New Hampshire, with gentle stretches and ripply patches flowing by white steepled churches, under red covered bridges, alongside quiet, open meadows of grass and flowers and deep woods with sunlight filtering through the trees. It's a good river for canoeing inn-to-inn. A prime reason to canoe on this river, however, is the outfitter's special trips. **Battenkill Canoe** (Box 65, Historic Rte. 7A, Arlington, 05250, tel. 802/362–2800 or 800/421–5268) provides maps and information on all the best spots to picnic, swim, and explore, along with rental canoes ($45 per day, discounts for kids). For families new to canoeing the best bet is a guided instructional day ($47.50 per person plus discounts for kids). Several longer guided canoe trips—overnighting at inns or camping—are suitable for families with kids under 13 ($350–$1,000 per person); they also put together custom family trips.

Fishing

There are several kinds of fishing kids can do in the Northeast—fly-fishing, ocean fishing from the shore or a boat, bait fishing in lakes and streams, and even lobstering, though the last is not, strictly speaking, fishing. The aim of most young kids, and plenty of older ones, is hauling in something, no matter what its size, as quickly as possible. So our most satisfactory excursions have been to small, stocked ponds and trout hatcheries or preserves where you are almost guaranteed a bite. On the coast, fish usually cluster at the bottom of rock jetties, another place to be sure of catching something fairly quickly. Fly-fishing, best for kids 11–12 and up, requires patience, technique, and muscle control. Instruction for kids is available in both of the Northeast's most famous trout river areas—the Battenkill in Vermont and New York's Catskills, as well as at some large resorts. Usually, preserves rent simple poles, but shops only rent more expensive fly-fishing or surf-casting rods. The most inexpensive introductions to fishing for families are the free fishing days in each state, usually on a weekend in the beginning of June during or just before National Fishing Week, when state fish and wildlife divisions offer family instructional clinics and free use of equipment at several sites, and waive the license requirement for adults. In the Northeast, kids under 15 do not need a fishing license.

Connecticut

The 500 lakes and ponds, 300 mi of streams, and 250 miles of coastline in the state ensure ample nooks and crannies for all kinds of fishing. For ocean fishing, we recommend the stone jetty in **Rocky Neck State Park** (see Chapter 5). For easy and accessible pond fishing, **Maltby Lakes** (Rte. 34, West Haven, tel. 203/624–6671, ext. 357), three ponds filled with native sunfish and stocked trout and surrounded by hiking trails, are in the southwestern part of the state. A "fishing park," **Paradise Valley Farm** (376 Nonnewaug Rd., Bethlehem 06751, tel. 203/266–7800; $5 adults, $3 kids under 12) opened in 1996; it's a 3-acre trout pond with picnic tables and benches on its grassy banks. A concession sells cold drinks, rents poles ($5), and charges $4.50 per pound for the fish you catch. The setting is lovely, but you can't grill here as you can at the Red Wing Meadow ponds in Massachusetts.

Maine

Lobstering Boat Trips

(**👫 5 – 15**) Lobstering is unique to the Northeast, and there are only a few places where families get a chance to actually see how it's done up close. **Finestkind Scenic Cruises** (Perkins Cove, Ogunquit 03907, tel. 207/646–5227; $8 adults, $6 kids), which depart from the dock at Barnacle Billy's, take up to 44 passengers for 50-minute cruises on a genuine lobster boat. The licensed lob-sterman on board hauls in lobster traps for everyone to see, explains why some lob-sters have to be thrown back, and shows kids how to bait the traps; passengers can buy lobsters that are "keepers." Cruises fill up quickly, so it's wise to make a reservation.

L. L. Bean Outdoor Discovery School

(👫 12+) An excellent family workshop on fly-fishing is given three times each sum-mer. This is a great way to introduce kids to the sport; the staff is particularly patient and the two-day course includes many activi-ties from fly-casting to collecting bugs. The school also offers wingshooting and canoe-ing workshops as well as short kids-only classes in fly-casting and fly-tying (also in mountain biking, kayaking, orienteering skills, and more). Kids must be 14 to participate in regular workshops.
🏠 Freeport 04033, tel. 800/341–4341, ext. 2666. Cost: $595 parent and child, includes use of equipment, snacks and lunches but not accommodations.

Massachusetts

Cape Cod

(👫 4–15) Just about everyone we know on the Cape has a favorite fishing hole among the hundreds of freshwater ponds ideal for family fishing. The ponds are easy to get to and are stocked with fish; kids can fish from the shore, which many kids like best, as well as from a boat. Wellfleet's Gull Pond, loaded with trout, native perch, pick-erel, and sunfish, and Cliff Pond in Nickerson State Park in Brewster, which also boasts "landlocked" salmon, are currently consid-ered the best spots on the Outer and Lower Cape. **Goose Hummock Shop** (Rte. 6A, Orleans 02653, tel. 508/255–0455) has licenses, gear, tackle, bait, and maps of the best fishing holes in the area. Licenses for older kids are also available at the town halls in Wellfleet and Brewster. Ocean fishing is

good from the jetties at Red River Beach in Harwich, but for safety, parents should accompany kids.

At low tide, feet squishing in the shellfish beds along the shoreline in Wellfleet, you can dig up steamers and mussels, oysters and scallops. Bring a bucket and invest in an inexpensive clam rake. You need a license from the town shellfish offices near Mayo Beach or from the town hall, where they'll give you advice on where to dig. To catch blue crabs, head for the public dock on North Dennis Road in Yarmouth. Tie a length of string around a chicken bone with some meat on it, lower it into the water, and wait for a bite.

Waterfield Farms Recreational Fishing at Bioshelters

(👫 3–14) These four calm, stocked ponds in a big grassy meadow are just about the simplest way for families (espe-cially with little kids) to start fishing because you don't have to bring anything except a picnic. You can rent fishing rods ($1), pur-chase nightcrawlers ($2 per dozen), and obtain fishing pointers from a staff member if you or your kids need it. Well-kept picnic tables are placed to catch sun and shade. You must purchase all trout you catch at $4.50 a pound.
🏠 500 Sunderland Rd., Amherst 01002, tel. 413/549–3558. Cost: $2.50 per person, $6 family of 4. Open Apr.–late June and Labor Day–mid-Oct., weekends (weather permitting) 9–5; late July–Labor Day, daily 9–5.

New York

The Catskills

(👫 9–15) The bright, winding, rocky streams of Sullivan County, especially the Beaverkill and Willowemoc Creek, are cele-brated for fly-fishing, and even though the banks of these rivers can be packed on a spring weekend morning, it's still a great place for kids to learn the necessary skills. The friendly, informal **Catskill Fly Fishing Center and Museum** (Old Rte. 17, Livingston Manor 12758, tel. 914/439–4810; open daily Apr.–Oct., 10–4, Nov.–Mar., Tues.–Fri. 10–1, Sat. 10–4), right on Willowemoc Creek between Roscoe (nicknamed "Trout Town") and Livingston Manor, has information on everything from the best fishing spots that week to trout preserves where your kids won't be frustrated. On four summer weekends it offers instruction ($50–$65) for kids of different age groups in the fine arts of fly-fishing and tying. The platforms above the water for anglers with disabilities are also ideal safe places for little kids to fish. Public fishing throughout the county in lakes and ponds and streams is well marked with bright yellow signs and parking areas. The **Eldred Preserve** (Rte. 55, Eldred, tel. 914/557–8316) is a private resort of log cabins, a restaurant, and nature trails with four trout ponds open to the public ($2.50 per person; $3.90 per pound for fish caught). Rental rods ($6) and tackle are available. The **Beaverkill Angler** (Roscoe, tel. 607/498–5194) is the only spot that rents fly rods ($25 per day).

Rhode Island

Clustered at Point Judith and around Narragansett Bay is the greatest concentration of ocean-fishing charter boats in the Northeast. It's much closer to good fishing grounds than places like Montauk on Long Island, so you don't have to spend the whole day on the water motoring to and from the fishing site. Many charter boats welcome kids and structure the day to suit them by fishing for blues off Block Island, taking time to go ashore, and even teaching kids how to fish. The **Rhode Island Party & Charter Boat Association** (Box 3198, Narragansett 02882, tel. 401/737–5812; ½-day trip $250–$300) has 47 boats of all sizes. Opt for a smaller one; boats that take 40–100 passengers usually stay out too long. **Rhode Island Yacht Charters** (8 Pond View Ct., West Greenwich 02817, tel. 401/397–9253; $80–

$125 per hr), with 10 boats, including a sailboat, take a personal interest in families and are particularly flexible.

Vermont

Battenkill River

(**👪 11 – 15**) The other famous trout river in the Northeast is the lively, clear Battenkill in southern Vermont; it's of particular interest to families because one of the best fly-fishing schools in the country, the **Orvis Company** (Rte. 7A, Manchester, tel. 800/235–9763; $340 per person), where my husband and I both learned to fly-fish, is on the river. I'm still hoping that sometime Gavin will want to attend one of their weekend parent and child courses, which follow a curriculum of fly-casting, fly-tying, stream ecology, and more, with field trips on the river.

Freeman's Brook (Kid's Brook)

(**👪 4 – 12**) This burbling brook flows through the middle of the town of Warren; one section is reserved for children's fishing and stocked with brook trout.
🏠 *For information, Sugarbush Chamber of Commerce, Rte. 100, Waitsfield 05673, tel. 802/496–3409.*

The Seyon Fly-Fishing Recreation Area

(**👪 9 – 15**) Unique in the Northeast, this area within Groton State Forest shelters a pond restricted to fly-fishing. Next to the pond is a large rustic farmhouse, which functions as bed-and-breakfast and restaurant (breakfast, lunch, dinner, and box lunches). You can also rent boats ($5.25–$15.75) here. *See also* Chapter 5, Groton State Forest.
🏠 *Seyon Recreation Area, Groton 05046, tel. 802/584–3829.*

Hiking, Walking, and Climbing

The Northeast has several thousand miles of trails of all kinds, so the locations and specific hikes below reflect our family's preferences for open vistas, big rocks, waterfalls and ponds, and spots where we're likely to see animals. Picking a hike of reasonable length and difficulty and being willing to stop usually make the difference between a pleasant day and one that ends in fights and grumps. By age 5 many kids can manage a ½- to 1-mi or an hour's hike, but before that, you'll probably have to carry them for at least a short bit. When hiking with a child in a backpack beware of trails with a steep downhill pitch or streams you have to leap across. Especially important on long hikes with kids is taking extra food and water, clothing, and a first-aid kit, a flashlight, matches in a waterproof container, a map, and a compass. Make sure your kids have good hiking shoes (sneakers are not recommended). Be aware that weather can change rapidly in this region. When hiking, you should also take precautions against poison ivy and Lyme disease. See Staying Healthy in Chapter 1.

For years our hiking bibles have been the excellent "50 Hikes" series published by Backcountry Publications (The Countryman Press, Woodstock, Vermont). Three other excellent guides are *Best Hikes with Children in Vermont, New Hampshire, & Maine* (1991); *Best Hikes with Children in Connecticut, Massachusetts, & Rhode Island* (1998); and *Best Hikes with Children in the Catskills & Hudson River Valley* (1992), all by Cynthia and Thomas Lewis (The Mountaineers). See also Chapter 5 for parks and forests and other green spaces with excellent trails.

Connecticut

The northwest corner of Connecticut, in the Litchfield Hills, is the most interesting in the state for hikers. It has many short,

scenic, easy paths perfect for toddlers, preschoolers, and older kids who enjoy a variety of diversions on a short hike.

Maine

Acadia National Park

(**††** 2–15) The park's free guided hikes and walks for children and families on the enormous network of trails are especially rewarding. We have many favorite hikes here, from the easy paths to Witch Hole Pond and Sargent Pond (good for swimming) to strenuous climbs. Don't forget a stop for popovers at the Jordan Pond House! The visitor center has good maps. *See also* Chapter 5.

🏠 *Superintendent, Box 177, Bar Harbor 04609, tel. 207/288–3338. Park Headquarters, Rte. 233, Eagle Lake. Open daily 8–4:30.*

Monhegan Island

(**††** 6–15) Remote and beautiful, this small rocky island 10 mi from the mainland is mostly wild, crisscrossed with 17 mi of varied trails that circle the island's rock-and-cliff coastline and traverse the pine woods in its center. It has all the best features of coastal hikes: a pebble-strewn beach with the remains of a shipwreck to explore, views of the open sea, coves with rocks to skip and climb on, plunging cliffs to beware of, grassy spots by rock faces for picnic lunches, and a small village, where the boat from the mainland docks, with ice-cream and souvenir shops. If you have younger kids, don't miss the Cathedral Woods trail, which seemed like a magic forest to Gavin when he was younger because of the tiny huts built at the bases of trees from sticks and bark, a tradition carried on by children on the island and visiting kids. Day-trippers have only a few hours on the island because of ferry schedules; it's most fun to spend the night at one of the island hotels. Ferries from Port Clyde Harbor (Monhegan Boat Line, tel. 207/372–8848) run throughout the year. Ferries also depart from Boothbay

Harbor (800/298–2284) and New Harbor on the Pemiquid peninsula (800/278–3346) from late June to Labor Day.

Mt. Kineo

(**††† 7+**) For a relatively short hike, this one has drama. The trails up Mt. Kineo, a towering sheer rock face thrust straight up from Moosewood Lake, are only accessible by boat. From Rockwood, on the lake's western shore, it's about a ½-mi canoe paddle (don't attempt it in bad weather). The mountain itself is named for an Indian chief, who, as legend has it, went to live alone here after being banished by his tribe. The bridle trail is the easiest climb (about three hours round-trip). Canoes for the trip can be rented at many Rockwood lodging spots, including Moose River Landing (tel. 207/534–7577); a shuttle leaves from the public landing every hour from 8 to 5 (tel. 207/534–8812; $5 per person).

Step Falls

(**††† 3–15**) This is one of the most satisfying short hikes we know, just outside the south end of Grafton Notch State Park on Nature Conservancy land. A trail along the brook leads to icy pools for a dip and rocks from which you can slide down into loud rushing water. Flat rock slabs overlooking deep, wide pools make a fine perch for lunch. *See also* Chapter 5, Grafton Notch State Park.
🏠 *Rte. 26, 7½ mi from Bethel near Grafton Notch State Park (turn right on gravel road just before metal guardrails that border both sides of road).*

Massachusetts

When it comes to picking the most enticing hiking trails for families in this varied state, we're torn between the sheltering forest and rounded hill landscape of the Berkshires and the otherworldly sand dunes and salt marshes of Cape Cod National Seashore and Plum Island.

Bartholomew's Cobble

(**††† 3–12**) A National Natural Landmark, the Cobble reminds me of a rock garden, with limestone and marble outcroppings (the cobbles) that provide the right environment, unique in the Northeast, for an amazing array of wildflowers and ferns, especially in the spring and early summer. Within its 300 acres of diverse landscape are many easy trails that even preschoolers enjoy. Try the trail along the burbling Housatonic River and a stop at the natural history museum. Each weekend there are many kids' programs, family hikes, and canoe trips; in winter, try a snowshoe trek.
🏠 *Weatogue Rd. (From Rte. 7A, turn right onto Rannapo Rd. and follow it 1½ mi to Weatogue Rd.; turn right, entrance on left), Ashley Falls 01222, tel. 413/229–8600. Cost: $3 adults, $1 kids 6–12. Office open daily 9–5, trails dawn–dusk.*

Massachusetts Audubon Society Sanctuaries

(**††† ALL**) Wide trails, easy terrain, benches to rest on, bird observation blinds, boardwalks across swamps or salt marshes that make noise as you clatter across them, and well-organized guided hikes are all reasons why hiking in the society's well-run sanctuaries continue to attract us. Ipswich River in Topsfield, Wachusett Meadow in Princeton, Laughing Brook in Hampden, and Wellfleet Bay on Cape Cod all have excellent naturalist-led hikes, many for children. For information contact the Massachusetts Audubon Society (208 S. Great Rd., Lincoln 01773, tel. 781/259–9500 or 800/283–8266).

Parker River National Wildlife Refuge

(**††† 4–13**) You're almost guaranteed sightings of deer, rabbits, ducks, geese, and many other kinds of birds in the marshes and dunes of this sanctuary. The beach walking is easy and excellent; Hellcat Swamp Trail cuts through a variety of habitats. A plus if you come after Labor Day is picking beach plums and cranberries.

🏠 *Plum Island, off Rte. 1A, Newburyport, tel. 508/465–5753. Cost: $5 parking, $2 walkers or bikers. Open daily ½ hr before sunrise–½ hr after sunset; beach closed Apr. 1–June 30 for nesting.*

Wellfleet Bay Wildlife Sanctuary

(🏃 **ALL**) We spied muskrats and all sorts of birds from each of the three trails that wind through the 1,000 acres because well-placed birdhouses draw wildlife close to the trails.

🏠 *West side Rte. 6, Wellfleet, tel. 508/349–2615. Cost: $3 adults, $2 kids under 16. Open daylight hrs.*

New Hampshire

Mt. Monadnock

(🏃 **9 – 15**) Mt. Monadnock's huge bald summit, looming over the surrounding landscape of low mountains, is the reason we've climbed it five times and love climbing it more than any other mountain in the Northeast. The last third of each of the six trails to the top is bare, open rock to clamber over. The shortest route, the White Dot Trail, is the toughest, rather like a stone stairway going straight up. The Marlboro trail is the best first-time route (take Rte. 124 for 5 mi from Marlboro; turn left and follow Shaker Rd. for ½ mi to the parking area; the trail begins across a gravel road; blazes are white). Be sure to purchase the *Monadnock Guide*, which includes a map, at the visitor center.

🏠 *Off Rte. 124 (4 mi north of Jaffrey), Jaffrey Center 03453, tel. 603/532–8862. Cost: $2.50 kids 12 and up.*

Pitcher Mountain

(🏃 **4 – 15**) The ½-mi trail up this mountain to a wide, flat, rock-covered summit is the shortest and easiest one we know to such incredible views of other peaks, lakes, and forests. Thickets of blueberry bushes (see Apple- and Berry-Picking, *above*), safe ledges to sit on and climb, and a fire tower open to the public are other attractions.

🏠 *Just off Rte. 123 between Marlow and Stoddard.*

White Mountain National Forest

(🏃 **ALL**) Higher, rockier peaks with more open vistas than any other mountain area in the Northeast, a wide variety of trails from easy to highly challenging, and the Appalachian Mountain Club's (AMC) guided hikes and system of huts all draw our family here for mountain hiking. The hiking hub of the area, the place to stop for information on trails and trail conditions, is the Appalachian Mountain Club's Pinkham Notch Camp at the base of Mount Washington. The lodge and dining room (not fancy) welcome guests, while the Pinkham Notch Visitor Center has educational displays and a store where you can buy books, maps, and hiking gear. It's the starting point for many of the AMC's family programs.

In addition to the guides mentioned in the introduction to this section, *The AMC White Mountain Guide* (26th edition, 1998) and *Waterfalls of the White Mountains* by Bruce and Doreen Bolnick (Backcountry Publications, 1990) highlight many easy to moderate hikes perfect for families. Maps are also available from the Forest Supervisor (Box 638, White Mountain National Forest, Laconia 03247, tel. 603/528–8721). *See also* Chapter 5.

🏠 *Forest Supervisor, Box 638, White Mountain National Forest, Laconia 03247, tel. 603/528–8721.*

Some of our favorite trails in this area include the following:

(🏃 **5 – 12**) **Greeley Ponds Trail.** Plank walks, bridges, and gravelly beaches around two wilderness ponds, as well as frog-catching and perhaps even beaver-watching, keep kids absorbed on this 4-mi, fairly level hike. 🚶 *Off Kancamagus Hwy. (Rte. 112, 9½ mi east of town at parking lot marked with name of trail), Lincoln.*

👫 6–15 **Lonesome Lake Trail.** One of the most popular family destinations in the White Mountains is remote and beautiful Lonesome Lake, edged with dark pine trees and in the shadow of the high Franconia Ridge. You can spend the night at the AMC's Lonesome Lake hut. The 3½-mi round-trip hike has some steep parts. Be sure at least to wade in the lake and take the trail around it. 🚶 *Off Rte. 93, Lafayette Campground, Franconia Notch State Park, Franconia.*

👫 4–15 **Loon Mountain.** If you want to take interesting trails along a mountain summit without having to hike for six hours to get there, you can access Loon Mountain by gondola; it runs from 9 AM to 7 PM. At the top we found boardwalks and trails leading through the nooks and crannies of hollowed-out glacial caves. 🚶 *Loon Mountain Park, Kancamagus Hwy., Lincoln 03251, tel. 603/745–8111. Cost: $9.50 adults, $5.50 kids 6–16.*

👫 3–10 **Lost Pond Trail.** A short 1½-mi (one-hour) round-trip to a scenic wilderness pond with views of Mt. Washington is one of the easiest trails in the Pinkham Notch area. It passes a beaver dam and lodge as well as the pointed stumps of trees chewed by beaver teeth. Gavin at 7 was also captivated by the boulder fields at the far end of the pond. 🚶 *Rte. 16 (sign near pond across from Pinkham Notch Camp).*

New York

Adirondack Park

👫 8–15 More than 2,000 mi of marked trails leading to mountain peaks, ice caves, and waterfalls cross the wild, forested land of this park in northern New York State. Though you can find many easy hikes scat-

tered through the park, it's a place that draws serious hikers and climbers. The High Peaks district near Lake Placid concentrates rugged climbs and challenging trails. Many trails, though well marked, well maintained, and easily accessible from main roads (look for wood signs with yellow lettering), are rough, steep, and rocky, and as we learned on one ill-fated hike, sometimes lead straight up to the summit by way of an old, rutted, rock-strewn streambed. For kids under 13, the **Adirondack Mountain Club**'s (ADK) well-organized family events and guided hikes offer satisfying introductions to the region. They're similar to the AMC's programs in New Hampshire. On the High Peaks Traverse (for older kids), you get a taste of the wilderness without having to backpack; you hike in 3½ mi to the ADK's fairly comfortable but rustic **Johns Brook Lodge** and use that as your base for three to five days of hiking. Other family programs originate at ADK's wilderness center on the shore of Heart Lake. Contact the **Adirondack Loj** (off Rte. 73, Box 867, Lake Placid 12946, tel. 518/523–3441), which also has a campground, for information. The ADK in Lake George (Luzerne Rd., Lake George 12845, tel. 518/668–4447) provides information and sells guidebooks. The best guidebook to hiking in the Adirondacks with children is ADK's *Kids on the Trail* (1997), which describes 62 hikes and gives plenty of practical tips on hiking with kids of different ages.

Mohonk Mountain House and Mohonk Preserve

👫 3–15 These are two separate but adjoining areas for fabulous hiking (and biking, too). The 6,400-acre nature preserve (Mohonk Preserve) that surrounds the 2,000 acres owned by the Mohonk Mountain House resort (see Chapter 9) has easy paths and 25 mi of old carriage roads that even a stroller can negotiate, as well as more challenging hiking. Guided hikes are held each weekend, but reserve in advance, as they fill up quickly. The new interpretive center has indoor and outdoor exhibits, trail maps, and a gift shop. On the Mountain House resort property are some fantastic rock formations and open cliff hikes, especially the exciting Labyrinth (ages 10–15), with ladders up cliff walls, tunnels and bridges, and caves.

🏨 *Rte. 4455, Gardiner, tel. 914/255–0919 (preserve) or 914/255–1000 (Mohonk Mountain House). Cost: Preserve, weekends, $7, kids under 12 free; Mountain House $9–$12.*

Vermont

Green Mountain National Forest

(👫 **ALL**) In this huge forest we favor the special recreation areas designed to provide easy access to the backcountry. They have many good, short trails with much to see along the way; easy-to-read map brochures highlight sights appealing to kids. As part of their new watchable wildlife program, trail-head posts with a picture of a set of binoculars list the animals to watch for on your hike. Another great way for families to get out on the trail is with one of the Green Mountain Club's family outings (tel. 802/ 244–7037; $7 nonmembers, $5 members). See also Chapter 5.

🏨 *Forest Supervisor, Green Mountain National Forest, 231 N. Main St., Rutland 05701, tel. 802/747–6700.*

Grout Pond

(👫 **0 – 15**) A flat 2-mi loop trail, with camping shelters and picnic tables, circles this pretty pond frequented by canoers and beavers. Swimming is excellent.

🏨 *Kelley Stand Rd. (off Rte. 6 between Stratton and Arlington), Stratton.*

White Rocks Recreation Area

(👫 **3 – 15**) Among the most fascinating and easy trails we've hiked anywhere are the White Rocks and Ice Beds Trails in this area. The "white rocks," rock slides of shattered

quartzite deposited during the ice age, once served as a meeting place for Native Americans. The trail snakes along a ridge, past ledge outcroppings and overlooks of the huge boulder fields, and eventually comes to the base of the largest rock slide. If you look carefully, you'll be able to see snow and ice in the crevices even in August.

🏨 *Rte. 140, Wallingford 05773. Take Rte. 140 from Wallingford to Sugarhill Rd., then right on U.S. Forest Service Rd. 52 to White Rocks Picnic Area.*

Horseback Riding

Riding horseback through the woods on a crisp fall day, when the air smells sharp and red and yellow leaves surround you, is one of the great pleasures of the region. Five is not too young to begin learning, but many stables will not take kids younger than 8 on trail rides.

Among the best places for families to ride are ranches in New York's Catskills and stables and resorts in Vermont's Green Mountains, as well as the area around New York's Lake George. Horseback riding on cross-country trails is usually also available at ski resorts off-season. Late summer and fall, when days are a bit cooler, are the most comfortable times.

New Hampshire

Castle in the Clouds

(👫 **8 – 15**) Eccentric multimillionaire Thomas Gustave Plant's quirky stone mansion, built high above Lake Winnipesaukee in the Ossipee Mountain Range, is surrounded by 6,000 acres networked with 85 mi of bridle paths and carriage trails on which you can take one-hour guided rides.

🏨 *Rte. 171, Moultonborough 03254, tel. 603/476–2352 or 800/729–2468. Cost: $10 adults, $7 kids 11–17; $25 trail rides. Reservations required. Open May–Labor Day, daily 9– 5; Labor Day–mid-Oct., daily 9–4.*

New York

Ranch resorts lure families with trail rides for all levels of ability, pony rides for kids, and a welcoming attitude toward young kids. Two in the Catskills, Pine Grove Ranch Resort and Rocking Horse Ranch, have a large selection of horses, and trail rides and lessons are included in the price of lodging. They also have many other activities if not every child in your family wants to ride (see Chapter 9). **Pine Grove Ranch** (Lower Chestertown Rd., Kerhonkson 12446, tel. 914/626–7345 or 800/346–4626) breeds its own purebred and half-bred registered Arabian saddle horses, of which 85 are available to ride. There are ponies for little kids and western riding lessons eight times a day. **Rocking Horse Ranch** (600 Rte. 44–55, Highland 12528, tel. 914/691–2927 or 800/647–2624) has 120 horses, 500 acres of woods and orchards to ride in, and many half-hour trail rides a day.

Vermont

Kedron Valley Stables

(🚶‍♀️ 10 – 15) One of the prettiest villages in New England, Woodstock has been a center for riding for generations and seems, even today, to have more horses than cars. Kedron Valley Stables ranks high for families with older kids who know how to ride. The well-designed itineraries cover an 85-mi network of trails and paths—through flower-filled meadows, by lakes and streams, and up and down hills. As inn-to-inn trips require five or six hours per day in the saddle, kids should be keen, experienced older riders. 🏠 Rte. 106, South Woodstock 05071, tel. 802/457–1480. Cost: Trail rides $100 per hr for family of 4; lessons available; inn-to-inn treks $400–$1,550.

Mountain Top Inn and Resort

(🚶‍♀️ 6 – 15) You don't have to stay at this resort known for its cross-country skiing to take advantage of their excellent kids' riding lessons and trail rides during the warmer half of the year. Kids as young as 5 can learn to ride; those 8 (at least 54 inches) and up can go on one-hour, half-day, and full-day trail rides on 80 mi of trails. The stable has kid-size helmets. This is a friendly place where kids hang over the fence and help feed the horses. 🏠 Mountain Top Rd., Rte. 108, Chittenden 05737, tel. 802/483–2311 or 800/445–2100. Cost: Lessons $30–$40; trail rides $30 per hr; riding vacation packages available.

Vermont Icelandic Horse Farm

(🚶‍♀️ 9 – 15) These affectionate, sturdy, pony-size (12–14 hands) mounts brought from Iceland are less intimidating to kids and easy to ride because of their surefootedness and smooth gaits—you don't have to post. They were brought to Iceland more than 1,000 years ago by the Vikings and are now considered the purest breed of horse in the world. This farm's friendliness to kids is another reason to try a lesson or the one-hour and half-day guided trail rides that climb into high meadows and woods in the Mad River valley; longer rides make time for a swim. The farm has inn-to-inn treks in the valley, on which kids are allowed to help out with feeding and grooming. 🏠 Waitsfield 05673, tel. 802/496–7141. Cost: $40 per hr; small group rates for 3 or more; inn-to-inn treks $335–$1,095.

Llama Trekking

On a guided camping trip on which gentle-natured llamas carry the gear, you can hike over high trails into backcountry that might be too rugged and remote for a family to carry their own equipment. More approachable than packhorses, llamas don't bite or kick, though they've been known to spit.

Maine

Telemark Inn

(👫 4–15) Treks into even wilder country from this remote, rather deluxe Adirondack-style lodge perched in the peaks of the White Mountain National Forest seem designed to make families with little kids feel at home in the wilderness. You hike in along the spectacular Wild River to a base camp with a good swimming hole, then make daily forays up trails that have kid-pleasing features such as bear claw marks on tree trunks. No cramped tents or freeze-dried packets of mystery food on these treks; hot towels greet you in the morning, and food is good. (If three days with llamas seems too much, one-day treks are available as part of packages where you stay in the lodge.) *See also* Chapter 9.
🏨 *RFD 2, Box 800, Bethel 04217, tel. 207/ 836–2703. Cost: 3-day trek $475 adults, $350 kids 14 and under. Open May–Sept.*

Mountain Biking

With easy-to-difficult grassy trails already in place for cross-country skiing, old logging and access roads through the woods, and lifts to take you and your bike to the top of the mountain for thrilling rides down, ski areas offer the most extensive networks of safe off-road mountain-bike trails in the region. Many now not only maintain the trails in summer, but also offer rentals, races, guided tours, and instruction (usually for older kids and adults only), in addition to lodging and a host of other activities. Though 7- or 8-year-olds can ride many of the easier trails, kids need to be substantially older to use the high-performance bikes required to ride up or down from mountain summits. All areas below require the use of helmets and rent both adult and kid sizes, along with standard mountain and superperformance bikes. Besides those mentioned below, Smuggler's Notch offers trails easy

enough for younger kids. State parks and forests also have designated loops of uncharted logging roads and cross-country trails as mountain-bike paths.

Maine

Sunday River Mountain Bike Park

(👫 8+) A new beginner mountain bike park of wide gentle trails and its own chairlift opened at this ski resort in the summer of 1998. It's perfect for kids who are just learning and makes Sunday River a good mountain-biking destination for a family with widely varying biking abilities; besides the beginner area are 60 mi of marked and patrolled trails of varying difficulty. Access to all mountain biking plus rentals and instruction is conveniently centered on White Cap Base Lodge.
🏨 *Box 450, Bethel 04217, tel. 207/824– 3000. Cost: $8 trail fee, rentals (includes trail fee) $39–$50 adults, $35–$40 kids 12 and under; helmets included. Open late May– mid-Oct.*

New Hampshire

Information about biking in the state is conveniently listed on the New Hampshire highway map, which also mentions places to rent bikes.

The Balsams Mountain Bike and Nature Center

(👫 8–15) The Balsams Grand Resort Hotel has added fabulous mountain biking to its many superbly organized activities. From the end of May through mid-October you can ride the 33 mi of marked trails on their 15,000 acres, rent bikes, and take their guided biking tours even if you aren't a hotel guest. *See also* Chapter 9, Balsams Grand Resort Hotel.
🏨 *Dixville Notch 03576, tel. 603/255– 3921. Cost: $5 trail fee, bikes $10–$15, junior rate $5–$10; helmets included. Open late May–mid-Oct.*

Great Glen Trails Biking Center

(**⚥ 6 – 15**) At the foot of Mount Washington, this outdoor activity center maintains a network of biking trails that have great views as well as many easy short trails suitable for younger kids and a one-hour introduction to mountain biking. Trail descriptions are especially complete, with details about animals and plants you might see along the way. A deli where you can purchase prepared picnic lunches makes an outing here a snap. Kiddie cart trailers are available.

🏠 *Rte. 16, Pinkham Notch, Gorham NH 03581, tel. 603/466–2333. Cost: $5 trail fee, bikes $17 adults, $12 kids 6–12 (2 hrs). Open Memorial Day–mid-Oct.*

Loon Mountain Park

(**⚥ 6 – 15**) Right on the scenic Kancamagus Highway in the heart of the rugged White Mountains, Loon Mountain in summer feels more like a family and kid place than many other ski resorts with mountain-bike rentals and trails and is an especially good place if you have children of widely different ages. Its easy cross-country trails near the rushing Pemigewasset River even have picnic tables; a beginner loop is 3 mi long. The shop sponsors an exciting downhill four-hour guided bike tour on the Franconia Notch Bike Path.

🏠 *Rte. 112 (Kancamagus Hwy.), Lincoln 03251, tel. 603/745–8111. Cost: $15 per 2 hrs adult bikes, $12 kids 6–12; kid-size helmets available. Open Memorial Day–late Nov., daily 9–5.*

Waterville Valley

(**⚥ 6 – 15**) In this ski resort's mountain bike park on Snow's Mountain in the White Mountain National Forest, miles and miles of marked trails and bumps and jumps have been set aside only for bikers, so kids don't run the risk of hitting hikers. All sorts of lessons, guided tours, and spe-

cial events are offered throughout the summer (tel. 800/468–2553). **Adventure Center** (tel. 603/236–4666; trail passes $6 adults, $4 kids; bike rentals $10–$40 per hr adults, $8–$28 per hr kids) rents bikes as small as 20 inches.

Vermont

Catamount Family Center

(**⚥ 6 – 15**) Not far from Burlington is a 500-acre family outdoor sports playground (called Outdoor Experience in summer) where you can do orienteering, cross-country running, nature hiking, and especially mountain biking. Easy to hard trails, mostly pine bed or grass, crisscross the hilly land; once-a-week mountain-bike races are held, even for kids in the 8-and-under group. The smallest bike they rent will fit a 6-year-old. Kids can also attend regular weeklong, half-day mountain-bike camps.

🏠 *421 Chittenden Rd., Williston 05494, tel. 802/879–6001. Cost: Rentals $10 per 2 hrs for all performance bikes; helmets to borrow. Open weekdays 3–8, weekends 9–6.*

Craftsbury Outdoor Center

(**⚥ 12 – 15**) This unusual resort sits in northeast Vermont's high, rolling farm country in the midst of miles and miles of winding dirt farm roads and grassy cross-country ski and snowshoe trails perfect for mountain biking. Bikes are rented, self-guided bike tours ensure that you won't get lost, and flexible and informal instruction is available. Accommodations at the resort, once a boys' boarding school, are basic (mostly shared baths, simple furnishings) but comfortable, and meals are the healthy yet delicious whole-wheat pizza, homemade pudding kind. It attracts a very broad spectrum of people, from singles to families, serious athletes to grandparents.

🏠 *Box 31, Craftsbury Common 05827, tel. 802/586–7767 or 800/729–7751. Cost: $10 (2 hrs); longer rates available. Open daily 9–5.*

Mt. Snow Adventure Center

(**†† 7 – 15**) This friendly southern Vermont ski area is called the mountain bike center of the East because of the serious and intensive instruction it has long offered for highly athletic and competitive older teens and adults and because it has one of the most varied and extensive mountain-biking trail systems in the region. Yet many very easy trails that take off from the Carinthia lodge suit even young kids. Those who really want to learn may like being part of the all-day sports camp ($40); only kids 15 and up are eligible for the all-day bike school.

🏔 *400 Mountain Rd., Mount Snow, Dover 05356, tel. 800/464–3333 for information. Cost: half-day, $25 adults, $15 kids; full day, $40 adults, $25 kids; helmets included.*

Rockhounding and Fossil Hunting

Abandoned quarries and mines abound in the Northeast, but the safest places to prospect for minerals are at those monitored by a mineral shop, museum, or state park. (Do not go inside an abandoned mine unless experts have determined that it is safe.) At the least you need a small hammer, several small plastic or cloth bags in which to squirrel away each child's samples, and plastic safety glasses because chips do fly. A mineral pick and chisel are useful additions. Damp surfaces of sharp rock are the norm, so you need jeans and sturdy shoes with rubber soles.

Maine

Perham's

(**†† 5 – 13**) In the midst of a region thick with mineral and gem deposits, Perham's, the prime mineral store catering to the state's rockhounders, owns four quarries within 8 to 10 mi that are open to the public and provides a map. The sites are mostly big pits in the woods, each with its own specialty—rose quartz, mica, feldspar, and more. The store sells equipment (also for gold panning) and a guidebook to other quarries in Maine.

🏔 *194 Bethel Rd., Rte. 26, West Paris 04289, tel. 207/674–2341 or 800/371–4367. Open daily 9–5.*

New Hampshire

Gilsum

(**†† 5 – 13**) Tiny Gilsum, once a thriving mining town, sponsors an annual Rock Swap at the end of June that's great for kids who are serious rockhounders. Though the town library sells maps pinpointing the 60 abandoned mines in the area, the Rock Swap doesn't sponsor mine tours on which you can prospect. If you write, however, they may be able to get you permission to visit and prospect at a local one (Gilsum Recreation Committee, Box 76, Gilsum 03448, tel. 603/352–2472).

Ruggles Mine

(**†† 6 – 13**) At the oldest mine in the Northeast, on top of Isinglass Mountain, caves and tunnels with arched rock formations and floors slick with water lead off from the less eerie open pit. Bring a flashlight. The most common of the 150 different types of minerals and gems that you may find here are mica, feldspar, garnet, and quartz. If you're lucky, you might hit upon some golden beryl or tourmaline. In the small shop where you pay admission, you can buy or rent equipment and buy samples of minerals you want but don't find.

🏔 *Isinglass Mountain (off Rte. 4), Grafton 03748, tel. 603/523–4275. Cost: $15 adults, $5 kids 4–11. Open mid-May–mid-June, weekends 9–5; mid-June–mid-Oct., daily 9–5 (July–Aug. until 6).*

New York

Barton Garnet Mines

(**👫 6 – 13**) After a tour of the large open-pit mine where most of the world's industrial garnets (they're a dark red color) come from, you can look for stones yourself. In contrast to other mines, here site guides are available to answer questions about how to find stones. You do have to pay for the gems you take with you. You can also see gem cutters demonstrate how to polish and shape garnets.

🏠 *Rte. 28, North Creek 12853, tel. 518/ 251–2706. Cost: $6 adults, $4.75 kids 3–11. Open late June–Labor Day, Mon.–Sat. 9–5, Sun. 11–5.*

John Boyd Thacher State Park

(**👫 8 – 13**) This park covers some of the richest fossil-bearing terrain in the world; it's also a prime hunting ground for Indian arrowheads. The trail to take is the Indian Ladder Geological Trail, which is open to kids ages 8 and up.

🏠 *Rte. 157, 15 mi southwest of Albany, 12186, tel. 518/872–1237. Cost: Parking $4. Open daily 8 AM–dusk.*

Rollerblading and Skateboarding

Unlike California, the Northeast doesn't have a skate park in every single community. Nonetheless, in-line skating and, to a lesser extent, skateboarding are popular here, especially among teens in cities. On roads in city parks that are closed to traffic we've often seen more skaters than bike riders on a sunny weekend. The big problem elsewhere is traffic; however, several new skateboard parks at ski resorts have opened in the past year. The places below are among the indoor and outdoor centers in the Northeast strictly reserved for these two sports. Be aware that all require parents to sign a waiver before kids will be allowed to skate, and none will let kids skate without protective gear and a helmet.

Maine

Sunday River

(**👫 8+**) The new (1998) summer Adventure Center at this innovative ski resort houses a great skateboard/in-line park that welcomes kids from beginner to expert. It's not just the half-pipe, quarter-pipe, and fun boxes that attract kids but also the chance to hit the water slide nearby when you get tired of skating. *See also* Mountain Biking, *above,* and Chapter 7.

🏠 *Box 450, Bethel 04217, tel. 207/824–3000. Cost: $10 in-line skate or skateboard rental, includes helmet; 2-hr pass valid for skate park and water slide, $20. Open weekdays 9–3, weekends 9–4.*

Massachusetts

Charles River Esplanade

(**👫 9+**) For the best rollerblading in Boston, try the Esplanade along the Charles River in Boston. Skaters also congregate at Frog Pond on Boston Common and at Government Center. For rentals, **Eric Flaim's Motion Sports** (349A Newbury St., Boston 02116, tel. 617/247–3284; $15 per day including protective gear) specializes in in-line skates and offers lessons.

Maximus

(**👫 12 – 15**) The atmosphere at this huge, old, 4,000-square-ft warehouse, a mecca for Boston area skateboarders and in-line skaters, is friendly, and more experienced skaters readily offer tips to younger kids. It's a hangout for kids serious about the sports, with a street course of ramps and mini-ramps and a 10-ft half-pipe. Bring your own skateboard or skates; though helmets

(required) can be borrowed, these are "gross" according to one local skater.
🏠 *324 Rindge Ave. (off Massachusetts Ave., Alewife stop on Red Line T), Cambridge 02140, tel. 617/576–4723. Cost: $10. Open daily noon–8, girls only Wed. 8–10.*

New Hampshire

Waterville Valley

(🏃 8–15) Skaters of all ages enjoy tooling around at a leisurely pace on Waterville Valley's extensive network of paved roads, sidewalks, and parking lots with no pass-through traffic. Now, however, the center offers lessons and has a sports dome with an official in-line skate and skateboard area that features a half-pipe in summer. Small-size skates (size 1 and 2) are available.
🏠 *Waterville Valley 03215, tel. 603/236–8311. Cost: Skate area $5 per day; rentals $10–$28; includes helmets and protective pads, including small sizes. Rental center open daily 9–5, pavilion (indoor blading) weekends 10–5.*

New York

Central Park

(🏃 8–15) New York City's skating mecca is Central Park. Streets throughout the park are closed to traffic on weekends; if your kids are younger and just learning, **Wollman Rink**, near the southern end of Central Park, may be a better bet. Trick skateboarders congregate on the West Drive between 66th and 70th streets. Two convenient places to rent skates: **Blades Board & Skate** (120 W. 72nd St., tel. 212/787–3911; and 160 E. 86th St., tel. 212/996–1644; they'll give you instructions), or at **Wollman Rink** (midpark at 63rd St., tel. 212/517–4800), which also gives lessons.
🏠 *5th Ave. and 59th St. to Central Park West and 110th St., New York.*

Vermont

Stowe In-Line Skate Park

(🏃 10–15) In summer, most of the huge parking lot at the base of Spruce Peak ski area is transformed into a big in-line skate park. The setup, next to the Alpine Slide, has everything from a half-pipe to ramps, a downhill slalom course served by a lift, and a snack bar. Now a large flat area has been set aside for beginners to practice. Serious attention is paid to safety; rentals include helmets, elbow and knee pads, and wrist guards; in-line skates rented are top quality; and certified instructors give group and private lessons.
🏠 *Spruce Peak Base Lodge, Stowe Mountain Resort, 5781 Mountain Rd. (Rte. 108), Stowe 05672, tel. 802/253–3000. Cost: $6.50–$15; skates and protective gear $11–$20 (kids' sizes available). Open Memorial Day–Columbus Day, daily 10–7.*

Sailing and Windsurfing

To me sailing is the sport that best captures the essence of the Northeast. As you drive along the coastline of sheltered bays on a summer afternoon, you see harbor after picturesque harbor sprinkled with white sails and, beyond, beckoning, open blue water swept by wind. If you want to get out on the waves, the region offers sailing schools, bareboat charters of day sailers and cruising boats, and captained boats of all kinds where you can relax and let a skipper and crew do the work. Besides the ocean sailing areas that most appeal to us, large lakes, such as Lake Champlain, Lake Winnipesaukee, and Lake George have active sailing communities despite heavy powerboat traffic. We discovered that the most inexpensive way for a family to learn to sail or rent a boat is through one of the many community sailing programs; the U.S. Sailing Association (Box 1260, Portsmouth, RI 02871, tel. 401/683–0800 or 849–5200) publishes a free directory to all the programs in the United States.

You'll find rental Windsurfers and lessons at many beaches, but not all have conditions appropriate for beginners—you must have the right angle of wind to windsurf safely. Beginners (kids as young as 7 can learn if they are strong) need large inland ponds or bays with flat water and steady light winds like the kettle ponds on Cape Cod; those more advanced want the thrill of rolling wave action that you find at ocean beaches. Besides the Cape and Nantucket, Martha's Vineyard and Block Island offer limited but good windsurfing. Taking a lesson from someone with experience is important.

Connecticut

Longshore Sailing School

(👫 8 – 15) Known for its successful junior sailing program, the largest in the country, this school also offers private sailing lessons for families in a calm, protected bay of Long Island Sound, an easy place to learn. It also rents boats and Windsurfers.

🏠 *260 S. Compo Rd., Westport 06880, tel. 203/226–4646. Cost: $40 per 1-hr lesson.*

SoundWaters

(👫 8 – 15) A combination of sailing and environmental education, three-hour trips on this three-masted schooner give opportunities to steer the boat and hoist the sails as well as trawl for sea creatures and learn about the ecology of Long Island Sound.

🏠 *Brewer's Yacht Haven, Washington Blvd., Stamford 06902, tel. 203/323–1978. Cost: $25 adults, $15 kids 12 and under.*

Maine

Boothbay Harbor

(👫 5 – 15) This is boat country; it has the greatest number and variety of pay-as-you-go boat excursions in Maine. Seal watches,

puffin watches, lighthouse watches, lobster fishing, up the Kennebec River, out to a misty island, just sailing around the bay, a water taxi from one side of the bay to the other—whatever intrigues you is leaving in half an hour at most. Cruising the coves, circling the islands, rocking on waves is the only way to really know Maine, and the trips, as if planned for young children, are mostly short and skirt coastlines with much to see. A boat tour of the harbor and a short sail on a Friendship sloop (a type of one-masted sailboat) are musts. **Cap'n Fish's Boat Trips** (Pier 1, tel. 207/633–3244) offers many one-hour (and longer) choices; *Bay Lady* (Pier 8, tel. 207/633–2284), a 31-ft Friendship sloop, leaves Fisherman's Wharf for one and ½-hour cruises.

Windjammer Cruises

(👫 8 – 15) Windjammers are the classic tall-ship schooners rigged with many sails to accommodate the variable winds characteristic of the East Coast and flexible enough to change course quickly. An impressive fleet of them lies in Camden's picturesque harbor and elsewhere in huge Penobscot Bay. On a three- or six-day cruise, adventure combines with quiet relaxation, good food, and a chance to explore the pine-covered islands of the rocky coast and bay the way sailors did more than 100 years ago. Kids can help hoist sails and steer the ship. Each night you anchor in a different cove or village harbor; in July many of these sponsor street dances and races. The **Maine Windjammer Association** (Box 1144P, Blue Hill 04614, tel. 207/374–2955 or 800/807–9463; $350–$745 per person), with 10 ships, sets aside several large ones each summer for family trips. **Maine Windjammer Cruises** (Box 617, Camden 04843, tel. 207/236–2938 or 888/692–7245; $295–$745 per person) has three ships. The *Mistress* is ideal for a large family.

Massachusetts

Cape Cod

(**☆☆ 6 – 15**) What makes the Cape an ideal place for kids to learn to windsurf is the large number of bays and ponds with different angles and intensities of wind. Among the prime places to learn and experiment are large, freshwater kettle ponds, such as Great Pond in Eastham, and protected bays, such as Pleasant Bay in Chatham. At calm Gull Pond in Wellfleet (which connects with three other ponds) and Flax Pond in Nickerson State Park, numerous different kinds of boats are available to rent. **Jack's Boat Rentals** (Rte. 6, Wellfleet, tel. 508/349–9808; $20–$35 per hr) has concessions at both Gull Pond (tel. 508/349–7553) and Flax Pond (tel. 508/896–8556), offering rental canoes, kayaks, boogie-, sail-, and surfboards, Sunfish, and even kid-size Windsurfers that can be used by 6- and 7-year-olds, in addition to lessons. Yet private lessons offered by Eric at **Fun Seekers** (tel. 508/349–1429), usually held at Great Pond or Pleasant Bay, are much more thorough; a two-hour introductory lesson includes Windsurfer rental. Eric also conducts 2½-hour family kayak tours of salt marshes ($30 per person).

The Cape's shifting winds require a different kind of sailing. **Arey's Pond Boat Yard** (Arey's La., Box 222, off Rte. 28, South Orleans 02662, tel. 508/255–0994; 5 morning group lessons, $160; private lessons, $100 per 2 hrs) is one of the Cape's few sailing schools outside a yacht club; it offers group and private lessons for kids and adults.

Nantucket

(**☆☆ 7 – 15**) The most popular beach on Nantucket for families, **Jetties Beach** is an easy place to learn to windsurf and sail because windsurfing is safe no matter what the wind direction. *See also* Chapter 14, Boating.

Rhode Island

Newport

It's one of the yachting capitals of the world, the site of the America's Cup race, and on a sunny day with the steady southwest breezes for which it is famous, Narragansett Bay is thick with sailboats of every size billowing white sails and colorful spinnakers. Even if you sail for only an hour or two, doing it here is interesting for kids because the bay is full of other boats; if you spend half a day or more, there are easy-to-sail-to destinations such as Block Island, Sakonnet Point, and Cuttyhunk, where you can go ashore. If you want to learn to sail, this city has more sailing schools than any other in the Northeast to choose from. Try one of the following:

(**☆☆ 12 – 15**) **J. World Sailing School**. After talking to a number of sailors and yacht-club members, I've satisfied myself that this is the ultimate sailing school in Newport, the one I'd most like my family to attend if I could afford it. They are flexible, offering instruction for a weekend or five days for just adults or a family; families can also make special arrangements for a day or for several days on a cruising boat. Kids need to be old enough and interested enough to put up with six-hour days on the water. **🏠** *Box 1509, Newport 02840, tel. 401/849–5492 or 800/343–2255. Cost: $325 and up per person.*

(**☆☆ 7 – 15**) **Sail Newport Sailing Center**. The whole purpose of community sailing organizations such as this one based at Fort Adams State Park is to make sailing more available and affordable, especially for kids and families. Kids 7–15 can join a two-week all-day sailing school, adults and kids 13 and up can take a three-day series of sailing lessons, a family can hire a private instructor to teach them all, or you can just rent 19- or 22-ft sailboats by the half or full day. **🏠** *60 Fort Adams Dr., Newport 02840, tel. 401/849–8385 or 401/846–1983.*

Swimming

In the Northeast there are five areas that we think have the very best ocean beaches: the southern shores of Long Island and Rhode Island, the islands of Nantucket and Block Island, and Cape Cod. Not all beaches are equally safe for kids, however; those with riptides, sudden drop-offs, and heavy surf may be okay for older kids and adults familiar with the ocean, but little kids need shallow, warm water, low wave action, and no undertow. It's important to realize that two beaches only ½ mi apart can have widely different conditions.

As everyone in our fair-skinned family burns quickly and few ocean beaches offer shade, we usually haul a portable umbrella just in case we can't find one to rent. In July and August, the biggest problem at just about any beach in the Northeast is parking. As the parking cost can be as high as $10 per day, whenever possible we stay at a hotel or in a cottage within walking or biking distance of at least one attractive beach.

I should say a word about swimming in lakes and rivers. Maine's Sebago Lake is sand bottomed, fringed with pines and sand beaches (though except for the state park, all are privately owned by individuals and resorts), and crystal clear. Lake Champlain's shoreline in both Vermont and New York offers few sand beaches (except in Vermont's Grand Islands area) but clean and delicious water.

Massachusetts

Cape Cod

The choice of different kinds of beaches on the Cape is staggering (there are 150): On protected Cape Cod Bay, the surf is gentle, the shallow water seems to stretch forever, and it's warm; southside beaches on Nantucket Sound have rolling surf and are warmed by the Gulf Stream; at the round, deep freshwater kettle ponds tucked away behind ocean beaches, water is warm and calm, too, like big swimming pools; at open ocean beaches, waves of cold water curl in and vigorously slap the beach. A beach sticker is usually required for parking; rates range from $7 to $12 per day, cheaper by the week. See also Chapters 5 and 14.

Some of our favorite beaches are these:

(**ᵗᵗ ALL**) **Cape Cod National Seashore**. The park's ocean beaches are spectacular. Nauset Beach in East Orleans (tel. 508/240–3780), in the seashore but managed by the town, is a 10-mi long barrier beach with big waves and a special surfing area, and is great for older kids who want to boogie board. But for families, Herring Cove Beach, which faces the bay, and Race Point Beach in Provincetown are more protected; Race Point Beach is prettier, with more sun, dunes, and a feeling of remoteness. ⬥ *South Wellfleet 02663, tel. 508/349–3785. Open weekdays 8–4:30.*

(**ᵗᵗ ALL**) **Flax Pond**. Located in Nickerson State Park (Rte. 6A, Brewster 02631, tel. 508/896–3491. Cost: Free), this pond is warm and calm, ideal for toddlers, with a nice beach and picnic areas, lifeguards, a snack bar, a playground, and boat and Windsurfer rentals plus instruction.

(**ᵗᵗ ALL**) **Old Silver Beach**. North Falmouth's long crescent of soft white sand is kept shallow at one end by a sandbar, which makes tide pools with crabs and minnows. The beach has lifeguards, bathrooms, showers, a snack bar, and lots of parking, but is sometimes crowded.

(**ᵗᵗ ALL**) **Sandy Neck Beach**. West Barnstable's (Sandy Neck Rd. off Rte. 6A) 6-mi barrier beach between the bay and marshland is one of the Cape's most beautiful, with sand dunes and a sand and pebble beach that looks like it goes on forever. At low tide shallow pools form for splashing and paddling, but stay away from the area where four-wheel-drive vehicles are allowed. Just before dusk musicians, storytellers, and mimes perform around a campfire. It has a snack bar and full facilities.

☆☆ ALL **Skaket Beach.** In Orleans (off Skaket Rd.), which faces warmer Cape Cod Bay, you'll find one of the nicest and most peaceful beaches on the Cape for families with young kids; when the tide recedes, you'll find nearly a mile of tide pools to explore.

☆☆ ALL **West Dennis Beach.** In West Dennis, on the warmer south shore, this beach has an open feeling and extensive parking, as well as Windsurfer rentals, bathhouses, a playground, and food. A beach parking pass in this town is good at any beach.

Nantucket

Believe it or not, the waters around Nantucket are warm from mid-June through September, and the warmest, calmest water is on the north shore. *See also* Chapter 15, Beaches.

New York

Long Island

The traffic on this island drives us wild, especially on summer weekends. The reason everyone, including us, is willing to put up with it is the fringe of magnificent wide beaches along Long Island's south shore that run practically its entire 103-mi length from (incredibly crowded) Jones Beach all the way to Montauk Point.

Ocean swimming on these beaches requires some skill, so when Gavin was small, we searched out bay beaches and those that border both the ocean and a large pond. A major difficulty is finding a beach where you can park for just the day. Although anyone can simply walk onto a beach, parking at many is restricted to Nassau and Suffolk county residents and nonresidents who have paid an expensive full-season fee for a sticker, and this requirement is strictly enforced. Cars are towed. Only state parks and some town beaches have one-day-use

parking fees (as much as $15), and lots fill up quickly.

The two areas we head for, for different reasons, are Fire Island and the South Fork, at the tip of the island, which include the following beaches:

☆☆ 4–12 **Fire Island National Seashore.** Two hours from New York City, Fire Island is the beach area we come to when we want to feel cut off from everything but sand and water and sky. There are no cars here, just boardwalks across the dunes. All the visitor center areas have splendid beaches; the best swimming for little kids is at high tide when shallow water extends far, far out into the Atlantic. *See also* Chapter 5.
🏠 *Park Headquarters, 120 Laurel St., Patchogue 11772, tel. 516/289–4810; Sailors Haven Visitor Center, tel. 516/597–6183.*

☆☆ 0–15 **Foster's Memorial Beach** (Long Beach). On Noyac Bay west of Sag Harbor, Long Beach is safe enough for kids ages 3–4 to sit in the water with a bucket and shovel while you watch from 5 ft away. Lots of families eat dinner here while watching the sunset.
🏠 *Southampton. Cost: Parking $10.*

☆☆ 8–15 **Hither Hills State Park.** Montauk is wilder and more windswept than Easthampton, and this beach is sometimes swathed in mysterious mists (see Camping, *above*).

☆☆ 3–15 **Main Beach.** There's a casual elegance to this white-sand beach on the South Fork that makes it one of the most beautiful in the world; even the weathered wood pavilion has charm. Everything you want is here—snacks, Windsurfers, swimming lessons—but if you have little kids, you can't let them just frolic about in the water unless you are right next to them. Note that daily parking is only permitted on weekdays.
🏠 *End of Ocean Ave., Easthampton. Cost: Parking $15 (at beach or at Easthampton Village Hall, 27 Main St., tel. 516/324–4150). Open weekdays 9–4.*

Rhode Island

Block Island

In contrast to the flat or rolling landscape of many other beach areas, this one is hilly, with breathtaking bluffs and moors, and small beaches in coves. A long, curved swath of beautiful sand beaches on the island's east side, known collectively as Crescent Beach, runs from Old Harbor to Jerry's Point, an easy walk up Corn Neck Road. For more beaches, see also Chapter 15, Beaches.

South County

The stretch of coastline from Watch Hill at the Connecticut border to Narragansett, which Route 1 parallels, consists almost entirely of town- or state-owned sandy beaches, some of which are restricted to town residents with a sticker. These are mostly wide, flat beaches with the merest hint of dune, more accessible than those on Long Island. These are some of our preferred spots:

5+ **Misquamicut State Beach and Atlantic Beach**. For people-watching, teen action, and bodysurfing, this 7-mi-long, very wide beach park is it. There's even an amusement park with miniature golf, kiddie rides, and a Ferris wheel right here. Expect crowds and loud music from boom boxes. The water is very clean, although occasionally August can bring in an excess of seaweed. Surf is usually mild to moderate, and there's little undertow.
Atlantic Ave. (off Rte. I; follow signs), Westerly, tel. 401/596–9097.

6–15 **Narragansett Town Beach**. A highly accessible, yet perfect New England beach of miles of fine white sand that you can walk to from town, it has some of the best surfing on the East Coast; for older teens who want to learn, free lessons are given by the pros once a week in summer. There's little undertow and a gradual drop here.
Rte. IA, Narragansett, tel. 401/783–6430.

6+ **Ninigret Conservation Area/East Beach**. Outstandingly beautiful, this undeveloped barrier beach lies between Ninigret Pond, Rhode Island's largest salt pond, and Block Island Sound and borders the Ninigret National Wildlife Refuge. With few amenities (only a lifeguard and portable toilets in the tiny parking lot), a steep drop-off, and moderate surf, it's best for families who want a long, uncrowded beach; 2 mi away, Blue Shutters Town Beach has many family amenities. Ninigret Pond is ideal for windsurfers. See also Chapter 5.
Conservation Area, end of East Beach Rd., off Rte. I, Charlestown 12813, tel. 401/322–0450, in winter 401/322–8910.

1–10 **Roger W. Wheeler State Beach**. It is safe for kids to romp in the surf at this clean beach protected by a jetty because there is no rough surf or undertow, and shallow water extends out quite a way. Swimming lessons, a playground, and picnic areas are added family attractions.
Off Sand Hill Cove Rd., Narragansett, tel. 401/789–3563. Cost: Parking $8–$10.

Vermont

Sandbar State Park

ALL This long, wide sandy beach on a natural sandbar in Lake Champlain is the very best family beach in Vermont. What makes it so great for little kids is that you can wade out 50 to 100 ft before you get to deep water. Naturally there is a playground, bathhouse, and snack bar, plus views across the lake. You'll also see geese, gulls, terns, and many other birds because the beach borders a Fish & Wildlife refuge.
Rte. 2, Milton, tel. 802/893–2825. Cost: $2 weekdays, $3 weekends adults, $1.50 kids 4–15. No pets.

Tennis

In nearly every community we've visited in the Northeast we've tracked down at least one or two tennis courts, and at many resorts, tennis is a major sport, with tennis lessons and clinics for both parents and kids. Rockywold-Deephaven Camps and the Balsams in New Hampshire, the Sagamore in New York State, and Basin Harbor Club in Vermont all have excellent programs. Tennis fanatics who crave a total family weekend or weeklong tennis immersion also swear by the summertime tennis programs at ski resorts. Bolton Valley and Smuggler's Notch in Vermont have family-oriented programs.

Bridges Resort and Racquet Club

(**ii 3+**) In the serene Mad River valley with the Green Mountains on the west, this resort offers both superb tennis for families and easy access to a variety of other sports, from hiking to horseback riding. What makes it special for kids are the small racquets, lower nets, and well-supervised group lessons. See also Chapter 9.
i Sugarbush Access Rd., Warren 05674, tel. 802/583–2922 or 800/451–4213.

New England Tennis Holidays at Sugarbush Resort

(**ii 3 – 15**) Centered at the Pavilion Sports Center right across from the Sugarbush Inn, this is one of the top tennis schools in the country for adults. The choices for younger children are diverse; kids can join a tennis and swimming program, attend every-other-day or afternoon clinics, play matches, or enter the Sugarbush Day School camp program of ropes courses, hiking, swimming, and field trips. I'm convinced the kids' lessons are successful because the instructors have been specially trained to teach kids and lessons have humor and informality.
i R.R. 1, Box 350, Warren 05674, tel. 800/869–0949. Facilities: inn or condominium lodging, ½- and full-day kids' camp, regular kids' clinics and matches, nursery, 27 outdoor

courts, 3 indoor courts, 18-hole golf course, indoor and many outdoor pools.

Tubing

The kind of tubing our family has done is the easy kind, simply sprawling on an inner tube in bathing suits and drifting lazily downstream with the current for an hour or two on flat, calm rivers. For that, all we need are basic tubes, life jackets, towels, a pair of old sneakers, a pleasant stream—and someone with a car to pick us up at an agreed-upon take-out point. Even younger kids can manage such an outing if the stream is shallow and slow, with few rocks. Tubing in a Class II river (see White-Water Rafting, below, for explanation of class categories), where you contend with 1- to 3-ft waves, is exciting but too challenging and scary for those much under 12. Either way, expect to get wet and wear a T-shirt and hat and plenty of sunblock. Go in July and August, when the water is warmer.

Connecticut

Farmington River, New Hartford to Canton

(**ii 10 – 15**) Similar to New York's Esopus Creek in exciting rapids, the 2½-mi stretch popular for tubing on this river strikes me as safer because there are fewer rocks, and lifeguards are stationed at the biggest rapids to ensure that those who overturn get to shore safely. On a hot day, the three sets of rapids are thick with shrieking teenagers, who, we observed, sometimes climb out and hike back to do them again. **Farmington River Tubing** (Satan's Kingdom State Recreation Area, Rte. 44, New Hartford 06057, seasonal tel. 860/739–0791; main office in Niantic, tel. 860/693–6465; $12, including life jacket and shuttle) rents heavy-duty tubes. Kids must be at least 10, 4' 5" tall, and know how to swim.

Maine/New Hampshire

Saco River, North Conway to Hiram Falls

(7–12) The slow-moving Saco, ideal for family canoers (see Canoeing, *above*), is almost too slow for tubing, though you'll see many trying it. Bring your own tube, as shops in the area do not rent them. There are many entry points along the river; check with **Saco Bound** (Box 119, Rte. 302, Center Conway 03813, tel. 603/447–2177; Main St., North Conway 03860, tel. 603/447–3801) for information.

New York

Delaware River, Sullivan County

(8–15) Floating and bobbing over a 3-mi Class I section of gentle riffles on this river boundary between New York State and Pennsylvania (see also Canoeing, *above, and* White-Water Rafting, *below*) is just exciting enough to be fun, but relaxing compared to tubing the Esopus (see *below*). With time out for a swim, it takes about two to three hours, and the best time is after lunch. **Kittatinny Canoes** (Dingmans Ferry, PA 18328, tel. 800/356–2852; $16.50 per day), with six outposts along 135 mi of river, three in New York State, rents custom-made tubes and provides life jackets.

Esopus Creek

(12+) Tubing on the rapids of the fast-flowing, rocky Esopus Creek, a Class II waterway in the Catskill Forest Preserve, is a hot summer afternoon adventure for families with kids over 12 who won't be daunted by the 1- to 3-ft-high waves. You bounce along on huge truck-size inner tubes; if the water isn't high enough (check with the shop below) you're likely to bump on rocks; if too high, the water may be too fast and rough. A few caveats: Wear helmets, life jackets, and canvas shoes for protection; kids shouldn't tube without an adult. **Town Tinker Tube Rental** (Bridge St., Phoenicia 12464, tel. 914/688–5553; $10 tubes with seats, $2 life jackets, $3 helmets) rents tubes and equipment and provides bus shuttle service ($3) regularly on weekends.

Whale-Watching

If you want to whale-watch in the Northeast you can catch a boat from any number of town wharves in five states, from the tip of Long Island to northern Maine. Kids agree that seeing a whale is incredibly exciting, especially if it swims around the boat, but they don't like gazing out over expanses of water while waiting and waiting for one to appear. A little pre-trip education helps, though whale-watch boats usually carry a naturalist who spouts some amazing facts about whale habits on the way out so kids know what to look for.

Consider trips that take four hours or less and keep in mind that larger boats minimize rolling. Some trips guarantee whale sightings (if you don't see one, you get a repeat trip) and offer food, drink, and a sheltered, preferably heated, cabin area. The whale-watching season is April to October, but the best months are the warmer ones, mid-June through September. Only four kinds of whales appear in the Northeast—fin, right, minke, and humpback—and you rarely see all kinds.

Out on the water, the temperature will be at least 10°F, sometimes 20°F cooler that on land, and kids may get wet from the spray. Wear long pants and rubber-soled shoes, and bring sunglasses, sunscreen, a hat, a sweatshirt, a waterproof windbreaker, and binoculars. If kids start to feel sick, stay out in open air; keep eyes on the horizon; nibble on plain crackers. *Where the Whales Are* by Patricia Corrigan (Globe Pequot, 1991) lists all the trips in North America.

Maine

Bar Harbor

(**†† 8–15**) When you travel out from Bar Harbor to Mount Desert Rock, where the whales' feeding grounds are, you sail around Acadia National Park. Fewer whale-watch vessels ply these waters than ply the Stellwagen Bank. You may want to try the *Acadian Whale Watcher* or *Sea Bird Watcher,* a fast 70-ft boat that offers a four-hour trip on which you'll also see puffins. Both boats have heated cabins and carry naturalists. Midweek is busiest. Dress warmly.

🏠 *Golden Anchor Pier, 52 West St., Bar Harbor 04644, tel. 207/288–9794. Cost: $26–$34 adults, $16–$18 kids 7–15. Trips depart late Apr.–mid-Oct.*

Massachusetts

Massachusetts Bay

Whales travel the length of the Gulf of Maine, but the greatest number congregate in the Stellwagen Bank, a huge, watery feeding ground of plankton that attracts some 500 whales annually for a summer-long dinner party in Massachusetts Bay just between Provincetown and Gloucester.

This is the prime East Coast whale-watching territory, yet it's only 6 mi from Provincetown Harbor. You won't necessarily see more whales than you will in Maine, but it will be warmer on the ocean. Though I've included boat trips from other points below, taking off from Provincetown is ideal for kids; because you're already 30 mi out at sea, it takes far less time before you actually see a whale.

(**†† 8–15**) **Captain John Boats.** Of the several boats of this modern fleet, one is quite large, with a spacious, enclosed cabin that has seats, tables, and a big snack bar, as well as an upper deck. Onboard naturalists are research scientists who track these whales all year long and know most by

name. Though sightings are not guaranteed, in practice the company gives rain checks if no whale is sighted. Trips are four hours long; it usually takes about 45 minutes to an hour before whales are spotted.

🏠 *Town Wharf, 117 Standish Ave., Plymouth 02360 (about 40 mins from Cape Cod), tel. 508/746–2643 or 800/242–2469. Cost: $24 adults, $15 kids under 12. Trips depart Apr.–Oct., weekdays at 11, weekends at 9 and 2.*

(**†† 8–15**) **Hyannis Whale Watcher Cruises.** The only excursions from the mid-Cape use a large boat that accommodates 300.

🏠 *Millway Marina, Barnstable Harbor, Hyannis 02630, tel. 508/362–6088 or 800/287–0374. Cost: $24 adults, $15 kids 4–12. Open Apr.–Oct.; 2 to 3 3½-hr trips a day.*

(**†† 8–15**) *Ranger V.* This is my pick for the best trip for kids—the largest whale-watching boat on the Cape, it carries 415 passengers. The size guarantees minimal rocking and virtually eliminates seasickness. Family-owned and run, it appreciates young passengers.

🏠 *MacMillan Pier; ticket office, Bradford St. at Standish St., Provincetown 02657, tel. 508/487–3322 or 800/992–9333. Cost: $18, kids 9 and under free. Open mid-Apr.–mid-Nov.; several 2-hr trips a day.*

(**†† 10–15**) *Voyager.* This is a long trip (the boat leaves from Boston), five hours, but for kids the big draws are the naturalists from the aquarium staff on board, one of whom presides over an onboard tide pool with creatures that can be touched, plus equipment to check out—using instruments to record wind speed, for example.

🏠 *New England Aquarium, Central Wharf, Boston, tel. 617/973–5277 for information, 617/973–5281 for reservations. Cost: $24 adults, $17.50 kids 12–18, $16.50 kids 3–11. Open Apr.–Oct.; several trips a day.*

White-Water Rafting

White-water rafting can be exhilarating for families without being totally terrifying and can be appropriate for kids as long as they know how to swim, like boats and the water, and are old enough—at least 8 (50 pounds). Some rafting companies will take younger kids; I don't advise it. Rivers differ in how dangerous and difficult they are to maneuver; that depends on both the time of year (wilder in April than in August) and also on the intensity and nature of the rapids. A classification system that ranks their difficulty from I (flat water with no more than riffles) to V (for experts only) gives you some guidance. Kids under the age of 13 should stick pretty much to Class II and III, but even on a Class II river, expect to get wet.

Maine and Massachusetts have very strict regulations about guide licensing and quality and condition of equipment. Outfitters listed here give safety talks prior to the trip and cater to families. Forget April (the water is too high), May, and even the beginning of June, when the water is still so cold you have to wear a wet suit to stay warm.

Maine

Kennebec River & Dead River

(**♔♕ 8 – 15**) These two rivers rushing through a landscape of wild northern forest wilderness converge at the Forks, where many rafting companies are based. In the upper gorge of Kennebec River you'll find water in the Class III and IV categories; adventurous kids 12 and up (weighing 90 or more pounds) are permitted; below it is Carry Brook, 6 mi of easy, gentle rapids even 8-year-olds might enjoy, but with just as much wilderness scenery. Outfitters offer families various possibilities—a split trip for adults and kids or a half-day trip on the easy section. Among the best family trips for those with kids under 12 are Northern

Outdoors' full-day Family Rafting Adventure on the Dead River, held on two Saturdays in June and August when the river is lower, and their Family Overnight Adventure, which combines swimming and tubing with a run in Kennebec Gorge. **Northern Outdoors** (Box 100, Rte. 201, The Forks 04985, tel. 207/663–4466) maintains an entire resort center with cabins and other activities. Another good outfitter is family-run **Crab Apple Whitewater, Inc.** (Crab Apple Acres Inn, Rte. 201, HC63 Box 25, The Forks 04985, tel. 207/663–2218 or 800/553–7238), which has been in the business since 1981 and is very family-oriented, with guides who are especially friendly to kids. Both outfitters trips cost between $60 and $80 per person including lunch, less for half-day trips.

Massachusetts

Deerfield River, Fife Brook

(**♔♕ 8 – 15**) The 12 mi of fast-flowing river, mostly Class II, with one Class III rapids, that pass through Mohawk Trail State Forest make a good introductory guided raft trip for kids because of the easy rapids, pleasant swimming spots, and abundance of wildlife. Six-hour-long trips include time for lunch and plenty of swimming. **Crab Apple Whitewater, Inc.** (see *above*) runs trips for $52 to $72, including lunch.

New York

Delaware River, Sullivan County

(**♔♕ 8 – 15**) The combination of relatively tame rafting, with the spectacular scenery more common to intense gorge rapids, draws many families to this wide, swiftly flowing Class I+ and II river, where you need no guide to accompany you. Along the most scenic section, from Pond Eddy to Mata-moras, high shale cliffs with ribbon waterfalls and unusual rock formations rise straight up from water so clear you can look down and see fish. Your kids will probably spot beaver lodges and birds of all kinds, from blue herons to bald eagles. **Kittatinny Canoes** (Dingmans Ferry, PA 18328, tel. 800/356–2852; $24–$27 per person; children under 12 free when 4th, 5th, or 6th in a raft) offers continuous daily trips on six-person rafts from three locations on the upper Delaware at bargain prices, especially for families with several children. Shuttle service and life jackets are included but lunch is not.

Sacandaga River

(👫 8 – 15) This short, fun-filled, and exciting, but not intimidating, introduction to rafting takes under two hours and travels 3½ mi over Class II and some Class III rapids. It's for families who just want a taste of white water; the trip doesn't have the wild and adventurous flavor of longer trips on more spectacular rivers. **W.I.L.D. W.A.T.E.R.S.** (Rte. 28, Warrensburg, NY 12885, tel. 518/494–7478 or 800/867–2335; $16 adults, $14 kids 12 and under) runs regular trips daily. Reservations are not necessary, though they are advisable.

. . . And Just in Case: Rainy-Day Action Adventures

Into the life of every family on vacation in the Northeast, unless you are very, very lucky (not us), come those days and weekends when the rain washes out everyone's outdoor plans. We've found that a museum will rarely suffice as a substitute, but indoor miniature golf or video games may. For younger kids, the ubiquitous Discovery Zone centers, in every northeastern state except Vermont and New Hampshire, are a good choice. The choices that follow are especially unusual.

Connecticut

Stew Leonard's Dairy

(👫 2 – 12) It's the Disneyland of supermarkets, a cross between an amusement park and a country fair that's now the world's most entertaining and largest (it covers 8½ acres) supermarket. In the parking lot, goat kids amble in the petting zoo; inside, animated milk cartons sing, a mechanical chicken in a cage shoots out plastic eggs, and employees dressed as cows and chickens wander the aisles.
🏠 *100 Westport Ave., Norwalk 06851, tel. 203/847–7213. Open daily 7 AM–11 PM.*

Maine

L. L. Bean & L. L. Bean Kids

(👫 12 – 15) Wandering around here on a rainy day or boring evening (it's open 24 hours a day, 365 days a year) is great fun. The store, housed in a rehabilitated version of Leon Leonwood Bean's original boot factory, is still the center of the company's mail-order business. Better yet is the new kids-only store right across the parking lot, a well-supervised space with a climbing wall, stationary bikes, and much more. The free horse-drawn carriage outside will take you to the 100-plus factory outlets in town.
🏠 *Rte. 1, Freeport 04033, tel. 207/865–4761 or 800/341–4341.*

New Hampshire

Funspot Amusement Center

(👫 12 – 15) The ultimate game and bowling spot in the Northeast for kids, this one has 500 electronic games and both regular and candlepin bowling.
🏠 *Rte. 3 (1 mi north of town), Weirs Beach 03247, tel. 603/366–4377. Cost: 25¢ tokens (discounts for bulk purchases). Open Sept.–*

June, Sun.–Thurs. 10–10, Fri.–Sat. 10 AM–11 PM; July–Aug., daily 9 AM–1 AM.

Perpetual Motion Indoor Playground

(**†† 1–6**) More like an actual indoor version of an outdoor playground than Discovery Zone centers, Perpetual Motion is also more personal, individual, and charming, with a huge wooden train of four brightly painted cars designed by its engineer-owner. Kids seem to get an extra kick out of the fact that swings, a huge sandbox, and a minicarousel with three horses are all indoors.

🏠 *16 Haverhill St., Rte. 133, Andover 01810, tel. 978/474–4424. Cost: $5.50. Open Mon.–Wed. and Fri.–Sat. 9:30–5, Thurs. 9:30–7:30, Sun. noon–5.*

New York

Doubleday Batting Range

(**†† 6–15**) Nowhere are kids so much in the mood to test out their own batting and pitching abilities as in Cooperstown, home of the Baseball Hall of Fame. Luckily, right near it is a building filled with batting cages and a machine that measures the speed of your pitch with radar, where kids can indulge their need for action. Although most batting ranges don't have anything for little kids, here the machine in one batting cage pitches just tennis balls and in another softballs.

🏠 *Doubleday Plaza, Cooperstown 13326, tel. 607/547–5168. Cost: $2 per machine. Open late June–Labor Day, daily 10–5; Memorial Day–late June and Labor Day–Columbus Day, weekends noon–6.*

OUTDOOR ACTION IN THE SNOW
SKIING, SKATING, SNOWSHOEING, BOBSLEDDING, AND MORE

Winter in the Northeast is usually cold, sometimes brutally cold, and snowy. But the mountainous landscape, quaint towns, and cozy lodges of northern New England and New York lend themselves to family vacations that embrace the ice and snow. To us the season means skiing, sledding, ice-skating, snowshoeing, and the justly famous snow sculpture contests at the area's winter carnivals. Most downhill areas I've included offer all of the above as well as cross-country skiing and sleigh rides.

Ski trips are ideal family vacations in the Northeast because skiing is fun for everyone, from beginner to expert, and because in an effort to attract families New England ski areas offer excellent baby-sitting facilities, kids' lessons, teen centers, bargain family packages, discount lift tickets, and many other lures. Various types of multiple-area lift passes (either season, day, or several-day) and frequent skier programs (you accumulate points toward a day of free skiing) can be true family bargains. The American Ski Company, for example, has a Magnificent 7 card, which is good at all its resorts—Sugarloaf, Sunday River, Killington, Mt. Snow, Sugarbush, and Attitash/Bear Peak—as well as the Edge Card frequent skier program. With this card you can also purchase lift tickets right at a lift instead of standing in line.

Among the nearly 100 downhill ski areas in the Northeast, I've chosen those that my family or skiing families I know have found particularly family-friendly and that offer the most for families with kids of all ages and abilities. All described here have good nursery facilities and excellent ski school programs for children as well as adults, a casual atmosphere, and other family amenities. Most nurseries, for example, rent pagers; if your child is having a hard day, the staff will contact you. The ski schools have teaching programs that rely on games and other fun activities and have a teacher/student ratio of no more than 1:6 for kids under 7, and no more than 1:10 for older kids. I used to favor areas that offered SKIwee, but that program is fading and new good kids' programs are emerging, such as the American Ski Company's Perfect Kids and the programs at Smuggler's Notch (**see below**, Vermont). Snowboarding instruction for younger kids (ages 6 and up) is now available at most ski areas in the Northeast. Besides the expansion of snowboard parks, the latest trend is terrain parks whose trails include a host of features that can be used by skiers as well as snowboarders. Snowshoeing and snow tubing are also growing in popularity, and many ski areas are setting aside special snowshoe trails and a lighted slope for tubing at night.

All areas rent ski equipment; areas with ice-skating also rent skates. Remember that it's essential to make reservations for the nursery, children's programs, and children's rental equipment well in advance, especially for holidays and weekends. Although there are many lovely places to cross-country ski, I've deliberately chosen only those that rent kids' equipment, give kids' lessons, and have some super-easy, well-groomed, and patrolled trails.

Good guides to skiing with kids include **The Best Family Ski Vacations in America** by Laura Sutherland (St. Martin's Press, 1997) and **Ski Vacations with Kids in the U.S. & Canada** by Candace Stapen (Prima, 1997). **Family Travel Times** has an annual issue with up-to-date information on ski areas (tel. 888/822–4388), but also check the September, October, and November issues of **Ski, Skiing,** and **Snow Country** magazines and a great ski Web site: www.skinet.com.

Maine

Maine's big pluses are a long season, usually with more natural snow than other states, generally lower prices for everything from lodging to all-day children's programs, and smaller crowds and shorter lift lines at most areas. The drawback is the driving time to get from southern New England and New York to west-central Maine. Small resorts like Saddleback (tel. 207/864–5671) and Shawnee Peak (tel. 207/647–8444) are friendly, rustic, and inexpensive—appealing for families. Nevertheless, as most of them have what I call layer-cake skiing—experts at the top, intermediates in the middle, and beginners at the bottom—and limited options for some age groups, I've opted to include only Maine's two major ski resorts; both are owned by the American Skiing Company and offer the frequent skier card and multiple-area lift pass mentioned above.

Sugarloaf/USA

The modern village at the base of Sugarloaf Mountain in western Maine is the largest on-mountain ski village in the Northeast. The area is a hit with families because it's compact and convenient—facilities, lodgings, restaurants, grocery stores, and an indoor sports center are clustered by the central lifts. You can walk or ski almost everywhere. And unlike many other ski areas Sugarloaf has varied activities for kids six nights a week. Other pluses: the only above-the-timberline skiing in New England; rock concerts for teens; excellent day care for little ones; a kids-only ski slope; hard-to-easy slopes; even half-hour dogsled rides (tel. 207/246–4461) through pines and over mountains on sleds pulled by 12 all-white Samoyeds.

This is a big area with a lot for all skiers—beginning, intermediate, or expert—with great tree skiing as well as an especially good beginners' program. The novice area has three chairlifts that lead to three beginners-only trails. The $10-a-day ticket for these lifts is a special bargain for all riders. Some slopes are designated family areas reserved for slow skiers and are ideal for family runs with younger children—hot-doggers caught bombing around on them must forfeit their lift tickets until they watch a film on safe skiing. More than 50% of the trails are easy or intermediate (long runs wind down the face of the mountain offering wonderful views), but unlike some family-friendly New England areas, Sugarloaf also satisfies families that include expert downhill skiers, adult or teenager: The vertical is higher than that of any peak in the Northeast other than Killington's in Vermont (much more crowded) and Whiteface's at Lake Placid, New York. From the steep, open snowfields that cover the summit you can take some of the most challenging black-diamond runs in the East. If you love bumps, try Sugarloaf's bone-rattling Skidder. The trails, which do include a few easy runs from high elevations, spread out like a fan from the snowfields. With one of the largest halfpipes in the country and host to the qualifier for the 1998 Olympics, snowboarding facilities at Sugarloaf are superb.

The best deals for families are the annual Children's Week in January (kids 12 and under stay free in their parents' room and get lessons, lift tickets, equipment, and use of the health club free) and Family Fling weeks in February and March, when kids are half-price and special races, movies, and evening events are planned.

A bright, cheery nursery takes kids from 6 weeks to 6 years daily and on Wednesday and Saturday nights from 6 PM to 10 PM. Three-year-olds who want to try skiing use equipment free. Kids 4–6 (Mountain Magic) and 7–12 (Mountain Adventure) can participate in half- or full-day programs. The intermediate kids' adventure slope, Moose Alley, has a ½-mi-long trail with a secret entrance and a warming lodge where you can get hot chocolate and cookies.

Sugarloaf also has an excellent fast-paced daily ski clinic for kids 13–6, who can hang out later at the alcohol-free Avalanche Club. Primarily frequented by kids who can't yet drive, it has video games, Ping-Pong, and movies. One night a week teens take over the health club.

On-mountain lodging includes condos, an inn, and a hotel, which are moderate to very expensive; the older condos are closer to the lifts. Lodging packages include use of the resort's health club. The access road (Rte. 27) has some attractive, informal, friendly, and inexpensive lodges.

🏨 R.R. 1, Box 5000 (off Rte. 27), Carrabassett Valley 04947-9799, tel. 207/237–2000; 207/237–2000 snow report; 800/843–5623 on-mountain lodging; 800/843–2732 area-wide reservations. Facilities: 126 trails, 14 lifts, 20 restaurants, 3 pools, health club, ski school, nursery, teen center, laundry, hotel, condos, shuttle buses. AE, MC, V.

CROSS-COUNTRY SKIING AND SNOWSHOEING. Sugarloaf's **Touring Center** (tel. 207/237–2000) is the terminus for 62 mi of cross-country trails along old logging roads, through pine forests, and down an old narrow-gauge railway track that loops through the Carrabassett Valley. Because Sugarloaf gets so much snow, cross-country skiing is usually good even fairly late in the season. A few trails are lighted at night.

Sunday River

Sunday River, the first ski area owned by the American Ski Company, is a combination of the West and New England. It's a huge complex of interconnected trails (including an open snow bowl) that sprawl across eight mountains with slope-side lodging in modern, low condos, a couple of luxury hotels, and a few country inns. You'll find more diversity of terrain here than at any other ski area in New England: long runs and varied trail configurations for experts and intermediates; snowboard "playgrounds" on every mountain for snowboarders; and a huge learning area. Trails and lodging (including a massive four-story wood-frame hotel and conference center that has both old-fashioned shutters and contemporary sleekness) have been added at a rapid pace since the 1980s, but the atmosphere remains low-key and focused on the slopes rather than the glitz. Five miles away, down a level road, is Bethel, a historic New England village so perfect that it was once featured in a Christmas-card commercial.

A surprising number of easy and intermediate trails start from the peaks, though most of the highest trails are for experts. Although the wide variety of slopes spread out over several mountains is a plus, it's also a drawback for families: Lifts start from several different base areas in the valley, making it easy to lose kids unless you all stick together.

The key attractions for families are the teaching program at the excellent children's ski school (ranked No. 1 in the East by readers of *Ski* magazine), the child care, the snowboard parks and clinics and nighttime activities for teens, and for parents a Learn-to-Ski program that virtually guarantees you'll learn to ski before you leave. If you and your children are learning to ski or trying to get to the next level, Sunday River is a great place. There is free skiing and instruction (tel. 207/824–3018) for anyone with a physical disability. At Nite Cap, the new nighttime entertainment center at the White Cap Base Lodge, you can eat at a family-friendly Italian restaurant, go on a snowshoe hike, ice-skate, play the latest video games, or try snow tubing under lights. Many teens spend their evenings riding the lighted halfpipe open every evening of the week.

All the kids' programs, including a day-care center for ages 6 weeks to 6 years, are conveniently based at the South Ridge Learning Area, as is the kids' rental shop. The ski school program for ages 3–12, Perfect Kids, has been so successful that now all American Ski Company resorts use it and others have bought it. Instructors receive extensive training in learning styles; they find out just what works with each child and teach accordingly. Kids seem to progress faster here because extra instructors shuttle among groups to whisk away those who are about to make the leap to the next level of skill for an hour or two of one-on-one coaching. Tiny Turns (ages 3–4) includes an hour of private coaching; Mogul Munchkins is for 4- to 6-year-olds; Mogul Meisters (skiing) and Low Riders (snowboarding) are for 7- to 12-year-olds. For kids over 12 there

are daily clinics in both skiing (More Terrain and Vertical) and snowboarding (Black and Blue Crew); these hook kids up with others their age. The popular teen nightclub, MVP's, open from 7 to 11:30 PM on weekends and during holiday weeks, offers music, videos, and pizza.

On-mountain lodging includes two hotels, trailside condos, and town houses that range from moderate to very expensive, plus an inexpensive inn and ski dorm. For families with older kids, the White Cap Condos are next to Nite Cap and its teen evening activities. Families with younger ones can opt for condos in the South Ridge area. Nearby are several inexpensive, old-fashioned ski lodges.

🏠 *Box 450, Bethel 04217, tel. 207/824–3000 information; 207/824–6400 snow conditions; 800/543–2754 lodging reservations. Facilities: 126 trails and glades, 18 lifts, 9 restaurants, 7 pools, health club (at hotel), ice-skating, ski school, sleigh rides, snowmobiling, snowshoeing, 3 day-care centers. AE, D, MC, V.*

CROSS-COUNTRY SKIING. Sunday River Inn and Cross-Country Ski Center (tel. 207/824–2410), ½ mi from the ski area's main entrance, has 40 km (25 mi) of groomed trails. Nearby are several other centers, including Telemark Inn (see Chapter 9).

Massachusetts

The Berkshire hills of western Massachusetts shelter a number of friendly ski areas; the hills are gentler than those farther north and offer mostly beginner and intermediate slopes. Several are just right for an introduction to skiing, a family day trip, or a weekend outing, especially when it's very cold up north. An excellent, comprehensive guide to all winter sports in this area, including some wonderful off-the-beaten-path cross-country trails, is *Skiing Downhill and Cross-Country in the Berkshire Hills* by Lauren Stevens and Lewis Cuyler (Berkshire House, 1990).

Butternut Basin

Butternut has neither on-mountain lodging nor the flavor of a charming, cohesive ski town or resort, nor the size and variety of places farther north. But for a day trip or even a weekend it offers a friendly family atmosphere; very clean, modern, attractive and sunny base lodges with old-fashioned, tasty fast food (in the spring bring your lunch and eat on the sunny deck overlooking the slopes); a strong SKIwee program on weekends; and two completely separate beginner lifts and slopes for kids. It's only a two-hour drive from most of Connecticut, Westchester County, and the Springfield area.

The biggest drawbacks are the weekend crowds and lift lines, though kids who are in beginner SKIwee classes won't have to wait long at their lifts. If you can, get here early, ski, and eat lunch by 11:30. There's not a lot for teens—no night skiing, for example— but there is a snowboard park and two smaller terrain parks that even intermediate skiers can enjoy, and the ski shop has a wide (though pricey) selection of ski wear and junior racing wear to browse through. The trails are mostly broad, open, well-configured beginner and intermediate runs; you can enjoy a panoramic view of the Berkshires from the summit.

The best bet here for kids 4–12 is the weekend SKIwee program, which offers a half-day option. The beginner area has wide, gentle slopes and is right by the main base lodge, so it's easy to ski over from other slopes periodically to check on how your child is doing. Instructors are warm and friendly. A sweet nursery in a three-room log cabin takes up to 25 kids ages 2½–6 but will accept younger ones, even babies, if you reserve. The number of caretakers varies, but the ratio is one adult to four or five kids.

Since the area is small and compact, kids who are good skiers can explore Butternut Basin by themselves; many kids head for the coin-operated slalom run (free on weekdays), where you can race against the clock or another skier on a parallel course.

Motels and inns on Route 23 are closest to the ski area; you'll also find places ranging from moderate to very expensive in nearby Great Barrington, South Egremont, and Stockbridge.

🏨 Rte. 23 (2 mi east of town), Great Barrington 01230, tel. 413/528–2000 information and lodging suggestions; 800/438–7669 snow conditions. Facilities: 22 trails, 8-km (5-mi) cross-country trails, 8 lifts, 2 cafeterias. AE, D, MC, V.

Jiminy Peak

Jiminy Peak is small, but its atmosphere and amenities are similar to those at more major resorts in Vermont—and it's only 2½ hours from New York City. We like the convenience of the handsome neocolonial clapboard condominiums and suite hotel clustered at the base of the lifts; the clean, roomy cafeterias; and the variety of beginner, intermediate, and black-diamond trails. It's ideal for a weekend, especially for a family of low to good intermediate skiers who want to ski together. Because of the area's small size, congenial atmosphere, and converging trail layout, this is also a place to let kids explore the mountain on their own. One drawback, though: The slopes here tend to ice up in the afternoon, more so than at Butternut.

The two-room nursery with a staff of one adult for five kids and lots of toys in a big room takes babies from 6 months, and the ski school program accepts children ages 4–12. Though there's a beginner J-bar lift and a separate beginner slope, I think the beginner area and program at Butternut are superior. The facilities for small ones here are a bit out of the way, and the ski-school meeting area can be congested.

The best bet for kids is the Mountain Adventure program—eight weekends of instruction for kids 6–17 with the same teacher. Night skiing and a snowboard park are about it for teen action, but the black-diamond trails are pretty challenging. One bargain for ages 7–22 is the student ticket available midweek during nonholiday weeks.

The resort's expensive to very expensive on-mountain hotels and condos are the most convenient; less expensive inns and motels are nearby in Hancock and Pittsfield. 🏨 *Corey Rd., Hancock 01267, tel. 413/738–5500 or 888/454–6469 information and on-mountain lodging; 413/443–9186 or 800/237–5747 area lodging (Berkshire Visitor's Bureau); 413/738–7325 snow conditions. Facilities: 28 trails, 7 lifts, 2 restaurants, 2 cafeterias, bar, ice-skating, ski school, nursery. AE, D, MC, V.*

New Hampshire

New Hampshire's White Mountains, dominated by looming 6,288-ft Mt. Washington, thrust up high, beautiful, rugged peaks in the northern part of the state. That's where you'll find the biggest ski areas, many of which are easily accessible from Interstate 93. Direct national flights land at Manchester Airport, an hour from many of the slopes. By car, Boston is two to three hours away from most areas; New York is six. New Hampshire's ski areas have a casual, friendly feel, making them great for families. For general and lodging information and up-to-date snow conditions at all resorts in the state, call Ski New Hampshire, tel. 800/887–5464, which has an actual person to answer questions and give recommendations seven days a week during ski season, or access www.skinh.com.

Bretton Woods

Bretton Woods has the sociable, intimate atmosphere of a small, old-fashioned area, yet it has plenty of family amenities—and spectacular views of Mt. Washington. It's not glitzy or hectic with activities, and it has a variety of gentle yet interesting and winding runs that are perfect for kids who are just learning to ski. The terrain makes it easy for the whole family to ski together or for kids to explore the mountain on their own, sheltered from wind by surrounding mountains. The junior ticket rate extends to 15-year-olds (as opposed to 12 at most areas). A limited lift-ticket policy keeps the area generally uncrowded, plus it offers night skiing, convenience, comfort (superior food compared to other ski areas), and good value. An attractive three-level base lodge houses a nursery, parking is easy, and the resort's on-mountain town houses offer good packages for families. The grand Mt. Washington Hotel (see also Chapter 18), the area's new owner, plans to remain open in winter in December 1999 and to double the number of trails by 2000.

During Family Fest Weeks (between Christmas and New Year's and Presidents' holiday week in February) kids can take sleigh rides, play games, and see movies. Most activities are geared to younger kids; however, snowboard movies hosted by an extreme skier (whose daredevil antics kids love to hear about), pizza and sub parties, and night skiing are the attractions for teens.

Most of the slopes are beginner and intermediate, among them several long, gentle runs from the top, but there is an expert glade skiing area at the top of the mountain. Try eating at the mountaintop restaurant at the end of the high-speed quad chairlift; glass, china, and silverware are used to cut down on waste.

The Babes in the Woods nursery in the base lodge is open for 2-month-old infants to 5-year-olds from 8 AM to 5 PM. If your children seem ready, they can spend part of the day in the hour-long snow play and ski readiness program, in which a ski instructor works with just two kids (equipment is included in the price). Children 3 to 12 can attend the excellent Hobbit Ski and Snowboard School's all-day (8:30 to 4) programs based on the SKIwee model; kids 8–12 can opt for the new snowboard program. Lifts, lunch, equipment, two outdoor sessions, and supervised play are all included. Kids 5 and under ski free everywhere when with their parents.

Convenient on-mountain town houses have good family packages; a lovely, moderately priced lodge and a motor inn owned by Bretton Woods are nearby. The Mt. Washington Hotel is one of the grand old resorts of the region. You'll find inexpensive, clean, and functional motels in the town of Twin Mountain 5 mi away—some of these offer their own family packages.

🏨 *Rte. 302, Bretton Woods 03575, tel. 603/ 278–5000; 800/232–2972 information; 603/ 278–1000 Bretton Woods lodging; 800/245– 8946 Twin Mountain Chamber of Commerce. Facilities: 33 trails, 7 lifts, 2 restaurants, cafeteria, ice-skating, sleigh rides nearby. AE, D, DC, MC, V.*

CROSS-COUNTRY SKIING AND SNOW-SHOEING. Bretton Woods has superb cross-country skiing on its 90 km (56 mi) of groomed trails. These go through the woods and over bridges, are well maintained and easygoing, and afford great views of Crawford Notch. The cross-country center (tel. 603/278–5181 or 800/232–2972) is at the hotel, a few miles from the base lodge.

Jackson Ski Touring Foundation

In Jackson, New Hampshire—a charming, traditional New England village below Mt. Washington, with a population of about 800—cross-country skiing is as good as it gets. The Jackson Ski Touring Foundation maintains a vast (the largest in the East), well-groomed and -marked (according to difficulty) trail network surrounding the town. There is a moderate fee for use of the trails, which wander up three river valleys in the White Mountain National Forest, but kids 9 and under ski free. You can set out on a ski tour from the door of your inn or ski to a restaurant for lunch. A large, new, friendly base lodge provides a fireplace to warm up, tables where you can eat a bag lunch, storage for skis, lessons, and rentals. A few trails

are set aside for snowshoeing, but most are skiing only. The town has a lighted ice-skating rink. And if you want shopping and nightlife, North Conway is not far away.

Nestlenook Farms Recreation Center (tel. 603/383–0845) also has ice-skating as well as sleigh rides in the country, over arched bridges and along a river. On the sleighs, drawn by Clydesdales, are cushioned benches, brass lamps, and sleigh bells. Kids can feed reindeer in the woods and warm up with hot cider and hot chocolate afterward.

The 15 or so places to stay in town range from condos to cozy inns and from inexpensive to very expensive. Some are much more appropriate than others for families, but the local Chamber of Commerce is very helpful and knowledgeable.

🏨 *Jackson Ski Touring Foundation, Box 216, Main St., Jackson 03846, tel. 603/383–9355 or 800/927–6697 information and snow conditions; 800/866–3334 area reservations (Jackson Resort Association); 603/356–3171 or 800/367–3364 (Mt. Washington Chamber of Commerce). Facilities: 156 km (100 mi) of trails. MC, V.*

DOWNHILL SKIING. Two small nearby areas are particularly good for families with small children. **Black Mountain** (tel. 603/383–4490) in Jackson has bargain midweek lift tickets and a special weekend family ticket for two parents and two kids 15 or under. **King Pine Ski Area** (tel. 603/367–8896) at Purity Spring Resort, 25 minutes south of Jackson, with 50% beginner runs, offers excellent beginner instruction and great snowshoeing.

Loon Mountain

Just off the Kancamagus Highway, only a few miles from Interstate 93 and Lincoln, Loon is a nice, friendly family mountain that doesn't cost the earth. It has a wide variety of terrain, many lodging choices in each price range, some after-ski activities for kids—a Wildlife Theater that presents live animal shows and a Children's Theatre that puts on fairy-tale productions. In the nearby towns of Lincoln and Woodstock there's a cinema and an arcade. Condos (and a resort hotel) are right on the mountain—some really are ski-in/ski-out. The friendly staff (who have a special rapport with kids) and the food on the mountain (especially the barbecue on the deck at Summit Lodge) all contribute to Loon's appeal. A free and funky steam train links one base lodge with the other. Condos and parking lots form a long strip at the foot of the mountain between the two clusters of lifts. You can also ice-skate on the lighted rink by the cross-country ski center, where you can rent skates and snowshoes.

Beginner slopes and trails are set off from other trails, so slow-skiing families don't have to worry about hotshots; one long, 2½-mi run from the very top of the mountain has enforced slow skiing. All the wide, easy intermediate, and beginner trails make this area a good one for a family of beginning or low intermediate skiers, but a separate sector of Loon mountain boasts expert slopes, accessible from a gondola from the base lodge. One new attraction is tubing at night in the beginner area; Loon plans to introduce lift service to haul you and your tube up one slope.

Loon Mountain limits lift tickets to reduce lines, so it's important to reserve a ticket in advance by phone or stay in lodging that includes a guaranteed lift ticket; otherwise you probably won't get one on weekends or holidays. Though the arrangement of the lifts generally spreads skiers well, they end up jostling a bit on big holiday weekends.

The Honeybear nursery takes children from 6 weeks to 8 years; 3- and 4-year-olds have their own ski camp program, as do 5- and 6-year-olds. Kids 7–12 can join the Adventure Ski Camp.

On-mountain lodging includes both condominiums and a hotel with a pool. Accommodation at both ranges from moderate to very expensive and includes guaranteed lift tickets. Nearby Lincoln has inexpensive

motels, many of which offer packages that also include guaranteed weekend lift tickets. 🏠 *Kancamagus Hwy., Lincoln 03251, tel. 603/745–8111; 603/745–8100 snow conditions; 800/227–4191 lodging. Facilities: 43 trails, 8 lifts, 7 restaurants, ice-skating, night tubing, kids' theater. AE, D, DC, MC, V.*

CROSS-COUNTRY SKIING AND SNOW-SHOEING. Check at Loon's cross-country skiing headquarters near the base lodge for information (and lessons and rentals) on the 35 km (21 mi) of trails. Be sure to try the logging road that parallels the East Branch of the Pemigewasset River, where two kids we know spotted lots of small wild animals and dramatic ice formations.

Waterville Valley

This self-contained resort in the White Mountain National Forest with a 4,000-ft mountain as a backdrop is one of the best-value ski areas for families in the Northeast. In a cup surrounded by mountains, one of which is laced with ski trails, this modern version of a cozy New England town centers on Town Square. Here families climb aboard horse-drawn sleighs for daily afternoon and evening rides, set out on the cross-country trail system, or just skate on the big, covered skating rink. The interconnected clapboard buildings around the square house shops, restaurants, lodgings, entertainment, and a sports center; inns, lodges, and condos spread out beyond. Whether you want excellent child care, highly rated ski instruction, the best snowboard parks for beginners to experts, superb cross-country skiing with good instruction for kids, kids' and family activities, or plenty for teens to do, all of it is here—and at great prices. Lift tickets for kids 12 and under are a mere $10 and teens get a discount. Snowshoe rentals in all sizes and many miles of snowshoe trails beckon those who want to try this growing sport. There's even a program for children with physical disabilities. The town recreation department schedules family and children's activities, including movies and gym times, on a regular basis.

No lodging is ski-in/ski-out, but all is within 1½ mi of the Town Center and 2 mi of the base lodge. A free shuttle bus travels through the valley all day long picking up and dropping off skiers. With a five-day mid-week package, you can store your equipment at the base lodge free.

Most trails are intermediate; there are no long beginner runs, and the expert runs don't offer the variety, challenge, or length of those at Sugarloaf. They converge at the base lodge, making it easy to find your kids, especially as the lodge houses everything—ski school, nursery, lift ticket office, cafeteria, and pizza corner. (A new quad lift has cut down on the congestion that used to arise.) Adult and kids' beginning trails and lifts are helpfully set off from the main runs; little kids even have their own easy-to-use surface lift.

The nursery, several cheerful and well-equipped rooms in the base lodge, takes 6-week-old infants to 4-year-olds; it opens up onto a children's terrain garden. Infants and toddlers have their own rooms, and there's even a separate area for nursing mothers.

In the excellent ski and snowboard school kids 3–12 have both half- and full-day options that include indoor games and a rest time for younger kids. Three- to 5-year-olds have their own ski slope, Kinderpark, accessible only from the ski school. Kids as young as 6 can opt for snowboarding, provided they wear at least a size 2 boot. Kids 9–12 (Mountain Scouts) stay with one instructor the entire day, eating lunch in one of the mountain restaurants, or they can sign up for Nastar race clinics.

Unlike many other ski areas, Waterville Valley has much for teens: a discounted lift ticket; teen ski and snowboard camps during holiday weeks that spill over into after-ski sleigh rides and ice-skating parties; and snowboard parks that are ranked among the best in the East by *Snowboarder* magazine.

The yurt in Boneyard is a real teen hangout; inside is a video camera so you can watch your friends take the jumps. It's easy to walk everywhere, and because of the resort's secluded location, it's safe for older kids to get around by themselves. The resort's busiest weeks, between Christmas and New Year's, February President's Day, and the first week in March, are the most fun for teens.

Most of the valley's lodging is in moderate to very expensive condominiums and all-suite hotels; many have swimming pools. Family packages make them more reasonable, but the town also has moderately priced lodges and country inns. Children 12 and under ski and stay free with some lodging packages. Nearby Campton has inexpensive bed-and-breakfasts.

🏔 *Waterville Valley 03215, tel. 603/236–8311 or 800/468–2553 information and lodging; 603/236–4144 snow report. Facilities: 52 trails, 11 lifts, 5 restaurants, sports center (with indoor pool, hot tub, indoor tennis courts, indoor track), ice-skating, sleigh rides. AE, D, DC, MC, V.*

CROSS-COUNTRY SKIING AND SNOW-SHOEING. Waterville Valley's cross-country network, ranked among the 10 best in America by *Snow Country* magazine, has 105 km (65 mi) of graded trails, of which 70 km (43 mi) are groomed and patrolled; the rest are marked wilderness trails. Kids get their own special lessons. The rental center for snowshoeing is at the downhill base lodge. Trails from there hook up with the cross-country network.

New York

The Catskills and the Adirondacks contain numerous small and large ski areas. For information on small areas that are family-oriented, fun, and inexpensive for a day trip, see *Let's Take the Kids! Great Places to Go with Children in New York's Hudson Valley* by Mary Barile and Joanne Michaels (St. Martin's Press, 1990).

Garnet Hill Lodge Ski Touring Center

Perched high in the southern Adirondacks, this comfortable, cozy, family-friendly lodge and touring center (*see also* Chapter 9), ranked one of the 10 best in North America by *Snow Country* magazine, maintains the largest privately operated cross-country trail system in the region, a fully equipped shop, and a special kids' ski program, even for kids 3–5 on weekends and holiday weeks. If your kids are too young, they rent pulks (small sleds) so you can pull them as you ski. Among the easy trails for beginners are scenic ones on the shore of Thirteenth Lake, which is down the mountain from the lodge; in the spring you can ski to a working sugarhouse. Because of its high elevation (2,000 ft) there is snow cover very late in the winter. You don't have to stay here to ski, but it's much more fun to just walk out the door to a trail; besides, free ski lessons and trail fees are included and staying here is fun. Combination packages provide a day or more of downhill skiing at nearby Gore Mountain.
🏠 *Thirteenth Lake Rd., North River 12856, tel. 518/251–2444. Facilities: 55 km (33 mi) of groomed trails, hot tub and sauna, snowshoeing, sledding. AE, D, MC, V.*

Whiteface/Lake Placid

Yes, Whiteface Mountain is terrific for downhill skiing—and very uncrowded—but it's quite cold and often icy up here. This classic, rugged eastern mountain, site of the 1932 and 1980 Olympic Winter Games alpine events, is 3,216 ft high and offers very long (for the East), challenging runs as well as a good beginner area and lower prices, including lift tickets, than other major Northeast ski areas. There's a good kids' ski school and day care. But the real reason for families to come here in the winter is that it and the village of Lake Placid, 9 mi away, are a center for off-slope winter activities that are unavailable at other ski resorts: bobsled rides on America's only Olympic bobsled run (you ride with two or three people, a

driver, and a brakeman; it's for adventurous kids 12 and up); luge rides; skating on the outdoor Olympic Speed Skating Oval and on all the Olympic indoor rinks; and watching such competitions as the World Junior Alpine Skiing Championships. A special $39 ticket lets you try many of these activities once. All the facilities used for the 1980 Olympics are still here and in use. For information, contact the Olympic Regional Development Authority (tel. 800/462–6236; *see also* Chapter 17).

The town, which borders Mirror Lake, has an old-fashioned, European flavor; it's full of restaurants, shops, and movie theaters yet small enough so that a 12- and a 14-year-old we know could explore the town's many kitschy souvenir shops on their own.

Whiteface has runs spread out over two peaks; many steep, twisting trails lure advanced skiers, but the majority of runs satisfy intermediates or beginners. Nonetheless, this area is best for experts or intermediates (except children under 10) because those are the longer, more interesting trails; the beginner slopes are confined to the bottom of the mountain.

Kids Kampus, a sector of the mountain reserved for kids 1–12, has its own base lodge and cafeteria, a snow playground, a chairlift, and a handle tow. You can park here and then, after dropping your kids off, catch a shuttle to the base lodge. The nursery is open for kids 1–6 from 8 AM to 4 PM; kids 3–6 can join a play-and-ski program of indoor and outdoor activities for a half or full day. Kids 7–12 can also attend a half or full day, something many areas don't offer.

Several teens we know praise the brand-new Stimilon-designed halfpipe in the snowboard park; what they like best, though, is trying all the other activities in the area, including shopping and exploring the town on their own.

A wide variety of inexpensive to expensive lodging in individual houses, condos, lodges, hotels, cabins, motels, and B&Bs is available in Lake Placid and as close to Whiteface as across the road from the ski area. But this is one area where I recommend staying in the town, preferably right on Mirror Lake and with indoor parking so you don't have to scrape ice and snow off your car in the morning. In February, a highlight is the nearly 100-year-old Saranac Lake Winter Carnival nearby, which has an ice palace you can walk through (tel. 518/891–1990).

♠♠ *Whiteface Mountain Ski Area, Rte. 86, Wilmington 12997, tel. 518/946–2223, or Olympic Regional Development Authority, Lake Placid 12946; 800/462–6236 information and ski conditions; Lake Placid Visitors Bureau 800/447–5224 (reservations). Facilities: 65 trails, 10 lifts. Nearby: bobsled rides, dogsled rides, ice-skating, luge rides, ski jumping clinics, snowmobiling, tobogganing. AE, D, DC, MC, V.*

CROSS-COUNTRY SKIING AND SNOW-SHOEING. The Mt. Van Hoevenberg Cross-Country Center (tel. 518/523–2811) has 50 km (31 mi) of very wide, groomed, patrolled, and marked trails, including many easy but scenic ones good for children. Unlike at most areas, the trails here are kept covered with snowmaking equipment. Intrepid families who want wilderness skiing can easily hook up with the Adirondack Park's trails.

Vermont

Most of Vermont's 20 alpine ski areas and most of its cross-country areas are on or not far from Route 100, a north–south highway roughly near the center of the state that parallels the Green Mountains. Keep in mind that there can be great differences in temperature between the most southern resort, Mount Snow and the most northern one Jay Peak, almost at the Canadian border. If you have young children, opt for the more southern resorts in the coldest months. In addition to the areas below, I want to mention a small one that is adding more and more amenities for families and younger children. Ascutney (Rte. 44, Brownsville 05037, tel.

802/484-7711), a friendly area almost on the New Hampshire border, is modeling itself on Smuggler's Notch (*see below*). With mostly beginner and intermediate trails, all ski-in/ski-off slope-side condominiums with fireplaces, and extremely reasonable family packages, this is a place to consider. For information on Vermont skiing, check with the Vermont Ski Area Association (26 State St., Box 368, Montpelier 05601, tel. 802/223–2439 for mountain conditions and information; 800/837–6668 for reservations; or access www.skivermont.com).

Killington

In the past few years this seven-mountain area known for having the best party scene for singles in the East has added so many draws for families that *Family Fun* rated it one of the 10 best family areas in the United States. The reason behind the transformation is the American Ski Company, which now owns it. What's great: An entire mountain with all novice and intermediate terrain, Ram's Head, has now been set aside just for families; no hotshots and party types allowed—slow skiing is enforced. The big family center contains all the kids' facilities—ski school, a day-care center, kids' rentals, and a food court that's filled with other families. Family activities, like slalom races, and free snowboarding and skiing for kids under 12 are regular features of well-priced family packages available midweek throughout the entire season.

Yet this resort will challenge the most expert teen or adult; the largest ski resort in the East, it also has the longest alpine trail, a total of 205 trails, the steepest vertical rise, and the longest ski season in the East. Whatever you want, it's here, except for Western-style powder—glade trails; the steepest mogul run in New England; long, long beginner trails that wind down Killington Peak; three halfpipes, including one of the best in America; the world's first heated lift; two snowboard parks; and six alpine parks. A few other pluses include snowboard instruction specially geared for the 4 to 6 age group, an introduction to skiing for kids 2–3, and two special teen weeks annually with evening events and activities.

But although I know plenty of families who love to ski Killington, I still have a doubt or two about it as a great family resort for all age groups, especially for preteens who like to go off on their own. For older teens, yes, it's great. But the biggest drawback remains the size and complexity of the place—I once "lost" a group of preteens who were supposed to be skiing with us, and that can easily happen to anyone. So if you plan to ski outside Ram's Head, be sure to take the complimentary tour; it's essential to orient yourself. And make sure your kids know where to go if they get separated from you.

The American Ski Company has also added its characteristic family-friendly features, such as the Ground Zero Fun Park, a lighted area by the Killington Base Lodge that contains a tubing run, skating rink, halfpipe, and luge run, plus fireworks.

You can find accommodations in condominiums a few steps from the slopes, a huge new luxury slope-side Grand Resort Hotel that resembles the ones at other American Ski Company resorts, budget to expensive motels and condos on the access road, and nearby old-fashioned country ski lodges. Our favorite is Trailside Lodge (tel. 802/ 422–3532 or 800/447–2209), a classic ski lodge with moderate prices (breakfast and dinner included). Nearby Rutland has very inexpensive motels.
🏠 *Killington Rd., Killington 05751, tel. 802/ 422–3333 information; 800/621–6867 lodging; 802/422–3261 snow conditions. Facilities: 205 trails, 33 lifts, 4 restaurants, 7 cafeterias, health club (for hotel guests only), ice-skating, snowmobiling, snowshoeing. AE, D, DC, MC, V.*

CROSS-COUNTRY SKIING AND SNOW-SHOEING. Killington offers snowshoeing tours with a naturalist guide (tel. 802/621– 6867). Mountain Top Inn Touring Center (*see below*) is 15 minutes by car. Nearby is

also Mountain Meadows Lodge ski touring center (Thundering Brook Rd., Killington 05751, tel. 802/775–1010) with 60 km (36 mi) of trails, rentals, and instruction.

Mountain Top Inn Touring Center

Mountain Top has been a center of ski touring for more than 30 years. Now, with 110 km (66 mi) of wide, double-tracked trails and another 72 km (45 mi) of single-track backcountry trails, it is an outstanding place to learn how to cross-country ski or take up snowshoeing. Families can take advantage of the skating rink, sledding, tobogganing, saunas, a hot tub, horse-drawn sleigh rides, and winter horseback riding. You don't have to stay at the inn, but it turns out to be a good deal because all the activities and a ski-touring pass are included in the price. *See also* Chapter 9.
🏠 *Box 521, Mountain Top Rd., Chittenden 05737, tel. 800/445–2100 or 802/483– 2311; 800/372–2007 area lodging. Facilities: restaurant, bar. AE, MC, V.*

Mount Snow–Haystack

Mount Snow and neighboring Haystack, now owned by the American Ski Company, constitute the southernmost big ski area in New England. The area is relatively close to the Northeast's urban centers—four hours by car from New York City and the Connecticut coast, less from Albany, Boston, and Hartford—which makes it good for a weekend. The southern location also means that in midwinter Mount Snow can be as much as 15°F warmer than areas farther north—a real plus for families with small kids—but extensive snowmaking installations give it a long season (November to May). Families of beginning skiers and those with preteens and teens who love to snowboard will find it offers much more than other resorts.

Mt. Snow is comfortable, unpretentious, and very family-oriented, with a lot of new-in-1998 improvements, such as a Welcome Center in the Main Lodge, where you purchase all tickets and sign up for clinics and rentals, and a new lodge, the Discovery Center, that's just for beginning skiers only a few steps away. Here you'll find rentals, the kids' ski school, and clinics for beginning adults. Just out the door are the learning slopes, with kids on one side and adults on the other, and an easy Magic Carpet lift (like a conveyor belt on snow) to haul you up. As at all other American Ski Company resorts, the ski school teaches the Perfect Kids and Perfect Turn methods. Little kids (and parents who worry about hotshot snowboarders running into their kids) love the new terrain park just for them and the other Magic Carpet lift that looks like a covered bridge. The cheerful, well-equipped, and extremely well run nursery has been expanded; besides separate rooms for infants, toddlers, and preschoolers, plus one for naps, you'll find a large indoor playground with climbing structures, video games, air hockey, and even a parents' lounge.

Families can ski together easily here because more than two-thirds of the trails (on five mountain faces) are for beginners or intermediates, including most of the wide, sunny runs from the summit. In fact, the area has started offering a two-hour family clinic in which kids and their parents can ski and learn together. Yet you'll also find some challenging steep slopes and bump trails, including the scary Ripcord.

If you have preteens or teens who board, this is the place to come. Several we know rate the snowboard parks here "awesome." The Gut, Mt. Snow's renowned competition halfpipe, is Vermont's longest, served by its own lift. Each of the five large terrain parks is geared to a different ability level—two are for intermediate riders and a new extreme park caters to real experts. The Cave Club in the basement of the Main Base Lodge caters to the 10-to-14 crowd with games, including Ping-Pong. Teens tend to spend evenings at the Carinthia lodge, where there's a lighted outdoor ice-skating rink, sledding on the Ski Baba Trail, and a lighted

snowboarding area; now that a lighted tubing slope has opened in the Main Base area, kids may begin to congregate there.

The one big drawback at Mount Snow is the crowds of day-trippers on weekends, especially in the cafeterias. If your family plans to ski together, head for the Carinthia Base Lodge or Haystack. Ideal for families with young children just learning to ski, Haystack has a special learning area with its own lodge and an inexpensive weekend family-of-four lift ticket. Though accessible from Mount Snow by shuttle bus, Haystack does have a condominium village of its own.

The several Fun Factor Five Ski Weeks include special activities each evening for kids 12 and under, but throughout the season (except holiday weeks) a child 12 and under can ski free when a parent purchases a midweek package. Many nearby inns offer a variety of lodging packages—usually free accommodations and meals for children sharing a room with parents.

Mount Snow has no central sports facility. At Adams Farm (tel. 802/464–3762) in Wilmington you can take a 1½-hour sleigh ride through meadows to a log cabin in the woods, where you'll warm up with hot chocolate by an old-fashioned woodstove. Some lodges have their own small pools.

The resort has several on-mountain lodging options, from relatively expensive condominiums (except during special package weeks) to the typical American Ski Company luxury hotel with an outdoor ice-skating rink, and a less expensive lodge with suites. Several inexpensive inns border Route 100 just south of the mountain. 🏨 *400 Mountain Rd., Mount Snow 05356, tel. 800/245–7669 or 802/464–8501 information and lodging; 802/464–2151 snow reports. Facilities: 134 trails, 26 lifts, 5 restaurants, 7 cafeterias, 5 bars, health club (for hotel guests only), nursery. AE, D, DC, MC, V.*

CROSS-COUNTRY SKIING. Timber Creek (tel. 802/464–0999) is right across the road from Mount Snow. Nearby West Dover and

Wilmington have four cross-country centers: the **Hermitage Inn** (Box 457, Wilmington 05363, tel. 802/464–3511), **Prospect Touring Center** (tel. 802/442–2575), the **Sitzmark Lodge** (E. Dover Rd., Wilmington 05363, tel. 802/464–3384), and the **White House Touring Center** (Box 757, Wilmington 05363, tel. 802/464–2135).

Okemo Mountain Resort

For families, Okemo's attractions lie in its convenience and cozy atmosphere: All the facilities at the bottom of the mountain are close together, so it's easy to drop kids off and to find one another at the end of the day; the 800 slope-side condominiums with their cost-cutting family packages (on specially designated family weeks) really are ski-in/ski-out. One problem, however, is that the cluster of several-story buildings at the bottom of the mountain and the arrangement of the condos on the mountainside make you feel you're surrounded by high-rises instead of out in the wild. Another drawback is that to reach the top, skiers must take a beginner lift and then transfer to other lifts partway up the mountain.

Unlike most other ski areas, Okemo is right next to a town. Ludlow has specialty shops with kid appeal, restaurants and pizza places that deliver, sleigh rides, a cross-country skiing center, lots of lodging choices (if the aesthetics of the on-mountain condos bother you, several old-fashioned, out-in-the-country inns are nearby), and a good program of town activities for kids. It's fun to try snowshoeing as a family here; the new 5-km (3-mi) snowshoe trail around the mountain is easy enough for even young kids.

The skiing is also family friendly, particularly the long, wide beginner slope and two beginner lifts right across from the base lodge. The trails are mostly intermediate, with many long runs that kids and parents can ski together, and even a 4½-mi-long beginner trail from the top of the mountain. All the lifts and trails eventually funnel people into the same small area at the bottom,

which has some advantages, but when the resort is very crowded, the lift lines are long, and you feel like you're skiing out of and into a traffic jam. In 1999, however, Okemo will start expanding its base area and add some new trails. One drawback for very good skiers is that many trails have the same configuration. Teen snowboarders praise the huge, 1-mi long snowboard park, with its 900-watt sound system, 420-ft halfpipe and a brand-new 280-ft one. As at several other areas, they've created smaller parks intended for different ability levels within the bigger park and installed a yurt with a deck, bleacher-seating, and a video playback system; this has become a teen hangout.

The nursery, convenient in the lower level of the base lodge, is open daily and on some holiday evenings. Kids 1–6 play indoors and out. One bargain: Midweek day care is half price. Kids 3–4 can take an easygoing, very basic—no lift riding—introduction to skiing.

The award-winning Snow Star Skiers and Riders program for kids includes regular guided treks to nature zones (you get to see bear claw marks on trees). Beginners learn the basics before they even hit the slopes, then head for the children-only teaching slope and an easy-to-use poma lift—especially valuable when the mountain is crowded. You can watch your kids from the bleacher seats overlooking the beginner slope. The daylong program for kids 8–12 with average or better skills skis the main mountain. All the programs lunch in the ski school center, where there are also after-ski activities. The all-season junior racing team trains competitors ages 8–18—the largest program in the country. The best time to come with teens is on weekends or during holiday periods when the town of Ludlow offers ice-skating, volleyball, and dances in the new teen center in a renovated old-fashioned movie theater.

On-mountain accommodations include hundreds of fairly expensive ski-in/ski-out condos (midweek packages are the best bet) plus a lodge, but there are many inexpensive country inns and motels in Ludlow and within a 10-mi radius.

🏨 *RFD 1, Ludlow 05149, tel. 802/228–4041; 802/228–5571 or 800/786–5366 reservations and area lodging; 802/228–5222 snow conditions. Facilities: 96 trails, 13 lifts, restaurant, 4 cafeterias, bar. AE, D, MC, V.*

Stowe Mountain Resort

Established in the 1930s as one of the country's first ski areas, Stowe is a quaint yet cosmopolitan village with excellent, challenging downhill skiing and some of the best cross-country touring centers in the Northeast for families. We like skiing here because it's not a planned community at the base of the lifts; rather, there's a sense of tradition and history and an almost European flavor to this oldest New England ski town. Mountain Road between the town and the downhill ski area is lined with restaurants, inns of various sizes and price ranges, ice cream parlors, and shops. The Village Trolley travels along it all day long, dropping off and picking up people and skis. There's ice-skating at Edson Hill Manor's (tel. 802/253–7371 or 802/253–8954) rink or the town public rink and sleigh rides at Edson Hill Manor, Topnotch Resort & Spa (tel. 802/253–8585), or Pristine Meadows (tel. 802/253–9877).

Serious skiing—or snowboarding—families who like a more sophisticated atmosphere and food, and have kids over 8, will find Stowe especially appealing. In the past several years, however, the resort has really improved its facilities for younger kids, and the annual January winter carnival has many activities for them.

Stowe's downhill skiing area is divided between Spruce Peak for beginners and intermediates, where the ski school is located and which functions somewhat like a family center, and Mt. Mansfield (4,393 ft), where trails range from long, easy glides from the summit to intermediate runs to the steep, famous, Front Four double-black-diamond runs. The two base lodges are linked by a shuttle bus.

The cozy, cheerful day-care center for babies (2 months old minimum) to 3-year-olds in a renovated house just to the left of the Spruce Base Lodge has floor-to-ceiling windows. The well-run Children's Adventure Center ski school at the lodge has instructors hired specifically to teach children and a variety of programs. The flexible Kid's Adventure (3–5) is a combination ski lesson/child-care program (up to four hours of skiing depending on a child's interest and a large toy-filled indoor play area). Those beyond that stage use several open, gentle slopes and a slow, close-to-the ground chairlift. Kids 6–8 (Mini-Mountain Adventure) have their own base camp where they eat lunch together and store their equipment if they're skiing all week; kids 9–12 join Mountain Adventure and ski all over both mountains with their instructor.

During holiday weeks intermediate and advanced skiers 13–16 have a special full-day program, Teen Extreme; some days they break at five or six for pizza and then ski at night together. The challenging snowboard park (one of the best in Vermont) has specially designed jumps, pipes, and obstacles all over Mt. Mansfield, which are highlighted on the regular trail map, available where you buy lift tickets. Teens hang out in the yurt on the slopes, where they can watch video replays of themselves and their friends taking on the halfpipe and by the computers in the Octagon Café at the top of Mt. Mansfield, where you can send e-mail to your friends.

Stowe has inexpensive to expensive, casual to elegant motels, country inns, full-service resorts, bed-and-breakfast options, and even houses to rent within a short drive of downhill and cross-country centers. The best bet for downhill skiers is somewhere along Mountain Road; for cross-country skiers, we recommend the Trapp Family Lodge (tel. 802/253–8511). It's the classic inn where cross-country skiing was introduced in the United States.

🏨 *5781 Mountain Rd., Stowe 05672, tel. 802/253–3000 or 800/247–8693 informa-*

tion or reservations; 800/253–4754 slope-side lodging; 802/253–2222 snow conditions. Facilities: 47 trails, 11 lifts, 2 restaurants, 4 cafeterias, 3 bars, health club, 4 ski shops. AE, D, DC, MC, V.

CROSS-COUNTRY SKIING AND SNOW-SHOEING. The nearly 200 km (124 mi) of trails at the four cross-country centers— **Edson Hill Manor** (tel. 802/253–7371), **Stowe Mountain Resort** (tel. 802/253–3000), **Topnotch Resort and Spa** (tel. 802/253–8585), and the **Trapp Family Lodge** (tel. 802/253–8511)—in Stowe are linked (though only experts can really manage to ski from one to another). The best choices for families are skiing Stowe's 4½-km (3-mi) recreational path that meanders through town or the Trapp Family Lodge's groomed, well-patrolled trails on the outskirts of town.

Smuggler's Notch

This self-contained resort village at the bottom of Morse Mountain is simply one of the very best ski resorts in the Northeast for families, with a superb child-care center and award-winning children's ski school and programs, a well-thought-out teen program, and reasonably priced family packages. The number of planned evening family activities—bingo, etc.—rivals what you find on a cruise ship. Commitment to families is evident in every aspect of the resort. For example, it's the only ski area with a kid's trail map and a family learning center to explain how snowmaking works. Convenience is a huge plus here: The village houses restaurants (you'll see families at all of them), sports facilities, shops, and entertainment, all within walking distance of the condos, slopes, and chairlifts. The levels of service (for example, you can reserve cribs, potty seats, high chairs, and so on), friendliness to and enthusiasm for kids, and organization are unsurpassed at any ski area in the Northeast.

The food and activities are all appropriate for kids, and nearby restaurants share the easy tone. A small, lighted outdoor ice-skat-ing rink is just the right size for kids. Across the road from the resort is Vermont Horse Park (tel. 802/644–5347), which offers sleigh rides.

Ski trails spread out over three mountains: Morse for beginners, Madonna and Sterling for experts and intermediates. One drawback is that you have to take a lift to the top of Morse and ski across to the other mountains; you can ski or take a shuttle back to the village. Though this area is small in comparison to, say, Killington, there are several long beginner runs, a trail over the mountain to Stowe (you can purchase a one-time lift ticket there to get back), challenging bump runs and glade skiing, a Nastar race course, and now a triple black-diamond trail and Stimilon-approved terrain park with the usual table tops, spines, rolls, and a halfpipe. A night school for boarding even encourages families to learn on a beginner's teaching slope.

The five- and seven-day family ski packages, available all winter long, are your best bet here: They include lift ticket, accommodations, use of the pool and hot tub, and family and teen evening activities. Smuggler's even offers a Family Fun Guarantee—if your family doesn't have fun, your program fees will be refunded. Free lessons, rentals, and dinner for kids 3–12 are an added feature during the two annual Family Fest weeks.

The Alice's Wonderland Child Care Center for kids 6 weeks to 6 years is a model to be emulated. Warm and welcoming, its large rooms (one for infants, with a special sleeping room; one for toddlers; and one for older kids) are filled with a pleasant disorder of colorful toys, climbing apparatuses, blocks, huge fish tanks, and rocking chairs. Kids spend the day both indoors and out at the roomy outdoor playground behind the center, which has a petting zoo.

The kids' ski school is really clued in to what motivates kids to learn. The Mogul Mouse's Magic Lift for beginners is low to the ground and runs at half speed. More than two-thirds of the 280 instructors are specially trained to teach kids. In the Discovery Camp for kids 3–6, a horse-drawn wagon sometimes takes kids up to the lift, and kids learn through fun and games—playing Simon Says on skis, skiing under hoops, and participating in a cookie race at the end of the week. The Adventure Camp for kids 7–12 is similar. There's even a special one-hour family program, Mom and Me or Dad and Me, in which a specially trained instructor shows you how to teach your child to ski.

Evenings bring free family activities—bingo, Pictionary, sledding, ice-skating, fireworks; Tuesday is Parents' Night Out, when kids up to 12 can eat dinner and join in special activities at Alice's.

The innovative teen program was one of the first in the Northeast. The Explorer Program for ages 13–17 features challenging instruction—racing development, glade and bump ski techniques, or snowboarding; during holiday weeks a full-day program includes opportunities to sample these and snowshoeing. Scheduled evening teen activities here (karaoke, sledding, volleyball, dances) actually are well attended because the ski instructors go, too, inviting kids to come along after the ski program ends. The pool table is a big attraction at the alcohol-free teen center Outer Limits (busiest after 7:30, deserted during the dinner hour); it has couches, magazines, video games, and an experienced counselor, who introduces kids to each other. A new popular event is the weekly Saturday-night Millennium Zone, a nightclub with a DJ, ski and snowboard movies, and a giant pillow-fight game called the Joust.

The condominiums on the mountain are the best choice because of the resort's ski packages and their convenience, but inexpensive lodging is available on Route 108 between the resort and the town of Jeffersonville. 🏨 Rte. 108, R.R. 2, Box 5290, Smuggler's Notch 05464–9531, tel. 802/644–8851 or 800/451–8752 information, reservations, snow report. Facilities: 60 trails, 8 lifts, 2 terrain parks, half-pipe, 435 studio–5 bedroom condominiums, 5 restaurants, 3 bars, cafeteria, indoor pool with sauna and hot tub, exercise room, 2 indoor tennis courts, ice-skating, general store, sports shops, teen club. AE, DC, MC, V.

CROSS-COUNTRY SKIING AND SNOW-SHOEING. Smuggler's has 23 km (14 mi) of trails winding through woods and along a stream and up into the Notch itself. On Wednesday and Saturday nights, the Nordic Tour skis the trails and the Owl Tour, on snowshoes or skis, takes you hooting around for owls and into the Notch for history about the place.

Stratton

I find Stratton expensive and crowded, and its extensive village complex and covered parking lot for 700 cars remind me of a mall. But my son and his friends love it—and so do a lot of families we know, particularly those that include good intermediate or expert skiers or snowboarders. Why? For one thing, they appreciate its warmer southern location. For another, they like that Stratton is one big mountain, so everyone in a family can take the gondola to the top, ski down a different slope (including some bumps and super-challenging black diamonds), and meet at the bottom. Add to this convenient on-mountain lodging, a sports center, an excellent kids' ski school, and a huge ski learning park where beginners can ski on their own. Young teens like to hang out in the 25 shops and restaurants in a minimall at the base, where they can play Ping-Pong and avail themselves of excellent snowboarding facilities and instruction. This is the birthplace of the snowboard, and the U.S. Open Snowboard championships are held here. Stratton has several special packages for families throughout the season.

Stratton's trails fan out from the summit, the most difficult plunging down the front face of the upper mountain. Several easy long runs wind along either side, and the Ski Learning Park beginner area of 10 trails (and a terrain garden) and several short lifts lies on the lower mountain directly in front of the village square complex. It's an easy mountain to master and to ski together as a family; you can also let your kids explore on their own in the learning park, which has its own less-expensive lift ticket. Another good place for families to ski is the less-crowded and sunnier Sun Bowl area on the other side of the mountain; you can ski to it on an easy trail or drive to the Sun Bowl Base Lodge. On the main face of the mountain, the high-speed, 12-passenger gondola is exciting to ride, but lines are generally long on weekends.

The sports center is a bit of a hike from most condos. The country club a mile away has a lighted ice-skating rink. Don't look for special planned evening activities for kids and families here—many are chilling out in a condo watching a rental video—but Mulligan's restaurant does have a big video arcade. Nearby Manchester is filled with sophisticated shopping (including lots of outlets) and restaurants.

In the base lodge, a fresh, spacious center for infants and children age 6 weeks to 12 years has a downstairs crib and infant section that includes a private room for nursing mothers; upstairs you'll find a room full of the small tables, toys, and climbers that make toddlers and preschoolers feel at home. The SKIwee Little Cub program (ages 4–6) has its own building on the slopes across from the main base lodge and also teaches little ones to snowboard with the new small boards. The flexibility of the combined play-and-ski program is an asset for families. Not only can you choose half- or full-day, but if children don't want to go back out to ski, they can stay inside and paint or play.

The Big Cubs (ages 7–12), including snowboarders as well as skiers, have their own space in the lower level of the main base lodge, equipped with indoor training equipment, picnic tables, videos, and more. For kids who come to Stratton every weekend, the Stratton Mountain Training Center

offers regular recreational and racing training in which kids ski or snowboard with the same group; the snowboard race training here is the very best.

The only special teen programs are through the Stratton Mountain Training Center. Good skiers can join one of these for a day or weekend, but the evening casual learn-to-snowboard program on one lighted trail has become a hot teen event.

On-mountain lodging includes moderate to very expensive houses, condos, an inn, a lodge, and a hotel. Less-expensive motels and lodges are 15 minutes away on Route 11. ⚐ *R.R. 1, Box 145, Stratton Mountain 05115, tel. 802/297–2200 or 800/787–2886; 802/297–4211 snow conditions; 802/297–4000 or 800/787–2886 on-mountain and area lodging reservations. Facilities: 92 trails, 12 lifts, 9 restaurants, 7 bars, indoor lap pool, indoor tennis court, exercise room, racquetball, ski instruction, ski shop. AE, D, DC, MC, V.*

CROSS-COUNTRY SKIING AND SNOW-SHOEING. Stratton's cross-country center (tel. 802/297–2200) is in the Sun Bowl area; 25 km (15 mi) of trails are groomed; 50 km (30 mi) are backcountry skiing. Three other cross-country touring centers are based nearby: the **Hildene Inn** (Manchester, tel. 802/362–1788); **Viking Ski Touring Center** (Londonderry, tel. 802/824–3933); and **Wild Wings Ski Touring Center** (Peru, tel. 802/824–6793).

Sugarbush

Since its purchase by the American Ski Company in 1995, this 40-year-old area nestled in beautiful Mad River valley has changed and expanded dramatically, adding many attractions for families, from a huge but appealing kids' learning area to a family mountain dedicated to slower skiers. But what we love about it is the atmosphere of the whole valley, which remains the unspoiled, old-fashioned Vermont of covered bridges and white churches. No fast-food restaurants, strip malls, or even traffic lights here, and the charming villages of Waitsfield (6 mi away) and Warren (3 mi away) provide a wider variety of interesting and sophisticated dining and lodging than do most ski areas.

Sugarbush encompasses two mountain areas, Lincoln Peak and Mt. Ellen, connected by a high-speed quad, the Slide Brook Express; even kids who are novices enjoy the 10-minute-long ride, which feels like a roller coaster. The best area for families is Lincoln Peak, where you'll find the Family Adventureland, a mountain with 22 beginner and intermediate trails where fast skiing and snowboarding are banned. In the Adventureland you'll find Sugarbear Forest, a football-field-size kids-only learning area with kid-friendly terrain features like a covered bridge to ski through and bumps and rolls to ski over. Beginning kids (and others) love the Magic Carpet, a slow-moving conveyor lift that you can ride on with or without your skis; it even has a canopy over it so it feels like a tunnel. A new lighted tubing park takes over this area after dark.

Yet if you have an expert or two in your family you'll also find some of the most challenging skiing in the East here, including the classic narrow, twisting Castlerock trails, which follow the natural topography, unique adventure trails through the trees, and guided backcountry skiing. Teens praise the new snowboard park, Mountain Rage, with a precision-cut killer halfpipe, the intermediate glade skiing, the arcade in the Sports Center, and the races and movies held during school holidays.

All the trails in the Lincoln Peak area funnel conveniently down to two central lodges and a village of condominiums, restaurants, shops, and a sports center. The problem is that only a limited amount of the condo lodging is ski-in/ski-out, but a pleasant free shuttle links all the condos to the lifts and base lodges and even makes regular runs to restaurants in Warren and Waitsfield.

Just about all the kids' facilities are brand new and shiny. Two playrooms, across from the main lodge, house babies 6 weeks to 3 years; the 2- and 3-year-olds have their own mini ski slope here. Other kids' programs are equally well-thought out, based on the acclaimed teaching program at Sunday River. Each age group—4 to 6, 7 to 12—has its own space, which also dispenses rentals. (Picking up and dropping off kids was a complicated nightmare in 1997, but that's been corrected.) There's also a full-day teen program. Nearby Waitsfield has a covered skating rink (tel. 802/496–9199).

On-mountain lodging includes condominiums, both plush and plain, and the elegant Sugarbush Inn; less-expensive lodges with personality are at the bottom of the access road, and the nearby towns of Warren and Waitsfield have a wide variety of accommodations at all prices. Our favorite family bargain: the Inn at Mad River Barn (tel. 800/631–0466) next to the nearby small but historic Mad River Ski Area, which has been around since the 1940s and still feels like a real old-time friendly ski lodge.
🏠 *R.R. 1, Box 350 Warren 05674-9993, tel. 802/583–2381; 800/537–8427 lodging; 802/583–7669 snow conditions. Facilities: 112 trails, 18 lifts, 4 cafeterias, 3 restaurants, sports center (with exercise room, indoor pool, and indoor tennis), ice-skating, sleigh rides, ski and snowboard shops. AE, D, MC, V.*

CROSS-COUNTRY SKIING AND SNOWSHOEING. Adjacent to the Sugarbush Inn are 25 km (15 mi) of groomed trails; the Round Barn Cross Country Ski & Snowshoe Center in Waitsfield (tel. 802/496–6111) also has 25 km (15 mi); both also rent snowshoes. There's yet another center in nearby Warren.

Suicide Six and the Woodstock Inn and Resort

Among the greatest ski bargains for families in the Northeast are the Family Ski Weeks (offered five weeks January–February) at the plush and historic 144-room Woodstock Inn, which owns this small ski area that's more appropriate for families than its name suggests. The packages are the reason to come here. They include outstanding lodging (uniquely decorated rooms in various configurations with luxurious marble baths) in the large white clapboard-and-brick, distinctly New England–style inn, as well as free lift tickets, ski rentals, and group lessons for the entire family. Believe it or not, it also includes two connecting rooms, one of which will hold as many as four kids, and free breakfasts and dinners for kids under 14. Now there's also a kids' game room on the second floor filled with board games, books, puzzles, and a couple of arcade games. Those who can take the best advantage of the Ski Weeks are families with kids over 6 who are beginning or intermediate skiers—or snowboarders, as there's a snowboard park.

🏠 *Woodstock 05091, tel. 802/457–1100 or 800/448–7900 for inn, fax 802/457–6699; 802/457–6666 snow conditions; 802/457–6661 Suicide Six area. Facilities: 22 trails, 3 lifts, sports center (1½ mi from inn; with exercise room, indoor pool, sauna, and indoor tennis courts), baby-sitting. AE, MC, V.*

CROSS-COUNTRY SKIING AND SNOW-SHOEING. The ski touring center nearby has 60 km (37 mi) of trails. Equipment and lessons are available free with the family package.

BIG-TIME SPORTS FOR SPECTATORS
HOOPS, HITS, HAT TRICKS, AND TOUCHDOWNS

The Northeast has some of the best teams and players in the country, some of the most historic stadiums and arenas, such as Yankee Stadium, and a wide variety of sports to view, from baseball to horse racing.

We always had the most successful sports outings when we took Gavin's age and current sports passions into account, not just our own. Though I've seen 2-year-olds at major-league baseball games and have some football-fanatic friends who always take their twin 5-year-olds along, I've found that before kids turn 7 and 8 they aren't all that interested in watching sports at stadiums and arenas with enormous crowds and rarely understand the intricacies of game rules. (Hockey and baseball seem easiest for kids to understand.) The four years from 10 through 13 are when most kids want to attend just about any sports event; at older ages they often prefer seeing a sport they like to play themselves.

Minor-league baseball games and Ivy League college football are usually more fun than major-league events for little kids—the seats are much cheaper, the smaller stadiums have better viewing and more places to run around, the players are friendlier and more approachable, and the crowd is rarely combative or rowdy.

When my son was little, we sat as close as possible to the action in the bigger stadiums to keep his interest and we made sure he knew what he was going to see before we went. Great sports movies such as *Field of Dreams* (1989) and *Rookie of the Year* (1993) may spark interest. We also aimed for events that had something special—baseball games on promotional days when kids are treated to a special souvenir like a helmet, a poster, or even a bat.

Expect what happens on the rink or field in the Northeast to trigger strong passions among adult fans and players. You're liable to see plenty of drinking and obnoxious behavior at both baseball and hockey big-league games—in Madison Square Garden players and spectators sometimes draw applause for starting fights. When you can, opt for seats in the family-oriented, alcohol-free sections some stadiums now have. And make sure you tell your kids to head for the game announcing booth if they can't find you.

Auto Racing

Connecticut

Lime Rock Park

(👫 5+) We live only about 20 minutes from this racetrack, known for the best road racing in the Northeast, and our family has spent many sunny weekend afternoons watching races here. Perhaps the two most exciting race weekends for families are Memorial Day and the Vintage Festival with historic sports-car races and a swap meet on Labor Day. What's unique here is the parklike atmosphere. Along with many other families, we bring picnics and view the events from the natural amphitheater seating of the grassy spectator hillsides while the little kids roll down the gentle incline. Kids under 12 are admitted free, and families are welcome to camp for free (inside the track) and explore the park's 300 acres in the rolling Litchfield Hills.
🏠 *Rte. 112, Lakeville 06039, tel. 860/435–2571 or 800/722–3577. Cost: $5–$65; parking free. Season: mid-Apr.–mid-Oct. (not all weekends).*

Baseball

Maine

Portland Sea Dogs

(👫 7+) This minor-league team, a class AA franchise of the Florida Marlins, plays in a beautiful ballpark that is part of the new Portland Sports Complex. The highlight of attending a game here is what happens when a player hits a home run or the Sea Dogs win—a lighthouse pops up above the fence in center field and emits a whistle and shoots off fireworks. Games here have all the usual virtues of minor-league games. One player always signs autographs in the concourse 45 minutes before the game. Be

warned: The Sea Dogs are very popular locally and some games are sold out in advance. Call first. General admission tickets are okay if you get there early enough. Seats beyond third base are the best; they're closer to the field and don't face afternoon sun.
🏠 *271 Park Ave., Portland 04102 (mailing address: Box 636, Portland 04104), tel. 207/874–9300. Cost: $4–$6 adults, $2–$5 kids under 17. Season: Apr.–Sept.*

Massachusetts

Boston Red Sox

(👫 7+) I think seeing a game at Fenway Park, where the Boston Red Sox (American League) have played since 1912, is more fun for kids than at any other major sports stadium in the Northeast because it's small and idiosyncratic and seating areas are totally smoke-free. Afternoon games here capture the spirit of baseball as it should be. No matter where you sit, you almost always have a good view—though we favor the family sections on the field line; they're alcohol-free and have an overhang in case of rain. Fenway also has a quirky, personal, offbeat charm that even young kids seem to pick up on; its unique many-sided shape, the 37-ft-high green wall nicknamed "The Green Monster" in left field, the old-fashioned scoreboard, and the animated neon Citgo sign all make it special to us. Along with the Yankees, the Boston Red Sox have had some of the most famous players in baseball, such as Ted Williams, Mo Vaughn, and Roger Clemens. Fenway welcomes families, offering regular family discount days (listed on ticket brochure), "Youth" days on which kids 15 and under get free promotion items, and even a special kids' opening day (after the first home opening game) with kids' music. For autographs, arrive about an hour and a half before the game and hang out by the dugout. Tickets are usually easy to get, even just before game time, except when the Red Sox are playing the Yankees (their arch rival) or the Blue Jays. For a snack don't miss the clam chowder from Legal Seafoods.

🏟 *Fenway Park, 4 Yawkey Way (Fenway stop on Green Line T), Boston 02215, tel. 617/ 267–1700. Cost: $10–$30. Season: 1st wk Apr.–Sept.; day games 1:05 PM, night games 7:05 PM.*

Cape Cod Baseball League

(👫 **3–14**) Since 1885, the nation's most talented college baseball players have been recruited to make up the 10 town teams of the oldest summer league in the country. Major-league scouts are at all the games; 80% of the Cape League players go on to play ball professionally—the way Carlton Fisk, Ron Darling, Mo Vaughn, and Will Clark did. There are games most days of the week at 5 or 7 o'clock, usually at high school ball fields in the various towns, which conveniently solves the problem of what to do in the evening on a beach vacation. Wherever you happen to be staying, you'll find a game near you. Admission is pass-the-hat. Bring a blanket or lawn chairs. Players also hold baseball clinics for kids on a weekly basis. 🏟 *Box 164, South Harwich 02661, tel. 508/ 362–3036. Check with the Chamber of Commerce in the town in which you are staying for a schedule. Season: mid-June–Sept.*

Pittsfield Mets

(👫 **3+**) To us a baseball game at Wahconah Park on a warm summer night is the perfect place to introduce young kids to the sport. Cozy, charming, and intimate, with a backdrop of mountains, this old-fashioned ball field where minor leagues have played since 1919 has no AstroTurf, electronic scoreboard, or grandstand seating 50,000 people. Instead, plastic owls swing from the rafters to scare away pigeons, and the wooden seats are so close to the field you feel as if you could touch the players. You can even get (and afford) front-row seats, but it's also fun to watch while you picnic at the tables on the third-base side. Though the Mets are a short-season Class A New York–Penn League team, the first rung for rookies on their route to the major leagues,

you'll see lots of talent at these games: Curtis Pride, Jeromy Burnitz, David Telcheder, and Tito Navarro are just some of the Pittsfield Mets who have made it to the majors.

Kids rush down for the on-field contests between innings and have time to shake hands with and get autographs from the ballplayers. Home games are held three or four times a week, weekdays at 7 PM, Sunday at 6 PM. Some weeks they're on the road, so call for a schedule. 🏟 *Wahconah St. (North St. ½ mi then left to Wahconah St.), Box 328, Pittsfield 01202, tel. 413/499–6387. Cost: $1–$6.75. Season: mid-June–1st wk Sept.*

New York

New York Mets

(👫 **7+**) If you live in New York City, you're a Mets or a Yankees fan, not both. In contrast to the Yankees, the Mets are a relatively new team; they started out in 1962 with a collection of losers—players tossed out by other teams. In fact they were perennial losers for seven years until they finally won the World Series in 1969 (they were nicknamed the Miracle Mets for that year). Since then they've only won again in 1986— though the sixth game in that series (versus the Boston Red Sox) has become one of the most famous games in history because of an error by a Red Sox player that allowed the Mets to win that game, the next game, and the Series. Shea Stadium is not as impressive as Yankee Stadium, nor does it have an illustrious history. Still, the horseshoe-shape stadium with no centerfield seats seems more family-oriented than Yankee Stadium. No smoking is permitted in the seating sections, no-alcohol sections are scattered throughout the stands, and after selected home games, kids can line up to run around the bases in the Dynamets Dash. Best of all, a big apple pops up when the Mets hit a homer. You won't have much trouble getting a baseball card autographed before the game; gate C opens at 5:10. Tickets are usually available right up until game time for virtually all games.

🏟 *Shea Stadium, 126th St. and Roosevelt Ave. (Willets Point/Shea Stadium stop on Subway 7), Flushing 11368, tel. 718/507–6387. Cost: $9–$35. Season: Apr.–Sept.*

New York Yankees

(👫 **7+**) The history of great baseball in America is inextricably linked with the history of the Yankees, as many of the sport's most famous names—Babe Ruth, Lou Gehrig, Joe DiMaggio, Mickey Mantle, Yogi Berra—have played for the team. Watching a game at Yankee Stadium, where the team has played since 1923, is exciting partly because of its past. The Yankees have won 24 World Series, more than any other team; in 1998 their victory over the San Diego Padres was followed by an extravagant parade in New York City. The stadium is huge and impressive; we find night games more exciting because of the lights. If your kids are autograph seekers, get here an hour or two before the gates open because the only time the players will sign baseballs or cards (if they do at all) is as they're coming off the field during batting practice. All seating sections are now smoke-free and consumption of alcohol is prohibited in several areas of the stands, but bleachers are not recommended for families. Main box seats and field box seats are best. Eat at the Sidewalk Cafe on field level of section 15, the only spot where you can get a kid's meal, and if your kids are real baseball fans, stop to see the stone monuments to Babe Ruth, Mickey Mantle, and other legends in Monument Park. Though Yankee Stadium is not in a great neighborhood, riding the subway to this location is okay (even for night games—if you go home with the crowd).

🏟 *Yankee Stadium, 161st St. and River Ave. (Subway 4, D, or C to 161st St./Yankee Stadium), Bronx 10451, tel. 718/293–6000. Cost: $7–$45. Season: Apr.–Sept.*

Rhode Island

Pawtucket Red Sox

(👫 **4+**) The playing is pretty close to what you'd see at any major-league ballpark (this Class AAA affiliate of the Boston Red Sox is the last step on the minor-league ladder before the major leagues and it sends about 60% of its players to the majors; Ellis Burks and Mike Greenwell are alumni). The longest game in the history of baseball was played here in 1981; it started on April 18 and ended on June 23. The communal atmosphere at small, cozy 7,000-seat McCoy Stadium (compare with Yankee Stadium's 57,000 seats) draws everyone in. We love the winding staircases with huge paintings of baseball stars. Regular promotional nights, with such giveaways for kids as posters, baseball cards, caps, and coloring books, are scheduled throughout the summer; kids can also take advantage of free baseball clinics on the baseball field, with hands-on instruction from PawSox players. If you attend a summer evening game, sit on the first-base side so you don't face the sometimes blinding setting sun.

🏟 *McCoy Stadium (I–95 south to Exit 2A; Newport Ave. 2 mi, then right on Columbus Ave. at light), Box 2365, Pawtucket 02861, tel. 401/724–7300; Ticketmaster 401/331–2211. Cost: General admission $4 adults, $3 kids 12 and under; box seats $6 adults, $5 kids 12 and under. Season: Apr.–Sept.*

Basketball

Massachusetts

Boston Celtics

(👫 **8+**) Going to a Celtics game in Boston is still an exciting sports viewing experience even though the team now plays in the new (and 4,000 seats bigger) Fleet-Center instead of the historic Boston Garden next door. However, the Garden's famous parquet wood floor, with irregularities only the home team knows, and the colorful championship banners and numbers of all the retired stars have been moved to the new arena. The Celtics have been the National Basketball Association's top team 16 times, and world champions 16 times. The electricity in the atmosphere is partly due to the enthusiasm of Boston's basketball fans, who are among the most knowledgeable and pleasant around. If you ask them about any player, you're likely to hear a complete biography. Tickets are difficult to get, especially to games with the most popular teams. Your best bet is to call as soon as they go on sale in October.

🏠 *FleetCenter, 150 Causeway St. (North Station stop on Green or Orange Line T), Boston 02114, tel. 617/523–3030 (information, season tickets); Ticketmaster 617/931–2222 (individual tickets). Cost: $10–$72. Season: Nov.–Apr., sometimes as late as June.*

New York

New York Knickerbockers

(👫 **9+**) Going to a New York Knicks game in Madison Square Garden is exciting. The team is one of the leaders in the NBA, with a long list of previous players now in the Hall of Fame—Walt "Clyde" Frazier, Earl "the Pearl" Monroe, Bill Bradley, Harry Gallatin, Willis Reed—and current stars like Patrick Ewing. The fast-paced games are full of action but last just over two hours (less than football, baseball, or hockey). During time-outs and halftime the Knicks City Dancers perform short routines to music. Knicks games rarely become rowdy, and the fans, though wild about the team, are more sedate. The only problems are the high price of tickets and how to get seats close to the action. Center court is where we like to sit, but we've rarely been able to. Your best bet is to order tickets as far in advance as possible. Tickets for the play-offs are almost impossible to get, even if you're willing to pay scalpers' prices; a limited number of tickets are available in late August and early September.

🏠 *Madison Square Garden, 7th Ave. between 31st and 33rd Sts., New York 10001, box office tel. 212/465–6000; Ticketmaster 212/307–7171. Cost: $20–$200. Season: late Oct.–Apr.*

Football

Massachusetts

Harvard Crimson

(👫 **7+**) Though the Boston College Eagles (Alumni Stadium, Chestnut Hill, Brookline, tel. 617/552–2000) have a long tradition of playing great football, our favorite place to see football in Boston is at Harvard University's Soldier's Field on a Saturday afternoon. We like to come here for the atmosphere; though the stands are rarely full, we find the energy and enthusiasm of the almost totally youthful crowd more appealing than that of the audience at a professional game. The stadium is smaller and easier to get to, and the tickets are less expensive. The Harvard-Yale game is still the most exciting.

🏠 *North Harvard St. and Soldier's Field Rd., Allston, tel. 617/495–2212 or 617/495–2211. Cost: $10; Harvard-Yale game $25. Season: Sept.–Nov.*

New England Patriots

(👫 **9+**) Boston's professional football team plays at the Foxboro Stadium 25 mi from Boston. There are no tiers, poles, or pillars, so you can see well from everywhere, and there is a special no-alcohol, patrolled family section. The giant scoreboard shows replays and more. On the other hand, bathrooms and water fountains are few in number. Traffic on Route 1 for the two hours before and after the game is horrendous (there are buses during the season, but no subway line). That may be the reason for the tradition of tailgate picnics before and after the game in the huge parking lot. Individual tickets do go on sale in mid-June and usually sell out by the time the season begins, but occasionally individual tickets are available during the season. Your best bet, though, is to attend one of the pre-season games in August.

🏠 *Foxboro Stadium, Rte. 1, Foxboro 02035, tel. 508/543–1776 or 800/543–1776; Ticketmaster 617/931–2222. Cost: $26–$60. Season: Sun.-afternoon games Sept.–Dec.*

New York

New York Giants and New York Jets

(👫 **9+**) Ranked among the major NFL teams ever since their start in 1925, the Giants have won two Super Bowls. The New York Jets (American Football League) had their heyday in the '60s and early '70s when Joe Namath was their big star. Neither of these teams is easy to see. The trouble is that all seats for Giants games and most of the Jets games at this huge 77,000-seat stadium are sold on a season-ticket basis, and there's a waiting list for those. Every family we know who has attended a game has a friend or an employer with a season pass; individual Jets tickets are snapped up as soon as they go on sale in August. Giants tickets are sometimes available on the day of the game. If you go at the beginning of the season, get there early to see the team warm up. At halftime, high school bands play and dogs chase Frisbees. The Giants and the Jets play at Giants Stadium alternate weeks depending on the leagues' schedules.

🏠 *Giants Stadium (off Rte. 3), East Rutherford, NJ 07073, Giants tel. 201/935–8111; Jets 516/560–8200. Cost: $40–$45. Season: Sept.–Dec.*

West Point

(👫 **8+**) Michie Stadium at the United States Military Academy is among the most beautiful stadiums in the country. It's also a great place for families to see a football game. There's a pregame parade of bands

and hundreds of cadets in full dress uniforms, complete with tall hats and feathers, and four army mules run up and down the end zone each time the Black Knights make a touchdown. Before or after the game, there's plenty to see at this historic military site. *See also* Chapter 2.

🏠 *U.S. Military Academy, Visitors Center, West Point 10996, tel. 914/938–2638; tickets 914/446–4996. Cost: $21; on Kids' Day kids' tickets are half-price. Season: Sept.–Nov.*

Hockey

Massachusetts

Boston Bruins

(👫 **9+**) One of the National Hockey League's most consistently good teams, the Bruins share the FleetCenter with the NBA's Celtics. Two Hall of Famers, Phil Esposito and Bobby Orr, were once on the team, and two excellent current players are Jason Allison and Ray Borque. There's an undeniable excitement to a Bruins game, partly because most of the audience are total hockey buffs who are ready to share their knowledge with kids. As at most hockey games, there's sometimes as much action in the stands as on the ice, which usually means fights. Games are usually sold out by game time, but you can get tickets if you call far enough in advance.

🏠 *FleetCenter, 150 Causeway St. (North Station stop on Green or Orange Line T), Boston 02114, tel. 617/624–1000 (FleetCenter); for tickets, call Ticketmaster 617/931–2222. Cost: $20–$75. Season: Oct.–Mar.*

New York

New York Islanders

(👫 **9+**) The Islanders games simply do not have the same excitement as the Rangers games in Madison Square Garden, unless the team is playing exceptionally well;

nor is Nassau Coliseum, on Long Island, easy to get to except by car. But because tickets are sold out only when the Islanders are playing one of the league's star teams, you're more likely to be able to get tickets. It's also easier for kid fans to get autographs here before the game. The Islanders haven't yet equaled their incredible team of the early 1980s, when they won four Stanley Cup trophies, but they do have some exciting players, including top-scoring Zig Palffy.

🏛 *Nassau Veterans Memorial Coliseum, Uniondale, Long Island 11553, tel. 516/794–4100. Cost: $19–$60. Season: Oct.–Apr.*

New York Rangers

(👬 **9+**) The Rangers, who share Madison Square Garden with the NBA's Knicks, are exciting to watch. The crowd at Rangers games is sometimes rowdy, shouting and chanting obscenities at opposing teams or specific players—this upsets some kids and delights others. If you see a fan wearing a Rangers jersey, ask any hockey questions you have; in our experience the more obscure the better. Tickets have been sold out fairly far in advance since the Rangers won the Stanley Cup in 1994.

🏛 *Madison Square Garden, 7th Ave. between 31st and 33rd Sts., New York 10001; box office tel. 212/465–6040; Rangers' hot line 212/308–6977. Cost: $22–$75. Season: Oct.–Apr.*

Horse Racing

New York

Saratoga Racetrack

(👬 **6+**) Saratoga's 36-day Thoroughbred racing season each August has the best atmosphere for families of any racetrack in the Northeast; it's the cleanest and most pleasant, and children are welcome despite the fact that the season is a major social as well as sporting event. Kids who already

love horses have the most fun, but you may be able to inspire enthusiasm in any who don't by reading one of Marguerite Henry's books about horses, especially *King of the Wind*. Post time for the first race is 1 PM, but a horse-loving family we know likes eating breakfast here (offered daily except Tuesday from 7 to 9:30) so they can watch horses work out. Soak up the atmosphere on a free tour of the barn and paddock areas on a "people train" (no strollers), where grooms, trainers, jockeys, and owners care for the horses. Whatever races you attend will be fast, exciting, and colorful. The best place for families to sit, especially those with little ones in strollers and small kids who need to run around, is the big open picnic area near the grandstand where you can see the race on the closed-circuit TVs on every tree. On big festival days the atmosphere is like that of a fair, with clog dancers and other entertainment.

🏛 *Rte. 9P, Saratoga Springs 12866; Aug. tel. 518/584–6200; Sept.–July 718/641–4700. Cost: $2 grandstand; $4 clubhouse (dress code). Season: last wk in July and Aug.*

Polo

Massachusetts

Myopia Polo

(👬 **5+**) A polo match has many things kids find exciting—there's lots of speed and action as the horses thunder up and down the field and bump one another, and kids can jump up and down as they watch from a grassy sideline. For two horse-loving kids on my Boston panel, the big treat at halftime is stamping down the divots of turf kicked up by the horses on the field. Bring an elegant picnic, not fast food. The grounds open at 1:30 PM (match begins at 3) if you want to picnic first.

🏛 *435 Bay Rd., Rte. 1A (Exit 20A off Rte. 128), South Hamilton 01982, tel. 978/468–7956 or 978/872–2077. Cost: $5 adults, kids under 12 free. Season: late May–Oct.*

Running

Massachusetts

Boston Marathon

(**††** 6+) Since 1897, the country's oldest marathon has been run annually on the third Monday in April—Patriot's Day—drawing both world-class runners and amateurs. To us this marathon is the Northeast's most interesting to watch because of the celebratory atmosphere generated by the spectators, including lots of kids, who regard this day as the beginning of spring. Boston families we know traditionally gather early at the starting point on the Common in Hopkinton, the finish in Copley Square (our favorite), or other good viewing points—along Commonwealth Avenue, Boylston Street, or Beacon Street, or at Wellesley College or on Heartbreak Hill in Newton, 6 mi from the finish. Many kids enjoy handing out cups of water, which most runners accept gratefully. Front runners reach the finish at about 2 PM; an awards ceremony and live entertainment start at 6 PM. The route of the marathon is printed in the *Boston Globe* and on page 19 of the *Boston Yellow Pages*.

🏠 *Boston Athletic Association, 131 Clarendon St., Boston 02116, tel. 617/236–1652.*

Soccer

Massachusetts

New England Revolution

(**††** 9+) Not only are more and more kids playing soccer, but during the 1998 World Cup in France it also became clear that more and more families are watching professional soccer. New England's professional soccer team, composed of both American and foreign players, celebrated its first season in 1996. It's the only major-league soccer team in New England. Three hot scorers are Joe-Max Moore, Raul Díaz Arce, and Mike Burns. Soccer games and skills competitions for kids 16 and under, face painting, and many other activities are part of a celebration that is held two hours before the game.

🏠 *Foxboro Stadium, Rte. 1, Foxboro 02035, tel. 508/543–0350; Ticketmaster 617/931–2000. Cost: $10–$35. Season: late Apr.–Sept.*

New York

New York Metrostars

(**††** 9+) The other major-league soccer team in the Northeast, the Metrostars, also celebrated their first season in 1996. We give our highest marks to the New England Revolution for all the pregame festivities for families.

🏠 *Giants Stadium, Meadowlands Sports Complex, East Rutherford, NJ 07073, tel. 201/935–3900. Season: late Mar.–Sept.*

Tennis

New York

U.S. Open

(**††** 10+) Everyone in our family is a passionate tennis player, so we grab any chance to see incredible playing up close. It's very difficult to get tickets to the U.S. Open, one of the four prime tournaments of U.S. tennis, unless you're a season subscriber (members of the U.S.T.A. have priority for remaining tickets), but we think attending the qualifying matches the week before it starts (the third week in August) is even more fun for families—and they're free. Besides the matches between the hottest players in two of the stadiums (including the Arthur Ashe Stadium), there are matches on all the side courts; you can wander from one to another, stopping to watch whoever catches your fancy. The

Sunday before the Open, now called Arthur Ashe Day, features matches with celebrities like Bill Cosby. The setting is pretty, near the New York Hall of Science. All kinds of food are available; we like the outdoor café. Tickets to early matches are easier to get; those for the semifinals and finals sell out as soon as they go on sale in May.

🏠 *United States Tennis Association, Flushing Meadows–Corona Park, Flushing 11365, tel. 914/696–7000 (information), 718/760–6200 (tickets). Cost: $20–$60. Season: late Aug.–early Sept.*

FAMILY FARMS, RESORTS, INNS, AND RANCHES

9

SADDLE UP, TEE OFF, AND LIE AROUND

Over the years we've discovered that the Northeast has a wide range of family-friendly places to stay: grand historic resorts that have sheltered presidents; new ones with first-class golf courses; tranquil, picturesque farms; ranches with nonstop activities; and nature and music camps that provide education as well as entertainment. Resorts, whether luxurious and expensive or informal and a bargain, usually ensure that you'll have the easiest vacation imaginable, with accommodations, meals, supervised kids' and adult programs, and extensive sports facilities all included in the price. But it's important to decide just what kind of atmosphere and how much pampering your family wants. We don't like nonstop activities or constant interaction with other adults, for example, and we don't mind roughing it as long as we're in a beautiful place with great views.

In recent years most of the larger ski resorts in the Northeast have become true four-season destinations, catering to families by offering not just an outstanding variety of outdoor activities that few other resorts can match but also extremely reasonably priced family packages, child care, and ways for kids to connect easily with other kids (see also Chapter 7). That makes these particularly good choices for families with teens, who tend to be happiest among a large-enough group of peers in a space where they can hang out together; they also have to be able to get around easily on their own by bike or foot. Add to that either challenging activities like rock climbing, waterskiing, or participating in organized sports activities. If all this can be near a town with shops, too, you've got it made. The family lodges and inns listed below provide amenities similar to those of the resorts but on a smaller scale.

Unlike resorts and lodges, farms tend to be quite low-key, a way for families to enter into a simpler way of life that's been an integral part of New England since Colonial times. When it comes to ranches, there aren't many here compared with in western states, and most are in New York State.

Nature camps offer the joy of living close to the wild. We feel that a family will have a good time only at a nature camp that truly understands a kid's way of exploring—these camps do. We learned the hard way that you should bring exactly what the camp suggests you bring. Don't expect your kids to blossom into lovers of the outdoors overnight: Prepare them by taking short hikes or treks *before* you go camping.

It's hard to compare costs, because some places include all meals, kids' programs, and recreational facilities, even the use of boats, in the price, while others do not. The latter may appear less expensive, but in our experience they usually end up costing more when you add up what you spent at the golf course, the tennis courts, and the restaurants. If your accommodations include a kitchen, you can save money by cooking for yourself. Resorts tend to be the most expensive. The price categories below are based on what a family of four with two school-age children would spend on an average day: $$$$, over $400 a day; $$$, $300–$400; $$, $200–$300; $, under $200. Weekly rates are lower. Cribs and cots are available in all the places listed here. Lessons, whether tennis, golf, or sailing, and boat usage usually cost extra.

It's best to stay one week if you're going to sign up for a kids' program; that way, you can take advantage of all the facilities and your kids can make some friends. If you stay longer, you may find, as we have, that all the newfound friends leave, and your child is miserable for the following week. Most places charge more in July and August, while June and September are bargains. For more ideas, look at *New England Farm Vacations* by Lisa Angowski Rogak (Country Roads Press, 1994), *The Best Bargain Family Vacations in the U.S.A.*, Revised Edition, by Laura Sutherland and Valerie Wolf Deutsch (St. Martin's, 1997), and *The 100 Best Family Resorts in North America*, 4th Edition, by Janet Tice, et al. (Globe Pequot, 1998).

Connecticut

Sunrise Resort

(👫 2–14) This 400-acre family-owned resort on the Salmon River in a picturesque landscape of rolling green hills and tiny villages of white houses hums with constant activity, from nightly movies to organized sports, dance lessons, luaus, rubber ducky contests, and much more every hour of the day and evening. It is truly a family place; you're liable to see three generations of an extended family eating, playing, and talking together. Softball games attract players of all ages as do horseshoes and shuffleboard. Accommodations, food, and the golf course are no-frills—rooms and cabins are plain but comfortable, have air-conditioning but no TV or phone; food is ample and decent but no more. For toddlers, though, the facilities are amazing—a wading pool with kid-size

lounges and chairs, a scaled-down mock western village and merry-go-round, all supervised by well-trained counselors. Kids who love Ping-Pong will can play in the game rooms and even outside the dining room by the river. Most of the families are from the New York and Boston areas. This is not a place for families who want a sophisticated atmosphere or outdoor adventures.

🏠 *Box 415, Rte. 151, Moodus 06469, tel. 860/873–8681 or 800/225–9033. 1- to 4-room cottages and cabins, some waterfront, 50 motel-style rooms. Facilities: restaurant, snack bar, barbecue pavilion, badminton, basketball, boccie, beach boating, croquet, evening family activities, fishing, 18-hole golf course, horseback riding, kids' program and activities, miniature golf, mountain biking, nightclub, Ping-Pong, outdoor pool, recreation center, shuffleboard, softball diamond, spa, teen activities, 4 tennis courts. Open Memorial Day–Labor Day. MC, V. $*

Maine

Attean Lake Lodge

(**ii 2 – 12**) These 15 hewn-log cabins and lodge founded in 1900 are on Birch Island, a 10-minute boat ride from the shore of pristine, 6-mi-long Attean Lake. Cabins nestle cozily and privately among the trees and have wonderful views of the lake. Each has a broad, partly screened deck and a woodstove or fireplace. Playing cards at night in front of a fire by kerosene lamplight really makes you feel like you're out in the wilderness; be sure to bring several flashlights and extra batteries. Three meals a day of simple New England fare are served on real tablecloths at the main lodge, but the cookouts twice a week are more fun, since you eat at picnic tables overlooking the lake while little kids run around. Canoes and kayaks are stashed conveniently at spots along the shore and by ponds adjacent to the trails, so you don't have to portage. For toddlers, the resort's own fairly long, sandy beach, well equipped with sand toys and beach chairs, is right near the lodge. Kids can gather in a games and library room in the main lodge, but many families tend to spend their days together.
🏠 *Jackman 04945, tel. 207/668–3792 (May–Oct.). 15 cabins. Facilities: hiking, beach, boating, fishing, library. AP. AE, MC, V. Closed late Sept.–Memorial Day. $$*

Chewonki Wilderness Programs

(**ii 8+**) The Chewonki Foundation is dedicated to environmental education and still operates the oldest ecologically oriented kids' camp in the country, once attended by bird expert Roger Tory Peterson. Now it also has weeklong (and sometimes three-day) summer and winter family programs that teach about the environment through an encounter with nature somewhere in Maine, whether canoeing, kayaking, hiking,

snowshoeing, or sailing. What's special is their hands-on way of teaching about the natural world (such as night walks to listen to owls hooting, trees rustling, and raccoons snuffling) and the emphasis on group participation. Every trip produces a journal (a compilation of poems, essays, drawings, and accounts of each day's activities by all the adults and kids in the group), which is copied so everyone has a record of the trip. Food is healthy—no dehydrated packets—and even kids learn how to make pancakes and other easy dishes over open fires. It's important to know just how much your kids are able to do and not overestimate their capacities. Are they ready for a six-day hiking trip that culminates in a climb of Mt. Katahdin?
🏠 *485 Chewonki Neck Rd., Wiscasset 04578, tel. 207/882–7323, fax 207/882–4074. MC, V. Rates include camping equipment, boating, meals, and instruction; kids' rates. $–$$$*

Goose Cove Lodge

(**ii 0 – 12**) This secluded lodge and 13 cottages with a quintessential Maine coastal view of pine-covered islands and the open ocean beyond has been rated one of the best family cabin resorts in the Northeast by *Family Circle* magazine. The combination of the friendly staff, the casual yet sophisticated atmosphere, and the way activities and meals promote intimacy among the guests makes this place special. One advantage if you have small children is that kids eat at 5 PM, before the adults, and are involved in activities until 8. It's blissful to engage in animated adult conversation over drinks in a cozy lounge, then consume delicious adult food like white bean and escarole salad or rhubarb pudding in a spectacular, windowed half-octagon dining room overlooking a deck and the ocean—all while your kids go on supervised scavenger hunts. This place is best for families with portable babies or kids who love nature and who want a few activities during the day but not a structured program. Here there's just enough—a one-afternoon-a-week nature camp and a crafts hour. Families like hiking on the many short trails, especially to Barred Island, a bird sanctuary accessible by foot only at low tide. It helps if your kids are the hardy type—the water at the beach is pretty cold and there's no swimming pool.

⚓ Goose Cove Rd., Deer Isle, Sunset 04683, tel. 207/348–2508, fax 207/348–2624. 4 rooms, 8 suites in main inn and annexes; 13 cottages, all with refrigerator or kitchenette. Facilities: dining room, baby-sitting, beach, boating, biking, hiking, supervised kids' dinner, kids' menu, library with children's books, Ping-Pong, recreation room, sailing lessons. MAP. MC, V. Closed mid-Oct.–mid-May. $$–$$$

Kawahnee Inn

(**👫 2–14**) Nestled in pines overlooking beautiful Webb Lake, this classic homey lakeside lodge in the Rangeley Lakes region of northwest Maine has everything: mountains to climb, a fine white-sand beach that's perfect for little kids, pure lake water that's cold enough to be bracing but not too cold, good fishing, rustic cabins with stone fireplaces, rockers, and screened-in porches, fabulous views across the lake, even fine moose watching. In the main lodge you can stay in one of the spartan rooms upstairs, gather downstairs around the huge fieldstone fireplace to read or play cards, and eat simple home-cooked food (they offer three meals a day) in a pleasant dining room or screened-in porch with log furniture. We think the best bet for families is a two-bedroom cottage with a kitchen—you'll still have the option to eat at the lodge whenever you want. Don't expect anything fancy or sophisticated; time spent in this wonderfully worn and relaxing place is what lake vacations used to be like. There's plenty to do, but none of it is highly organized. Nearby Mt. Blue State Park (see also Chapter 5) will set up a guided hike or trip to pan for gold. The most satisfying for kids, however, is just paddling around in a canoe, swimming at the beach, or hiking a real

mountain. If you want a two-bedroom cottage in August, reserve very early. Avoid late May and the first two weeks in June, when black flies are at their peak.

⚓ Rte. 142, Box 119, Weld 04285, tel. 207/585–2000, fax 207/585–5545 (summer); 7 Broadway, Farmington 04938, tel. 207/778–4306, fax 207/778–3809 (mid-Oct.–mid-May). 9 rooms (5 with private bath, 4 with shared) in main lodge (2-night minimum mid-July–Aug.), 12 1- to 3-bedroom cabins, some with kitchen or kitchenette (1-wk minimum mid-July–Aug.). Facilities: restaurant (mid-June–Labor Day), beach, boating, fishing, goldpanning, nearby golf, hiking, swimming, nearby tennis. EP or B&B. MC, V. Closed mid-Oct.–mid-May. $

Samoset Resort

(**👫 3–12**) Set on a couple of hundred acres next to Maine's picturesque Penobscot Bay, this resort is a good place to combine a golf and family vacation, even though the sleekly modern wood hotel and condominiums with gabled roofs do have a conference-center feel. Unfortunately, to get from the hotel to the ocean, you have to walk around the golf course on a long public access road. Families may wish to opt for the plush-contemporary condos, which have kitchenettes and views of the bay, or the two-bedroom cottage right on the ocean next to the 15th fairway. Fishing off the nearby mile-long lighthouse-tipped granite breakwater is a thrill for kids. Meals in the dining room tend to drag; eating burgers at umbrella-topped picnic tables outside or in the café may be preferable.

⚓ 220 Warrenton St. (off Rte. 1), Rockport 04856, tel. 207/594–2511 or 800/341–1650, fax 207/594–0722. 132 double rooms, 18 suites; 72 time-share condos in 3 buildings. Facilities: 3 restaurants, snack bars, indoor and outdoor pools, 18-hole golf course, 4 outdoor tennis courts, badminton, basketball, croquet, health club, horseshoes, racquetball, shuffleboard, volleyball, fishing, bicycles, kids' programs in summer and holidays, playground. MAP or EP (kids' program, bikes, golf not included). AE, D, DC, MC, V. Kids under 16 free; package plans. $$–$$$$

Sebasco Harbor Resort

(🏃🏃 4–12) Simple, 1950s-style cottages, a main inn, and a lighthouse are clustered within walking distance of each other on a rocky and beautiful 660-acre peninsula on the Maine coast. Many organized family activities, from folk concerts and line dancing to bingo games, and reasonable prices draw families back here year after year. You can park your car and not use it again until you leave. Since the resort was purchased by a new owner in 1997, much-needed redecoration and remodeling have taken place—all the cottages and many of the inn rooms have new paint and furnishings, as well as TVs. The cottages are the best bet for families. This is a fairly casual and sociable place, even though the new formal dining room prefers jackets; it's crammed with stuff for kids to do, and signing up is easy. When you arrive, you receive a list of all the activities and clear instructions. Two-year-olds wade happily in the shallow end of the saltwater pool that looks out over the bay while 12-year-olds take turns doing corkscrew jumps into the deep end. *Ruth*, the resort's boat, takes a weekly hour-long "pirate trip" in Casco Bay (about halfway through the cruise, menacing-looking but friendly costumed pirates complete with eye patches come on board). After dinner, young teenagers can play Candlepins, New England's old-fashioned version of bowling, at the resort's four-lane alley in the funky barnlike recreation building. Don't worry about the food. The blueberry pancakes and lobster are the best, along with the BLTs at the snack bar, which overlooks the water. If you want more privacy and sophistication, you can stay at the nearby Rock Gardens Inn and Cottages (tel. 207/389–1339) and still use the recreational facilities here.

🏡 *Sebasco Estates 04565–0075, tel. 207/389–1161 or 800/225–3819, fax 207/389–2004. 47 rooms in main inn and lodges; 21 1-*

to 4-bedroom cottages, some with fireplace and/or kitchenette. Facilities: dining room, pub, beach 1 mi away, boating, daily boat excursions, bowling, fishing, 9-hole golf course, hiking, kids' program (ages 3–15; extra charge), Ping-Pong, playground, outdoor saltwater pool, recreation room, 2 tennis courts, video games. MAP or B&B. AE, MC, V. Closed Nov.–Apr. Kids 10 and under stay and eat free. $–$$

The Telemark Inn

(🏃🏃 4+) Though this small, Adirondack-style lodge is only 10 mi from the picturesque town of Bethel, it's surrounded by the White Mountain National Forest and feels very remote, more like a comfortable private wilderness camp than an inn so close to civilization. Owner Steve Crone, a real outdoorsman, shares his commitment to and knowledge of the environment with families (and others) four seasons of the year, introducing them to adventures such as llama treks (see also Chapter 6); nature hikes in the summer, fall, and spring; and skijoring (being pulled by a dog while on skis) in winter. For families who want some guidance into the natural world, the packages here are ideal, especially since you can pick from a variety of guided adventures. But you can just stay here, too. Kids can feed the llamas; you can relax on the wonderful long front porch to read a book, listen to birds, and watch the sunset; or you can all head out the door for a wilderness hike on your own. Built in the 1920s by a multimillionaire, the inn has hand-built wood cabinetry and furniture, pine-paneled walls, and a huge mineral stone fireplace, but this is an outdoorsy, informal place where kids feel at home. Rooms are attractive but not filled with antiques; baths are shared. The food is particularly healthy and good, featuring vegetables grown in the inn's organic garden.

🏡 *RFD 2, Box 800, Bethel 04217, tel. 207/836–2703. 6 rooms, shared baths. Facilities: canoeing, educational day trips (natural history, birds, etc.), nearby golf, hiking, horseback riding, llama treks, mountain biking, swimming, nearby tennis; in winter: cross-country skiing,* *ice-skating, skijoring, snowshoeing. FAP (packages) or B&B. AE, D, MC, V. $–$$$*

Washburn-Norlands Living History Center

(**†† 8+**) If your kids are fascinated by how children lived long ago, they might jump at the chance to spend a three-day weekend at this living-history center, living in the year 1779 or 1870. Norlands, a traditional Maine farmhouse with a connected cottage, a shed, and an enormous barn, was the summer home of the Washburns, a prominent New England family. All of it is pretty much as it was in the last half of the 19th century. If you opt for the 1870 program, you'll sleep in the attached seven-room, hired-man's cottage (the farmhouse in front is now a museum) under fairly primitive conditions: no private bedrooms and an outhouse behind the barn or a chamber pot under your bed. There is a wood-burning stove. As soon as you arrive, you are given the name of a real adult or child close to your age in the Pray or Waters family (the Washburns' nearest neighbors), and that's the role you play for the rest of your stay during a make-believe family reunion. The staff and everyone else stay in character as they pitch in together to milk cows, cook meals from recipes used 100 years ago, or play an old-fashioned game. At dinner, when the president is discussed, his name is Ulysses S. Grant, and current events means the recent purchase of Alaska. Your assumptions about modern living may be rearranged (toilet paper, window screens, and modern mattresses are the only contemporary concessions). For the 1779 program, you'll stay in an early Cape one-third of a mile away on a pond, haul water from the pond in a canvas bucket, cook supper over the fireplace, and eat with only a knife. Staying here can leave a more profound impression about life in the past on your kids than any visit to Sturbridge or Mystic, but it is not for every family. It's best to come in summer or early fall before it gets too cold. Read the information they send before you make reservations.

🏠 *Billie Gammon, 42 Hathaway Hill Rd., Livermore Falls 04253, tel. 207/897–2236, fax 207/897–7064. 5 bedrooms for 16 participants. Facilities: 2 dining rooms. AP, MC, V. Discounts for kids up to 17. $*

Massachusetts

Chatham Bars Inn

(**†† 4–10**) This is one of the last of America's grand oceanfront resorts; its gracious, elegant, shingled World War I–vintage inn and group of Cape-style shingled cottages sit on a low hill across from the beach, a three-minute walk from Chatham village. To me this luxurious and soothing place feels very much like Cape Cod a generation ago—spacious, quiet, private, slightly formal, with spectacular views of a bay teeming with fishing boats. The bay and beach (there's also a beachfront pool) are somewhat sheltered from the open Atlantic by a long outer sandbar across the mouth of the bay. A five-minute trip on the inn's launch brings you to the bar, where the surf crashes in on the ocean side and the currents on the bay side create warm, shallow pools perfect for wading.

You may rent single rooms or suites in cottages that have up to 18 bedrooms. Smaller cottages with one or two suites are fine for a family—rooms in all cottages are particularly spacious. Furnishings vary, from opulent master suites with chintz and heavy Victorian wood in the Main Inn to the antique wicker, paned windows, and pine furniture in cottages—my choice for families. A few cottages are still being renovated. Many of the shore cottages are far enough from the inn that you'll have to drive to meals and activities; even at the closest ones you have to cross a road.

🏠 *Chatham 02633, tel. 508/945–0096 or 800/527–4884, fax 508/945–5491. 172* *rooms and suites in main inn (40 rooms) and in 29 cottages. Facilities: 3 restaurants, beach, croquet, 9-hole golf course nearby, health club, pool, shuffleboard, supervised kids' programs (ages 4–12) mid-June–Labor Day, 3 tennis courts, volleyball. AE, DC, MC, V. $$$–$$$$*

Lighthouse Inn

(✟✟ **ALL**) The center section of the white clapboard main inn that looks out on Nantucket Sound was once a lighthouse (in 1850), and the light in the tower is still lit every night. Small and informal, this resort welcomes children with a miniature golf course and two playrooms equipped with games, sand toys, art supplies, and kid-size furniture. Lunch is served on a deck and you can watch sunsets from the porches. For more privacy, families can choose the classic, weathered shake cottages and guest houses where roses climb white trellises and scrubby pines remind you that the ocean wind here blows hard all winter long. These cottages have a homey decor but come with unexpected conveniences like cable TV and hair dryers in the bathrooms. Though the water may be warm at the two small beaches on either side of a long stone breakwall in front of the inn, kids, including toddlers, like to splash in the solar-heated pool. The snack bar has kid-size tables.

🏠 *Box 128, West Dennis 02690, tel. 508/ 398–2244, fax 508/398–5658. 32 rooms, 7 suites, 13 cottages. Facilities: dining room, pool, miniature golf, tennis court, Ping-Pong, shuffle-board, beach, recreation room, video games, kids' program (ages 3–12), kids' lunch, dinner, and evening entertainment. MAP or B&B. MC, V. Closed mid-Oct.–mid-May. Free for kids under 3. $$*

New Seabury Resort

(✟✟ **2–15**) Though we're not fans of planned communities and question the wis-dom of siting a golf course on fragile wet-lands, we have to admit that this complex of tasteful small villages, each with a different architectural style, and private homes on

2,000 acres of a beach-fringed peninsula overlooking Nantucket Sound does evoke something of a Cape Cod feel. Curving roads and secluded paths wind through piney woods out to small beaches and dunes, as well as to a fabulous 3-mi-long beach. Most of the more than 1,600 houses and attached villas here are privately owned second homes. That and its size mean New Seabury doesn't have the immediate friendly intimacy of many of the Northeast's family resorts. Nor does it have a central dining building to pull people together. On the other hand, as all lodging includes kitchens, this is a good place for a very comfortable extended family vacation at the beach. Kids ride their bikes everywhere on the network of bike trails. The wide, sandy bathing beach has tame surf, warm water, shady cabanas, and even a beachfront pool. The big plus for teenagers at this resort is the Popponessett Marketplace, the spot for a variety of family and kid activities, from concerts to pony rides; it features a shopping area of weath-ered shingle buildings, crushed seashell walk-ways, climbing roses, and, more importantly, a pizza parlor, a Ben & Jerry's, miniature golf, and 20 shops.

🏠 *Box 550, Rock Landing Rd., New Seabury 02649, tel. 508/477–9111 or 800/999– 9033, fax 508/477–9790. 165 studio, 1-bed-room, and 2-bedroom villas with kitchens, some with air-conditioning. Facilities: 7 restau-rants (in summer), snack bar, beach, boating, bicycles, baby-sitting, hiking, health club, 2 18-hole golf courses, 2 pools, 16 tennis courts. AE, D, DC, MC, V. $$–$$$*

Pinewoods Camp

(✟✟ **3–12**) Our friends Curtis and Louise, who never miss an opportunity to square dance, have been to the annual Pinewoods family music and dance camp near Plymouth several times with their three children. The camp, one of several in the eastern United States sponsored by the Country Dance and Song Society, offers accommodations in a variety of buildings, from houses with several rooms to individual cabins. Campers age 5 and up help with meals or housekeeping. The buildings stand on 23 acres of pine-covered hills near two lakes; the clear water at the larger (1 mi long) is good for swimming. Everyone gets to know one another here, and a real camaraderie develops from singing and dancing together. Two classes a day are organized by age, one is organized by interest, and some are for families together. It's not all music and dance—there are crafts classes, for instance.

🏠 *Country Dance and Song Society, 132 Main St., Haydenville 01039–0338, tel. 413/ 268–7426, ext. 3, fax 413/268–7471. 140 beds in cabins, some with bath nearby. Facilities: dining room, boating, family and adult dance programs, kids' program (combining music, dance, crafts, songs, storytelling). AP (includes all classes, activities). MC, V. 2-wk programs, July and/or Aug. $–$$*

New Hampshire

Appalachian Mountain Club Family Education Programs

(🏃 5–13) Sleeping in bunks at Lonesome Lake Hut, the AMC's most popular family destination in the White Mountains, was a peak outing for our family. The hike up to it is a short and easy 1.8 mi, but the view made us feel we'd come much, much farther. At the Zealand Falls Hut at the edge of the Pemigewasset Wilderness, you can swim in very cold pools by a waterfall. Staff naturalists lead hikes, teach map and compass reading, and use nature games to help kids—and their parents—learn about animals as well as the importance of treating the earth with respect. Be sure to ask the age range of a particular program before signing up. One thing John and I appreciate about the AMC huts is the fact that they are a big step up from camping: breakfast and a hot dinner, basic but filling, are provided. The meeting point (and sometimes the main accommodations) for many of the family programs in July and August is the larger Pinkham Notch Lodge, a brown wood building rather like a barn. The Lodge has comfortable rooms, hot showers, a library and visitor center, and the AMC Trading Post, where you can buy gear and maps. It's essential to reserve, especially for prime times in late July and August. AMC members get a discount.

The AMC also maintains a number of other camps; one waterfront nature camp that we think is splendid for families is Three Mile Island Camp on Lake Winnipesaukee. You live in cabins (kerosene lamps, outhouses, and sun-heated showers) on a 43-acre rocky island; a main building has a game room, a fireplace, and electricity, as well as sailboats and canoes that campers can use.

🏠 *Pinkham Notch Visitor Center, Box 298, Gorham 03581, tel. 603/466–2721 (Appalachian Mountain Club, 5 Joy St., Boston, MA 02108; membership and information, tel. 617/523–0636; reservations 603/466–2727, fax 603/466–3871). Lodge at Pinkham Notch: 23 bunk rooms with sheets and blankets for 2, 3, 4, or 5; 4 family rooms; 2 large shared baths; facilities: snack bar, library, store, visitor center with exhibits. Lonesome Lake Hut: 2 bunkhouses with 9 rooms for 4, 6, or 8; facilities: canoes, kids' program. MAP. MC, V. $*

Balsams Grand Resort Hotel

(🏃 5+) This huge, gracious 100-year-old resort seems transplanted from a hillside above Lake Lugano in Switzerland to the banks of this perfect lake in the middle of a 15,000-acre New World mountain wilderness. In the late-19th century, when steam trains whisked well-to-do city folk to the mountains each summer, there were dozens of grand hotels like the Balsams in the White Mountains; this is one of the few survivors, and with good reason. It still has one employee for every guest, which means the service is as deluxe as the surroundings.

The resort's oldest part is a white-frame four-story building with a long wraparound porch; it is joined by an entrance portico to a fantasy Mediterranean-style seven-story pale-brown stucco wing that was built in 1918 and has reddish-orange tiles on its roofs and cupolas. Kids love exploring the endless covered porches, corridors, and public rooms filled with ornately carved Victorian furniture; they'll find a vintage Coca-Cola machine in the game room. In the formal dining room, they can view the entrées at a central table before ordering. Unlike that at most family resorts, the food here is superb. The spacious rooms have been completely renovated in the past few years; now all have traditional New England–style decor—four-poster beds, wicker chairs, pastel walls, wall-to-wall carpeting, ruffled tieback curtains, and huge walk-in closets— yet each has an individual look. Many have fireplaces and deep tubs.

Activities for all ages but infants seem limit-less—a mountain-biking program attracts teens, a staff naturalist leads small groups to a moose-watching site, kids can even take conga lessons from the hotel's ballroom musicians, and you can all catch an evening feature film in the hotel's theater. Rooms come equipped with long lists of activities and careful instructions on how to sign up. 🏨 *Dixville Notch 03576, tel. 603/255–3400 or 800/255–0600; in NH, 800/255–0800; fax 603/255–4221. 204 rooms, 75 connect-ing rooms; no TV in rooms. Facilities: dining room, baby-sitting, badminton, cinema, cro-quet, exercise room, fly-fishing, 18- and 9-hole golf courses, hiking, ice-skating, mountain bik-ing, nursery and day camp, playground, pool, recreation rooms, shuffleboard, cross-country skiing, downhill skiing, sleigh rides, snowshoe-ing, lake swimming, 6 tennis courts, volleyball, supervised kids' dinner. MAP (late Dec.–Mar.), AP (late May–mid-Oct.; includes all facilities and programs). AE, D, MC, V. Closed Apr.– early May and Nov.–early Dec. Kids under 18 pay their age times $7.50 per night. $$$–$$$$*

Inn at East Hill Farm

(👫 1–9) Have your kids ever collected eggs, then brought them into the kitchen to have them cooked for breakfast? They can do this every morning at this unposh work-ing family farm and resort. Quarters are diverse; you can stay in cottages with knotty-pine furniture, motel-type rooms with a basic Scandinavian look, or even a five-bedroom house that looks like a repro-duction maple sugaring house with a porch at each end. In the absence of a structured program, young school-age kids are free here to explore nooks and crannies and join in making ice cream in an old crank ice cream maker. They can hang over a wooden slat fence to pet horses, feed chicks, or just poke around one of the many barns any time of year. There's also a pond with pad-dleboats and rowboats. For toddlers and young school-age kids, it feels very comfort-able and down-home, especially with stacks of muffins and cookies and juice waiting just in case they get hungry in the afternoon. 🏨 *460 Monadnock St. (watch for signs to Mt. Monadnock on Rte. 12 in town), Troy 03465, tel. 603/242–6495 or 800/242– 6495, fax 603/242–7709. 9 double rooms with bath (2 connect) and deluxe 3-bedroom, 3-bath suite in main inn; 7 2-bedroom cot-tages; 4 3-bedroom, 2-bath cottages; 18 rooms with bath (all connect) in modern motel-style unit; 1 deluxe 5-bedroom, 5-bath house. Facilities: horseback riding, ice-skating, daily organized kids' activities, pony rides, 2 outdoor pools, indoor pool, wading pool, sauna, cross-country skiing, sledding, sleigh rides, snowshoeing, tennis court, 2 hot tubs, waterski-ing. AP (includes activities). D, MC, V. Kids under 2 free, special rates for ages 2–18. $*

Loch Lyme Lodge and Cottages

(👫 1–13) Families have been coming to this peaceful, relaxing, friendly, and inexpen-sive resort in the Connecticut River valley for more than 70 years, many booking a year or more in advance. Though the main lodge is 18th century, this is not a fancy place. The office is in the red barn. The roomy, old-fashioned, stained-lumber-sided cabins with red trim (some have screened porches and fireplaces) face the lake or the lawn or nestle in the woods. Cabins facing the lake are booked way, way ahead; several are taken for the first week in August until 2010! As you sit in one of the white Adirondack chairs by the lake at dusk, watching your kids catch fireflies or play flashlight tag with a bunch of other kids, you may be gratified to observe that filling unstructured time with country pleasures is just what kids need on a summer vacation. One of those pleasures is talking to the lodge's friendly international college-student staff.

🏠 *70 Orford Rd., Rte. 10, Lyme 03768, tel. 603/795–2141 or 800/423–2141, fax 603/795–2141. 4 rooms with shared bath in main lodge, 12 1- to 4-bedroom cabins with kitchens; 11 1- to 2-bedroom cabins with meals or breakfast only. Facilities: badminton, baseball, basketball, beach, boating, bicycles, playground, 2 tennis courts, volleyball. No TV. MAP or CP (includes boats). No credit cards. Closed Sept.–June. Kids 4 and under free, special rates for ages 5–15; other discounts and packages. $*

Purity Spring Resort

(👫 1–15) This old New England farmstead turned resort on a winding road seems to be exactly what a summer camp for families should be. The onslaught of adult and family events includes canoe races, island breakfast cookouts, and Trivial Pursuit tournaments. Everything is about "family fun": beaches (three are roped off so it's easy to keep track of kids), a drop-in childcare center, weekly all-day family hikes in the White Mountains, and evening campfires. Two big maples frame the modest white farmhouse with green shutters that serves as the main inn; unadorned cottages and lodges are gathered nearby, on the flat expanse of green lawn brightened with flower beds. Rooms are basic and functional. In the lodges, which we liked best, the rooms, each with private bath, have a common lounge with TV and VCR.

🏠 *HC63 Box 40, Rte. 153, East Madison 03849, tel. 603/367–8896 or 800/367–8897, fax 603/367–8664. 45 rooms in summer, 77 in winter, some with shared bath, in cottages (some with fireplace), main inn, and lodges open year-round; 1 lodge is at King Pine Ski Area. Facilities: air-conditioning, baby-sitting, badminton, basketball, beaches, boating, daily child care, croquet, health club, hiking, ice-skating, kids' programs, coin laundry, Ping-Pong, playground, indoor pool, recreation room, shuffleboard, downhill and cross-country skiing, snowshoeing and rentals, 5 tennis courts, waterskiing, TV with VCR in each building. AP (late June–Aug.); MAP (Sept.–Oct.); B&B (late Mar.–late June, mid-Oct.–mid-Dec.). AE, D, MC, V. Discount for kids. $–$$*

Rockhouse Mountain Farm

(👫 3–12) This lovely 450-acre farm lies in the foothills of the White Mountains. The old New England farmhouse with small and medium-size rooms filled with Welsh pine is a refreshing contrast to the area's more commercial amusement attractions. A treat for kids 6 and older is the chance to sleep with other kids in the kids' bunk rooms. They can hang out in the barn, where there's actually a swing hanging from the rafters, and help milk cows, feed chickens and ducks, sit on tractors, go haying, pat dogs and cats and llamas, and be impressed by peacocks strutting about with spread tails. If your kids are at least 6, don't miss the half-hour hike to an ancient Indian cave on Rockhouse Mountain on the farm's property.

🏠 *Rockhouse Mt. Rd. (6 mi south of Conway, off Rte. 153), Eaton Center 03832, tel. 603/447–2880. 15 rooms with shared or private bath, 3 kids' bunk rooms (4 bunks per room). Facilities: 2 dining rooms, separate kids' dining room, beach ½ mi away, boating, hiking, Ping-Pong, recreation room. MAP (includes boats). No credit cards. Closed late Oct.–mid-June. Discount for kids. $*

Rockywold-Deephaven Camp

(**†† ALL**)   This is a special place, the only resort on scenic, island-filled Squam Lake, the film site of *On Golden Pond*. Nearly 100 years old, it has always struck me as a quintessentially Yankee resort—a combination of wonderful service (your "cottage girl" [read maid] will wash your laundry; the *New York Times* will appear upon request; the kitchen will clean and cook fish you catch), rustic but private accommodations in unique individual cottages of dark, weathered wood along a craggy shore, serious tennis playing and sailing, and a very strong respect for nature. Little changes here: Blocks of ice harvested from the lake in winter are still delivered daily to each cottage and stored in an old wood icebox. Everything is rural and camplike—no TV, no radio, no phone, just unpainted walls, individual short wooden docks, and the essential screen porch overlooking the lake, where you sit at twilight to avoid getting eaten by mosquitoes. Time-tested activities like square dances, hikes, fishing, softball games, or capture the flag include everyone from infants to white-haired great-grandparents. A building geared for teens provides Ping-Pong, pool, snacks, and companions. The food is hearty—hot soup, roast beef, tortellini, and a big salad bar—but always includes a vegetarian dish. Like Purity Spring, this is a big summer camp, but more sophisticated, intellectual, and upscale despite its underplayed accommodations. Kids over 8 can roam just about everywhere themselves, but there are no lifeguards.

Now for the drawback: It's very hard for newcomers to rent a cottage here, almost impossible in August. Get on the waiting list, accept a late-June or early July week, then keep coming back until you're promoted to high season via their complicated seniority system.

🏠 *Box B, Squam Lake, Pinehurst Rd. (off Rte. 113), Holderness 03245, tel. 603/968–3313, fax 603/968–3438. 60 cottages. Facilities: 2 small beaches for toddlers, boating, 2 docks,* hiking, hydrobikes, mountain bikes, recreation room, indoor play areas, playground, morning play group (ages 3–5), sailing, 8 tennis courts. AP (includes all activities but boating, bikes, and lessons). No credit cards. Closed mid-Sept.–early June. Free for kids under 2; reduced rate for kids 2–5. $$$

Whitney's Inn at Jackson

(**†† 4–13**)   Whitney's, a little more than a mile from the center of town, is a classic mid-19th-century inn, a sky-blue farmhouse with additions that ramble on and on. The setting, though, reminds us of the Alps, especially in summer, when, if you walk up the hill by the pond across the road, you'll be treated to a stunning view of the entire Presidential Range. We know this place best in winter because it's right next to the Black Mountain ski area and is surrounded by one of the best cross-country trail systems in the Northeast, a network that meanders all over this valley; conveniently for families, one trail starts by the pond. Though the inn and service are gracious, it is not at all stuffy. Such thoughtful touches as the huge, three-ring binder at the desk that catalogs all the inn's board games and puzzles by age category or the decidedly informal rec and game room in the big wood barn next door let you know just how welcome families are. Guest rooms in the inn (they're named after trees) are spacious but also filled with breakable-looking collectibles. For families with young children the family suites (like motel units) and cottages, which also have living rooms with day beds, are more appropriate. *See also* Chapter 7, Jackson Ski Touring Foundation.

🏠 *Box 822, Rte. 16B (1½ mi from town and covered bridge), Jackson 03846, tel. 603/383–8916 or 800/677–5737, fax 603/383–6886. 14 rooms in main inn, 8 family suites in chalet, 4 rooms in Brookside House, 2 cottages. Facilities: dining room, optional kids' dinner, badminton, ice-skating, picnic area, Ping-Pong, recreation room, shuffleboard, cross-country skiing, downhill skiing, swimming pond, tennis court, volleyball. MAP or CP. AE, D, MC, V. Kids* under 12 stay and eat free in family suites. Mar. 26–Labor Day. $–$$

New York

Fieldstone Farm Resort

(👫 4 – 15) About 9 mi from the National Baseball Hall of Fame is this friendly, informal farm with 170 acres of fields, big ponds with islands, and woods that are safe for kids to explore after a hard day of total immersion in baseball. The fieldstone barn, the house, and the two-story stone town-house apartments are clustered together by a pond and swimming pool on a huge expanse of mown grass and trees; farther up the driveway past the meadow are the wood-frame cottages, some set back in the woods, some right in a field on top of the hill, with space and light around them. Furnishings are eclectic. We really felt kids were welcome here when we saw the 80-ft-long rec room on the top level of the barn—some kids were shooting baskets; others had set up a volleyball net for a game. Outside, kids were petting one of the two cats. Many guests come back year after year, initially because the farm is close to the Baseball Hall of Fame, but then just because it's a place to sink into the natural world.

🏠 201 Rose's Hill Rd., Richfield Springs 13439, tel. 315/858–0295 or 888/353–3276. Rte. 28 north from Cooperstown to Fly Creek, right on Rte. 26 and watch for signs, 9 mi from Cooperstown. 7 apartments, 13 studio–large 3-bedroom cottages, all with kitchen. Some sleep 8. Facilities: basketball, boating, fishing, hiking, coin laundry, Ping-Pong, pool, recreation room, shuffleboard, store, tennis court, volleyball. D, MC, V. Weekly stays given priority July–Aug. $

Garnet Hill Lodge

(👫 2 – 14) High above Thirteenth Lake is this wonderfully friendly and informal mountain lodge, where families are completely at home. Noted primarily for cross-country skiing in winter (see also Chapter 7), it's also a great place to stay in summer, when the cross-country trails become mountain biking and hiking trails. You feel as though you are in the middle of wilderness—the lodge is surrounded by tree-covered mountains and borders one of the largest wilderness tracts in the Adirondacks. The 2-mi-long lake is pristine, with cool, very clear water and a completely undeveloped shoreline, except for the Garnet Hill private sand beach. Canoeing here is especially fun for kids because distances are short and you can easily pull up by big rocks. Naturalist-led hikes a couple of times a week and biking excursions are the extent of the organized activities, but kids get to know one another quickly, gathering in the afternoon to swing on the tire swing or in the hammock and running around the lawn after dinner with a flashlight on searches for bats. Later families play Ping-Pong and pool, or they gather for Monopoly or cards in front of the massive stone fireplace. August is when you'll find the most families.

This is a relatively small lodge, with rooms in five different buildings; we like to stay in the main lodge, the Log House, which was built in 1936, because the restaurant, games room, and Ping-Pong and pool tables are on the main floor. The nine balcony rooms upstairs have views of the lake, mountains, and beautiful rolling lawn; they're preferable to the seven lower-priced regular rooms across the hall. Also good for families are the five spacious rooms (and a common room) in the Birches, just down the hill in the woods. Furnishings are comfortable and contemporary.

🏠 Thirteenth Lake Rd., North River 12856, tel. 518/251–2444. 30 rooms with private bath in main lodge and 3 smaller buildings, most with private bath; also 23 2- to 4-bedroom vacation homes, all with kitchen. Facilities: beach, boating, fishing, hiking, hot tub, mountain biking, Ping-Pong, sauna, 3 tennis courts, TV and games room, white-water rafting and tubing nearby. MAP. AE, D, MC, V. $$

Mohonk Mountain House

(👫 **ALL**) We love staying at this huge, rambling stone and painted-wood hotel with towers and cupolas. It was built in the late-19th century and is now a National Historic Landmark and one of the best big resorts for families in the Northeast. The gigantic fireplaces, carved dark woodwork, and Victorian antiques everywhere make us feel we're in some grand, European castle. The setting is spectacular, too—perched at the rocky edge of a deep, clean, blue mountaintop lake in the Shawangunk range about two hours north of New York City. Most of the rooms also have antiques and fireplaces; we prefer the tower rooms, which have fabulous views of the mountains. The hotel does not feel too stuffy or formal. There are "a zillion things to do here, so it's hard to choose" is the assessment of many kids. You can hike on 85 mi of trails through woods, by ponds, and up to peaks in the 8,500 acres (belonging to the hotel and to the Mohonk Preserve; see Chapter 6) surrounding the hotel. You can have tea on the porch, walk on a bridge to a sunbathing float in the lake, visit the blacksmith shop, hunt for arrowheads, and much more. If you come in the winter, there's snowshoeing, ice-skating, and great cross-country skiing.

🏠 *Lake Mohonk, New Paltz 12561, tel. 914/255–1000 or 800/772–6646 (reservations), fax 914/256–2161. 261 rooms, 16 connecting rooms. Facilities: restaurant, snack bar, baby-sitting, basketball, beach, boating, croquet, evening activities for kids and teens, fishing, 9-hole golf course, health club, hiking, horseback riding, kids' buffet at 6 (summer and holidays), kids' programs (ages 2–12, mid-June–Labor Day and most weekends), laundry, library, shuffleboard, softball, 6 tennis courts, volleyball; in winter: ice-skating, cross-country skiing, snowshoeing. AP. AE, D, DC, MC, V. Kids stay free in parents' room during special family wks. $$$–$$$$*

Rocking Horse Ranch

(👫 **4+**) Despite the deer with antlers over the fireplace and the steer skulls, wagon wheels, and colorful Native American blankets on the barn-board walls in the modern, motel-style main building and rooms, this ranch has a Long Island or Hudson Valley flavor overlaid with folksiness. It does have the largest stables in the East, with 120 horses, 500 acres of woods and orchards to ride in, and literally hundreds of activities for every age group and interest, from infants up. If you are an experienced rider, you may be able to go on several hour-long trail rides a day, though trail-ride sign-up lines are often long. All rides are accompanied by several experienced members of the ranch staff; one friend of Gavin's, looking for some excitement, was disappointed by how quickly staffers controlled a beginner's runaway horse.

Younger kids especially enjoy the petting zoo; older kids go for the video parlor. Supervision of kids is superb.

🏠 *600 Rte. 44–55 (intersection of Rtes. 44 and 55 off Rte. 9W, 75 mi north of New York City), Highland 12528, tel. 914/691–2927 or 800/647–2624, fax 914/691–6434. 120 rooms. Facilities: air-conditioning, archery, badminton, basketball, boating, boccie, croquet, evening entertainment for families and teens, fishing, health club, hiking, horseback riding, kids' program day and evening, miniature golf, nursery, Ping-Pong, playground, indoor and outdoor pools including wading pool, shuffleboard, tennis, video games, volleyball, waterskiing; in winter: ice-skating, skiing, sleigh rides, snow tubing. MAP (includes all activities and facilities). AE, D, DC, MC, V. Free for kids under 4, less than ½ price for ages 4–16. $$–$$$*

Sagamore Resort

(👫 **3–15**) Built in 1883 on Green Island in Lake George, just across a short bridge from Bolton Landing, the Sagamore was restored to grand resort status in the 1980s and came under the management of the Omni chain. A long stairway leads to the porticoed entrance of the Victorian-style hotel, which is flanked by two several-story white clapboard wings. The suites in the stained-wood-and-glass lakefront lodge buildings (a short walk from the main hotel) are just right for families; they have a more Adirondack-country feel and are filled with sturdy Adirondack twig-style furniture, cushy sectional couches, quilts on the walls, fireplaces, and small kitchens with round wooden tables for eating.

Service is impeccable, food is excellent; at breakfast younger kids are welcomed with a special kid-height buffet table, stocked with bite-size French toast, tiny pancakes, chocolate milk, Frosted Flakes, and coloring books. The well-organized kids' program is best for preschoolers and school-age children. The lake beach, mostly encircled with a wood deck, is too deep for very young children; though they can play in the sand behind it, they can't walk into the water themselves. For teenagers, the big attractions are hanging out in the game room, the tennis and golf clinics, and going to the nearby amusement parks.
🏨 *Bolton Landing 12814, tel. 518/644– 9400 or 800/358–3585, fax 518/644–2626. 54 rooms, 46 suites in main hotel; 120 rooms, 120 suites in 7 lodge buildings; all have fireplace, terrace, or balcony. Facilities: 2 dining rooms, café, grill room, baby-sitting, basketball, beach, boating, fishing, 18-hole award-winning golf course and driving range, health club, allday kids' program and dinner, Ping-Pong, playground, indoor pool, racquetball, recreation room, sailing, 5 outdoor and 2 indoor teen activities and parties, tennis courts, video games, volleyball, windsurfing. AE, DC, MC, V. Fee for some activities. $$$–$$$$*

Silver Bay Association

(👫 **ALL**) This enormous 600-acre national conference center for the YMCA on Lake George is simply an astonishing bargain for vacationing families. Picture long, flat grassy fields, turn-of-the-century Adirondack wood-and-stone buildings, and a massive four-story clapboard inn, a timber boathouse, and many more buildings, all set on one of the most beautiful bays on the lake. The inn's

peaked dormer windows and covered porch hung with plants are both on the National Register of Historic Places. The real bargains here are the recreational facilities, which are like those at a grand resort, and the kids' program and playgrounds for infants and up, which are among the best we've seen anywhere. Do check out the spacious parent-child center. Rooms in the inn, on the other hand, are pretty basic: Scandinavian style with clean, functional bathrooms; the rooms in lodges with shared baths, which are quite large, holding a double and a single bed, have that old-furniture look and are decorated with amateur watercolors painted by guests. On the plus side, if your kids leave their wet bathing suits on the floor, it doesn't matter. Food is no-frills but includes things kids like. It's an easy drive to Lake George attractions, but your kids probably won't want to leave.
🏨 *Silver Bay 12874, tel. 518/543–8833, fax 518/543–6733. 103 rooms (15 adjoining rooms) in main inn, 27 rooms (4 adjoining) in Bayview Lodge; 125 rooms with shared baths in 6 other lodges; 23 1- to 4-bedroom cottages with kitchens. Facilities: snack bar, archery, arts center, baby-sitting, baseball, basketball, 2 beaches, boating, exercise room, hiking, kids' programs (infants–high school), lessons (swimming, sailing, tennis), library, nature center, softball, teen programs, 6 tennis courts; in winter: ice-skating, cross-country skiing, snowshoeing. AE, MC, V. Kids under 4 free, kids 4–12 pay ½ price when sharing room with parents. $*

Rhode Island

Weekapaug Inn

(👫 **3 – 15**) On first sight it looks like an unpretentious, rambling, weathered barn with dormer windows and expansive decks. It's set on a flat peninsula poking out into a huge saltwater pond behind a long barrier beach. The simplicity is the sophisticated, proper, old New England–family kind (no bathing suits in the public rooms, please, and jackets at dinner). The inn does not advertise. It is in a very quiet colony of large, privately owned summer cottages on a stretch of beautiful white-sand beaches that are as glorious as any in the Northeast. This is not a "family place" in the sense that the Tyler Place or the Basin Harbor Club in Vermont is (see below). Instead, it has room for a few families and extends its warm, personal, attentive service to them. Relaxing, playing tennis, or boating on the big saltwater pond behind the tennis courts, and enjoying the beach and the ocean are the key attractions. The kids' morning program is also low-key: playing at the beach (nearby private Fenway Beach is shallower and has more young kids than the beach in front of the inn), going crabbing, and arts and crafts. If older kids get bored, you're not too far from Mystic Seaport or the new Pequot Museum (see also Chapter 2).

In contrast to the antiques-filled common rooms on the first two floors, which resemble an old private club, the bedrooms are simple, with small baths, but you won't spend much time in them. For older children and teens who want independence, there are 10 reduced-rate small rooms on the top floor, with two shared baths that are most often rented to the children of guests. The food is really good, especially the fish.
🏠 *25 Spring Ave., Weekapaug 02891, tel. 401/322–0301, fax 401/322–1016. 55 rooms, plus 6 family suites and 10 rooms that share 2 baths. Facilities: dining room, snack bar, 2 beaches, biking, boating, croquet, nearby golf, jungle gym, morning kids' program (ages 3–10), lawn bowling, library, Ping-Pong, recreation room, sailing, shuffleboard, 2 tennis courts, TV room, windsurfing. AP. No credit cards. Closed Labor Day–early June. Special rates for kids. $$$*

Vermont

Basin Harbor Club

👫 3–15 This 700-acre lakefront resort around secluded Basin Harbor on Lake Champlain's eastern shore just oozes the comfortable, conservative New England style and tradition favored by well-to-do families who like to wear blue blazers and bow ties to dinner on their vacations. It really does feel like a club—and you can fly in on your private plane. White sailboats and speedboats dot the lake; brightly painted Adirondack chairs in red, blue, and yellow line the expansive, well-manicured lawn in front of the main lodge, a red-roofed white farmhouse nestled among colorful flower beds near the lake. Families, sometimes three generations, gather on the veranda for a drink. The whole place seems bright and timeless, as though summers here have not changed in the hundred-odd years the Beach family has owned and run it. This is a more formal, upscale spot than the Tyler Place (see below) farther north on the lake and not as appropriate for families with toddlers.

The food in the main dining room is good and the wine list is superb. Sweet-toothed kids recommend the desserts and especially the make-your-own sundae bar laid out at the lunch buffet. Kids of all ages can choose to eat with their own families or with their peers. Alternatives to a formal dinner are the once-a-week family picnics and the Red Mill, a casual place for hamburger fare with bare wood beams and tables in an old restored barn that also houses a game room, usually full of teens. The airy cottages furnished in pine, wicker, and chintz may be preferable to the slightly stuffier, country-house feel of the main lodge. All the cottages are different— one- or two-story white frame, some fronted with cut Vermont stone, some with decks or screened porches, some in the woods, by a garden, or even perched on pillars at the edge of the water. The sheltered sandy beaches are much nicer than the one at the Tyler Place; they're better for little kids than the pool. The growing numbers of 13-, 14-, and 15-year-olds enjoy the programs with the Lake Champlain Maritime Museum at the edge of the property; the agenda includes nautical archaeology, snorkeling, and scuba diving, and the excellent golf and tennis clinics for teens. (The top four teen golfers in Vermont were taught by their pro.) August and the Fourth of July are still the times when you'll find the most kids, but there are kids' programs on weekends in the fall.

🏨 *Basin Rd., Vergennes 05491, tel. 802/ 475–2311 or 800/622–4000, fax 802/475– 6545. 43 hotel rooms in 2 main buildings; 77 cottages, all with phone, most with refrigerator, ½ with fireplace. Facilities: 3 restaurants, snack bar, baby-sitting, badminton, beach, biking, boating, afternoon crafts, croquet, family activities, golf, hiking, morning kids' program (ages 3–15) and kids' dinner, library with kids' books, Ping-Pong, playground, pool, private airstrip, recreation room, tennis, volleyball, waterskiing, windsurfing. AP (includes all facilities) July–Aug. MC, V. Closed mid-Oct.–mid-May. Kids' rates and packages. $$$*

Bridges Resort and Racquet Club

(👬 **3+**) With a mountain backdrop and towering pines near the Sugarbush ski area, this is ski-season condo-land, but in summer it becomes a tennis-playing family's heaven. It's my pick for a strictly tennis destination because of the well-run, extensive program that even teaches tennis to 3-year-olds, using regular junior racquets but a lower net. Youngest kids in families of tennis players often feel left out, I've observed—here they don't. *See also* Chapter 7, Sugarbush.

🏨 *Sugarbush Access Rd., Warren 05674, tel. 802/583–2922 or 800/453–2922, fax 802/ 583–1018. 100 1-, 2-, and 3-bedroom condominiums. Facilities: 1 indoor and 2 outdoor pools, 2 indoor and 10 outdoor tennis courts, health club, volleyball, recreation room, playground, kids' activity center, kids' programs, tennis instruction. AE, MC, V. Family packages. $$–$$$*

Mountain Top Inn and Resort

(👬 **ALL**) Though this is a small country inn, it has as many things to do as a much bigger, more expensive, even grand resort.

And the views of the Green Mountains and the Chittenden Reservoir are absolutely sensational. The real draw for us are the extensive cross-country ski trails on the inn's 1,300 acres, but horse-loving friends tell us that this is also an especially good place to introduce young (8 and up) kids to horseback riding and for more experienced families to take a riding vacation. In winter, it's most convenient to stay at the main inn, a modern post-and-beam farmhouse with comfortable sofas and stacks of board games in the two main sitting areas. The rooms here, unfortunately, could use more soundproofing. In summer, try one of the cottages just up the hill; they're close to the kidney-shape pool.

🏨 *Mountain Top Rd., Rte. 108, Chittenden 05737, tel. 802/483–2311 or 800/445– 2100, fax 802/483–6373. 35 rooms, 22 cottages and chalets. Facilities: restaurant, outdoor café, beach, boating, croquet, fishing, 5-hole golf course, hiking, horseback riding, pool, sauna, shuffleboard, tennis court; in winter: ice-skating, cross-country skiing, sledding, sleigh rides, snowshoeing. EP or MAP (includes all activities without instruction). AE, MC, V. Free for kids under 6; discount for kids under 18. $$$*

Rodgers' Country Inn

(👬 **3–9**) In the high, rolling country of northeastern Vermont, down a rutted dirt road, is this small, off-the-beaten-path farm. It takes only two families at a time, so coming here is more like visiting an aunt or a grandma than going to a resort. For city-bred kids it's a peaceful, quiet place where they can take a break from their overscheduled lives and easily entertain themselves with all the animals they'd like to have but don't. They pet goats as well as 10 or so cats and kittens.

🏨 *RFD 3, Box 57, West Glover 06875, tel. 802/525–6677 or 800/729–1704. 5 rooms with shared bath. Facilities: playground, swimming 4 mi away. AP or CP. AE, MC, V. Closed Dec. Discount for kids under 12. $*

Tyler Place

(ħħ 0–13) You feel as though you're at a cheerful, simple, and informal (but not rustic) summer cottage colony at this terrific 60-year-old resort. It holds about 58 families and is spread out along a mile of Lake Champlain's wooded shoreline. All the lodgings are different: Some are basic, square white-frame 1930s-style cottages with a fireplace, chenille bedspreads, painted old furniture, and a screen porch, overlooking the lake or set back on the lawn; others are suites in a Victorian farmhouse with its own small playground or in the big, modern stained-wood inn that also houses the two-story dining room hung with patchwork quilts. All provide separate bedrooms for parents, something we've always viewed as important. Families return year after year for the infant care in the form of parents' helpers and the structured, well-supervised morning and evening programs for six separate age groups of kids from 2 to 17 led by adventurous and wonderfully outgoing and nurturing college students. This is one of the few places that really cater to people with infants and toddlers, but for many kids over 14 it may be too sedate.

During the summer it's not a place for an intimate family vacation—kids eat lunch and dinner with their peers and counselors (a nice touch for teens is the extra-late breakfast), and parents eat at tables of six in the adult dining room. (In May, June, and September, though, themed family retreats for families with younger kids—family wellness, the French language, etc.—are held here.) You'll find whatever kind of sports activity you want. The only drawback is the lack of a good beach for small children; use the L-shape lifeguarded pool and the little kids' wading pool instead.

ĦĦ *Box 1, Highgate Springs 05460, tel. 802/868–4000 or 802/868–3301, fax 802/868–7602. 29 3- to 6-room cottages with fireplace, 29 suites. Facilities: dining room, adult activities, baby-sitting, beach, biking, boating, evening entertainment, family events, fishing, kids' programs (infants–teens), playgrounds,* indoor and outdoor pools, softball, 6 tennis courts, volleyball. AP (includes all sports and lessons). D, MC, V. Closed mid-Sept.–May. Special rates May, June, Sept. $$–$$$*

Wildflower Inn

(ħħ 1–14) There's no doubt that kids are welcome at this country farmhouse on 500 beautiful acres: Teddy-bear pancakes with chocolate chips appear at breakfast; the children's playroom has dress-up clothes and an oval mirror, a reading loft, and air hockey; and outside you'll find a batting cage with a pitching machine. Animal-lovers will have a blast in the barn petting the rabbits, a calf, horses, and assorted dogs and cats. The owners have eight children themselves, ranging from toddlers to teens, so they understand what will keep kids of all ages happy, such as the family dinner hour at 5:30, for which you can preorder so your food is ready the moment you sit down.

The several buildings—a main farmhouse, a large carriage house, the Meadows building, which was once a blacksmith shop, and a honeymoon cottage—are conveniently grouped together; the rooms and suites all have a country feel, with bright rag rugs and different lovely touches, such as fresh flowers, Shaker rockers, a canopy bed, and sturdy oak antiques. (The most popular is a family suite of two bedrooms, sitting room, and kitchenette in the carriage house.) Although primarily a place for families who want to engage in outdoor activities together—hiking, fishing, tennis, and more—a daily two-hour activity program after breakfast gives parents of 3- to 10-year-olds a break.

ĦĦ *Darling Hill Rd., Lyndonville, VT 05851, tel. 802/626–8310 or 800/627–8310, fax 802/626–3039. 11 rooms, 9 suites (with kitchenettes), 1 cottage. Facilities: dining room, baby-sitting, basketball, fishing, hiking, kids' menu, kids' program in summer, mountain biking, nightly kids' movie, playroom, pool and wading pool, soccer, tennis court; in winter: ice-skating, snowshoeing. CP. MC, V. Closed Nov. and Apr. $–$$*

MUSIC, DANCE, THEATER, AND THE CIRCUS
BRASS BANDS, PUPPETS, AND *THE NUTCRACKER*

10

I n the cities of the Northeast, especially New York and Boston, you can find truly fantastic music, dance, and theater performances for families throughout the year. In summer, the Berkshires of Massachusetts also offer an exceptional selection. Many companies tour throughout the Northeast, especially during holiday seasons and summer, so check with major arts centers, theaters, and symphonies as well as with performing groups for schedules of children's events.

It's difficult for most kids—even young teens—to sit and listen to or watch a long performance without squirming. Kids 3–8 like very short puppet shows, plays, and music where they can be part of the action; kids of all ages like outdoor concerts and festivals where they can get up and move around. Other good bets are circuses. A chance to meet and talk with performers after a show and learn how instruments and scenery or special theatrical effects work make a performance more intriguing, and being as close to the action as possible makes a big difference to kids, no matter what their age.

Music, Dance, and Theater Events

Many of the troupes and performances that appeal to kids don't fit neatly into one category—music, dance, or theater—but are a combination of several.

Connecticut

International Festival of Arts and Ideas

⛑ 5+ Dozens of first-class events and performances, about half of which are intended for families, take place around New Haven's town green in this two-year-old, four-day, five-night festival with performers from many different cultures. You might

see the Bread and Puppet Theater or the famous Paris circus-theater Cirque Baroque or hear some of the greatest salsa music in the world. Be sure to hear at least one of the free concerts on the New Haven Green and try out the free arts and science activities for kids.

🏠 *On Town Green, New Haven (mailing address: 227 Church St., New Haven 06521), tel. 888/278–4332 or 203/498–1212. Cost: Free for most events; others $10–$20. When: late June.*

Maine

Maine Festival

⛑ ALL This four-day showcase of Maine artists is probably the best arts festival for families in the Northeast. Seven tents, spread out over 23 acres on a promontory overlooking a beach, shelter stages for music, dance, theater, poetry, storytelling, 1,000 performers. Though one stage is set aside for performances and activities for children, just about everything here is appropriate for families. Don't miss the traditional Maine fiddle music.

🏠 *Thomas Point Beach (Rte. 1 to Cook's Corner exit, then Rte. 24 South), Brunswick 04011 (mailing address: 582 Congress St., Portland 04101–3311), tel. 207/772–9012 or 800/639–4212. Cost: $12 adults, $9 kids 13–17, $6 kids 12 and under, $25 family pass (for family of 5), discounted tickets in advance. When: 1st or 2nd weekend in Aug.*

Massachusetts

New England Folk Festival

(👫 4+)   The big daddy of folk festivals in New England is a 54-year-old three-day gathering with dancing, storytelling, folk singing, dulcimer playing, and more in seven dance halls and performing areas under one roof. Saturday and Sunday are the best days for families, but be warned that the event draws a big crowd.

🏠 *Held at Natick High School, 15 West St., Natick, tel. 617/354–1340 (information). Cost: $10–$12 per session. When: late Apr.*

The Revels

(👫 4+)   The Revels produces exuberant pageants of folk dances, music, storytelling, and singing inspired by folk traditions of different cultures and times in three locations in the Northeast. The Christmas Revels, celebrating the winter solstice, is somewhat like a magical circus; some parts we love remain the same—the silly mummer's play and a spiral dance in which the performers join hands with the audience and weave through the theater. The Spring Revels, held in a different theater, in Boston, is similar; you might see Irish jigging and pipe music. Revels North, the New Hampshire branch, offers Coun-

try Revels and Shaker Revels in the summer. New York City has only the Christmas Revels, usually performed in Symphony Space.

🏠 *1 Kendall Sq., Bldg. 600, Cambridge 02139, tel. 617/621–0505. (Performances in Sanders Theatre, Cambridge 02138; Spring Revels in Emerson Majestic Theatre, Boston). Also Revels North in Hanover, NH 03755, tel. 603/298–8913, and in New York City, tel. 212/206–6875. Cost in Cambridge: $16–$30 adults, $9–$24 kids under 12. When: May, last 2 weeks of Dec.*

New Hampshire

International Children's Festival

(👫 3+)   Main Street is closed to accommodate the five canopy-covered stages of this well-produced entertainment fest that's been around since 1980. The stage for teenagers hums with rock bands and a karaoke machine; on another you may see a steel drum band or Polish folk dancers. Very young kids are entertained by magicians, jugglers, and puppeteers. The festivities start at night with a family concert and fireworks.

🏠 *On Main St., Somersworth 03878 (mailing address: Somersworth International Children's Festival, Box 255, Somersworth 03878), tel. 603/692–5869. Cost: Free (food and some activities extra). When: 3rd Sat. in June.*

The Revels

See Massachusetts, *above.*

New York

Bardavon Opera House

(👫 5+)   This intimate old-time opera house has seats upholstered in plush blue velvet, a sweeping 40-ft dome decorated with curving plasterwork, and a pipe organ like those in 1920s movie palaces. It's the best place in the Hudson Valley to see good family theater, music, dance, and puppets at both kids' daytime shows and evening performances—you might see the comic Flying Karamazov Brothers juggle plates of spaghetti. The Hudson Valley Philharmonic also presents a children's concert series. A once-a-month classic film series draws lots of families; when *Robin Hood* was shown, kids came in costume.

🏠 *35 Market St., Poughkeepsie 12601, tel. 914/473–2072. Off-season tel. 914/473–5288. Cost: $4.50–$6 kids' daytime shows, $5–$28 evening shows (price varies by show); students and kids under 12 sometimes get a discount. When: Sept.–June.*

High Five

(👫 10 – 18) This New York City organization provides a way for teenagers to get low-cost ($5) tickets to a wide variety of great music, dance, theater, art, and film performances in New York City; you can see Alvin Ailey, the New York City Ballet, the New York Philharmonic, the Pan-Asian Theater, and many, many more. High Five tickets are one of the great bargains in the Northeast, and for midweek events a teenager can get two tickets for the price of one, so you can come along, too. To obtain them, however, your teen must go in person to a New York City (there are also a few in New Jersey) Ticketmaster outlet. Lists of these and available performances are in their seasonal mailing.

🏠 *High Five Tickets to the Arts, 1 E. 53rd St., 5th floor, 10022–4200, tel. 212/445–8587. Cost: $5.*

The Revels

See Massachusetts, *above.*

Saratoga Performing Arts Center

(👫 8+) The Arts Center in Spa State Park is the summer home of the New York City Ballet and the Philadelphia Orchestra. Though lawn seating for evening opera and

orchestra concerts and dance performances is free for kids under 12, for dance we'd opt for the inexpensive ballet matinees that feature story ballets such as *A Midsummer Night's Dream*. Call the National Museum of the Dance (South Broadway, Saratoga Springs, tel. 518/584–2225, ext. 3204) to reserve a spot on the special behind-the-scenes tour offered to kids before the performance.

🏠 *Spa State Park, Saratoga Springs 12866, tel. 518/587–3330 (box office). Cost: $5–$20 ballet matinees; other performances $10–$45. When: June–Aug.*

Strictly Music

Massachusetts

For kids who like traditional folk and fiddle music, check with the Folk Arts Center (Box 867, Cambridge, MA 02238, tel. 617/491–6084).

Boston Pops Orchestra

(👫 8+) At the Boston Pops concerts in Symphony Hall an air of boisterous festivity fits with the mix of popular classics and movie scores that everyone recognizes. Round tables and chairs replace the hard wooden seats, and kids can eat sandwiches and drink sodas while listening. The Pops also performs free outdoor concerts at the Esplanade Hatch band shell by the Charles River, including one on the 4th of July followed by fireworks, and one at Tanglewood (see below).

🏠 *301 Massachusetts Ave., Boston 02115, tel. 617/266–1492 or 888/266–1200 (ticket office). Cost: $13–$47. When: mid-Dec.–Jan. 1 and mid-May–early July.*

Boston Symphony Orchestra

(👫 5 – 12) The Boston Symphony is one of the country's great orchestras, but attending a regular concert is best for older kids who love music. For younger kids, subscribe to the one-hour Youth and Family Concerts designed to appeal specifically to families. Pre-concert activities include tours of the hall and a chance to play an oboe and ask musicians questions; music is usually something colorful, like *The Firebird.* Single tickets are very hard to get. Another great family event is the once-a-year Salute to Symphony, an all-day open house at which you can also see instruments and ask musicians questions.

🏠 *301 Massachusetts Ave., Boston 02115, tel. 617/266–1492. Cost: $7.50–$27.50. When: Oct., Jan., Mar.*

New England Conservatory of Music

(🧍🏼 **5+**)   The free concerts at this renowned music school are among the great music bargains for families in the Northeast. A wide variety of music is presented in both informal and formal settings; a monthly calendar conveniently lists it all. In the spring a lively annual music festival features the music of one country. You don't need tickets; just show up.

🏠 *290 Huntington Ave., Boston 02115, tel. 617/262–1120, ext. 700 (auditorium in Jordan Hall, 30 Gainsborough St., Boston 02115; subway Symphony on Arborway/Green Line). Cost: Free. When: Sept.–June.*

Tanglewood Music Festival

(🧍🏼 **5+**)   The best seats at this 210-acre summer home of the Boston Symphony Orchestra are on the maple-shaded lawn— and lawn tickets are free for kids under 12. The premier summer musical festival in the Northeast, it presents three particularly family-friendly special events: a day of entertainment and fireworks on the Fourth of July; two free family concerts (shorter, more playful pieces) on Saturday mornings; and Tanglewood on Parade, an afternoon and evening of demonstrations and concerts that ends with booming cannons and fireworks. Traffic can be terrible on weekend evenings.

🏠 *Rte. 183, West St., Lenox 01240, tel. 413/ 637–5165 (June–Sept.) or 617/266–1492 (Sept.–June). Cost: $15–$79; lawn tickets $12– $16 adults, kids under 12 free. When: June–Sept.*

New Hampshire

Temple Town Band

(🧍🏼 **ALL**)   Listening to band music on a town green on a hot summer night is a true New England experience. The Temple Town Band, whose concerts we've always enjoyed, has been around since 1799 and performs in many New Hampshire towns each summer; the ideal place to hear the band is on the rectangular green in Walpole, surrounded by shade trees and white frame houses. The band members dress in white muslin shirts and three-cornered hats and play all the best oompah as well as jazz, swing, show tunes, and more.

🏠 *Various locations; for schedule, write The Temple Town Band, Box 66, Temple 03084. Cost: Donation requested. When: July–Aug.*

New York

Carnegie Hall

(🧍🏼 **6–13**)   This celebrated century-old hall hosts an annual series of family concerts that feature renowned performers who relate well to kids. You'll see everything from jazz bands to the Empire Brass group to pianist Emmanuel Ax; during the 45 minutes of activities before the concert you might have a chance to see what's inside a cello or try a clarinet. The price is a bargain.

🏠 *154 W. 57th St., at 7th Ave., New York 10019, tel. 212/247–7800. Cost: $5. When: Once a month, Oct., Nov., Jan., Feb., Mar., Apr.*

Little Orchestra Society

(🧍🏼 **3–12**)   Since 1947, this organization's concerts for children at Avery Fisher Hall in New York City provide lots of action along with the music. Nine 40- to 50-minute Lollipop Concerts, held in the small Florence

Gould Hall (50 E. 59th St.), are for ages 3–5; you might hear short pieces that single out instruments in particular sections of the orchestra. The slightly longer Happy Concerts for Young People (for ages 5–12) usually have scenery and a story, as in the annual production of *Amahl and the Night Visitors*. Although you can purchase single tickets the week of the performance, some years most are sold through subscription. 🏛 *330 W. 42nd St., 12th floor, New York 10036, tel. 212/971–9500. Cost: $15–$32. When: Sept.–May.*

Metropolitan Opera

(👫 4–13) The three annual hour-long Growing Up with Opera productions, designed especially for families, are in English and include audience participation. Produced by the Metropolitan Opera Guild, they're shown in two small theaters. The first program of the season, *My First Trip to the Opera*, is a half-hour introduction to opera for ages 4–6; the second, for ages 6–12, is a more sophisticated and longer introduction. In 1998 both were staged in a 90-seat theater in SoHo where kids were so close to the action that attention never lagged. The other production is usually a shortened, updated classic like *The Barber of Seville* at a bigger theater at John Jay College. At the cast party after the last performance, kids can obtain autographs. The 1½-hour backstage tour of the Met (Sept.–June, Mon.–Sat.) for kids 10 and up visits the wig shop, the scenery shop, and the huge and fabulous sets for current productions. 🏛 *70 Lincoln Center Plaza, New York 10023–6593. Growing Up with Opera, tel. 212/769–7008 reservations, 212/769–7020 backstage tour. Cost: Opera $10–$15. When: Nov. and Mar. Backstage tour $8 adults, $4 students with valid ID.*

New York Philharmonic Orchestra

(👫 6–16) One of the great orchestras of the world, it gives regular performances in Lincoln Center's Avery Fisher Hall and free concerts in various New York City parks in summer. Most fun for kids are the one-hour-long Young People's Concerts and the two free programs held at Barnes & Noble bookstores. Children's Promenades—giving kids an opportunity to do some hands-on musical activities—are held before each concert. One good book to read before attending, especially for younger kids, is *The Philharmonic Gets Dressed*, by Karla Kuskin (HarperTrophy, 1986). The Philharmonic is also now reaching out to teenagers with "Philharmonic Teens" (tel. 212/875–5732 for pre-concert info), a special one-hour concert for a mere $15. The Fourth of July concert in Central Park, accompanied by fireworks, is crowded but fun to attend if you have older children. 🏛 *Avery Fisher Hall, 10 Lincoln Center Plaza, New York 10023, tel. 212/875–5732 education office, 212/875–5656 audience service. Cost: $6–$21. When: year-round.*

Radio City Music Hall

(👫 6+) If your kids like spectacles, they'll love to see one on this vast stage, especially during the annual Christmas show. The costumes are lavish, there's lots of music and action, the laser lighting effects are spectacular, and the Rockettes are as impressive as ever in their precision dancing. We also admire the Art Deco interior of this huge 6,000-seat theater. Though the 45-minute backstage tours are expensive ($13.75 adults, $9 kids 12 and under), you do get to see all the backstage workings. The theater is scheduled to reopen after restorations in September 1999. 🏛 *1260 6th Ave., between 50th and 51st Sts., New York 10020, tel. 212/247–4777; tickets at box office or Ticketmaster 212/307–7171. Cost: $27–$72, depending on date and seat location. When: Christmas Spectacular, Nov.–Jan.*

CHAPTER 10

Rhode Island

Rhythm & Roots at Escoheag

(👫 **ALL**) Unusual instruments and rollicking fiddle and accordion music animate this annual three-day music and dance festival. Be sure to hear the strange Creole instrument, the *frottoir*. You make music by pulling spoons, bottle openers, and other metal scrapers across this instrument, which looks like a corrugated metal vest. A family stage presents music especially for kids as well as storytelling and costume-making for the Mardi Gras parade.

🏠 *Stepping Stone Ranch, Escoheag (mailing address: Rhythm & Roots at Escoheag, 239½ Genesee St., Utica, NY 13501), tel. 888/855–6940. Cost: $15 Fri., $30 Sat. or Sun. adults ($65 for all 3 days); discounts for advance purchase; kids 12 and under free. When: Labor Day weekend.*

Dance

Massachusetts

For folk dance events, contact the Country Dance and Song Society (17 New South St., Northampton, MA 01060, tel. 413/584–9913) or the Folk Arts Network (Box 867, Cambridge, MA 02238, tel. 617/491–6083 or 617/491–6084).

Boston Ballet Company

(👫 **5+**) The Boston Ballet's annual production of *The Nutcracker* is a lavish, traditional show, more fanciful and lighthearted than the New York City Ballet's version. Numerous *Nutcracker*-related activities in Boston add to the pleasure of the season. Visit the Ritz-Carlton hotel's specially decorated lobby, restaurant, and "Nutcracker suite." *Cinderella* is another Boston Ballet favorite. Best bets for families are the Saturday and Sunday matinees.

🏠 *19 Clarendon St., Boston 02116, tel. 617/695–6950. (Performances held at Wang Center for the Performing Arts, 270 Tremont St.) Cost: $12–$59. When: Oct.–mid-May.*

Jacob's Pillow Dance Festival

(👫 **5+**) High on a farm hillside perches the oldest contemporary dance center in the United States. Innovative and colorful modern troupes, such as the American Indian Dance Theatre, come here to perform the kind of dances that pique the interest of kids. Head also for the outdoor Inside/Out Stage, a raised platform surrounded by wooden benches and picnic tables, where families watch free performances while eating lunch or dinner. The view is pretty good from anywhere in the 600-seat barn-style main theater.

🏠 *Rte. 20, Becket 01223 (mailing address: Box 287, Lee 01238), tel. 413/243–0745. Cost: $15–$45. When: June–Sept.*

New York

Joyce Theater

(👫 **7+**) Many renowned small dance companies, such as the wild, acrobatic group Pilobolus, perform at this small theater each year. Most offer something for kids—the Ballet Tech company (formerly the Eliot Feld company) features child dancers at some performances. The best bets for kids are the Saturday family matinees at 2 PM; troupes perform kid-friendly selections from their regular repertory, and after the performance kids get to meet the dancers and receive autographs. Kids who attend two matinees automatically become Joyce Junior members; they get a third matinee free. Regular tickets cost about half what you pay for good seats at the New York City Ballet.

🏠 *175 8th Ave., New York 10001, tel. 212/242–0800. Cost: $26–$35 adults, $10 kids at family matinees. When: year-round.*

New York City Ballet

(♀♂ 4+) The New York City Ballet's annual production of *The Nutcracker* has spectacular sets and special effects (a tree that grows 40 ft tall) that impress even kids reared on *Jurassic Park* and *Independence Day*. With little ones, pick the matinee performances, because almost the entire audience will be families. The theater is big; if you can, spring for orchestra seats no farther back than row P for the best views. Be sure your kids go to the bathroom before you arrive, because intermission is a madhouse.

The company's Family Matinees, which features more kid-friendly ballets such as the comic *Harlequinade*, are also fun for kids because before the performance dancers demonstrate steps, give autographs, and answer questions such as "Why don't guys wear toe shoes?" Additional family matinees are planned for 1999, the 50th anniversary of the company.

🏠 *New York State Theater, Lincoln Center Plaza, New York 10023, tel. 212/870–5570. Cost: $20–$80. When: The Nutcracker late Nov.–Jan.; matinee series Jan.–Mar.*

New York Theatre Ballet

(♀♂ 3–12) Each year this small company performs several enchanting one-hour abridged versions of classical ballets such as *The Nutcracker* and *Cinderella* specifically for families. They are the best introduction to ballet for younger kids; productions zip along, plenty of comedic elements are introduced, and costumes and scenery are simply scaled-down versions of those flaunted by bigger companies. In New York City, *Nutcracker* performances take place in Florence Gould Hall, an intimate theater with red velvet seats. The company also performs elsewhere in New York City and tours throughout the United States.

🏠 *30 E. 31st St., New York 10016, tel. 212/679–0401. (Florence Gould Hall, 55 E. 59th St., New York 10022, tel. 212/355–6160.) Cost: $20 adults, $12.50 kids under 14. When: fall, winter, spring seasons.*

Vermont

Marlboro Morris Ale

(♀♂ 3–14) For more than 20 years morris dancers have gathered in Brattleboro and neighboring towns on Memorial Day weekend to celebrate spring the way people have for centuries in England—with intricate stepping, hopping, and leaping morris dances, performed in white and crimson costumes that have bells jingling from their knees and streamers flying. The music is spirited accordions, fiddles, and pipes.

🏠 *Mailing address: The Marlboro Morris Ale, c/o Rachel Popowich, Ashfield, MA 01330, tel. 413/625–9863. Cost: Donation. When: Memorial Day weekend; Sat. in Brattleboro; Sun. in various towns, ending in Newfane.*

Theater

Connecticut

Garde Arts Center

(♀♂ 6+) The interior of the state's last remaining vaudeville cinema house still looks like the movie palace it was in the 1920s, with marble floors and reliefs of a Moroccan parade on the walls. Just being here is as much fun as the family movie program or the children's theater and musicals, most by Theatreworks (*see below*) and the excellent Missoula Children's Theatre.

🏠 *312–329 State St., New London 06320, tel. 860/444–7373. Cost: $6 movies, $8–$10 productions. When: Sept.–June.*

Massachusetts

Boston Children's Theatre

(♀♂ 5–12) The fine actors in the 12 to 15 productions of classic children's literature and musicals each year are all between ages 10–18. Besides the main productions they give free performances in Boston parks during the summer. Our favorite show, *The Fairy Tale Forest & Enchanted Castle,* is presented in October at the George Wright Golf Course in Hyde Park; scenes take place in several locations and the audience walks to them. Dress warmly.

🏛 *647 Boylston St., Boston 02116, tel. 617/ 424–6634 info and tickets. (Performances in the C. Walsh Theatre, at Suffolk University, 55 Temple St., Boston.) Cost: $5–$15. When: Dec., Feb., Apr. Free outdoor performances June–Aug.*

Marco the Magi's "Le Grand David and His Own Spectacular Magic Company"

(👫 6+) This vaudeville-style magic show is a one-of-a-kind extravaganza of showmanship that's been around for 22 years. A tuxedoed doorman ushers you into the ornate lobby, where a clown sells goodies at the candy counter and magicians circulate, demonstrating tricks. The show is a fast-paced kaleidoscope of constantly changing props, gorgeous backdrops, brocaded costumes, disappearing and reappearing people, and goldfish reeled in from the audience. Sitting up front is crucial if you want to catch the intricate magic maneuvers. There's no reserved seating, so arrive early. The 2¼-hour performance has only one intermission, which makes it too long for very little kids. After the show members of the cast sign autographs and shake kids' hands in the lobby.

🏛 *Cabot Street Cinema Theatre, 286 Cabot St. (Rte. 128 to Rte. 62 [Exit 22E], then 2½ mi to Cabot St.), Beverly 01915, tel. 978/ 927–3677. Cost: $15 adults, $10 kids 11 and under. When: weekends, mid-Sept.–early Aug.; Larcom Theatre 2 Sat. a month mid-Oct.–May.*

Puppet Showplace

(👫 5–12) A resident company, visiting puppet troupes, and workshops for kids make this the place for puppets. Resident company shows (45 minutes–1 hour) are usually lively adaptations from folk and fairy tales. Arrive early so your kids can try out puppets on the little stage in the lobby. The brick-walled theater is small and friendly, the stage a basic platform with lights. After some performances kids have a chance to make their own puppet.

🏛 *32 Station St. (Boston T to Brookline Village on Green Line), Brookline 02146, tel. 617/731–6400. Cost: $6. When: year-round.*

Shakespeare and Company

(👫 13+) If you want your kids to see a Shakespeare play—and enjoy it—Edith Wharton's palatial estate, the Mount, with its four separate theaters is the place to come. The productions are lighthearted and fun, making the most of Shakespeare's fools, clowns, and wit. Most inexpensive are the noon performances in the Stables. Evening Main Stage productions outdoors on the rolling lawn are staged more elaborately.

🏛 *The Mount, Plunkett St. (junction Rtes. 7 and 7A), Box 865, Lenox 01240, tel. 413/ 637–3353. Cost: $6.50–$35, depending on production and time. When: July–Aug.*

Wheelock Family Theatre

(👫 ALL) Kids feel thoroughly comfortable in this 650-seat auditorium on the Wheelock College campus—and at all the theater productions, which are intended to appeal to the whole family, not just kids. Casts are a mirror of the world: Superman may be an African-American, Peter Pan may be Chinese, and there's a combination of old and young, students and (mostly) professional actors. Sets, costumes, and acting for the annual musical, the young children's show (usually an adaptation of a children's classic such as *Stuart Little*), and all the dramas are far superior to those in most family theaters.

🏛 *Wheelock Family Theatre, 180 The Riverway, Boston 02215, tel. 617/734–5200, ext. 2147. Cost: $10–$15. When: weekends Nov.– May.*

New Hampshire

New England Marionette Theatre

(**†† 7+**) Marionette versions of operas are the specialty here; two charming one-hour productions, one in spring, one in winter, are adapted or written for kids and sung in English, and after the performance kids can meet the puppeteers. In *Magic Fantasy*, a version of Mozart's *The Magic Flute*, a little girl searches for the flute. Another regular production is *Amahl and the Night Visitors*. The 2-ft-tall classic marionettes are meticulously hand-carved and the seats are plush. Regular shows are for kids 12 and up; they're 2½ hours long and sung in the original language with projected subtitles.
🏠 *24–26 Main St., Peterborough 03458 (mailing address: Box 141, Peterborough 03458), tel. 603/924–4333 or 888/636–7372. Cost: $14 adults, $10 kids under 12 for family shows; $22–$24 adults, $20 students for regular shows. When: weekends May–Dec.*

New York

Broadway and Off-Broadway

(**†† 4+**) The excitement and electricity of attending a performance on Broadway or elsewhere in New York City are paralleled nowhere else in the world. Kids under 10 seem to like many of the musicals, such as *Les Misérables* and *Cats*. The New Amsterdam Theatre (214 W. 42nd St., tel. 212/282–2900), which was refurbished and revitalized by Disney and reopened in 1997, plans to show family musicals, like the big hit of 1998, *The Lion King*. The big drawback to all Broadway shows is cost; an orchestra ticket can be $60 or more. Try to get half-priced tickets at TKTS the day of performance. *See also* Chapter 12.

International Festival of Puppet Theater

(**†† ALL**) The very best puppet troupes from as many as 16 countries perform at various theaters around New York City in this three-week-long biennial festival started by Jim Henson. (Several also tour to other U.S. cities.) The next one is scheduled for the year 2000. Be aware that some productions are strictly adult fare, but appropriate performances for kids are clearly designated. Special films of puppet performances are scheduled at the Guggenheim Museum (*see also* Chapter 12) in conjunction with the festival.
🏠 *The Jim Henson Foundation, 117 E. 69th St., New York 10021, tel. 212/279–4200 (Ticket Central box office). Cost: $12–$30 adults, $10–$20 kids. When: Last 3 wks in Sept.*

Mac-Haydn Theatre

(**†† 5–9**) You can take advantage of in-the-round seating to see the well-produced musicals for children and adults performed by this theater's resident troupe. No seat is more than 30 ft from the stage, so when it really rained in *Singin' in the Rain*, we got the full effect. The scripts and music of the children's shows are original, and the stories are more substantive than in many folk and fairy-tale theater productions. Each one includes audience participation and a photograph session with the cast afterward.
🏠 *Rte. 203 (½ mi west of village), Chatham 12037 (mailing address: Box 204, Chatham 12037), tel. 518/392–9292. Cost: $16.90–$18.90 adults, $9 kids 12 and under; kids' shows $7. When: late May–mid-Sept.; kids shows July–Labor Day.*

New Victory Theater

(**†† 7+**) The historic Victory theater reopened in 1995 as New York City's first performing-arts theater on Broadway strictly for kids and families. Performances, which range from a classic film series to vaudeville artists to fantastical musicals to the theatrical Canadian circus, Cirque Eloize, are the very best. The interior is splendid—carved plaster covered in gold leaf, ornate boxes that seat four, and a fancy domed ceiling. A yearly family membership ($25) entitles you to 40% discounts on tickets and coupons for parking and restaurants.

🏠 209 W. 42nd St., New York 10036 (mailing address: Box 21158, New York 10129), tel. 212/239–6255. Cost: $8 films, $10–$25 regular performances. When: year-round.

The Paper Bag Players

(👫 3–8) The hour-long original productions of this award-winning children's theater company are fast-paced shows of skits, dances, and mime, accompanied by electric harpsichord and kazoo. The gaily painted scenery and costumes are ingeniously made from cardboard boxes and brown paper bags—the company's trademark. Young kids especially like the chances to shout warnings, join in songs, even scream as loud as they can. The company travels throughout the Northeast.

🏠 50 Riverside Dr., tel. 212/362–0431 or 800/777–2247. Cost: $15–$20 When: Jan.–Mar. at Sylvia and Danny Kaye Playhouse, 68th St. between Park and Lexington Aves., tel. 212/772–4448. Elsewhere in the Northeast on tour.

The Puppetworks

(👫 3–11) The classic marionettes this company uses in their 45-minute shows are made right in the basement of the small, 75-seat theater, a few blocks west of Prospect Park in Brooklyn. Each year three 19th-century fairy tales are produced. The theater displays hundreds of marionettes from past performances on the walls. On Sundays six months of the year the company also puts on shows at the Children's Aid Society in Manhattan.

🏠 338 6th Ave., Brooklyn 11251, tel. 718/965–3391. Cost: $8 adults, $5 kids 12 and under. When: year-round, weekends.

Theatreworks USA

(👫 6–13) Each year this award-winning theater group puts on 14 different one-hour plays and musicals for children, in New York City and elsewhere on tour. They are among the very best productions around for kids, with top-class scripts, music, sets, and acting. Some shows are based on beloved kids' books, stories, and classics, such as Beverly Cleary's Ramona Quimby, The Three Little Pigs, and Oliver Twist; others take on historical subjects, as in The Color of Justice, a play about Thurgood Marshall and Brown vs. Board of Education, or their new play about Paul Robeson. Historical plays are best for kids 8 and up. In New York City they offer theater parties after the 10:30 AM performance.

🏠 890 Broadway, New York 10003, tel. 212/677–5959 (performances held at Promenade Theatre, 2162 Broadway at 76th St.). Cost: $18.50. When: New York Oct.–Apr. and July (July performances free; at Tribeca Performing Arts Center at Manhattan Community College, 199 Chambers St., tel. 212/642–6754).

Rhode Island

All-Childrens Theatre Ensemble

(👫 3+) The talented 8- to 17-year-olds who make up this ensemble put on some fabulous productions; those for younger kids call for much participation from the audience. A series of 40-minute plays based on familiar stories is for kids 3 to 11, but the group also performs plays for the entire family. Some are written especially for them; others, like Annie, are standard fare. One of the most interesting series are the winning plays by teenagers who compete in the annual playwriting contest. Some productions tour.

🏠 1 Allens Ave., Providence 02903, tel. 401/331—7174 (performances at Vartan Gregorian School Theatre, 455 Wickenden St., 02903). Cost: $6–$8 adults, $4–$5 kids 3–17. When: year-round.

Vermont

Bread and Puppet Theater

(👫 **ALL**) This troupe is known internationally for performances of social and political commentary, which feature towering,
20-ft-tall puppets parading on stilts. You can
see them at many festivals in the Northeast
and on September weekends and during
their own annual festival they perform in a
natural outdoor amphitheater on the farm
where they live.
🏠 *Rte. 122 (1 mi east of Rte. 16; Exit 25 off
I–91), Glover 05839, tel. 802/525–3031.
Cost: Donation for museum and performances
at the farm; price varies elsewhere, usually not
more than $10. When: Museum open May–
Oct., daily 10–5; weekend performances Sept.;
major festival weekend usually in Aug.*

Spectacles

New York

The Big Apple Circus

(👫 **2 – 12**) The Big Apple is the best circus in the country for young kids because
it's small—only one ring—but still has top-
class international performers. Each season
a brand-new theme and show thread
together the many phenomenal acts of
clowns, aerialists, acrobats, and animals.
We like to attend during the Christmas
season, when the big circus tent is at New
York City's Lincoln Center, and the color
inside contrasts with the snow outside; it
also has seasons in Boston; Hanover, New
Hampshire; Great Barrington, Massachusetts; and at the Shelburne Museum in Vermont. This is a circus kids eventually grow
out of.
🏠 *35 W. 35th St., New York 10001-2205,
tel. 212/268–2500. Cost: $15–$55, depending on seat location. When: New York City late
Oct.–Jan.; call for schedule at other locations.*

Ringling Brothers and Barnum & Bailey Circus

(👫 **8+**) It's a huge, three-ring spectacle,
with more animal acts (including 15–20 elephants) and more performers (150) than
the Big Apple Circus. It's almost too big for
very little kids, but they will have fun in the
new kids' programs before the performance, when they can meet the clowns and
have their faces painted. In the past, trapeze
artists, the Flying Vargas, and Ariana—the
human arrow projected from a giant cross-
bow—have wowed us. Each year there's a
new show with new performers.
🏠 *For schedule: 8607 Westwood Center Dr.,
Vienna, VA 22182, tel. 703/448–4000, or call
Madison Square Garden, tel. 212/465–6741.
Cost: $10–$30. Many discounts. When: usually
New York, Mar.–Apr.; Boston, Oct.; Providence
and Hartford, spring.*

Vermont

Circus Smirkus

(👫 **ALL**) The fast-paced two-hour show
of this charming little youth circus (the only
touring youth circus in the world) features
the most talented and accomplished 9- to
18-year-olds from circus schools all over the
world, including Circus Smirkus's own summer circus camp. The circus performs in small
towns across New England (call for schedule)
but starts and ends the season with shows at
the circus camp in Greensboro.
🏠 *1 Circus Rd., Greensboro 05841, tel. 802/
533–7125, 802/533–7443, or 800/532–
7443. Cost: $10 adults, $8 kids 4–12. When:
July–late Aug.*

Herrmann's Royal Lipizzan Stallions

(👫 **3+**) These famous white horses,
bred since the 16th century to be the world's
most fabulous horses for exhibition and battle maneuvers, parade around the sand ring
in Lipizzan Park, on an island in Lake Champlain, their summer residence. They keep
time to music, perform astonishing acrobatic

leaps, rear up on their hind legs, and perform military dressage. After the show, you can meet the riders and pat the horses at the stables. If you can, obtain a video of Disney's movie *The Miracle of the White Stallions*, which tells the story of how they were rescued at the end of World War II.

🏠 *Lipizzan Park, Rte. 2 (Take Exit 17 off I–89), North Hero 05474 (for information, Lake Champlain Islands Chamber of Commerce, Box 213, North Hero 05474, tel. 802/372–5683). Cost: $15 adults, $8 kids 6–12. Fri. night ½ price. When: mid-July–Aug.*

PART III

PLACES

Cities and Family-Friendly Resort Areas

BOSTON

11

ON THE TRAIL OF PAUL REVERE, SWAN BOATS AND DUCKS, AND THE COUNTRY'S BEST ICE CREAM

To Gavin and my panel of kids who live in and around it, Boston is much more than a city where the country's history comes alive, even though its crooked streets are packed with sites they have learned about in school. To them, the home of the Boston Tea Party, Paul Revere's midnight ride, and the "shot heard round the world" is also a place of harbors and rivers and boats of all sizes tied up at wharves designed for walking and exploring. Kids like Boston's contrast of old and new, the many kid-oriented museums and theaters, and the fact that it's a small, clean, cheerful, cozy city.

Though our family loves New York City, we do find Boston more manageable and pleasant and welcoming to families. The one danger (for us, anyway) is concentrating too much on the educational possibilities of its historic sites and museums. You're missing much of Boston's pleasure if you don't picnic in one of the beautiful parks and stroll in one of its fascinating neighborhoods: the North End, the waterfront, Beacon Hill, Downtown, Chinatown, Back Bay, Charlestown, and, across the Charles River, Cambridge. Each has a distinct flavor, and because Boston is so compact, you can visit more than one in a day if you wish. A weekend is barely enough time to get started; with a week you can begin to know the city.

Boston's suburbs, such as Brookline, also have many attractions for kids and are easy to get to by public transportation. Several towns close to Boston are worth visiting for a day of your trip: Lexington and Concord for revolutionary sites; Salem for witch museums; Plymouth for Plimoth Plantation and, of course, the Rock.

Boston feels safer than New York, but families should realize that they need to use the same kind of caution they would in any large city—stick to well-lighted streets at night, stay alert, and don't consider walking through Boston Common and the Boston Public Garden after dark. You will not see as many homeless people sleeping or begging for money as you do in New York City. I'm not sure that I would let young teenagers travel all around the city by themselves during the day, but I didn't feel worried when my son (at a younger age) walked a few blocks back to the hotel by himself or confined his explorations to busy Faneuil Hall Marketplace. With small children, your main concern is Boston's crazy drivers; when crossing streets, hang on to energetic little ones. Kids should know what to do and where to go in case they're separated from you.

The Basics

How to Find Out What's Going On

The **Greater Boston Convention & Visitors Bureau** (Two Copley Place, Suite 105, Boston 02116–6501, tel. 617/536–4100 or 800/888–5515; open weekdays 9–5) is your best source of information on everything from events to maps to hotel packages; it's the most helpful and well-organized city visitor bureau I've ever dealt with. The travel planner includes a list of family-friendly hotel packages, an events calendar, and attractions. For $5.25, they'll send you the comprehensive Official Visitor Information Kit. Don't forget to ask about the Family ValuePass, which offers discounts at museums, shops, and restaurants. They even publish (for $2.50) *Kids Love Boston,* an entertaining large-type guidebook written for kids. They also sell the Boston CityPass, a book of discount tickets (half-price) to six attractions and museums with plenty of kid appeal ($26.50 adults; $13.50 kids 13–18); these include the New England Aquarium, the Museum of Science, the Museum of Fine Arts, the Isabella Gardner Museum, the John Hancock Observatory, and the John F. Kennedy Library and Museum. Be aware, though, that some hotels in Boston offer family discounts to some of these destinations, so the pass may not be as useful to you as the New York CityPass is. The Visitors Bureau Web site is www.bostonusa.com.

Boston by Phone (tel. 888/733–2678) is a telephone line sponsored by the Visitor Bureau that connects your call for free to hotels, restaurants, shops, and more.

VISITOR INFORMATION CENTERS.
Boston Common Information Center (147 Tremont St., no phone; Park St. stop on Red Line T; open weekdays 9–5, weekends summer only), on the Tremont Street side of Boston Common, has brochures, free maps,

and information on sightseeing tours; here you can purchase subway and bus tourist passes. **Prudential Center Visitor Information Center** (800 Boylston St.; open weekdays 8:30–5, Sat. 10–6, Sun. 11–6), in the Center Court of the Prudential Center, offers similar information. **Cambridge Visitor Information Booth** (Harvard Sq. [booth, call for hours], office at 18 Brattle St., Cambridge 02238, tel. 800/862–5678; open weekdays 9–5) will help you plan your time in Cambridge. At the **Boston National Historical Park Visitor Center** (15 State St., tel. 617/242–5642; open daily 9–5) knowledgeable park rangers can answer your questions about historic Boston; there are also very clean public bathrooms—important, as many of the buildings on the Freedom Trail have no rest rooms.

NEWSPAPERS, MAGAZINES, AND BOOKS. The following publications are available on newsstands, in supermarkets, and in bookstores:

The *Boston Globe* (135 William T. Morrissey Blvd., tel. 617/929–2000), Boston's main newspaper, publishes a "Calendar" section every Thursday that highlights family-oriented activities.

The *Boston Parents' Paper* (Box 1777, Boston 02130, tel. 617/522–1515), published monthly, has a calendar of events and happenings for kids. It is available free at libraries, supermarkets, museums, and children's shops.

BOOKS FOR KIDS. *Kidding Around Boston* by Helen Byers (John Muir Publications, 1997), for kids 8–12, contains simple maps and combines a history and sightseeing overview of the various neighborhoods, along with lots of interesting facts.

Kids Love Boston, published by the Greater Boston Convention & Visitors Bureau (see *above*) for the same age group, is shorter, organized by subject (museums, open space, cool for kids, and so on), and includes a short glossary of Boston lingo.

Boston's historic sites meant more to Gavin when he visited them because he'd read up on the Revolution. *Sam the Minuteman* by Nathaniel Benchley (HarperCollins, 1987) is an easy-to-read book for 4- to 8-year-olds. *And Then What Happened, Paul Revere?* by Jean Fritz (Scholastic, 1996), for kids 6–10, tells the story of Revere's life and famous ride in an amusing way. *Johnny Tremain* by Esther Forbes (Dell, 1987), for kids 8–13, is an exciting novel set in Boston at the time of the Revolution. Chances are younger kids (3–7) have already read Robert McCloskey's beloved *Make Way for Ducklings* (Puffin Books, 1993), about a duck family's search for a home, which they find at the pond in Boston's Public Garden.

Arriving and Departing

BY BUS. Greyhound (2 South Station, tel. 800/231–2222) offers direct trips or connections to all major cities in North America. **Peter Pan Trailways** (700 Atlantic Ave. by South Station, tel. 800/343–9999) connects Boston with cities in Massachusetts, Connecticut, New Hampshire, and New York.

BY CAR. Three major highways funnel into Boston. Interstate 95 links it with New York City, southern Connecticut, and Providence, and continues north through the city to New Hampshire and Maine. The Massachusetts Turnpike (a toll road known as the "Mass Pike"), I–90, runs east–west through the middle of the state, intersecting with I–91, which goes north to Vermont, and the New York Thruway. In Boston the Mass Pike intersects with I–93, the main route from Boston to northwest New England.

BY PLANE. Some 40 major airlines fly to Boston's Logan International Airport (tel. 800/235–6426), about 3 mi northeast of central Boston on the other side of Boston Harbor. If you can, choose a carrier that arrives at either Terminal A (Cape Air, Continental, Continental Express, East Wind, and MidWest) or Terminal C (Delta, TWA,

and United) because both terminals offer a special kids' play space, Kidport. The one at Terminal C is much bigger.

Between the Airport and Boston: Traffic from the airport to Downtown Boston is not quite as bad now that there are three harbor tunnels (except during rush hour), but there's still the construction of the new central artery tunnel between Downtown Boston and the waterfront to consider. The fastest and easiest (and most appealing) way to get into the city remains the **Airport Water Shuttle** (tel. 617/439–3131 or 800/235–6426), comfortable commuter boats that take seven minutes to cross the harbor between the airport's Boat Dock and Rowes Wharf in Downtown Boston. Buses from each terminal transport passengers to the water shuttle. The cost is $10 for adults; children under 12 travel free. A bargain choice is the subway (MBTA, the "T") from Airport Station to Downtown, which costs only cents. Free shuttle buses (Nos. 22 and 33) connect terminals to the T station. Either of these is my choice over taxis (available in queues outside each terminal, tel. 617/561–1769), which cost about $17 if traffic is light. For general information on all ground transportation call Massachusetts Ground Transportation Information Line (tel. 800/235–6426).

BY TRAIN. On Amtrak (tel. 617/482–3660 or 800/872–7245), the northeast corridor route from Washington, D.C., New York, and Philadelphia ends at Boston's South Station (Atlantic Ave. and Summer St., ticket office tel. 617/345–7451), with its big, light-filled concourse busy with food vendors. New high-speed train service from New York City to Boston (only 2¾ hours) will begin in the fall of 1999. The "Lake Shore Limited," Amtrak's service to and from the Midwest and western New York State destinations, also terminates here. Some trains also stop at Back Bay Station. Commuter trains serving points north and west of the city come into North Station (Causeway and Friend Sts., tel. 617/722–3200).

Getting Around Boston

Forget about driving a car in this city; the central Downtown area consists of crooked, narrow streets, mostly one-way (many were originally cow paths leading to and from the Boston Common). In addition, until 2004 traffic will be even worse than usual because of what the city refers to as "the Big Dig." This project involves building a central artery tunnel with an eight-lane highway beneath the existing elevated highway that divides Downtown and the waterfront. While the city is doing a good job of re-routing both cars and pedestrians, don't take a car when going to the waterfront if you don't have to; take the T instead. With the exception of several public garages, parking lots are expensive. Two central places to park are the underground garage at Boston Common and at the Prudential Center.

TAKE A WALK. Boston is relatively small and compact, with many parks, a long accessible harbor front, and several pedestrian-only marketplaces. Two walking routes are even marked on the sidewalk with a red stripe (the **Freedom Trail**) and a blue stripe (the **Harborwalk**). Sturdy shoes are a must, however, especially on the brick sidewalks of Beacon Hill and the cobblestones of open market spaces such as Faneuil Hall Marketplace. The other pedestrian problem here is the traffic. Beware of aggressive drivers when crossing streets, even if the light is with you.

The oldest part of Boston is a peninsula shaped like a fist, bounded by Boston Harbor to the north and east; the Fort Point Channel to the east; and the Charles River to the west, separating Boston from Cambridge. The focal point of the peninsula is **Boston Common and the Public Garden**, at the center. To the northeast lies the **North End**, the city's oldest section, whose hodgepodge of streets is the home of the Italian community, with colorful cafés, good-smelling bakeries, and frequent summer festivals. **Beacon Hill**, to the west, has cobblestone streets lined with trees and elegant

brick town houses; it's largely a residential area. To the east, wedged between the Common and the waterfront, is **Downtown**, comprising several distinct areas—the department stores of Downtown Crossing, a pedestrian mall, historic sites on the Freedom Trail, Faneuil Hall Marketplace, and the financial district. Just south of it sits **Chinatown**, only a few blocks long, much smaller and less crowded than its New York City counterpart, yet still the third-largest in the United States. The **Waterfront**, with boats docked at every wharf, small parks, the aquarium, and several museums appealing to kids, borders Boston Harbor. Trees, cafés, boutiques, elegant town houses, the library, Symphony Hall, and a couple of malls line the grid of fashionable **Back Bay**, which begins at the west end of the Public Garden and extends north to the Esplanade. To its west is the **Fenway**, a place of world-class museums, a sprawling park, and the Red Sox ballpark.

Charlestown, across the Charlestown Bridge from the North End, harbors one of the city's highlights for kids, the Charlestown Navy Yard, where the USS *Constitution* is permanently docked. Across the Charles River to the west is **Cambridge**, actually a separate city, home to Harvard University; it's good for people-watching and shopping, especially for teens.

RIDE THE T. Boston's subway is called the "T" (short for MBTA, Massachusetts Bay Transit Authority), and large signs with a black T in a circle mark the stations. The four lines—green, blue, orange, and red—radiate outward from central Boston, connecting at the hub of Downtown stations. Tokens, available at booths or vending machines in each station, cost 85¢ for adults and 40¢, twice for children 5–11, but additional fares are charged for destinations outside a central zone. You may save money by buying one-, three-, or seven-day Boston Passport Tourist Passes ($5, $9, and $18 respectively, available at visitor information centers, many Downtown hotels, train stations, and the airport T station); they offer unlimited travel on the subway and local buses.

If you have a baby or toddler, be aware that on the Green Line trains you must climb several steps to board and must collapse strollers; on all other lines, you can wheel them right on. Note also that in some stations tracks are flush with the platform, so little kids don't realize when they are too close; hold their hands tightly and keep them well back.

Riding the T, except during rush hour, is our preferred way to get around Boston besides walking; kids find it nicer and more fun than the subway in New York. A large subway map is posted in each station; you can also pick up a pocket copy at the Park Street Station, visitor centers, and some hotels. Most stations seem safe, although, as in all cities, be alert, especially at night, and don't board deserted cars. In our experience the T's token clerks and other passengers are friendly and helpful. You can also call the Massachusetts Bay Transportation Authority's 24-hour travel information line (tel. 617/222–3200) for trip-planning directions.

TAKE THE BUS. Boston's bus system provides crosstown service and routes that extend farther into the suburbs than the T does; I find it relatively complicated, though efficient. Rather than poring over bus maps (available at the Park Street T station information booth, Downtown Crossing and Government Center stations), call the MBTA's travel information line (see *above*) for bus numbers, schedules, and stop locations. Buses charge 60¢, 30¢ for kids 5–11; you must have exact change. The one-, three-, and seven-day tourist pass (see *above*) is also accepted on Downtown buses.

HIRE A TAXI. Unlike New York, Boston is not a taxi town. You need to head for a hotel taxi stand or telephone for a cab. Two companies that offer 24-hour service are **Checker** (tel. 617/536–7000) and **ITOA** (Independent Taxi Operators Association; tel. 617/426–8700). Boston's one-way streets

and tangled traffic make for convoluted routes that add up; the current rate is $1.50 for the first ¼ mi, 25¢ per ⅛ mi thereafter.

Family-Friendly Tours

(👫 7 – 12) **Boston by Little Feet.** Games, activities, and amazing facts (we learned that the City Hall Plaza contains 2½ million bricks) fill these one-hour Downtown walking tours that introduce kids to history and architecture. Stops at both new and historic buildings (some on the Freedom Trail) give kids a sense of more than just the "old stuff," as one 10-year-old put it. Children must be accompanied by an adult.
🏠 *Boston by Foot, 77 N. Washington St., tel. 617/367–2345 or 617/367–3766. Meet on Congress St. at Statue of Samuel Adams in front of Faneuil Hall. Cost: $8 adults, $6 kids 12 and under. Reservations advised holidays and peak weekends. May–Oct., Sat. and Mon. at 10, Sun. at 2.*

(👫 5 – 15) **Boston Duck Tours.** The hottest tours in Boston are the 80-minute city-and-river excursions aboard brightly colored restored World War II amphibious landing vehicles. This is the most entertaining overall tour of the city—the vehicle cruises by major sights on land, then plunges into the Charles River for a view of it all from the water. You won't escape without purchasing something from the line of souvenir "Duck-ware." Get tickets early—they often sell out by noon.
🏠 *Pick up at 101 Huntington Ave. by the Prudential Center, tickets inside next to Levi Store, tel. 617/723–3825. Cost: $20 adults, $16 students, $10 kids 4–12, 25¢ kids 3 and under, plus tax. Reservations for groups only. Season Apr.–Nov., every ½ hr 9 AM–5:30.*

(👫 7 – 15) **Boston Harbor Cruises.** Viewing Boston and all its piers and fishing boats from the water gave us a totally new sense of the city. For kids we favor one of the shortest tours: Boston Harbor Cruise's 45-minute USS *Constitution* trip, a narrated trip around the inner harbor that stops at the

Charlestown Navy Yard. You can get off to explore the *Constitution*, then board another boat an hour or so later.

🏛 *Boston Harbor Cruises, Long Wharf (blue ticket booth), Boston 02110, tel. 617/227–4321. Cost: $8 adults, $6 kids 3–12. Open daily May–mid Oct.*

👫 4–15 **Charles River Boat Company Tours**. We boarded one of these single-deck boats for a 50-minute narrated ride up the Cambridge side of the Charles River and back down the Boston side. The views of the two skylines are truly special.

🏛 *Pickup at CambridgeSide Galleria, tel. 617/621–3001. Cost: $8 adults, $5 kids 12 and under. Open May, Sept. weekends only noon–5; Memorial Day–Labor Day, daily noon–5.*

👫 7–15 **Freedom Trail**. If your kids are history buffs, they may enjoy the 90-minute guided tour of five sites on the Freedom Trail led by the national park's rangers. How interesting it is depends partly on the ranger leading the tour, but it is free.

🏛 *National Historical Park Visitor Center, 15 State St., 02109, tel. 617/242–5642.*

👫 5–10 **Historic Neighborhood Foundation**. Several 90-minute walking tours geared for kids focus on things like how cobblestone walks were built. The Make Way for Ducklings walk, our favorite (for kids 5–8), follows the route taken by Mr. and Mrs. Mallard in Robert McCloskey's book from Boston Common through Beacon Hill and around to the Public Garden.

🏛 *99 Bedford St., 02111, tel. 617/426–1885. Cost: $7 adults, $5 children. Reservations essential. Open May–June, Sat. weather permitting; July–Aug., Fri.–Sat.*

Pit Stops

The best places to find clean, pleasant bathrooms: all museums, though only the Children's Museum and the Museum of Science have diaper-changing facilities; National Park Visitor Centers at the Charlestown Navy Yard and along the Freedom Trail Down-town (no bathrooms in most historic buildings along the trail); major department stores; shopping malls and markets such as the Prudential Center, Copley Place, City Place in the Transportation Building, CambridgeSide Galleria, and Faneuil Hall Marketplace; the Christian Science Center; the Boston Public Library on Boylston Street; and South Station. In Cambridge your best bet, outside of museums, are the second-floor rest rooms in the Coop in Harvard Square. If you're desperate, most shops will allow children to use their private facilities.

Emergencies

Children's Hospital (300 Longwood Ave., tel. 617/355–6000, emergency room 617/355–6611) is the best place to call. **Inn-House Doctor** (tel. 617/859–1776) is a 24-hour, seven-day-a-week service that provides doctors (including pediatricians) who make house calls to hotels, apartments, and bed-and-breakfasts. A doctor returns your call in 15 minutes and arrives within an hour. Expect to pay between $150 and $250. Referrals for emergency dental services are available through the Metropolitan District Dental Society (tel. 508/651–3521). **CVS Pharmacy** (155 Charles St., Boston, tel. 617/523–4372) is open until midnight; CVS Pharmacy in Cambridge (Porter Square, tel. 617/876–5519) is open 24 hours.

Baby-Sitters

At many of Boston's hotels the concierge keeps a list of screened staff members willing to baby-sit when not on duty. Often this is the least expensive route to go. Two agencies are **Personal Touch** (87 Summer St., tel. 617/451–2052), which uses screened college students and professional women and charges $12.60 per hour for one to three children, with a four-hour minimum, billed to rooms in some hotels; and **Parents in a Pinch** (45 Bartlett Crescent, Brookline, tel. 617/739–5437), which has trained and screened sitters, many of them students, and charges about $30 (half day or evening) to $40 (full day) plus $8.50 per hour for two children (the office is only open weekdays from 8 to 4).

When to Go

Boston has so many museums and indoor attractions for kids that there's plenty to do here even in the coldest winter months. In early April there's still a possibility of a blizzard. From mid-April, when the Swan Boats return to the Public Garden, through June, and in September and October, the temperature is generally delightful for walking around. For festivals, especially those in the North End, summer is the best time, though the city can be very hot and muggy, with occasional heat waves in the 90s. When that happens, there are many pleasant ways to get out on the water where it's cooler, or head for beaches.

Scoping Out Boston

Serendipities

Of the sights my Boston kids' panel consider most "Boston," a surprising number turn out to be free or very inexpensive.

IN THE PUBLIC GARDEN AND ON THE COMMON

(**ii 0 – 8**) Ride on a Swan Boat. The oldest and most famous children's attractions in the city are the pedal-powered Swan Boats that circle the Public Garden's Lagoon, a hit ever since they debuted in 1877. Rides last 12 minutes, just long enough for little kids to want a second one. Other Make Way for Ducklings landmarks hereabouts: the shiny bronze statues of the mallard brood just through the gates at the corner of Beacon and Charles streets; and the banks of the Lagoon, where well-behaved and well-fed ducks will soon gather if you arrive with a bag of bread crumbs (one prime spot is by the large weeping willow at the base of the bridge).

🏠 *On the Lagoon, Boston Public Gardens, near Boylston and Charles Sts., tel. 617/522–1966. Park St. stop on Red Line. Cost: $1.75 adults, 95¢ kids under 13. Open July–mid-Aug., daily 10–5; mid-Apr.–June and late Aug.–mid-Sept., daily 10–4.*

(**ii 1 – 10**) Wade in the Frog Pond. On a hot summer day, it's a Boston tradition for kids to wade and splash in this large, shallow concrete depression in the Common below the Soldiers and Sailors monument. Just about every little kid on my Boston panel listed this as one of the "most fun things to do" in the city.

🏠 *North side of the Common, just in from Beacon St. and the State House.*

BACK BAY

(**ii 5 – 12**) Old John Hancock Building weather forecast. A column of light panels on the Old John Hancock Building (not the new Hancock skyscraper) will give you the weather prediction if you can interpret the code. A simple rhyme helps kids remember it: "Steady blue, clear view/ Flashing blue, clouds due/Steady red, rain ahead/Flashing red, snow instead." In baseball season, flashing red means the Red Sox game is postponed.

🏠 *Corner of Berkeley and Stuart Sts.*

TRAINS AND SUBWAYS

(**ii 3 – 10**) Five-Minute Train Ride. An incredibly cheap (85¢ adults, 45¢ kids 5–11, free under 5) and short real train excursion is the five-minute ride from refurbished South Station (near the Children's Museum) to Back Bay Station (not far from the Swan Boats at the Public Garden).

(**ii 2 – 13**) Ride in the First Subway Car. Kids who've never traveled by subway usually find staring down the dark tunnel and glimpsing a lighted station ahead fun. Avoid rush hours if you can.

NEIGHBORHOODS

(**ii ALL**) North End. Boston's Italian-American district starts at Hanover Street or Salem Street and spreads north. Zigzag up the side streets until a good bakery smell draws you into a café. Food and festivals pull us to this neighborhood, along with a few Freedom Trail sites such as Paul Revere's House and Old North Church. Hanover Street is lined with cafés, all with different atmospheres. Dairy Fresh Candies (57 Salem St.) displays all manner of sweets, and on Prince Street, one door in from Salem Street, Parizale's Bakery sells all shapes and sizes of bread. You can watch cheese being made at Purity Cheese (corner of Cross and Endicott Sts., Tues.–Fri. mornings). Don't come on a Sunday, when many shops are closed, unless there's a festival on. Two of our favorites are the festivals of St. Joseph at the end of July and St. Anthony (the largest) at the end of August (for festival information, tel. 617/635–3911).

(👫👫 10 – 15) **Harvard Square, Cambridge**. The place where teenagers hanker to hang out is around Harvard Square, which isn't a square at all but the chaotic intersection of Massachusetts Avenue, Brattle Street, and John F. Kennedy Street. It's right outside the gates of Harvard University, and the atmosphere is youthful and eccentric; teens may ask you, "Do you have to walk around with us? Couldn't we meet you someplace in an hour or two? . . ." For funky used clothing and T-shirt shops, bookstores (we last counted 25), cafés, and street performers from bagpipers to magicians, it can't be beat. Don't miss the zany Harvard Lampoon building on Mt. Auburn Street or the Harvard Coop (see Shopping, below) across from the Red Line T station.

ALL AROUND THE TOWN

(👫👫 2 – 12) **Animal statues**. Boston's public sculptures include many animals. In front of F.A.O. Schwarz (corner of Boylston and Berkeley Sts.; Arlington stop on Green Line T) you can't miss the 12-ft-tall **bronze bear**, which weighs 6,112 pounds. Atop Faneuil Hall (in Dock Square; State St. stop on Orange or Blue Line T) is a copper-gilded **grasshopper weather vane** that's been spin-

ning since 1742, supposedly a symbol of good luck. The four huge **marble Foo dogs** (to us they look like lions) at the base of the 36-ft-high gate at the entrance to Chinatown (Beach and Edinboro Sts.) are said to guard Chinatown against evil spirits. And of course there are the **ducklings** in the Public Garden (see above).

Monuments, Markets, and Historic Sites

See the appropriate chapters in Part II, Pleasures, for sites whose costs and hours are not given below.

IN BOSTON

(👫👫 10 – 15) **African Meeting House and Black Heritage Trail**. The oldest African-American church in the United States helped escaped slaves find safe houses along the Underground Railroad. Boston has a surprising wealth of sites important in black history—in 1790, Massachusetts was the only state with free black citizens and no slaves—and the National Park Service offers a guided walking tour, called the Black Heritage Trail. 🏛 *8 Smith Court at Joy St., tel. 617/742–5415. Bowdoin stop on Blue Line T. Cost: Free.*

(👫👫 ALL) **Boston Waterfront**. The renovated waterfront, where clipper ships once docked, is now a place for watching boats, sitting in cafés and parks, visiting the aquarium, and just strolling. Until "the Big Dig" is finished in 2004 there will be construction between Downtown Boston and the waterfront. To get there, your best bet, if you are not staying on the waterfront, is taking the T. See also Chapter 2. 🏛 *Follow Atlantic Ave.*

(👫👫 ALL) **Faneuil Hall Marketplace** (also called **Quincy Market**). A shop-lined cobblestoned plaza, facing Faneuil Hall, is one of our favorite places for people-watching, free entertainment, and food stalls. See also Chapter 2. 🏛 *State and Congress Sts., tel. 617/523–1300. State St. stop on Blue Line T.*

★★ 7 – 15 **Freedom Trail.** A prominent red line in the sidewalk marks a 3-mi walking route past 16 Colonial or revolutionary landmarks. It's one of the city's chief attractions; we found the walk tiring, however. You can pick up brochures on the trail from the National Park Service Visitor Center (see above). See also Chapter 2.

★★ 5 – 15 **John Hancock Tower Observatory.** The observation deck on the 60th floor of the tallest skyscraper in New England is a good place to get an overview of Boston. See also Chapter 2.
🏠 200 Clarendon St., tel. 617/572–6429.

★★ 8 – 15 **Old Granary Burying Ground.** Old shady graveyards appeal to my family; wedged between buildings on a busy modern street is this historic one, where Paul Revere, Sam Adams, and John Hancock are buried. The tilting slate headstones, some from as early as 1660, are gruesomely decorated with old-fashioned skulls and crossbones (no rubbings permitted).
🏠 Tremont and Park Sts. Park St. stop on Red Line T.

★★ 7 – 15 **Old North Church.** The code was "One if by land, two if by sea," and when two lanterns were hung in the steeple of this church in April 1775, Paul Revere galloped off on his midnight ride, warning the militia that the British were arriving by sea. A brief stop to sit in the box pews here will interest even kids who aren't mad about history. Make sure you visit the small shop and museum next door, which displays an old musket actually fired in the battle at Lexington, and the little garden in back.
🏠 193 Salem St., tel. 617/523–6676. Haymarket stop on Orange or Green Line T, then 10-min walk. Cost: Free. Open daily 9–5; Sun. services at 9, 11, and 4.

★★ 10 – 15 **Old South Meetinghouse.** Built in 1729 as a Puritan Church, this meetinghouse on the Freedom Trail was where issues of the day were argued in public; revolutionists gathered here to disguise themselves as "Indians" on the night of the Boston

Tea Party. Now completely renovated, it contains many interactive, kid-friendly exhibits and regularly sponsors interesting events and tours. You can still hear the dramatic recorded versions of the Tea Party debate via headphones as you sit in one of the box pews. The large gift shop has the best selection of good kids' books about the Revolution. Prep your kids with some history before visiting here—and don't stay too long.
🏠 310 Washington St., at Milk St., tel. 617/ 482–6439. State St. stop on Orange or Blue Line T. Cost: $3 adults, $1 kids under 18. Open daily 9:30–5.

★★ 5 – 15 **Paul Revere's House.** The tiny house—the oldest house in Boston—where Paul Revere lived when he made his famous ride is worth a stop. See also Chapter 2.
🏠 19 North Sq., tel. 617/523–2338.

★★ 5 – 15 **Skywalk View and Exhibit.** Though the renovated Skywalk, on the 50th floor of the Prudential Tower, isn't as high up as the John Hancock Observatory, it offers a stunning 360-degree view of Boston and superior exhibits. Most fun of the 30 displays are the Faces Wall—you open the door on which a portrait is mounted to discover more about the person—and the videos of famous events.
🏠 800 Boylston St., Boston 02116, tel. 617/ 859–0648. Cost: $4 adults, $3 kids 2–10. Open daily 10–10.

★★ 8 – 15 **State House.** Built in 1795 on land that was once John Hancock's pasture, this impressive gold-domed building with marble staircases is still Massachusetts's capitol building. Kids on my Boston panel, however, rated it "not very interesting" except when they could watch the legislature in session (for a schedule, tel. 617/727–2860). A huge wooden fish, called the Sacred Cod, hangs in the Senate Chamber. Self-guided tour brochures are available at the information desk; ask for the special children's guide that tells about the legislature and how the ladybug came to be the state insect.
🏠 Beacon St. at Park St. (across from the Common), tel. 617/727–3676. Across from

the Boston Common. Park St. stop on Red Line T. Cost: Free. Open weekdays 9–5.

CHARLESTOWN

(**ii** 6+) **Bunker Hill Monument.** The site of the first major battle of the American Revolution, the Battle of Bunker Hill (a misnomer—the site is actually named Breed's Hill), has a small museum and a panoramic view. If you can, visit during the summer when there are musket firing demonstrations. *See also* Chapter 2.

🏠 *Breed's Hill, Monument Ave., Charlestown, tel. 617/242–5641.*

(**ii** ALL) **Charlestown Navy Yard.** At the Navy Yard, where warships were built for more than 170 years, you can spend a couple of hours savoring the waterfront sights and it won't be enough. The original Yard, now a National Park, is a virtual museum of American shipbuilding; the other 100 acres include gardens, old granite buildings converted to offices and condominiums, and a beautiful 1½-mi waterfront walk. Stop first at the National Park Service Visitor Center (good bathrooms) for a free map. Friendly park rangers will help you plan your time, or you can take their free 50-minute tour in summer (it involves a lot of walking and seems geared to older kids). You can go aboard two ships: the **USS Constitution**, Boston's number one attraction (*see* Museums, *below*), and a World War II destroyer, the **USS Cassin Young**. Also, don't miss the display of ship models at the **Boston Marine Society** in Building 32. The best place for lunch?: the light-filled Atrium Cafe in Building 149 opposite the parking garage. In summer, "The Whites of Their Eyes," an exciting half-hour multimedia reenactment of the Battle of Bunker Hill, is presented in the **Bunker Hill Pavilion** (tel. 617/241–7575) not far from the USS **Constitution**. Between April and October the easiest (and most enjoyable) way to get here is by water shuttles, which cost just $1 and are run by Boston Harbor Cruises from Long Wharf; the Navy Yard is a stop on their *Constitution* trip and harbor tour (see

above). You can also take Bus 93 from Haymarket.

🏠 *Constitution Rd., Charlestown, tel. 617/242–5601. Cost: Free, except for "The Whites of Their Eyes" ($3 adults, $1.50 under 18, $8 family) and USS* **Constitution** *Museum ($4 adults, $2 kids 6–16). Visitor center and most attractions open daily 10–5 (until 6 in summer). Parking.*

LEXINGTON AND CONCORD

The first battle of the American Revolution took place in these two towns, respectively 12 and 20 mi from Boston.

(**ii** 8–15) **Battle Green.** A number of sites are clustered in the center of Lexington, on Lexington Green: the **Minuteman Statue**; yellow wood-framed **Buckman Tavern** (tel. 781/862–5598), where the Minutemen met on April 19, 1775; and the small **Lexington Visitor Center** (1875 Massachusetts Ave., tel. 781/862–1450) with rest rooms and a diorama of the April 19 battle.

(**ii** 10–15) **Minuteman National Historical Park.** The first battles in the Revolution were fought along this 20-mi route. *See also* Chapter 2.

🏠 *Minuteman Visitor Center, 1 mi from Battle Green, off Rte. 2A, Concord, tel. 781/862–7753; North Bridge Visitor Center, 171 Liberty St., Concord, tel. 978/369–6993.*

(**ii** 8–14) **Orchard House.** Fans of Louisa May Alcott's books may want to make a pilgrimage to her home. Do take the informative tour. *See also* Chapter 2.

🏠 *399 Lexington Rd., Box 353, Concord, tel. 978/369–4118.*

(**ii** 10–15) **Walden Pond State Reservation.** Little of Thoreau's solitude is left: The nature trails are crowded, and in summer boaters, fishermen, and swimmers swarm over the pond. To our disappointment only a cairn of stones marks Thoreau's cabin site, but we added to the pile, created by travelers from all corners of the globe.

🏠 *Rte. 126 off Rte. 2, Concord, tel. 978/369–3254. Cost: $2 per car. Open daily 5 AM–8 PM.*

SALEM

Twenty miles northeast of Boston (drive Rte. IA north, or take Bus 450 or 455 from Haymarket, or Rockport train from North Station), Salem is a good place for a day trip. See Museums, *below*, for all the witch-related attractions, which are the real draw here for kids.

(👫 10 – 15) House of the Seven Gables. The inspiration for Nathaniel Hawthorne's famous novel of the same name, this dark, almost black house with imposing peaked gables is brooding and compelling from out-side, cozy inside. The 10-minute video retelling of the novel is worthwhile even if you have read the book. Climbing up the twisting secret staircase is the main attrac-tion for kids on my Boston panel. A shuttle bus will take you to the Salem 1630 Pioneer Village (*see below*). The last three weekends in October bring Spirits of the Gables, a ghostly Halloween event.
🏠 *54 Turner St., tel. 978/744–0991. Cost: $7 adults, $4 kids 6–17; combination ticket with Pioneer Village available. Open Jan.–Mar., Mon.–Sat. 10–4:30, Sun. noon–4:30; July–Oct., daily 9–6.*

(👫 5 – 13) Salem 1630 Pioneer Village. Some kids on my Boston panel prefer this smaller-scale living-history village, with its live animals to feed, to Plimoth Plantation (*see below*). A fitting time to come is during Salem's Haunted Happenings weekends in October; at night this becomes a spooky haunted village—but it's too scary for the very little ones. See *also* Chapter 2.
🏠 *Forest River Park, Salem, tel. 978/745–0525 or 978/744–0991.*

PLYMOUTH

Expect to see many tour buses crammed into this small town 41 mi southeast of Boston. Cranberries, Pilgrim sites, unique living-history museums, and tacky souvenir shops make up its wide appeal. The infor-mation booth at 130 Water Street has walking tour maps. For information, con-tact **Destination Plymouth** (225 Water St.,

Suite 202, Plymouth 02361, tel. 800/872–1620).

(👫 5 – 13) Cranberry World. The Ocean Spray Visitor Center in the midst of the Massachusetts cranberry bogs turned out to be both fun and educational for us. See *also* Chapter 2.
🏠 *225 Water St., tel. 508/747–2350.*

(👫 7 – 14) Plimoth Plantation, *Mayflower II*, and Hobbamock's Homesite. More than any other living-history museum in the Northeast, this village—thatched-roof dwellings, a replica of the *Mayflower*, and an Indian settlement—tries to be completely authentic. See *also* Chapter 2.
🏠 *Warren Ave., Rte. 3A, tel. 508/746–1622. Take Rte. 3 south to Exit 4, then follow signs.*

(👫 5 – 15) Plymouth Rock. The rock marking the spot where the Pilgrims landed is small and disappointing, but, says Gavin, "you have to see it." See *also* Chapter 2.
🏠 *Water St., Plymouth, no phone.*

Museums

IN BOSTON

(👫 4 – 10) Boston Tea Party Ship and Museum. Anchored at the Congress Street Bridge, the *Beaver II* is a fairly authentic replica of one of the British ships made famous by the Boston Tea Party in 1773. See *also* Chapter 3.
🏠 *Congress St. Bridge, tel. 617/338–1773. South Station stop on Red Line T.*

(👫 ALL) Children's Museum. Plan on spending at least several hours in this, the very best children's museum in the North-east, with four floors full of imaginative touch-look-discover-play exhibits. It's very crowded on a rainy Sunday. See *also* Chap-ter 3. The Computer Museum is next door.
🏠 *Museum Wharf, 300 Congress St., tel. 617/426–6500, 617/426–8855 for event info. South Station stop on Red Line T.*

(👫 8+) Computer Museum. A con-verted wool warehouse next to the Children's Museum houses two floors of hands-on exhibits in the world's only museum devoted to the computer—a must for computer lovers, especially those over 10. *See also* Chapter 3.

🏛 *Museum Wharf, 300 Congress St., tel. 617/426–2800. South Station stop on Red Line T.*

(👫 **7+**) **Isabella Stewart Gardner Museum.** This museum, designed to look like a 15th-century Italian palace, has plenty of treasures that appeal to children, including many paintings and ceramics of animals and even an entire room with leather walls. *See also* Chapter 3.

🏛 *280 The Fenway, tel. 617/566–1401. Ruggles/Museum stop on Green Line T.*

(👫 **13+**) **John F. Kennedy Library and Museum.** Better than any other museum dedicated to a president, this one conveys the reality of an exciting election campaign and Kennedy's presidency—through televised commercials, speeches, and debates; displays of newspapers and magazines of the day; and re-created settings of campaign headquarters and offices. The building itself is spectacular, and beautiful willows shade the grounds on the University of Massachusetts campus.

🏛 *Columbia Point, tel. 617/929–4567. Take Red Line T to JFK/UMass stop, then free shuttle to museum. Cost: $8 adults, $4 kids 13–17, 12 and under free. Open daily 9–5.*

(👫 **8+**) **Museum of Fine Arts.** The MFA, Boston's counterpart to New York's Metropolitan Museum (though not quite as great), has almost 200 galleries of masterpieces and excellent art programs for kids and families. *See also* Chapter 3.

🏛 *465 Huntington Ave., tel. 617/267–9300. Ruggles/Museum stop on Green Line T.*

(👫 **2+**) **Museum of Science.** We spent about three hours at this huge museum of 400 interactive exhibits on the Charles River between Cambridge and Boston. We consider it one of the best science museums in the Northeast. *See also* Chapter 3.

🏛 *Science Park, tel. 617/723–2500. Science Park stop on Green Line T.*

(👫 **6+**) **Sports Museum of New England.** This museum of interactive exhibits about all sports, including candlepin bowling, now has two locations. The largest is on the fifth and sixth floors of FleetCenter, where the Bruins and Celtics play. The other branch is outside the city in Lowell. *See also* Chapter 3.

🏛 *150 Causeway St., tel. 617/624–1234. North Station stop on Green or Orange Line T.*

ACTON

(👫 **ALL**) **Discovery Museums.** Out front, Bessie, a green dinosaur sculpture, announces these two special museums 40 mi from Boston. The **Children's Museum** (ages 1–6), set in a converted Victorian house, is like a huge playhouse, with a whale video in a closet, a room full of Legos for building, and much more. The small, light-filled **Science Museum** (ages 6 and up) is modern, its tower shows off octagonal windows, and the staff has a hands-on philosophy. Unfortunately, it tends to get busy here—many school groups visit—and there can be a line to get in. It's a good idea to call ahead to verify opening times.

🏛 *177 Main St., Rte. 27, Acton, tel. 978/264–4200. Cost: $6 to visit 1 museum, $9 for both. Both museums open late June–mid-Oct., Tues.–Sun. 9–4:30; late Oct.–mid-June, Tues., Thurs., Fri. 1–4:30, Wed. 9–6, weekends 9–4:30.*

CHARLESTOWN

(👫 **4+**) **USS *Constitution* and Museum.** The USS *Constitution*, nicknamed "Old Ironsides," has a regular tour that fascinates kids. The museum's hands-on exhibits present the ship's history and much more. *See also* Chapter 3.

🏛 *Charlestown Navy Yard, Charlestown, tel. 617/426–1812.*

SALEM

(👫 **6+**) **New England Pirate Museum.** A guide-storyteller introduces tales of famous pirates such as Captain Kidd through

a tour into a stage-set seaside village, down into an 80-ft man-made cave, and past various scenes. There is plenty of drama and a good gift shop full of such stuff as treasure chests and replica gold doubloons.
🏠 *274 Derby St., Salem, tel. 978/741–2800. Cost: $4 adults, $2.50 kids 3–14. Open mid-May–Oct., daily 10–5, Nov. weekends only.*

(👫 8+) **Salem Wax Museum of Witches and Seafarers**. The most interesting wax museum in the Northeast offers activities for kids. *See also* Chapter 3.
🏠 *Derby St., Salem, tel. 978/740–2929.*

(👫 7+) **Salem Witch Museum.** Figures in stage sets dramatize the history of the famous witch trials in this imposing museum—not for little kids. The Witch Dungeon Museum nearby (16 Lynde St., tel. 978/744–9812) presents a live reenactment of a witch trial and tour of a dungeon. *See also* Chapter 3.
🏠 *Washington Sq., off Washington St., Salem, tel. 978/744–1692.*

WENHAM

(👫 4–13) **Wenham Museum**. This museum houses a delightful collection of dolls and dollhouses. It also sponsors special events for kids, such as a teddy-bear parade. *See also* Chapter 3.
🏠 *132 Main St. (Rte. 1A), Wenham, tel. 978/468–2377.*

Animals

IN BOSTON

(👫 ALL) **Franklin Park Zoo.** Covering 72 acres, this zoo has among its exhibits the world-class African Tropical Forest, with gorillas, hippos, baboons, and crocodiles, and an Australian Outback Trail, with kangaroos and wallabies. The Children's Zoo is best for kids 3–8. *See also* Chapter 4.
🏠 *Circuit Dr., Franklin Park, Dorchester, tel. 617/541–5466.*

(👫 ALL) **New England Aquarium.** This enormously popular aquarium on the

waterfront is easy to get to, air-conditioned, and all indoors. Best features: the four-story main tank, circled by spiraling ramps, and the touch tank. *See also* Chapter 4.
🏠 *Central Wharf, Boston, tel. 607/973–5200.*

AROUND BOSTON

(👫 2–11) **Drumlin Farm Education Center and Wildlife Sanctuary.** This demonstration farm and nature center 22 mi west of Boston is a place to see farm animals as well as New England wildlife exhibits; its big grassy fields are ideal for running and kite-flying. *See also* Chapter 4.
🏠 *South Great Rd. (Rte. 117), South Lincoln, tel. 781/259–9807.*

(👫 1–12) **New England Alive.** Though treating injured and orphaned animals is the center's main purpose, kids can pat baby animals and view New England wildlife. *See also* Chapter 4.
🏠 *185 High St. (Rtes. 1A and 133), Ipswich, tel. 978/356–7013.*

Green Space

A chain of parks stretching from Boston Common west, many of which were designed by Frederick Law Olmsted, are called the "Emerald Necklace." For other parks outside but near the city, *see also* Chapter 5.

IN BOSTON

(👫 ALL) **Arnold Arboretum.** More than 6,000 varieties of trees and shrubs (all labeled) adorn 265 beautiful acres of open spaces and ponds, hills, and ravines in this Harvard-run botanical garden designed by Frederick Law Olmsted. On a sunny day its roads (closed to cars) and paths are filled with families promenading and pushing strollers. Don't miss a visit to the bonsai trees. Kids interested in models may enjoy the 8- by 16-ft model of the arboretum, complete with individual trees. Best times to come are in May and June, especially on Lilac Sunday, when morris dancers perform.

🏛 *125 Arborway (Rtes. 1 and 203), Jamaica Plain 02310, tel. 617/524–1718. Forest Hills stop on Orange Line T, then walk 2 blocks northeast to main gate. Cost: Free. Open daily dawn–dusk; building open weekdays 9–4, weekends noon–4.*

👫 **ALL**　**Boston Common.** The 50-acre Common, the oldest public park in the United States (since 1634), has big old trees and grass fields. It began as a cow pasture, and for nearly 200 years it was the site of public executions; today, the central Downtown location makes it a traditional play spot for kids in all seasons. It felt small and cramped to our family, though, and it isn't as pretty as the Public Garden across Charles Street. A small fenced playground has picnic tables and a climber with a big blue tube to slide through; nearby, the Frog Pond lets kids splash and wade in summer, ice-skate in winter. There's also a good sledding hill. Regular concerts are held at the bandstand, including outdoor performances of Shakespeare. This is not a place to walk after dark.
🏛 *Bounded by Beacon, Park, Tremont, Boylston, and Charles Sts. For information, call Boston Parks and Recreation Dept., tel. 617/ 635–4505; for performances, ext. 6400; for tours by Boston Park Rangers, tel. 617/635– 7383. Park St. stop on Red Line T.*

👫 **ALL**　**Boston Harbor Islands State Park.** Seventeen islands scattered across Boston Harbor constitute this park, where we love to picnic on a hot summer day. *See also* Chapter 5.
🏛 *Water shuttle: Boston Harbor Cruises, Long Wharf, tel. 617/227–4321. The islands: Dept. of Environmental Management, 349 Lincoln St., Bldg. 45, Hingham 02043, tel. 617/727–5290.*

👫 **ALL**　**Boston Public Garden.** Across Charles Street from the Common lies the lovely 24-acre Public Garden. No child under 10 should miss riding in the Swan Boats (*see Serendipities, above*). Meandering short pathways under drooping willows, a miniature suspension bridge crossing over a 4-acre pond with ducks, and statues of

ducks and George Washington make it ideal for small children.
🏛 *Bounded by Arlington, Boylston, Beacon, and Charles Sts. For information, call Boston Parks and Recreation Dept., tel. 617/635– 4505. Arlington stop on Green Line T.*

👫 **ALL**　**Lower Basin and the Esplanade.** Along the Charles River from the Museum of Science to Harvard Bridge (Massachusetts Ave.) runs a stretch of grassy spaces, winding paths, duck-filled lagoons, and several playgrounds. In July the Boston Pops perform at Hatch Shell. From the open, grassy Cambridge side of the river you have a good view of Harvard's rowing crews skimming by; there's fine biking and in-line skating along the sidewalk. Take the Red Line T to either Charles Street on the Boston side or Harvard Square on the Cambridge side.

PLAYGROUNDS. Favorites of our family and my Boston panel: **Christopher Columbus/Waterfront Park** (Atlantic Ave. between Mercantile St. and Long Wharf), which has an excellent view of boats in the busy harbor, a long vine-covered colonnade that's fun to run through, wading in summer, and a clean, modern play area with a large, boatlike wooden climbing structure; **Clarendon Street Playground** (corner of Commonwealth Ave. and Clarendon St., Back Bay), a small shady playground with a big wooden climbing structure and a grassy hill that's fun to roll down; **Charlestown Waterfront Playground** (facing Pier 4 across from USS *Constitution* Museum, Charlestown Navy Yard), a fabulous playground with an imaginatively designed wading pool and a shiplike wooden climbing structure that has decks, a steering wheel, and a slide; **Cambridge Common** (off Waterhouse St., between Massachusetts Ave. and Garden St., Cambridge), a delightful fenced playground that's accessible to people with disabilities.

AROUND BOSTON

👫 **ALL**　**Blue Hills zReservation.** Only about 10 mi south of the city in Milton, this 7,000-acre reservation is a haven for hikers, pond swimmers, berry pickers, cross-country skiers, mountain bikers, and ice-skaters. The winding, steep, rocky trails are best for older kids with hiking experience. Don't miss the Trailside Museum, run by the Massachusetts Audubon Society, where kids can see some animals.

🏦 *Park headquarters: tel. 617/698–1802. Trailside Museum, 1904 Canton Ave., Milton, tel. 617/333–0690. By car: I–93 to Rte. 128, take Exit 3 and follow signs for Houghton's Pond. Cost: Park free; museum $3 adults, $1.50 kids 3–15. Museum open Tues.–Sun. 10–5.*

(👬 **ALL**) **Ipswich River Wildlife Sanctuary.** This well-maintained Audubon Sanctuary just 24 mi from Downtown Boston offers excellent kids' programs and guided hikes. *See also* Chapter 5.

🏦 *87 Perkins Row, Topsfield, tel. 978/887–9264.*

(👬 **2 – 15**) **Larz Anderson Park.** Thanks to its combination of hills and lawns, a pond with ducks to feed, picnic areas and playgrounds, and the Museum of Transportation filled with cars in an old carriage house, this 63-acre park is an excellent destination for an afternoon outing—and it's only 15 to 20 minutes from Boston. On a nice day the hill where the Anderson mansion once stood attracts kite flyers; on a snowy one it's thick with sledders. The easiest way to get here from Downtown Boston is by car.

🏦 *Entrances on Goddard Ave. and Newton St., Brookline, tel. 617/730–2069. By car: Rte. 9 west to Lee St., then turn left. By T: Cleveland Circle stop on Green Line T, then Bus 51 to museum. Museum tel. 617/522–6547 or 617/522–6140.*

Sports

Big-Time for Spectators

Spectator sports are a major obsession for many Bostonians, and they have unswerving loyalty to their home teams. Arrive early and don't cheer too loudly for the visitors, even if

they're your own home team. (Definitely do not let your kids wear Yankees T-shirts at a Red Sox game.) When they're available, opt for seats in family sections where no alcohol is permitted. The *Boston Globe's* Friday edition lists college and professional sports schedules. *See also* Chapter 8.

BASEBALL. The baseball season runs from April to October.

Boston Red Sox. The Sox (American League) have played in charming, relatively small, old-fashioned Fenway Park since 1912. Tickets are usually easy to get, except when the Sox are playing the Yankees (their arch rival) or the Blue Jays.

🏦 *4 Yawkey Way, tel. 617/267–1700 (tickets). Fenway stop on Riverside/Green Line T.*

BASKETBALL. Basketball season is late October through April.

Boston Celtics. Tickets to home games on the famous parquet floors, now moved to the larger FleetCenter, are still very hard to get.

🏦 *150 Causeway St., tel. 617/523–3030 (information, season tickets), Ticketmaster 617/931–2222. North Station stop on Orange or Green Line T.*

FOOTBALL. Football season is from early September through December. Pro games are usually on Sunday afternoons, college games on Saturday afternoons.

New England Patriots. Though the Patriots' home, Foxboro Stadium, is sometimes sold out to season ticket holders, individual tickets do go on sale. Traffic is horrendous.

🏦 *Rte. 1 (25 mi south of Boston), Foxboro, tel. 508/543–1776, 800/543–1776, or Ticketmaster 617/931–2222. Take Rte. 1 south off I–95 for 3 mi.*

Various college teams popular with Boston families include the **Boston College Eagles** (Alumni Stadium, Chestnut Hill, Brookline, tel. 617/552–2000); the **Boston University Terriers** (Nickerson Field, off Commonwealth Ave., tel. 617/353–3838); the **Harvard University Crimson** (Harvard University Stadium, N. Harvard St. and Soldiers Field Rd., Allston; tel. 617/495–2212).

HOCKEY. The season is from October through April, with games mostly on Thursday and Saturday evenings.

Boston Bruins. The Bruins share FleetCenter with the NBA's Celtics. Tickets are usually sold out by game time.

🏛 *150 Causeway St., tel. 617/624–1900 or 617/624–1000, Ticketmaster 617/931–2222. North Station stop on Green and Orange Line T.*

RUNNING. Boston Marathon. Held every year on Patriot's Day, the third Monday in April, this is one event that the families on my Boston panel love to watch.

🏛 *For information, contact Boston Athletic Association, 131 Clarendon St., 02116, tel. 617/236–1652.*

SOCCER. New England Revolution. This new major-league soccer team shares Foxboro Stadium with the Patriots.

🏛 *Rte. 1 (25 mi south of Boston), Foxboro, tel. 508/543–0350 or 508/543–5001, Ticketmaster 617/931–2222. Take Rte. 1 south off I–95 for 3 mi.*

Outdoor Action

BICYCLING

(👪 **8+**) The best place (with the nicest views) to ride bikes in the city is along both sides of the Charles River on the 18-mi-long **Dr. Paul Dudley White Bike Path**, which runs from the Museum of Science to Watertown Square and up to Cambridge. On Sundays in summer, when it's closed to traffic, we also like **Memorial Drive** on the Cambridge side of the river. **Back Bay Bikes and Boards** (336 Newbury St., tel. 617/247–2336) rents adult-size bikes but also has one small kid's bike ($20 per day, $10 for two hours, including helmet). No maps are provided, however. **Community Bike** (496 Tremont St., tel. 617/542–8623) rents adult-size bikes ($20 per day plus deposit) and helmets, but it does not have small frame bikes for young kids. It does carry good maps.

BOATING

(👪 **6–15**) It's easy for a family to sail in Boston, on either the **Charles River** or Boston Harbor. On the Charles River, sailing dinghies can be rented at low rates through Community Boating (21 Embankment Rd. along the Esplanade just below Longfellow Bridge, tel. 617/523–1038, mid-June through Aug.). After passing a sailing test, experienced families can purchase a two-day (or 45-day) visitor membership allowing them to use boats; you can also hire an instructor. Summer group lessons for kids cost only $1. On Boston Harbor, the Courageous Sailing Center in Charlestown Navy Yard (Pier 4, tel. 617/242–3821, take $1 water shuttle from Long Wharf), with one of the best sailing schools in the Northeast and dozens of boats of various sizes, offers classes, private lessons, and rentals for visitors (only on weekdays) in **Boston Harbor**. Unlike the Boston Sailing Center on Lewis Wharf, the Courageous allows you to use boats for just one day. You can also row or sail on beautiful **Jamaica Pond** in Jamaica Plain.

ICE-SKATING

(👪 **6–15**) Among the many parks where you can skate on weekends in winter, we favor two. Skating on the **Lagoon** in the Public Garden remains a Boston family tradition, though in many years the ice doesn't solidly freeze until late in the season—if at all. You must bring your own skates or you can rent them at the Boston Skate Shop (135 Charles St. S, tel. 617/482–7400). More reliable ice can be found at the renovated Frog Pond in Boston Common, where you can rent both adult- and kid-size skates at bargain prices ($5 for the whole day) and sip on hot chocolate at the concession pavilion (tel. 617/635–4505). You can also skate at Larz Anderson Park (see above), which has rentals.

KITE FLYING

(👪 **3+**) Franklin Park's annual **kite festival** in mid-May (for information call Parks Dept., tel. 617/635–4500) draws thousands of kids and adults, as kites fill the sky in a mind-boggling array of shapes, sizes, and colors. Festivities include kite-making clinics. My Boston panelists also favor areas along the Cambridge side of the Charles River and the hill above the Museum of Transportation in Larz Anderson Park, both of which are open and usually breezy.

ROLLER-SKATING

(👭 **10+**) In-line skating is a key spring, summer, and fall sport for kids in the city. One highly favored spot is the long paved path through the **Esplanade** along the Charles River (wider than those across the river in Cambridge); around the **Christian Science Center** (intersection of Massachusetts Ave. and Huntington Ave.), the smooth brick pedestrian plaza by the reflecting pool is a good place for beginners to practice. For rentals, **Eric Flaim's Motion Sports** (349 Newbury St. near Tower Records, tel. 617/247–3284) rents in-line skates for kids and adults. Rentals include protective gear. It also has a skate school that offers lessons to kids. The **Beacon Hill Skate Shop** (135 Charles St. S, tel. 617/482–7400) near the Boston Common gives lessons and has a limited selection of small size in-line skates; it also rents ice skates and sell skateboards.

WHALE-WATCHING

(👭 **10–15**) Traveling out to the Stellwagen Bank in Massachusetts Bay to spot whales is a popular activity for families, particularly when the weather is hot and sticky, though it makes for a long trip, usually five to six hours. Of the regularly scheduled trips, we like the New England Aquarium's trips aboard *The Voyager* best (tel. 617/973–5277 or 617/973–5281). *See also* Chapter 6.

Indoor Action

BOWLING

(👭 **10+**) At **Ryan Family Amusement Center** (64 Brookline Ave. across from Fenway Park, tel. 617/267–8495) you can try candlepin bowling, a traditional New England sport that uses small, slender pins and a smaller ball. There are plenty of video games here, too. Come in the afternoon after a Red Sox game.

INDOOR PLAYGROUND

(👭 **0–5**) **Tot Stop**, a large three-level play area located in a former school, has ride-on toys, special areas for toddlers and infants, a large barn with nooks and crannies and slides, and an indoor "beach" and a snack bar with lunch stuff and coffee for adults.

🏠 *41 Foster St., off Massachusetts Ave., East Arlington, tel. 781/643–8687. Cost: $5.50 for kids over 12 months; maximum $12.95 per family; discounts for kids 6–12 months. Open Mon.–Sat. 9:30–5:30, Fri. 9:30–8.*

ROLLERBLADING AND SKATEBOARDING

(👭 **10–15**) A huge old warehouse in Cambridge has been converted into **Maximus**, the indoor mecca for Boston-area skateboarders and in-line skaters. *See also* Chapter 6.

🏠 *324 Rindge Ave. (off Massachusetts Ave.), Cambridge, tel. 617/576–4723.*

Shopping

Because of their significant population of college kids, Boston and Cambridge offer more than enough teen-appealing shops to occupy visitors for several weeks. It's also a book lover's heaven, with an amazing number of colorful, quirky, and often huge bookstores. Around **Harvard Square**, more than 100 shops are crammed into a several-block area, including lots of music and book stores, the best spots for antique clothing, and branches of chains such as the Body Shop and Urban Outfitters. The Back Bay's wide, elegant **Newbury Street** is another prime zone, starting from the stylish clothing boutiques at the Public Garden end and going on to the trendier, more youth-oriented clothing shops toward Massachusetts Avenue. Nearby, on Boylston Street, the **Prudential Center**, connected to the upscale, glitzy Copley Place mall, also attracts clothes-browsing teenage girls.

Malls and Marketplaces

ALL   CambridgeSide Galleria. This is a favored shopping and eating and just hanging-out spot. Among its 100 shops and restaurants, **Benetton**, **Gap**, **J. Crew**, the **Original Levi's Store**, and **Banana Republic** are hot spots for clothes, **Pappa-Razzi** (see Eats, below) and the **Food Festival** on the Charles River for lunch or dinner. In summer, cruise boats dock here and paddleboats are for rent on the lagoon. The mall stays open until 9:30, and a free shuttle bus carries shoppers to and from the Kendall Square T station. The mall is also one block away from the Lechmere station on the Green Line T.
🏠 *100 CambridgeSide Pl., tel. 617/621–8666.*

ALL   Faneuil Hall Marketplace. If you're going to shop in only one place in Boston, this is it. The more than 70 shops are joined by ranks of pushcarts under the canopies fanning out from the central building, Quincy Market. It's more a bustling open-air market than a mall. A sampling of kid-friendly shops: At **Purple Pizazz**, everything from stuffed animals to T-shirts is purple. You'll find a good selection of children's books at the branch of **Waterstone's Book Store**. You can create your own cap at **Custom Caps** and find a wide variety of magic and juggling items at **Magic Studio**. Teens recommend a stop at the **Wall**, a music store loaded with CDs, and soccer fans say visiting the **World Soccer Shop**, which carries shirts, hats, mugs, and more with logos of soccer teams around the world, is a must. For younger kids, **Mama Bear's Shop** is filled with every conceivable teddy bear. See *also* Chapter 2.
🏠 *Between Commercial and Congress Sts., tel. 617/338–2323.*

Books and Music

0 – 14   Children's Book Shop. In contrast to those of most children's bookstores, this shop's large selection (some 20,000 books) includes plenty of young adult fiction and even a few racks of parenting books where adults can browse.
🏠 *237 Washington St., Brookline, tel. 617/734–7323.*

11+   Harvard Coop. This gigantic three-floor store of games, toys, housewares, and clothing also stocks an astonishing selection of books (250,000 different titles from Stephen King to the most obscure scholarly tome), plus CDs, posters, and computer stuff.
🏠 *1400 Massachusetts Ave., Cambridge, tel. 617/499–2000.*

12+   HMV. The biggest record store in Cambridge, HMV attracts a diverse clientele with its huge stock (particularly of classical music), in-store DJ on Friday and Saturday nights, and regular live performances.
🏠 *1 Brattle St., Cambridge, tel. 617/868–9696.*

13+   Newbury Comics. Though the name makes it sound like a comic book shop (the store does have a few shelves of new comics, sold at a 20% discount), most of the business of this 20-store chain is rock CDS, especially those of alternative music groups. The Harvard Square store (36 JFK St., 2nd floor of Garage Mall, Cambridge, tel. 617/491–0337), with its hip environment, is a teen and student hangout, with occasional in-store concerts.

10+   Tower Records. This chain's second-largest U.S. branch (three floors, 46,000 square ft, a shade smaller than the downtown New York City branch) hums with electronic entertainment: TV monitors, listening posts, and computer screens where you can punch up all sorts of music information.
🏠 *360 Newbury St. (corner of Massachusetts Ave.), tel. 617/247–5900.*

👭 ALL Waterstone's Booksellers. An oversize Curious George doll and a huge selection of kids' books attract families to the store's second-floor children's section, a carpeted loft area marked off by brightly painted glass dividers and railings. Story hour is Wednesday at 4.
🏠 26 Exeter St. (at Newbury St.), tel. 617/ 859–7300.

Comics

👭 10–15 Comicopia. This clean, well-lighted store carries a comprehensive selection of new comics, plus comic book T-shirts and posters and the Japanese Anime videos popular with many teenagers; it also sells Magic the Gathering, including single cards (most stores don't).
🏠 464 Commonwealth Ave., Kenmore Sq., tel. 617/266–4266.

👭 10+ Million Year Picnic. The collection—more than 25,000 comics, both new and vintage—is the oldest in New England, and the store also stocks comic-related T-shirts and posters.
🏠 99 Mt. Auburn St., Harvard Sq., Cambridge, tel. 617/492–6763.

Stuff to Wear

👭 12+ Mass Army Navy Store. One room is devoted exclusively to worldwide military surplus goodies, but the rest of the two floors are stocked with a wide selection of teen staples: jeans, khakis, boots, and shirts.
🏠 1436 Massachusetts Ave., Harvard Sq., Cambridge, tel. 617/497–1250.

👭 12+ Oona's Experienced Clothing. Crammed onto racks in four tiny rooms is an excellent selection of the recycled clothes that are so appealing to many teens, all at relatively low prices.
🏠 1210 Massachusetts Ave., Cambridge, tel. 617/491–2654.

Toys and Games

👭 ALL Children's Museum. The big first-floor museum shop sells new books, educational toys, and crafts kits, but we gravitate instead to the Recycle shop on the second floor, where you can find wonderful cheap materials for crafts projects.
🏠 300 Congress St., Museum Wharf, tel. 617/426–6500, ext. 210.

👭 10+ Complete Strategist. A mecca for kids who are fascinated by role-playing games and miniatures, this small branch of the New York City store is frequented by many college kids.
🏠 201 Massachusetts Ave. (near the Christian Science Center), tel. 617/267–2451.

👭 6–12 Enchanted Cottage. Everything a dollhouse owner needs is for sale here. Thirty or more dollhouses decorated with miniature furnishings and light fixtures are usually set up for viewing.
🏠 2512 Massachusetts Ave., Cambridge, tel. 617/491–8818.

👭 ALL F.A.O. Schwarz. A huge bronze teddy bear outside marks Boston's branch of the famous toy store, which is more cozy and fanciful in layout and design than the original in New York City. Its two floors brim with touch-and-play possibilities, wonderful animated displays, fabulous stuffed animals (some bigger than the little kids patting them), all at very high prices. The library section has an excellent selection of kids' books.
🏠 440 Boylston St. (in Back Bay), tel. 617/ 266–5101.

👭 ALL Museum of Science. This museum gift shop stocks a wide selection of kids' science books and toys.
🏠 Science Park, tel. 617/589–0320.

Unusual Stores

👭 8+ Beadworks. The Newbury Street store of this nationwide chain has one of the biggest (as many as 3,000 different beads) and most organized selections

I've seen, enticingly sorted out in lovely oak boxes. There's a supervised worktable right in the store, and displays of sample projects hang on the walls. The Cambridge branch is smaller and has no work area.

M *349 Newbury St., tel. 617/247–7227; 23 Church St., Cambridge, tel. 617/868–9777.*

(👬 4+) **Cybersmith.** Though this two-level shop sells software and books about computers, it's primarily a hip technology center where you can try out all the latest software or plonk down with the latest video gaming systems. Some CD-ROM stations are set up just for the littlest ones. Kids 8 and up gravitate toward the virtual reality stations—Virtual Skiing and Virtual Skate-boarding—on 50-inch monitors, and the creativity station where you can put cool effects on a picture of yourself. You get a cybercard and pay for a set amount of usage time (1 hour costs $9.95, for example), but you have to pay separately for time at the virtual reality stations and simulators (4 for $10, for example). The friendly staff members, trained to help all ages master new technology, are patient and approachable.

M *42 Church St. in Harvard Sq., tel. 617/ 492–5857. Open until midnight Fri.*

(👬 8–15) **Jack's Joke Shop.** This shop (it's still here!) stocks all the appallingly corny stuff—hand buzzers, fake cockroaches and rats, crazy glasses, Halloween masks—that delights kids who are still in the practical-joke stage.

M *38 Boylston St., tel. 617/426–9640.*

(👬 ALL) **Learningsmith.** On the main floor, 12 different colorful "try it out" sections (crafts, games, astronomy, math, etc.) hold fascinating books, calendars, toys, and all manner of learning products to stimulate the mind. A carpeted area at the back of the store is just for the under-6 crowd. On the mezzanine eight computers let shoppers experiment with the latest in software.

M *25 Brattle St., Harvard Sq., Cambridge, tel. 617/661–6008.*

Eats

Because about a third of the population of Boston and Cambridge are students, many of the city's restaurants are casual, inexpensive, and noisy—all of which make them appealing to families.

The food specialty of Boston is fresh fish of all kinds: clams, fried and steamed and in chowder; baked scrod; codfish cakes; and lobsters every which way. Many of Boston's seafood restaurants offer kids' menus with appealing alternatives as well. Kids may be more interested in other quintessential Boston tastes: baked beans, Indian pudding, and apple pandowdy at Durgin-Park; dim sum in Chinatown; Italian pastries and gelato in North End cafés; and marvelous ice cream, its quality kept high by fierce local competition.

Cambridge, with its diversity of students from every corner of the globe, is the place to try any ethnic cuisine that interests your kids, from Thai to Indian to Greek to Korean.

Boston's malls and indoor atriums contain food courts with many casual snacking spots: the concourse in light-filled **South Station**, where you can watch rushing people and see the train tracks; the Terrace Food Court in the **Prudential Center**; the brass-and-marble food court in upscale **Copley Place**, where kids can toss pennies into waterfalls; and the **CambridgeSide Galleria**'s Food Festival court, overlooking the Charles River. You can eat alfresco at one of the city's two open-air markets. Colorful, untouristy **Haymarket Square** (bounded by Blackstone, Hanover, and North Sts.) teems with outdoor fruit and vegetable stalls and tiny shops behind opened shutters wafting the smell of fresh bread. It's open Friday and Saturday mornings. Haymarket Pizzeria (100 Blackstone St., tel. 617/723–8585) sells pizza slices that you can eat sitting at sawhorse tables under big skylights. At **Faneuil Hall Marketplace** (bounded by Commercial and Congress Sts.), head for the center building, Quincy Market, where more than three dozen food stalls compose an exotic buffet. Don't miss the New England chowder at the Bay State Chowda Co. (tel. 617/742–4441). Beware noontime, however, when the crowds fill the aisle between the stalls. Eat a picnic on a bench outside in the plaza, or head for one of the cafés under the canopies on either side.

Boston is a picnicker's paradise. In the **Public Garden**, we spread a blanket near the Lagoon and save our sandwich crusts for the ducks. Just below the **Science Museum** are lovely picnic tables overlooking the Charles River. In the plaza in front of the **aquarium**, you can picnic by the wave pool near the cavorting harbor seals. From the grassy banks of the **Esplanade**, you can watch sailboats and Harvard's rowing shells. Along the harbor front are benches and views in **Christopher Columbus Park**, just beyond the **Charlestown Navy Yard**, and at the tip of Long Wharf. For a unique picnic spot try beautifully landscaped **Post Office Square Park** (bounded by Franklin, Pearl, Milk, and Congress Sts.), where atop a parking garage you'll find a wildflower garden, an expanse of grass, and chairs and tables by a café with take-out treats. Weekdays at lunchtime, it's crowded with office workers.

If your kids can't live without a Big Mac, try the McDonald's branch on the first floor of the Children's Museum (tel. 617/482–1746), which is usually crammed with families; if you get your burgers to go, you can picnic outside on benches by the water.

Category	Cost*
$$$	over $25
$$	$15–$25
$	under $15

per person for a three-course meal, excluding drinks, service, and sales tax

American Eclectic

(👬 12+) **Casablanca Restaurant**. This restaurant scores high for its inventive food

and informal, with-it atmosphere. The booths in front are comfortable, but the more spacious back room, with slow ceiling fans and the bar, is livelier. Both are decorated with potted palms and murals of characters from the movie *Casablanca*. The food is an eclectic mix of juicy burgers, grilled pizza, and delicious Moroccan and Middle Eastern specialties.

🏠 *40 Brattle St., Harvard Sq., Cambridge, tel. 617/876–0999. AE, D, MC, V. $$–$$$*

(👬 ALL) **Durgin-Park**. Climb a flight of wooden stairs to this Boston institution, here since 1827. The no-frills second-floor dining hall seats everybody at long communal tables. Waitresses treat you like family—which means they may exhort kids to finish their vegetables. Kids happily chow down on the good straightforward Yankee food: baked beans, prime rib, Indian pudding. Chicken fingers, franks and beans, and ice cream are on the menu also.

🏠 *340 Faneuil Hall Marketplace, North Market Bldg., tel. 617/227–2038. Reservations not accepted. AE, D, DC, MC, V. $$*

(👬 9–15) **Hard Rock Cafe**. Outside, half a Cadillac thrusts out from the facade below the words MASSACHUSETTS INSTITUTE OF ROCK. Inside, rock-and-roll music plays loudly and rock memorabilia decorates the walls (look for Stevie Ray Vaughn's guitar and Jim Morrison's leather pants). Besides the ubiquitous burgers and sandwiches, this member of the chain serves an okay New England clam chowder.

🏠 *131 Clarendon St. (between Columbus and Boylston Sts.), tel. 617/424–7625 or 617/353–1400. Reservations not accepted. AE, D, MC, V. $$*

(👬 10+) **Harvest**. Just reopened in fall 1998 by the team who made a success of Grill 23, this restaurant in Harvard Square satisfies demanding adult taste buds and offers a pleasant outdoor terrace café that appeals to kids. On the inventive menu, especially at lunch, are dishes that will appeal to kids, like a Harvest Burger with Boston baked beans and fries. Lunch is cheaper, too, and it's always nice to sit on a terrace in Harvard Square.

🏔 *44 Brattle St., Cambridge, tel. 617/868–2255. Reservations recommended. AE, D, DC, MC, V. $$–$$$*

(👫 **ALL**) **Marketplace Cafe.** An outdoor garden in front, a winter garden inside, and tables with paper tablecloths and crayons for the kids make this one of the most enjoyable lunch places in Faneuil Hall Marketplace. The chowder is spicy with cayenne pepper; there's also a good selection of sandwiches and pastas.

🏔 *Faneuil Hall Marketplace, end of North Market Bldg., Cafe tel. 617/227–9660. AE, DC, MC, V. $$$*

Chinese and Japanese

(👫 **ALL**) **Goemon's Japanese Noodle Restaurant.** The fun lies in choosing from a long list of meats and/or vegetables to top off your noodles (three kinds). Served in a big, deep bowl in steamy broth, it smells good, it's filling, and it's a bargain. At the counter, you can watch the chefs at work. The atmosphere is relaxed and okay for kids. Up a flight of stairs is the well-known sushi spot Tatsukichi.

🏔 *189 State St., tel. 617/742–1441. AE, D, DC, MC, V. $*

(👫 **ALL**) **Golden Palace.** This second-floor banquet hall in Chinatown has fancy pagoda-style overhangs, great golden dragons on the walls, and a fish tank with goldfish. Many families, mostly Chinese, come at lunchtime for dim sum: individual servings of tidbits or snacks (dumplings, spareribs, spicy shrimp, and more) offered from wheeled carts. You pay for each serving you choose; most are around $1 to $2. Kids like the excitement of choosing and nibbling, though there can be a long wait on crowded Sundays.

🏔 *14 Tyler St., between Beach and Kneeland Sts., tel. 617/423–4565. Dim sum served 9–3. AE, DC, MC, V. $–$$*

(👫 **ALL**) **Imperial Teahouse.** A rival to the Golden Palace (see above) for the best dim sum in Chinatown, this big, airy, noisy second-floor dining room has less in the way of decor, but its open fish tank is irresistible to kids. We give the dishes at the Golden Palace a slight edge, but the selection is larger here. Though the line moves fast, expect at least a 15-minute wait for dim sum on weekends.

🏔 *70 Beach St., tel. 617/426–8439. AE, DC, MC, V. $–$$*

Fish

(👫 **2+**) **Barking Crab.** Old buoys and crab traps decorate this funky place, which most resembles a waterside clam shack. Lobster, peel-and-eat shrimp, tender crab cakes—all the fish is fresh and good. If your kids are willing to try lobster the waiters will give them rocks to crack open the claws. In warm weather you can sit outside at picnic tables, and if kids are bored, ask for one of the games the restaurant keeps on hand. This place is not far from the Children's and Computer Museums.

🏔 *88 Sleeper St. (Northern Avenue Bridge), tel. 617/426–2722. No reservations. High chairs. AE, D, DC, MC, V. $$*

(👫 **3+**) **Legal Sea Foods.** Fresh, fresh, fresh fish, as many as 30 varieties simply and deliciously prepared, keeps families coming back, despite the inevitable long waits. At the Columbus Avenue location, we skip the line for the dining room and sit in the bar, which is more informal—paper place mats on imitation-granite Formica; kids can color their place mats, hang out next to the salt-water aquarium, and watch sports on the TVs above the bar. There's even fish-shape ravioli on the kids' menu.

🏔 *5 Cambridge Center, tel. 617/864–3400; 35 Columbus Ave. (in the Boston Park Plaza Hotel), tel. 617/426–4444; and several other Boston locations. Kids' menu. AE, DC, MC, V. $$–$$$*

(👫 **6–15**) **Union Oyster House.** A friend tells me that Marshall House, a few doors down, is better for steamers and oysters, but the truth is I'm charmed by the history of this tourist-packed spot (a revolutionary newspaper was printed upstairs in the 1770s, and it claims to be the oldest restaurant in America, with the oldest wooden booths). Kids too young to appreciate history were nevertheless mesmerized by the big lobsters in the aquarium under the stairs. 🏠 *41 Union St., tel. 617/227–2750. Kids' menu, high chairs, booster seats. AE, DC, MC, V. $$–$$$*

Italian

(👫 **ALL**) **Caffe Paradiso.** Less colorful than the Caffe Vittoria (see *below*), this North End café is a lively espresso bar where you can get homemade spumoni, gelato, Italian ices, and a sandwich if you're hungry. Tiny tables and hanging plants are the decor. The atmosphere is more authentically Italian than the Cambridge branch, which is filled with students. 🏠 *255 Hanover St., tel. 617/742–1768. I Eliot Sq., Cambridge. tel. 617/868–3240. Reservations not accepted. AE, MC, V. $$*

(👫 **ALL**) **Caffe Vittoria.** Despite the cramped seating, this North End café is worth a stop for great cappuccino, cannoli, and Italian ices that are tart but delicious. A massive polished espresso machine, marble floors, a mural of Italy, and lively music from the jukebox add up to what we think a café ought to be. 🏠 *296 Hanover St., tel. 617/227–7606. Reservations not accepted. No credit cards. $*

(👫 **ALL**) **Pappa-Razzi Trattoria/Bar.** These two branches of the chain are a step up from a pizza joint, with their wood-and-brass decor, low lighting, and casual, almost California-style atmosphere. There are pizzas, inventive pasta dishes (star and rocket pasta on the kids' menu), and Italian-style sandwiches. 🏠 *271 Dartmouth St., tel. 617/536–9200; CambridgeSide Galleria, Cambridge. tel. 617/ 577–0009. Kids' menu, high chairs, booster seats. AE, D, DC, MC, V. $$*

(👫 **ALL**) **Trattoria Il Panino.** At the Faneuil Hall Marketplace branch of this stylish and reliable local chain (there's one Downtown and three small ones in the North End) you can eat outside and service is fast. A wide variety of well-prepared, reasonably priced pasta dishes and the pizzas appeal to kids, but there's also much for adults. The restaurants have no kids' menu, but they will do smaller portions for kids at reduced prices. 🏠 *Faneuil Hall Marketplace, tel. 617/573– 9700. High chairs. AE, DC, MC, V. $$*

Mexican

(👫 **9+**) **Border Cafe.** Big portions of cheap but good burritos and other Tex-Mex specialties with Caribbean touches draw teens on my Boston panel. The chips and salsa are standard but good; bright advertising murals cover the walls. Expect hordes of students, noise, and slow service. 🏠 *32 Church St., Cambridge, tel. 617/864– 6100. High chairs, booster seats. Reservations not accepted. AE, DC, MC, V. $–$$*

(👫 **ALL**) **Fajitas & 'Ritas.** It's easygoing, fun, and lively; at the Boston branch you can even write on the walls with crayons while sitting at your table. The menu offers assorted fajitas and a few other simple Mexican dishes. Service is fast. The Brookline branch has more kids. 🏠 *25 West St., between Tremont and Washington Sts., tel. 617/426–1222; 48 Boylston St., Brookline, tel. 617/566–1222. High chairs, booster seats. Reservations not accepted. AE, D, DC, MC, V. $–$$*

Mainly Hamburgers and Hot Dogs

(👫 **4–15**) **Fuddruckers.** Cheap burgers served with many toppings are just about all there is at this theater-district branch of a Texas-style chain. 🏠 *8 Park Pl., at Stuart St., tel. 617/723– 3833. High chairs, booster seats. Reservations not accepted. AE, D, DC, MC, V. $*

ALL **Hood Milk Bottle.** In front of the Children's Museum, this 40-ft-tall white wooden milk bottle is a Boston landmark. Salads, long hot dogs wrapped in a taco, and other to-go fare is dispensed from open windows hooded by red awnings.
🏠 *300 Congress St., Museum Wharf, no phone. No credit cards. $*

Pizza Places

ALL **Bertucci's Brick Oven Pizzeria.** At this friendly, informal chain, you can watch your pizza be lifted out of the huge brick ovens with big wooden paddles. There's a floor-to-ceiling chalkboard to draw on and pizza play dough to mold. The open kitchen produces fair pastas, thin- and thick-crusted pizzas with a choice of 20-odd toppings; a kids' menu featuring plain pasta caters to finicky eaters.
🏠 *Faneuil Hall Marketplace, 22 Merchant's Row, tel. 617/227–7889; 39–45 Stanhope St., near Copley Sq., tel. 617/247–6161; 21 Brattle St., Harvard Sq., Cambridge, tel. 617/ 864–4748. Kids' menu, high chairs, booster seats. Reservations not accepted. AE, DC, MC, V. $–$$*

5+ **Pizzeria Regina.** We thought the pizza here was very good, and the pitchers of soft drinks are a plus. The original North End location is a Boston landmark, an authentic old-time pizza joint; neither the pizza nor the atmosphere at the Faneuil Hall or Brookline branches is quite as good.
🏠 *11½ Thatcher St., tel. 617/227–0765; Faneuil Hall Marketplace, tel. 617/227–8180. High chairs, booster seats. Reservations not accepted. No credit cards. $*

Sweet Stuff

6–12 **Emack & Bolio's.** Just a storefront in a Victorian town house, this place sells perhaps the best smoothies and ice cream cake in town. We go for the hand-rolled cones filled with flavors like Chocolate Moose, dipped in chocolate sprinkles or coconut.

🏠 *290 Newbury St., tel. 617/247–8772. No credit cards. $*

ALL **Herrell's Ice Cream.** A major player in Boston's competition for the best ice cream shop, Herrell's is owned by Steve Herrell, founder and former owner of Steve's Homemade Ice Cream (*see below*). Come for the famed rich and creamy-smooth chocolate pudding ice cream. One room here used to be a bank vault—it still has a vault door with a dial that works.
🏠 *15 Dunster St., Harvard Sq., tel. 617/ 497–2179. No credit cards. $*

3+ **Hing Shing Pastry.** On a visit to Chinatown, stop at this bakery store for a bag of freshly made fortune cookies for just $1, or some delicious almond cookies.
🏠 *67 Beach St., tel. 617/451–1162. No credit cards. $*

Outside the City

3–12 **Bonkers Fun House Pizza.** A good stop for energetic kids after visiting Salem's museums, this is a combination pizza-and-hot-dog place and noisy amusement park.
🏠 *Lowell St., Peabody, tel. 978/535–8355. High chairs, booster seats. Reservations not accepted. AE, DC, MC, V. $*

ALL **Clam Box of Ipswich.** With jaunty red-and-white striped awnings outside, this classic self-serve fish place has been selling fried clams and shrimp, lobsters, and more for 60 years. Portions are so large that two people can share one dinner. The outside deck, shaded by trees, draws families of noisy kids; the inside dining room has a wonderful mural of Wingersheek beach.
🏠 *246 High St., Rte. 1A, Ipswich, tel. 978/ 356–9707. Kids' portions, high chairs, booster seats. Reservations not accepted. No credit cards. $*

Where to Stay

As in New York, hotels here are expensive. The difference in Boston is that many more, including the luxurious ones, not only welcome families but cater to them with all manner of special treats: child-friendly rooms, story hours, game rooms with videos and Nintendo, and discount coupons to children's attractions. The *Boston Travel Planner*, available from the Greater Boston Convention & Visitors Bureau (*see* How to Find Out What's Going On, *above*), includes a list of Family-Friendly Hotel Packages with some two dozen hotel family packages; be sure to ask specifically for the family rate when you reserve.

There are practically no budget hotel alternatives in either Boston or Harvard Square. You can stay in an outlying area—convenient enough if you plan to spend time in Lexington and Concord, Salem, or the North Shore, but awkward if you plan to spend most of your time in the heart of the city. Boston can be hot in summer, so I've favored hotels with pools over those without. Because of the number of colleges and conventions in this city, hotels are often booked far in advance, including weekends of special events such as the Boston Marathon; if you're calling at the last minute, try the Visitor's Bureau Hotel Hot Line (tel. 800/777–6001).

All the hotels below offer some special family rate, which cuts as much as $100—sometimes more—off the posted rate. Best rates for most of these hotels are on weekends, for summer packages, and from January through March. Generally the highest rates are in the fall. Unless otherwise noted, parking will be $15 and up per night. The hotels listed below do not charge for cribs, but most charge $10 and up for a roll-away bed.

Category	Cost*
$$$$	over $300
$$$	$200–$300
$$	$125–$200
$	under $125

*All prices are for a standard double room, excluding 9.7% tax.

$$$$

Four Seasons Hotel. A luxurious, 16-story brick hotel in a perfect location overlooking Boston Public Garden, this is one of the city's two best hotels for families (the other is the Ritz-Carlton; *see below*). The wonderful little luxuries for kids here include fluffy child-size bathrobes (a big hit with one well-traveled 6-year-old), bedtime milk, cookies, balloons, kids' shampoo, in-room VCR, and children's videos. It's less formal than the Ritz-Carlton, and the staff is friendly and considerate. The regular double rooms are large and elegant, but best bets for families are the corner rooms with two king-size beds, the double rooms that connect to a second room with twin beds (a special rate is available for the second room), or the executive suites, consisting of a bedroom and a sitting area that can be closed off with French doors. The 51-ft-long pool on the eighth floor, which overlooks the garden, has a shallow end (2½ ft deep); unlike many other hotel pools, it has a full-time lifeguard and kids are welcome anytime it's open (6 AM–10 PM).
🏨 *200 Boylston St., 02116, tel. 617/338–4400 or 800/332–3442, fax 617/423–0154. 213 rooms, 75 suites. Kids under 18 free. Facilities: 2 restaurants, fitness center, no-smoking rooms, parking (fee), pool. AE, DC, MC, V.*

Ritz-Carlton. Rich with tradition and with impeccable service, this 16-story hotel facing the Public Garden exudes the air of an earlier era; I expect to see little girls in dresses with velvet collars and shiny Mary Jane shoes in the lobby. During the Christmas season, the lobby and restaurants are festively decorated; other kids' events year-round include lunches with kids' book authors, cooking classes, and a weekend of etiquette instruction. All rooms are grandly spacious and traditionally furnished, but the ultimate in family suites anywhere is the hotel's very expensive Junior Presidential Suite, a colorful, childproof kids' bedroom-playroom filled with toys, books, stuffed animals, and a TV with video games, all connected to a room for parents. The Ritz, as befits a great hotel, provides everything families need, even lending ice skates to use on the pond in the Public Garden.

🏨 *15 Arlington St., 02117, tel. 617/536–5700 or 800/241–3333, fax 617/536–1335. 231 rooms, 44 suites. Facilities: 4 restaurants, baby-sitting, fitness center, no-smoking floors, parking (fee). AE, DC, MC, V.*

$$$

Colonnade Hotel. To me, personal service and the large "baby-safe" rooms (rubber stops on table corners, covered electrical outlets, playpens), and the rooftop pool where you can get burgers for lunch and gaze out over the city are the most appealing features of this small, 11-story modern hotel adjacent to the Prudential Center. Rooms are large. The hotel's restaurant, Brasserie Jo, serves delicious food, including kid-pleasers like roast chicken and home-made ice cream. The several family packages, good any day of the week, brings it into this price range.

🏨 *120 Huntington Ave., 02116, tel. 617/424–7000 or 800/962–3030, fax 617/424–1717. 285 rooms, 12 suites. Facilities: restaurant, baby-sitting, health club, outdoor pool, room service. AE, DC, MC, V.*

Eliot Suite Hotel. There's a warm, homey, European feeling to this small but elegant nine-floor suite hotel in the Back Bay, near Newbury Street shopping. The building is old, so the suites (one or two bedrooms) have slightly different layouts, but all are comfortable and spacious, with traditional

decor and marble baths. Corner suites have views of the Charles River. A typical family suite includes a bedroom, a large living room with a fold-out queen-size sofa, a TV in both rooms, and a kitchenette with a microwave, a small refrigerator, and a cof-feemaker. The hotel serves breakfast in the award-winning restaurant, Clio's, and soup and sandwich fare is available through room service. The location on Commonwealth Avenue makes it a good base for walking around town.

🏨 *370 Commonwealth Ave., 02215, tel. 617/267–1607 or 800/443–5468, fax 617/536–9114. 95 suites. Kids under 16 free (limit 2 to a family). Facilities: restaurant, baby-sitting, no-smoking rooms, parking (fee). AE, DC, MC, V.*

Marriott Long Wharf. For a summer week-end, this modern chain hotel on the water-front would be our choice—first, because it's only a block from the shopping scene at Faneuil Hall Marketplace, and second, because it has a large shallow swimming pool, usually filled with kids of all ages, and a harbor-view sundeck where you can order poolside lunches. You have the aquarium practically next door, Columbus/Waterfront Park just outside, and a T stop in front of the hotel. The regular weekend specials really bring down the price for a family of four. The green-accented rooms are in tradi-tional Early American decor, with closets big enough to hide in; most have some view of the harbor. Weekend packages are the best bet.

🏨 *296 State St., Long Wharf, 02109, tel. 617/227–0800 or 800/228–9290, fax 617/227–2867. 400 rooms. Kids under 18 free. Facilities: 2 restaurants, game room, health club, pool, in-room VCRs. AE, D, DC, MC, V.*

$$–$$$

Embassy Suites Hotel. This 16-story brick atrium hotel on the Charles River offers all suites and an indoor swimming pool, some-thing other all-suite hotels in town don't have. The one-bedroom suites, decorated in soft colors and corduroy, have space for kids to cavort; the bathroom, with marble and mirrors and a telephone, is luxurious. Video games are in each suite. It's rather far off the Downtown tourist path and closer to Cambridge than Boston proper, but a courtesy van to Downtown is provided, and the amenities and family packages here make up for that.

🏨 *400 Soldiers Field Rd., 02134, tel. 617/783–0090 or 800/362–2779, fax 617/783–0897. 310 suites. Kids under 18 free. Facilities: restaurant, baby-sitting, free parking, pool. CP. AE, D, DC, MC, V.*

Royal Sonesta. This modern two-tower hotel with recently refurbished bright, spacious rooms is right on the Charles River in Cambridge. Many rooms have a river view (costs extra). You can walk and bicycle along the riverside promenade right by the hotel, the Museum of Science is next door, and the CambridgeSide Galleria is just across the street. It is far from other Boston attractions, though it does offer courtesy van service to and from many Boston and Cambridge points of interest. The weekend family fun package gives you larger rooms and brings rates down into the next lower price range; extra amenities include use of bicycles, Polaroid cameras, tickets to the Museum of Science, boat rides on the Charles River, and all the ice cream you can eat from a cart in the lobby. The new restaurant, Gallery Café, has a patio; the Continental breakfast buffet is great for impatient and hungry kids.

🏨 *5 Cambridge Pkwy., Cambridge 02142, tel. 617/806–4200 or 800/766–3782, fax 617/806–4232. 400 rooms. Kids under 18 free. Facilities: 2 restaurants (kids' menu), baby-sitting, bicycling, health club, indoor pool with retractable roof. AE, D, DC, MC, V.*

$$

Harvard Square Hotel. This modern, five-story brick motel is right off Harvard Square—a perfect location if you have teens—and the price is pretty reasonable

compared with that of other hotels nearby. Rooms are still smallish, decorated in a more with-it contemporary style with pleasant pinks and greens; if your family requires quiet, be sure to ask for a room that doesn't face the street. Though it doesn't have a pool, guests have free use of the pool and other facilities at the Cambridge YMCA about 15 minutes away. They can also dine at the nearby Inn at Harvard and charge it to their room.

🏨 *110 Mt. Auburn St., tel. 617/864–5200 or 800/458–5886, fax 617/864–2409. 73 rooms. Kids under 16 free. Facilities: coffee shop, parking (fee). AE, DC, MC, V.*

The MidTown Hotel. Comfortable oversize rooms for families at very reasonable rates (the low end of this category), an attractive outdoor pool with lifeguard, and a good location not far from the Prudential Center are the reasons to stay at this motel-style spot atop an underground garage, especially in summer. About 40 of the rooms had undergone a much-needed renovation at press time; all should be renovated by spring 1999, but make sure you request a renovated one.

🏨 *220 Huntington Ave. 02115, tel. 617/262–1000 or 800/543–1177, fax 617/262–8739. 159 rooms. Kids under 18 stay free. Facilities: restaurant, free parking, pool. AE, D, DC, MC, V.*

$–$$

Eliot and Pickett Houses. Families are welcome at this lovely 20-room B&B in 19th-century brick town houses adjacent to the Boston Common and the State House lawns. This is an ideal location for kids of all ages. Rooms are spacious and elegant, wallpapered, furnished with attractive kid-friendly antiques; some have two four poster-beds and fireplaces. Two kitchens on the first floor are stocked with breakfast supplies; you can even make lunch and dinner here if you wish. Though rooms are TV-less there is a TV in the communal living room downstairs; in summer you're liable to see a group of kids watching cartoons on Saturday morning. The parking lot under Boston Common charges only $5 a day on weekends.

🏠 6 Mt. Vernon Place, 02109–2800, tel. 617/248–8707. 20 rooms, 18 with private bath. Facilities: kitchens. AE, D, DC, MC, V.

$

Susse Chalet Motor Lodge. There are two buildings here: a motor lodge fashioned after a ski lodge, where rooms have few frills, and a newer, more modern hotel-style inn next door. There's an outdoor pool, an indoor kids' center with video games and activities like the toddlers' ball crawl, and an adjacent bowling alley. Decent-size rooms are pleasant but bland motel style; you can reserve a microwave and fridge. From the center of Boston it's a 10-minute drive; the Alewife stop on the Red Line T is just under a mile away. Ask for family package rates, offered year-round.

🏠 800–900 Morrissey Blvd., Dorchester 02122, tel. 617/287–9200 or 800/524–2538, fax 617/282–2365. 309 rooms, 1 family suite. Kids under 18 free. Facilities: 3 restaurants, pool, free parking. AE, DC, MC, V.

Terrace Inn Best Western. It looks like a highway motel plunked down on a city street, but the two-room family suites here, which include kitchenettes, are a big bargain. Close to Boston University and Boston College, it's only a few blocks from a public ice rink and a ball field, and within walking distance of the Green Line T.

🏠 1650 Commonwealth Ave., 02135, tel. 617/566–6260 or 800/242–8377, fax 617/731–3543. 72 rooms. Kids under 18 free. Facilities: free parking. CP. AE, DC, MC, V.

Bed-and-Breakfasts

Many B&Bs in Boston, unlike those in New York City, actually welcome children. **Bed and Breakfast Associates/Bay Colony Ltd.** (Box 57166, Babson Park, Boston 02157–0166, tel. 617/449–5302 or 800/347–5088, fax 617/449–5958) represents about 400 rooms throughout the city and surrounding

area. During the off-season—winter and early spring—hosts often offer family discounts. Expect to pay anywhere from $60 (if your kids are under 5 and stay in your room) to about $175 (for two rooms). When you reserve, ask detailed questions about locations, and check the deposit and refund policy.

Apartment Rentals

AAA Corporate Rentals. Totally furnished one- or two-bedroom condos with fully equipped kitchens and bathrooms—sometimes even fireplaces and cable TV—can be rented. For a weeklong stay, a family of four will spend about $775.

🏠 120 Milk St., 02109, tel. 617/536–6900 or 800/487–5020, fax 617/357–7330.

Entertainment and the Arts

Amusement Parks

👫 2+ **Canobie Lake Park.** Only a 35-minute drive from Boston, this big, shady park offers original turn-of-the-century buildings and 40 rides set against the backdrop of a lake. The exuberant spirit of the place hits you from the moment you park your car, and it has something for everyone, from the Yankee Cannonball, a classic old wooden roller coaster, to the Psycho-Drome, an indoor scrambler with light and sound effects (older kids only), a huge swimming pool, and 20-minute rides on a paddle-wheeler. Throughout the summer several shows are presented daily; Saturday night means fireworks.

🏠 N. Policy St., Salem, NH, tel. 603/893–3506. Take Exit 2 off Rte. 93, then left on Policy St. ½ mi. Cost: $19 adults, $12 kids under 48". Open mid-Apr.–Labor Day, daily noon–10.

👫 2+ **Salem Willows Park.** Beloved by several kids on my Boston panel, this oceanfront park is a nostalgic reminder of another era with a funky arcade, rides for little ones, the best popcorn in the world, free concerts, and a pier for strolling and fishing. Cappy's Seafood has fried clams, scallops, and lobster rolls; the Chinese restaurant still has chop suey sandwiches.

🏨 173 Fort Ave., Salem, tel. 978/745–0251 (the Arcade). Cost: Park entrance free; arcade games 25¢ each. Open Apr.–Oct., Mon.–Sat. 11–11, Sun. noon–11.

Film

(👫 3–6) **Boston Public Library.** A regular series of free films for younger kids is held in this historic library filled with statues and paintings—don't miss the marble lions guarding the impressive main stairway.
🏨 Copley Sq., tel. 617/536–5400. Film showings Sept.–June, 1st Fri. of month, 10:15 AM; July–Aug., every Fri. 10:15 AM.

(👫 8+) **Hatch Shell on the Esplanade.** Bring a blanket and a picnic for the urban version of a drive-in: free Friday-night flicks on a big screen (only in summer from the end of June to the end of Aug.). Cross the Arthur Fiedler footbridge at Arlington and Beacon streets.
🏨 Tel. 617/727–9547.

(👫 6+) **Loews Copley Theater.** Set in an upscale mall with expensive shops, this 12-screen theater always has at least one or two films appropriate for younger kids. Occasionally it joins with the Hard Rock Cafe to offer dinner and a movie for $14.99.
🏨 100 Huntington Ave., in Copley Place, tel. 617/266–1300; ticket charge 617/333–3456.

Performing Spaces and Performers: Theater, Music, Dance

Considering its size, Boston and the surrounding towns have a significant number of performances for kids, many of them inexpensive events at college and university theaters. For folk music, Boston even beats out New York. The most complete listings

appear in the Thursday edition of the Boston Globe and the monthly calendar in Boston Parents' Paper (see How to Find Out What's Going On, above).

DISCOUNT TICKETS. Bostix, Boston's best ticket source, sells half-price tickets for same-day performances at an octagonal booth by Faneuil Hall (open Tues.–Sat. 10–6, Sun. 11–4) and in Copley Square (same hours). Telephone for both is 617/723–5181. A "menu board" in front tells you which events are available. The line is always long on weekends, and you must pay cash. Half-price tickets don't go on sale until 11. Bostix also sells full-price tickets (like Ticketmaster) and has information on many events and attractions. Advance half-price tickets are available by mail through **Arts/Boston** (100 Boylston St., Suite 735, tel. 617/482–2849 or 617/423–0372).

THEATER AND PUPPET SHOWS

(👫 5–12) **Boston Children's Theatre.** See Chapter 10.

(👫 6+) **Marco the Magi's "Le Grand David and His Own Spectacular Magic Company."** See Chapter 10.

(👫 5+) **North Shore Music Theatre.** Celebrity concerts, Broadway musicals, and kids' musicals are performed in the round, so you can see easily from any seat. Special children's performances are held Saturdays in May and Friday mornings in July and August.
🏨 62 Dunham Rd. (Exit 19 off Rte. 128), Beverly, tel. 978/922–8500. Cost: $27–$44 adults, $13.50–$17.50 kids 18 and under for regular shows, $6.75–$7.25 all tickets for kids' shows.

(👫 5–12) **Puppet Showplace.** See Chapter 10.

(👫 4+) **The Revels.** See Chapter 10.

(👫 9+) **Shear Madness.** A long-running humorous mystery play is performed cabaret-style. Playing at the Charles Playhouse's main stage is Blue Man Group: Tubes, the same show that appears off-Broadway in New York City, an extravaganza of physical stunts, visual gags, music, and much more. Teens find it "awesome."

🏛 *Charles Playhouse/Stage II, 74 Warrentown St., tel. 617/426–5225. Cost: Tues.–Thurs. and Sun. $30; Fri.–Sat. $34.*

👫 **6+**   **Theatre in the Open at Maudslay State Park.** Innovative family-oriented theater is performed in a gorgeous outdoor setting on an old estate. All is informal, and kids are welcome to come backstage after the performance, see how the scenery was constructed, and meet the cast.

🏛 *Curzon Mill Rd., Newburyport, tel. 508/465–2572. Take Exit 57 off Rte. 95, go right on Rte. 113, turn left at cemetery onto unmarked Noble St., then follow signs. Cost: $5; 1st performance of each show free. When: weekends mid-May–Sept.*

👫 **ALL**   **Wheelock Family Theater.** *See Chapter 10.*

MUSIC. In summer, Boston rings with free outdoor concerts in parks and plazas. We have the most fun at the concerts at the Esplanade (*see below*), but other good ones for kids are the free outdoor concerts and events such as a dance festival at Downtown Crossing (tel. 617/482–2139) and jazz concerts in Columbus Park on Friday nights (tel. 617/635–3911). If you have teenagers, check at Newbury Comics (*see Shopping, above*) for information on store-sponsored rock music events.

👫 **8+**   **Boston Pops.** *See Chapter 10.*

👫 **5–12**   **Boston Symphony Orchestra.** *See Chapter 10.*

👫 **8+**   **Esplanade Concerts.** Picnicking on the grass above the Charles River while music wafts out from the Hatch Band Shell is a summertime must for us. In addition to the Boston Pops, a range of internationally known dance, opera, and music groups, including youth orchestras, appears. A moderately priced snack bar is near the Shell, which also has rest rooms.

🏛 *Hatch Shell, tel. 617/727–9547, ext. 550.*

👫 **5+**   **New England Conservatory.** *See Chapter 10.*

DANCE

👫 **5+**   **Boston Ballet Company.** *See Chapter 10.*

👫 **9+**   **Dance Umbrella.** This organization, like Jacob's Pillow in the Berkshires, presents the very best contemporary dance troupes, such as the wild and acrobatic Pilobolus. Many special performances for families, usually Sunday matinees, are scheduled each year; kids under 12 are usually half-price.

🏛 *515 Washington St., Boston 02111, tel. 617/482–7570. (Many performances at the Emerson Majestic Theatre, 219 Tremont St., tel. 617/824–8000.) Cost: $14–$65. When: Sept.–June, Thurs.–Sun.*

CIRCUS

👫 **3–12**   **Big Apple Circus.** In April and May, this splendid one-ring show performs in a heated tent near the Children's Museum. *See also Chapter 10.*

🏛 *Children's Museum, 300 Congress St., Museum Wharf, tel. 617/426–8855.*

👫 **6–15**   **Ringling Brothers and Barnum & Bailey Circus.** The three-ring big-top circus plays at FleetCenter every October; on arrival, a circus parade treks through the North End. *See also Chapter 10.*

🏛 *150 Causeway St., tel. 617/624–1000.*

MUSEUM PROGRAMS

👫 **2+**   **Children's Museum.** Every weekend there's something—a Japanese mime, Puerto Rican dancers, a workshop to learn hip-hop—and kids are invited to participate.

🏛 *300 Congress St., Museum Wharf, tel. 617/426–6500. Cost: Free with museum admission.*

👫 **4–12**   **Museum of Fine Arts.** Two regular year-round programs involve kids in observing artwork and then creating something based on what they've seen. The Children's Room, for kids 6–12, is a free drop-in workshop every weekday afternoon; Family Place, held once a month on a Sunday ($5 per family), is for kids 4 and older with their parents. **ᴍ** *465 Huntington Ave., tel. 617/267–9300.*

FESTIVALS AND STREET PERFORMERS. First Night (tel. 617/542–1399), a citywide, no-alcohol New Year's Eve celebration of 250 performances, fireworks, and a special kids' afternoon festival, is the oldest of these events in the country. At the end of April each year, the **New England Folk Festival** (tel. 617/354–1340) attracts families for dance and music; Saturday and Sunday are the best days for kids. On weekends in late spring, summer, and early fall **Faneuil Hall Marketplace** and **Harvard Square** (particularly at Brattle Square, where Mt. Auburn and Brattle Sts. join) are thick with magicians, jugglers, musicians, and acrobats. In late May, the **Street Performers Festival** (tel. 617/523–1300) in Faneuil Hall Marketplace is a time to stick bottle caps to the bottom of your shoes and join the marchers in the Kazoo Parade or simply enjoy gazing at the continuous free entertainment. It ends with a fantastic fireworks show.

NEW YORK CITY

12

SKYSCRAPERS, THE STATUE OF LIBERTY,
AND THE BEST TOY STORE IN THE COUNTRY

My son Gavin, who grew up in New York and now visits regularly, has always thought of it as the most exciting city in the world—despite visits to Paris, Rome, Milan, Boston, and San Francisco. To him and my panel of New York City kids it has the biggest and best of everything—skyscrapers, ferryboats, lights, crowds, energy, 7 million people who represent almost every nationality in the world, and tons of things to do that you can't do anywhere else. Here's what they love about New York: Chinese restaurants, climbing to the crown of the Statue of Liberty, the dinosaurs at the American Museum of Natural History, eating at outdoor cafés and in tiny midtown parks with man-made waterfalls, the Staten Island Ferry, the Paper Bag Players productions, flagging down taxis, bagels, the world's greatest pizza, the Knicks at Madison Square Garden, visiting a real aircraft carrier, and on and on and on.

In fact, when we visit New York, choosing what to do is our family's biggest problem. I've learned that the most important thing you can do for your kids—and yourself—on a visit to this city is to resist the frenetic pace and slow down. Plan to see no more than two major attractions in one day and be flexible: To really enjoy this city with kids you have to build into your daily sightseeing plans a visit to a playground, a walk down just one street in a neighborhood, and a stop for ice cream at a café where you can people-watch. Take a list of the attractions or events that most appeal to your kids, and make their first choice the highlight of your first day.

To most people, Manhattan is synonymous with New York City; that's where most of the city's attractions are. But the other four boroughs—Queens, Brooklyn, Staten Island, and the Bronx—are worth visiting, too. Each offers something unique for families: the Bronx Zoo, the Brooklyn Botanical Garden, the New York Hall of Science in Queens, and Historic Richmond Town on Staten Island.

It helps to think of Manhattan as a collection of small neighborhoods: the Lower East Side, Chinatown, Little Italy, SoHo, Greenwich Village, Murray Hill, Chelsea, Lincoln Center, the Upper West Side, the Upper East Side. Each has its own flavor, attractions, and restaurants. The best way to see and appreciate New York City with kids is to adopt a neighborhood for a day or a weekend and explore its sights, shops, restaurants, and parks.

The city also has its share of problems that families need to know about. The main question most families have: Is it safe for children? My answer is: Most areas of Manhattan are as safe as—if not safer than—neighborhoods in any other major city. This means using the kind of caution required in any large city: sticking to well-lighted and well-traveled streets at night and being alert to what is going on wherever you are. I would not let young teenagers travel around the city by themselves even during the day, because they often don't have the street savvy to anticipate a problem. With small children, your main concern is street traffic and crowds. When crossing streets, watch out for bicyclists, who often ignore traffic lights, and hang on to rambunctious little kids in crowded stores, streets, and subways. Kids should know what to do and where to go in case they get separated from you.

The Basics

How to Find Out What's Going On

The **New York Convention and Visitors Bureau** (810 7th Ave., New York, NY 10019, tel. 800/692–8474 or 212/397–8222 from outside North America; personalized assistance, 212/484–1222) publishes a seasonal "Official NYC Guide," which lists hotels, restaurants, events, attractions, performing arts, and more, though in very small type; it also includes useful discount coupons. Send away for it and inquire about other discount passes available; in the past the various Visitors Centers around the city sponsored by the Bureau have offered a free pass that entitled holders to special rates at hotels, discounts at selected restaurants, and two-for-one admissions to attractions. You'll find drop-in Visitors Centers at JFK Airport, Grand Central, Penn Station, Macy's, the World Trade Center, and in Times Square. The NYCVB Web site is www.nycvisit.com.

One new valuable discount coupon is **New York CityPass**, a ticket book that admits you to six of the city's top attractions with kid-appeal for about half-price: the Empire State Building Observatory and the Top of the World Trade Center; and four museums: the American Museum of Natural His-

tory, the *Intrepid* Sea/Air/Space Museum, the Metropolitan Museum of Art, and the Museum of Modern Art. You can purchase these at any one of the six attractions and they're good for nine days. Since kids under 13 get in most places for a significantly reduced rate, CityPass wisely offers only adult ($26.75) and youth ages 13–18 ($21) passes.

NEWSPAPERS, MAGAZINES, AND BOOKS. Look for the following publications on newsstands, in supermarkets, and in bookstores, or request them by phone.

Two local parents' monthlies with good information are *Big Apple Parents Paper* (Family Communications, 36 E. 12th St., New York 10003, tel. 212/533–2277), which includes a calendar of events as well as articles and reviews of restaurants, and *New York Family* (Family Publishing Group, 141 Halstead Ave., Suite 3D, Mamaroneck 10543, tel. 914/381–7474), which has the most easy-to-use listings of current performances, museum exhibits, and the like. When in New York, you can pick up free copies.

Local newspapers and magazines also have good listings of events and performances for children: The *New York Times* has columns "Family Fare" and "Spare Times for Children" on current attractions for kids in the Friday "Weekend" section; *New York Newsday* has kids' features every day and events listings for kids on Friday; *TimeOut New York*, published weekly, also has a special section listing shows, films, and things to do for kids; in *New York* magazine, also a weekly, check the sections "Other Events" and "Children."

Another useful source of information is the *Central Park Calendar of Events* (Central Park Conservancy, 830 5th Ave., at 64th St., New York 10021, tel. 212/360–2766). Published quarterly, it lists walks, special activities, and performances for kids in Central Park.

BOOKS FOR KIDS. Many books for kids have New York City as a backdrop; here are a few of our favorites: *Eloise* by Kay Thompson (ages 4–8), a classic humorous story of a little girl's life at the Plaza Hotel; *Cricket in Times Square* by George Selden (ages 6–10), in which a cricket from Connecticut turns up in the subway station in Times Square; *Stuart Little* by E. B. White (ages 6–10), about mouse-size Stuart's adventures in and around Central Park; *Harriet the Spy* by Louise Fitzhugh (ages 8–11); and *From the Mixed Up Files of Mrs. Basil E. Frankweiler* by E. Konigsburg (ages 8–13), about children who hide out in the Metropolitan Museum of Art to solve an art mystery.

MOVIES. So many films have been set in New York that your child has probably seen at least one, but if not, rent *Ghostbusters, Home Alone II, Superman, King Kong, Big,* or *The Muppets Take Manhattan* to provide a preview of the city.

Arriving and Departing

BY BUS. All lines arrive at and depart from Port Authority Bus Terminal. Prepare your kids to see some vagrants and hustlers.

BY CAR. The major interstates that come into New York are I–495 from Long Island; I–95 from Connecticut and New England to the Bruckner Expressway (I–278) and across the Triborough Bridge; the Lincoln Tunnel (I–495), Holland Tunnel, and George Washington Bridge (I–95) connect New York City with New Jersey.

BY PLANE. Try to land at La Guardia Airport (in Queens) or Newark International Airport (in New Jersey) if you can; John F. Kennedy International Airport (in Queens) is hard to get around. (International travelers should be aware that Air France has installed an extremely pleasant family lounge at JFK.) All airports do have nurseries where you can easily change diapers, as well as a variety of restaurants, from Pizza Hut to cafeterias.

Between the Airport and New York: The easiest way for your family to get to a hotel is by **limousine service**. Limos can pick up riders only by prior arrangement; call at least 24 hours in advance to reserve. Prices are generally very slightly higher than taxi rates. **Carmel Car and Limousine Service** (tel. 212/666–6666 or 800/922–7635) has station wagons that are larger than taxis at very good rates. Other limo services are **Absolute Limousine** (tel. 800/222–6588 or 212/227–6588) and **Tel-Aviv Private Car & Limousine Service** (tel. 212/777–7777). Plan on about $20–$26 plus tolls and tip from La Guardia; it will take 30 to 45 minutes. A flat cab rate fare—$30 plus tolls and tips—from JFK has been in effect for the past few years; the trip takes about an hour. From Newark, flat rate fares—$30–$50 plus toll and tip—depend on where you are going in Manhattan or the other boroughs. The **Delta Water Shuttle** (tel. 800/543–3779) is a ferry you can catch at La Guardia that docks at 34th Street and Wall Street in Manhattan; it's faster than a taxi ($15). **New York Airport Service** (tel. 718/706–9658) buses go into Manhattan from JFK ($13 one way/$20 round-trip) and La Guardia ($10/$15) frequently; as children under 12 ride free when accompanied by an adult, they're worth it for a single parent if you don't have much luggage. **Olympia Trails Airport Express** (tel. 212/964–6233) buses leave from Newark for Grand Central, Penn Station, and the World Trade Center; the fare is $10, and children under 3 ft tall are free.

BY TRAIN. If you take **Amtrak** (tel. 800/872–7245), which offers frequent service between Washington, D.C., and New York, and Boston and New York, you will arrive at and depart from Pennsylvania Station (31st–33rd Sts. between 7th and 8th Aves.). **Long Island Railroad** trains (tel. 718/217–5477) and **New Jersey Transit** trains (tel. 201/762–5100) also come into this station. **Metro-North Commuter Railroad** (tel. 212/532–4900) serves the northern suburbs and Connecticut as far east as New Haven from Grand Central Terminal.

Getting Around New York

Take a cue from New Yorkers, who rarely use cars to get anywhere in the city. It's much easier (and more fun) to use public transportation or a taxi. Although some hotels do offer parking, it is usually expensive (as much as $25–$35 a day; see Lodging, *below*, for hotels that offer free parking), and many charge each time you take your car out. If you do drive to New York, plan to park your car for your entire stay.

TAKE A WALK. The easiest and most interesting way to see New York with children is on foot, provided that you have a stroller for children under 5. Do not try to go too far, and stop frequently. Sturdy shoes are important; pounding the pavement, stepping in potholes, and walking on cracked sidewalks is tiring. But walking offers kids a chance to notice typical New York sights: the man walking six huge dogs, bread shaped like a large turtle and an alligator in a bakery window, a juggler on a street corner. Our family likes to keep walking until we're all ready to go back to the hotel—then we take a taxi, subway, or bus and rest our feet.

The city streets above 14th Street are designed like a grid: Numbered streets run east and west; numbered and named avenues run north and south. Fifth Avenue divides the east side from the west side. The avenue west of 5th is labeled Avenue of the Americas, but no New Yorker calls it that.

To us it's still 6th Avenue. Below 14th Street the streets are a crooked hodgepodge, so you need a map. Manhattan is bounded on the west by the Hudson (or North) River and on the east by the East River.

Where to walk? Just explore a neighborhood. Downtown includes all the neighborhoods south of 14th Street. At the very tip of this island is Lower Manhattan, sometimes just called Wall Street or the Financial District. The oldest part of the city, it houses skyscrapers, the financial center, South Street Seaport, and parks right on the water. Chinatown, just north of it, has crowded streets filled with people speaking Chinese, fascinating shops, and dozens of Chinese restaurants. TriBeCa and SoHo, which border Chinatown on the west, are trendy and chic; you'll find the hippest art galleries, shops—especially clothing stores—and cafés here. Just north of Chinatown is Little Italy, a small neighborhood of Italian cafés, restaurants, and frequent festivals. Above these are Greenwich Village (called "the Village"), whose lovely tree-lined streets and brownstones, cafés, and shops reflect its history as home to writers and artists, and the East Village, whose funkier (and dirtier) streets spill over with a younger, more punk-looking crowd. Chelsea (on the west side) and Gramercy Park and Murray Hill (on the east side) are largely residential. Midtown, bounded on the north by the bottom of Central Park, is like a big square in the center of the city that's primarily commercial—hotels, restaurants, department stores, and landmark office towers like the Empire State Building.

Everything above 59th Street is Uptown. On the west side of Central Park is the Upper West Side, a very family-oriented, primarily residential area with some important museums—the American Museum of Natural History, for example, as well as the Lincoln Center complex, and many family-welcoming restaurants. Just to the north of it is Morningside Heights, where Columbia University is located, and above it is Harlem,

a historic center for African-American culture, politics, and music for nearly a century,
perhaps best explored on a tour (see Family-Friendly Tours, below). The Upper East
Side, on the east side of Central Park, is
dominated by expensive, elegant apartment
buildings and shops and the greatest concentration of art museums in the city. Above
it is East Harlem (or Spanish Harlem),
where the population is almost entirely
Latino.

RIDE THE SUBWAY. Subway tokens, available at booths or machines in each subway
station, are $1.50; children under 6 ride free.
Put in a token to go through the turnstile;
little kids under 6 just duck below it. However, if you'll be in the city for several days
and plan to take the subway frequently, purchase the Metropolitan Transit Authority's
(MTA) MetroCard, a thin plastic card with a
magnetic strip that you swipe through an
electronic reader to pass through the turnstile; the reader deducts the fare from the
card and displays how much remains.
MetroCards are available at station token
booths in a variety of amounts. More than
one person can use the same card, just
swipe it through the reader once for each
rider.

It's true that subways are noisy, crowded,
and sometimes filled with unsavory characters. It's also true that they are usually the
quickest way to get somewhere and that
many children—mine included—enjoy riding them.

A few caveats. Avoid rush hours. Take a bus
or taxi if you have a stroller and are alone;
carrying a stroller up and down the flights of
steps to the subway platforms is very tiring
and dangerous—platforms slant toward the
track and unattended strollers will roll. Hold
your children's hands tightly on the platform
and stand well back from the edge. During
off-peak hours wait in the designated safe
area. Don't get into deserted cars.

Check the large subway maps by the token
booth to figure out your route, ask the

token clerk or another passenger, or consult
a folding map from the New York Convention and Visitors Bureau. Most New Yorkers
are friendly and are happy to help you. You
can also call the Metropolitan Transit
Authority (MTA) (tel. 718/330–1234 or
718/330–4847) from 6 AM to 9 PM for bus
or subway directions in more than 140 lan-
guages and dialects.

TAKE THE BUS. Buses charge the same
fare as the subway, $1.50; children under 6
ride free. You must have a subway token,
exact change in coins (no pennies), or, better yet, a MetroCard. Bus routes usually go
north and south or east and west; if your
route requires two buses, get a free transfer
from the bus driver when you board. Before
you wait at a bus stop, check to make sure
the bus you want stops there, as not all
buses stop at every stop along the route. It's
important to have a bus map; you can get
subway and bus maps at all subway token
booths, unless they've run out, or at the
New York Convention and Visitors Bureau,
Grand Central Station Information booth,
or Penn Station Information booth, because
buses often don't have them. You can call
the MTA for route information (see Ride the
Subway, above). Take note that when traffic
is heavy, buses are very slow, and during
rush hours they're packed.

HAIL A TAXI. Because a family of four with
two children over 6 will pay $6 for one ride
on a subway or bus, if you're not going far, a
taxi ride may actually cost less (they charge
per ride, not per passenger—$2 for the first
⅕ mi, 30¢ for each additional ⅕ mi, and 30¢
for each 75 seconds you're not moving). A
50¢ charge is added after 8 PM). Tip about
15%. It's usually pretty easy to find a taxi, but
not when it's raining, at rush hour, or when
theaters let out.

Family-Friendly Tours

Most kids I know do not like long tours on
which adults drone on about events or
buildings, so I've included only a few special
tours.

👪 5+ **Big Apple Greeters**. The "greeters" are New York City residents who volunteer to spend a few hours with visitors to welcome them to the city. They'll show you how to use the subway and bus systems, give you a MetroCard, answer questions, help orient you to sights you're interested in, and generally make you feel comfortable in the city. This is one of New York City's bargains—it's free. After you make your reservation (at least a week in advance) you'll be matched with a guide who shares your interests.
🏠 *1 Centre St., tel. 212/669–8159, fax 212/669–3685.*

👪 5+ **Circle Line Cruise**. New York is so packed with buildings that it's hard to get a picture of it as a whole, much less visualize it as an island, unless you get out on the water. This company offers three different ways to do that. The classic 35-mi circumnavigation of Manhattan takes three hours; there is also a two-hour trip, a semicircle tour that doesn't go completely around the island. A one-hour seaport Liberty cruise leaving from the South Street Seaport goes by the Statue of Liberty and the Brooklyn Bridge. If your kids want more excitement, try one of the 30-minute Seaport Speedboat rides in *The Beast*, a fast boat that looks like a huge yellow alligator. We like the long trip, but with younger kids my vote is for the two-hour trip. The boats for the two longer cruises are big, so you don't feel cramped unless it's very crowded, as it is on holiday weekends when the weather is good. You can bring lunch, but hot dogs and sodas are sold on board; there are bathrooms. Each guide has his own patter; some tell very funny jokes. Ours have always welcomed lots of questions from kids. Don't go unless it's a nice day, which means not too hot or too cold or too rainy, and make sure your child is up to the length of trip you choose.
🏠 *Pier 83, 42nd St. at Hudson River, tel. 212/563–3200. Cost: 3-hr cruise, $22 adults, $12 kids 2–12; 2-hr, $18 adults, $10 kids 2–*

12. Cruises Mar.–Nov., 10, 11, noon, 1:30, 2:30, 4; in winter reduced schedule. 1-hr cruise and speedboat rides leave from Pier 16, South Street Seaport, tel. 212/630–8888. Cost: 1-hr cruise, $12 adults, $6 kids 2–12. Open Mar.– mid-Dec., 12, 1:30, 3, 4:30 weekdays, weekends also at 6. Cost: speedboat rides, $15 adults, $10 kids 2–12. Open June–mid-Oct., every hr 11:15–7:15.

👪 9+ **Harlem Spirituals**. Of this friendly company's various bus tours in and around Harlem, those on Wednesday and Sunday mornings, which include attending a vivid one-hour gospel service of music, singing, and clapping as well as stops at historic buildings, are best for kids. Soul-food lunches afterward are optional and cost extra (but they're worth it). Tours begin at their midtown office.
🏠 *690 Eighth Ave., tel. 212/391–0900. Cost: $33–$75 adults, $27–$60 kids 12 and under. Wed. and Sun. tours begin at 9 AM.*

👪 6+ **New York Skyride**. Of course this isn't really a tour; rather a simulated, eight-minute wild roller-coaster-like ride around New York City landmarks (on a big screen), complete with ear-splitting sound effects. To me it's overpriced, but many kids love it. Expect to wait in line, sometimes as long as 30 minutes.
🏠 *In the Empire State Building, 5th Ave. and 34th St., tel. 212/279–9777. Cost: $11.50 adults, $9.50 kids 4–12. Combination tickets for a visit to the Empire State Building Observation Deck are $14 adults and a bargain $9 for kids 4–12. Open 10 AM–10 PM.*

👪 5+ **Small Journeys, Inc**. If you are in New York with several other families, consider taking a custom tour with this group, which designs walking (and other) tours especially geared to children's interests. Guides are entertaining and flexible.
🏠 *114 W. 86th St., tel. 212/874–7300. Cost: $210 for 4 hrs, with a suggested maximum of 15 people.*

👪 5+ **Urban Park Rangers**. Rangers lead free walking tours every Saturday and

Sunday rain or shine (call for specific times and for theme) in Central Park and at a variety of other parks in the five boroughs. You don't have to reserve in advance, but call to ask about the themes of the tours to make sure your kids will be interested. Tours last about 90 minutes and are full of action—kids can look for insects beneath leaves and logs during the Central Park "bug out" walk or participate in an afternoon of Ranger nature games.

🔒 *North Meadow, Central Park, tel. 212/988–4952; park events hot line, 888/697–2758 or 212/360–3456. Cost: Free.*

Pit Stops

The best places to find clean, pleasant bathrooms in New York City: all museums; libraries; major department stores; lobbies of big hotels; and public atriums. Go before you leave for the theater or movies to avoid long lines. Don't use the bathrooms in subway stations—they are usually filthy. Rest rooms in city parks can be iffy, too; don't ever send a child in alone.

Emergencies

FOR MINOR PROBLEMS. New York Hospital's Urgent Care Center (525 E. 70th St., tel. 212/746–0795); or Roosevelt Hospital's Urgent Care Center (58th St. at 9th Ave., tel. 212/523–6765).

FOR SERIOUS EMERGENCIES. Call 911 for police, fire, and ambulance. For Poison Control, call 212/340–4494. Pediatricians are on duty in the emergency rooms at Bellevue Hospital Center (1st Ave. and 29th St., tel. 212/562–3025 or 212/562–4141) and at Columbia Presbyterian Medical Center (622 W. 168th St., tel. 212/305–6628 or 212/305–2500). There are 24-hour full-service emergency rooms at New York Hospital (510 E. 70th St., tel. 212/746–5050), New York University Medical Center (550 1st Ave., at 33rd St., tel. 212/263–7300), and St. Luke's–Roosevelt Hospital (58th St. at 9th Ave., tel. 212/523–6800).

New York Hotel Urgent Medical Services (tel. 212/737–1212) is open 24 hours for both house calls and office visits. Dial-A-Doctor is a 24-hour house-call service (tel. 212/971–9692). Physicians Home Care is a house-call service available until midnight (tel. 212/737–2333).

24-Hour Pharmacy: Several branches of the Duane Reade chain are open all night: at Broadway and 57th Street (tel. 212/541–9708), at 3rd Avenue and 74th Street (tel. 212/744–2668), and at Lexington Avenue and 47th Street (tel. 212/682–5338). Genovese (2nd Ave. and 68th St., tel. 212/772–0104) also provides free delivery.

Baby-Sitters

Most hotels have a list of baby-sitters or bonded baby-sitting agencies that they know and use regularly. The agency that many recommend is the Babysitter's Guild (60 E. 42nd St., Suite 912, tel. 212/682–0227), which has been in business for more than 50 years. Other baby-sitting agencies are listed in the Yellow Pages. Most charge $12 and up per hour, with a four-hour minimum.

When to Go

New York is a year-round destination, with special attractions indoors and outdoors during each season. In the coldest months, January and February (as well as any time the weather is miserable), New York's museums and indoor atriums provide plenty to occupy kids—and there's outdoor ice-skating. December is exciting: The Christmas decorations are up, stores are crowded with shoppers, and there are free holiday concerts and performances all over the city that are geared toward children. But our favorite times are the early fall, late spring, and early summer, the most pleasant seasons for walking and outdoor sightseeing. These are also the seasons with the most parades and street fairs. Summer, especially July and August, can be brutally hot and humid; temperatures are often above 90°F, and though museums, buses, and shops are air-conditioned, just getting from place to place can be extremely unpleasant. On the plus side are the large number of free outdoor concerts, plays, and performances of all kinds.

Scoping Out New York

Serendipities

Some of the sights our family views as "quintessentially New York" are free—or at least very inexpensive.

IN CENTRAL PARK

(**👫 2 – 6**) **Climb on the Alice in Wonderland statue.** You'll see little kids climbing all over this bronze statue of Alice sitting on a giant mushroom with a grinning Cheshire cat and flanked by the White Rabbit and the Mad Hatter. **🏠** *North side of Conservatory Water, near 5th Ave. and 76th St.*

(**👫 3 – 12**) **Watch sailboats on the Conservatory Water.** On Saturday at 10 AM you can watch people sailing very expensive and elaborate model boats on this small round pond many New Yorkers refer to as "the sailboat pond" (just in from 5th Ave. and 74th St.). You can bring your own toy sailboat to sail after the official races are over.

(**👫 2 – 10**) **Listen to the Delacorte Music Clock.** Near the Central Park Zoo is a whimsical clock (just in from 5th Ave. and E. 65th St.) set on top of a redbrick arch. Stand in front of it on the hour or half hour and you'll see and hear the six-animal band play a tune as they turn.

(**👫 ½–10**) **Ride the carousel.** This merry-go-round is a staple of childhood for many New York kids—an antique carousel with 58 painted, hand-carved horses and bouncy music. The carousel does go fast; timid 2- and 3-year-olds may prefer to ride in one of the stationary sleighs.

🏠 *Midpark, off 65th St. transverse, tel. 212/ 879–0244. Cost: 90¢. Open May–Sept., weekdays 10:30–5:30, weekends and holidays 10:30–6:30; Oct.–Apr., daily 10:30–5, weather permitting.*

(**👫 ALL**) **Ride in a horse-drawn carriage.** Most kids are fascinated by the horse-drawn carriages at Grand Army Plaza (59th St. and 5th Ave.); you'll also find them along 59th St. and at Columbus Circle (59th St. and Central Park West). All the carriages are different, some completely open, some covered; their drivers dress in top hats or other appropriate garb. You can hire a carriage for a ride through the park for $34 for 20 minutes or so, $10 for each additional 15 minutes (agree on a price in advance).

BOATS, TRAMS, AND SUBWAYS

(**👫 ALL**) **Staten Island Ferry.** One of New York City's major freebies is the 20-to-30-minute ferry ride from the tip of Manhattan across New York Harbor to Staten Island in one of these big orange ferries. You have good views of the Statue of Liberty and the New York skyline. Our family likes to take the ferry on a warm summer night and see the city lit up; no matter how hot it is, there's usually a breeze on the water. **🏠** *Battery Park and Whitehall St. (Subway 1 or 9 to South Ferry), tel. 718/727–2508. Cost: Free. Open daily 24 hrs.*

(**👫 3+**) **Roosevelt Island Tram.** Another way to get a splendid—and cheap—view of the Manhattan skyline is by riding the city's only aerial tram, from 59th Street to Roosevelt Island. It takes just a few minutes. Kids afraid of heights should avoid it, but those who like gondola rides or Ferris wheels think it's terrific. Get there early to nab one of the few seats. **🏠** *2nd Ave. between 59th and 60th Sts. (Subway 6, N, or R to 59th St.), tel. 212/832– 4543. Cost: $1.50 each way. Open Sun.– Thurs. 6 AM–2 AM, Fri.–Sat. 6 AM–3:30 AM.*

(**👫 2 – 13**) **Ride in the first subway car.** Most kids love peering through the front window of the first subway car at the tracks and lighted tunnel, zooming through the darkness, and suddenly pulling into a lighted station.

NEIGHBORHOODS

(**👫 4–15**) Watch for murals on buildings. New York is full of surprises. When you go to the South Street Seaport or the Fulton Fish Market, walk north on Front Street to Peck's Slip; then face north and look at the trompe l'oeil mural of the Brooklyn Bridge by Richard Haas on the building opposite. When you're in SoHo, find the "Knowledge is Power" graffiti mural (my son's favorite) at West Houston and Broadway and another Richard Haas mural of windows, one with a cat sitting on the windowsill, at the corner of Prince and Greene streets.

(**👫 ALL**) Neighborhoods. Our family is happy to spend an afternoon just wandering through one of New York's neighborhoods. Here are the two we like best:

In **Chinatown**, walk down Mott Street from Canal Street to Chatham Square. Most kids like the pagoda-shape telephone kiosks and buildings, the twisty streets crammed with residents chatting in Chinese, and the restaurant windows where you can look in on chefs slicing and dicing. You can browse for Chinese toys and souvenirs displayed outside shops and markets. Chinatown Fair (8 Mott St.) is a video game arcade with more than 50 video and pinball games. It's a little dingy but filled with young kids having fun.

In **SoHo**, walk down West Broadway, Wooster Street, and Prince Street. This 26-block gallery neighborhood of cast-iron buildings is especially entertaining on a crowded sunny Saturday. You'll see lots of New Yorkers with babies in strollers as well as teens and preteens.

Skyscrapers, Statues, and a Historic Seaport

(**👫 3–13**) Cathedral of St. John the Divine. When finished, this glorious cathedral will be the largest in the western hemi-

sphere; with an outrageous fountain, playground, peacocks, and many kid-pleasing sculptures you can touch, it's very kid-friendly. Buy the "Kids' Cathedral" booklet (for kids 3–9) and look at David Macauley's book *Cathedral* before you come. **🏠** *Amsterdam Ave. between 110th and 112th Sts., tel. 212/316–7540.*

(**👫 5–15**) Chrysler Building. Though not as tall as the Empire State Building, this shiny skyscraper, built as the home of the Chrysler Corporation, looks like Flash Gordon's idea of a rocket. Look up at the car designs at each setback—the gargoyles at the fourth one are in the style of radiator caps—and the wheel designs carved right in the brick. If you go into the marble lobby, check out the ceiling mural. **🏠** *405 Lexington Ave., between 42nd and 43rd Sts. Open weekdays.*

(**👫 ALL**) Empire State Building. This landmark is probably the best known of the city's skyscrapers, even to kids. See also Chapter 2 and above, Family-Friendly Tours, for the New York Skyride on the second floor. **🏠** *34th St. and 5th Ave., tel. 212/736–3100. Accepts CityPass.*

(**👫 5+**) Grand Central Terminal. Of the two main train stations in Manhattan, this one's the more spectacular, especially now that it has undergone massive renovation. Climb the wide marble stairs at rush hour and watch the commuters, and look up at the constellations illustrated on the teal-blue ceiling. If you can, take the Municipal Arts Society free tour, given every Wednesday at 12:30; walk across one of the "skybridges" inside the windows at the top of the building. Look down and you'll have a view of the whole terminal. Among the many shops in the terminal is one for kids, the Children's General Store. **🏠** *42nd St. and Lexington Ave. For tours, Municipal Arts Society, tel. 212/935–3960.*

(**👫 10+**) New York Stock Exchange. The view from the visitor's gallery of brokers noisily trading shares on the 90- by 90-ft floor and of the electronic screens on the walls were more interesting to kids we know than the exhibits in the visitor center. During school vacations, get in line early.

🏠 *Visitor center, 20 Broad St. (Subway 2, 3, 4, or 5 to Wall St.; or J, M, or Z to Broad St.), 3rd floor, tel. 212/656–5165. Free tickets distributed starting at 8:45; arrive before 10 to be certain of getting in. Open weekdays 9–4:30, but trading ends at 4.*

(👫 **ALL**) **Rockefeller Center**. This complex of buildings, including Radio City Music Hall and NBC, public plazas, and an ice rink on 5th Avenue, is a great place for walking around. *See also* Chapter 2.

🏠 *47th–52nd Sts. between 5th and 6th Aves., tel. 212/698–2950. NBC tours, tel. 212/664–7174.*

(👫 **7+**) **Sony Wonder Technology Lab**. The futuristic technology exhibits here are really an ad for Sony, but so what? It's still fun to zoom up the glass outside elevator, log in and receive your own key card, explore the many exhibits (like pressing buttons to create a music video and work the robots)—and it's free. Aim for an afternoon visit; school groups predominate in the morning.

🏠 *Sony Plaza, 550 Madison Ave., between 55th and 56th Sts., tel. 212/833–8100. Free. Open Tues.–Sat. 10–6, Thurs. 10–8, Sun. noon–6.*

(👫 **ALL**) **South Street Seaport**. Besides a museum with historic ships, this 11-block district has boat rides and street performances. *See also* Chapter 2.

🏠 *19 Fulton St., at East River, tel. 212/748–8600 or 212/732–7678.*

(👫 **ALL**) **Statue of Liberty**. This 151-ft-tall symbol of freedom, known to even very small children, is on all my New York kids' lists as one of the sights in the city they've liked best. *See also* Chapter 2.

🏠 *Liberty Island (ticket office at Castle Clinton for Statue of Liberty ferry), tel. 212/363–3200, ferry 212/269–5755.*

(👫 **9+**) **United Nations**. It's the flags of all the nations flying outside the Secretariat, one of the three main U.N. buildings, and the numbers of people from many different countries that appeal to kids under 9. Older kids like the meditation room in the main lobby and the daily tours—in the visitor's gallery kids can listen on headphones and press a button to hear a translation into another language. Because of security reasons, you can only sometimes visit the General Assembly when it's in session from September to Christmas (call first, then arrive early, as only a limited number of seats are available). The gift shops downstairs have international souvenirs, books of all countries, and U.N. stamp collections. Adjacent to the U.N. headquarters are lovely lawns and trees and a pretty garden. Older kids may find it fun to eat at the Delegates Dining Room (reservations tel. 212/963–7625), with its sweeping views of the East River.

🏠 *East River between 45th and 46th Sts. (Subway 4, 5, 6, 7, or S to Grand Central Station, then walk east), tel. 212/963–7713. Cost: $7.50 adults, $4.50 students, $3.50 8th graders and under; no kids under 5 permitted. Open for tours daily 9:15–4:45; closed weekends Jan.–Feb.*

(👫 **ALL**) **World Financial Center**. The four buildings are joined by corridors lined with shops and restaurants; the Courtyard and Winter Garden Atrium overlooking the Hudson are places to run to in rainy weather or to buy take-out sandwiches or ice cream to eat while strolling on the Esplanade (see Green Spaces, *below*). Weekends and holidays bring scheduled free entertainment, most of it for children.

🏠 *Battery Park City, on Hudson River at Liberty and Vesey Sts., tel. 212/945–0505.*

(👫 **ALL**) **World Trade Center and Observation Deck**. The view and the ride to the top of one of the city's two tallest skyscrapers still thrill us. *See also* Chapter 2.

🏠 *Church and Cortlandt Sts., tel. 212/435–4170 information and kids' events, 212/323–2340 observation deck. Accepts CityPass.*

Museums

MANHATTAN

🏛 *40 W. 53rd St., between 5th and 6th Aves., tel. 212/956–3535. Cost: $5 adults, $2.50 students over 12. Open Tues.–Sun. 10–6, Thurs. 10–8.*

(👫 ALL) **American Museum of Natural History.** The best natural history museum in the country and the largest in the world, it's on the top-10 list of every kid on my New York City panel, regardless of age. The Hayden Planetarium is closed for renovation and will reopen in 2000. *See also* Chapter 3.
🏛 *Central Park West at 79th St., tel. 212/769–5100. Accepts CityPass.*

(👫 1–9) **Children's Museum of Manhattan.** At this four-floor interactive museum of environments toddlers and preschoolers can explore a playroom with a great climbing structure; changing exhibits are lively and imaginative, often based on kids' books. Older (meaning 7 and up) kids should check out the Urban Tree House, the electronic sound studio where you can compose and record your own music, and a high-tech TV studio where you can produce, direct, or act.
🏛 *212 W. 83rd St. (Subway 1 or 9 to 86th St.), tel. 212/721–1224. Cost: $5, kids under 2 free. Open Sept.–May, Wed.–Sun. 10–5; July–Aug., Tues.–Sun. 10–5.*

(👫 ALL) **Cloisters.** We've always loved walking around this branch of the Metropolitan Museum of Art; its medieval buildings, cloistered walkways, and gardens remind us of a medieval monastery. Toddlers gravitate to the flowers and statues in the small courtyards. Older kids enjoy the Unicorn Tapestries and walks on the parapet. Quiet and peaceful, it has a wonderful view of the Hudson River.
🏛 *Fort Tryon Park (Bus M4 from midtown, or Subway A to 190th St.), tel. 212/923–3700. Cost: Suggested donation $8 adults, $4 students, 12 and under free. Open Mar.–Oct., Tues.–Sun. 9:30–5:15; Nov.–Feb., Tues.–Sun. 9:30–4:45.*

(👫 10+) **Ellis Island Immigration Museum.** Touring this national museum on a historic island in New York Harbor can be a moving experience for families. *See also* Chapter 3.
🏛 *Ellis Island (Statue of Liberty boat from Battery Park), tel. 212/363–3200.*

(👫 4–12) **Forbes Magazine Galleries.** This museum in Greenwich Village is small and special, with a wonderful collection of 500 toy boats and 10,000 toy soldiers.
🏛 *62 5th Ave., at 12th St., tel. 212/206–5548. Cost: Free. Open Tues., Wed., Fri., Sat. 10–4.*

(👫 5+) **Guggenheim Museum.** Though this Frank Lloyd Wright–designed museum has an extensive collection of European and American paintings and sculpture and regularly schedules interesting special exhibits, the real reason to see it with children is the building's spiral shape. Take the elevator to the top and follow the ¼-mi-long ramp past the paintings on the way down. The once-a-month Family Day, on a Sunday, combines activities and a tour for kids 5–12 (reservations are essential, tel. 212/423–3587). Family films are also shown regularly.
🏛 *1071 5th Ave., at 88th St. (Subway 4 or 6 to 86th St.), tel. 212/423–3500. Cost: $12 adults, $7 students, children under 12 free; family tour and workshop $10 per child. Combination tickets that include the SoHo branch are $16 adults, $10 students; your visit to the second must take place within 7 days. Open Sun.–Wed. 10–6, Fri.–Sat. 10–8.*

(👫 3+) **Guggenheim Museum SoHo.** This downtown museum now shows a lot of video art and multimedia installations, which usually intrigue most kids more than staid paintings on the wall. SoHo Tots, a tour and hands-on activity for kids 3–5, is held every Friday morning at 11. Also be sure to stop in the huge gift shop, which is full of interesting things.
🏛 *575 Broadway at Prince St. (Subway N/R to Prince St.), tel. 212/423–3500. Cost: $8 adults, $5 students, kids under 12 free. SoHo*

Tots, $10 per child. Open Wed.–Fri. and Sun. 11–6, Sat. 11–8.

✝✝ 4–15 *Intrepid* Sea/Air/Space **Museum.** A must-see on several boys' and girls' lists, this is the world's only museum in an aircraft carrier. Here you'll see a spy plane, space vehicles, and rockets. *See also* Chapter 3.
🏠 *Pier 86, W. 46th St. at 12th Ave. (Subway A, E, or C to 42nd St.; or Bus M42 to last stop), tel. 212/245–0072. Accepts CityPass.*

✝✝ 5+ **Liberty Science Center.** A five-minute ferry ride across the Hudson from lower Manhattan is New Jersey's enormous science museum; its four floors of intriguing interactive exhibits include a six-story IMAX screen. Be warned that it is often crowded with school groups during school hours. *See also* Chapter 3.
🏠 *251 Philip St., Jersey City, tel. 201/200–1000. NY Waterway ferry, tel. 800/533–3779.*

✝✝ 7–15 **Lower East Side Tenement Museum.** This urban living-history museum on the Lower East Side portrays the lives of immigrants in New York City in the 19th and early 20th centuries. The exhibits in the gallery, which include a 6-ft model tenement filled with tiny figures representing families who lived in the building, are worth seeing. But taking a tour of the restored apartments in the 1863 tenement building across the street is the real reason to come. There are two different tours. The best for families is a 30-minute visit (at 12, 1, and 3 on weekends only) to the Sephardic Jewish Confino family's apartment—you can actually touch things. A costumed guide plays the part of a 17-year-old immigrant girl; she tells you about her life, lets you help out with her chores, and even turns on a working Victrola.
🏠 *90 Orchard St., between Broome and Delancey Sts. (Subway F to Delancey St.), tel. 212/431–0233. Cost: Gallery free; tour $8 adults, $6 students, kids 5 and under free. Open Tues.–Fri. noon–5, Thurs. noon–9 PM, tours every half hr 1–4; Sat.–Sun. 11–6; tours every half hr 11–4:15.*

✝✝ 4+ **Metropolitan Museum of Art.** One of the greatest art museums in the world, the Met (as it's known to New Yorkers) is filled with gallery after gallery of masterpieces. Surprisingly, many kids say they like this better than any other art museum in the city. *See also* Chapter 3.
🏠 *1000 5th Ave., between 82nd and 84th Sts., tel. 212/535–7710. Accepts CityPass.*

✝✝ 3+ **Museum of the City of New York.** A favorite destination of some kids, this museum devoted to the history of New York City houses a permanent collection of dollhouses and antique toys on the third floor and models of ships and dioramas of life in early New York on the second. It's best to time a visit so you can attend their Saturday-morning storytelling sessions or one of their free-with-admission family weekend programs and workshops. These are fairly active; kids can go on a treasure hunt in the toy gallery, make dollhouse furniture from found objects, or participate in a jazz concert.
🏠 *5th Ave. at 103rd St. (Subway 6 to 103rd St., or Bus M1, M3, or M4), tel. 212/534–1672. Cost: Suggested donation $10 per family, $5 adults, $4 kids. Open Wed.–Sat. 10–5, Sun. noon–5.*

✝✝ 4+ **Museum of Modern Art.** On Saturday mornings from 10 to 11, kids 5–10 and their parents can catch a guided tour of this world-famous collection of modern paintings at a special rate of $5 per family (including a return pass); each week you explore a different aspect of MoMA's collections (enter through the Edward John Noble Education Center at 18 W. 54th St.; doors open at 9:30). The galleries are big and bright, and many kids also love the wonderful outdoor sculpture garden. A special Family Package for one adult and up to four kids ($11.50) includes the museum guidebook for families, "Art Safari." Request it when you enter. Hour-long family movie programs of classic short films are shown on Saturday from 12 to 1, and there are periodic activity workshops designed for families.

🏢 *11 W. 53rd St. (Subway E or F to 5th Ave.), tel. 212/708–9400. Cost: $9.50 adults, $6.50 students, kids under 16 free with adult; pay what you wish Fri. after 4:30. Open Sat.–Tues. and Thurs. 10:30–6, Fri. 10:30–8:30. Accepts CityPass.*

👫 5 – 15   **Museum of Television and Radio.** This library has a collection of 98,000 TV and radio programs for viewing and listening that spans broadcast history. See also Chapter 3.

🏢 *25 W. 52nd St., tel. 212/621–6600.*

👫 6+   **National Museum of the American Indian.** The largest collection of Native American artifacts in the world is now at the Heye Center on the lower floors of the ornate Alexander Hamilton Customs House in downtown Manhattan; the building appeared in *Ghostbusters II*. Although much here is for adults, kids find the Great Rotunda and its painted dome "pretty awesome" and like wandering through the exhibits looking for drums, moccasins, or bison hides. Occasional special dance and music performances are often highly appropriate for kids.

🏢 *1 Bowling Green, tel. 212/668–6624. Cost: Free. Open daily 10–5.*

👫 3 – 10   **New York City Fire Museum.** The two floors of horse-drawn fire wagons, fire buckets, sliding poles, and fireproof uniforms in this turn-of-the-century firehouse fascinated Gavin and his friends when they were about 5. The only drawback is that you can't climb on any of the fire engines. Call to make sure a school tour isn't scheduled for the day of your visit or it's a madhouse.

🏢 *278 Spring St., between Hudson and Varick Sts., tel. 212/691–1303. Cost: Suggested donation $4 adults, $2 students, $1 kids under 12. Open Tues.–Sat. 10–4.*

👫 ALL   **South Street Seaport Museum.** Much of the seaport complex is an actual museum, including the four historic ships, a gallery with changing exhibits, a working 19th-century print shop, and a chil-

dren's center with hands-on workshops. Ask about the nearby archaeology site, New York Unearthed (tel. 212/748–8628), too. See also Chapter 2.

🏢 *16 Fulton St., at East River, tel. 212/748–8600.*

👫 7+   **Studio Museum of Harlem.** The center of Harlem's art community, this small but world-class museum features both paintings and sculpture of African-American, African, and Caribbean artists and exhibits of crafts that appeal to kids. Events like the December Kwanzaa celebration attract many families. The gift shop has an excellent selection of books on and by African-Americans.

🏢 *144 W. 125th St., between Malcolm X and Adam Clayton Powell Blvds. (also called Lenox Ave. and 7th Ave.), tel. 212/864–4500. Cost: $5 adults, $3 students 12 and over, $1 kids under 12. Open Wed.–Fri. 10–5, weekends 1–6.*

BROOKLYN

👫 2 – 12   **Brooklyn Children's Museum.** A multilevel hands-on play-and-learn museum with an imaginative tunnel entrance, this wildly exuberant place is hard to get to but worth it. See also Chapter 3.

🏢 *145 Brooklyn Ave., tel. 718/735–4432.*

👫 4+   **Brooklyn Museum.** The superb and extensive collection of mummies is only one of the reasons to come to this huge place, New York City's second-largest art museum, located near Prospect Park and the Brooklyn Botanical Garden. There is much to see here, from extensive permanent exhibits of European and American painting to an outdoor Sculpture Garden and American period rooms. Plus it is never crowded. One gift shop is just for kids; weekend kids' programs are excellent.

🏢 *200 Eastern Parkway, tel. 718/638–5000; Subway 2, 3 to Eastern Pkwy.-Brooklyn Museum. Cost: $4 adults, $2 students, kids 11 and under free. Open Wed.–Fri. 10–5, Sat. 11–9, Sun. 11–6.*

👫 4+ New York Transit Museum. Housed in an actual 1930s subway station, the museum has 18 restored vintage subway cars—some 90 years old— that you can climb aboard. In the gift shop you'll even find subway-token jewelry.

🏠 Beneath Boerum Pl. and Schermerhorn St., Brooklyn Heights (Subway G to Schermerhorn; A or F to Jay St./Borough Hall; M, N, or R to Court St.; or 2, 3, or 4 to Borough Hall), tel. 718/243–8601. Cost: $3 adults, $1.50 kids under 17. Open Tues.–Fri. 10–4, weekends noon–5.

STATEN ISLAND

👫 ALL Historic Richmond Town. The 27 restored 17th- to 19th-century buildings in this 90-acre museum village include the oldest (300 years old) standing elementary school in the United States. Three streets seem just like an old-time village, and kids can run in and out of the buildings exploring. Craftsmen in period costumes, such as the harness maker, give demonstrations at special events on weekends; the most fun for kids is the county fair in August. A museum displays antique dolls and toys.

🏠 441 Clarke Ave., Staten Island (Staten Island Ferry, then Bus S74), tel. 718/351–1611. Cost: $5 adults, $2.50 kids 6–18. Open Sept.–June, Wed.–Sun. 1–5; July–Aug., Wed.–Fri. 10–5, weekends 1–5.

👫 1–10 Staten Island Children's Museum. Kids can walk through, touch, and sometimes play in the exhibits at this children's museum, which is part of the Snug Harbor Cultural Center, a group of landmark buildings on 80 acres overlooking New York Harbor. Bugs are the focus upstairs. Outside, big and interesting sculptures dot the spacious lawns; some, like the huge wooden grasshopper, are ideal for climbing kids. The ducks on the pond will appreciate the crumbs from your picnic lunch.

🏠 1000 Richmond Terr. (Staten Island Ferry, then S40 bus), tel. 718/273–2060. Cost: $4, kids under 2 free. Open Tues.–Sun. noon–5.

QUEENS

👫 9+ American Museum of the Moving Image. If your kids are media buffs, don't miss this museum devoted to film, television, and radio. Besides the wonderful costume gallery, we also recommend the makeup exhibit and one of our favorite sights, Tut's Fever Movie Palace, a spoof of 1920s movie palaces, complete with life-size cutouts created by artist Red Grooms. Upstairs are the interactive exhibits that so attract kids; you can experiment with the sound effects in movies, create an animated short, and project your own face into movie scenes. Movies are shown here, too, and there's a café.

🏠 35th Ave. and 36th St., Astoria, Queens (Subway N to Broadway, Queens), tel. 718/784–0077 or 718/784–4520. Cost: $8.50 adults, $4.50 kids 5–18. Open Tues.–Fri. noon–5, weekends 11–6.

👫 3–15 New York Hall of Science. New York City's only science museum is definitely worth the trek to Queens. It has 185 hands-on exhibits where kids can learn about optical illusions, atoms, and the science of sounds; kids 6 and up can frolic in the huge new science playground. See also Chapter 3.

🏠 47-01 111th St., Flushing Meadows, Queens, tel. 718/699–0005.

Animals

New York boasts four zoos and one aquarium, all managed by the New York Zoological Society's Wildlife Conservation Society.

MANHATTAN

👫 0–12 Central Park Wildlife Conservation Center. The 5½-acre Central Park zoo, small and manageable, is a delight, especially for toddlers and preschoolers. See also Chapter 4.

🏠 64th St. and 5th Ave., tel. 212/861–6030.

THE BRONX

👫 ALL Bronx Zoo/International Wildlife Conservation Park. Plan to spend an entire day at the largest zoo in any United States city. Its naturalistic habitats, home to some 4,000 creatures, substitute moats for cages to separate people from the animals. There's also a Children's Zoo where kids can pet and feed domestic animals. *See also* Chapter 4.

🏠 *Bronx Park, Bronx, tel. 718/367–1010.*

BROOKLYN

(👫 **ALL**) **New York Aquarium for Wildlife Conservation.** This is one of the Northeast's top aquariums, with 300 species of fish and outdoor habitats with penguins and seals. Make your visit part of a day-long excursion to Coney Island—walk along the beach and the 2½-mi boardwalk and stop at the Astroland Amusement Park (see Outdoor Action, *below*). *See also* Chapter 4.

🏠 *Coney Island at W. 8th St., off Surf Ave., Brooklyn, tel. 718/265–3474.*

(👫 **0–12**) **Prospect Park Wildlife Conservation Center.** Opened in 1993, this zoo in Prospect Park is geared for children, with exhibits on animal lifestyles and a sweet petting zoo. Highlights are the baboons—you can sit right in front of their glass-enclosed environment and watch them play—and a Discovery Trail where you can pretend to be a turtle inside your giant shell. Combine a visit here with some time in lovely Prospect Park (the historic Carousel is close to the zoo's entrance) and the Lefferts Homestead (tel. 718/965–6505; free), a Dutch farmhouse with exhibits kids can touch.

🏠 *450 Flatbush Ave., Brooklyn, tel. 718/399–7339. Cost: $2.50 adults, 50¢ kids 3–12, kids under 3 free. Open Apr.–Oct., weekdays 10–5, weekends 10–5:30; Nov.–Mar., daily 10–4:30.*

QUEENS

(👫 **0–12**) **Queens Wildlife Conservation Center.** This small, 11-acre zoo next to the Hall of Science specializes in North American animals, all cleverly arranged so you see them from a walking trail. The

aviary is in Buckminster Fuller's geodesic dome, designed for the 1964 World's Fair; the spectacle bears (so-called for the rings around their eyes), known for climbing trees, are a treat to watch. Don't come to Queens just to see the zoo, but do schedule time to visit when you go to the Hall of Science. The nearby Queens Museum of Art in the New York City Building (tel. 718/592–9700; open Wed.–Sun.) is also worth a stop to see the scale model of the whole city, which contains 895,000 tiny buildings and other landmarks.

🏠 *Flushing Meadows–Corona Park, 53-51 111th St., Queens, tel. 718/271–1500. Cost: $2.50 adults, 50¢ kids 3–12. Open Apr.–Oct., weekdays 10–5, weekends 10–5:30; Nov.–Mar., daily 10–4:30.*

Green Spaces

(👫 **ALL**) **Battery Park Esplanade/Hudson River Park.** The Esplanade, a 25-acre park along the Hudson River starts south of Battery Park City, a complex of apartments and shops, and extends north to the World Financial Center. Strolling along on a nice day you'll see tugboats, ferries, and barges on the river, sailboats in the North Cove harbor, and the Statue of Liberty from South Cove. The fences along the river are toddler-proof, and the small playground at the south side of North Cove is exceptionally clean; it's only a few steps to enter the Winter Garden Atrium of the World Financial Center. Skateboarding and rollerblading are permitted along one of the Esplanade's walkways. Just north of the World Financial Center is Hudson River Park, which has one of the nicest playgrounds in the city. Metal-chain climbing nets for the adventurous, miniature slides for toddlers, a pedal-driven red carousel, even a raised sand-table for kids using wheelchairs fill the enormous playground space. A waterfall pool, sculptures kids can climb on, and an expanse of green lawn make this a great place to spend a sunny afternoon.

🏠 *From Chambers St. to Battery Park at Hudson River (Subway 1, 2, 3, or 9 to Cham-*

bers St. or C or E to World Trade Center). Special programs tel. 212/267–9700. Open daily dawn–dusk.

(👫 **ALL**) **Central Park.** This 853-acre haven designed by Frederick Law Olmsted in the heart of Manhattan is one of the great city parks of the world. Home to a zoo, a model sailboat pond, a children's marionette theater, baseball fields, adventure playgrounds, a carousel, places to feed ducks, a rink for rollerblading and ice-skating, a lake for rowboating and another for fishing, statues to climb on, and bike and horseback riding, it provides so much for families that your visit to the city won't be complete without at least one stop. The visitor center at the Dairy (64th St., midpark, tel. 212/794–6564; open Tues.–Sun. 10–5) is the most convenient place to pick up a good map of the park and a calendar of events (there are many for kids); newly renovated Belvedere Castle (79th St., midpark, tel. 212/772–0210) offers nature exhibits, including crayfish to examine with microscopes; at the Dana Discovery Center (110th St., midpark, tel. 212/860–1370) you'll find family workshops and fishing. For the best people- (and skateboarder-) watching, head for Bethesda Terrace (72nd St., midpark). Playgrounds abound on both the east and west sides of the park. On the West Side we like Spector Playground at 85th Street, with a fenced-off toddler area and a big wooden tree house, and the Wild West Playground at 93rd, with four wood towers and lots of sprinklers in summer. Others are at 62nd, 67th, 81st, 84th, 96th, and 99th streets. On the East Side our favorite is the Rustic Playground at 67th Street—it has a tree house with a slide down into the huge sandbox area, a stone bridge, picnic tables, and a rock to climb. Others are at 72nd, 76th, 79th, 84th, 96th, 100th, and 108th streets.

🏠 *Bordered by 5th Ave., Central Park West, 59th St., and 110th St., tel. 212/360–3444. Events hot line 212/360–3456.*

Other Manhattan Parks and Playgrounds. Among the smaller parks scattered all over the borough, our favorites are Abingdon Square Park (in Greenwich Village at the corner of Bleecker and Hudson Sts.), which has a big sandbox and climbing equipment; Mercer Street Park (also in the Village, just north of Houston St.), which has a big sand area, a climbing area with a bridge, and a spray fountain when it's hot; the shady playground in Carl Schurz Park (on the Upper East Side at 84th St. and East End Ave.), which has several good climbing structures in its shady playground, a sprinkler area and a lovely riverside promenade; the P.S. 87 School Playground (on the Upper West Side at Amsterdam Ave. and 77th St.), which has a fabulous, architect-designed, parent-built climbing space. Riverside Park (on the Upper West Side just west of Riverside Dr.), a long, narrow park along the Hudson River, has a great playground at 91st Street, with hippo sculptures, swings, and drop-in crafts classes in summer. Some parts of this park are cleaner and more pleasant than others. Walk along the Promenade, a walkway that goes north from 80th Street. The Asser Levy Playground (23rd St., one block from the East River) caters to kids with disabilities; slides have wheelchair stations and pavement is textured for kids who are blind.

BROOKLYN

(👫 **ALL**) **Brooklyn Botanic Garden.** When you need a break from the city environment, visit the garden's 52 acres with more than 12,000 different kinds of plants. For kids there is an indoor plant fun house in the Discovery Center and a huge outdoor garden divided into four zones. Most children also like the ducks and bridges in the Japanese Garden, where the pond (in the shape of the Chinese character for "heart") has turtles and goldfish and a Japanese teahouse.

🏠 *1000 Washington Ave. (Subway 2 or 3 to Eastern Pkwy., or D to Prospect Park), tel. 718/622–4433. Cost: $3 adults, $1.50 students with ID, 50¢ kids 6–16; free Tues. Open Apr.–Sept., Tues.–Fri. 8–6, weekends and holidays*

10–6; Oct.–Mar., Tues.–Fri. 8–4:30, weekends and holidays 10–4:30. Conservatory closes ½ hr earlier.

👫 ALL **Prospect Park.** At 536 acres, this stretch of green, also designed by Olmsted, is nearly two-thirds the size of Central Park, after which it's modeled, though it has no streets crossing it. The 90-acre Long Meadow is great for picnics and kite flying; feed the ducks or paddle a boat on the 60-acre lake; see puppet shows and more at the Picnic stage; in winter, ice-skate on the rink; stop at the zoo (*see Animals, above*). Right by the zoo are a lovely old-fashioned carousel with dragon chariots and giraffes; the Lefferts Homestead, where kids can play with reproductions of 19th-century toys; and a playground with a tree house.
🏕 *Eastern Pkwy. and Grand Army Plaza (Subway 2 or 3 to Grand Army Plaza, or D to Prospect Park), tel. 718/965–8999 (events hot line). Open daily dawn–midnight.*

The Bronx

👫 ALL **New York Botanical Garden.** One of the world's largest botanic gardens (250 acres), with a huge, glass conservatory filled with changing exhibits, this garden is a good reason to make another trip to the Bronx. For kids, the new 12-acre Everett Children's Adventure Garden finally opened in the spring of 1998; it's the largest and most ambitious such project in the world. And what a great place this is! It borders a marshy pond where you can look for frogs, cross a bridge into the oldest forest in New York City, pretend to be lost on a kids-only path, climb in a boulder maze, study tree rings of a 100-year-old oak, look through a telescope, and use the microscope in the sunny lab housed in an Adirondack-style cottage. The weekend programs for kids and families are superb.
🏕 *Bronx Park (Metro North train from Grand Central Terminal to Botanical Garden station), tel. 718/817–8700. Cost: General entrance $3 adults, $2 students with ID, $1 kids 2–12; Children's Garden $3 adults, $2 students with*

ID, $1 kids 2–12. Free Wed. all day and Sat. 10–noon. Parking $4. Open Tues.–Sun. 10–6.

Roosevelt Island

👫 3–12 **Lighthouse Park.** Perched on the northern tip of an island in the middle of the East River is the lighthouse that gives its name to this lovely, clean small park with picnic tables, lots of open space, barbecue grills, and a fine view of the Manhattan skyline, bridges, and tugboats. Just south of it is a new park, Octagon Park, which has soccer fields, tennis courts, a baseball diamond, and 200 community gardens. Coming here for a picnic is a good excuse to take the tram.
🏕 *Roosevelt Island tram from 2nd Ave. between 59th and 60th Sts., then 25¢ bus trip to park.*

Sports

Big-Time for Spectators

New York is home to six major-league teams, but only two of them actually play in Manhattan. When you buy tickets, check the stadium diagrams near the front of the Manhattan Yellow Pages. Ticketmaster (tel. 212/307–7171) has tickets for all but football games. *See also* Chapter 8.

BASEBALL. The baseball season runs from April to October.

New York Mets. The Mets (National League) play at Shea Stadium in Queens. Tickets are usually easy to get. *126th St. and Roosevelt Ave. (Subway 7 from 42nd St. to Willets Point/Shea Stadium stop), Flushing 11368, tel. 718/507–6387.*

New York Yankees. The home of the Yankees (American League) is Yankee Stadium in the Bronx, where they've played since 1923. Tickets are usually easy to get. *161st St. and River Ave. (Subway 4, C, or D to 161st St./Yankee Stadium), Bronx 10451, tel. 718/293–6000.*

BASKETBALL. Basketball season is late October to April.

New York Knickerbockers. The "Knicks," an NBA team, play at Madison Square Garden. Tickets are sometimes hard to get. *7th Ave. between 31st and 33rd Sts.; box office tel. 212/465–6000; Ticketmaster 212/307–7171.*

FOOTBALL. Football season is September to December.

The New York Giants (National Football Conference) and the **New York Jets** (American Football Conference) both play at Meadowlands (East Rutherford, NJ 07073). It's nearly impossible to get tickets for either one, but a few individual Jets game tickets go on sale at the end of August. *Giants tel. 201/935–8111; Jets 516/538–6600.*

HOCKEY. Hockey season is October–April.

New York Islanders. The Islanders (tel. 516/794–4100) play at Nassau Veterans Memorial Coliseum (tel. 516/794–9300) in Uniondale, Long Island (1255 Hempstead Turnpike, Uniondale, NY 11553).

New York Rangers. The Rangers (National Hockey League) play at Madison Square Garden. *7th Ave. between 31st and 33rd Sts.; box office tel. 212/465–6040; Rangers hot line 212/308–6977.*

SOCCER. Soccer season is late March–September.

New York Metrostars. The Metrostars play at Giants Stadium. *Meadowlands Sports Complex, East Rutherford, NJ 07073, tel. 201/583–7000.*

TENNIS. U.S. Open. One of the four prime tennis tournaments in the United States is held at the U.S.T.A. National Tennis Center in Flushing Meadows–Corona Park in Queens during the end of August and in early September. Tickets to early matches are sometimes easy to get; those for the semifinals and finals sell out as soon as they go on sale in May. *United States Tennis Asso-*

ciation, Flushing Meadows–Corona Park, Flushing, Queens 11365, tel. 914/696–7000.

Outdoor Action

AMUSEMENT PARKS

(👫 **3+**) Coney Island is where amusement parks started, and even though **Astroland Amusement Park** is a bit shabby today, it's worth a stop, particularly if you're visiting the New York Aquarium, which is just a short walk away. (Its parking lot is adjacent to Astroland.)
🏠 *1000 Surf Ave., Coney Island, Brooklyn, tel. 718/372–0275. By subway, F train to W. 8th St. and walk across overpass; by car, Exit 7, Ocean Pkwy., south from Belt Pkwy. onto Surf Ave. Open daily noon–midnight.*

(👫 **3+**) **Deno's Wonder Wheel Park** is a short walk from Astroland. This smaller park has 18 rides for kids and the beach is visible just across the boardwalk.
🏠 *1025 Boardwalk (adjacent to Astroland), Coney Island, Brooklyn, tel. 718/372–2592. Open daily 11 AM–midnight.*

BICYCLING

(👫 **8+**) The best place to ride bikes with kids is in **Central Park**. The long, drive is closed to car traffic for several hours during the day and evening on weekdays and all weekends and on holidays. The most convenient place to rent bikes is Central Park Bike Rentals (Loeb Boathouse, midpark near E. 74th St., tel. 212/861–4137); they have kids' bikes, too. Expect to leave a credit card or a large deposit. Brooklyn's **Prospect Park** is also a lovely place to bike; its winding roads are closed to cars.

BOATING

(👫 **3+**) Rowing a boat on the 18-acre lake in the middle of **Central Park** is fun even when the lake is very crowded. We still talk about the time we saw a fairly hefty man stand up, lose his balance, and go overboard, his arms waving while a dozen boatloads of people looked on. Let young teenagers have their own boat (if they can swim). Go early on a nice weekend morning or you'll wait and wait. *Loeb Boathouse, mid-park near 74th St., tel. 212/517–2233.*

ICE-SKATING

(**††** 4+) In winter, the two best places to skate outdoors are **Rockefeller Center** (50th St. at 5th Ave., lower plaza, tel. 212/332–7654) and **Wollman Rink** (Central Park, midpark near 63rd St., tel. 212/396–1010). Both have lockers, skate rentals, music, and places to eat, and both are crowded on weekends. Wollman Rink is larger and has special teen rates. Don't go at night with little kids—the teens skate fast. Rockefeller Center is the place to come at Christmastime, when the big Christmas tree there is all lit up. **Lasker Rink** (in Central Park at 110th St., tel. 212/534–7639) is cheaper and less crowded than Wollman Rink and attracts many families on weekends, but the ice is not maintained as regularly.

IN-LINE SKATING AND SKATEBOARDING

(**†† 8+**) The traditional spring, summer, and fall sport for kids 8 and up in New York City is in-line skating, and the best place to do it is in **Central Park**. On weekends, when the loop road in the park is closed to traffic all day, it's filled with skaters. **Blades Board & Skate** (120 W. 72nd St., tel. 212/787–3911; 160 E. 86th St., tel. 212/996–1644) rents kid-size skates and will give instructions. At **Wollman Rink** (midpark at 63rd St., tel. 212/396–1010), you can skate to music in the rink during the warm months—there are inexpensive special family nights here and it's rarely crowded. Skate rental here also includes protective gear. Skateboarders congregate on Central Park's West Drive. Blades Board & Skate has skateboards for rent, too. In lower Manhattan, skaters like the riverside promenade by Battery Park City; rent skates at **Blades Board & Skate** (128 Chambers St., at West Broadway, tel. 212/964–1944). You can also

skate along the **Riverside Park Esplanade** and in **Brooklyn's Prospect Park** (*see* Green Spaces, *above*). The **Roller Rink at Chelsea Piers** (*see* Sports Centers, *below*) has two rinks on a pier that juts out into the Hudson River (Pier 62, 23rd St. at the Hudson River, tel. 212/336–6200). One is open to general skating all day. A small skate park for trick skating is between the two rinks. Instruction and rentals are offered.

KITE FLYING

(**†† 2+**) Sheep Meadow in **Central Park** near West 67th Street is a huge expanse of lawn. On a windy day, we like flying kites here along with multitudes of other kids and their parents.

Indoor Action

BOWLING

(**†† 8+**) **Leisure Time Bowling and Recreation Center** has 30 lanes, hot video games, and good fast food. What's great for kids is the "bumper bowling"; special padding keeps balls out of the gutter.
🏠 *625 8th Ave., at Port Authority Bus Terminal, tel. 212/268–6909.*

ICE-SKATING

(**†† 5+**) **Sky Rink at Chelsea Piers** (*see below*), has two large rinks, open year-round, that overlook the Hudson River. Serious competitive skaters practice here, but it's fine for kids. You can rent skates and snack on pizza.
🏠 *23rd St. and the Hudson River, tel. 212/336–6100.*

INDOOR PLAYGROUNDS

(**†† ½–6**) Even though more indoor playgrounds have opened in Manhattan, **Playspace** is still the best one. This 7,500-square-ft play area has lots of light, safe climbing equipment, a huge sandbox with very clean sand, blocks and other toys, an infant area, a snack bar, and art and music activities. It's even air-conditioned. Parents must supervise their children (2473 Broadway, at 92nd St., tel. 212/769–2300; $5.50 per person; open Mon.–Sat. 9:30–6, Sun. 10–6). Another pleasant spot for toddlers is **My Favorite Place**, right below a fine toy store (*see below*). Cozier for little ones than Playspace, it has blocks of all kinds, a play kitchen, dress-ups, and a climbing structure. Three is really the top age here (265 W. 87th St., at Broadway, tel. 212/362–5320; $8 per child; open weekdays 9:30–5:30, weekends only if no birthday party scheduled).

SPORTS CENTERS

👫 2+ **Chelsea Piers**, the massive sports complex right on the Hudson River, is the most impressive center in the city. It has a 23,000-square-ft Field House with open basketball games for older kids, batting cages, an indoor climbing wall designed just for kids, an incredible gymnastics area with an in-ground trampoline, and a special toddler gym. Much is in use for ongoing classes and teams, but there are open gym times. Here you'll also find a picnic area and promenade (tip of Pier 62), a skateboard park, and rinks for in-line skating and ice-skating. There's even bumper bowling for kids (Hudson River between 17th and 23rd Sts., Field House, tel. 212/336–6500; gym open weekends 5–6:30, $15; toddler gym daily 10–2, weekends also 2–4, $8). At **Hackers, Hitters, and Hoops**, whether your kids want to play miniature golf, Ping-Pong, basketball, or bat a baseball in a batting cage, they can do it here. Go during the day; at night the bar opens and the place is full of twentysomethings (123 W. 18th St., tel. 212/929–7482; free admission Wed.–Sat. 11–5 and Sun.–Tues. all day, tokens for activities 50¢; opens at 11 AM).

Shopping

New York is a shopper's paradise. This selection of stops represents a small fraction of places that appeal to kids. I've concentrated on the unique and unusual.

Flea Markets

A favorite activity of young New York teens is shopping for clothes and jewelry at some of the city's regular flea markets. Here are our family's picks:

The **P.S. 44 Flea Market** (Columbus Ave. between 76th and 77th Sts.) is held inside and outside this school building on Sundays from 10 to 5:30. There's a real teen scene here. **Tower Market** (Broadway between W. 4th and Great Jones Sts.), on weekends from 10 to 7, is full of crafts and funky ethnic clothes.

Comics and Baseball Cards

👫 6+ **Cosmic Comics.** Voted best comic store in Manhattan by NYPress, it stocks both new and old comics, plus action figures, models, nonsport trading cards, and even T-shirts. It's great for kids because new comics are half-price to the under-16 group on Sundays.
🏠 *36 E. 23rd St., 2nd floor, tel. 212/460–5322.*

👫 6+ **Forbidden Planet.** When we lived in New York, no week was complete for my son without a trip to this store full of vintage and new comic books, a fabulous—and huge—selection of science fiction and fantasy books and posters, and displays of games and collectible toy action figures, robots, and spaceships from the United States and Japan.
🏠 *840 Broadway, at 13th St., tel. 212/473–1576.*

👫 6+ **New York Mets Clubhouse Shop** (575 5th Ave., at 47th St., tel. 212/986–4887) and the **New York Yankees Clubhouse** (110 E. 59th St., between Park and Lexington Aves., tel. 212/758–7844) both have baseball cards, memorabilia that belonged to former players, sweatshirts, hats, and so on. You can also purchase tickets for games in both shops.

👫 6+ **Village Comics.** Half of this store is full of new and collector comics; the other half has an outstanding selection of science-fiction books and science-fiction posters.

🏠 *214 Sullivan St., tel. 212/777–2770.*

Books

(👫 2+) **Barnes & Noble.** Several of this citywide chain of huge bookstores have excellent selections of kids' books and offer regular story hours, kids' author appearances, and even activities. We like best the two stores listed below, but also check on the new megastore on 86th Street between 2nd and 3rd avenues.

🏠 *2289 Broadway at 82nd St., tel. 212/362–8835; 33 E. 17th St., at Union Square, tel. 212/253–0810; 240 E. 86th St., tel. 212/794–1962.*

(👫 2+) **Books of Wonder.** With 5,000 books including out-of-print bargains and any Oz book you want, our favorite children's bookstore in New York is the largest, but it doesn't feel like a warehouse. People who work here really like kids and know their books. Story hour is Sunday at 11:45.

🏠 *16 W. 18th St., tel. 212/989–3270.*

(👫 1–13) **Tootsie's Children's Books.** Their new location in a charming town house is bigger and better, with more of everything, both books and toys, and more activities and story hours for kids, too. You'll find books for all age groups, from picture books to paperbacks for older kids, plus a good selection of *Goosebumps, Baby Sitters' Club,* etc.

🏠 *555 Hudson St., at Perry St., tel. 212/242–0182.*

Music

(👫 10+) **HMV U.S.A.** These huge CD and cassette superstores with their high-tech decor are where teenagers like to buy—or just to listen through headphones. Our favorite locations are these two.

🏠 *1280 Lexington Ave., at 86th St., tel. 212/348–0800; 2018 Broadway, at 72nd St., tel. 212/721–5900.*

(👫 10+) **Tower Records.** HMV's rival in terms of size, selection, and appeal to the preteen and teenage market, it's crowded, busy, and noisy. There are now several stores in Manhattan, but the two original ones listed below are the most fun.

🏠 *692 Broadway, at 4th St., tel. 212/505–1500; 1961 Broadway, at 66th St., tel. 212/799–2500.*

Virgin Megastore. These new three-story megastores are the latest hot places to buy CDs and tapes; with a café, bookstore, and movieplex, teens don't want to leave. Many listening posts are scattered throughout the store. The neighborhood in Times Square still isn't great, however.

🏠 *1540 Broadway, at 45th St., tel. 212/921–1020; 14th St. and Broadway, tel. 212/598–4666.*

Stuff to Wear

(👫 12+) **Antique Boutique.** A number of 14-year-old girls we know recommend this place, with its racks and racks of recycled clothing, including suede jackets, sweaters, prom dresses, and Hawaiian shirts.

🏠 *712 Broadway, between Astor Pl. and 4th St., tel. 212/460–8830.*

(👫 12+) **Canal Jean.** Bins of inexpensive sweaters and jeans, motorcycle jackets, funky clothing from the '40s and '50s, plus a trendy SoHo atmosphere attract lots of New York teenagers.

🏠 *504 Broadway, near Spring St., tel. 212/226–3663.*

(👫 5+) **Capezio Dance Theatre Shop.** Girls and boys taking dance lessons like to stop in this shop, which carries tights, leotards, and ballet shoes.

🏠 *1650 Broadway, at 51st St., tel. 212/245–2130.*

Toys and Games

(👫 4+) **Big City Kites and Darts.** This store for the enthusiast participates in kite

festivals and exhibitions and will help you choose something for a beginner. There are old-fashioned box kites, animal kites, and a kite that looks like a comet, plus other toys that fly—Frisbees, gliders, and so on.
🏠 *1210 Lexington Ave., at 82nd St., tel. 212/472–2623.*

(👫 10+) **Compleat Strategist.** For role-playing games (Advanced Dungeons and Dragons, and such) and role-playing minia-tures, this is a must-stop. The 33rd Street branch has the best collection of miniatures and paints; the 57th Street branch has the most extensive selection of role-playing kits.
🏠 *11 E. 33rd St., at 5th Ave., tel. 212/685–3880; 342 W. 57th St., between 8th and 9th Aves., tel. 212/582–1272.*

(👫 8+) **Dollhouse Antics.** Though serious dollhouse collectors shop here, the miniature furniture, rugs, lamps (complete with wiring), doll families, and dollhouses all on a 1-inch scale delighted some 8-year-old girls we know.
🏠 *1343 Madison Ave., at 94th St., tel. 212/876–2288.*

(👫 1+) **Enchanted Forest.** This charm-ing SoHo store looks like a whimsical the-atrical stage set of a forest. Handmade stuffed animals in baskets stand on a tree-house-like platform. Even if you don't buy any of the handmade toys or books of fairy tales, this is an essential place to visit.
🏠 *85 Mercer St., near Spring St., tel. 212/925–6677.*

(👫 1–10) **My Favorite Place.** Besides a good selection of top-class toys like Playmo-bil sets you'll find a corner bin with items under $5 and a host of activities—drop-in art classes in the back room, family gather-ings, and events in a toddler playroom.
🏠 *265 W. 87th St. at Broadway, tel. 212/362–5320.*

(👫 1–11) **Pennywhistle Toys.** Bears blowing soap bubbles stand outside both locations of this upscale shop; kids want to stop even if you don't go inside. Do, though, because they carry the kinds of quality

imported toys that you can't get at big chains. The selections show a real kid-sensi-bility on the part of the owner, meaning that even the educational toys look like fun. We like the Columbus Avenue store best because it's close to other neat shops and the Museum of Natural History.
🏠 *448 Columbus Ave., at 81st St., tel. 212/893–9090; 1283 Madison Ave., at 91st St., tel. 212/369–3868.*

(👫 ALL) **F.A.O. Schwarz.** This is many kids' favorite toy store to visit and a must-see place for those who've never been here. Its two floors have everything from trains to dolls to baby toys arranged in small bou-tique shops. On the first floor, the collection of stuffed animals of all sizes, some twice as big as small children (or even grown-ups), is the best anywhere. The enormous Lego section has a table of Legos to play with; the Brio train setup is wonderful to look at. The best part is that you can touch and try everything. Prices are very high, and week-ends before Christmas it's jammed, with a line extending into the street by afternoon.
🏠 *767 5th Ave., at 58th St., tel. 212/644–9400.*

Unusual Stores

(👫 5+) **Louis Tannen's.** With more than 8,000 items, this is the world's largest magic store. Wands, crystal balls, top hats with rabbits—there are lots of things for kids. It publishes a catalog and sponsors a one-week summer magic camp.
🏠 *24 W. 25th St., 2nd floor, tel. 212/929–4500.*

(👫 6+) **Maxilla & Mandible Ltd.** This is a strange store that intrigued my son when he was 9, 10, and 11 and collecting speci-mens. It's full of all kinds of animal skeletons, fossils, antlers, teeth, butterflies, and seashells. Most are too expensive for sou-venirs, but the porcupine quills, fossils, and shark teeth, and fish vertebrae are less than $3.
🏠 *451–455 Columbus Ave., between 81st and 82nd Sts., tel. 212/724–6173.*

👫 5+   **Star Magic.** The space-age environment—black ceiling, spacecraftlike walls, suspended spheres and spaceships—means just walking into these shops is fun. But there's plenty to buy: New Age futuristic music tapes, high-tech toys, and scientific items like minerals and prisms and star charts.

🏠 *745 Broadway, between 8th St. and Astor Pl., tel. 212/228–7770; 275 Amsterdam Ave., at 73rd St., tel. 212/769–2020; 1256 Lexington Ave., between 84th and 85th Sts., tel. 212/988–0300.*

👫 ALL   **Warner Bros. Studio Store.** This cartoon lover's heaven—three floors of Bugs Bunny, Tweety Bird, Daffy Duck, and other Looney Tunes characters and DC comics heroes on clothes, in artwork, on toys, posters, even golf balls—is the most interesting of New York's theme stores. It's fun just to look around and watch the continuous cartoons on huge monitors.

🏠 *5th Ave. and 57th St., tel. 212/754–0300.*

Eats

Believe it or not, there are more than 17,000 restaurants in New York. I've chosen from among the many reasonably priced ones that welcome children. Though not all have high chairs, booster seats, or a kids' menu, they do have food and atmosphere that my family and my New York City kids' panel (ages 2–15) and their parents like, and most represent something unique for kids in atmosphere, type of food, or history. (I'm not including regular McDonald's, Burger King, or Pizza Hut; if your kids have to go there, check the Yellow Pages; however, if you're desperate, the McDonald's at 136 W. 3rd St., tel. 212/674–2566, is big and bright and has an outdoor children's play area.) The fanciest McDonald's in the world (at 160 Broadway, between Maiden La. and Liberty St., tel. 212/385–2063) has a doorman, a pianist, marble tables, mirrors, real flowers, and table settings. For additional suggestions,

I recommend *Kids Eat New York*, written by a New York City fifth grader and his mom, Sam Freund and Elizabeth Carpenter; it reviews more than 150 restaurants for both adult and kid appeal (available from bookstores or the publisher, the Little Bookroom, 5 St. Luke's Pl., New York 10014, tel. 212/691–3321).

There are some New York food experiences that our family thinks no visitor should miss—eating bagels and drinking egg creams, going to a New York deli for a pastrami sandwich, buying a bag of hot roasted chestnuts or a big salty pretzel from a street vendor, eating an Italian ice, and having dim sum in Chinatown. In New York you can try food from almost any culture in the world—Italian, Jewish, Mexican, Ethiopian, Chinese, Korean, Thai, Indian—so if there is an ethnic cuisine your child has ever wanted to sample, now is the time.

But don't eat only at restaurants in New York. Among the eating places we liked best when our son was small, especially on a rainy day, were the city's indoor atriums. The **Garden Plaza** at 56th Street and Madison Avenue has towering bamboo trees, tables, a snack bar that sells good sandwiches, and free concerts on Wednesdays at 12:30; the renovated **Market at Citicorp** at Lexington Avenue and 53rd Street has take-out food places in its three levels beneath a huge skylight, café chairs and tables where you can eat, and occasional musical entertainment for children. In the **World Financial Center** (across from the World Trade Center on the Hudson River between Liberty and Vesey Sts., tel. 212/945–0505) you can get take-out sandwiches or ice cream to eat along the Esplanade or choose something simple at one of the Winter Garden's several cafés.

Despite the fact that New York is filled with skyscrapers, there are good places to picnic, even in midtown. In the city's outdoor "pocket parks," which are about the width of a small building, you'll see lots of parents and kids, especially on weekends. Our favorites are **Paley Park** (53rd St. between 5th and Madison Aves.), **Greenacre Park** (51st St. between 2nd and 3rd Aves.), and the **McGraw-Hill Park** (48th St. between 6th and 7th Aves.). All have waterfalls more than 20 ft high (you can walk under the one in the McGraw-Hill Park), snack bars, and tables and chairs or benches.

Then there's Central Park. Spread a picnic out by the baseball playing fields on the park's west side and eat while watching one of the many weekend baseball games. Or take a picnic to the **Statue of Liberty** or to the **Lighthouse Park** on Roosevelt Island, which even has picnic tables.

A few restaurant hints: Remember that during the week midtown and Wall Street area restaurants will be jammed between noon and 2 PM; the same is true on weekends in more residential neighborhoods like the Upper West Side. If you have very small children, eat early.

Category	Cost*
$$$	over $25
$$	$15–$25
$	under $15

per person for a three-course meal, excluding drinks, service, and sales tax

American Eclectic

(**ALL**) **America.** Among our preteen friends, this noisy restaurant regularly wins four stars for its USA-theme food and decor. Paintings of New York Harbor cover the walls, and in one corner of the bar figures of Washington and Lincoln preside over a table. Young, punk-looking waiters serve you from a fun menu of several hundred items, each assigned an American home—from Georgia peach pancakes to Buffalo chicken wings to New Mexican black bean cakes to New England roast turkey to hamburgers, pizza, and PB&J. On Saturdays and Sundays they give kids coloring books

and crayons; a storyteller performs Saturdays, and Sunday brings magic shows and a balloon artist.

9 E. 18th St., between 5th Ave. and Broadway, tel. 212/505–2110. High chairs, booster seats. Reservations recommended. AE, D, DC, MC, V. $–$$

(**4+**) **American Festival Café.** Eat lunch or dinner here, right next to the Rockefeller Center skating rink, in winter; be sure to ask for a table by the window so you can watch the skaters. Hamburgers and prime rib are your best bets. Two bargains for families: the pretheater dinner (not during holiday season) and our pick—the Skaters' Specials (usually in February), which include skate rentals and rink admission along with dinner; on weekends, with breakfast and lunch.

20 W. 50th St., between 5th and 6th Aves., tel. 212/332–7620. Kids' menu, high chairs, booster seats. Reservations essential. AE, DC, MC, V. $$–$$$

(**ALL**) **Boathouse Café.** On a warm and beautiful summer evening we love dining at this somewhat expensive terrace restaurant overlooking the lake in Central Park. Tables outside have flowered umbrellas and white tablecloths, and a canvas tent shelters you in case of rain. It's dressy but casual, and you can bring a stroller right to the table. The food—like roast chicken and pasta and grilled fish—is elegant but usually appeals to kids, and hot dogs and hamburgers are available if your kids won't eat anything else. Sometimes a jazz trio entertains. If you want something less expensive for breakfast or lunch, try the take-out counter of Boathouse Express, which shares the kitchen. There are picnic tables, but bring a blanket so you can picnic with a view of the lake.

In Central Park's Loeb Boathouse, near 72nd St., tel. 212/517–2233. Kids' menu. AE, D, DC, MC, V. Open year-round. $$$

(**8+**) **Mickey Mantle's.** No matter where you sit in this informal contemporary restaurant, you're surrounded by baseball. The friendly, gregarious waiters wear baseball shirts. You can watch one of the eight oversize TV screens tuned to baseball games while you eat and check out the hats and uniforms that belonged to baseball stars of yore, like Joe DiMaggio—though the memorabilia is updated from time to time. The food—burgers, chicken fried steak, Southern fried chicken fingers, ribs—is good and portions are large.

🏨 *42 Central Park South, between 5th and 6th Aves., tel. 212/688–7777. Reservations essential. Kids' menu/portions, high chairs, booster seats. AE, D, DC, MC, V. $–$$*

(👫 **7+**)   **Tavern on the Green.** If you want to take your children over 6 to dinner at one fancy restaurant in New York, this is the place. In Central Park, it's a magical extravaganza of twinkling lights and glass that one 7-year-old we know dubs "the fairyland restaurant." My family prefers the glitzy Crystal Room with its glass walls and ceiling, especially at sunset, but in warm weather some kids favor dining in the garden with its twinkling lights. Look for animal shapes in the topiary that borders it.

🏨 *Central Park West and 67th St., tel. 212/873–3200. Reservations essential. Kids' menu, high chairs, booster seats. AE, DC, MC, V. $$$*

(👫 **ALL**)   **Two Boots.** They love kids here, and kids reciprocate the sentiment, but the crowd includes artists from this East Village neighborhood as well. The food is Cajun and Italian (the boot shapes of Louisiana and Italy are the inspiration for the name), and pizza, too. Cowboy boots, old movie posters, kids' artwork, and funky little plastic lights adorn the walls. Cups with animal handles, crayons, coloring books, and paper tablecloths all add to the kid appeal. Kids' food here is more imaginative than at most places and includes a Pizza Face, an individual pizza with vegetables standing in for eyes, mouth, and nose. The branches at 75 Greenwich Avenue (tel. 212/633–9096), 74 Bleecker Street (tel. 212/777–1033), and 44 Avenue A (tel. 212/254–1919) are take-out pizzerias; the one on Avenue A across the street from the main restaurant now has

a sidewalk café. In early 1999 they plan to open a Two Boots in Grand Central Station.

🏨 *37 Ave. A, between 2nd and 3rd Sts., tel. 212/505–2276. Kids' menu, high chairs, booster seats. Diaper-changing table in rest room. Reservations only for 6 or more. AE, MC, V. $–$$*

Bagels

(👫 **2+**)   **H & H Bagels.** Are these the best bagels in New York? Several kids we know think so. They recommend getting a hot one at these stores and munching on the street. Among their various locations, the following are very convenient.

🏨 *2239 Broadway, at 80th St., tel. 212/595–8003; 1551 2nd Ave., tel. 212/734–7441. $*

Barbecue

(👫 **ALL**)   **Brother Jimmy's BBQ.** The price is right at this laid-back spot with meaty St. Louis–style ribs, fried chicken, and cornbread—every night of the week two kids under 12 eat free with each adult. Plus early-bird dinners for adults are half-price. Expect to see lots of families and hear noisy old-time rock music.

🏨 *1461 1st Ave., at 76th St., tel. 212/288–0999. Kids' menu, booster seats. Reservations not accepted. AE, D, DC, MC, V. No lunch weekdays. $*

(👫 **ALL**)   **Cowgirl Hall of Fame.** This place is a fantasy old-time western saloon, with wooden booths, antler chandeliers with colored lights, and Tex-Mex fare. Better barbecue can definitely be found elsewhere, but the Wednesday night $10.95 all-you-can-eat catfish and chicken fry is a bargain; kids eat for $5.95. That includes music, too. There are crayons and paper to keep kids busy and a general store at the front where you can buy kitschy western stuff. Adults often find it all slick and hokey, but kids say they like this restaurant "a lot." Their funny-looking baked potato ice cream is a must at least once!

519 Hudson St., at 10th St., tel. 212/ 633–1133. Kids' menu, high chairs, booster seats. AE, MC, V. $

(ALL) **Dallas BBQ**. Early-bird specials—two people eat for $7.95—make family eating cheap at this reliable Texas-style barbecue chain.
1265 3rd Ave., at 73rd St., tel. 212/772– 9393; 27 W. 72nd St., between Central Park West and Columbus Ave., tel. 212/873–2004; 21 University Pl. and 8th St., tel. 212/674– 4450; 132 2nd Ave., at St. Mark's Pl., tel. 212/ 777–5574. Reservations not accepted. High chairs. AE, DC, MC, V. $

(ALL) **Virgil's Real Barbecue**. Portions are huge at this immense but authentic barbecue joint designed to look like a real southern roadside shack (upstairs) and '50s diner (downstairs). Service is southern-style friendly, and plenty of families we know claim the ribs and pulled-pork sandwiches are the best in the city.
152 W. 44th St., tel. 212/921–9494. Kids' menu, high chairs, booster seats. Reservations recommended. AE, D, DC, MC, V. $

Breakfast

(ALL) **Royal Canadian Pancake House**. Fifty-odd varieties of pancakes are served all day. Flapjacks (so-so quality) are so big they drape over the huge plates; think about splitting orders. All three locations also serve eggs, sausage, and omelets. The staff is friendly and there are crayons on the tables. Expect a wait on weekends, especially at the Broadway location, which is always full of families.
1004 2nd Ave., at 53rd St., tel. 212/980– 4131; 2286 Broadway, between 82nd and 83rd Sts., tel. 212/873–6052; 180 3rd Ave., at 17th St., tel. 212/777–9703. High chairs, booster seats. No credit cards. $–$$

Chinese and Japanese

(5+) **Benihana West**. Watching the Japanese chef dice and slice chicken and steak, twirling and tossing the knife in the air

in between chops, and then cook the pieces on the grill at your table wows many kids. You sit on three sides of a big square table for seven diners; your chef stands at the fourth side in front of the center grill. Everything is ready quickly, and you're entertained while you wait. The Japanese food isn't the best in the city, but it's okay. Yes, it's a little slick and touristy, but it's fun.
47 W. 56th St., between 5th and 6th Aves., tel. 212/581–0930. Booster seats. AE, DC, MC, V. $$$

(ALL) **Mandarin Court**. You'll see lots of families, mostly Chinese, between 11 and 4 on weekends at this wildly popular dim sum parlor, which is much smaller than some of this area's huge dim sum emporia. You may have to wait a few minutes on Sunday. Dim sum are individual servings of dumplings of all kinds, noodle and rice dishes, egg custards, and more. Chinese waiters wheel carts full of new servings every 10 or 15 minutes; everyone points, choosing and trying different dishes; and you sit at a big round table with people you don't know. You pay according to the number of plates on your table at the end of the meal.
61 Mott St., near Canal St., tel. 212/608– 3838. Booster seats. AE, MC, V. $

(3+) **20 Mott Street**. For dim sum we like this three-story restaurant, which has a fish tank to look at in the downstairs room, tables with tablecloths, and a wide variety of dim sum. Try the wonton soup, vegetable dumplings, and the sticky rice in a lotus leaf.
20 Mott St., tel. 212/964–0380. Reservations recommended. Booster seats. AE, MC, V. $

(3+) **Ollie's Noodle Shop and Grille**. Both these branches look like busy luncheonettes; the one on Broadway and 84th Street, across the street from a good movie theater, attracts more families. The portions of mandarin noodle soup and other noodle dishes are large, and the good flavors even appeal to fussy eaters. Service is fast.

🏨 *200 W. 44th St., between Broadway and 8th Ave., tel. 212/921–5988; 2315 Broadway, at 84th St., tel. 212/362–3111. Reservations not accepted. AE, MC, V. $*

Delicatessen/Jewish

(👫 ALL) **Carnegie Delicatessen and Restaurant**. It's noisy and crowded and you have to wait in this quintessential New York deli with a take-out counter in front and small tables in the back. But we think it's a real slice of New York—and they like kids, too. Try their egg creams. The best and thickest pastrami sandwiches, chicken soup, and potato pancakes are what we go for, but they also have burgers and franks—and even Jell-O. The menu is huge. You can even come here for breakfast.

🏨 *854 7th Ave., between 54th and 55th Sts., tel. 212/757–2245. Reservations recommended. High chairs, booster seats. AE, D, DC, MC, V. $–$$*

(👫 3+) **Yonah Schimmel's Knishery**. This Lower East Side Jewish institution started out as a pushcart 100 years ago. Eating potato latkes (pancakes) here or any of their dozen delicious knishes (pastries stuffed with potatoes, cheese, fruit, or meat, then deep fried) is like entering the New York immigrant world of the early 20th century. If you go to the Lower East Side Tenement Museum, be sure to come here.

🏨 *137 E. Houston St., near 2nd Ave., tel. 212/477–2858. AE, MC, V. $*

Diners

(👫 ALL) **E J's Luncheonette**. A '50s-style diner with funky plastic statues of Marilyn Monroe and old-fashioned chrome-rimmed counter stools, it's open for breakfast, lunch, and dinner every day and has great malteds, french fries, and blue-plate specials. Lunch on weekends is crowded.

🏨 *447 Amsterdam Ave., near 81st St., tel. 212/873–3444; 73rd and 3rd Ave., tel. 212/472–0600; 6th Ave. between 9th and 10th*

Sts., tel. 212/473–5555. Reservations not accepted. Kids' menu, high chairs, booster seats. No credit cards. $

(👫 4+) **Ellen's Stardust Diner**. The front of this '50s diner is a red subway car; inside are a regulation '50s soda fountain, complete with chrome trim, vintage movie posters, and a model train zipping around on a track above your head. Kids groove on the loud doo-wop music, the black-cow drink (a root-beer float), the TV monitors with black-and-white movies, and the waiters' cool nicknames—our last one was Boogaloo. Weekend evenings are variety shows in which the waiters sing.

🏨 *1650 Broadway, at 51st St., tel. 212/956–5151. Reservations not accepted. AE, D, DC, MC, V. $–$$*

Italian

(👫 ALL) **Carmine's**. Eating at these big, informal, noisy Italian family restaurants is "like going to Grandma's" says one family of regulars. Service is family style, with huge platters of old-fashioned Italian-American food, like spaghetti and meatballs and chicken Parmesan. Six people, even hungry teenagers, can split three or four entrées and eat for about $90. You'll see more families at the Upper West Side branch. So that you don't have to wait an hour or more, put your name down, ask how long the wait will be, and then come back.

🏨 *2450 Broadway, between 90th and 91st Sts., tel. 212/362–2200; 200 W. 44th St., between 7th and 8th Aves., tel. 212/221–3800. Reservations essential for lunch and pretheater before 6 PM. Booster seats. AE, MC, V. $–$$*

(👫 3+) **Mimi's Macaroni**. Though this place is completely family friendly—kids can pick a toy from a large box to play with at the table—adults who like sophisticated Italian dishes will also be happy here. And despite the number of families, this small restaurant is fairly calm and even looks elegant. The kids' menu of pasta dishes is more interesting than most.

🏠 *718 Amsterdam Ave. at 95th St., tel. 212/866–6311. Reservations not accepted. Kids' menu, high chairs, booster seats. D, DC, MC, V. $–$$*

Mainly Hamburgers and Sandwiches

(👫 **3+**) **Hamburger Harry's**. It's busy and casual but a definite cut above the usual burger joint. The mesquite-grilled hamburgers are good, there are curly french fries, and they do special things for children—like pass out crayons and paper (though sometimes you have to ask).
🏠 *157 Chambers St., between W. Broadway and Greenwich St., tel. 212/267–4446; 145 W. 45th St., between 6th Ave. and Broadway, tel. 212/840–2756. Booster seats. AE, DC, MC, V. $*

(👫 **10+**) **Internet Café**. The reason to come here with older kids is so they can surf the net and eat; you'll also see little ones in strollers. Food is sandwiches and salads; you can eat in the long, narrow restaurant (there's a gallery in front) or, in nice weather, in the courtyard out back.
🏠 *82 E. 3rd St., tel. 212/614–0747. MC, V. $*

(👫 **ALL**) **Jackson Hole**. The five branches of this citywide chain not only have the very best—and maybe the broadest selection of—hamburgers in town, they're also hip, funky, and cheap and have great fries, onion rings, salads, and real hot chocolate. Teenagers hang out at the Columbus Avenue branch (which has outdoor seating) and the 2nd Avenue and Madison Avenue branches after school and on weekends.
🏠 *232 E. 64th St., tel. 212/311–7187; 521 3rd Ave., at 35th St., tel. 212/679–3264; 1611 2nd Ave., at 84th St., tel. 212/737–8788; 517 Columbus Ave., at 85th St., tel. 212/362–5177; 1270 Madison Ave., at 91st St., tel. 212/427–2820. AE. $*

Mexican

(👫 **ALL**) **Benny's Burritos**. It's just a storefront with a few tables inside (and

out, when the weather is nice), but as you walk by, the smell of Mexican beans and beef assaults you. Several families we know swear these are the best burritos in New York.
🏠 *113 Greenwich Ave., near Jane St., tel. 212/727–0584; 93 Ave. A, at 6th St., tel. 212/254–3286. Reservations not accepted. No credit cards. $*

(👫 **4+**) **Manhattan Chili Company**. Brightly colored murals of Manhattan as "Chili town" spread over the walls; the Statue of Liberty is holding a chili pepper. If you're with a crowd reserve the red table in the shape of a chili in the center of the restaurant. The children's menu includes hot dogs and delicious frozen drinks in many flavors. Be sure to inquire how spicy a particular dish is before you order. This Times Square restaurant is right around the corner from the New Victory Theater.
🏠 *500 Broadway, on 43rd St., tel. 212/730–8666. Reservations recommended. Kids' menu, high chairs, booster seats. AE, D, DC, MC, V. $*

(👫 **ALL**) **Mary Ann's**. The several branches of this Mexican chain are highly reliable; if you like homemade, traditional Mexican fare you won't be disappointed in the burritos, tamales, and grilled meats with mole sauce you'll find here. Decor is the Mexican blanket, stucco walls and tiles variety, with La Bamba–style music in the background. The Upper West Side and East Side branches have more families, but we like the original one in Chelsea, too.
🏠 *2452 Broadway at 91st St., tel. 212/877–0132; 1501 2nd Ave. between 78th and 79th Sts., tel. 212/249–6165; 116 8th Ave. at 16th St., tel. 212/633–0877. Kids' menu, high chairs, booster seats. MC, V. $*

Pizza Places

In New York you can get several kinds of pizza—New York style with a puffy crust (also called Sicilian style); Roman style with a thin, crisp crust; and deep-dish Chicago style.

4+ John's Pizzeria. The crust on John's pizza is crisp and slightly charred, there are 55 different topping choices, and the ingredients are truly fresh. Even the plain cheese with fresh tomatoes is a gourmet treat—and kids like it, too. You can't buy by the slice here and there are lines, but it's worth the wait. We like the downtown branch best; the uptown ones feel more like restaurants than the original no-frills spot with bare tables in the Village. But you can watch the pizzas being made in all of them, and the huge, skylit Times Square branch is spectacular.
🏠 *278 Bleecker St., between 6th and 7th Aves., tel. 212/243–1680; 260 W. 44th St., between Broadway and 8th Ave., tel. 212/391–7560; 408 E. 64th St., between 1st and York Aves., tel. 212/935–2895; 48 W. 65th St., between Broadway and Central Park West, tel. 212/721–7001. Reservations not accepted. No credit cards. $–$$*

2+ Lombardi's Pizza. The huge pizza oven at this restaurant in Little Italy was the first one in America. Chefs here like kids and frequently let them throw a piece of coal on the fire. Thin-crusted pizzas are excellent; the toppings are fresh ingredients.
🏠 *32 Spring St., at Mott St., tel. 212/941–7994. Reservations not accepted. No credit cards. $–$$*

Sweet Stuff

ALL Ferrara's. My husband and I like the smaller, less touristy, turn-of-the-century Caffè Roma down the block (383 Broome St., at Mulberry St., tel. 212/326–8413), where many Italian families come after church on Sunday, but my son and his friends have always preferred this spacious, shiny, and expensive Italian café because of the long, fancy glass case where you can see the huge selection of cookies and pastries. Strollers are welcome.
🏠 *195 Grand St., between Mulberry and Mott Sts., tel. 212/226–6150. Booster seats. AE, D, DC, MC, V. $$*

2+ Serendipity 3. This kid-size spot in a cozy brownstone oozes charm. Though it is noted for its fabulous desserts, foot-long hot dogs, and whimsical gifts and funky jewelry in the tiny shop in front, you can get a basic omelet, vegetable pizza, hamburgers, crepes, and more. Try the huge, old-fashioned drugstore sundaes and the frozen hot chocolate.
🏠 *225 E. 60th St., between 2nd and 3rd Aves., tel. 212/838–3531. Booster seats. AE, D, DC, MC, V. $$*

Theme Restaurants

9+ Hard Rock Cafe. The music is loud and the walls of the two-level dining area are festooned with rock-and-roll memorabilia—guitars, clothing, even John Lennon's wire-rimmed glasses; ask your waiter for the free guide to their locations. Favorite items: BLTs, cheeseburgers, Caesar salads, virgin strawberry daiquiris, hot fudge brownies, and old-fashioned shakes and sodas. You usually don't wait more than 15 minutes, except during school breaks.
🏠 *221 W. 57th St., between Broadway and 7th Ave., tel. 212/489–6565. Reservations not accepted. AE, DC, MC, V. $$*

9+ Jekyll & Hyde Club. Many kids say it's worth the usual 45-minute wait to see the bizarre and scary-to-little-kids ghoulish decorations of this action-oriented theme restaurant. Skeletons, creepy artwork, skull mugs, and spooky black-and-white movies are only part of it; try to sit in the first- or second-floor rooms so you can have the best views of the ongoing floor show of, say, Dr. Jekyll transforming himself into Mr. Hyde. Go for the least expensive and most basic food.
🏠 *1409 6th Ave., tel. 212/541–9517. AE, DC, MC, V. $$*

5+ Planet Hollywood. The food isn't the reason to come to this movie-theme spot—changing displays of props and costumes from movies, like Terminator's ripped-apart head, are what intrigue kids. The menu is mainly pizzas, salads, pastas, fajitas, sandwiches, and very good desserts; while you eat you can watch videos of movie trailers. The wait is usually longer than at the Hard Rock down the street. 🏨 *140 W. 57th St., between 6th and 7th Aves., tel. 212/333–7827. Reservations not accepted. AE, MC, V. $–$$*

Where to Stay

In New York City the ideal family hotel just doesn't exist; it's a matter of trade-offs. The biggest problem is price: Hotels here are very expensive. The best way to get a bargain is to take advantage of special weekend packages; many expensive ($$$) hotels listed below fall into the moderate ($$) category on weekends. Another way to save money in New York is to stay in a room or suite with a kitchenette where you can make breakfast, pack a lunch, or indulge in late-night snacks at a reasonable price. Most hotels in New York charge $20 to $30 for rollaways, and few provide the family packages and amenities (story hour, kids' toiletries, and so on) that are a matter of course in Boston's hotels. Frolicking around in a pool is one good way for kids to relax after a day of sightseeing, but be aware that some New York hotels with pools restrict the hours kids can use them.

The following hotels offer families something special—and actually want families to stay. For additional suggestions, check the Sunday travel section of the *New York Times* for special family-rate packages tied to particular events.

Category	Cost*
$$$$	over $350
$$$	$250–$350
$$	$150–$250
$	under $150

*All prices are for a standard double room, excluding $2 occupancy charge and 13¼% tax.

$$$$

Le Parker Meridien. This subdued but classic and elegant French hotel, with its soaring lobby linking 56th and 57th streets, has a 20- by 40-ft pool on the 42nd floor where you can order lunch or just ice cream; a sundeck with lounge chairs where you view the Hudson River; a fitness center with a basketball court; and a special pass that gets you into the restaurant Planet Hollywood (see Eats, *above*) next door and the Harley Davidson Café across the street without waiting in line. It's also centrally located—a short walk from Central Park, Rockefeller Center, and the F.A.O. Schwarz toy store. Plus, they really like families here. The rooms, with a brown, black, and cream color scheme and Biedermeier-style furniture, look a little formal, but they're good sized for Manhattan—a double would work for a family of four with two small children. A better choice for families, though, is one of the small suites, which contains a queen-size sofa and has lots of drawers and shelf space; many suites have full kitchens. Their new restaurant, Norma's, serves fancy breakfasts—Molten Chocolate French Toast, etc.—all day. 🏨 *118 W. 57th St., between 6th and 7th Aves., 10019, tel. 212/245–5000 or 800/543–4300, fax 212/708–7477. 600 rooms, 100 suites. Kids under 12 free; under 18 free on weekends, $30 weekdays. Facilities: 2 restaurants, lobby lounge, health club, jogging track, no-smoking floors, parking (fee), indoor pool (swimming classes), crib free, VCRs, rentals, and CD players. AE, D, DC, MC, V.*

Regal U.N. Plaza. The kid appeal at this modern, luxury hotel is the 22- by 44-ft glass-enclosed pool on the 27th floor (a lifeguard is on duty when it is open). What parents like is the exceptionally accommodating service, including complimentary limousine service to the theater district, the nearby U.N. gardens, and the hotel's family plan, which allows them to rent a connecting room for the kids at 50% off, something I'd do as the rooms are not really big enough for two parents and two school-age children. The U.N. Plaza offers good weekend and holiday packages; it's a terrific place to stay on the Fourth of July because you have a fabulous view of the fireworks over the East River. Hotel rooms start on the 28th floor; request one that has floor-to-ceiling windows. Our family calls the furnishings "plush contemporary."

🏨 ⎮ *United Nations Plaza, 44th St. and 1st Ave., 10017, tel. 212/758–1234 or 800/ 233–1234, fax 212/702–5051. 427 rooms, 44 suites. Kids under 16 free. Facilities: restaurant, health club, no-smoking rooms, pool, indoor tennis court, garage with unlimited access on weekends. AE, D, DC, MC, V.*

$$$

Doubletree Guest Suites Hotel. Although this 43-story, all-suite hotel is in the busy—and sometimes slightly unsavory—theater district (but right across from TKTS, the discount ticket office), it has so many features attractive to parents and kids that it may be the most family-friendly hotel in New York. For example: Suites on the eighth and ninth floors are childproofed with electrical outlet covers, unbreakable dishes and glasses, corner guards for furniture, and spout covers; the spacious kids' playroom (Kids' Club) on the fourth floor has brand-new toys, games, stuffed animals, and books and is open daily from 9:30 AM to 11 PM; kids receive a welcome pack with a coupon book of discounts for meals, attractions, and even a game of laser tag at nearby Lazer Park. You can borrow many family essentials, too—a stroller, a baby bathtub, and you can even get diapers! And now Doubletree has begun offering family theater packages, including tough-to-get tickets to *The Lion King*. All the rooms are suites, which are always great for families. Here the standard one has a private bedroom, a living room with a queen-size sofa bed, a desk that doubles as a dining table, and a kitchenette with a sink, microwave, coffeemaker, and wet bar (refrigerators are available on request). Furnishings

are attractively modern and sturdy; colors are warm earth tones. The bathrooms are basic and small but new. The only drawback is the lack of closet space. In case you're worried about the neighborhood, let me assure you that security is good; the small street lobby has a doorman and guard on duty at all times. The restaurant serves breakfast, lunch, and dinner.

🏨 ⎮ *1568 Broadway, at 47th St., 10036, tel. 212/719–1600 or 800/325–9033, fax 212/ 921–5212. 460 suites. Kids under 17 free. Facilities: restaurant, fitness room, coin laundry, kids' playroom, VCRs and rentals. Family packages. AE, D, DC, MC, V.*

Manhattan East Suite Hotels. All the units in this group of small hotels on Manhattan's East Side are studio, one- or two-bedroom suites with real kitchens that contain a microwave, a four-burner stove, a full-size refrigerator, a toaster, a sink, a coffeemaker, a dishwasher, and all the dishes and cookware you need. Rooms are huge compared to usual hotel rooms, with plenty of space for kids to color, curl up and read, or have a snack. Staying in one is like having your own apartment in New York. Best of all, they offer families a wonderful weekend (Friday–Sunday) package year-round that includes a family guide to the city, discount admission to the Children's Museum of Manhattan, a baby-sitting referral service, a special rate on one- and two-bedroom suites, and even a grocery shopping service, for a fee, of course. Of the 10 hotels, we especially like the following one.

Surrey Hotel (20 E. 76th St., tel. 212/288–3700, fax 212/629–1549; 130 suites) on the Upper East Side feels more like a residence than a hotel and has a wonderful location a half a block from good playgrounds in Central Park. Nearby are the Central Park Zoo, museums such as the Metropolitan Museum of Art, and appealing Madison Avenue kids' toy and book stores. You'll find tasteful, European-style traditional Chippendale-ish furnishings covered in pinks and dark greens and pleasant but not new bathrooms. Adjacent to the hotel is Café Boulud, owned by the famous chef Daniel Boulud.

🏨 *All hotels, tel. 800/637–8483. Kids under 12 free. Facilities: restaurant (at most hotels), health club, coin laundry, free parking. AE, D, DC, MC, V.*

$$

Loews New York. An excellent midtown location, an array of services for family travelers, and reasonable prices are the attractions of this large, refurbished, unstuffy hotel. In fact, the kid offerings indicate just how welcome families are: The staff will supply a gift bag when kids arrive, kids' bathrobes, and a variety of kid items to use during your stay such as games, books, strollers, potty seats, baby bath tubs, outlet protectors, even car seats and night-lights and Nintendo on request. Furnishings are comfortable contemporary, in browns and dark greens, with sleek wooden built-ins. Rooms are reasonably sized—the double room with two double beds is the best bet for families.

🏨 *569 Lexington Ave., at 51st St., tel. 212/752–5000 or 800/836–6471, fax 212/752–3817. 726 rooms, 37 suites. Kids under 18 free. Facilities: restaurant (kids' menu, high chairs, booster seats), complimentary cribs and roll-away beds, health club, no-smoking floors, on-site parking, mini-refrigerators, room service, VCRs and kids' videos. AE, D, DC, MC, V.*

Mayflower on the Park. This stately and gracious yet warm and homey hotel just across the street from Central Park is within walking distance of midtown and Lincoln Center. In fact, every weekend complimentary cookies, brownies, and hot chocolate or lemonade (depending on the season) are available to guests at a table in the lobby. Unlike rooms at most hotels, even the basic doubles here are high ceilinged, light-filled (especially the ones that face the park; $25 extra), and exceptionally spacious. Most rooms have an alcove pantry with refrigerator and sink. No microwaves, but a few hot plates are available on request. In keeping

with the flavor of the hotel, dark wood furniture is comfortable and traditional; print drapes and bedspreads are greens and blues, and carpeting is thick. Some doubles connect, but suites may be a better deal for your family. One-bedroom suites are enormous; ask for one with a large table and chairs. The Thanksgiving Day parade goes right by the hotel and there's a cute petting zoo in the lobby. The hotel maintains a list of approved baby-sitters and restaurants in the area for kids. You can gain admission to the nearby YMCA pool on request.

🏨 *15 Central Park West, at 61st St., 10023, tel. 212/265–0060 or 800/223–4164, fax 212/265–5098. 165 rooms, 200 suites. Kids under 16 free. Facilities: restaurant (kids' menu, high chairs), health club, 12 no-smoking floors, VCRs (for rent). AE, D, DC, MC, V.*

$

Excelsior Hotel. The key attractions to this hotel are its low price and excellent Upper West Side location—it's right across the street from the American Museum of Natural history, with good shops and restaurants nearby. This also happens to be the street where they blow up the huge float balloons the night before the Macy's Thanksgiving Day parade. The one-bedroom suites (most appropriate for families; the double rooms are not really big enough for four people) have two good-size rooms (including two closets) with fold-out couch, TV, table and chairs, and full kitchenette with stove, refrigerator, and sink. Definitely not as nice as the rooms at the Beacon (see below), the accommodations have, however, been renovated over the past few years. Make sure you reserve (three weeks to a month in advance) a park view and get a renovated room—others are dingy and have old and unattractive bathrooms.

🏨 *45 W. 81st St., 10024, tel. 212/362–9200 or 800/368–4575, fax 212/721–2994. 160 rooms, 95 1-bedroom suites, 6 2-bedroom suites. Facilities: coffee shop. AE, DC, MC, V.*

Hotel Beacon. Out of the bustle of midtown on the family-friendly Upper West Side, this hotel is convenient to many attractions for children—the Children's Museum, the American Museum of Natural History, and Central Park—and the hotel truly welcomes families with such details as a wide selection of family videos. All the rooms in this small combined apartment house and hotel are large and pleasant, with framed botanical prints and attractive Queen Anne–style dark wood furnishings, and all have kitchenettes with a full-size refrigerator, a sink, and a four-burner stove. Doubles easily accommodate a family of four, and suites are large enough to accommodate three or four children. Although it's not as luxurious as the more expensive Manhattan East Suite hotels (see above), it's one of the city's best bargains, especially on weekends, so reserve early.

🏨 *2130 Broadway, at 75th St., 10023, tel. 212/787–1100 or 800/572–4969, fax 212/724–0839. 101 rooms, 82 suites. Kids under 17 free. Facilities: coffee shop, in-room VCR on request (no charge), high chairs, strollers. AE, D, DC, MC, V.*

Travel Inn. The best things about this hotel are the Olympic-size pool and the price. The rooms are large, bright, and sparkling clean, just like those in a good motor inn, and easily accommodate a four-person family. Many overlook the pool; opt for one of these instead of looking out over the street. Now for the bad news: location. Though it's within walking distance of the *Intrepid* Sea/Air/Space Museum and the Circle Line tour, this far-west area is primarily warehouses and parking lots. The 42nd Street crosstown bus stops across the street, but you may find yourself, as one family we know did, taking a lot of taxis back in the late afternoon and evening.

🏨 *515 W. 42nd St., between 10th and 11th Aves., 10036, tel. 212/695–7171 or 800/869–4630, fax 212/967–5025. 160 rooms, 1 suite. Kids under 15 free. Facilities: deli, free on-site parking, pool, restaurant (will deliver to rooms). AE, D, DC, MC, V.*

Bed-and-Breakfasts

If your family wants to feel like natives and see what it's like to live in a SoHo loft or a Village brownstone, or if you're planning a long stay in the city, you might want to try an "unhosted" apartment offered through a bed-and-breakfast referral service. (Unlike at a regular B&B, the owner does not stay on the premises, and you are responsible for the housekeeping; few "hosted" apartments in New York City accept children.) Most apartments cost from $140 up for a family of four. Be as complete as possible in describing your family's requirements (if you have very small children, ask if the apartment has window guards, for example) when you reserve, and ask detailed questions about locations. Check the deposit and refund policy.

City Lights Bed & Breakfast Ltd. (Box 20355 Cherokee Station, 10021, tel. 212/737–7049, fax 212/535–2755; DC, MC, V) is particularly accommodating to families and follows up with questionnaires.

Urban Ventures (38 W. 32nd St., 10001, tel. 212/594–5650, fax 212/947–9320; AE, MC, DC, V), in business for 25 years, represents more than 900 unhosted apartments.

Entertainment and the Arts

Film

You don't have to wait in line to buy a ticket for any movie in New York. Just call **MovieFone** (tel. 212/777–3456) to charge a ticket to your credit card. One movie theater frequented by families and teens is **Sony 84th Street Theater** (84th St. and Broadway, tel. 212/887–3892), which has a good selection of video games.

(👫 6+) **Sony Theatres Lincoln Square.** So far this 12-screen theater complex is the ultimate movie-viewing spot in New York

City, a combination of modern comfort, new technology, and a dash of the ambience of old-style movie palaces. The top attraction for kids is the IMAX theater, with a screen eight stories high and super-advanced 3-D technology.

🏠 *Broadway and 68th St., tel. 212/336–5000 or 212/595–6391.*

The following are special movie programs for kids and families.

👫 6+ **Bryant Park Summer Film Festival.** Every Monday evening in summer (from mid-June to the end of Aug.) classic films, preceded by Looney Tunes cartoons, are projected onto a giant screen in this recently restored midtown park. In a city version of a drive-in, chairs are set up on the lawn. Seats are free; popcorn and hot dogs are available. Or you can bring a blanket and a picnic. There's usually a large crowd, though, so get there early to stake your claim.

🏠 *42nd St. between 5th and 6th Aves., behind New York Public Library, tel. 212/512–5700.*

👫 6–12 **Family Film Series.** A half hour of short films for families are shown Saturdays at 12:30 and again at 2 PM in the fall and spring at the Metropolitan Museum of Art. Families we know like to tour a few galleries in the morning, have lunch, and then see a film.

🏠 *Metropolitan Museum of Art, 5th Ave. at 82nd St., tel. 212/570–3932.*

👫 5–13 **Movies for Kids, Walter Reade Theater.** The Lincoln Center Film Society puts on a regular series for kids every weekend at 2 PM at rock-bottom prices ($3) for Manhattan. American classics, films set in New York City, and musicals are just some of the themes of choices over the past year. Occasionally foreign films are shown; subtitles are read aloud.

🏠 *In Lincoln Center, 165 W. 65th St., tel. 212/875–5610.*

Performing Spaces and Performers

There are excellent performances just for children in New York City every weekend; be sure to check under "Family Fare" and "Spare Times for Children" in the *New York Times* "Weekend" section on Friday and in *New York Family* (*see* How to Find Out What's Going On, *above*).

DISCOUNT TICKETS. TKTS. This is the source for almost half-price tickets for same-day Broadway theater performances. Of the two locations, the Lower Manhattan booth is often better for families than the one centrally placed on Broadway. Downtown lines tend to be shorter, you can wait indoors, and tickets for Wednesday, Saturday, and Sunday matinees are sold a day in advance.

🏠 *Mezzanine level of 2 World Trade Center or Broadway at 47th St., tel. 212/768–1818.*

Hot Seats. If you'll be in the city in the spring, obtain a copy of the spring issue of this organization's newspaper, *Passport to Off Broadway*, which contains discount coupons for an amazing number of performances. The rest of the year they provide listings of performances. Call 212/989–5257 for information.

High Five Tickets to the Arts. This organization provides a way for teenagers to get low-cost tickets to many performances. *See* Chapter 10.

THEATER AND PUPPET SHOWS

👫 4+ **Broadway and Off-Broadway.** Kids often enjoy plays, performances, and especially musicals that are not intended for children. Long-running shows kids recommend include *Cats, Beauty and the Beast, Blue Man Group: Tubes,* and *The Fantasticks*. The big drawback for families is the cost; an orchestra ticket on Broadway can be as much as $70 or more. Try to get half-price tickets the day of performance if you can (*see above*) and order the free *Family Guide to Broadway* (tel. 212/764–1122 or 800/

832–8440); it describes plots of musicals and plays and includes age guidelines for kids.

(👪 8+) *A Christmas Carol.* The extravagant musical version of this classic Christmas story appears annually from mid-November through the beginning of January at the Theater at Madison Square Garden; though the theater seats 5,600, the seating area fans out so most seats have a good view.

🏠 *Theater at Madison Square Garden, 7th Ave. between 31st and 33rd Sts., tel. 212/465–6741 information, 212/307–7171 Ticketmaster. Cost: $19–$78, depending on seat.*

(👪 3–12) **International Festival of Puppet Theater.** Twenty or more puppeteers perform in various city locations during this biannual fall festival sponsored by the Jim Henson Foundation. *See also* Chapter 10.
🏠 *Jim Henson Foundation, 117 E. 69th St., tel. 212/794–2400.*

(👪 2–9) **Miss Majesty's Lollipop Playhouse.** Kids like these performances of classic fairy-tale adaptations such as *Snow White* and *Sleeping Beauty* because the company's versions of the stories contain lots of comic elements and give kids the opportunity to participate.
🏠 *Grove St. Playhouse, 39 Grove St., tel. 212/741–6436. Cost: $8. Performances Sept.–June., weekends at 1:30 and 3:30.*

(👪 6–15) **New Victory Theater.** The performances at this Broadway theater dedicated to presenting the best for families range from theater to dance and music. This is the very best theater in New York for kids. *See also* Chapter 10.
🏠 *209 W. 42nd St., tel. 212/239–6200 or 800/432–7250 (Telecharge).*

(👪 4–9) **Paper Bag Players.** See Chapter 10.

(👪 3–5) **Puppet Playhouse.** Different talented puppet groups or magic acts, many from Russia and Eastern Europe, perform here every Saturday and Sunday from October through May. The tiny 91-seat theater

makes viewing easy for even the smallest kids. Theater and music groups also perform here from time to time.
🏠 *Mazur Theater at Asphalt Green, 555 E. 90th St., tel. 212/369–8890. Cost: $8. Performances Oct.–May, weekends.*

(👪 3–7) **Puppetworks.** See Chapter 10.

(👪 5+) **Shakespeare in Brooklyn.** The outdoor rooftop theater of the Brooklyn Children's Museum (*see above*) is the setting for this annual children's introduction to the Bard. In July, seasoned Shakespearean actors from the Joseph Papp Public Theater present an hour of short scenes and monologues from the comedies and romances—*The Tempest,* and so on—and answer questions afterward.
🏠 *Brooklyn Children's Museum. 145 Brooklyn Ave., Brooklyn, tel. 718/735–4402.*

(👪 3+) **Swedish Cottage Marionette Theater.** The small (85 seats) theater in a little cottage in the middle of Central Park behind the Delacorte Theater is a great introduction to the theater for little ones. The one-hour productions of fairy tales feature large marionettes in great costumes with fancy sets and lively music. Saturday performances during the winter are very, very popular; reserve a week in advance if you can. Weekdays in winter school groups dominate, but usually there's extra space for a few individuals.
🏠 *Near Central Park West and 79th St., tel. 212/988–9093. Cost: $5 adults, $4 kids. Performances July–Aug., weekdays; Oct.–June, Tues.–Sat. Reservations essential.*

(👪 4+) **TADA!** This unique musical theater group composed of New York City kids ages 6–17 puts on two lively, original one-hour family productions each year, one during July and August and another in December and January. Some are based on kids' experiences; others are adaptations of children's books, like the recent show "Little Moon Christmas," adapted from the story about a theater that grants wishes. All have catchy songs and easily graspable plots.

🏠 *120 W. 28th St., tel. 212/627–1732. Cost: $12 adults, $6 kids under 15. Performances July–Aug., Tues.–Thurs. and weekend matinees (call for times); Dec.–Jan., Fri. 7:30, weekend and holiday matinees; also a new spring show in March. Reservations essential.*

👫 6–12 **Theatreworks USA**. See Chapter 10.

MUSIC. One of the great things about New York is the variety of free concerts that are held in Central Park, at the World Financial Center, at South Street Seaport, and at many other places around the city, especially in summer.

👫 5+ **Arts Connection**. Just about every Saturday afternoon at 3 PM during the school year, this organization presents bargain ($6 per person) one-hour shows of famous dance, theater, or music groups or individual performers designed specifically for families, such as an Andre Watts special piano concert or the New York City Ballet's introduction to dance. The 45-minute Saturday morning shows are for 3- to 5-year-olds. The 250-seat theater is just the right size for kids. Reserve at least a week or two in advance. 🏠 *120 W. 46th St., tel. 212/302–7433. Performances Oct.–May.*

👫 8+ **Bryant Park Young Performers Series.** From May through September one-hour lunchtime concerts on Monday and Friday feature young, up-and-coming jazz and classical musicians playing with established artists. 🏠 *Bryant Park, W. 42nd St., east of 6th Ave., tel. 212/983–4142.*

👫 6–13 **Carnegie Hall.** The family concert series, which features such well-known performers as Yo-Yo Ma, is a great bargain. See also Chapter 10. 🏠 *154 W. 57th St., at 7th Ave., tel. 212/247–7800.*

👫 8+ **Jazzmobile.** During July and August this group dedicated to introducing people to jazz performs about 40 free concerts in the five boroughs.

🏠 *154 W. 127th St., tel. 212/866–3616 (information line for concert locations; in use July and Aug. only).*

👫 7+ **Juilliard School.** Great bargains for families are the free recitals and concerts given by precollege students at this world-famous music school in Lincoln Center. On Saturdays from about 11 to 6, for example, you can hear one-hour recitals by students ages 7–17 in the main recital hall. There's a wide range of accomplishment; some of the older kids are already under management. Attending is all very informal: Just walk in, listen as long as you like, then leave. The regular student orchestra concerts are also free, but you must pick up a ticket at the box office for some of them. Be prepared to see a few homeless people in the audience. The school will send you a schedule if you send a stamped self-addressed envelope or tell you what is playing over the phone, but you can also check the bulletin board in the lobby. 🏠 *60 Lincoln Center Plaza, tel. 212/799–5000, ext. 241.*

👫 3–12 **Little Orchestra Society.** See Chapter 10.

👫 6–14 **Metropolitan Opera.** The Growing Up with Opera performances are produced especially for families by the Metropolitan Opera Guild. See also Chapter 10. 🏠 *70 Lincoln Center Plaza; Growing up with Opera reservations tel. 212/769–7008.*

👫 6+ **New York Philharmonic.** One of the great orchestras of the world, the Philharmonic performs two annual series of children's concerts. See also Chapter 10. 🏠 *10 Lincoln Center Plaza, tel. 212/875–5732 information, 212/875–5656 tickets.*

👫 6+ **Radio City Music Hall.** The vast stage is the setting for the annual Christmas Spectacular that wows kids with music and action. 🏠 *1260 6th Ave., at 50th St. in Rockefeller Center, tel. 212/247–4777 information, 212/307–7171 Ticketmaster.*

👫 10+   **SummerStage**. A wide variety of free concerts from rock to reggae to bagpipes and more appears here each summer. Have a picnic while you listen.
🏠 *Rumsey Playfield, Central Park, tel. 212/ 360–2777.*

DANCE. Besides performances in the museum programs (listed below) and at Arts Connection (listed above), the following are good bets for kids.

👫 6+   **American Ballet Theater.** The story ballets (*Swan Lake, Coppelia, Giselle*, and so on) for which this company's dancers are world renowned tend to be more accessible to kids. The costumes, dancing, and stage sets are uniformly superb. Unfortunately they perform in the huge Metropolitan Opera House; if you can't get seats in the front of the orchestra or in the grand tier, which are closer to the stage, don't bring younger kids. Best bets are the Wednesday and Saturday matinees. The company performs from April through June.
🏠 *70 Lincoln Center Plaza, tel. 212/477– 3030. Cost: $15–$65, depending on seat location.*

👫 8+   **Joyce Theater.** See Chapter 10.

👫 4+   **New York City Ballet.** See Chapter 10.

👫 3–12   **New York Theater Ballet.** See Chapter 10.

STORYTELLING. Barnes & Noble, Books of Wonder, and Tootsie's bookstores (see Shopping, *above*) have regular story hours for kids.

👫 5–9   **Central Park's Hans Christian Andersen Statue.** During the late spring, summer, and early fall, storytellers entertain kids on Saturday from 11 to 12. If you can, hear the beguiling Diane Wolkstein, author of several books of folktales. A storyteller will be there even if it's raining lightly.
🏠 *Near 72nd St. and 5th Ave. on west side of sailboat pond, tel. 212/368–3444.*

👫 3–12   **New York Public Library.** There's something for every kid at one of the world's largest branch library systems. The Central Children's Room at the Donnell Library Center (20 W. 53rd St., between 5th and 6th Aves., tel. 212/621– 0636), the largest children's room in the system, always has a program.

CIRCUS

👫 1–12   **Big Apple Circus.** See Chapter 10.

👫 6+   **Ringling Brothers and Barnum & Bailey Circus.** See Chapter 10.

MUSEUM PROGRAMS. Almost all museums in New York have regular events for children; some offer both performances and workshops that fall into more than one category. Those I've chosen are ones that we and my kids' panel have particularly enjoyed.

👫 6+   **American Museum of Natural History.** Check out what's on in the Leonhardt People Center on the second floor. In this small theater space it's easy for kids to see and hear—and it's not hard to leave if you lose interest. Most of the performances involve dance or music from another culture. Other terrific performances (we've seen Native American dances and drumming) take place in the galleries. If you're in New York before Christmas, be sure to attend one of the museum's origami workshops. The huge screen ($13 adults, $9 students with ID, $7 kids 2–12; includes museum admission) shows visually spectacular films such as *Amazon. See also* Chapter 3.
🏠 *Central Park West and 79th St., tel. 212/ 769–5100.*

👫 2–10   **Brooklyn Children's Museum.** In addition to all-day activities on weekends, there's usually a performance on Saturday or Sunday. We've seen the colorful Chinese Folk Dance company as well as a puppet show featuring African-American popular music.

Workshops and performances here tend to be very multicultural. *See also* Chapter 3.
🏛 *145 Brooklyn Ave., tel. 718/735–4400.*

(👫 2–10) **Children's Museum of Manhattan.** Weekends here are chockablock with activities for kids. Most performances are for ages 5 and up; the theater is small, participation is encouraged, and kids have a chance to talk with the performers. You'll see everything from an Irish music group playing bagpipes and harps to clog dancers. The art studio also has regular workshops. *See Museums, above.*
🏛 *212 W. 83rd St., tel. 212/721–1234.*

(👫 6+) **Metropolitan Museum of Art.** Every Friday and Saturday night the Met is open until 8:45. Between 5 and 8, the Great Hall Balcony Quintet plays on the second-floor balcony. Children often like to sit on benches across from the musicians, listen for a while, then explore the surrounding galleries. Stay to have dinner in the museum cafeteria; then attend the excellent one-hour family lecture and sketching workshop for parents and kids 6–12 at 6 or at 7:30 on Friday. The museum also has a good family film series (*see above*) and children's concerts several times a year. *See also* Chapter 3.
🏛 *1000 5th Ave., at 82nd St., tel. 212/535–7710.*

(👫 6+) **Museum of the City of New York.** Nearly every Saturday there's a special family performance of dance, theater, or music or a workshop related to a special exhibit. We've found the puppet shows here among the very best in the city. There's a special family rate for museum admission that includes performances. *See Museums, above.*
🏛 *5th Ave. and 103rd St., tel. 212/534–1672.*

CLASSES. There are an enormous number of classes in music, dance, and art for children in the city, but most of them require you to sign up for a certain number of sessions. Those below (and under Museum Programs, *above*) do not; though some of them don't require reservations, it's best to call before going.

(👫 5+) **Arts Connection.** From 12:30 to 2:30 on Saturday afternoon, prior to the regular 3 PM performance (*see Music, above*), there's always a fascinating, activity-packed family workshop—you might make Mexican masks for the Day of the Dead, learn to hula, or build instruments from paper tubes and bottles. The artists, architects, musicians, and dancers who lead them are adept at finding ways to involve kids of all ages and parents. Be sure to make reservations.
🏛 *120 W. 46th St., tel. 212/302–7433. Cost: $2.*

(👫 4–12) **Brooklyn Museum.** This huge museum offers free weekend art classes. "Arty Facts" is a 1½-hour family workshop (kids 4–7) in which you view some aspect of an exhibition, then create related artwork. The instructors here are especially tuned in to kids.
🏛 *200 Eastern Pkwy., tel. 718/638–5000. Cost: Suggested contribution $4 adults, $2 students, under 12 free. Open Wed.–Fri. 10–5, weekends 11–5.*

(👫 2–10) **Children's Museum of the Arts.** The space in this ground-floor SoHo loft is an environment for making art rather than a traditional museum. When there's a special "exhibit" kids make art related to it. The atmosphere is informal and fun; the highlight for a 6-year-old we know was decorating a vest with buttons and beads in a costume collage workshop.
🏛 *182 Lafayette St., between Broome and Grand Sts., tel. 212/274–0986. Cost: $4 weekdays, $5 weekends. Open Thurs.–Fri. 1–7, weekends 11–5.*

CAPE COD, MASSACHUSETTS █13
HIGH DUNES AND 150 BEACHES

Cape Cod is an especially great place for kids of all ages, from babies to teens. This 70-mi-long arm of land has an amazingly diverse assortment of beautiful white-sand beaches and dunes, and its many towns each have their own personality. You'll find wonderful playgrounds, shops, miniature golf, day camps, and nature programs for kids all over the place, and concerts and movies prevent the boring-evening syndrome that dooms many beach vacations.

Though there is undeniably a commercial, shopping-mall side to the Cape, at least in its bustling larger towns, the creation of the Cape Cod National Seashore preserved most of the land in what's known as the Lower Cape—from the "elbow" of the arm, around Chatham, up to the "fist" at Provincetown, the area my family prefers. Families with young kids may prefer the south-shore beaches, where the water is warmest.

One thing to keep in mind when scheduling your trip is that the Cape's summer traffic jams are legendary. On Friday nights it can sometimes take two hours just to cross the bridge over the canal that separates the Cape from mainland Massachusetts. Try to base yourself in the area where you want to spend most of your time, because although distances are not great, there can be traffic tie-ups on the Cape itself, too. To us, though, Cape Cod has so many attractions that braving the traffic is definitely worth it.

The Basics

How to Find Out What's Going On

The **Cape Cod Chamber of Commerce & Visitor Bureau** (Rtes. 6 and 132, Box 16, Hyannis 02601, tel. 508/362–3225 or 888/896–2732) is open year-round. Besides the main location, look for information booths at the Sagamore Bridge rotary (tel. 508/888–2438), just over the Bourne Bridge on Route 28 (tel. 508/759–3814) heading toward Falmouth, and a large center on Route 3, Exit 5. We've found that local chambers of commerce usually provide more and better information; they include **Brewster** (74 Locust La., 02631, tel. 508/896–3500); **Chatham** (533 Main St., Box 793, 02633-0793, tel. 508/945–5199 or 800/715–5567); **Dennis** (242 Swan River Rd., West Dennis 02670, tel. 508/398–3568 or 800/243–9920); **Eastham** (Box 1329, 02653, tel. 508/240–7211); **Orleans** (44 Main St., Box 153, 02653, tel. 508/255–1386 or 800/255–1386); **Truro** (Rte. 6 at head of the Meadow Rd., Box 26, North Truro 02666, tel. 508/487–1288); and **Wellfleet** (Rte. 6, Box 571, 02663, tel. 508/349–2510). **Best Web site**: www.capecod.com.

Kids on the Cape (Sandcastle Publishing Co., Box 1341, Orleans, MA 02653, tel. 508/

255–6900), a free booklet published during the summer season, is the best resource for families on current activities, events, and sights on the Cape.

Arriving and Departing

BY BOAT. **Bay State Cruise Company** (tel. 617/723–7800) runs a three-hour trip by ferry from Boston to Provincetown (summer only). This is too long for all but older kids.

BY BUS. **Bonanza Bus Lines** (tel. 800/556–3815) offers direct and frequent service to Falmouth, Bourne, and Woods Hole from Boston and Logan Airport, as well as daily service from New York, Connecticut, and Providence. **Plymouth & Brockton Company** (tel. 508/775–5524 or 508/746–0378) runs buses from Boston to a number of Cape communities, including Provincetown. The **Cape Cod Regional Transit Authority** (tel. 800/352–7155 or 508/548–7588) provides local service, including a route between Barnstable and Woods Hole that stops at popular destinations.

BY CAR. Route 6 (the Mid-Cape Highway), which connects to Route 3 from Boston, runs the length of the Cape to Provincetown, but it has no view of the water. Route 28, which connects to Route 195 and then to I–95, goes along the south shore and is usually full of traffic. Route 6A along the north shore is the scenic route. On all roads in summer, eastbound lanes are jammed afternoons and evenings on Friday, and westbound traffic is jammed from noon to 9 on Sunday. The biggest tie-up is at the bridges across the Cape Cod Canal.

BY PLANE. **Barnstable Municipal Airport** (Rte. 28 rotary, Hyannis, tel. 508/775–2020) offers service from Boston year-round via Cape Air; there's also year-round service from New York City (La Guardia) via Colgan Air/Continental Connection and US Airways Express.

Family-Friendly Tours

👫 4+ **Cape Cod Duckmobile.** The 30-minute tours in this giant "duck," a 28-passenger blue amphibious craft with a bright yellow top, please even teens. First it goes up and down the streets and back roads of Hyannis, letting out loud quacks; then it heads for the harbor. Kids love going along the boat ramp and splashing into the harbor. It's expensive, but kids say it's worth it.
🏠 447 Main St., Hyannis, tel. 508/362–1117. Cost: $12 adults, $10 students, $8 kids 12 and under. Tours Apr.–mid-Oct., daily; tours every hr on weekends.

👫 4–13 **P-Town Trolley Tour.** If your kids have never traveled on an old-fashioned trolley, they might enjoy this 45-minute narrated tour of Provincetown. You can get on and off at four locations (including the National Seashore's visitor center), wander around, then board another trolley a half hour later.
🏠 In front of Town Hall, Provincetown, tel. 508/487–9483. Cost: $8 adults, $5 kids under 13. Open May–Oct., daily 10–5.

Emergencies

Cape Cod Hospital (27 Park St., Hyannis 02601, tel. 508/771–1800) and **Falmouth Hospital** (100 Ter Heun Dr., Falmouth 02540, tel. 508/457–3524) both have 24-hour emergency rooms, though these are jammed in summer. For **fire** or **ambulance** anywhere on the Cape, call 911. **Poison Hot-line** (tel. 800/682–9211). Omni Dentix (Cape Cod Mall, Hyannis 02601, tel. 508/778–1200) is a dental clinic that accepts emergency walk-ins. Most of the Cape's 20 CVS drugstores (there's one in the Cape Cod Mall, Hyannis, tel. 508/771–1774) are open until 9 PM Monday through Saturday, Sunday until 6; the Stop 'n Shop Pharmacy (65 Independence Dr., Hyannis, tel. 508/790–2149) is open from 8 AM to 8 PM Monday through Friday, to 7 PM Saturday and 5 PM Sunday.

When to Go

Since the main reason to go to the Cape with kids is the beach, the water, and outdoor action, summer is the time to be here. Tourists swarm in the first week in July and August; the second and third weeks in July tend to be less crowded; however, the last half of June and early September are the best choice if it doesn't conflict with your kids' school calendar. Early fall is still balmy, the water is warmer than it is in June, and prices drop dramatically. Most attractions on the Cape are open from Memorial Day through September, sometimes to the end of October.

Scoping Out Cape Cod

Cape Cod is commonly divided into three sections, yet the names are counter-intuitive and may seem confusing: the Upper Cape (the first section you drive through as you come from the mainland), Mid-Cape, and the Lower Cape, also called the Outer Cape. The Upper Cape includes such towns as quaint Sandwich on the north shore and, on the south shore, New England-y Falmouth and Woods Hole (home of the famous oceanographic institute and docking point for ferries to the island of Martha's Vineyard). In the Mid-Cape, Hyannis, a village made famous by the Kennedys, is the business hub of the Cape. Though it's crowded and noisy, families usually end up here at some point or other, either to visit attractions, go shopping, or catch a ferry to Martha's Vineyard or Nantucket. Dennis, with its charming Colonial center, encompasses four towns and some 15 beaches on both Cape Cod Bay and the south shore.

The Lower Cape begins where the peninsula abruptly hooks northward. On the bay, Brewster, an old New England town of shade trees, captains' houses, and country roads, is a good place for outdoor action, including freshwater swimming, camping, and walking across miles of tidal flats. We love Chatham, situated on the elbow of the Cape and surrounded by water on three sides; it has gray-shingle cottages and the smell of honeysuckle and the sea. Pleasant, unassuming Orleans has activities such as roller-skating, sailing, kayaking, and swimming at beaches on both the bay and ocean. At Eastham the Cape becomes wilder and less populated, a place of high dunes and windswept ocean beaches. Uncrowded Wellfleet, tucked into a sheltered spot on Cape Cod Bay, has a meandering coastline of watery green salt marshes, hidden freshwater ponds, a wildlife sanctuary, and the National Seashore. Truro is also untouristy, surrounded by high dunes, rolling moors, and houses in tiny valleys. Provincetown, nestled on a hill above the bay at the Cape's tip, has a diverse mix of people—families, fishermen, flamboyant gays, assorted sightseers. We come to shop, climb the Pilgrim monument, go on a whale watch, people-watch on the wharf, and marvel at the 60-ft-high dunes.

Attractions below have been grouped by town, beginning at the Cape Cod Canal and proceeding out along the Cape to its tip.

Museums, Famous Sites, and Other Attractions

(👫 3 – 13) **Heritage Plantation.** At this museum complex you'll find a Shaker round barn full of classic and historic cars, including a 1931 yellow-and-green Duesenberg built for Gary Cooper. There's also a collection of 2,000 hand-painted miniature soldiers and an old-fashioned carousel with hand-carved horses on this 76-acre property of gardens and wooded groves along Shawme Pond. Kids like their regular outdoor concerts.
🏛 *Grove and Pine Sts., Sandwich, tel. 508/ 888–3300. Cost: $9 adults, $4.50 kids 6–18. Open mid-May–mid-Oct., daily 10–5.*

(👫 3 – 10) **Thornton W. Burgess Museum.** This homey little cottage by a willow-edged duck pond houses books and memorabilia of children's book author Thornton Burgess. *See also* Chapter 3.

🏨 *4 Water St., edge of Shawme Pond, Sand-wich, tel. 508/888–4668.*

(👫 **0–9**) **Cape Cod Discovery Museum.** There are 4,000 square ft of inter-active exhibits here, including Jake's Interna-tional Diner, where kids can pretend to be waiters, waitresses, and chefs.

🏨 *444 Main St. (Rte. 28), Dennisport, tel. 508/398–1600. Cost: $2.50 adults, $4.50 kids 1–15. Open mid-June–Labor Day, daily 9:30–7:30; Labor Day–mid-June, daily 9:30–5:30.*

(👫 **3–12**) **Cape Cod Museum of Natural History.** This museum set on 82 acres taught us much about how the Cape's native creatures survive, with exhibits, family programs, and short nature trails through marshes. The museum also organizes family excursions to Monomoy Wildlife Refuge and Nauset Marsh.

🏨 *896 Main St., Brewster, tel. 508/896–3867 or 800/479–3867. Cost: $5 adults, $2 kids 5–12. Open Mon.–Sat. 9:30–4:30, Sun. 11–4:30.*

(👫 **3–12**) **New England Fire and History Museum.** Kids can climb on engines and a fireboat here, at one of the world's biggest collections of fire engines and memorabilia. The museum's six buildings on Brewster's common also house a historic blacksmith shop and an animated diorama of the Great Chicago Fire; movies are shown regularly.

🏨 *Rte. 6A, Brewster, tel. 508/896–5711. Cost: $5 adults, $2.50 kids 5–12. Open Memorial Day–Labor Day, weekdays 10–4, weekends noon–4; Labor Day–Columbus Day weekends, noon–4.*

(👫 **3–8**) **Stony Brook Grist Mill.** At this weathered-shingle mill with turning water-wheel, little kids like to clatter across the small wooden bridges out back. Inside you can watch cornmeal being ground and buy some; upstairs, in the museum, a weaver is working at a loom.

🏨 *Stoney Brook Rd., Brewster, tel. 508/896–6745. Cost: Donations accepted. Open May–June, Fri. 2–5; July–Aug., Thurs.–Sat. 2–5.*

(👫 **6–15**) **Highland Light.** The Cape's oldest lighthouse, Highland Light (also called Cape Cod Light), is still active, and now you can climb to the top with a guide, though only kids 51″ or taller can do so. Before you climb, you'll see a short and interesting doc-umentary of how they moved the light-house back from the shore to save it. Be sure to take a look in the Truro Historical Museum in the old house next door; it has a gift shop, period rooms with old toys, and exhibits on the many shipwrecks caused by the treacherous sandbars to the north.

🏨 *Off Lighthouse Rd., off Rte. 6, North Truro. Museum tel. 508/487–3397. Cost: lighthouse or museum $3, combination ticket $5. Open Memorial Day–mid-Oct., daily 10–6; after mid-Oct., call for hrs.*

(👫 **6+**) **Expedition *Whydah* Sea Lab & Learning Center.** Pirates and shipwrecks fascinate most kids, and this center displays weapons, clothing, and coins recovered from the pirate ship *Whydah*, which was wrecked in the 18th century. This is the only pirate wreck ever recovered. Interactive exhibits illustrate some of the archaeological techniques used to salvage the treasure in the 1980s.

🏨 *16 MacMillan Wharf, Provincetown, tel. 508/487–8899. Cost: $5 adults, $3.50 kids 6–12. Open mid-Apr.–mid-Oct., daily 10–5 (July–Aug., daily 10–7); mid-Oct.–Christmas, weekends 10–5.*

(👫 **6–15**) **Pilgrim Monument and Museum.** A granite tower honors the Pil-grims, who landed here in 1620 before pushing on to Plymouth. *See also* Chapter 2.

🏨 *High Pole Hill on Winslow St., off Bradford St., Provincetown, tel. 508/487–1310.*

Animals and Marine Life

(👫 **4–10**) **Green Briar Nature Center and Jam Kitchen.** In the center, you'll find live frogs, turtles, a rabbit in a hutch, shells, and aquariums; the gardens and an adjoining 57 acres dubbed the Old Briar Patch are laced with the finest nature paths in this part of the Cape. You can also buy some beach-plum jelly at the old-fashioned kitchen in the woods next to a pond.

🏠 *6 Discovery Hill Rd., off Rte. 6A, East Sandwich, tel. 508/888–6870. Cost: Donation requested. Open Apr.–Dec., Mon.–Sat. 10–4, Sun. 1–4; Jan.–Mar., Tues.–Sat. 10–4.*

(👬 **3 – 12**) **Fisheries Aquarium.** Kids can touch and see lobsters, starfish, and other species native to Cape Cod's waters here at the public aquarium of the Northeast Fisheries Science Center. *See also* Chapter 4.

🏠 *Albatross and Water Sts., Woods Hole, tel. 508/495–2000.*

(👬 **2 – 12**) **ZooQuarium.** This combination petting zoo, discovery center, aquarium, and sea-lion show also offers regular educational programs. *See also* Chapter 4.

🏠 *Rte. 28, West Yarmouth, tel. 508/775–8883.*

(👬 **2 – 10**) **Bassett Wild Animal Farm.** When kids are little, no trip is usually complete without a stop to see exotic wild critters and pet domestic animals.

🏠 *620 Tubman Rd., between Rtes. 124 and 137, Brewster, tel. 508/896–3224. Cost: $5.75 adults, $4 kids 2–11. Open mid-May–mid-Sept., daily 10–5.*

(👬 **ALL**) **Chatham Fish Pier.** After 2 PM, wiggly little kids and grown-ups crowd the pier's observation deck to watch the returning fishing boats unload their catch; the action reaches its peak between 4 and 5.

🏠 *Shore Rd. and Barcliff Ave., Chatham.*

(👬 **6 – 14**) **Monomoy National Wildlife Refuge.** This 2,750-acre preserve on Monomoy Island, a barrier beach of tidal flats, dunes, marshes, and ponds, provides a resting and nesting place for migrating birds. From a ¾-mi interpretive trail along the beach on the mainland, you and your kids can enjoy a good view of the refuge and its birds. The Cape Cod Museum of Natural History (*see* Museums, *above*) has regular guided tours that are very appropriate for kids. If you want to go on your own, call one of the three ferry services: Monomoy Island

Ferry, tel. 508/945–5450; Outermost Marine, tel. 508/945–2030; or Stage Ferry, tel. 508/945–1860.

🏠 *Morris Island, Chatham, tel. 508/945–0594.*

(👬 **ALL**) **Wellfleet Bay Wildlife Sanctuary.** The appeal of this 1,000-acre haven of salt marshes, moors, ponds, and woods are the animals (muskrats, turtles, and others) and 250 species of birds, which appear even when kids are making lots of noise. We like the mile-long Goose Pond Trail; an inexpensive guide shows the birds and plants you will encounter. A nature center has hands-on exhibits; activities for kids include walks, workshops, evening slide shows, and a day camp. It's run by the Massachusetts Audubon Society; if you've been an Audubon member for at least a year, you can camp here.

🏠 *West side of Rte. 6, off West Rd., Box 236, South Wellfleet, tel. 508/349–2615. Cost: $3 adults, $2 kids 6–12. Open daily dawn–dusk.*

Beaches

The Cape's 150 salt- and freshwater beaches provide an amazing variety of sand, water, and amenities. The Cape Cod Visitor's Guide details costs; hefty parking fees ranging from $8 to $12 per day are charged at town beaches unless you purchase a weekly or season-long sticker (check at individual town halls). Parking lots at the most popular beaches fill up quickly.

The beaches facing the Atlantic Ocean along the National Seashore are beautiful and less crowded, but they're not for young kids; serious, rough surf rolls in, sometimes with a strong undertow, and the water temperature is cold. Instead, head for the gentle swells and dune landscape of beaches along Cape Cod Bay, or the big, wide south Cape beaches facing Nantucket Sound, where the water is warmed by the gulf stream. Here is a town-by-town rundown of kid-friendly spots.

CAPE COD NATIONAL SEASHORE. This beach park stretches 40 mi from Chatham to Provincetown, offering beaches, dunes, hiking paths, bike trails, and beachcombing. The headquarters are in Wellfleet (Wellfleet, MA 02667, tel. 508/349–3785). Two visitor centers—the Salt Pond Visitor Center (tel. 508/255–3421), off Route 6 just outside Eastham, and the Province Lands Area Visitor's Center (tel. 508/487–1256), on Race Point Road, off Route 6 in Provincetown—provide information and some of the best guided walks and family nature programs on the Cape. See *also* Chapter 5.

NORTH FALMOUTH. See Chapter 6, Swimming.

WEST BARNSTABLE. See Chapter 6, Swimming.

HYANNIS. Wide **Kalmus Beach** (Ocean Street), nearly a mile long, has fine sand, warm water, no undertow, a very gradual drop-off, and a sheltered area good for little kids; you'll find a snack bar, showers, life-guards, and rest rooms. Along Lewis Bay, smaller **Veteran's Park Beach** (Ocean Street) is also good for little kids, with similar water and wave conditions and a tree-shaded picnic table. It has rest rooms, life-guards, and a snack bar. Active young teens may prefer **Craigville Beach.**

WEST DENNIS. See Chapter 6, Swimming.

HARWICH. On the Sound, **Red River Beach** has amenities and a pleasant expanse of sand.

BREWSTER. Eight miles of bay beach here are washed with calm, warm water, and tidal flats stretch as far as a mile into the bay. At **Paine's Creek Beach** a gentle stream winds through a salt-marsh meadow to a small beach surrounded by coves and inlets (no rest rooms), but keep an eye out for the incoming tide. **Breakwater Beach** has the largest parking area, better swimming, and rest rooms. For freshwater swimming, as well as boating and windsurfing, try **Flax Pond** in Nickerson State Park (see Chapter 6, Swimming).

CHATHAM. A curving strip of barrier beach that protects Chatham's harbor, **South Beach** can be reached only by a five-minute water taxi shuttle (Outermost Harbor Marine, Morris Island Rd., tel. 508/945–3030). On the ocean side of the sandbar, surf crashes in; currents on the bay side create shallow pools for wading. There are no rest rooms. You can walk from town to spectacular **Chatham Light Beach**, newly formed by storms. **Ridgevale Beach** (Ridgevale Rd. off Rte. 28) along Nantucket Sound shelters an inlet whose protected waters are always calm and warm; an open ocean side is for kids who love waves. There are rest rooms, lifeguards, and a snack bar.

ORLEANS. With its large tidal flats and warm water, **Skaket Beach** is one of best beaches for kids on the Lower Cape. The snack bar sells butterfly and minnow-catching nets. Ten-mile-long **Nauset Beach** has the most exciting surf.

EASTHAM. On the spot where the *Mayflower* Pilgrims first met the local Indians, **First Encounter Beach** is a lovely quiet beach on the bay, bordered by a vast marsh meadow. There are rest rooms. The National Seashore's beaches begin in Eastham, with **Coast Guard Beach** and **Nauset Light Beach**. Their imposing cliffs, long rolling waves, and roaring surf draw avid bodysurfers and board surfers; though riptides and cold waters make them unsuitable for smaller kids to swim, the beach is wide and the sand inviting, and they're conveniently close to the Salt Pond Visitor Center. There are lifeguards, showers, and a food concession.

WELLFLEET. A small sand beach on fresh-water **Long Pond** (take Long Pond Rd. off E. Main St.) is a lovely place for younger kids to swim; it has a shaded grassy area with picnic tables, a float to swim to, and good fishing. You need a town sticker to park at any of Wellfleet's beaches, and to get one you have to prove you are staying in Wellfleet.

TRURO. On the bay, **Corn Hill Beach** is where the Pilgrims first found corn. It's a good place for shelling. Off-road vehicles take over after 5 PM.

PROVINCETOWN. Two National Seashore beaches here are great for families: **Herring Cove** and **Race Point Beach**, both near easy hiking trails and equipped with showers, lifeguards, and rest rooms. Parking lots fill early. Herring Cove has slightly warmer bayside water, gentler waves, a snack bar, and a parking lot closer to the beach; it draws both a gay crowd and families. We prefer Race Point Beach because it's near massive sand dunes and feels more remote.

Sports

Recreation departments and public libraries in towns all over the Cape offer a profusion of day camps and town activity programs for kids, including tennis, swimming, and sailing lessons. If you're going to be here at least a week, they're well worth checking out, especially if your kids want to get together with other kids. Also try the nature programs offered by the Cape Cod National Seashore and Wellfleet Bay Wildlife Sanctuary.

Big-Time for Spectators

BASEBALL. Cape Cod Baseball League. Teams play regularly in 10 towns, including Hyannis, Chatham, Brewster, Harwich, and Orleans, at hours early enough for even little kids to enjoy the games. (For information, tel. 508/996–5004.) *See also* Chapter 8.

SOCCER. The **Cape Cod Crusaders**, a professional soccer team, play exciting games at the Barnstable High School Field, mostly on Friday and Saturday nights. Call 508/790–4782 for a schedule. Ticket prices are modest: $6 adults, $4 kids under 12, $19.95 family package.

Indoor and Outdoor Action

AMUSEMENTS. Much of the arcade and miniature golf action is clustered along

Route 28 between Yarmouth and Harwich Port.

Cape Cod Storyland Golf. This 2-acre, 18-hole miniature-golf course is set up as a mini–Cape Cod; each hole is a town on the Cape, with reproductions of historic buildings, ponds, waterfalls, and a mill.
🏠 *70 Center St., by railroad depot, Hyannis, tel. 508/778–4339. Cost: $6 adults, $5 kids under 12. Open mid-Apr.–Oct., daily 8 AM– midnight.*

Charles Moore Arena. Roller-skating and rollerblading go on here Tuesday through Friday during the day. Friday night is Rock Night, just for kids 9–14 (no parents) from 8 to 10. And there's ice-skating, too!
🏠 *O'Connor Way, Orleans, tel. 508/255– 2971. Cost: $4, $3 kids under 13, $2 skate rentals; Rock Night $5. Open year-round; call for hrs.*

Pirate's Cove. The most elaborate of the Cape's dozen miniature golf emporiums, this place with two courses has a great pirate ship in a fake pond surrounded by cliffs and waterfalls.
🏠 *728 Main St. (Rte. 28), South Yarmouth, tel. 508/394–6200. Cost: $6 adults, $5 kids under 13. Open Apr.–May and Sept.–Oct., call for hrs; June, daily 10–9:30; July–Aug., daily 9 AM–11 PM.*

Ryan Family Amusement Centers. Everything from candlepin bowling (using a lighter ball) to pinball to video games is offered at three locations on the Cape.
🏠 *Cape Cod Mall (game room only), Rte. 132, Hyannis, tel. 508/775–5566; 1067 Rte. 28, South Yarmouth (the biggest), tel. 508/ 394–5644; 200 Main St., Buzzards Bay, tel. 508/759–9892. Open daily 9:30 AM–10 PM; Cape Cod Mall stays open later.*

Water Wizz Water Park. It's the best water park in New England, with incredible slides and pools for all ages. Little ones love sitting under the mushroom sculptures that "rain" water like sprinklers, while older kids enjoy sliding down the three tubes, including the longest (six-story) tube slide in New England.

Rtes. 6 and 28, Wareham (near Buzzard's Bay), tel. 508/295–3255. Cost: $20 adults, $11 kids under 48". Open late June–Labor Day, daily 10–6:30; Memorial Day–late June, weekends 10–4.

BIKING. What a great place Cape Cod is for family biking! The paths on the Lower Cape are mostly flat, some ideal even for kids with training wheels, and lead to beaches, picnic spots, and wonderful views. The 20-mi Cape Cod Rail Trail, the longest, runs from South Dennis to Eastham. See also Chapter 6.

BIRD-WATCHING. The **Wellfleet Bay Wildlife Sanctuary** (see Scoping Out Cape Cod, above) has extensive kids' birding activities. For books and bird paraphernalia, check out the **Bird Watcher's General Store** (see Shopping, below).

BOATING. The Cape's calm ocean bays and kettle ponds are prime locations for all types of boating, and instruction for kids is readily available, both on a onetime-lesson basis and as part of a series. **Nickerson State Park** off Route 6A in Brewster (tel. 508/896–3491), a large, forested park that almost seems more like the Berkshires than Cape Cod, is dotted with kettle ponds for swimming, fishing, and boating, including windsurfing. Chatham, Wellfleet, and Eastham also offer good windsurfing; sailing is best in South Orleans (see also Chapter 6). One of the most captivating trips for kids is the **Nauset Marsh Family Cruise** in a small, glass-bottom boat; run by the Cape Cod Museum of Natural History, they provide many hands-on activities (tel. 800/479–3867). Also wonderful are **OceanQuest's** 90-minute marine research trips aboard a converted 60-ft fishing vessel (tel. 800/376–2326 or 508/457–0508), which leaves from Woods Hole. For canoeing and kayaking, **Cape Cod Coastal Canoe & Kayak** (tel. 888/226–6393 or 508/564–4051) rents boats and runs naturalist-led trips all over the Cape sponsored by the Cape Cod Museum of Natural History. One of the nicest places to explore is the Waquoit Bay

National Estuarine Research Reserve (off Rte. 28, East Falmouth, tel. 508/457–0495), which has marshland, open water, and a wilderness island.

FISHING. The Friday Cape Cod Times "Fishing Around" column tells the latest on what's being caught and where. Many kids find clam digging and catching blue crabs most absorbing, but it's also fun to cast a line off busy MacMillan Wharf in Provincetown. The bridge on Mill Pond in Chatham is another spot for kids to drop in a line. For clam digging, we head for Wellfleet. See also Chapter 6.

HIKES AND WALKS. We think the best hikes in the Lower Cape are in the **Cape Cod National Seashore**, **Wellfleet Bay Wildlife Sanctuary**, and at the **Cape Cod Museum of Natural History** (see Scoping Out Cape Cod, above). Another of our favorites is the half-mile **Parmet Cranberry Bog Trail** off North Parmet Road in Truro, where a wooden boardwalk and trail lead past a pond, the cranberry vines grow down to the sea, and birdsong fills the air. **Nickerson State Park** in Brewster (Rte. 6A, tel. 508/896–3491) has regular nature walks geared for kids.

PLAYGROUNDS AND SKATEBOARD PARKS. The Lower Cape has three splendid playgrounds—in Harwich, Chatham, and Orleans, each adjacent to the local elementary school. Nauset Regional Middle School on Eldredge Parkway in Orleans has its own skateboard park.

WHALE-WATCHING. Taking kids on a whale watch is easier on Cape Cod than anywhere else in the Northeast because you don't have to go far to get to prime whale-watching waters. See also Chapter 6.

Shopping

HYANNIS. Main Street is lined with touristy T-shirt shops, ice cream and candy stores, cheerful eating places, souvenir shops, and miniature golf, the kind of atmosphere favored by teens. The air-conditioned **Cape Cod Mall** (between Rtes. 132 and 28, Hyannis, tel. 508/771–0200) is the Cape's largest, with 90 shops, a food court, and stroller rentals.

ORLEANS. The **Baseball Shop** (26 Main St., tel. 508/240–1063) sells everything related to baseball (and other sports), including baseball cards, hats, and clothing. **Compass Rose Book Shop** (45 Main St., tel. 508/255–1545) has an excellent selection of kids' titles plus toys and games. The **Bird Watcher's General Store** (36 Rte. 6A, tel. 508/255–6974 or 800/562–1512) is full of interesting bird-related stuff. **Nauset Sports** in Orleans (Rte. 6A at the rotary, tel. 508/255–4742) is huge, the source for beach games, kids' wet suits, and boogieboard rentals.

CHATHAM. A great place for kids, the **Chatham Nature Shoppe** (637 Main St., tel. 508/945–7700) sells meteorites, fossils, and gemstone jewelry.

WELLFLEET. Throughout July and August, the **Wellfleet Drive-In Theater** (Rte. 6, Eastham–Wellfleet line, tel. 508/349–2520) becomes a giant flea market on Mondays, Wednesdays, Thursdays, weekends, and holidays during the summer (open 8–4; $1 per car weekdays, $2 weekends), weekends only after Labor Day ($1 per car). A snack bar and playground and a carnival atmosphere make it a worthy destination for a family with kids of widely varying ages.

PROVINCETOWN. Commercial Street, the main drag, has shops of nostalgic memorabilia and oddball items jammed alongside restaurants and cafés; it's great for people-watching. Stop by the **Provincetown Fudge Factory** (210 Commercial St., tel. 508/487–2850), which sells what we believe are the best peanut-butter cups in the world, among other sweet treats. The barnlike **Marine Specialties** (235 Commercial St., tel. 508/487–1730) is loaded with odd inexpensive items kids like to collect. Head down to the honky-tonk wharf off Commercial Street for T-shirt and souvenir outlets.

Eats

Chowder, clams, lobster (try lobster rolls), scallops, and fish of all kinds are the Cape's specialties, though most seafood restaurants offer alternatives; ideal for families with young kids are the many informal clam shacks where you can sit outside at picnic tables. Several restaurants have early bird specials—low-priced dinners in early evening, usually before 6 PM. A local chain that can be counted on for good home cooking, friendly service, and informality is **Hearth & Kettle**, which serves breakfast, lunch, and dinner.

Category	Cost*
$$$	over $25
$$	$15–$25
$	under $15

*per person for a three-course meal, excluding drinks, service, and sales tax

Low-Price Lobsters and Picnic Fare

⚭ ALL **Baxter's Fish N' Chips.** Sitting at picnic tables on an outdoor deck, you can watch the boats on busy Lewis Bay as you eat delicious fresh fish and maybe the best fried clams on the Cape. Occasionally a seaplane lands nearby, to the delight of kids. The menu includes burgers as well.
🏠 117 Pleasant St. Wharf, Hyannis, tel. 508/775–4490. High chairs, booster seats. Reservations not accepted. AE, MC, V. Closed mid-Oct.–Apr. $–$$

⚭ ALL **Bayside Lobster Hutt.** At this noisy, friendly place on a country road leading to the harbor, everyone sits at long picnic tables. The fish is fresh and good; cheeseburgers and hot dogs are also available.
🏠 Commercial St., Wellfleet, tel. 508/349–6333. AE, D, MC, V. $

ŤŤ ALL Lobster Claw. A step up from lobster-in-the-rough places, this popular rustic spot with a menu shaped like a lobster claw is generally considered the best family restaurant on Cape Cod. Fish dinners, lobster, mussels, steamers, and superb fried clams are the best bets. Come early (before 5:30) to beat the crowds—and save money with the early bird menu. More than 250 lobster items are available in the gift shop.

ŤŤ Rte. 6A, Orleans, tel. 508/255–1800. Kids' menu, high chairs, booster seats. AE, D, MC, V. $

Sweet Stuff

ŤŤ ALL Four Seas. Eating homemade ice cream (35 flavors) in this old-fashioned parlor has been a Cape tradition since 1934.

ŤŤ 360 S. Main St., Centerville, tel. 508/775–1394. Booster seats. No credit cards. $

ŤŤ ALL Sundae School Ice Cream Parlor. The working nickelodeon and other memorabilia in this 19th-century barn capture kids' interest while they wait for their cones. Dollops of real whipped cream and homemade ice cream plus toppings are served from an antique marble soda fountain. The East Orleans and Harwichport locations have the same ice cream but less interesting interiors.

ŤŤ Lower County Rd., Dennisport, tel. 508/394–9122; 210 Main St., East Orleans, tel. 508/255–5473; 606 Main St., Harwichport, tel. 508/430–2444. $

Picnics

The Lower Cape has hundreds of picnic places with views, tables, beaches, and rest rooms, all easily accessible by car; good picnic spots are listed under each town in Kids on the Cape (see How to Find Out What's Going On, above). **Pilgrim Lake**, off Monument Road in Orleans, has plenty of parking, warm swimming waters, and picnic tables.

Doane Rock Picnic Area in Eastham, off the Cape Cod Rail Trail bike path, is marked by a huge glacial boulder. Gavin loved the view of both bay and ocean from the **Pilgrim Heights** picnic area off Route 6 in North Truro. Off the beaten path, crowd-free **North Beach**, a barrier beach off Chatham reached by water taxi from Chatham Harbor (tel. 508/945–9378), is one of our favorites. For dinner picnics we head to one of the Cape Cod Baseball League's games (see Sports, above).

Where to Stay

The Cape Cod Chamber of Commerce's Resort Directory lists hundreds of accommodations, plus real-estate agencies. For summer stays the most popular cottages must be booked far, far in advance; most accommodations insist on weeklong minimums. The Chamber's information booths can help with last-minute accommodations. After Labor Day, rates drop markedly.

If you want to rent a private house, cottage, or condominium, **Great Vacations, Inc.** (Box 1748, Brewster 02631, tel. 508/896–2090) is the place to contact. It's an agency run by a group of mothers who truly understand the needs of vacationing families. They manage nearly 300 properties in Brewster, Dennis, and Orleans, from a five-bedroom mini-estate with swimming pool to simpler spots well under $1,000 a week. They provide a 40-page Help Book with local restaurant recommendations as well as many services, including housekeeping and advice on where to buy a birthday cake.

For more expensive, full-service resorts on Cape Cod that offer meals and children's activities, see also Chapter 9, the Chatham Bars Inn, the Lighthouse Inn, and the New Seabury.

Category	Cost*
$$$$	over $160
$$$	$110–$160
$$	$70–$110
$	under $70

*All prices are for a standard double room in high-season, excluding 9.7% tax.

Capt. Gosnold Village. The gray-shingle one- to three-bedroom cottages and motel units stand in a shady complex with a large pool at its center. Some furnishings have a clean, modern look; we like best the simple and pleasant cottages (these contain more than one unit) decorated in Colonial-country style that have private entrances and decks or patios (complete with grills). The quiet residential neighborhood is safe for biking and only a short walk from three beaches. The fenced-in pool has a lifeguard. 🏨 *230 Gosnold St., Hyannis 02601, tel. 508/775–9111. 28 units. Facilities: pool, basketball, baby-sitting, playground. MC, V. Closed Nov.–Apr. $$–$$$$*

Even'Tide Motel. Regularly voted the best motel on the Outer Cape, this friendly compound of cottages and a motel is set back from the road on 11 acres that border the Cape Cod National Seashore (a 1-mi path through the woods leads to Marconi Beach) and the Cape Cod Rail Trail. At the center is a 60-ft heated indoor pool that's great for rainy days. You'll find plenty of other families here. 🏨 *Rte. 6, Box 41, South Wellfleet 02663, tel. 508/349–3410. 30 motel rooms, some with kitchenette, 9 1-, 2-, and 3-bedroom cottages. Facilities: grills, picnic area, playground, indoor pool. AE, D, DC, MC, V. $$–$$$*

Hostelling International Mid-Cape. Two cozy but very basic family cabins are part of this 60-bed hostel surrounded by woods where you can barbecue. It's just a step up from camping, at the rock-bottom price of $45 per cabin. The location is superb: easy biking distance from the Cape Cod Rail Trail,

1½ mi from a bay beach, 4 mi from the Salt Pond Visitor Center, and only 3 mi from the National Seashore's Nauset Beach. Yet although families can return to their cabin at any time during the day, the standard lockout rule (closed 10–5) applies to the main building where the bathrooms and kitchen are located. 🏨 *75 Goody Hallet Dr., Eastham 02642, tel. 508/255–2785, fax 508/255–9752. 60 beds, 2 family cabins. Facilities: kitchen privileges, basketball, Ping-Pong, volleyball. Reservations essential July–Aug. MC, V. $*

Kalmar Village. On a quiet strip of bayfront south of Provincetown, close to dunes and grassy hills and wide open spaces, this family-owned cottage resort is a great place for swimming in the bay and communing with nature. The housekeeping cottages, grouped around green lawns with picnic tables, grills, and a large pool, are authentically Cape Cod—cheerful, white-and-bright, with lots of windows and blond wood. The newer two-bedroom cottages, closest to the water, are the nicest. 🏨 *Shore Rd. (Rte. 6A), Box 745, North Truro 02652, tel. 508/487–0585, fax 508/487–5827. Winter mailing address: 246 Newbury St., Boston 02116, tel. 617/247–0211. 50 cottages, 6 efficiencies, 4 motel rooms. Facilities: pool, beach, laundry, baby-sitting. AE, D, MC, V. Closed late Oct.–mid-May. $$*

Surf Side Cottages. For families who want to enjoy the Cape's simple pleasures of biking and relaxing at the beach, these cottages within the National Seashore and just 250 paces down to the beach are ideal. Some of the charming beach cottages have gray shingles, some have slanted roofs and pastel siding, and others have flat roof decks. Each has a kitchen with dishwasher, fireplace, screen porch, and its own yard with picnic table and barbecue. Inside, they're rustic, decorated with knotty pine and rattan furniture. 🏨 *Box 937, Oceanview Dr. and Wilson Ave., South Wellfleet 02663, tel. 508/349–3959. 18 1-, 2-, and 3-bedroom cottages. MC, V. $$–$$$*

CAMPING. There are many private family campgrounds on the Lower Cape; the Chamber of Commerce has a brochure listing them.

Nickerson State Park Campground. Just outside your tent flap (or RV door) are all the recreational opportunities of this beautiful 2,000-acre park. Breakwater Beach in Brewster and Skaket Beach in Orleans are not far. *See also* Chapter 5.

🏠 *Rte. 6A, Brewster 02631, tel. 508/896–3491. 418 sites; no hookups. Advance reservation, tel. 413/443–0011. 168 first-come, first-served sites. Facilities: showers, water, flush toilets, dumping station. No credit cards. Closed late Oct.–early Apr. Cost: $6 per night.*

Entertainment and the Arts

For nighttime activities, don't ignore the many outdoor options—beach walks, campfires with sing-alongs, and concerts under velvety black skies. Check out the programs offered by the **Wellfleet Bay Wildlife Sanctuary** and the **Cape Cod National Seashore** (*see* Scoping Out Cape Cod, *above*).

(👫 **4–10**) **Cape Playhouse.** This renowned historic theater presents children's concerts, plays, and puppet shows by the best touring performers on Friday mornings in July and August. If you can, see a production by David Syrotiak's National Marionette Theatre; they are filled with incredible special effects. Reserve early.

🏠 *Rte. 6A, East Dennis 02638, tel. 508/385–3911. Cost: $6 all ages for kids' performances, $15–$28 for adult performances. Closed Labor Day–mid-June. MC, V.*

(👫 **ALL**) **Chatham Band Concerts.** These traditional, free Friday-evening band

concerts feel like a lively town party. Families carrying sweatshirts (it gets cold), blankets, folding chairs, and picnic baskets spread out their dinner beforehand. Then the 40-piece band, resplendent in blue-and-red uniforms, plays while folks keep time on the roped-off dance floor. Younger kids energetically join the sing-alongs and special children's dances; when they get too sleepy, their parents carry them off to the car. Come early to get a parking space. (Band concerts are also held in Sandwich, Falmouth, Hyannis, Yarmouth, and Harwich.)

🏠 *Kate Gould Park, Main St., tel. 508/945–0342.*

(👫 **4+**) **Harwich Junior Theatre.** Founded in 1952 by the then drama director of the Wheelock Family Theatre in Boston, this theater gives drama classes for children year-round and presents four summer productions.

🏠 *Division St., Harwich Box 168, West Harwich 02671, tel. 508/432–2002.*

(👫 **3–10**) **Pirate Adventures.** The *Sea Gypsy* sails off on an adventure five times daily in the summer; pirate hats, painted faces, a secret map, and a water cannon are all part of it. Kids even get to help haul up an underwater treasure.

🏠 *Frequent trips daily from Ocean Street Dock, Hyannis, tel. 508/775–5565, and from Town Cove in Orleans, tel. 508/255–4250; or call 888/729–2500.*

(👫 **ALL**) **Wellfleet Drive-In Theater.** A Cape landmark since 1957, this is the last drive-in left here. There's also a miniature golf course, a playground, a dairy bar, and a place to buy burgers and other good stuff to eat.

🏠 *Rte. 6, tel. 508/255–4250. Cost: $6 adults, $3.50 kids 5–11. Open June–mid-Oct.*

NANTUCKET, MASSACHUSETTS
BIKE PATHS AND COBBLESTONE STREETS

14

It's the postcard-perfect summer vacation spot: an island removed from time, guarding its historic cobblestone streets, quaint gray-shingle cottages, proud whaling captains' houses, and miles of clean white-sand beaches, to serve them up annually to visiting summer families. This 12- by 3-mi island 30 mi from Cape Cod is self-contained and cozy—big enough to offer activities for every age group but small enough that everything is easy to get to. Older kids can be independent, biking off in the morning to the beach, going to the movies by themselves, learning to sail and windsurf—and you don't have to drive them. The water is warm, the broad flat beaches invite sand castles and bare feet, and the land is delightfully breezy and wide open.

There's also lots of history here. This little island was the foremost whaling port in the world in the mid-19th century, and the town of Nantucket preserves the atmosphere of that past almost too faithfully. Little kids may enjoy reading the Obediah books by Brinton Turkle (published by Puffin/Penguin), about a boy who lived on Nantucket at that time; older kids may have read or seen the movie *Moby Dick*, the story of a whaling captain who lived on Nantucket.

Summer crowds can be a problem, as honking traffic clogs the town's streets and people flood the beaches. Everything is expensive, in keeping with the upscale group who summer here regularly and the fact that everyone and everything must be ferried from the mainland. Still, it's a marvelous island.

The Basics

How to Find Out What's Going On

The **Chamber of Commerce** (Pacific Club Bldg., 48 Main St., tel. 508/228–1700; open Memorial Day–Labor Day, weekdays 9–5, Sat. 11–5; weekdays only rest of yr), publishes *The Official Guide to Nantucket* and pamphlets on seasonal events. The **Nantucket Visitor Services and Information Bureau** (25 Federal St., tel. 508/228–0925; open July–Labor Day, daily 9–5; Labor Day–July, Mon.–Sat. 9–4) will provide a free *Nantucket Vacation Guide* and help you find a room for the night if you have not reserved, but will not make advance reservations for you. The most useful **Web site** is www.nantucket.net. Other invaluable resources: The **Nantucket Concierge** (Box 1257, tel. 508/228–8400) handles everything from lodging and dining reservations to fishing-trip information to baby-sitting arrangements. **Nantucket Rent All** (135 Old South Rd., tel. 508/228–1525) rents everything from playpens to beach umbrellas.

Guide to Nantucket by Polly Burroughs (Globe Pequot, 1991) has good historic information on the island and the island's buildings. *What's So Special About Nantucket* by Mary Miles introduces kids 4–8 to all Nantucket's sights through a story about a little boy who visits. *Kids Play on Nantucket,* a book published annually by the *Nantucket Journal* (Box 779, Nantucket 02554, tel. 508/228–8700), can be purchased on the island. It is filled with excellent information.

Arriving, Departing, and Getting Around

BY BIKE. Everyone on the island seems to bike—we've seen whole families strung out along paths, their descending bike sizes making them resemble a family of ducks. Good paved paths lead to most beaches, and rentals are readily available. An energetic family could bike around the entire island in one day. Helmets must be worn by kids under 12.

BY BUS. Plymouth & Brockton Company (tel. 508/746–0378) runs buses from Boston to Hyannis, with stops en route. In Hyannis you can catch a ferry to Nantucket (*see below*). On Nantucket, the NRTA Shuttle (fares 50¢–$1; 3-day, 7-day, and 1-month passes available; June–Sept.) makes five loops; these go to 'Sconset and major beaches in town from June through September. Check at the **NRTA** office (22 Federal St., upstairs, tel. 508/228–7025 or 508/325–9571). Passes and route information are available at **Nantucket Visitor Services and Information Bureau** (25 Federal St., tel. 508/228–0925).

BY CAR. Not only are ferry reservations hard to get for a car, but Nantucket's main streets are clogged with traffic in summer and there are no in-town parking lots. For short visits of a weekend or several days, it's best not to bring a car; for longer vacations when you're staying farther out, you may want one, but it's easier to rent a car on the island than bring your own (just make sure you reserve a car in advance). Besides, there

are some beaches you can get to only in a four-wheel-drive vehicle (you must have a permit to drive off-road; check with the Chamber of Commerce for current regulations). Both cars and Jeeps can be rented at the airport from **Budget** (tel. 508/228–5666 or 888/228–5666), **Hertz** (tel. 508/228–9421 or 800/654–3131), **Thrifty** (tel. 508/325–4616 or 800/367–2277), **Nantucket Windmill** (tel. 508/228–1227 or 800/228–1227), and **Nantucket Jeep Rental** (tel. 508/228–1618). **Don Allen** (508/228–0134) specializes in Ford cars, including Explorers. Preston's Rent-A-Car (tel. 508/228–0047) delivers cars to wherever you're staying. **Young's 4 X 4 & Car Rental** (Steamship Wharf, tel. 508/228–1151) is right in town.

BY FERRY. You MUST have reservations far, far in advance if you want to bring your car over in summer; we know people who have shaped their entire vacation around the dates of their ferry reservations. The highway distance to Hyannis from New York City is 271 mi (6 hrs or more), from Boston 80 mi (2 hrs or more); be sure to account for summer traffic jams on the Cape (we know people who have missed their precious car reservation because of them). It's much easier if you only bring people and bicycles on the boat.

The **Steamship Authority**'s car-and-passenger ferries leave South Street dock in Hyannis year-round. The trip takes 2¼ hours.
🐴 *For reservations, call 508/477–8600. Cost: Round-trip fare mid-May–mid-Oct. $22 adults, $11 kids 5–12; cars $220. Lower rates mid-Oct.–Dec.*

Hy-Line ferries carry only passengers (and bikes) and operate from May through October, leaving from Ocean Street dock in Hyannis; their trip is shorter, 1¾ or two hours. The high-speed catamaran ferry (tel. 508/778–0404) takes a mere hour.
🐴 *For information and reservations, call in Hyannis, 508/778–2600 or 800/492–8082, 508/778–2602 for parking; in Nantucket, 508/228–3949. Cost: One-way fare $11 adults, $5.50 kids 3–12; $21 for first-class*

ticket; high-speed catamaran $29 adults, $23 kids 1–12.

BY PLANE. A number of airlines fly year-round into **Nantucket Memorial Airport** (tel. 508/325–5300) from Boston, Hyannis, Martha's Vineyard, New Bedford, New York (La Guardia and Newark), and Providence. Business Express/Delta Connection (tel. 800/345–3400) flies from Boston (year-round) and New York (in summer); Cape Air (tel. 800/352–0714) flies from Boston, Providence, and New Bedford; Continental Connection (tel. 800/523–3273) flies year-round from New York (La Guardia and Newark) and Martha's Vineyard. US Airways Express (tel. 800/428–4322) flies from Boston and New York (La Guardia). The airport is about 3½ mi from town.

BY TAXI. You can usually find a taxi waiting at the airport or at the foot of Main Street by the ferry, or call one of the many taxi companies, such as **All Point Taxi** (tel. 508/325–6550) and **Betty's Tour & Taxi Service** (tel. 508/228–5786). Fares are flat fee, based on one person: $3–$15, plus $1 for each additional passenger.

Family-Friendly Tours

Most taxi companies also provide private guided tours.

(**⚥ 8+**) **Gail's Tours.** Gail Johnson, a seventh-generation native, is knowledgeable, lively, enthusiastic, and flexible enough to stop for photos and a picnic, and she likes kids. Regular 1½-hour van tours are scheduled; Gail even picks you up at your hotel or cottage. This is a great way for kids to get a sense of the whole island.
🏨 *Tel. 508/257–6557. Cost: $12 per person. Open year-round. Departures in summer, daily 10, 1, and 3. Winter tours by appointment. Call ahead for reservations.*

Pit Stops

You'll find public bathrooms at the end of Main Street on Straight Wharf, on the

waterfront at Children's Beach, and at the Nantucket Visitor Service and Information Bureau. Almost all beaches have rest rooms.

Emergencies

The **Nantucket Cottage Hospital** (57 Prospect St., tel. 508/228–1200) has a 24-hour emergency room. **Congdon's** pharmacy (47 Main St., tel. 508/228–0020) is open until 10 PM mid-June–September; **Nantucket Pharmacy** (45 Main St., tel. 508/228–0180) stays open until 10 PM Memorial Day–Labor Day; and **Island Pharmacy** (Finast Plaza, 31 Sparks Ave., tel. 508/228–6400) is open until 8:30 PM year-round.

Baby-Sitters

Most resorts and hotels maintain lists of baby-sitters. **Nantucket Babysitters' Service** (tel. 508/228–4970) provides well-screened student baby-sitters for either summer-long jobs or evenings.

When to Go

Summer is the prime season here, with July and August the most crowded; more kids seem to be here in July than in August. The sun's heat is tempered by ocean breezes, making the island more pleasant than mainland beaches in summer. Nantucket's waters are warm enough for swimming as early as mid-June and sometimes as late as October, though the waves get rough after Labor Day. Biking, hiking, and hanging out in town are all pleasant long after the tourist crush has left after Labor Day; museums and restaurants usually stay open until Columbus Day. The spring is iffy, often wet and dreary. The following events are among the most fun for families.

(**⚥ ALL**) **Fourth of July.** It's fun to join the crowds at Jetties Beach for games, then a band concert, then fireworks at dusk. For information, call 508/228–7213.

(**⚥ 3+**) **Sandcastle Sculpture Day.** In August, the most unusual and fun-filled family event on the island includes competitions for kids and adults. For information, check with the Chamber of Commerce, tel. 508/228–1700.

Scoping Out Nantucket

Nantucket is basically a one-town island, with all the shops and most restaurants clustered in a few blocks by the waterfront at the entrance to Nantucket Harbor. The twisting lanes and brick alleyways of Nantucket town are best explored on foot; sneakers are best for little kids because of the bumpy cobblestones and high curbs. Fourteen historic buildings are open to the public; you can buy a visitor pass that admits you to all, at a cost much lower than paying separate admissions. A walking-tour guidebook is available from the Nantucket Historical Association (tel. 508/228–1894), which offers wonderful regular Living History for Children programs such as the one at the Old Mill (*see below*). Besides their two properties listed below, kids also like the spooky Old Gaol on Vestal Street (free) and a peek in the Oldest House (16 Sunset Hill), which was built in 1686. Kids also pick up plenty of history just from strolling around and absorbing the 17th- and 18th-century atmosphere.

Roads and bike paths lead from this hub off across the island's moors to small villages near beaches to the west, east, and south. The biggest of these is Siasconset, called 'Sconset, 7 mi from town—mostly a summer community with a post office, a few stores, restaurants, and cottages. The village of Madaket has little more than a restaurant and good sunsets.

A Museum, Mill, and More

(👫 8–12) **First Congregational Church & Old North Church Vestry.** When you climb the 92 steps to the tower of Nantucket's largest church, you have the best view of the island—ponds, beaches, winding streets, and rooftops.

🏠 *62 Centre St., tel. 508/228–0950. Cost: $2 adults, 50¢ kids under 15. Open Mon.–Sat. 10–4.*

(👫 3–14) **Maria Mitchell Science Center.** Nantucket-born Maria Mitchell became the first person to discover a comet with a telescope, in 1847. She went on to become the first woman astronomy professor in the United States, at Vassar College. The cluster of buildings named for her includes two **observatories** (open for public viewing Mon., Wed., and Fri. nights in summer); a **library** (2 Vestal St., tel. 508/228–9219; it has books for both adults and kids); the **house** in which she lived (1 Vestal St., tel. 508/228–2896; it has the only public roofwalk on the island); and a tiny **aquarium** on the wharf (28 Washington St., tel. 508/228–5387), which offers marine ecology workshops and field trips. **Hinchman House** (7 Milk St., tel. 508/228–0898), a natural-history museum with a collection of live reptiles and a huge insect display, offers regular bird-watching field trips and nature walks. The association also offers science, history, and art classes throughout the summer for kids 4–12.

🏠 *Maria Mitchell Association, 2 Vestal St., tel. 508/228–9198. Cost: Combined admission pass $7 adults, $4 kids 6–14; annual family membership $35. Museums open mid-June–Aug., Tues.–Sat. 10–4. Limited fall hrs.*

(👫 ALL) **Nantucket Atheneum.** One of the oldest libraries in the United States, the Greek Revival–style Atheneum has been recently restored and expanded. The new, light-filled Weezie Wing for Children hosts regular story hours and activities; the adjoining park has a lovely play space.

🏠 *Corner of Federal and India Sts., tel. 508/228–1110. Open Mon.–Sat. 9:30–5 (Tues. to 8 PM); shorter hrs in winter.*

(👫 5–12) **Old Mill.** This red-and-gray shingled mill is one of the last working wind-powered mills in the country, still grinding corn to cornmeal when the wind is blowing. In the summer the Nantucket Historical Association sponsors a weekly program in which kids can help grind the cornmeal, then take it to the oldest house on the island to bake it into corn bread.

🏠 *Prospect, W. York and S. Mill Sts., tel. 508/228–1894. Cost: $2 adults, $1 kids 5–14; visitor pass to 14 historic buildings $10 adults, $5 kids 5–14. Program: $20. Open May–mid-June and Sept.–Oct., daily 11–3; mid-June–Sept., daily 10–5.*

👫 5+) **Sanford Farm/Ram Pasture and the Woods.** Much of Nantucket is flat heath that blooms with wildflowers in summer; on these 900 acres at the island's west end a meandering trail passes Hummock Pond, a long silvery finger of water where you can spot turtles and, at dusk, deer.

🏠 *Off Madaket Rd. near intersection of Cliff Rd.*

👫 ALL) **Straight Wharf.** At the foot of Main Street, along a wharf where some ferries from Hyannis and Martha's Vineyard pull in, gift shops and restaurants are crammed side by side and teens hang out—shopping, eating ice cream, sitting on the benches, and talking.

👫 6–15) **Whaling Museum.** It's set in a historic factory built for refining spermaceti (a wax made from whale oil) and making candles; the enthusiastic guides (call for tour times) give vivid descriptions of whaling days. The rustic old building holds a whale skeleton, harpoons, and a rigged whaleboat, giving kids a real feel for Nantucket's whaling past.

🏠 *Broad St., head of Steamboat Wharf, tel. 508/228–1736. Cost: $5 adults, $3 kids 5–14; visitor pass to 14 historic buildings (permits 1 visit to each) $10 adults, $5 kids 5–14. Open summer, daily 10–5; spring and fall, daily 11–3.*

Beaches

Nantucket's long, wide beaches circle the island like a big golden wreath, one overlapping the other; kids can bike or take a shuttle bus to almost all of them, and all are open to any visitor—no parking permits are required. Beaches on the north shore facing

Nantucket Sound have the calmest and warmest water; the best waves for surfing roll into the popular south-shore beaches and those to the east, where the undertow is stronger.

NORTH-SHORE BEACHES. Great for the littlest kids, **Children's Beach** has lovely sand for sand castles and calm, warm water. Close to town—just a short walk down South Beach Street from Steamboat Wharf—it's next to a grassy park with benches and picnic tables, a playground, rest rooms, a bandstand, take-out food, lifeguards, and showers. A T-shirt tie-dying workshop takes place Friday at noon. Dune-sheltered **Dionis Beach** (3 mi west of town via the Madaket bike path and Eel Point Rd.; look for a white rock pointing to the entrance) has calm water and a long sandbar stretching out during low tide, which make it good for swimming, picnicking, and shell collecting; it does, however, have pebbly areas and occasional seaweed. There are lifeguards and rest rooms. **Jetties Beach**, just a mile north of town, is the best all-around family beach, with the most activities for all ages: windsurfing, sailing, tennis, volleyball, swim lessons for little kids, and a playground and skateboard park. There are lifeguards, changing rooms, rest rooms, showers, phones, restaurant and take-out food, a boardwalk to the beach, and water-sports rentals—but on a sunny day it is busy, busy, busy. Scenic **Brant Point** (take Hulbert Ave. from Jetties Beach), by a lighthouse where you can watch boats, is best for picnicking and shell collecting; the current is strong, the drop-off sudden, and there are no lifeguards.

SOUTH-SHORE BEACHES. One of the most popular beaches with teens is **Surfside Beach**, which has the best surf on the island; little kids like exploring the small rolling dunes and playing on the long, wide beach, which is great for kite-flying. A 3-mi bike or bus ride south from town, it gets crowded in summer (to escape, walk east toward 'Sconset). There are lifeguards, rest rooms, showers, phones, and a snack bar. Just west of Surfside is **Miacomet Pond**, a small, warm freshwater pond separated from the ocean by a strip of sand where little kids can wade. At out-of-the-way **Cisco Beach** (4 mi from town via Hummock Pond Rd.), the hot teen surfing beach, you can walk for miles, surf in the big waves, fish, and feel the wind. About the only facilities here are lifeguards. **Madaket Beach** is my idea of a perfect beach—clean white sand, humongous waves, and the best sunsets on the island, all reached by a scenic 6-mi bike path over gentle hills. It has lifeguards, rest rooms, and a gourmet take-out shop on the bike path.

OTHER BEACHES. Seven miles east of town, **'Sconset Beach** makes for a full day's outing, with its grassy dunes and cliffs, the picturesque nearby village, and the Sankaty Lighthouse. It's not always good for swimming—the surf can be heavy and the wind blows in seaweed—but it has lifeguards and a playground.

Coatue–Coskata–Great Point is an empty spit of dune and beach separating Nantucket Harbor from Nantucket Sound; you have to take a boat or four-wheel-drive vehicle (permits at Wauwinet Gate House, tel. 508/228–0006).

Sports

Indoor and Outdoor Action

AMUSEMENTS. Nobadeer MiniGolf. In such a carefully preserved, picturesque environment you eventually end up saying "Thank God for minigolf." This 18-hole miniature golf course has wonderfully landscaped holes including lagoons; a casual Mexican restaurant, Patio J's, is on site.
🏕 *Nobadeer Farm and Sun Island Rds., off Milestone Rd., tel. 508/228–8977. Open late June–Sept., daily 9 AM–11 PM.*

BIKING. For kids, Nantucket is nicer than the Cape for biking, because they can safely bike to all the best beaches themselves. In the busy summer months they should stick to the five paved official bike paths, described below, which are only open to foot and bicycle traffic. It's possible to ride on the island's many dirt roads if you rent a mountain bike, but these are also open to speedy mopeds. A rudimentary bike trail map is in *The Official Guide to Nantucket*, but it's better to get the detailed maps available from rental places.

The 6½-mi-long **Milestone Bike Path** parallels Milestone Road across the center of the island to the village of 'Sconset and 'Sconset Beach. **Surfside Bike Path**, 3 mi of flat terrain ending at Surfside Beach, is the easiest for young kids; along the way, stop at the Shack, a snack bar with hot dogs and picnic baskets. **Cliff Road Bike Path**, 2½ mi of rolling terrain, takes you alongside Cliff Road, past a small pond. The 5½-mi-long **Madaket Bike Path** is the most beautiful—a winding path traversing gentle hills, skirting Long Pond (picnic tables), and ending at spectacular Madaket Beach. The new 7½-mi-long **Polpis Bike Path** parallels Polpis Road from Milestone Road to 'Sconset, where you'll find rest rooms and places to eat. There are about eight bike-rental shops on the island; we like **Young's Bicycle Shop** (Steamboat Wharf, tel. 508/228–1151; daily bike price, $20 adults, $10–$15 kids, helmets included), which has the best maps of the island's bike paths.

BIRD-WATCHING AND NATURE WALKS. The Natural History Museum at **Hinchman House** (see Scoping Out Nantucket, *above*) sponsors bird and nature walks for kids and adults in summer. If you want to feed ducks, head for **Consue Springs**, a small pond surrounded by reeds on Union Street, a 15-minute walk from downtown. The best place to see many different kinds of birds easily is **Eel Point**, on the northern side of Madaket Harbor, where the humps of a long sandbar create little islands on which gulls rest and scores of other birds perch, fly up, chatter, and sing to one another.
🏕 *Follow trail from Eel Point Rd. Cars must be left about ½ mi from beach on dirt road. Maps*

available at the Nantucket Conservation Foundation (118 Cliff Rd., tel. 508/228–2884).

BOATING. The best destination for kayaking and sailing is deserted **Coatue Beach**, a half-hour paddle from town. Kids can windsurf, sail Sunfish, or kayak at **Jetties Beach**, where you can get both rentals and lessons. *See also* Chapter 6, Sailing and Windsurfing.

Nantucket Island Community Sailing (tel. 508/228–6600), like other community sailing programs, offers lessons (including racing techniques) for kids and adults; members ($50 per year) who pay an additional fee can use the boats during open sail times. **Force 5** (Jetties Beach, tel. 508/228–5358; 37 Main St., tel. 508/228–0700) and **Indian Summer Sports** (Steamboat Wharf, tel. 508/228–3632) rent all kinds of boats; Force 5 maintains the only windsurfing school on the island. **Sea Nantucket** (tel. 508/228–7499) rents nonrollable kayaks and will arrange kayak tours for families. **Skip Willauer** (tel. 508/325–2120) gives private sailing lessons and cruises for all ages. On Straight and Steamboat wharves you'll find many charter sailboats to take you out for a few hours or the whole day. Our pick is the Friendship sloop the ***Endeavor*** (Straight Wharf, tel. 508/228–5585), which offers special sailing excursions for families and Pirate Adventures (*see* Entertainment and the Arts, *below*) for little kids. The sloop's skipper has added a re-created whaleboat; you can be part of a crew on a simulated whale-chasing adventure. With **Harbor Cruises** (Straight Wharf, tel. 508/228–1444) you can go on a lobstering excursion; children's ice cream cruises leave from the same dock every afternoon.

FISHING. The main island catch in summer is bluefish—if you go out on a small fishing boat, you can look down and see the fish just gliding in the waves. Charter boats dock at Straight Wharf; Bob DeCosta, owner of the ***Albacore*** (Straight Wharf, tel. 508/228–5074), schedules trips so you start fishing just 10 to 20 minutes from the dock. **All Over It** (tel. 508/325–6043), a fly-fishing and surf-cast-

ing guide service, has experience in teaching all members of a family—including kids.

Younger kids we know enjoy catching flounder from the dock; just drop in a line, using a quahog for bait. What you catch, you can eat. **Bill Fisher Tackle** (14 New La., tel. 508/228–2261) and **Barry Thurston Fishing Tackle** (at the Marina, tel. 508/228–9595; he also rents boats) rent equipment and welcome kids.

HIKES AND WALKS. The most magical places for quiet walks are the beaches, especially just before dusk, and the long trail in the **Sanford Farm/Ram Pasture** conservation area (*see* Scoping Out Nantucket, *above*). The **Nantucket Conservation Foundation** (118 Cliff Rd., tel. 508/228–2884) owns thousands of acres of open land, marked by maroon signs with a wave-and-seagull logo.

INDOOR SWIMMING. On rainy days kids congregate at the **Nantucket Community School**, which has a big pool with a lifeguard. Many activities are scheduled here, from water aerobics to kids' swim lessons, so check the schedule.

🏫 *10 Surfside Rd., tel. 508/228–7257 school, 508/228–7262 pool. Cost: Basic daily rate $6.50 adults, $5.50 kids. Open year-round.*

TENNIS. At the six tennis courts on **Jetties Beach**, the local parks and recreation department sponsors regular tennis clinics for kids as young as 4 (for adults, too; tel. 508/325–5334). **Brant Point Racquet Club** (48 N. Beach St., tel. 508/228–3700) has nine clay courts and group and private instruction for kids.

Shopping

In downtown Nantucket, **Mitchell's Book Corner** (54 Main St., tel. 508/228–1080) is a cozy, very personal bookstore noted for its huge collection of books on Nantucket and its big children's corner. If you write before you come, they'll send you a brochure listing kid and adult books related to the island. **Seven Seas Gifts** (46 Centre St., tel. 508/

228–0958) is filled with inexpensive gift and souvenir items such as shells, Nantucket jigsaw puzzles, and jewelry. Some older teens may be fascinated by the **Fragrance Bar** (5 Centre St., tel. 508/325–4740), an all-natural perfume-oils store carrying 420 different essences, which you can test on yourself to find your own special scent. For clothing, **Vis à Vis, Ltd.** (34 Main St., tel. 508/228–5527) has dresses and shoes that teens approve of. At **Force5 Watersports** (37 Main St., tel. 508/228–0700) you can peruse the latest in boogie boards, bathing suits, Windsurfers, and more, while listening to the latest in music, too. **Indian Summer** (above Young's Bike Shop, 6 Broad St., tel. 508/228–3632) is Nantucket's only surf- and skateboard shop, with a huge selection.

Along touristy Straight Wharf, check out the **Toy Boat** (tel. 508/228–4552). Chock-full of handmade toy boats and games, it hosts occasional kids' workshops. **Aunt Leah's Fudge** (Straight Wharf Courtyard, tel. 508/ 228–1017) sells more than 20 varieties of fudge and imaginatively packed goodies.

Eats

As at any beach resort in the Northeast, seafood is the specialty—chowder, bluefish, and, starting in the late fall, scallops. Gourmet take-out shops and deceptively simple white-walled restaurants serve sophisticated dishes like ravioli with chutney. Those below are tried and true.

Category	Cost*
$$$	over $25
$$	$15–$25
$	under $15

*per person for a three-course meal, excluding drinks, service, and sales tax

(ALL) **Atlantic Cafe.** Of the various burger spots, we'd pick this casual, sometimes noisy place with nautical art, wood

beams, and a good menu—finger food, salads, sandwiches, simple chicken and fish dishes, and, of course, burgers. Most families head for the hand-carved wooden booths in the quieter back room rather than the tables around the bar in front.
15 S. Water St., tel. 508/228–0570. Kids' menu, high chairs, booster seats. Reservations not accepted. AE, D, DC, MC, V. $

(ALL) **The Brotherhood of Thieves.** Curly fries, burgers, good soups, and good prices draw families to this authentic 1840s whaling bar with candlelight.
23 Broad St., no phone. Kids' menu, high chairs, booster seats. No reservations. No credit cards. $

(ALL) **DownyFlake.** A large doughnut-shape sign leads you to the best breakfast in town. Famous for homemade doughnuts, pancakes with blueberry or cranberry syrup, and pastries, this restaurant is also a good source for take-out sandwiches and picnic lunches.
Children's Beach, tel. 508/228–4533. Reservations not accepted. No credit cards. No dinner. $

(ALL) **Espresso Cafe.** A popular hangout for teens and college kids, this old-fashioned ice-cream soda fountain serves the best cappuccino, chewy brownies, and ice cream, along with soup, pasta, sandwiches, and thick gourmet pizza. Inside, you sit under paddle fans at round tables; you can also take a number, order, then eat under sea-green umbrellas on the tree-shaded brick patio.
40 Main St., tel. 508/228–6930. Booster seats. Reservations not accepted. No credit cards. $

(ALL) **Juice Bar.** Right on the wharf, it's a runner-up to the Espresso Cafe (see above) for the best ice cream on Nantucket, as the long lines will testify. Homemade flavors are served in waffle cones with lots of toppings. There are also yummy fresh-squeezed juices (try the guava) or coffee or muffins.
12 Broad St., tel. 508/228–5799. No credit cards. Closed end of Sept.–Mar. $

(♔♀ ALL) **Nantucket Lobster Trap.** Very casual and down home, this place has walls draped with fishnets and a big patio with a canopy. The lobster dinners are among the best on the island. You can save money by eating early.

🏠 *23 Washington St., tel. 508/228–4200. Kids' menu, booster seats. AE, MC, V. Closed Nov.–Apr. $–$$*

(♔♀ ALL) **Something Natural.** For a lunch stop en route to Madaket Beach, try this store's thick, delicious sandwiches (go for the turkey) on a variety of homemade breads; sample their chocolate-chip cookies and regular sodas, too. You can eat at the picnic tables here or have your food packed to take to the beach.

🏠 *50 Cliff Rd., next to bike path to Madaket Beach, tel. 508/228–0504. AE, MC, V. Closed mid-Oct.–early May. No dinner. $*

For Picnics

North-shore beaches are better for picnics, as they have less wind to blow sand on your food. For little kids, try the picnic tables at **Children's Beach**; at uncrowded **Brant Point** you can watch boats while you eat; and on **Long Pond**, which is right off the Madaket Bike Path, there are picnic tables by the water. For a major picnic expedition, rent a boat to cart family, food, and Frisbees over to **Coatue Beach**.

Where to Stay

The majority of accommodations on Nantucket are small inns and bed-and-breakfasts, better suited for romantic honeymooners or older couples than they are for families. The B&Bs that welcome children usually have at least one separate apartment or ground-floor suite that separates you from the guests looking for romance.

The island's several reservation services will help you book an appropriate inn, B&B, or cottage. If you'd prefer to stay in a cottage,

remember that on Nantucket in summer, weeklong stays are the minimum. The **Nantucket Concierge** (*see* How to Find Out What's Going On, *above*) is very personal, handling a small but highly select group of lodgings; their welcome package for families includes information on kids' activities and they will even stock your refrigerator before you arrive. **Nantucket Accommodations** (Box 217, Nantucket 02554, tel. 508/228–9559) is very large, representing some 1,300 rooms and 80 cottages. Realtors who handle rental houses and apartments are listed in *The Official Guide to Nantucket*; the **Maury People** (35 Main St., 02554, tel. 508/228–1881) is one company that's happy to work with families. For prime dates, reserve well in advance. In season, the Nantucket Visitors Services and Information Bureau keeps a current list of rooms available for last-minute bookings.

Most lodgings, except for some of the cottages, are in or close to town (handy to Children's and Jetties beaches). Kids are likely to prefer staying in town, or out toward Surfside and Madaket beaches, to 'Sconset, where the great attractions are peace, solitude, and the company of gulls.

Practically no places comfortable for families are available for much under $130 a night—which makes a $1,000-a-week cottage, where you can spread out and do your own cooking, look pretty good. There are no campgrounds on the island.

Category	Cost*
$$$$	over $240
$$$	$175–$240
$$	$130–$175
$	under $130

*All prices are for a standard double room in high season, excluding 9.7% tax.

Beachside at Nantucket. This two-story motel-style building with stylish rattan and wicker furniture is in an ideal location for families, a five-minute walk from Jetties Beach and all its activities and a 12-minute walk from Main Street. Rooms are a good size and bright with French prints and French doors; they have patios or decks that overlook a heated outdoor pool. There's a tennis club next door, too.

🏨 *30 N. Beach St., ¾-mi west of town center, 02554, tel. 508/228–2241 or 800/322–4433, fax 508/228–8901. 90 rooms and suites. Facilities: air-conditioning, pool. CP. AE, D, DC, MC, V. $$$*

Nantucket Settlements. Though some of the historic guest houses and cottages maintained by this agency are a good 10-minute walk from town, they also offer much that can make a family vacation very pleasant—full kitchens, access to washers and dryers, and patios and grills. The apartments in the guest houses are less expensive; we prefer the cottages. Some have two bedrooms, and a few have a loft as well. The Bayberry Upper, Bayberry Lower, and Honeysuckle cottages, the newest, are especially nice, bright, and modern.

🏨 *Box 1337, tel. 508/228–6597 or 800/462–6882, fax 508/228–6291. 18 studio, 1- and 2-bedroom apartments in 3 houses, 7 cottages. MC, V. $–$$$$*

Periwinkle Guest House and the Cottage. On North Water Street, not far from the Whaling Museum and Children's Beach, stands this big old Nantucket house and a small cottage next door. The family who owns them rents rooms in six buildings in town; these particular properties are especially welcoming to families. The cottage has a kitchen with a refrigerator but no cooking facilities. There's a big backyard with picnic tables and a back porch.

🏨 *Accommodations Et Al, 11 India St., Box 1436, 02554-1436, tel. 508/228–9009 or 800/992–2899. 18 rooms (some share baths), 1 cottage. CP. MC, V. $–$$*

White Elephant. This grand old-style resort away from the noisy wharf is separated from Nantucket Harbor only by a wide, grassy lawn. Decks with bright white tables, chairs,

and umbrellas wrap around the main hotel and look out on a swimming pool and boats bobbing in the bay. Gray-shingle cottages, done up in English country style—some with a small kitchen—are good for families. Here you can have privacy, super resort amenities, and top-notch service.

🏨 *Easton St., Box 359, 02554-0359, tel. 508/228–2500, reservations 800/475–2637, fax 508/228–3639. 48 rooms, 32 1- to 3-bedroom cottages. Facilities: restaurant, refrigerators, pool, croquet. CP. AE, D, DC, MC, V. Closed mid-Sept.–Memorial Day. $$$$*

Entertainment and the Arts

👫 7+ Actor's Theater of Nantucket. Many of the shows here are highly appropriate for kids, and some shows begin as early as 5 PM.

🏨 *Methodist Church, 2 Centre St., tel. 508/228–6325 or 508/228–5387. Open July–Aug.*

👫 8–13 InterNet Cafe. Friday and Saturday evenings from 6 PM to 9 PM are Kids Night Out here. Cruising the net with a guide and playing video games are the attraction. Light snacks are provided, too.

🏨 *2 Union St. (upstairs), tel. 508/228–9165. Reservations required. Cost: $30.*

👫 5–14 Murray Camp. Four evenings a week this kids' camp organizes Kids Night Out, three-hour fun adventure expeditions—a crabbing trip, beach games and contests, a ghost walk with scary stories—for kids only. It's possible to attend the daytime camp for just a week.

🏨 *Box 3437, tel. 508/325–4600. Cost: $40. Open July–Aug. Tues.–Fri. 6–9.*

👫 4–15 Nantucket Island School of Design and the Arts. In a funky old converted cow barn, this school holds kid-friendly classes in painting, collage, and more.

🏨 *23 Wauwinet Rd., tel. 508/228–9248.*

15

BLOCK ISLAND, RHODE ISLAND
HIKING, WALKING ALONG THE BLUFFS, AND BIRD-WATCHING

Nature-loving families looking for an old-fashioned, unsophisticated beach vacation gravitate to this small island 13 mi off the Rhode Island coast. All you really need are bikes, bathing suits, and a fishing rod, plus maybe a sweatshirt for a cold night. The Nature Conservancy calls it "one of the 12 last great places in the western hemisphere," and you can see why: though the island's only 7 mi long and 3 mi wide, its landscape is varied and dramatic, revealing 200-ft-high bluffs and cliffs, golden sand beaches, 365 freshwater ponds, high moors, rolling dunes, and gentle surf as well as ferocious waves.

The options at Block Island are limited—which is why it's not great for teens—but happily, everything is kid-size. The hikes are truly special but short; the bike rides are easy; the cliffs are an adventure to climb, but hardly El Capitan. Its two towns, Old Harbor and New Harbor, are tiny, low-key, and relaxed. Kids can walk down the street with a bucket of bait and go barefoot just about everywhere. Restaurants have big decks where kids can watch boats and make noise without bothering other customers. You don't need a car to get around unless you are staying far from the towns; distances are so small that even kids get used to walking or biking everywhere. And despite the summer crowds that flow off the ferry each day, Block Island is still less crowded—and less expensive—than most other beach areas in the Northeast.

The Basics

How to Find Out What's Going On

The **Block Island Chamber of Commerce** (23 Water St., Old Harbor, Block Island 02807, tel. 401/466–2982 or 800/383–2474) has an information booth right at the ferry landing and a larger office just up the hill. The **Block Island Tourism Council** (Box 356, Block Island 02807, tel. 401/466–5200; Web site www.blockisland.com) will also provide information. Their Official Visitor's Map is essential. Another good Web site is www.ultranet.com/block-island/.

The *Block Island Times* (Box 278, Block Island 02807, tel. 401/466–2222), published weekly in summer, lists community activities and special events and carries ads that alert you to dinner bargains. The map on the inside of the back page is highly detailed and useful. Pick up a free copy in town or send $1 plus your address to receive a copy before you arrive.

Arriving and Departing

BY CAR. A car is not essential unless you're staying in a house far from town. If you don't bring your own car over on the ferry, you can rent one from **Old Harbor Bike Shop** (tel. 401/466–2029) or **Block Island Bike & Car Rental** (tel. 401/466–2297).

BY FERRY. This is the easiest—and most enjoyable—way to get here, though if you want to bring your car in the summer, make reservations very, very far in advance. Block Island is 9 mi from Rhode Island's coast and 13 mi from the tip of Long Island. The shortest trip is from Point Judith, Rhode Island (1 hr, 10 mins), operated year-round by **Interstate Navigation Co.** (Galilee State Pier, Point Judith, tel. 401/783–4613; one-way fare $8.40 adults, $4.10 kids 5–11, $26.30 per car). In summer, Interstate also runs passenger-only ferryboats from Newport and Providence, Rhode Island, and passenger-and-car service on the two-hour trip from New London, Connecticut. **Viking Ferry Lines** (tel. 516/668–5709) takes passengers and bicycles (no cars) in summer from Montauk, Long Island (1 hr, 45 mins). There are always lots of taxis waiting at the ferry landing; it's worth it to take one to your hotel if you have kids and lots of gear. Two to call are **O. J.'s Taxi** (tel. 401/782–5826) and **Wolfie's Taxi Service** (tel. 401/466–5550).

BY PLANE. Block Island State Airport (tel. 401/466–5511) is a short distance from both Old and New Harbor, off Center Road. These airlines serve the island: **New England Airlines** (tel. 401/596–2460 or 800/243–2460) leaves hourly in summer from Westerly, Rhode Island, arriving in a mere 12 minutes; **Action Airlines** (tel. 800/243–8623) and **Resort Air** (tel. 800/683–9330) maintain charter services to the island. In foggy or stormy weather, flights will probably be canceled; schedule your flight so that you can catch a ferry if that happens. Some hotels offer van pickup at the airport; taxis are available there, too.

BY TRAIN. To take **Amtrak** (tel. 800/872–7245) to the ferry, the easiest connection is at New London; it's also possible to take the train to Kingston, Rhode Island, and then get a cab to the Point Judith ferry pier.

Family-Friendly Tours

O. J.'s Taxi (tel. 401/782–5826) gives a lively tour filled with anecdotes about the island's history. It's a good way to get an overview, especially with tots.

Pit Stops

You'll find public rest rooms on the Old Harbor ferry dock, at the town dock, at town hall on Old Town Road, at the public library, at North Light, and at Benson Town Beach Pavilion at State Beach.

Emergencies

There is no hospital on Block Island; serious medical emergencies require a flight to Westerly, Rhode Island, arranged through the **Block Island Medical Center** (Box 919, Payne Rd., tel. 401/466–2974), which has a resident physician. There is no longer a pharmacy on the island; however, the Medical Center has a list of mainland pharmacies to call, and the prescriptions will be brought on the next plane.

Baby-Sitters

Most resorts keep lists of individuals they've used before. The chamber of commerce also has a list of potential baby-sitters, but no one on it has been screened.

When to Go

The prime summer season here is from the end of June through Labor Day, and most hotels, many restaurants, and other businesses close for the winter after Labor Day or by the end of October. In autumn, the island is a famous stopover for many different migrating small birds. Check with the Block Island Chamber of Commerce (tel. 401/466–2982) for information on the following events.

(**ALL**) **Seafood Festival and Chowder Cookoff.** Lots of food to taste and vote on and a small circus are the highlights of this

June event, along with arts and crafts and kids' face painting.

(**ALL**) **Fourth of July.** A real small-town celebration in a spectacular and unique setting, it's the island's biggest event, with the usual concerts, picnics, parades, and fireworks.

Scoping Out Block Island

The two towns are in the center of the island, barely a mile apart. Old Harbor, the larger, is a cluster of streets around the water; New Harbor, facing onto Great Salt Pond, is just a grouping of restaurants, hotels, boat docks, and marinas. There is one lighthouse at each end of the island.

Outside the two towns, most of the island is open space: dunes and hummocks of grass, beach and high bluffs, salt ponds and sparkling kettle holes scraped out by glaciers 10,000 years ago. About one-third of it is preserved in several conservation areas; there are five wildlife refuges, some mainly dunes and grass and beach, some high bluffs and meadows. The three most interesting ones to us are **Clay Head,** along the north shore; **Rodman's Hollow,** a wildlife refuge in the center of the southern part of the island; and the **Greenway,** a network of trails in the island's center, west of Old Harbor. **Andy's Way,** a shallow tidal area and small beach on Great Salt Pond, is a favored place for younger kids to squish their feet in tidal flats. The **Nature Conservancy** (Ocean Ave., New Harbor, tel. 401/466–2129) can tell you everything you want to know, provides a map, and leads all sorts of hands-on exploring walks for families.

A Museum, Nature Center, and More

(**1–10**) **Animal Farm.** In the large meadow next to the 1661 Hotel and Hotel Manisses is a collection of llamas, emus,

goats, ducks, cows, and other animals to pet and watch.
 Spring St., tel. 401/466–2063. Cost: Free. Open dawn to dusk.

(**5+**) **Block Island Historical Society.** Once a hotel, this rambling structure is filled with permanent and special exhibits, some of which appeal to kids—such as Manissean Indian arrowheads and old fishing equipment.
 Old Town Rd., tel. 401/466–2481. Cost: $2 adults, $1 kids under 12. Open June, weekends 10–5; July–Sept., daily 10–5.

(**4–12**) **Block Island National Wildlife Refuge.** This stretch of dunes and grass at the northern tip of the island next to North Lighthouse is a primary summer nesting area for gulls. *See also* Chapter 5.
 Corn Neck Rd., 02807. Call the Nature Conservancy (tel. 401/466–2129) for information.

(**4–14**) **Great Salt Pond Channel.** As boats pass through this narrow channel by the Coast Guard Station to enter Great Salt Pond, it's fun to wave at the passengers and fish in the churned-up water.
 Follow Coast Guard Rd. past Charleston Beach.

(**ALL**) **North Light** and **North Light Interpretive Center.** Sturdy granite-block North Light looks more like a stone church; it stands lonely and deserted amid dune grass at the northernmost tip of Block Island. Inside is the island's most fascinating museum for kids. The first floor is an interpretive center of old lifesaving equipment—boats, ropes and pulleys—and huge photos of past storms, wrecks, and lifesaving expeditions. The original Fresnel lens used in the tower is displayed on a pedestal at kid height.
 Corn Neck Rd. There is no telephone, but you can get information from the Town Hall, tel. 401/466–3200. Cost: $2 kids over 12. Open Memorial Day–Columbus Day, weekends 10–5 (mid-June–mid-Sept., daily 10–5).

(**4–15**) **Southeast Light and Mohegan Bluffs.** Mohegan Bluffs is the most spectacular natural site on the island, with views of Montauk and big waves crashing impressively on the rocky shore far below. A sandy path through roses and daisies ends at the bluffs. Agile older kids can take the narrow stairway 200 ft down the cliff face (easier than the slog back up; expect groans) to the rock-strewn beach—the surging surf is simply awe-inspiring. From the bluffs you can walk to the working lighthouse, a picturesque brick house that was moved from the edge of the Bluffs in 1993.

🏠 *Southeast Light Rd., tel. 401/466–5009. Open June–Labor Day, daily 10–4, call for weekend hours Labor Day–Columbus Day.*

Beaches

You could practically walk all the way around the island on beach, but most areas are not for swimming or sand-castle building. Jellyfish, debris, and seaweed are swept onto the west coast by prevailing winds; the pebbly beaches below the Mohegan Bluffs and the Spring House Hotel are better for collecting rocks and beachcombing. Dangerous currents have swept people away at the northernmost point of the island. All beaches are free.

Nestled into the curve of the island's eastern shore, however, from Old Harbor to Jerry's Point, is a 2-mi-long string of perfect sand beaches collectively called **Crescent Beach**, the best on the island for swimming. Corn Neck Road roughly parallels them. **Fred Benson Town Beach** (tel. 401/466–7717), just north of the harbor, is often crowded with day-trippers straight off the ferry, but it has good amenities—a snack bar, picnic tables, rest rooms, and lifeguards. Above State Beach, **Scotch Beach** draws many young teens because a volleyball net is set up here and the waves are bigger. Farther north lies **Mansion Beach**, the island's prettiest beach, where the tang of the sea mingles with the scent of beach roses and bayberry bushes. It's good for little kids because the sandy bottom stays shallow a long way out; for older kids, the waves are

big enough for good bodysurfing and boogie-boarding. Tidal pools here are fun to explore; just north of the beach, rocky areas called pots and kettles attract many different kinds of fish, making it the top local spot for snorkeling. (Rent or buy snorkeling equipment from Island Outfitters and Dive Shop on Ocean Avenue, tel. 401/466–5502.) Parking is limited.

Ballard's Beach, a ½-mi stretch just below Ballard's Inn in Old Harbor, teems with action—lifeguards, volleyball, a self-service food court—but the crowd tends to be older. It's a fine place for kids to play while you are eating dinner.

Sports

Outdoor Action

BASEBALL. Visiting kids 6–12 are welcome to play at the regular summer baseball games two nights a week. Check game schedules in the *Block Island Times*.

BICYCLING. A bicycle ride on a blackberry-bordered lane past a tiny sparkling pond is a typical Block Island outing. All kinds of roads and paths suitable for bikes, from paved to dirt, traverse the fairly hilly terrain, though there are no paved paths set aside just for bikes. Watch out for traffic between about 11 and 3 on the roads around town; on the island's west side, hills are steeper but car traffic is lighter. If you want to explore dirt roads, you should rent a mountain bike. You can get maps at the Chamber of Commerce or from your bike rental stores. **Moped Man** (245 Main St., Box 125, Old Harbor 02807, tel. 401/466–5444), right across from the Point Judith ferry, has a wide variety of bikes for about $20 adults or kids (smallest is 14½ inches); helmets are included in the price. **Old Harbor Bike Shop** (Box 550, Water St., Old Harbor 02807, tel. 401/466–2029) has adults' and children's bikes ($10–$30 per day) and baby seats; helmets are included in the kids' price.

BIRD-WATCHING. The Atlantic Flyway, the path thousands of birds—more than 200 species—take in their migration along the Atlantic coast, passes right over Block Island. For perching birds, look near the ponds on the trails at **Clay Head** (see below).

BOATING. The calm Great Salt Pond has good conditions for kids to learn any kind of boating. Kayaks are stable enough to be used at the beach. The low-key **Block Island Club** (Corn Neck Rd., tel. 401/466–5939) offers a lifeguarded beach on calm Great Salt Pond with sailing and windsurfing (swimming, tennis lessons, and barbecues for kids and grown-ups, too). You can join for a week, 2 weeks, month, or summer. It's a great way to plug into a local community of families. **Oceans & Ponds** (Ocean Ave., Old Harbor, tel. 401/466–5131) has a large selection of canoes and kayaks to rent or buy, also offers lessons, and will pick up and deliver. Surfboards, boogie boards, and sailboards can be purchased at **Island Sport Shop** (995 Weldon's Way, tel. 401/466–5001).

FISHING. Fishing is big here, and much of it is the kind of fishing kids like—where they can catch a fish right away. **Payne's Dock**, which juts out into the Great Salt Pond in New Harbor, is a good spot to drop a line (nearby Payne's Dock Take Out has picnic tables where you can eat lunch). Some kids may prefer to go out on the water to fish from a rowboat; **Twin Maples** (Beach Ave. by New Harbor, tel. 401/466–5547) rents rowboats ($12.50 per day), fishing equipment, and tackle for boat fishing ($4 per day), and sells bait. **Oceans & Ponds** (see above) also rents fishing rods, shows you how to beach-fish, runs an excellent fly-fishing school, and has a boat charter service.

Thick populations of striped bass, bluefish, cod, and flounder hide in the ledges just off shore in Block Island Sound, and many families come to this island to catch them. In addition to the charter service of **Oceans & Ponds, Captain Bill Gould** and his crew

provide equipment and instruction for half-day and full-day trips, April to October; on the *G. Willie Makit* (Box 1010, Old Harbor, tel. 401/466–5151).

HIKES AND WALKS. Hiking on Block Island is tailor-made for kids—trails in nature areas are short but eventful, winding by ponds, opening up to sudden ocean views, skirting thickets where you can glimpse deer, passing an old stone wall strung with juicy blackberries. At **Clay Head**, one of the best places in North America to observe songbirds in the fall, we wandered a series of densely wooded paths called the Maze and then emerged at the top of a dramatic bluff above the beach. The Chamber of Commerce has several maps of hiking trails, including "Block Island Walking Trails," which you can also get from the Nature Conservancy (see Scoping Out Block Island, *above*). The Conservancy organizes many hikes for kids. Wherever you hike, be aware that Lyme disease is endemic to Block Island.

HORSEBACK RIDING. Rustic Rides Farm (West Side Rd., tel. 401/466–5060) offers an appealing guided trail ride of the rocky west coast, as well as pony rides for little kids.

KITE-FLYING. At the end of the day, when swimmers leave the beach, kids of all ages fly kites above the silvery water. Other breezy locations are the grassy field by Southeast Lighthouse above the Mohegan Bluffs or on the Spring House Hotel's property (see Where to Stay, *below*), if you're staying there. To buy kites, head for the **Block Island Kite Company** (Corn Neck Rd., tel. 401/466–2033).

PARA-SAILING. Cheaper than hot-air ballooning, para-sailing looks like an even more exciting way to go aloft. You launch and land on a boat deck, spending 12 minutes or longer in the air, 300 to 800 ft above the water. **Block Island Para-sail** (Box 216, tel. 401/466–2474) offers daily trips from Old Harbor Dock. Cost: $50–$70.

Shopping

Water Street in Old Harbor is the main shopping drag. **Esta's at Old Harbor** (tel. 401/466–2651) is filled with junky souvenirs and a slew of beach toys and supplies; teen girls should check out the jewelry. **Star Department Store** (tel. 401/466–5541), an old and wonderful "everything" store, keeps many kids happy on a rainy day. The **Book Nook** (tel. 401/466–2993) and **Island Bound** (tel. 401/466–8878) are the two bookstores on the island; both have a selection of kids' books. **Strings and Things** (Water St. at Fountain Sq., tel. 401/466–5666) has a crafts room where older kids can put together necklaces and earrings from a large assortment of beads.

Block Island Kite Company (tel. 401/466–2033), on Corn Neck Road across from Crescent Beach, is a must-stop for families. The third oldest kite store in New England, this spot has one of the best selections. Its neighboring store, **Boatworks**, carries all the essential air, sand, and water toys as well as games.

Eats

Specialties on the island are Block Island Chowder and fresh fish. Some of the restaurants in the grand old wooden hotels perched above the harbor serve elegant—and expensive—gourmet fare, but we also found many inexpensive, down-home establishments with booster seats.

Category	Cost*
$$$	over $25
$$	$15–$25
$	under $15

*per person for a three-course meal, excluding drinks, service, and sales tax

ALL **Aldo's Italian Seafood Restaurant.** This family-style refuge behind the Harborside Inn at Old Harbor serves good pasta and gourmet pizza. You can eat outside. *Weldon's Way, tel. 401/466–5871. High chairs, booster seats. Reservations not accepted. AE, MC, V. $–$$*

ALL **Ballard's Inn.** It's an island landmark, a place where the motto truly is "Bring the kids and come as you are." Huge family-style lobster dinners (there's also Italian food) are served up in stainless-steel bowls on oilcloth-covered tables in a noisy, lively—and enormous—dining room or out on a deck overlooking the beach. Kids run in the sand when they finish eating and return just in time for the family-style entertainment that includes silly songs. This is not for sophisticates, but it's great fun. *42 Water St., Old Harbor, tel. 401/466–2231. Kids' menu, high chairs, booster seats. Reservations not accepted. AE, MC, V. $–$$*

ALL **Bethany's Airport Diner.** Right next to the runway of the Block Island Airport, this diner is decorated with model airplanes, propellers, and other flying gear, and kids can watch planes take off while they eat. There are two small tables here just for kids. *State Airport, tel. 401/466–3100. Booster seats. Reservations not accepted. No credit cards. $*

ALL **Ernie's Old Harbor Restaurant.** Breakfast at this local hangout is a tradition among kids who summer here. Sitting on the broad deck, you can watch the ferries arrive. *Water St., Old Harbor, tel. 401/466–2473. Reservations not accepted. No credit cards. No dinner. $*

ALL **Finn's Seafood Restaurant.** Eat outside on the deck, where the panorama of the harbor keeps kids constantly entertained. The menu includes fish dinners, lobster rolls, smoked bluefish pâté, and fish-and-chips fresh from Finn's fish market next door, as well as burgers. There's also a take-out window. *Ferry Landing, Water St., Old Harbor, tel. 401/466–2473. Reservations not accepted. AE, MC, V. $$*

♀♀ ALL) **Ice Cream Place.** Yes there's a Ben & Jerry's on the island, but we think the best stuff in town is this shop's French Silk flavor, which tastes like frozen chocolate mousse.

🏠 *Weldon's Way, tel. 401/466–2145. No credit cards. $*

For Picnics

We usually choose to picnic at the beach. **State Beach** has picnic tables crowded with day-trippers. Head for scenic **Mansion Beach** farther north. **Negus Park,** a 2-acre square of green downtown behind the Fire Barn, is one of the few places on the island for a picnic under shade trees. At **Settler's Rock**, on the road to the North Light, there are some picnic tables with great views and bird-watching. A big grassy field by the **Southeast Light** is a good spot for picnicking and flying kites. For take-out delis, try **Payne's Dock Take Out** (tel. 401/466–5572) on Great Salt Pond in New Harbor or **Old Harbor Take Out** (tel. 401/466–2935) at the Ferry Landing in Old Harbor, which has blue picnic tables with big blue umbrellas, very good sandwiches, clam chowder, and a terrific view of the ferry dock.

Where to Stay

Block Island's lodging choices include sprawling wooden Victorian hotels (some refurbished and some not), smaller inns and B&Bs (sometimes with very thin walls), and clusters of small cottages, most close to the towns of New or Old Harbor. Many do not take children; each of the three listed below has something special for families. **Block Island Holidays** (Box 803, 02807, tel. 401/466–3137 or 800/905–05907) is like a reservation center; they will help you find everything from hotels to cottages or houses, for short or long stays, and even offer individual packages that include lodging, meals, a tour, and activities. For stays of a week or more, we like to rent a house (you must reserve several months in advance). Other places that have listings are **Phelan Real Estate** (Water St., 02807, tel. 401/466–2816), which has many rentals; the Phelans have children themselves and know about lots of activities. **Sullivan Real Estate** (Water St., 02807, tel. 401/466–5521) also has extensive listings. There is no camping on the island.

Category	Cost*
$$$	over $150
$$	$100–$150
$	under $100

*All prices are for a standard double room in high season, excluding 12% tax.

Bellevue House. This property offers two-bedroom apartments and three-bedroom cottages, a location about five minutes above the town and harbor, and a large grassy yard for kids to run around. The rooms have a beachy look, airy and pleasant, but they aren't big; two of the cottages are not heated (although generally not a problem, the owners like to let guests know). I lean toward the third-floor two-bedroom apartment, which has light coming in on all four sides. Small stoves, big refrigerators, picnic tables, and grills allow families to save some money on restaurant meals.

🏠 *Box 1198, 356 High St., 02807, tel. 401/466–2912. 8 B&B rooms, 3 with private bath. 5 apartments, 2 3-bed cottages. 1-wk minimum stay in apts. and cottages in summer. Cottage prices $$$. Facilities: grills, picnic tables, croquet. MC, V. Closed mid-Oct.–early May. $$*

Spring House Hotel. High on a hill above the ocean, but only a five-minute walk from town, the Spring House is a grand white Victorian hotel that's both warm and elegant. Staying here or in the annex behind it, you feel like you're living in the island's past. Big two-room suites are furnished with solid Victorian replicas; the wide green lawns are great for kite-flying or sprawling in Adirondack chairs. A regular all-you-can-eat family barbecue is laid out on the veranda in summer; in the dining room, parents can enjoy a truly gourmet meal while kids play flashlight tag outside. One drawback: Instead of the deep Victorian bathtubs you'd expect, the bathrooms here have meager shower stalls. 🏠 *Spring St., 02807, tel. 401/466–5844 or 800/234–9263, fax 401/466–5844. 39 rooms, 10 suites. Facilities: restaurant, croquet, volleyball, beach. Kids 7–12 $10; over 12, $20. CP. AE, MC, V. $$$*

Surf Hotel. Casual and funky, the Surf is a rambling old Victorian inn with white verandas and a cupola; rockers on the front porch look out on Old Harbor. It's filled with kid-friendly touches—a playground with a basketball hoop, a parakeet and dogs in the lobby, grills for barbecuing on the porch, and a communal refrigerator. Run out the back door and down a few steps and you're at the beach. The clean, colorful rooms line long corridors; most share baths; spring for an oceanside view ($10 extra). There is a six-night minimum in July and August. 🏠 *Dodge St., 02807, tel. 401/466–2241. 47 rooms, all with sink; 3 rooms with private*

bath. Facilities: playground. Kids in parents' room, $15. CP. MC, V. Closed Columbus Day.– Apr. $–$$

Entertainment and the Arts

(👫 **3 – 15**) **Empire Theater.** Exposed beams and rafters make this former roller-skating rink, built in 1882, look like a big barn dressed up as a theater. Families come here for more than just rainy-day matinees and evening screenings of first-run features. In summer there are weeklong kids' theater workshops and productions that are easy to sign up for. 🏠 *Water St., tel. 401/466–2555. Open Memorial Day–Labor Day.*

(👫 **3+**) **Oceanwest Theatre.** A first-run theater at Champlin's Marina in New Harbor, it offers rainy-day matinees for kids, as well as nightly movies. Nearby is the marina playground, with the usual swings and slide and a metal stagecoach to climb in. 🏠 *New Harbor, tel. 401/466–2971. Open Memorial Day–Labor Day.*

THE BERKSHIRES, MASSACHUSETTS

16

MUSIC AND OLD-FASHIONED BASEBALL

The Berkshires' green hills, spread over western Massachusetts, beckon families with an unsurpassed variety of cultural events, a landscape of kid-size New England towns, and ample recreational opportunities, from spying a beaver to dipping a candle to exploring a round stone barn. Moreover, all these attractions are within an hour's drive of one another. Each of the area's attractive towns has one or two—sometimes several—attractions for kids, but again, some towns have more to offer than others. My picks? Great Barrington, Lenox, and Williamstown.

The Basics

How to Find Out What's Going On

Berkshire Visitor's Bureau (Berkshire Common, Plaza Level, Pittsfield 01201, tel. 413/443–9186 or 800/237–5747; Web site, www.berkshires.org) provides an essential and excellent map, a free official guide to the region that includes restaurants and lodging options. The lodging list in the official guide indicates whether children are welcome at each spot. **Lenox Chamber of Commerce** (Lenox Academy Bldg., 65 Main St., 01240, tel. 413/637–3646 or 800/255–3669; Web site www.lenox.org.) has guides to local attractions. **Mohawk Trail Association** (Box 2031, Charlemont 01339, tel. 413/664–6256) publishes a visitor's guide to the region. Another useful Web site: www.berkshireweb.com.

The *Berkshire Eagle* (75 S. Church St., Pittsfield 01201, tel. 413/447–7311) is the area's main newspaper with ads for house rentals. It publishes a regular supplement in summer, *Berkshires Week*, that contains a calendar of events. *The Berkshire Book*, 5th edition by Jonathan Sternfield & Lauren Stevens (Berkshire House), is the most detailed guide to the region. *Adventures in the Berkshires: Places to Go with Children* by Patti Silver and Vivienne Jaffe (Berkshire Country Day School, Box 867, Lenox, MA 01240; 1991) is a terrific resource for visiting families, including everything from museums to berry farms to libraries. *A Guide to Natural Places in the Berkshire Hills* by Rene Laubach, *Hikes & Walks in the Berkshire Hills* by Lauren Stevens, and *Bike Rides in the Berkshire Hills* by Lewis C. Cuyler, all published by Berkshire House, are very detailed guides.

Arriving and Departing

BY BUS. Peter Pan Bus Lines (tel. 800/237–8747) links Boston, Albany, and New York City with Pittsfield, Lenox, and Lee; **Bonanza Bus Lines** (tel. 800/556–3815) connects New York City, Vermont, and Providence, Rhode Island, with the Berkshires and stops at several towns in the region.

BY CAR. The Massachusetts Turnpike (I–90) connects Boston with the central Berkshires area of Stockbridge and Lenox, continuing on to link with the New York State Thruway.

From Boston the trip takes about 2½ hours. The fastest route from New York City is on the Taconic State Parkway, which joins the Berkshire section of the Thruway at Chatham; to the central area around Lenox, it's about three hours. The main north–south highway through the Berkshires is Route 7, which runs north into Vermont and south into Connecticut. Route 23 cuts across the region in the south; Route 2 (the Mohawk Trail) is the main east–west route in the north.

BY PLANE. **Bradley International Airport** (Windsor Locks, CT, tel. 860/292–2000), between Hartford, Connecticut, and Springfield, Massachusetts, is the closest major airport to the Berkshires, about an hour by car. All major car-rental firms have desks at the airport. **Albany International Airport** (see Chapter 17), just west of the Berkshires, is also an access point.

BY TRAIN. It's possible to reach Pittsfield on **Amtrak's** (tel. 800/872–7245) once-a-day Lake Shore Limited from Boston to Chicago, or to reach Hudson, New York, on the north–south line.

Getting Around the Berkshires

BY CAR. Having a car is essential for visiting the area's back roads and attractions with kids. Towns are best explored on foot, especially during the trafficky summer months. Route 7 links all the major towns, from Great Barrington in the south to Williamstown in the north.

Family-Friendly Tours

You can get an overview of the region or a special insight into a particular aspect of it.

(** 8+) **Greylock Discovery Tours.** These experienced guides organize individual hiking or general sightseeing tours or canoe trips for groups of at least eight people, for example, a large family or two traveling together. And they're happy to include a stop at an alpine slide or for a round of minigolf.

🏠 *Box 2231, Lenox 01240, tel. 413/637–4442 or 413/637–4442.*

Pit Stops

Besides local gas stations, which can always be counted on, the town hall in each community has bathrooms open to the public.

Emergencies

The emergency number for police, fire, and ambulance is 911. **Berkshire Medical Center** (725 North St., Pittsfield, tel. 413/447–2000) is the largest and best-equipped hospital in the Berkshires. **Patrick's Pharmacy** (200 West St., Pittsfield, tel. 413/499–4063) maintains a 24-hour emergency service. **Village Pharmacy** (5 Walker St. at The Curtis Shops, Lenox, tel. 413/637–4700) also maintains a 24-hour emergency service.

When to Go

The Berkshires have something for families during every season. In winter, when it's cold and snowy, but not as icy as farther north in New England, downhill and cross-country skiing at one of the several ski areas and excellent outdoor ice-skating on small lakes are favored activities. March is maple sugaring time at several farms and at Hancock Shaker Village. Skip a visit in April, when wet weather and mud are the norm and ski areas are slush. Even though the weather can be iffy, the beginning of May is the month for kids' fishing derbies. During June, especially the last half, you can enjoy all outdoor activities, including baseball, but without the crowds. July and August, the best time for all music, dance, theater events, and country fairs, also brings traffic, crowds, very high prices, and hot and muggy days. September through October, when the leaves are a riot of color, are ideal for hiking and hayrides.

The following events are worth planning for:

(** 5 – 15) **Indian powwows** with dancing and native food are regularly held between May and October at Indian Plaza in Charlemont (tel. 413/339–4096).

👫 3 – 15 Pittsfield Mets baseball season starts in June (tel. 413/499–6387).

👫 5 – 15 The **Fourth of July** musical extravaganza at Tanglewood ends with fireworks over the waters of Stockbridge Bowl (tel. 413/637–5165; 617/266–1492 Sept.–June).

👫 8 – 15 Josh Billings RunAground in September is the Berkshires' greatest one-day party. Hundreds of teams compete in the oldest triathlon (bicycle, canoe, and running race) in New England (tel. 413/298–4992).

Scoping Out the Berkshires

Great Barrington is the southern Berkshires' big town, the place where families go to walk down a wide main street, see a matinee at an antique movie theater with painted loges and boxes, play indoor miniature golf on a rainy day, and eat at one of its many, many family-friendly restaurants. Lodgings here are less expensive and more available in the prime summer months.

Although **Lenox** and **Stockbridge** offer families a great deal of activities, the many local antiques-filled bed-and-breakfasts and restaurants really don't want their business. Still, within a 15-mi radius is the greatest concentration of attractions for families in the Berkshires. You'll find everything from museums to wildlife sanctuaries to our favorite place to watch baseball; above all, kids can attend free music, dance, and theater events at the many performing spaces. Lenox has historic mansions and many kids' activities; Stockbridge is glossy, a Norman Rockwell New England–postcard spot jammed with summer tourists.

Colonial **Williamstown**, dominated by Williams College, doesn't exude the touristy coziness of Stockbridge or the hum of culture of Lenox. This is a center for some of the most challenging hiking and canoeing, and the only white-water rafting in the region. Come here for spectacular views, a natural stone bridge to cross, Indian powwows, uncrowded swimming, the best state forest camping, a theater with great kids' programs, and a couple of first-rate museums.

Attractions below have been grouped by town, beginning in the south around Great Barrington and proceeding north to the Williamstown area.

Museums, Parks, and More

👫 3 – 10 Santarella (**Tyringham's Gingerbread House**). Often you'll see families stop just to look at this thatched-roof cottage with a witch's face built into the front of the roof. Once the studio for Sir Henry Hudson Kitson, the sculptor who created the Lexington Minuteman statue, it reminds us of something from "Hansel and Gretel." Inside you'll find a museum, but we most enjoy walking on the paths behind it, through gardens, around a pool, and across the little stone bridge.
🏠 75 Main Rd., Box 414, Tyringham 01264, tel. 413/243–3260. Cost: $3.75 kids over 6, kids under 6 free. Open Memorial Day–Oct., daily 10–4:30.

👫 3 – 15 Norman Rockwell Museum. Kids readily respond to Norman Rockwell's lively paintings of an earlier small-town New England, one peopled with freckle-faced kids skating, batting a ball, or ordering dinner on a train. This large building set on 36 acres above the Housatonic River holds the largest collection of his work in the world. It also houses his studio—he lived the last 25 years of his life in Stockbridge and plumbed its people and streets for subject matter. The beautiful grounds are dotted with sculptures designed for kids to climb on; we like the monster surrounded by monster benches. An excellent family program is held once a month.
🏠 Rte. 183, Stockbridge 01262, tel. 413/298–4100. Cost: $9 adults, $2 kids 6–18. Open year-round, daily 10–5.

★★ 0–8 **Berkshire Botanical Garden**. The 15 acres of the Berkshires' only botanical garden comprise a series of kid-size landscapes where little ones can let go of your hand and run freely. There are also paths and trails suitable for strollers. The growing vegetables, small ponds with water lilies and frogs, fragrances of blooming flowers, and enclosed herb garden all leave lasting impressions. Among the best events for kids of all ages are the scarecrow-making workshop and the wonderful fall Harvest Festival. *Rtes. 102 and 183, Stockbridge 01262, tel. 413/298–3926. Cost: $5 adults, $3 students, kids under 12 free. Open May–Oct., daily 10–5.*

★★ 5–10 **Berkshire Scenic Railway and Museum**. Two operating model railroads are the centerpiece of a museum in the old Lenox Station. You can take a 15-minute trip in a shiny 1920s Erie Lackawanna coach on the museum grounds. *Willow Creek Rd., Lenox 01240, tel. 413/637–2210. Cost: Museum free; train ride $2 adults, $1 kids under 14. Open weekends and holidays Memorial Day–Oct. and several weekends in Dec., 10–4.*

★★ ALL **Pleasant Valley Wildlife Sanctuary**. Here along Yokun Brook kids can see animals in natural settings, hike short trails to meadows and ponds, and participate in outdoor nature activities. The regular canoe trips (kids must be at least 10) are a bargain. In winter, you can rent snowshoes here (kids' sizes, too) and snowshoe on the sanctuary's paths. *472 W. Mountain Rd., Lenox 01240, tel. 413/637–0320. Cost: $3 adults, $2 kids 15 and under. Open Tues.–Sun. dawn–dusk and Mon. holidays.*

★★ 4–12 **Berkshire Museum**. You'll find glass made in the town of Berkshire, Native American artifacts, aquariums, and live animals on display at this family-friendly regional museum. There are behind-the-scenes tours as well as camping in an Indian tepee and daily activities in summer. Don't miss the room filled with miniature dioramas of animals of the world. *Rte. 7, Pittsfield 01201, tel. 413/443–7171. Cost: $6 adults, $4 kids 3–18. Open Sept.–June, Tues.–Sat. 10–5, Sun. 1–5; July–Aug., Mon.–Sat. 10–5, Sun. 1–5.*

★★ 8–13 **Hancock Shaker Village**. This restored village conveys the simple Shaker way of life through cooking and blacksmith demonstrations as well as visits to cows and sheep in the barn. *See also* Chapter 2. *Rte. 20, 5 mi west of Pittsfield, at junction of Rtes. 41 and 20, Box 898, Pittsfield 01202, tel. 413/443–0188.*

★★ 3–13 **Western Gateway Heritage State Park**. The big attraction for kids we know is the Tunnel Experience, a sight-and-sound-effects display about how the 4½-mi-long Hoosac Tunnel was built more than a century ago. Inside several railroad boxcars the sound of pickaxes striking stone, the feel of dripping water, and simulated explosions convey the drama. *B & M Freightyard, Rte. 8 South, North Adams 01247, tel. 413/663–8059. Cost: Donation requested. Open daily 10–5.*

★★ ALL **Mohawk Trail** (Route 2). A portion of the highway that follows the historic footpath known to the Indians in early American times passes through the northern Berkshires. Kids like Indian powwows of traditional dances, costumes, and food held periodically throughout the summer in Charlemont and the "trading post" stores of kitschy Indian souvenirs; they may not be as interested in the marked historic spots where Indian treaties were signed. If you go, stop at the Hail to the Sunrise monument to the Five Indian Nations of the Mohawk Trail.

Sports

Big-Time for Spectators

BASEBALL. The Berkshires are home to the ideal baseball experience for young fans.

👫 3+ Pittsfield Mets. The cozy, old-fashioned field in Wahconah Park where this minor-league team plays charms us all with its family atmosphere. *See also* Chapter 8.
🏠 *Box 328 (North St. ½ mi to Wahconah St. and turn left), Pittsfield 01202, tel. 413/499–6387.*

Indoor and Outdoor Action

AMUSEMENTS. Route 7 has a wide variety of good places for fun on rainy days.

👫 4–14 Alpine Slide. Most kids love a ride down an alpine slide. This is the only one in the region. Here you can also play minigolf and fish in a trout pond (*see below*, Fishing).
🏠 *Jiminy Peak, Corey Rd. off Rte. 7, Hancock 01237, tel. 413/738–5500. Cost: $4 per ride. Open Memorial Day–end of June and Labor Day–Oct., weekends only; end of June–Labor Day, daily.*

👫 4–15 Cove Lanes. You'll find great indoor entertainment here, including Rainbow's End, an indoor miniature golf course.
🏠 *Rte. 7, north of Great Barrington, 01230, tel. 413/528–1220.*

👫 4–15 Par-4 Family Fun Center. Go karts, batting cages, basketball, and a huge outdoor miniature golf course are what you'll find here.
🏠 *Rte. 7, Lanesboro 01237, tel. 413/499–0051. Open early May–mid-Oct.*

👫 2–11 Kids' World Playground. This large, multilevel wooden structure with a tower and a bridge is the most imaginative outdoor play space in the Berkshires. Check on hours when school is in session.
🏠 *96 School St., Williamstown 01267, tel. 413/499–5707.*

BIKING. Though the Berkshires have no paved bike paths like Cape Cod, the back-country roads through rolling farmland just outside Lenox—and elsewhere in the Berkshires—offer good family biking. In Lee, for example, most children ride their bikes

downtown. The **Arcadian Shop** (91 Pittsfield Rd., Lenox 01240, tel. 413/637–3010) rents mountain and hybrid bikes in all sizes and includes helmets, as well as a detailed map of the best bike routes. The shop also specializes in outdoor clothing and rents tents and snowshoes and cross-country skis, and even has a café. **Rick Moon Outdoor Adventures** (107 Stockbridge Rd., Great Barrington 01230, tel. 413/528–4666), which organizes and provides guides for all kinds of outdoor trips and adventures, rents top-of-the-line bikes in all sizes. **Plaine's Bike, Ski, Snowboard** (55 W. Housatonic St., Pittsfield 01201, tel. 413/499–0294) is a full-service bike shop.

BOATING. Onota Lake and Pontoosuc Lake, both near Pittsfield, are the best places for motorboating. Boat rentals (including sailboats and Jet Skis) are available at **Quirk's Marine** (990 Valentine Rd., Pittsfield 01201, tel. 413/447–7512). **Onota Lake Boat Livery** (463 Pecks Rd., Pittsfield 01201, tel. 413/442–1724) rents motorboats or canoes by the hour for use on Onota Lake. Pretty little Lake Garfield in South County is a good size for short boat ventures with kids—there are swimming ducks to feed as you go. **Kinne's Grove** (Rte. 23, Monterey, tel. 413/528–5417), right on the lake, rents rowboats and a canoe as well as motors and kid-size life jackets.

FISHING. Kids under 15 don't need fishing licenses in Massachusetts; older kids and adults can obtain them from town clerks and most outdoor sports stores. Bass, pickerel, several kinds of trout, and perch are some of the fish hiding in lakes, ponds, and streams. The **Green River** (stocked with trout) off Rte. 23 west of Great Barrington is easy to get to. **Benedict Pond** in Beartown State Forest has an open, grassy bank. For easy pier fishing, try Burbank Park on **Onota Lake** west of Pittsfield. Shops do not rent equipment, but in summer **Onota Boat Livery** (*see above*) sells bait and rod, reel, and tackle packages; the $15 package is perfect for kids. At **Berry Pond** in Pittsfield

State Forest (Cascade St., Pittsfield, tel. 413/442–8992) kids can throw in a line. Only kids 6–14 are permitted to fish **Wild Acres** (South Mountain Rd., Pittsfield, tel. 413/499–9344), a well-stocked trout pond in a pristine location near the Pittsfield Airport. Rick Moon Outdoor Adventures (see above) guides fly-fishing expeditions for families (including instruction and equipment).

👪 4 – 14 Jiminy Peak. The easiest place for kids to fish in the entire Berkshire area is in this resort's stocked trout pond; rental poles, buckets, and bait are right here.
🏔 *Corey Rd. off Rte. 7, Hancock 01237, tel. 413/738–5500.*

GREEN SPACES. The Berkshires are rich with parks and forests for exploring and enjoying nature. An annual pass ($15) allows you to park free in all state parks and forests that charge a fee.

👪 ALL Beartown State Forest. Outdoor family activities, from swimming and canoeing to camping to fishing in flowing brooks to hiking woodsy trails, are more easily accessible—even to families with little kids—in this state forest's thousands of acres than in others nearby.
🏔 *Blue Hill Rd. off Rte. 17 (access also from Beartown Mountain Rd. off Rte. 102 and Meadow Rd.), Monterey 01245, tel. 413/528–0904. Cost: $2 parking. Facilities: boating, camping, fishing, hiking, picnic area, cross-country skiing.*

👪 6+ Mt. Greylock State Reservation. From Massachusetts' highest peak you have a more spectacular view than from any other mountaintop in the Berkshires. See also Chapter 5.
🏔 *Rockwell Rd. (Massachusetts Turnpike to Exit 2, Rte. 20 West, Rte. 7 North to Lanesboro, follow signs to visitor center), Lanesboro 01237, tel. 413/499–4262 visitor center.*

👪 7+ Natural Bridge State Park. This 30-ft marble bridge is a geologic wonder. See also Chapter 5.
🏔 *Rte. 8 (Rte. 2 to Rte. 8 North, follow signs), North Adams 01247, tel. 413/663–6312.*

👪 ALL Savoy Mountain State Forest. The wild and beautiful forested landscape of these 11,000 acres is similar to Mt. Greylock's, but families with younger kids prefer it because of the uncrowded beaches on North and South Pond. Of the many hiking trails, the short route leads through a cool, dark forest to Tannery Falls, one of the prettiest waterfalls in the Berkshires.
🏔 *Rte. 116, Savoy 01247, tel. 413/663–8469. Cost: $2 parking. Facilities: boating, camping, fishing, hiking, nature center, cross-country skiing, snowmobiling, swimming.*

HIKING AND WALKING. One of the pleasures of this area is walking along the rolling lawns and gardens of historic houses such as **Naumkeag** (Prospect Hill, Stockbridge 01262, tel. 413/298–3239) and **Chesterwood** (off Rte. 183 between Glendale and Stockbridge, 01262, tel. 413/298–3579), which has a short nature trail and large sculptures kids climb on. Right in Lenox is town-maintained **Kennedy Park** (Rtes. 7 and 7A, tel. 413/637–3646 [Chamber of Commerce]), a lovely, large open space with many short hiking and cross-country ski trails and places for picnicking. The Appalachian Mountain Club, with headquarters at Bascom Lodge atop Mt. Greylock (Box 1800, Lanesboro 01237, tel. 413/443–0011), holds regular hikes and programs for families.

👪 3 – 12 Bartholomew's Cobble. Short, easy trails with rounded rocks to climb make this national natural landmark a delight for families. See also Chapter 6.
🏔 *Weatogue Rd. (from Rte. 7A going south, turn right on Rannapo Rd. 1½ mi to Weatogue Rd.; turn right; entrance on left), Ashley Falls 01222, tel. 413/229–8600.*

👪 4+ Bash Bish Falls. This cascade plunges 60 ft into a deep pool surrounded by flat rocks. The hike from the lower parking lot (actually in New York State) follows a gravel road to the falls (less than 1 mi) where you must climb down some stone steps to the view, which always seems a surprise. Guard rails keep you on the trails; swimming is not allowed, nor is picnicking.

🏔 *Mt. Washington State Forest (Rte. 41 to Bash Bish Rd., which becomes Rte. 344), Mt. Washington 01223, tel. 413/528–0330.*

👫 5 – 15 **Benedict Pond Trail.** Following the perimeter of the quiet small pond, the trail skirts a mix of boulders, hemlocks, and blueberry bushes. The Pond Loop Trail, just 1½ mi, lies right next to the shore but is rough in spots; a longer route follows an old road. End the day at the beach with a swim.
🏔 *Beartown State Forest.*

👫 5 – 15 **Field Farm.** Several miles of short hiking and cross-country ski trails on this 316-acre property are maintained by the Trustees of Reservations, a state land conservation organization. You don't have to stay at the farm's guest house to hike the trails, which have spectacular views of Mt. Greylock and are open daily from 8 AM to sunset.
🏔 *565 Sloan Rd. (at intersection of Rtes. 43 and 7, take Rte. 43 West, then right on Sloan Rd. 1 mi to entrance), South Williamstown, tel. 413/458–3144. Cost: free.*

👫 8 – 15 **Ice Glen Trail.** A clattery wooden suspension footbridge across the Housatonic River takes you to a shadowy trail through a mysterious boulder-strewn ravine edged with droopy hemlocks. The maze of rocks creates caves and crevices that retain ice long into spring and impart cool air even on a hot summer day. Climbing over these is difficult; make sure your kids are up to it and are wearing proper footwear.
🏔 *End of Park St., off Rte. 7, 2 mi south of Stockbridge.*

👫 7 – 15 **Monument Mountain Reservation.** This is a real mountain with a short (2.7-mi), circular trail to the Squaw Peak summit. The hike is easy enough for young children but offers everything a hike should have: spectacular views, a waterfall and a stream, open rocky ledges to scramble on, and rock towers, cliffs, and huge, white quartzite boulders at the top that glisten in the sun. It's one of the most memorable short hikes in the Berkshires, but, unfortu-

nately, the trail is packed with people on summer weekends. Beat the crowds by going early.
🏔 *Parking area off Rte. 7, 3 mi south of Stockbridge, tel. 413/298–3239.*

👫 5 – 15 **Tyringham Cobble.** A rewarding 2-mi loop leads up to rocky outcrops (a perfect picnic site) where you have views of the town and Goose Pond. Follow white, then blue blazes through a hillside meadow of blackberries (bring a plastic bucket in summer) and woods to the top.
🏔 *Jerusalem Rd. (watch for TRUSTEES OF RESERVATIONS sign), Tyringham 01262, tel. 413/298– 3239. Open daily sunrise–sunset.*

HORSEBACK RIDING. There are more horseback riding stables in Lenox than in any other Berkshire town. **Undermountain Farm** (Undermountain Rd., Lenox, tel. 413/ 637–3365) holds kid-oriented horse shows and gives lessons and trail rides. **Horsesense** (Golden Hill Farm, 87 Golden Hill Rd., Lenoxdale, tel. 413/637–1999) runs popular full-day and half-day children's camps four days a week throughout the summer. They fill up fast, so you must reserve early. Adults can also take jumping or trail riding lessons at any level, beginner or advanced. Trails are particularly scenic and in the spring kids can visit with baby chicks and lambs.

SKIING. For a day's outing with young kids who aren't hotshots, we prefer the tiny **Otis Ridge Ski Area** (tel. 413/269–4444), whose 11 trails lie a bit farther east along Route 23. It has the intimate family atmosphere of a club and is much less expensive. **Bucksteep Manor** (tel. 413/623–5555 or 800/645– 2825) in Washington and **Canterbury Farm** (tel. 413/623–0100) in Becket are good spots for family cross-country skiing, with lessons, rentals, and accommodation. **Butternut Basin,** a friendly but crowded mountain, is a 10-minute drive from Great Barrington. We'd rather ski at **Jiminy Peak Ski Area** than elsewhere in the Berkshires because of the more challenging trails and clean, spacious, uncrowded atmosphere. *See also Chapter 7.*

SWIMMING. Despite the number of lakes in the Berkshires, it's surprisingly hard to find a public lake beach with really good swimming. **Onota Lake**, west of Pittsfield (tel. 413/499–9344), has a variety of beaches, some very shallow, and lifeguards, bathhouses, picnic tables, and grills. For mountain ponds untouched by noisy powerboats, we prefer **Benedict Pond** (in Beartown State Forest), which we consider mountain pond swimming at its best—a small sandy beach, a sprinkling of picnic tables, no houses, and big pines, boulders, and mountain views.

(👫 4–15) **Green River Swimming Hole.** Here you can enjoy river swimming, with clear, albeit quite chilly water and a spot for sunbathing, but no lifeguards.
🏠 *Off Rte. 23 (1 mi west of town; watch for other cars parked on road), Great Barrington 01230.*

(👫 ALL) **Lake Mansfield.** Tucked into the northwest edge of Great Barrington, this lake has a pretty charm, plus warm water, a playground, and lifeguards.
🏠 *Off Christian Hill Rd., Great Barrington 01230, tel. 413/528–1619.*

(👫 3–15) **North Pond.** Uncrowded pond swimming in a beautiful forest environment draws families to this intimate, unspoiled pond in Savoy State Forest. Picnic tables and barbecue grills make this a good daylong destination.

(👫 ALL) **Otis Reservoir.** Sailboats and motorboats and very clean, clear water are the attractions here. The beach in Tolland State Forest is sandy.
🏠 *Rte. 8, Otis 01253, tel. 413/269–6002.*

(👫 ALL) **Sand Springs Pool and Spa.** The friendly atmosphere at these thermal mineral springs is laid-back. The naturally warm springs, a steady 74°F year-round, have been known since the mid-18th century, when Indian tribes gathered here. Now the water is channeled into a huge 50- by 75-ft swimming pool, an outdoor family-size hot tub with a shallow end for little ones,

and a toddlers' pool with a splashy fountain. Big trees and umbrellas shade the pool edge and picnic area, and there's a snack bar with delicious ethnic foods.
🏠 *Sand Springs Rd., Williamstown 01267, tel. 413/458–5205. Cost: $8 adults, $6.50 kids 4–14, $4 kids 2–3. Open Memorial Day– mid-Sept., weekdays 11–7:30, weekends 10– 8 (July weekdays until 8; mid-Aug.–mid-Sept. until 7).*

WHITE-WATER RAFTING. It's rare in the region, but you can do it.

(👫 8–15) **Deerfield River.** The only place for white-water rafting in Massachusetts, about 25 mi west of Williamstown, is also one of the best spots in the Northeast for families to try it. *See also* Chapter 6.

Shopping

Much of the Berkshires' shopping is antiques. However, there are a few places that kids usually find interesting.

MALLS AND MAIN STREETS. Berkshire **Mall** (Rte. 7 and Berkshire Mall Dr., Lanesboro 01237, tel. 413/445–4400) is the only enclosed shopping center in the Berkshires, with nearly 90 shops; there's also a cineplex theater with 10 movie choices. Great Barrington's **Railroad Street**, almost a pedestrian street in summer, has many shops worth kids' browsing.

STORES. Among the many stores in the Berkshires, these are especially interesting for children:

(👫 4+) **The Bookstore.** Little kids like the play area in the midst of a wide selection of great kids' books; the shop has been around for 22 years.
🏠 *9 Housatonic St., Lenox 01240, tel. 413/ 637–3390.*

(👫 0–8) **Gifted Child.** A selection of educational toys, crafts kits, dolls, clothes, and accessories for infants fills the shelves of these two stores.

🏠 72 Church St., Lenox 01240, tel. 413/637–1191; 28 Railroad St., Great Barrington, tel. 413/528–1395.

👨‍👧 **ALL** **Where Did You Get That?** A sense of humor and fun permeates this store carrying both hands-on educational toys and a corner of wonderful junky novelty items that kids love.

🏠 20A Spring St., Williamstown 01267, tel. 413/458–2206.

Eats

In this area, you'll find lots of restaurants with the typical fare that kids like—pizza, burgers, tacos. Nevertheless, I think our family has eaten more dinner picnics in the Berkshires than just about anywhere else.

Dress is casual in all the restaurants below.

Category	Cost*
$$$	over $25
$$	$15–$25
$	under $15

*per person for a three-course meal, excluding drinks, service, and sales tax

👨‍👧 **ALL** **Bev's Homemade Ice Cream.** We can never resist trying local ice cream parlors that make their own. Here there's much to try—creamy ice cream in yummy flavors, gelato, sherbet, sorbets, and smoothies, plus chewy brownies and espresso for the adults.

🏠 5 Railroad St., Great Barrington, tel. 413/528–6645; 38 Housatonic St., Lenox, tel. 413/637–0371. $

👨‍👧 **4–15** **Cheesecake Charlie's.** The 50-plus flavors of light but creamy cheesecake—the best our family has ever eaten—are the reason to come here. Only about six or seven flavors are available on any one day, which gives you a big reason to come back. You can also have a sandwich or pasta at one of the tables in the shop's center.

🏠 271 Main St., Great Barrington, tel. 413/528–7790. MC, V. $–$$

👨‍👧 **5+** **Dakota.** This restaurant has the fell of a grand but rustic hunting lodge; moose and elk heads gaze down from the pine walls, and a birch-bark canoe hangs from the ceiling. The fare includes steaks, chicken, and mesquite-grilled fish.

🏠 1035 South St., Rtes. 7 and 20, Pittsfield, tel. 413/499–7900. Kids' menu, high chairs, booster seats. AE, D, DC, MC, V. No lunch. $$

👨‍👧 **ALL** **Dos Amigos.** Mexican fare at this relaxed restaurant in an adobe-tan cottage ranges from simple tacos to a sophisticated seafood quesadilla and an extensive selection of vegetarian dishes (they use no lard at all). Inside you'll find open beams, dark wood, low lighting, a fish tank, and on Friday and Saturday nights, fine flamenco music. The kids' menu items are smaller, milder portions of just what's on the menu.

🏠 250 Stockbridge Rd. (Rte. 7), Great Barrington, tel. 413/528–2412. Kids' menu, high chairs, booster seats. AE, D, MC, V. $–$$

👨‍👧 **ALL** **Hobson's Choice.** Good grilled steaks, seafood, chicken, and Cajun specialties, as well as a homey, rustic atmosphere (barn-board walls and beams) appeal to us; from the salad bar you can look into the kitchen and talk to the chef about your order. You can get half orders for kids.

🏠 15 Water St., Williamstown, tel. 413/458–9101. High chairs, booster seats. AE, MC, V. Lunch Tues.–Fri., dinner daily. $$

👨‍👧 **ALL** **Jack's Grill.** This former hardware store with wood tables, wood floors, and a brick courtyard still has shelves that are loaded with interesting bric-a-brac—a pencil collection, old sports equipment—and tricycles dangle from the ceiling. Red Jell-O, chocolate pudding, and root beer floats are just some of the kid-friendly food served at this cozy American country–style restaurant; parents can order dishes like pot roast.

🏠 Main St., Housatonic, tel. 413/274–1000. Kids' menu, high chairs, booster seats. AE, D,

*DC, MC, V. Open May–Oct. (closed Mon.–
Tues. after Labor Day). $$*

(👫 **ALL**) **Miss Adams Diner.** This shiny
1949 Worcester Lunch Car in downtown
Adams serves breakfast and lunch. The
menu is classic (meat loaf). Our pick for
lunch is the homemade chili with a side
order of coleslaw, followed by luscious
banana cream pie; for breakfast, go for the
malted waffles with thick, glossy syrup.
🏠 *53 Park St., Adams, tel. 413/743–5300.
Booster seats. Reservations not accepted. AE,
D, MC, V. Dinner Thurs.–Fri. only. $*

(👫 **9 – 15**) **Red Lion Inn.** Even if you don't
stay at the most famous inn in the Berk-
shires, one dinner in its shady Courtyard of
white tables under green-and-white umbrel-
las or a cold drink with scones and biscuits
on its wide, rocker-filled veranda is a must in
summer. The regular weekly Courtyard bar-
becues are a treat; otherwise the food is
solid, traditional New England.
🏠 *Main St., Stockbridge, tel. 413/298–5545.
Kids' menu, high chairs, booster seats. AE, D,
DC, MC, V. $$$*

Picnics

With kids along, the best seats for a concert
at Tanglewood or a Shakespeare play at the
Mount are on a picnic blanket spread on the
grass. From the picnic tables by the Inside/
Out stage at Jacob's Pillow you have a good
view of dance works-in-progress performed
before the main evening event. Picnic cater-
ers (some too elegant for kids) will pack one
for you: The **Store at Five Corners** (Rtes. 7
and 43, Williamstown, tel. 413/458–3176) is
a gourmet shop whose sandwiches and salads satisfy adults and kids—and don't forget
the creamy homemade fudge. The **Deli** in
Great Barrington (343 Main St., tel. 413/
528–1482) accommodates our picnic style;
their sandwiches, some named for a famous
person, include a Jacques Cousteau shrimp
sandwich that's our favorite.

Throughout the region we've found picnic
tables attractively placed for family meals—

in the Berkshire Botanical Garden, in state
parks by ponds, and on the rolling grassy
lawns and gardens of the **Clark Art Institute** (225 South St., tel. 413/458–9545) in
Williamstown, from which you can hike a
pretty footpath up Stone Hill for a vista of
the town.

Where to Stay

The full range of condo resorts, inns, motels,
individual homes and cottages, and above all
bed-and-breakfasts can be found throughout the region. Route 7 is lined with motels,
especially between Great Barrington and
Stockbridge, north of Lenox, and just south
of Williamstown. Most seem very ordinary
and just too close to the road and the noise
of trucks. Three inexpensive ones that offer
something special: in Great Barrington,
Monument Mountain Motel (tel. 413/528–
3272) has a pool, woods, tennis, volleyball,
and family connecting rooms; in Williamstown, the **Maple Terrace Motel** (tel. 413/
458–9677) is right on Main Street but has a
secluded heated pool. All rooms have refrigerators and VCRs; some have microwaves
and two apartments have full kitchens.
Breakfast is included in the price.

In July and August, the prices for rooms in
Lenox and Stockbridge soar, and many inns
and B&Bs insist on a several-night minimum
stay on weekends, causing families to look
south to Great Barrington and north
toward Williamstown for cheaper accommodations. Do not come without reservations in summer.

Category	Cost*
$$$$	over $160
$$$	$110–$160
$$	$70–$110
$	under $70

*All prices are for a standard double room in
high season, excluding 9.7% tax.*

👫 6 – 15 **AMC Bascom Lodge.** When you stay at this rustic Appalachian Mountain Club lodge atop Mt. Greylock, its hand-hewn beams and stone fireplace will help you feel cut off from everything but views and woods when night falls. It's best for a hiking and sports-minded family who wants to make only a few treks to local cultural activities, preferably in nearby Williamstown. If you are in a private double room, mats are available for kids to sleep on. Advance reservations are essential.
🏠 *Box 1800, Lanesboro 01237, tel. 413/743–1591 or 413/443–0011; 413/684–3900 Oct.–May. 4 double rooms, 4 bunk rooms for 6 or 8, all with shared bath. Facilities: snack bar, hiking, kids' nature programs. MAP. MC, V. Closed Oct.–mid-May. $*

👫 4 – 13 **Blue Heron Farm.** The idea of staying on a working farm appeals to many families, and there are several in the Berkshires that welcome children (not all do). This one, a 200-year-old farm on 100 acres near Charlemont, breeds horses and sells goat's milk, blueberries, and maple syrup. Kids like to hang out in the barn and help milk the goats, pat the horses, and play with the owners' three dogs. Visitors stay in three outbuildings—a sugarhouse, cabin, and cottage; all have kitchens, fireplaces, TVs, and telephones, and more privacy than many other farm accommodations.
🏠 *Warner Hill Rd., Charlemont, tel. 413/339–4045. 3 units with 1–3 bedrooms in outbuildings. Facilities: blueberry picking, farm chores, hiking, wagon rides. $$–$$$*

👫 ALL **Eastover Resort.** Staying at this all-inclusive informal resort is like being on a cruise ship on land. It offers just about every activity a family might want, from horseback riding to live music and nightly dances for kids and adults; the atmosphere can get a bit noisy and corny, like glorified summer camp. It's a place you either love or hate. Totally kid-friendly, it has 1,000 acres to roam, built-in playmates, all-you-can-eat buffets, and buffalo to feed. Despite the exte-

rior grand-estate appearance, the motel-like accommodations lack phones, TVs, and air-conditioning.
🏠 *East St., off Rte. 7, Box 2160, Lenox 01240, tel. 413/637–0625 or 800/822–2386, fax 413/637–4939. 165 rooms, 120 with bath. Facilities: dining room, archery, badminton, driving range, exercise room, horseback riding (fee), kids' programs, mountain biking and bikes, putting green, indoor and outdoor pools, shuffleboard, softball, tennis courts, volleyball; in winter, cross-country and downhill skiing, tobogganing. AP. AE, DC, MC, V. Family wks and weekends offered. Closed Apr. $$–$$$*

👫 ALL **Jiminy Peak.** The tasteful gray clapboard country inn and condos nestled attractively at the base of the mountain have a ski-resort flavor even in summer—massive stone fireplaces, bright wood, views of hills, angled roofs, and a clock tower. There is a certain blandness to the decor, but rooms are light-filled.
🏠 *Corey Rd., off Rte. 7, Hancock 01237, tel. 413/738–5500 or 888/454–6469. 212 rooms. Facilities: restaurant, baby-sitting, fishing, miniature golf, pool, 6 tennis courts. AE, D, DC, MC, V. $$–$$$$*

👫 6 – 15 **Red Lion Inn.** It's the classic rambling New England inn, immortalized by Norman Rockwell, with a genteel small-town, Main Street flavor and rooms with antiques and Colonial charm. Rooms in the main inn vary in size and decor; for families we recommend the sets of two rooms connected through a bath or the larger suites in the annexes, some of which even have kitchens. They do welcome families. Come in the spring or early summer.
🏠 *Main St., Stockbridge 01262, tel. 413/298–5545, fax 413/298–5130. 110 rooms (78 with bath), 20 suites, 8 connecting rooms. Facilities: dining rooms, pool, baby-sitting. AE, D, DC, MC, V. $$$–$$$$*

👫 ALL **Sunset Farm Inn.** This friendly place, which produces maple syrup and sugar for its restaurant, has a real farm feel even though there are no animals left. Trails (including the Appalachian Trail) and a brook where kids can fish are out back. The farmhouse, filled with antiques that don't look worrisome for kids, also has a 10-table restaurant where lunch and dinner are served. The best unit for families is the apartment attached to the main house with an upstairs bedroom, a huge downstairs living room, and a full-size kitchen.

🏠 *Tyringham Rd. (mailing address: 74 Tyringham Rd., Lee 01238), Tyringham, tel. 413/243–0730 or 413/243–3229, fax 413/243–0730. 4 rooms with baths, 1 apartment. Facilities: restaurant, hiking. CP. AE, D, DC, MC, V. $$*

Entertainment and the Arts

Among the paramount attractions of the Berkshires are the performing arts—no other summer resort area in the Northeast can rival the excellence of music, theater, and dance performances for both adults and kids. Some shows are free for kids under 12 when you sit outside.

👫 10 – 15 **Berkshire Opera Company** productions in the auditorium of Berkshire Community College in Pittsfield and at Tanglewood highlight the funny and exciting elements of scores and librettos. Operas are sung in English. The community college performances are slightly less expensive.

🏠 *Mailing address: 314 Main St., Great Barrington 01230, tel. 413/528–4420. Cost: $20–$60.*

👫 8 – 14 **The Berkshire Theatre Festival,** with 70 seasons behind it, regularly puts on plays written specifically for middle-school-age kids in its Unicorn Theater, all with professional actors. On the Mainstage it shows off-Broadway fare.

🏠 *Main St., Stockbridge (mailing address: Box 797, Stockbridge 01262), tel. 413/298–5536 information; 413/298–5576 box office,*

late June–Aug. Cost: Children's theater Wed.–Sun. at noon, $5; other productions, $19–$37.

👫 6 – 15 **Jacob's Pillow** dance events include free works-in-progress. See Chapter 10.

🏠 *Rte. 20, Becket, tel. 413/637–1322 office, 413/243–0745 box office.*

👫 5 – 9 **Mac-Haydn Theatre** produces good musicals for both adults and kids in the round. See Chapter 10.

🏠 *Rte. 203, Chatham, NY 12037, tel. 518/392–9292.*

👫 4 – 15 **Massachusetts Museum of Contemporary Art,** called MoCa, is a visual and performing arts complex under construction in the massive buildings of an historic mill. It offers all sorts of performances for kids and families in the summer.

🏠 *87 Marshall St., North Adams 01247, tel. 413/664–4481.*

👫 3 – 15 **Robbins-Zust Family Marionettes** have presented a repertoire of familiar fairy tales—"Hansel and Gretel," "Sleeping Beauty," "Androcles and the Lion"—to audiences for more than 28 summers using their handcrafted puppets. Not only do they allow kids to touch the puppets and ask questions after the performance, but they also let older kids try working them.

🏠 *East Rd., Richmond 01254, tel. 413/698–2591. Cost: $3.50. Call for location of performances.*

👫 13+ **Shakespeare & Co.**'s productions of Shakespeare's plays are staged on the grounds of a palatial estate. See Chapter 10.

🏠 *The Mount, Plunkett St., Lenox, tel. 413/637–3353.*

👫 3 – 15 **Tanglewood,** the most renowned summer musical festival in the Northeast, has many family-friendly events and concerts. See Chapter 10.

🏠 *Rte. 183, West St., Lenox, 413/637–5165 or 617/266–1492.*

THE ADIRONDACKS, NEW YORK
HIGH PEAKS AND 3,000 LAKES

Entering the Adirondacks can be a bit like revisiting the 1950s. An inexpensive, uncrowded outdoorsy vacation is still here. Even in the most touristy areas, the region is refreshingly unsophisticated and has little of the restored-village-trendy-franchise syndrome that infects many parts of New England.

Much of the Adirondacks' landscape consists of rugged, dramatic, and wild (yes, there are bears) forests and mountains, but it also has nearly 3,000 lakes that range from 32-mi-long Lake George to small, pristine wilderness ponds. That makes it not only great hiking territory but also the place we've come for some of the best canoeing, fishing, and lake swimming in the East. Civilization, including its tackier aspects, is never far away. Even families with toddlers can find the ideal mix of activities.

The Basics

How to Find Out What's Going On

For the entire Adirondack region, the **New York State Travel Center** (1 Commerce Plaza, Albany, NY 12245, tel. 800/225–5698) and the **Adirondack Regional Tourism Council** (Box 2149, Plattsburgh, NY 12901, tel. 518/846–8016 or 800/487–6867) provide general information and travel guides. The **Department of Conservation** and its regional offices (50 Wolf Rd., Albany, NY 12233, tel. 518/457–2121 general information, 518/457–7433 hiking, 518/457–2500 campgrounds) runs the Adirondack Park's campgrounds and is a source of information on fishing, hunting, hiking, and more. For information specifically on the park, contact one of the two **Visitor Interpretive Centers**, the main one at **Paul Smiths** (tel. 518/327–3000) or the smaller one at **Newcomb** (tel. 518/582–2000); see information *below* under Museums. **Good**

Web sites: www.adirondacks.org and www.northnet.org/adirondackzic.

The **Adirondack Regional Chamber of Commerce** (Box 158, 136 Warren St., Glens Falls, NY 12801, tel. 518/798–1761) also has valuable information; local chambers of commerce have information on lodging, dining, attractions, and special events: **Warren County Tourism Department** (Municipal Center, Lake George, NY 12845, tel. 518/761–6468 or 800/365–1050, ext. 201; www.visitlakegeorge.com); **Lake George Chamber of Commerce** (Box 272, Lake George, NY 12845, tel. 518/668–5755); **Hamilton County Tourism** (County Office Bldg., White Birch La., Box 771, Indian Lake, NY 12842, tel. 518/648–5239 or 800/648–5239; be sure to ask for the "Blue Mountain Lake Information" brochure); **Indian Lake Chamber of Commerce** (Box 724, Indian Lake, NY 12842, tel. 518/648–5112); **Lake Placid-Essex County Visitors Bureau** (216 Main St., Olympic Center, Lake Placid, NY 12946, tel. 518/523–2445 or 800/447–5224; www.lakeplacid.com).

The Adirondack Book, 3rd edition by Elizabeth Folwell (Berkshire House, 1998), is the most complete guide to the entire region and a good resource when traveling with children. **The New York State Atlas & Gazetteer** (DeLorme Mapping, Box 298, Yarmouth, ME 04096, tel. 207/846–7000) is essential if you want to get off the beaten path. The best single road map I've found to the whole park is published by the **Adirondack North Country Association** (ANCA) (183 Broadway, Saranac Lake, NY 12983, tel. 518/891–6200).

Arriving and Departing

BY BUS. Though you can get to Lake Placid on **Adirondack Trailways** buses (tel. 800/225–6815) from Albany that connect to service from New York City, it's a hassle with kids.

BY CAR. The Adirondack Northway (I–87), which runs north and south on the eastern edge of the region, is the continuation of the New York State Thruway from New York City and is toll-free beyond Albany. It travels north just west of Lake George; for Lake Placid, take the exit for 9N and 73. Lake George is roughly 4½ hours from New York City; Lake Placid, 5½. Route 30 is the north–south road through the center of the region. The two primary east–west roads are Route 28 in the south (from Lake George to Blue Mountain Lake) and Routes 3 and 73 in the north. If you're coming from Vermont, ferries cross Lake Champlain at Ft. Ticonderoga and Burlington, and there is a bridge at Crown Point.

BY PLANE. The major airport closest to the entire region is **Albany International Airport** (tel. 518/869–9611), which is 50 mi south of Lake George and is served by most airlines. The only commercial airport in the area is the **Adirondack Airport** (tel. 518/891–4600 or 800/428–4322) at Lake Clear, about 30 minutes from Lake Placid. Car rentals are available at both airports.

BY TRAIN. Amtrak (tel. 800/872–7245) runs the *Adirondack* between New York City and Montreal with a stop in Westport, about 25 mi from Lake Placid. You have to arrange shuttle service (tel. 518/523–4431) in advance (some hotels have their own), and you'll have to rent a car when you get there.

Getting Around the Adirondacks

No matter where you base your family in the Adirondacks, a car is a must. Blue Mountain Lake is roughly in the center of the Adirondack Park, a little more than 50 mi northwest of Lake George and about 50 miles southwest of Lake Placid.

Family-Friendly Tours

Overlook Tours (tel. 518/743–1735) puts together theme tours in the Lake George region. **Lake Placid Carriage Rides** (1 Main St., Lake Placid, tel. 518/523–2483) offers a ride around Mirror Lake that's especially worthwhile right before it turns dark and the lights of the hotels are reflected on the water.

Pit Stops

At the corner of Canada Street (the main drag) and Beach Road in **Lake George** village are public bathrooms, and most public beaches also have them. Otherwise, head for a gas station. The municipal parking lot off Main Street in **Lake Placid** has public bathrooms.

Emergencies

Glens Falls Hospital (100 Park St., Glens Falls, tel. 518/792–3151, 518/761–5261 emergency room) has a 24-hour emergency room. **Hudson Headwaters Health Network** (Indian Lake, Rte. 28, tel. 518/648–5707) has a physician or physician's assistant on duty. **Adirondack Medical Center** (Church St., Lake Placid, tel. 518/523–3311) maintains a 24-hour emergency service with physicians on call. For **ambulance** and **fire**:

call 911 in Lake George, 518/352–7711 in Blue Mountain Lake, and 911 in Lake Placid. For **police** call 911 in Lake George, 518/585–6200 in Blue Mountain Lake, and 911 in Lake Placid. For **poison control** call 800/336–6997. **Rite Aid Pharmacy** in Warrensburg (147 Main St., tel. 518/623–3805) and in Lake Placid (85 Saranac Ave., tel. 518/523–5305) stay open until 9 PM weeknights, Sunday to 5 PM.

When to Go

Beginning at the end of June, the summer is prime boating, swimming, and hiking time in and around the region's lakes, and you're likely to find even the touristy places less crowded than the coast. Temperatures can be pleasantly warm, rarely too warm during the day, but they cool off considerably at night. The early fall is even better for hiking than the summer, with fewer mosquitoes and less humidity. In winter, the region comes alive with carnivals, snowmobiling, skiing, and ice-skating, but be prepared for very, very cold temperatures and a ton of snow. The spring is the one season not to come: It's basically mud and black flies, which last into mid-June.

The following holiday events are worth planning for:

(👫 **3+**)   **Winter Carnival**, Saranac Lake. The highlight of the February nine-day winter festival is the ice palace. Call 518/891–1990 or 800/347–1992 for information.

(👫 **ALL**)   The **July 4th Fireworks over Mirror Lake** in Lake Placid are the highlight after an afternoon and evening of music at the band shell and a parade.

(👫 **ALL**)   **Ice Shows and Figure Skating Competitions** take place at the Olympic Arena and **Ski Jumping Competitions** and demonstrations at the Ski Jumping Complex in July and August. For information, call 518/523–1655.

(👫 **ALL**)   **Lake George Family Festival Week** in August at Lake George's Shepard

Park includes concerts, puppet shows, and general festivities just for families. Call 518/668–5771.

Scoping Out the Adirondacks

The Adirondack Park has several distinct regions, but among those, three in particular stand out: busy, yet beautiful Lake George, with its mixture of amusement park attractions and exceptional boating; centrally located Blue Mountain Lake, ideal for canoe trips, a quiet lake vacation, and for exploration of the park; and Lake Placid, with its spectacular Olympic complex and proximity to High Peaks hiking.

The lower end of **Lake George** is an 8-year-old boy's idea of heaven: seven miniature golf courses, boat rides, a boardwalk with every conceivable kind of confection and junk food, games, and corny gewgaws. This is the most developed part of the Adirondacks, but the rest of the huge lake is still wonderful to explore by motorboat or sail.

For a lake vacation, **Blue Mountain Lake** is the opposite of Lake George, with just enough outdoor activity—short hikes, easy but diverse canoeing, a sprinkle of islands on a small lake, clear and clean but chilly swimming—to occupy families for at least a week. With its many connected lakes and ponds not too far from civilization (it's northwest of Lake George), it is one of the best areas in the Adirondacks for family canoeing.

Lake Placid has hosted the Winter Olympics twice, in 1932 and in 1980, and the complex, extensively used for training, is open to visitors. It's also on the edge of the High Peaks country, the center for not only some of the most difficult and challenging climbs in the East but also easygoing, simple climbs to great views that families with young kids can enjoy. Unlike Blue Mountain Lake and Lake George, it doesn't shut down on Columbus Day.

Attractions below have been grouped by region, starting with Lake George and ending with Lake Placid.

Museums, Forts, and More

👥 2–15 **Ft. Ticonderoga**. About 30 mi from the village of Lake George, this huge stone fort has booming cannon demonstrations and colorful marching music. *See also* Chapter 2.
🏠 *Rte. 74 (18 mi east of Exit 28 off I–87), Box 390B, Ticonderoga 12883, tel. 518/585–2821.*

👥 5–15 **Ft. William Henry**. This re-created log fort was an important outpost during the French and Indian War. *See also* Chapter 2.
🏠 *Canada St., Beach Rd. and Rte. 9 entrances, Lake George, tel. 518/668–5471.*

👥 6+ **Saratoga Racetrack**. Just 30 mi south of Lake George is the oldest and most famous Thoroughbred racetrack in the United States, open only in August. *See also* Chapter 8.
🏠 *Rte. 9P, Saratoga Springs, tel. in Aug. 518/584–6200.*

👥 6+ **National Museum of Racing**. At the entrance, you walk through a starting gate. The gallery exhibits are arranged in an oval to resemble a racecourse; on the tour of the Oklahoma Track next door, there's a demonstration of how to brush and curry a racehorse. Kids have a chance to don racing skills and ride a mechanical pony in the Children's Room (not open in August).
🏠 *191 Union Ave., Saratoga Springs, tel. 518/584–0400. Cost: $5 adults, $3 students, under 5 free. Open Mon.–Sat. 10–4:30, Sun. noon–4:30 (late July–Labor Day, daily 9–5).*

👥 3–12 **Lake George Steamboat Cruises**. A cruise on the lake is a must. The one-hour trip around the Lake George village end of the lake aboard the classic and colorful paddle wheeler, the *Minne-Ha-Ha*, is about the right length for young kids.
🏠 *Beach Rd., tel. 518/668–5777 or 800/*

553–2628. Cost: $7.75 adults, $5.25 kids 3–11. Open May–Labor Day, 6 one-hr trips daily.

👥 3+ **Adirondack Museum**. This great regional museum of Adirondack life has 22 exhibit areas that overlook the lake—and there's an old locomotive you can climb. *See also* Chapter 3.
🏠 *Rtes. 28N and 30 (past town), Blue Mountain Lake, tel. 518/352–7311.*

👥 4–15 **Adirondack Park Agency Visitor Interpretive Center** at Newcomb. Much more than a source of travel information, it is worth visiting for an introduction to the nature and history of the region through guided walks (some for kids), exhibits, and programs such as breakfast with the birds and an annual winter snowshoe event. Some of the lovely nature trails have paved surfaces, convenient if you have a baby in a stroller.
🏠 *Rte. 28N (Exit 29 off I–87), Box 101, Newcomb 12852, tel. 518/582–2000. Open daily 9–5.*

👥 4–12 **Bird's Boat Livery Mail Boat**. Tagging along on the pontoon boat (sometimes a 21-ft outboard instead) that has delivered mail to various cottages around Racquette Lake for more than 50 years is the best way to get to know the lake and much more fun than most lake tours for kids. The mail boy who hands over the mail is the youngest mail carrier in the United States. All you have to do is show up before the boat leaves at 10:15 AM, though you can reserve. The trip takes 2½ hours.
🏠 *Bird's Marina, Rte. 28, Racquette Lake, tel. 315/354–4441. Cost: $8 adults, $4 kids 6–12. Deliveries weekdays July–Labor Day.*

👥 4–15 **Paul Smiths Adirondack Interpretive Center**. Designed for kids and families, this center is a good stop to get an overview of the Lake Placid region's plants and animals. Try the guided short canoe explorations, special hiking trails (especially a new wilderness trail), and entertaining programs such as the one on birds of prey that make this center a must stop.

🏛 *Adirondack Park Visitor Center, Rte. 30 (12 mi north of Saranac Lake), Box 3000, Paul Smiths 12970, tel. 518/327–3000. Open daily 9–5.*

(👬 **6 – 15**) **Olympic Site Tour and Events.** For kids who find skiing and all winter sports more important than the World Series, a visit to the sites of the Olympic facilities in Lake Placid is vital.

The Olympic Jumping Complex and Kodak Sports Park (Rte. 73, tel. 518/523–2202) wowed us. A glass elevator takes you up 26 stories to an enclosed observation deck at the top of the jump tower. From there the jump looks like a giant's roller coaster that only goes down. Definitely visit it before you watch skiers train and compete; the freestyle aerialists zoom down jumps with special plastic matting and land skis first in a huge pool of water. It's much better than watching the Olympics on TV. The self-guided auto tour package is the best bet: We saved money and were able to spread our visits over two days. Expect lines and start early. The **Olympic Center** and **1932 and 1980 Lake Placid Winter Olympic Museum** (218 Main St., tel. 518/523–1655; $3 adults, $1 kids 7–12) are included in the tour price and are well worth a visit.
🏛 *Olympic Regional Development Authority, Olympic Center, Lake Placid 12946, tel. 518/523–1655 or 800/462–6236. Cost: Tour package (excluding admission on competition days): $18 adults, $12 kids 7–12. Open daily 9–4, some sites later.*

(👬 **ALL**) **Whiteface Mountain.** This mountain is a must, even though it's not the highest peak here. You can drive the 8-mi highway and climb the steep stone stairs to the summit, or you can take an elevator inside the mountain (better for little kids), reached by a long tunnel. The open summit affords an impressive view of many lakes. The cost, $8 plus $4 for each additional person in the car, is included in the Olympic site tour package (*see above*), as is a ride on the chairlifts over the Olympic Racing Trails.

Beaches

There's a wide selection of beaches in the Adirondacks, from sandy lakesides to secluded islands.

(👬 **5 – 15**) **Lake George Islands.** Forty-eight islands in the lake are open to the public for swimming, picnicking, and (on a few) camping, but you must have a boat and obtain a permit to get there. The Department of Environmental Conservation (Hudson Ave., Warrensburg, NY 12884, tel. 518/668–5441) has season permits ($4.50–$7.50) and information; stop at island headquarters, Glen Island, Narrow Island, or Long Island the day you plan to picnic.

(👬 **8 – 15**) **Million Dollar Beach.** The largest and most famous beach in Lake George, so-called because of the cost of construction back in the early days of the resort, has more action (volleyball) for older kids, as well as lifeguards, picnic tables, and other amenities. Behind the beach is a park with the remains of an old fort.
🏛 *Beach Rd., east of U.S. 9, tel. 518/668–3352. Cost: $1.*

(👬 **ALL**) **Shepard Park.** This is Lake George's family beach: a dock and a diving board, an enclosed swimming area, and so much free family entertainment in summer—regular fireworks on Thursday nights, puppet shows, and the special Family Fun Festival concerts in August—that you end up coming here even if you're staying somewhere with a private beach.
🏛 *Canada St., Lake George, tel. 518/668–2864. Cost: Free.*

Sports

Indoor and Outdoor Action

AMUSEMENTS. Cheerful honky-tonk sums up Lake George village. Its huge variety of fun parks, arcades, and wax museums has the advantage of small crowds and little expense. With 162 holes of miniature golf, Lake George has to be the capital of the sport in the Northeast. The oldest minia-ture golf course in the world is right here.

👫 5–15 Around the World in 18 Holes Mini-Golf. A huge statue of Paul Bun-yan towers over this old, classic course, where each hole lies in one of the world's famous buildings.
🏨 *Beach Rd., Lake George 12845, tel. 518/ 668–2531. Open mid-Apr.–Sept., daily.*

👫 ALL Great Escape and Splashwater Kingdom Fun Park. One hundred twenty-five wet and dry rides, shows, and attractions and six themed areas on 140 acres compose this biggest amusement park in New York State. Story Town and Jungle Land provide plenty of tame rides far from the screams of those strapped into the incredible Comet roller coaster. The only long lines were for the wet-and-wild attractions.
🏨 *Rte. 9, between Exits 19 and 20 off I–87, Lake George 12845, tel. 518/792–3500. Cost: $25.99 adults, $18.99 kids under 40". Open June–Labor Day, daily 9:30–6.*

👫 2–9 Magic Forest Family Fun Park. A 40-ft statue of Uncle Sam benignly over-sees this smaller, calmer park (25 rides), where kids stick their heads into the mouth of a huge lion's head sculpture for a drink of water and clap their hands on the train ride through a jungle of ferocious animal sculptures to keep the "beasts" from attacking.
🏨 *Rte. 9, Lake George, tel. 518/668–2448. Cost: $9.95. Open mid-June–Labor Day, daily 9:30–6.*

👫 ALL Water Slide World. It's a mix of terrifyingly high looping water-slick slides (35 of them!), a sweet toddler lagoon and pool, a giant wave pool, and the Lazy Adventure River, down which you float on huge tire tubes until the waterfall dunks you. This park is clean and the staff friendly. Expect long lines for the slides.
🏨 *Rtes. 9 and 9L, Lake George, tel. 518/ 668–4407. Cost: $19.95 adults, child rates*

according to height. Open late June–Labor Day, daily 10–6:30.

BOATING. The boats on Lake George are primarily powerboats and sailboats whose big wakes can make canoeing with kids a scary enterprise. You can explore some of the lake's many islands (see Lake George Islands, *above,* for information on obtaining permits to land on the islands). Rent a boat from a marina farther up the lake to avoid traffic jams. **Yankee Yacht Sales** (Rte. 9N, Diamond Point, tel. 518/668–2862) rents both motorboats and sailboats and even offers two-day weekend sailing courses in June and July and private sailing lessons throughout the summer. Even farther north, **Water's Edge Marina** (Sagamore Rd., Bolton Landing, tel. 518/644–2511) rents ski boats.

CAMPING. The campsites nearest to Blue Mountain Lake are on **Lake Durant** (Rte. 28, about 3 mi east of Blue Mountain Lake, tel. 518/352–7797). These have a swimming beach, canoe rentals, hiking trails, and show-ers. The most beautiful primitive campsites (best with older kids) are the 55 island sites on **Indian Lake** (off Rte. 30, 11 mi south of Indian Lake hamlet, tel. 518/648–5300). **Fish Creek Pond Campground** (Rte. 30, west of Saranac Lake, tel. 518/891–4560) is large and has all the amenities—showers, a recre-ational program, playground, and canoe rentals—but still feels like the wilderness. It's at the center of a short, easy canoe route. **Saranac Lake Islands Campsites** (tel. 518/ 891–3170) are beautiful and primitive, but not far from shore. The **Department of Environmental Conservation** (tel. 518/457–2500) will provide site maps and brochures. To reserve campsites, call 800/456–2267.

CANOEING. Essential reading is *Fun on Flatwater—An Introduction to Adirondack Canoeing* by Barbara McMartin (North Country Books, 1995), which describes 42 short, easy family canoe trips in the Adiron-dacks. Lake Durant (2 mi east on Rte. 28) is good for younger kids and beginning canoers because it's small. I can't imagine staying at Blue Mountain Lake and not spending some time in a canoe exploring the lake and its small, uninhabited islands of rock and pine. Most of the resorts provide canoes, but you can rent them from Blue Mountain Outfitters. *See also* Chapter 6, Canoeing.

👫 6–15 **Fish Creek Ponds Loop**. Seven different ponds and a creek make up this 12-mi canoe loop west of Saranac Lake, where you'll see lots of wildlife. Any part of this is good with younger kids. You can even spend a day with a guide here. **St. Regis Canoe Outfitters** (Box 318, Lake Clear 12945, tel. 518/891–1838) has experience with families; it runs a regular introduction to canoeing for kids.

FISHING. The **Steel Pier** in Lake George, where all the cruise boats dock, is a neat place for kids to throw in a line, something they can also do along the boardwalk. **Beach Road Outdoor Supply** (Beach Rd., Lake George, tel. 518/668–4040) sells bait.

Check with **Blue Mountain Lake Boat Livery** (tel. 518/352–7351) for bait and fishing tackle and information on the best fishing spots. At Long Lake, we pulled in some sunfish and perch fairly quickly at the town dock behind the post office.

It helps to have a guide tell you the most-up-to-date tips on what is biting where. **Jones Outfitters** (37 Main St., Lake Placid, tel. 518/523–3468) not only supplies guides (one guide to a family) but also has gear, rents various kinds of boats for fishing, and runs a fly-fishing school. For kids younger than 12, the owner suggests a one-hour private lesson.

👫 5–15 **High Peaks Base Camp, Fish Farm, and the Wood Parlor Restaurant** (Springfield Rd., Wilmington, tel. 518/946–2133) provides an easy way for kids to fish and then eat their catch without your having to clean it. The spring-fed pond is stocked; equipment is available.

HIKES AND WALKS. Lake George. With little kids, strolling Lake George's boardwalk

from the docks holds the delights of ducks to feed, benches to rest on, and boats to watch. The Adirondack Mountain Club (Rte. 9N, Lake George, tel. 518/668–4447) has an office that offers advice on hiking and other outdoor trips; its center in Lack Placid (tel. 518/523–3441) organizes many family and kid activities. The Adirondack Mountain Club guide to hiking the area with kids, **"Kids on the Trail"** (1997), describes 62 hikes that kids enjoy. The Department of Environmental Conservation (Hudson Ave., Warrensburg, tel. 518/623–3671) has free individual trail brochures.

👫 8+ **Prospect Mountain.** The view from the 2,100-ft summit is spectacular, but it tends to get crowded. If you have little kids and don't want to climb, free trams run regularly to the top, where you can see 100 mi into Vermont and New Hampshire.
🏔 *Prospect Mountain Memorial Hwy., off Rte. 9 (5½-mi drive from parking area to summit; trailhead begins on Montcalm St.), Lake George, tel. 518/668–5198. Cost: $5 per carload. Open daily 9–6.*

👫 4+ **Pack Demonstration Forest.** For little kids the diverse nature trails to ponds and by a river in this experimental forest (run by the Warrensburg campus of the State University of New York's Department of Environmental Science and Forestry) may be much more interesting than the Prospect Mountain climb and vista.
🏔 *Rte. 9, past Rte. 28 junction, Warrensburg, tel. 518/623–9679. Cost: Free.*

Blue Mountain Lake. Of the eight trails near Blue Mountain Lake, four are less than 1 mi long. Forget the trail to Blue Mountain's summit (2½ mi each way) with little ones; it is very steep, with rocky patches that are tough to navigate on the way down. The two easiest and most level are the trails off Route 28 to Rock Lake. The free "Woodland Trails of Blue Mountain Lake" map is available from shops in the town.

Lake Placid. One of the easiest walks in the Lake Placid region, ideal if you're pushing a stroller or eating ice cream cones, is the 2½-mi sidewalk around Mirror Lake. Early in the morning you may glimpse U.S. Olympic rowing and kayaking teams working out.

The High Peaks district directly south of Lake Placid has some rugged trails, but we've tried several short ones even younger kids can manage. The **Adirondack Mountain Club** (off Rte. 73, Box 867, Lake Placid 12946, tel. 518/523–3441) has trail maps, good suggestions, and great guided hikes and programs for families. See also Chapter 6, Hiking.

HORSEBACK RIDING. Warren County, right around Lake George, is noted for dude ranches and trail rides. The best bet for families who want to ride frequently is staying at a ranch resort (see Where to Stay, below). **Saddle Up** (tel. 518/668–4801) in Lake George offers family rides and trail rides for children with views of the lake. Wilson's Livery and Stables at the **Bark Eater Inn** (tel. 518/576–2221) in Keene, near Lake Placid, has 35 horses for trail rides, lessons, and hayrides for children as young as 3.

MOUNTAIN BIKING. A Mountain Bike Center at the Mt. Van Hoevenberg Olympic Cross-Country Area uses the network of ski trails through forest and by streams for mountain biking; many are easy family fun. **High Peaks Cyclery** (331 Main St., Lake Placid 12946, tel. 518/523–3764), which runs the Mountain Bike Center, rents bikes and helmets, including youth sizes, and also rents in-line skates and has pamphlets of good road and off-road trails in the area. **Garnet Hill Lodge**, about halfway between Lake George and Blue Mountain Lake (Thirteenth Lake Rd., North River 12856, tel. 518/251–2444; see also Chapter 9), rents bikes, has 30 mi of trails, including many easy ones, and regular "bike down-ride back" adventures. You don't have to stay at this friendly lodge to use the trails.

ROCK HOUNDING. Rock lovers can find good pickings halfway between Blue Mountain Lake and Lake George.

👫 6 – 13 **Barton Garnet Mines.** A 45-minute drive brings you to an open-pit mine where kids can pick up garnets and visit a great mineral shop. See also Chapter 6, Rockhounding.
🏠 Rte. 28, North Creek 12853, tel. 518/251–2706.

SWIMMING. The Adirondacks' lakes, whether surrounded by cottages or wilderness, provide refreshing, sometimes chilly swimming. All the recommended lodging spots are next to water. The **Lake George** area has good swimming, as does **Blue Mountain Lake**. In the **Lake Placid** region, calm **Mirror Lake** is fine for little kids, especially since it does not permit motorboats. For more remote swimming, **Heart Lake**, next to the Adirondack Mountain Club's lodge (see Where to Stay, below), is just at the edge of wilderness. The deep, chilly **Cascade Lakes** off Route 73, nestled into the chasm between Cascade and Pitchoff Mountain, are so narrow you can almost throw a stone across. It's a bit of a drive from Lake Placid to **Chapel Pond**, south of Keene Valley on Route 73, but above this glacial pond with good rocks to climb and sit on are crags favored by rock climbers.

WHITE-WATER RAFTING. In this region of the Upper Hudson River many of the rafting trips are too dangerous for kids.

👫 8 – 15 **Sacandaga River.** This short, safe trip on an easy river is one in the region I can recommend for families. Contact **W.I.L.D. W.A.T.E.R.S.** (Rte. 28, Box 197A, HCR01, Warrensburg 12885, tel. 518/494–7478). See also Chapter 6.

WINTER SPORTS. For skiing at Whiteface Mountain, cross-country skiing at Garnet Hill Lodge and in Lake Placid, and ice-skating, see Chapter 7.

Shopping

LAKE GEORGE. **Canada Street** in Lake George is souvenir street: T-shirt shops galore, Indian headdress schlock, kitschy postcards. **Million Dollar Half-Mile Factory Outlets** (Rte. 9, north of Exit 20 off I-87, Lake George) has more than 70 outlet stores arranged in four separate plazas next to and across the road from one another.

BLUE MOUNTAIN LAKE. There are only a few shops in this area. The **Adirondack Lakes Center for the Arts** (tel. 518/352-7715; see Entertainment, *below*) doesn't actually have a shop anymore but it still sells the birch-bark origami birds we love. The biggest shop is at the **Adirondack Museum** (*see* Scoping Out the Adirondacks, *above*), which carries tapes of famous Adirondack storytellers. In nearby Long Lake, **Hoss's Country Corner** (Rtes. 28N and 30, tel. 518/624-2481) has ice cream, worms, and an arcade across the street, not to mention a few magazines, books, and general picnic supplies.

LAKE PLACID. Main Street has some kitschy shops, and kids we know happily spend evenings browsing through them while their parents finish dinner. **Adirondack Trading Company** (tel. 518/523-3651) is full of doodads like cedar sachets. **Where'd You Get That Hat?** (tel. 518/523-3101) has wacky hats. Don't forget the **U.S. Olympic Spirit Store** (16 Main St., tel. 518/523-7207; U.S. Olympic Training Center, 421 Old Military Rd., Lake Placid, tel. 518/523-4856).

Eats

Adirondacks restaurants range from old-timey roadside diners to gourmet establishments with ironed white tablecloths; you'll find lots of fairly good family restaurants. Local food specialties are trout and game; atmosphere is what makes most of the restaurants listed below special. Dress is casual unless otherwise indicated.

Picnicking on a Lake George island can mean a picnic on a slab of rock, your boat rocking gently at anchor, and swimming afterward. To us Blue Mountain Lake's many

tiny islands, where you can beach a canoe on flat rocks and spread a blanket under pine trees, hold the best picnic places. At Buttermilk Falls, several miles north of town on North Point Road (left off Rte. 28N), you'll find picnic tables and fireplaces within a short walk of the falls.

Category	Cost*
$$$	over $25
$$	$15–$25
$	under $15

per person for a three-course meal, excluding drinks, service, and sales tax

(4–15) Boathouse. The wraparound deck above Mirror Lake plus food that pleases both kids and grown-ups (even a wine list) are reasons to come here. Pasta servings can be ordered in three sizes. *Lake Placid Club Dr., Lake Placid, tel. 518/ 523-4822. MC, V. $–$$*

(3–15) The Boathouse Restaurant. Among the many lakeside dining establishments around Lake George, we like this casual one in a historic turn-of-the-century blue boathouse about a mile and a half north of the village. Be sure to eat outside on the second-floor porch; from here you get a great view of the lake and boats. If you come by boat, you can tie up at the dock. The food is okay, especially the steaks. *Rte. 9N (at Cresthaven Resort Motel), Lake George, tel. 518/668-2389. Kids' menu. MC, V. $$*

(ALL) Papa's. An ice cream parlor with turn-of-the-century decor, comfy wooden booths, and outdoor seating on a back porch overlooking the Hudson River, it also serves reasonably priced soups, salads, and sandwiches. Spend some time looking at all the old photos and postcards of the Lake Luzerne area and the old-fashioned milk bottles. Whatever you eat, be sure to have one of the delicious ice cream sodas, malts, or chocolate egg creams.

🏨 *3–5 Main St., Lake Luzerne, tel. 518/ 696–3667. No credit cards. Open late May– Oct. Meals only to 8 PM; ice cream till 10 PM. $*

(👫 ALL) **S. J. Garcia's.** In the midst of T-shirt shops, wax museums, and more on Lake George's main drag is this fairly good Mexican restaurant with excellent nachos, fast service, and an outdoor deck out back. 🏨 *192 Canada St., Lake George, tel. 518/ 668–2190. Kids' menu, high chairs. Reservations not accepted. AE, DC, MC, V. $–$$*

(👫 ALL) **Tail o' the Pup.** When we spied the chrome-legged stools at the outside counters of this squat little building that flies the Stars and Stripes, we knew we'd found a classic roadside restaurant. For more than 50 years it's been serving great American road food like chicken and ribs in tangy barbecue sauce with waffle fries and coleslaw. 🏨 *Rte. 86, halfway between Lake Placid and Saranac Lake, Ray Brook, tel. 518/891–5092. Kids' menu, high chairs. Reservations not accepted. MC, V. $*

Where to Stay

The motels cramming the main road through Lake George village are a bit depressing. Try staying outside the town where you can really experience the lake— either farther up the lake in Diamond Point or Bolton Landing, or at an inexpensive lakeside cottage in nearby Lake Luzerne.

The tiny hamlet of Blue Mountain Lake has a handful of accommodations, most clustered around the eastern end of the lake alongside a few churches, a post office, a store, a boat livery, and a public beach.

A wide variety of inexpensive to expensive lodging in individual houses, condos, lodges, hotels, cabins, motels, and bed-and-breakfasts is available in Lake Placid; lists are available from the Lake Placid Visitors Bureau. *See also* Chapter 9, Sagamore Resort, the Silver Bay Association, and Garnet Hill Lodge.

The price categories that follow are based on summer-season rates and reflect what a family of four would spend for one night in a double room or the smallest appropriate accommodation available (sometimes a cottage): $$$, over $125; $$, $60–$125; $, under $60. When resorts are MAP or AP, categories are: $$$$, over $450; $$$, $350–$450; $$, $200–$350; $, under $200. Prices do not include 7% sales tax.

(👫 ALL) **Adirondack Loj.** This B&B lodge run by the Adirondack Mountain Club is a rustic, comfortable place perched at the edge of the wilderness with hiking trails up into the High Peaks and lake swimming right outside the door. We like the cozy bunk rooms with four built-in log beds that make you feel you're on board a ship. Meals are family style in a pine dining room at picnic tables. The High Peaks information center here has a nature museum with kids' programs and guided walks. 🏨 *Adirondack Loj Rd., Lake Placid 12946, tel. 518/523–3441. 9 family, double, and bunk rooms with shared bath; campground. Facilities: dining room, beach, camping, fishing, hiking. Kids under 2 free. CP. AE, D, MC, V. $$*

(👫 0–13) **Best Western Golden Arrow Hotel.** This casual, comfortable hotel has a modern European feel—and more atmosphere than most motels in the chain. You can't beat the location—right on the lake (you can just walk out the door to this hotel's private beach) and within walking distance of everything in town (across from the Olympic Center). 🏨 *150 Main St., Lake Placid 12946, tel. 518/523–3353 or 800/582–5540. 138 units, 5 with kitchen, 7 with fireplace. Facilities: baby-sitting, beach, boating, dock, indoor pool, wading pool, putting green. Kids under 12 free. Special summer packages. AE, D, DC, MC, V. $$–$$$*

(👫 5–15) **Canoe Island Lodge.** This carefully preserved lodge and assorted cottages on a Lake George hillside offer boating and a 4-mi-long private island for swimming and water sports. Flotillas of launches manned by college kids ferry families back and forth, a treat in itself. An air of casual elegance coexists with kids scrambling about the complex network of stone stairways, bridges, and paths. Rooms are in log cabins and cottages; they have modern baths, TV, and carpeting.

🏨 *Lake Shore Dr., Diamond Point 12824, tel. 518/668–5592. 72 rooms. Facilities: dining room, baby-sitting, beach, boating, Ping-Pong, playground, recreation room, tennis courts, windsurfing. Reduced rates for kids. MAP. No credit cards. $$$–$$$$*

👫 0–12 **Curry's Cottages.** We were charmed 20 years ago by these cute but simple barn-red cottages (some with fireplaces) with a straight line of white Adirondack chairs by their sandy beach; toddlers splashed in the shallow water then just as they do now. Opt for the cottages on the water rather than those across the road.

🏨 *Rte. 28, Blue Mountain Lake 12812, tel. 518/352–7354, 518/352–7355 in winter. 10 1- to 3-bedroom cottages. Facilities: beach, boating, dock. No credit cards. $–$$*

👫 ALL **Lakeview Fireplace Cottages.** The log-sided cabins with their big screened-in porches sit comfortably under pines by the shore of tiny Lake Vanare. The beach is a sunny peninsula with shallow water and canoes; a roped-in swimming area keeps kids safe. Furnishings are sturdy. Unlike many other cottages in the Lake George vicinity, all have big fireplaces and stacks of logs.

🏨 *3199 Lake Ave., Box 174, Lake Luzerne 12846, tel. 518/696–3197. 6 1-, 2-, and 3-bedroom cottages. Facilities: baby-sitting, beach, boating, playground. Rentals by wk only in summer. AE, D, MC, V. $–$$*

👫 0–12 **Prospect Point Cottages.** Away from the road on a private point with a big sandy beach, these cottages have fantastic views of the lake and a wide green lawn yet are within walking distance of town. Six of the cottages have been completely renovated, with new microwaves and other amenities.

🏨 *Rte. 28, Blue Mountain Lake 12812, tel. 518/352–7378. 10 1- and 2-bedroom cottages. Facilities: beach, boating, dock, playground. No credit cards. $$*

👫 ALL **Rydin' Hy Ranch Resort.** One of the several dude ranches in Warren County, the 800-acre Rydin' Hy Ranch is the least refined, the most kid-friendly, and the only one with its own shallow, sand-bottom lake. A couple of ponies are tied to a tree outside the main lodge so little kids can climb on and be led around any time. Kids whoop and holler in the lobby. If you want to ride morning and afternoon, you can. Rodeos are held here every Tuesday night in summer.

🏨 *Sherman Lake, Warrensburg 12885, tel. 518/494–2742. 12 cabins, 24 rooms in motel units, 4 2-room suites, 8 rooms in main lodge. Facilities: childproof rooms, baby-sitting, beach, boating, fishing, horseback riding, horseshoes, kids' programs, indoor pool, shuffleboard, tennis courts, volleyball, waterskiing. Many family packages. AP. AE, D, DC, MC, V. $$–$$$*

👫 6–14 **Sagamore Lodge.** Once a classic Adirondack camp, this complex of buildings on a private lake of a large estate is now a nonprofit organization that hosts weeklong and weekend workshops on Adirondack crafts and history, some of which are good for families. One unique program is their weeklong camp for grandparents and grandchildren; special family weeks include guided activities and a guided day trip to a accessible mountain. Expert guides will take you rafting, canoeing, mountain biking, hiking, and spelunking. Rooms vary in size and style, but are mostly pine-panelled with Adirondack furnishings. Don't forget to try the semi-outdoor bowling lane.

🏨 *Sagamore Rd., off Rte. 28 (about 12 mi from Blue Mountain Lake), Racquette Lake 13436, tel. 315/354–5303, fax 315/354–5851. 30 rooms with shared bath in 3 lodges and 3 cottages. Facilities: beach, boating, croquet, family programs, fishing, gift shop, hiking, tennis, volleyball. Family packages and discounts. AP. MC, V. $$*

(👫 6+) **Timberlock.** This is a place for families who want the authentic, unpretentious flavor of a small rustic Adirondack lake camp (unheated cabins have only propane lights and woodstoves; the oilcloth-topped dining table is on an open porch with plastic shades for bad weather) in a beautiful setting, but with myriad water sports for kids, including teens, that you usually find only at a bigger resort. It also has an excellent riding program, with three trail rides each morning and lessons. Here you'll find good hearty food, nightly campfires, naturalist-led hikes and canoe trips, and other thrilling activities for kids.
🏠 *Indian Lake, Sabael 12864, tel. 518/648–5494, 802/457–1621 in winter. 10 2- and 3-bedroom cottages, 4 1-room cabins with bath, 7 1-room cabins with shared bath; no electricity. Facilities: baby-sitting, beach, boating, horseback riding, nature programs, tennis courts, windsurfing, waterskiing. AP. No credit cards. $$–$$$*

Entertainment and the Arts

(👫 4–15) **Adirondack Lakes Center for the Arts.** It's the coziest-looking art center you can imagine—a former garage painted beige with white and barn-red trim and a long box of pink and white flowers outside. Come for the regular performances of everything from movies to zydeco music and fiddle jamborees, along with family arts and crafts workshops and storytelling.
🏠 *Rte. 28, Box 205, Blue Mountain Lake 12812, tel. 518/352–7715. Open year-round weekdays 10–4 (July and Aug. also Sat. 10–4 and Sun. noon–4).*

(👫 ALL) **Lake Placid Center for the Arts.** A regular Young and Fun series features the classic staples of good summer kids' theater programs (like the Mettawee Theater Company's larger-than-life puppet shows of myths) and a few comedy surprises. You'll also find films, theater for adults and older kids, and regular workshops here.
🏠 *91 Saranac Ave., Lake Placid, tel. 518/523–2512.*

(👫 0–12) **Lake Placid Sinfonietta.** The free Wednesday-night orchestra concerts at the village park band shell on the shore of Mirror Lake are a family affair. Adults sit on folding chairs, kids on the grass, and teens glide by in paddleboats with their dates. Bring insect repellent.
🏠 *Box 1303, Lake Placid, tel. 518/523–2051.*

(👫 8+) **Saratoga Performing Arts Center.** The summer home of the New York City Ballet, the Metropolitan Opera, and the Philadelphia Philharmonic, it's one of the best places to see first-class dance and music performances—including rock and popular bands—in July and August, and it's only a 30-minute drive from Lake George. *See also* Chapter 10.
🏠 *Saratoga Springs 12866, tel. 518/587–3330.*

THE WHITE MOUNTAINS, NEW HAMPSHIRE

GREAT HIKES, THE BEST CANOE ROUTE, AND A COG RAILWAY

Vistas of bare peaks roll on for miles, as though you're on a vast, bumpy sea. Among the region's many pleasures are pulling in a fish from an icy pool, riding the world's oldest mountain railway, canoeing a slow river, sleeping in a tent serenaded by owls, picnicking on a rock ledge, or spotting a moose by a boggy pond. Less spread out than the Adirondack region, it offers the same wild, mountainous terrain, but with a New England flavor.

The western White Mountains are linked to the less crowded, more diverse Mt. Washington Valley area to the east by the scenic Kancamagus Highway. My pick as the ideal base for a family stay in the White Mountains is the Mt. Washington Valley, especially the unspoiled village of Jackson and dramatic Pinkham Notch, near Mt. Washington itself. *See also* Chapter 5.

The Basics

How to Find Out What's Going On

Mt. Washington Valley Visitors Bureau (Box 2300, North Conway 03860, tel. 603/ 356–3171; Web site: www.whitemountains.com) puts out *The Official Guide to Mt. Washington Valley* and a "Tips and Tours" planning guide that lists everything from accommodations to where to find covered bridges. Also check with the **New Hampshire Office of Travel and Tourism Development** (Box 1856, Concord 03302–1856, tel. 603/271–2665; Web site: www.visitnh. gov). **Jackson Chamber of Commerce** (Box 304, Jackson 03846, tel. 603/383– 9356 or 800/866–3334 except New Hampshire and Canada) publishes a free travel guide and will book accommodations. For camping, biking, and hiking trails, and

canoeing, check with the **White Mountain National Forest** (719 Main St., Laconia 03246, tel. 603/528–8721), which also publishes a regular newsletter, and when you arrive, the **Saco Ranger Station** (on the Kancamagus Hwy. just off Rte. 16, Conway 03818, tel. 603/447–5448), which not only has comprehensive information, but also much experience in assessing White Mountains hikes and activities in terms of children. The **New Hampshire Division of Parks and Recreation** (172 Pembroke Rd., Concord 03301, tel. 603/271–3556 information, 603/271–3254 trails, 603/271– 3628 camping reservations; Web site: www.nhparks.state.nh.us) has information on state parks and forests. For other trail maps and hiking information *see* Hikes, Walks, and Climbs *in* Indoor and Outdoor Action, *below.*

The *Mountain Ear* (Box 530, Conway 03818, tel. 603/447–6336) is the local weekly newspaper; it lists happenings and events of interest to families and carries restaurant ads. Its regular "Summer Guide" is particularly useful.

The New Hampshire Atlas and Gazetteer (DeLorme Mapping, Box 298, Yarmouth, ME 04096, tel. 207/846–7000) has detailed maps of the region, a good fishing guide, plus listings of campgrounds, covered bridges, nature areas, and much more.

Arriving and Departing

BY BUS. Concord Trailways (tel. 800/639–3317) runs from Boston to various points in the valley.

BY CAR. The interstate nearest the Mt. Washington area, I–93, runs north and south through the western White Mountains; Route 112, the scenic Kancamagus Highway, links it with Route 16, the primary north–south highway through the Mt. Washington Valley; Route 302, which joins it for a short distance, branches off to the west and is always less crowded.

BY PLANE. The major airport closest to Jackson is **Portland Jetport** (tel. 207/775–5809) in Portland, Maine, about a 90-minute drive to the southwest. Major airlines flying to the **Manchester New Hampshire Municipal Airport** (tel. 603/624–6539) include United, US Airways, Continental Express, ComAir, and several commuter links. It is about 100 mi south of Jackson. Both airports have major car rental agencies.

Getting Around the White Mountains

To travel around the Mt. Washington and Jackson areas comfortably with a family, you must have a car. All airports have most major car rental agencies, including the small regional airport at Conway. Be warned that Route 16 between Conway and North Conway is often a matter of stopping and starting in traffic on weekends. You can try to bypass it by using the West Side Road in Conway to River Road, then Route 16 or Route 32.

Emergencies

Memorial Hospital (Rte. 16, North Conway, tel. 603/356–5461 emergency room). For **ambulance, fire,** and **police** in North Conway and Conway, call 911. For **ambulance** in other towns, call 603/539–6119. For **poison control,** call 800/562–8236. **CVS Pharmacy** (Rte. 16 next to Burger King, North Conway, tel. 603/356–6916) is centrally located and open until 9 PM Monday–Saturday, 6 PM Sunday.

When to Go

The White Mountains have family appeal in winter for skiing and in summer and early fall for hiking, canoeing, and everything else. Avoid arriving before mid-June because of the black fly season.

The following celebrations are worth planning for:

Winter carnivals and family ski weeks fill February in most of Mt. Washington Valley's five ski resorts.

Blueberry Festival features participating in a blueberry olympics, picking blueberries, and trying everything from blueberry syrup to muffins and pie. If you and your kids love horses, the **Equine Festival** is exciting, drawing world-class Olympic jumpers. Both these events are held at Attitash Bear Peak ski area (tel. 603/374–2368) in August.

Labor Day Weekend, look for the Jazz and Blues Festival (tel. 603/356–5251), which includes special children's concerts.

Scoping Out the White Mountains

The Mt. Washington Valley has attractions, action, and lodging to entertain families four seasons of the year. **Conway** and **North Conway** at its southern end are the commercial hub, with factory outlets, outdoor-equipment shops, miniature golf, and movie theaters—plus access to fine canoeing and a lake with a sandy beach. Farther north are **Glen**, which has several commercial attractions that appeal to kids, and **Jackson**, where we most like to stay for cross-country skiing. Still farther north is dramatic, less developed **Pinkham Notch**, home of the Appalachian Mountain Club, wonderful hiking, and the road up Mt. Washington. To the northwest of Jackson is **Crawford Notch**, the least developed and most magnificent of the White Mountains' narrow high passes, with the area's most scenic waterfalls, views, and more hikes; **Bretton Woods** to the north, a center for skiing, has the region's grandest hotel, and one of the world's oldest railways. *See also* Chapters 5, 6, and 7.

Train Rides, Gondolas, and More

(⚫ 6–15) Mt. Washington. At 6,288 ft, New Hampshire's highest peak is a real mountain even in western terms. From the distance it looks impressive, the summit often in clouds. Even if you don't get to the top (but you should) it's omnipresent as you drive and hike in the valley. It has incredible views (as far as the Atlantic Ocean) from the summit—if you're not fogged in, as happens 300 days of the year.

There are three ways to get to the top: hike, which is not recommended for families—it's a tough slog and the weather is too unpredictable and dangerous; take the 19th-century Mt. Washington Cog Railway, the second steepest railway in the world; or drive the steep, 8-mi-long Auto Road (begin at Glen House, off Rte. 16 in Pinkham Notch, 8 mi south of Gorham, tel. 603/466–3988; $15 car and driver, $6 adult, $4 kids 5–12), which climbs all the way up. You can drive your own car or take a guided tour.

(⚫ 7+) Mt. Washington Cog Railway. The train trestles and tracks snaking up to the top of Mt. Washington were the world's first mountain-climbing cog railway, built in 1869. The one-car train is pulled by a cute green-and-red coal-burning engine. On the way back, the engine backs down the steep 37% grade in front of the car to act as a brake. The cog wheels fit into slots between the rails. The round-trip takes three hours, with a break at the top to visit the observation center. Reservations are advised.

🏔 *Rte. 302, Bretton Woods 03575, tel. 603/ 278–5404, ext. 7, or 800/922–8825. Cost (round-trip): $39 adults, $24 kids, under 6 free; 8 AM and 5 PM fares discounted. Open May weekends, limited schedule; June–mid-Oct., daily 9–5 (mid-July–Labor Day and late Sept.– Columbus Day, daily 8–5), weather permitting.*

(⚫ 3–12) Conway Scenic Railroad. In contrast to the cog railway, these are soothing rather than exciting rides in old-fashioned trains. The shortest trip, from North Conway to Conway and back, takes about an hour and is the best one for younger kids. Twice a day the same train makes a longer trip to Bartlett. You can eat lunch in the dining car on either one or dinner on the Bartlett trip; kids under 4 eat and ride free at lunch. For added luxury, ride first class. Now another similar old-fashioned train makes a five-hour trip up to Crawford Notch; the views are spectacular but the trip is best for kids 8 and up who especially love trains.

🏔 *Rte. 16, North Conway 03860, tel. 603/ 356–5251 or 800/232–5251. Cost: $8.50– $42.95 adults, $6–$30.95 kids 4–12, free–$7 kids under 4. Higher rates include lunch or dinner. Open mid-May–late Oct., daily 9–6; Apr.– mid-May and Nov.–late Dec., weekends 9–6. Reserve early during foliage season.*

(⚫ 4–15) Wildcat Mountain Gondola. To us the view of the peaks of the Presidential Range made the 15-minute ride worth it even though we'd already been to the top of Mt. Washington. Little kids who can't climb a mountain this high (and older kids who don't want to) may truly enjoy the ride and the nature trails (you can walk part of the Appalachian Trail).

🏔 *Rte. 16, Jackson, tel. 603/466–3326 or 800/255–6439. Cost: $9 adults, $4.50 kids*

4–10. Open mid-June–late Sept., 9–4:30; mid-May–mid-June and late Sept.–Columbus Day, weekends 9:30–4:30.

Sports

Indoor and Outdoor Action

AMUSEMENTS. Places to go on rainy days or just for fun are sprinkled throughout the region.

(**★★ 6+**) **Attitash Bear Peak Alpine Slide and Outdoor Amusements**. This is one-stop amusement shopping with an all-you-can-eat price. An all-day ticket allows kids to ride three water slides, a ¾-mi alpine slide, and a scenic chairlift up and down until they're really tired of it. The ticket doesn't include the pony rides, golf driving range, Buddy Bear's pool for little kids (7 and under; $8 all day), the climbing wall and trampolinek, or mountain-bike trails nearby. **⚑** *Rte. 302, Bartlett 03812, tel. 603/374–2368. Cost: Day pass $19; single ticket (1 ticket good for 1 trip down alpine slide or ½ hr on the water slides) $8 ages 7 and up, kids under 7 free with parent. Open mid-June–Labor Day, daily 10–6; Memorial Day–mid-June and Labor Day–Columbus Day, weekends 10–5.*

(**★★ 4–13**) **Heritage New Hampshire.** A portrayal of New Hampshire's history through scenes and special effects is touristy but fun for an hour and a half on a rainy day. *See also Chapter 3.* **⚑** *Rte. 16 (6 mi north of North Conway), Glen, tel. 603/383–9776.*

(**★★ 4+**) **Pirate's Cove Adventure Golf.** The two courses here are definitely the best miniature golf in the area. Both have the same pirate theme, but one is slightly more challenging. Our vote for the best hole is the talking pirate head. **⚑** *Rte. 16, North Conway 03860, tel. 603/356–8807. Cost: $6 adults, $5 kids under 13. Open mid-May–Oct.*

(**★★ 2–11**) **Story Land.** This nursery rhyme and fairy-tale theme park in the woods has much more charm than most such places, especially the Oceans of Fun sprayground, which has a 30-ft submarine full of squirters to try, the life-size sand-castle maze, and the new loopy laboratory with 10,000 foam balls. There's even an area for infants. The price includes all rides, shows, parking, strollers, even a kennel service and loaner camera. **⚑** *Rte. 16 (6 mi north of Conway), Glen, tel. 603/383–9776. Cost: $18 kids 4 and up. Open mid-June–Labor Day, daily 9–6; Labor Day–Columbus Day, weekends 10–5.*

CAMPING. The White Mountains' wealth of camping opportunities includes a site especially suited to families (*see also* Chapter 6, Camping):

(**★★ 6–13**) **Crawford Notch General Store and Campground.** This is secluded wilderness camping in the most beautiful section of the Mt. Washington Valley. Unlike the primitive tent sites in Crawford Notch State Park, these have a store and showers. Sites are along the Saco River. **⚑** *Rte. 302, Hart's Location 03812, tel. 603/374–2779. 75 sites. Facilities: hot showers, swimming, hiking, fishing, mountain bikes, camp store. MC, V.*

CANOEING AND KAYAKING. Of the White Mountains' many waterways, one in particular offers good conditions.

(**★★ 3+**) **Saco River.** This shallow, sand-bottom river is one of the most perfect in the Northeast for both short and long family canoe or kayak trips, no matter how old your kids. **Saco Bound** (Center Conway, tel. 603/447–2177) has rentals. *See also* Chapter 6.

CLIMBING. North Conway is one of the two major centers for learning to rock climb in the Northeast. **Mt. Cranmore Resort Sports Center** (North Conway, tel. 603/356–6301) offers two-hour instruction sessions to a family of four for $100 using a large indoor climbing wall. Reservations are required.

FISHING. The cold, deep ponds, wide rivers, and winding streams in the White Mountains hold brown and brook trout, lake trout, bass, and salmon. You are more likely to actually catch fish on the Swift River along the Kancamagus Highway just west of North Conway, the Saco River, especially off West Side Road past Humphrey's Ledge and Route 302 in Hart's Location and Crawford Notch, and the Wildcat River just past the iron bridge in Jackson. Tiny Saco Lake in Crawford Notch, where we've been lucky, is very easy to get to and usually not crowded. For fly-fishing information and gear, **North Country Angler** (White Mountain Highway, Intervale, tel. 603/356–6000) rents rods ($25 a day) and teaches fly-fishing to kids (10 and up) as well as adults. The shop also has maps of good fishing spots in the area. For other types of bait and equipment, try Patch's Gun Shop (Glen, tel. 603/383–6545). The **New Hampshire Fish and Game Department** (tel. 603/271–3421) can give you additional information.

HIKES, WALKS, AND CLIMBS. Mt. Washington Valley's trails range from easygoing to highly challenging, up many peaks over 4,000 ft, as well as to waterfalls, along streams and rivers, and to high mountain lakes. The mountains here have more of an alpine feel than the dense woods of the Adirondacks. For families, the Appalachian Mountain Club's system of huts, guided hikes, lodges, and family programs helps even those with small children feel comfortable hiking farther afield. The AMC has the best information on trails and trail conditions; we always stop at the **Pinkham Notch Visitor Center** (Rte. 16, Box 29, Gorham 03581, tel. 603/466–2721) for advice, encouragement, and maps, and sometimes come back to have dinner. See also Chapter 9, Appalachian Mountain Club. A few walks follow.

When our son was small he was captivated by the **sidewalk loop in Jackson**, frequented by joggers, that goes through town and the covered bridge. The **Rob Brook Road Trail** (on left off Bear Notch Rd., 12 mi west of Conway off Kancamagus Hwy.) is great for viewing wildlife. **Crystal Cascade/Tuckerman Ravine Trail** (under 1 mi round-trip) begins from the AMC Pinkham Notch Camp; in less than half a mile you see the spectacular falls.

Arethusa Falls and Frankenstein Cliff trails (off Rte. 302; look for signs 15 mi from Rtes. 16 and 302 junction), a 4½-hour loop, take you to Arethusa Falls, the state's highest waterfall, 200-ft ribbons of water that plunge to a pool. You can lunch on Frankenstein Cliffs.

Diana's Baths Trail (on West Side Rd. between Conway and Bartlett, just north of Cathedral Ledge; follow Rte. 302 2 mi to the road, then follow it ½ mi past Bartlett-Conway line. Take gravel road to small sign indicating Moat Mountain Trailhead) is a fairly level ½-mi walk through the woods to a gorgeous waterfall and pools. You can swim below the falls, but not above them.

(**ALL**) **White Mountain National Forest.** Covering most of the upper half of New Hampshire and reaching in to Maine, the forest contains 750 mi of streams, 22 campgrounds, 50 lakes and ponds, and 1,200 mi of hiking trails. See also Chapters 5 and 6.

Forest Supervisor, 719 Main St., White Mountain National Forest, Laconia 03247, tel. 603/528–8721.

(**1+**) **Echo Lake State Park.** There's good swimming at the base of a dramatic rock cliff and hiking or biking on a scenic trail. See also Chapter 5.

Rte. 302 off Rte. 16, North Conway 03860, tel. 603/356–2672.

(**6 – 15**) **Crawford Notch State Park.** This pass harbors the highest waterfalls in the state and some of the most untamed forests and mountains in New Hampshire. See also Chapter 5.

Rte. 302, Bartlett 03812, tel. 603/374–2272.

MOUNTAIN BIKING. There's a surprising amount of fairly easy biking in this area of 82 peaks. In Conway a single sandy track parallels the Saco River. Start at the footbridge at the right end of the picnic area. In Jackson, the **Carter Notch Trail**, which crosses several brooks, begins at the end of Carter Notch Road off Route 16A. Cycle shops have a pamphlet listing easy rides. Excellent family biking plus rentals are available at several locations not far from Conway: **Bretton Woods Ski Area** (tel. 800/232–2972), the new **Great Glen Trails** (tel. 603/466–2333), and **Attitash Bear Peak** (tel. 603/374–2368). Farther west are **Loon Mountain Park** (tel. 603/745–8111, ext. 5400) and **Waterville Valley** (tel. 603/236–8311).

Other locations include **Moose Brook State Park** (off Rte. 2, 2 mi west of Gorham, tel. 603/466–3860) at the north end of the valley, which has good mountain-bike trails and serves as a base from which to hike the Crescent and Presidential ranges. The White Mountain National Forest is crisscrossed with logging roads mountain bikers can use (tel. 603/528–8721 for trail map). For bike rentals, **Joe Jones Shop** (Main St., North Conway, tel. 603/356–9411) carries sizes as small as 14 inches, sells bike maps with routes in the area, and charges $15 per day for a bike and helmet.

SWIMMING. You don't come to the White Mountains for great swimming of the serene, blue mountain-lake kind. Here you'll come across mostly cold, rocky pools under waterfalls. The ones we go back to are at **Jackson Falls** just above Jackson Village, where the Wildcat River has scoured out a series of fair-size pools and slides in a sunny spot.

Other favorites are **Diana's Baths** (see Hiking, *above*), the pools and slabs of rock for jumping above Rocky Gorge about 9 mi west of Conway on the Kancamagus Highway. Watch for the Rocky Gorge Picnic Area. Along Route 302, look for the confluence of the Sawyer and Saco rivers. The beach at **Echo Lake State Park** in North Conway can get very crowded at noon, but

even tots can enjoy it. In the southern part of the valley, there are two sandy beaches on the east side of **Chocorua Lake**.

WATCHING WILDLIFE. Moose are the exciting animal to spot here, and the surefire way to see one is to go on one of the 2½-hour tours that leave from **Main Information Booth** (Gorham, tel. 603/466–3103) at 6 PM ($15 adults, $10 kids 12 and under). They have a 95% success rate in spotting at least one moose. You travel in a 24-passenger bus. This is best for kids over 8 who are dying to see a moose.

WINTER SPORTS. For downhill and cross-country skiing in Jackson and at Black Mountain, Bretton Woods, and Waterville Valley, and sleigh rides and skating in the region, see Chapter 7.

Shopping

From Conway to North Conway 200-odd factory outlets are divided up among a series of centers like boxed chocolates, attracting tourists and teens with shopping addictions by the prospect of low prices and no sales tax on clothing. You could outfit everyone for school in a day. **OVP** (Settler's Green Outlet Village Plus, Rte. 16, North Conway, tel. 603/356–7031) is nice for kids because it's set around a large courtyard with grassy lawns, benches, and a gazebo and sometimes has free entertainment. The highlight among the stores at nearby **Tanger Outlet Centers** (Rte. 16, North Conway, tel. 603/356–7921 or 800/407–4078) is **L. L. Bean** (tel. 603/356–2100)—but it's not as neat as the original in Maine.

(👫 **7 – 12**) **Grand Slam Sports Cards** carries all kinds of sports memorabilia—jackets, caps, sweatshirts—as well as cards.
🏬 *Rte. 16 in Mt. Valley Mall, North Conway, tel. 603/356–2705.*

Eats

Our picnics are mostly on hikes—we try for a peak with a view or a waterfall, and the promise of food keeps us going. Down in the valley we found picnicking in the rain an unusual treat at the picnic tables inside the restored Swift River Covered Bridge (off West Side Rd. in Conway Village), now only used as a footbridge. Among the coziest eateries are those in the family farms and inns in the area. North Conway has a number of kid-friendly cafés, pizzerias, and burger spots; those below are something special.

Category	Cost*
$$$	over $25
$$	$15–$25
$	under $15

per person for a three-course meal, excluding drinks, service, and sales tax

★★ ALL **Elvio's Pizzeria.** Three types of pizza—thin crust baked in a stone deck oven, thick-crust Sicilian, and double dough—are the fare. Our vote goes to the thin crust.
🏠 *Main St., North Conway Village, tel. 603/356–3307. MC, V. $*

★★ 4+ **Fabyans Station.** Here you can feast on burgers and sandwiches in an old railroad depot next to the Cog Railway. The dining room serves full dinners, too.
🏠 *Rte. 302, Bretton Woods, tel. 603/846–2222. Kids' menu, high chairs. AE, MC, V. $–$$*

Horsefeathers. This casual neighborhood place serves good fresh fish, onion soup, and wine by the glass and microbrews for you and a kids' menu and free jellybeans for the kids.
🏠 *North Conway Village, tel. 603/356–2687. Kids' menu. AE, MC, V. $–$$*

★★ ALL **Red Parka Pub.** The bar scene here is lively, but there's also a terrific huge salad bar where kids can fill up plates and start eating immediately. A corny sense of humor that kids understand pervades—a menu in the form of a newspaper, chicken dishes listed as "Top Hen Hits," and appetizers like spudskins.
🏠 *Rte. 302, Glen, tel. 603/383–4344. Kids' menu. AE, D, MC, V. $–$$*

Where to Stay

This region has a wider range of places to stay than most resort areas, from hostel hiking lodges to grand hotel complexes. Most also have restaurants open to the public. We'd rather be out of the busyness of North Conway in summer, so all my choices, except the least expensive, are in the smaller, more New England–like towns farther north in the valley. *See also* Chapter 9: Rockhouse Mountain Farm, Purity Spring Resort, and Whitney's Inn at Jackson, and Chapter 7, Waterville Valley.

For the hostel below, $ means under $50; otherwise the prices correspond to the following chart:

Category	Cost*
$$$$	over $250
$$$	$175–$250
$$	$100–$175
$	under $100

All prices are for a standard double room in high season.

★★ ALL **Christmas Farm Inn.** The suites in the barn (a game room is downstairs) and the cottages are the best accommodations for families at this cheery country inn that has the facilities of a resort but the atmosphere of an intimate, friendly farm. Kids are welcome. Prices may seem high, but in fact they cover breakfast and dinner for a family of four as well as a suite. A golf course and tennis courts are just outside the door, as are cross-country ski trails in winter.

Rte. 16B, Jackson 03846, tel. 603/383–4313 or 800/443–5837, fax 603/383–6495. 34 rooms, 4 suites, 6 cottages with fireplaces. Facilities: restaurant, pool, outdoor hot tub, putting green, volleyball, cross-country skiing, recreation room, baby-sitting. MAP. AE, MC, V. $$$–$$$$

(ii ALL) **Hostelling International.** The Albert B. Lester Memorial Hostel. Much like a jolly do-it-yourself B&B in a country Victorian inn, this hostel is a renovated 100-year-old house with family rooms and small bunk rooms where families can save additional money by cooking their own dinners in the communal kitchen. There's a big backyard with grills and picnic tables.
36 Washington St., Conway 03813, tel. 603/447–1001, fax 603/447–1011. 6 bunk rooms; 3 family rooms, all share bath. Facilities: dining room. CP. Kids under 12, ½ price. MC, V. $

(ii ALL) **Mount Washington Hotel.** From a distance—and you can see it from miles away—the mammoth white building with its red roof framed by the highest peaks of the Presidential Range looks like a remote summer palace, every inch the grand resort it was at the turn of the century. All rooms have a Victorian theme—the most expensive are elegant with rich florals, and the smaller ones are decorated with wicker. By far the best bet for families with kids over 5 are the family chambers—two rooms joined by a bath, some with nice sitting rooms. Starting in November 1999, the hotel will be open year-round (see also Chapter 7, Bretton Woods Ski Area).
Rte. 302, Bretton Woods 03575, tel. 603/278–1000 or 800/258–0330. 200 rooms and suites in hotel, plus 34 in Bretton Arms

Country Inn and 50 in Bretton Woods Motor Inn; all use resort facilities. Facilities: 5 restaurants (7 in summer), baby-sitting, biking, fishing, 27-hole golf course, horseback riding (including pony rides), kids' programs at hotel (daily summer and winter; weekends spring and fall), indoor and outdoor pools, playground, recreation room, 12 tennis courts; in winter, cross-country skiing, downhill skiing, sleigh rides, snowshoeing. MAP. Special packages, including ski packages. Kids under 4 stay free in hotel; kids 5–12, $35; over 12, $70; kids under 18 stay free in Bretton Arms and Motor Inn. AE, D, MC, V. $$–$$$$

Entertainment and the Arts

Compared to the Berkshires or the Adirondacks, the arts are a minor attraction here. For families, the best is the summer concert series presented by the **Arts Jubilee** (Box 647, North Conway 03860, tel. 603/356–9393) under the stars in North Conway's Schouler Park. The highlight is the symphony pops concert with fireworks in July; a picnic dinner on the grass is the way to go. Bring your own seating.

The fine children's theater troupe at the **Papermill Theatre** (tel. 603/745–6032) at Loon Mountain performs short fairy-tale musicals; some years they travel to North Conway for a performance. The regular offerings are musicals with family appeal, like Annie and Damn Yankees; weekday family passes are a bargain. For movies, there are seven theaters among Conway Village, North Conway, and the Mountain Valley Mall.

Directory of Resources

No single travel resource can give you every detail about every topic that might interest or concern you. The following directory lists telephone numbers, helpful organizations, and other useful tips that will supplement the information given in this book.

Visitor Services

Connecticut Department of Economic Development (865 Brook St., Rocky Hill, CT 06067, tel. 860/258–4355 or 800/282–6863).

Maine Innkeepers Association (305 Commercial St., Portland, ME 04101, tel. 207/773–7670).

Maine Publicity Bureau (Box 2300, Hallowell, ME 04347, tel. 207/623–0363 or 800/533–9595).

Massachusetts Office of Travel and Tourism (100 Cambridge St., Boston, MA 02202, tel. 617/727–3201; for "Massachusetts Getaway Guide" only, 800/447–6277).

New Hampshire Office of Travel and Tourism (Box 1856, Concord, NH 03302-1856, tel. 603/271–2666 or 800/386–4664; for a recorded message about seasonal events, 800/258–3608).

New York State Division of Tourism (1 Commerce Plaza, Albany, NY 12245, tel. 518/474–4116 or 800/225–5697).

Rhode Island Department of Economic Development, Tourism Division (1 W. Exchange St., Providence, RI 02903, tel. 401/227–2601 or 800/556–2484).

Vermont Chamber of Commerce, Department of Travel and Tourism (Box 37, Montpelier, VT 05601, tel. 802/223–3443).

Vermont Department of Travel and Tourism (134 State St., Montpelier, VT 05602, tel. 802/828–3236 or 800/837–6668).

For local tourism offices, see Chapters 11–18.

Family-Oriented Tour Agencies

Family Explorations, Inc. (343 Dartmouth Ave., Swarthmore, PA 19081-1017, tel. 610/543–6200 or 800/934–6800, fax 610/543–6262).

Family Matters Travel (9944 Johnnycake Ridge, Concord, OH 44077, tel. 216/350–0550 or 800/850–0831).

Traveling with Children (2313 Valley St., Berkeley, CA 94702, tel. 510/848–0929 or 800/499–0929), though located on the West Coast, also offers consultation services to families planning trips to the Northeast.

Lodging

Bed-and-Breakfasts

Unfortunately no single bed-and-breakfast reservation service covers the entire Northeast. **The American Country Collection—Bed & Breakfast Vermont** (1353 Union St., Schenectady, NY 12308, tel. 518/370–4948) has visited all the more than 100 spots they list in western Massachusetts, Vermont, and eastern New York State. **Covered Bridge Bed & Breakfast Reservations** (69 Maple Ave., Norfolk, CT 06058, tel. 860/542–5944) covers Connecticut and the Berkshires in western Massachusetts; listings even include a working farm with horse and carriage rides, goats, sheep, and geese.

For ski resorts offering special kids' programs, see Chapter 7; for individual resorts, lodges, and guest ranches with special kids' programs, see Chapter 9.

Hotel Chains

Best Western (tel. 800/528–1234) allows kids to stay free in their parents' room in most locations, though the maximum age to qualify varies widely, from 2 to 17.

Choice Hotels (tel. 800/424–6423), which includes Comfort, Clarion, Quality, Sleep, Rodeway, EconoLodge, and Friendship Inns, allows kids 18 and under to stay free with parents at most locations.

Days Inn (tel. 800/325–2525) allows all kids 12 and under to stay free in their parents' room; at some locations the maximum age extends to 17.

Doubletree (tel. 800/424–2900) lets children 17 and under stay free with their parents. Some locations offer Family-Friendly Suites—baby- and childproof suites that come stocked with emergency baby supplies.

Four Seasons Hotels and Resorts (tel. 800/332–3442) features the V.I.K. (Very Important Kids) program, with amenity bags filled with goodies and other perks. Video games, toys, children's movies, baby supplies—even child-size furniture—are all available. Guest rooms can be childproofed upon request. Kids under 18 stay free with parents, and adjoining rooms are discounted for families through the Family Plan.

Holiday Inn (tel. 800/465–4329) allows kids 19 and under to stay free in their parents' room.

Howard Johnson Hotels (tel. 800/446–4656) lets kids under 18 stay free with their parents.

Hyatt (tel. 800/233–1234) lets kids under 18 stay free in their parents' room and offers 50% discounts on second rooms year-round at most hotels. At check-in kids are handed a welcoming pack, including a cap. Some locations offer Camp Hyatt, a program of supervised activities for younger kids.

Inter-Continental (tel. 800/327–0200) lets children under 14 stay free in their parents' room. In the Northeast, only New York City has a hotel in this chain.

Marriott (tel. 800/228–9290) lets kids 17 and under stay free at almost all locations. Recent seasonal promotions have included the Family Room program, offering discounts of up to 60% and free kids' meals for 21-day advance payment.

Radisson (tel. 800/333–3333) has a Family Magic program that includes free breakfasts, an adjoining room at a discount, and magic trick booklets and accessories for kids. About half participate in the Family Approved program, offering child-care services, cribs, child-proofing kits, and a library of kids' books, games, and videos. Some let kids as old as 18 stay free.

Ramada (tel. 800/272–6232) lets kids 18 and under stay free.

Ritz-Carlton Hotels (tel. 800/241–3333) allows kids up to age 12 or 18 (depending on location) to stay free; the Boston location has many unique kids' programs and events; see Chapter 11.

Sheraton (tel. 800/325–3535) lets kids 17 and under stay free in their parents' room. During occasional promotions and at some locations, kids 12 and under eat free or for 99.

Westin (tel. 800/228–3000) offers the year-round Westin Kids Club, with planned activities for kids age 12 and under. Kids receive gifts at check-in; parents receive safety kits. Children under 18 stay free in their parents' room. The only Westin hotels in the Northeast are in New York City and Boston. The New York hotel doesn't have the program; the Boston hotel does.

Money Matters

Many **automated-teller machines (ATMs)** are tied to international networks such as **Cirrus** and **Plus**. For specific Cirrus locations in the United States, call 800/424–7787. For Plus locations, call 800/843–7587 and press the area code and first three digits of the number you're calling from (or the calling area where you want an ATM).

Rental Cars

All major car-rental agencies serve the Northeast. Some of the top agencies include **Alamo** (tel. 800/327–9633; located at only the biggest airports), **Avis** (tel. 800/331–1212), **Budget** (tel. 800/527–0700), **Dollar** (tel. 800/800–4000), **Hertz** (tel. 800/654–3131), **National** (tel. 800/227–7368), and **Thrifty** (tel. 800/367–2277).

Directory of Attractions

Here is a list of the attractions covered in this book, each one followed by a **bold-face** age range and the *italic* number of the page on which you'll find a description.

Connecticut

Southwestern Connecticut

Barnum Museum, Bridgeport, **3–13**, *34*

Beardsley Park and Zoological Gardens, Bridgeport, **All**, *50*

Discovery Museum, Bridgeport, **3+**, *34–35*

Longshore Sailing School, Westport, **8–15**, *108*

Maritime Aquarium at Norwalk, Norwalk, **All**, *50*

Sheffield Island Lighthouse, South Norwalk, **6–13**, *18–19*

SoundWaters, Stamford, **8–15**, *108*

Stew Leonard's Dairy, Norwalk, **2–12**, *117*

The Connecticut River Valley

Gillette Castle State Park, East Haddam, **All**, *17*

Farmington River, Avon–Simsbury, New Hartford–Canton, **4–15**, *91, 113*

New Britain Youth Museum at Hungerford Park, Kensington, **3–12**, *51*

Old New-Gate Prison and Copper Mine, East Granby, **7–15**, *18*

Science Center of Connecticut, West Hartford, **3–12**, *51*

The Northwest Corner–the Litchfield Hills

Housatonic Meadows State Park, Cornwall Bridge, **7–15**, *87*

Housatonic River, Falls Village–Cornwall Bridge, **8–15**, *91*

Lake Waramaug State Park, New Preston, **0–12**, *62*

Lime Rock Park (auto racing), Lakeville, **5+**, *140*

Sharon Audubon Center, Sharon, **4–12**, *62*

White Memorial Foundation, Litchfield, **3–12**, *62–63*

New Haven and the Southeastern Coast

Children's Museum of Southeastern Connecticut, Niantic, **2–7**, *34*

Garde Arts Center, New London, **6+**, *171*

Historic Ship Nautilus and Submarine Force Museum, Groton, **6–15**, *35*

International Festival of Arts and Ideas, New Haven, **5+**, *165*

Mystic Marinelife Aquarium, Mystic, **All**, *50–51*

Mystic Seaport, Mystic, **All**, *18*

Rocky Neck State Park, Niantic, **2+**, *62, 87*

The Northeast Corner

Buell's Orchard, Eastford, **4–13**, *82*

Maine

The Coast South of Portland

Scarborough Marsh Nature Center, Scarborough, **5+**, *53, 66*

Portland to Pemaquid Point

Boothbay Harbor, **5–15**, *108*

Chewonki Wilderness Programs, Wiscasset, **8+**, *150*

Desert of Maine, Freeport, **5–14**, *65*

Ft. Popham, Phippsburg, **4–13**, *19*

Ft. William Henry and Colonial Pemaquid State Historic Site, New Harbor, **5–12**, *19*

L.L. Bean & L.L. Bean Kids, Freeport, **12–15**, *117*

L.L. Bean Outdoor Discovery School, Freeport, **12+**, *95*

Maine Department of Marine Resources Public Aquarium, West Boothbay Harbor, **2–12**, *52*

Maine Maritime Museum, Bath, **4–15**, *35–36*

Monhegan Island, **6–15**, *97–98*

Pemaquid Point Lighthouse and Fisherman's Museum, Pemaquid, **5–15**, *19–20*

Portland Sea Dogs (baseball team), Portland, **7+**, *140*

Railway Village, Boothbay, **3–9**, *36*

Reid State Park, Georgetown, **All**, *66*

Sebasco Harbor Resort, Sebasco Estates, **4–12**, *152*

Penobscot Bay

Ft. Knox State Park, Prospect Harbor, **3–15**, *19*

Goose Cove Lodge, Sunset, **0–12**, *150–151*

Samoset Resort, Rockport, **3–12**, *151–152*

Windjammer Cruises, Camden, **12–15**, *108*

Acadia

Acadia National Park, **2+**, *63–64, 84, 97*

Acadia Toddler Tromp, Acadia National Park, **1–5**, *87*

Acadia Zoological Park, Trenton, **1–12**, *52*

Bar Harbor, **8–15**, *115*

Lobster Hatchery, Southwest Harbor, **All**, *53*

Mt. Desert Oceanarium, Southwest Harbor, **All**, *52–53*

Western Lakes and Mountains

Grafton Notch State Park, Newry, **7**, *65*

Kawahnee Inn, Weld, **2–14**, *151*

Mt. Blue State Park, Weld, **6+**, *65–66, 87–88*

Perham's (rockhounding), West Paris, **5–13**, *105*

Sebago Lake State Park, Naples, **All**, *66, 88*

Step Falls, Bethel/Grafton Notch State Park, **3–15**, *98*

Sugarloaf/USA, Carrabassett Vallery, **All**, *120–121*

Ipswich, **1–12,** *54,* *191*

New England Pirate Museum, Salem, **6+,** *190–191*

North Shore Music Theatre, Beverly, **5+,** *207*

Paper House, Rockport, **5–12,** *24*

Parker River National Wildlife Refuge, Newburyport, **4–13,** *98–99*

Salem 1630 Pioneer Village, Salem, **5–13,** *25, 189*

Salem Wax Museum of Witches and Seafarers, Salem, **8+,** *39, 191*

Salem Willows Park (amusement park), Salem, **2+,** *206–207*

Salem Witch Museum, Salem, **7+,** *39–40, 191*

Theatre in the Open at Maudslay State Park, Newburyport, **6+,** *208*

Wenham Museum, Wenham, **4–13,** *41, 191*

The Pioneer Valley–Central Massachusetts

EcoTarium, Worcester, **3–15,** *39, 55*

Higgins Armory Museum, Worcester, **6–15,** *38*

Old Sturbridge Village, Sturbridge, **4–13,** *23*

Pinewoods Camp, Haydenville, **3–12,** *154–155*

Southwick's Wild Animal Farm, Mendon, **All,** *55*

Waterfield Farms Recreational Fishing at Bioshelters, Amherst, **3–14,** *95*

The Berkshires

Alpine Slide, Hancock, **4–14,** *282*

Bartholomew's Cobble, Ashley Falls, **3–12,** *98, 283*

Bash Bish Falls, Mt. Washington, **4+,** *283–284*

Basketball Hall of Fame, Springfield, **5–15,** *36*

Beartown State Forest, Monterey, **All,** *283*

Benedict Pond Trail, Beartown State Forest, **5–15,** *284*

Berkshire Botanical Garden, Stockbridge, **0–8,** *281*

Berkshire Museum, Pittsfield, **4–12,** *281*

Berkshire Opera Company, **12–15,** *289*

Berkshire Scenic Railway and Museum, Lenox, **5–10,** *281*

Berkshire Theatre Festival, Stockbridge, **8–14,** *289*

Butternut Basin, Great Barrington, **All,** *123*

Cove Lanes, Great Barrington, **4–15,** *282*

Deerfield River, Fife Brook, Charlemont, **10–15,** *92, 116, 285*

Field Farm, South Williamstown, **5–15,** *284*

Green River Swimming Hole, Great Barrington, **4–15,** *285*

Greylock Discovery Tours, Lenox, **8+,** *279*

Hancock Shaker Village, Pittsfield, **8–13,** *21–22, 281*

Ice Glen Trail, Stockbridge, **8–15,** *284*

Indian powwows, Charlemont, **5–15,** *279*

Jacob's Pillow (dance events), Becket, **5+,** *170, 289*

Josh Billings RunAground (triathlon), Berkshires, **8–15,** *280*

Kids' World Playground, Williamstown, **2–11,** *282*

Lake Mansfield, Great Barrington, **All,** *285*

Massachusetts Museum of Contemporary Art, North Adams, **4–15,** *289*

Mohawk Trail (Route 2), Berkshires, **All,** *281*

Monument Mountain Reservation, Stockbridge, **7–15,** *284*

Mt. Greylock State Reservation, Lanesborough, **6+,** *68–69, 283*

Natural Bridge State Park, North Adams, **7+,** *69, 283*

Norman Rockwell Museum, Stockbridge, **3–15,** *280*

North Pond, Savoy State Forest, **3–15,** *285*

Otis Reservoir, Otis, **All,** *285*

Par-4 Family Fun Center, Lanesborough, **4–15,** *282*

Pittsfield Mets (baseball team), Pittsfield, **3+,** *141, 280, 281–282*

Pleasant Valley Wildlife Sanctuary, Lenox, **All,** *281*

Robbins-Zust Family Marionettes, Richmond, **3–15,** *289*

Sand Springs Pool and Spa, Williamstown, **All,** *285*

Santarella (Tyringham's Gingerbread House), Tyringham, **3–10,** *280*

Savoy Mountain State Forest, Savoy, **All,** *283*

Shakespeare and Company, Lenox, **13+,** *172, 289*

Tanglewood Music Festival, Lenox, **5+,** *168, 289*

Tyringham Cobble, Tyringham, **5–15,** *284*

Western Gateway Heritage State Park, North Adams, **3–13,** *281*

New Hampshire

The Coast

Canobie Lake Park (amusement park), Salem, **2+,** *206*

Odiorne Point State Park, Rye, **2–15,** *71*

Strawbery Banke Museum, Portsmouth, **7–14,** *26*

The Lakes Region

Castle in the Clouds, Moultonborough, **8–15,** *101*

Funspot Amusement Center, Weirs Beach, **12–15,** *117–118*

Perpetual Motion Indoor Playground, Andover, **1–6,** *118*

Purity Spring Resort, East Madison, **1–15,** *157*

Rockywold-Deephaven Camp, Holderness, **All,** *158*

Ruggles Mine, Grafton, **6–13,** *105*

Science Center of New Hampshire, Holderness, **3–14,** *56*

The White Mountains

Appalachian Mountain Club, Pinkham's Grant, **4–15,** *88, 155*

Attitash Bear Peak Alpine Slide and Outdoor Amusements, Bartlett, **6+,** *305*

Balsams Grand Resort Hotel, Dixville Notch, **5+,** *155–156*

Fieldstone Farm
Resort, Richfield
Springs, **4–15**, *159*

John Boyd Thacher
State Park, Albany,
8–13, *106*

National Baseball Hall
of Fame, Cooperstown, **8+**, *46*

West of the Berkshires

Mac-Haydn Theatre,
Chatham, **5–9**, *173,
289*

Rhode Island

Providence

All-Children's Theater
Ensemble, Providence,
3+, *174*

Misquamicut State
Beach and Atlantic
Beach, Westerly, **5+**,
77, 112

Pawtucket Red Sox
(baseball team), Pawtucket, **4+**, *142*

Roger Williams Park
and Zoo, Providence,
All, *59*

The Coast–South County

Burlingame State Park,
Charlestown, **3–14**,
76, 89–90

Flying Horse Carousel,
Watch Hill Lighthouse, and Napatree
Point, Watch Hill,
3–10, *31*

Narragansett Town
Beach, Narragansett,
6–15, *112*

Ninigret Conservation
Area (East Beach),
Charlestown, **6+**, *77,
112*

Roger W. Wheeler
State Beach, Narragansett, **1–10**, *112*

Weekapaug Inn,
Weekapaug, **3–15**,
161–162

Newport

Astors' Beechwood
(historic house), Newport, **8+**, *30*

The Breakers (historic
house), Newport, **8+**,
30–31

Ft. Adams State Park,
Newport, **3+**, *76*

Green Animals (topiary
garden), Portsmouth,
2–12, *76*

J. World Sailing School,
Newport, **12–15**,
108

Norman Bird Sanctuary, Middletown, **7–12**,
77

Sail Newport Sailing
Center, Newport,
7–15, *109*

Block Island

Animal Farm, **1–10**,
272

Block Island Historical
Society, **5+**, *272*

Block Island National
Wildlife Refuge, **4–12**,
76, 272

Empire Theater, **3–15**,
277

Fourth of July, **All**,
272

Great Salt Pond Channel, **4–14**, *272*

North Light and North
Light Interpretive Center, **All**, *272*

Oceanwest Theatre,
3+, *277*

Seafood Festival and
Chowder Cookoff,
All, *271–272*

Southeast Light and
Mohegan Bluffs, **4–15**,
272–273

Vermont

Southern Vermont–South of Rutland

Battenkill River, **5–15**,
94, 96

Emerald Lake State
Park, East Dorset,
0–13, *78*

Green Mountain
National Forest, **All**,
78–79, 101

Grout Pond, Stratton,
0–15, *101*

Marlboro Morris Ale
(dance), Brattleboro,
3–14, *171*

Merck Forest and
Farmland Center,
Rupert, **3–12**, *79*

Montshire Museum of
Science, Norwich, **2+**,
47

Mt. Snow Adventure
Center, Dover, **7–15**,
105

Mount Snow–
Haystack, Mount
Snow, **All**, *130–132*

Okemo Mountain
Resort, Ludlow, **All**,
132–133

Stratton, Stratton
Mountain, **All**, *135–
136*

White Rocks Recreation Area, Wallingford, **3–15**, *101*

Central Vermont–Between Rutland and Montpelier

Basin Harbor Club,
Vergennes, **3–15**,
162–263

Bike Vermont, Woodstock, **10+**, *86*

Billings Farm and
Museum, Woodstock,
All, *31, 59*

Bridges Resort and
Racquet Club, Warren,
3+, *113, 163*

Freeman's Brook (Kid's
Brook), Warren, **4–
12**, *96*

Groton State Forest,
Groton, **3–15**, *79*

Kedron Valley Stables,
South Woodstock,
10–15, *102*

Mountain Top Inn and
Resort, Chittenden,
All, *102, 130, 163*

New England Tennis
Holidays at Sugarbush
Resort, Warren,
3–15, *113*

Quechee Gorge and
Quechee State Park,
Quechee, **6+**, *79–80*

Rock of Ages Granite
Quarry, Barre, **6–13**,
31–32

The Seyon Fly-Fishing
Recreation Area, Groton, **9–15**, *97*

Sugarbush, Warren,
All, *136–137*

Suicide Six and the
Woodstock Inn and
Resort, Woodstock,
All, *137–138*

UVM Morgan Horse
Farm, Middlebury, **4+**,
60

Vermont Icelandic
Horse Farm, Waitsfield, **9–15**, *102*

Vermont Institute of
Natural Science,
Woodstock, **3–15**,
60

Northern Vermont–North of Montpelier

Ben & Jerry's Ice
Cream Factory,
Waterbury, **3–15**, *31*

Bread and Puppet Theater, Glover, **All**, *175*

Burton Island State
Park, St. Alban's Bay,
All, *78*

Catamount Family
Center, Williston,
6–15, *104*

Circus Smirkus,
Greensboro, **All**, *175*

Craftsbury Outdoor
Center, Craftsbury
Common, **12–15**,
104

Fairbanks Museum and
Planetarium, St. Johnsbury, **5–13**, *47*

Index